Administering Freedom

DALE KRETZ

Administering Freedom

The State of Emancipation after the
Freedmen's Bureau

The University of North Carolina Press *Chapel Hill*

This book was published with the assistance of the Authors Fund of the University of North Carolina Press.

© 2022 The University of North Carolina Press
All rights reserved
Set in Arno Pro by Westchester Publishing Services
Manufactured in the United States of America

Library of Congress Cataloging-in-Publication Data
Names: Kretz, Dale, author.
Title: Administering freedom : the state of emancipation after the Freedmen's
    Bureau / Dale Kretz.
Description: Chapel Hill : University of North Carolina Press, [2022] |
    Includes bibliographical references and index.
Identifiers: LCCN 2022017149 | ISBN 9781469671017 (cloth) |
    ISBN 9781469671024 (paperback) | ISBN 9781469671031 (ebook)
Subjects: LCSH: United States. Bureau of Refugees, Freedmen, and Abandoned
    Lands—History. | United States. Pension Bureau—History. | African
    Americans—Government policy—History. | African Americans—
    Pensions—History. | Freed persons—United States—History.
Classification: LCC E185.86 .K72 2022 | DDC 973/.0496073—dc23/eng/20220518
LC record available at https://lccn.loc.gov/2022017149

Cover illustration: Alfred R. Waud, detail from drawing of Black soldiers mustering out in Little Rock, Arkansas, *Harper's Weekly*, May 19, 1866. Courtesy of Library of Congress Prints and Photographs Division (LC-DIG-ppmsca-21005).

To my parents,
David Kretz and June Kretz

Contents

Illustrations

Administering Freedom

Introduction

"This is a needle threader. I made it myself," chuckled the old man of Pine Bluff. "Watch me thread a needle." Nearly a century old by the late 1930s and feeling "like a poor old leaf left hangin' to a tree," William Baltimore still had enough energy to captivate his visitor with stories of ingenuity, hunger, and war. Covered in patchwork clothing stitched together himself, Baltimore spun tales of how he had once made a hacksaw from only a file, and a cotton scraper out of a piece of hardwood and a fragment of steel. He boasted he could build an entire wagon from scratch, save for the wheel hubs, and with tools of his own making, no less.

Baltimore's resourcefulness met well the hard necessities of an extraordinary, unsung life as a bondsman, soldier, and freedman on the cotton frontier of Arkansas. The outbreak of the Civil War found Baltimore working on his slave labor camp. By 1863, with the Union army nearby, Baltimore slipped his captors and followed the federal soldiers to Little Rock and enlisted, joining nearly two dozen of his fellow former slaves in the Fifty-Fourth U.S. Colored Troops (USCT). The freedman marched with his company all over the trans-Mississippi West, at one point going without food for three agonizing days. When the war ended, Baltimore returned to his farm. "I was free now," he recalled to his visitor, though "I didn't do so well on the land as I didn't have mules and money to live on." But soon something came along that secured him a steady means of support and, indeed, survival. During his interview, as he verbally composed his only autobiography, Baltimore used his self-made threader, a half arrow of tin, to pull the string through the needle's eye. "Can't I do it as fast as if I had a head full of keen eyes? My wife has been gone twenty years. She was blind too. I had to do something."[1]

Baltimore did what tens of thousands of his fellow freedpeople had been doing in the decades following the Civil War, apply for a federal pension. The U.S. Pension Bureau offered quarterly stipends to millions of qualified Union veterans and surviving heirs. Formerly enslaved veterans of the USCT were included in the program that many consider America's first welfare state. Yet formerly enslaved men and women accounted for only a fraction of the federal pension rolls, and they have long been overlooked by contemporaries and scholars alike.[2] In recent years, however, historians have devoted greater attention to the pension files of Black claimants, drawing on the rich documentary suite of each case, piecing together affidavits, depositions, and medical examinations of countless ordinary freedpeople constrained by illiteracy and poverty and otherwise lost to history. Beyond military exploits, the pension files hold revelatory potential for understanding everything from the intimate relationships of Black Southerners to the contours of Black neighborhoods and communities. Historians have used the pension files to great effect in reconstructing invaluable collective portraits of Black life in the tumult of the Civil War era.[3]

Yet the welter of documentation generated by the pension claims of freedpeople is a story in and of itself. Baltimore first applied for a pension in 1889 but failed to prove crucial aspects of his military service. His eyesight failed as well, and he fell on especially hard times until, as he put it, "friends dug up my record with the Yankees and got me a pension." Formerly enslaved men and women struggled to meet the evidentiary requirements for a successful pension, and many forfeited their claims altogether for lack of satisfactory proof of one's age, identity, service record, or family relations. But to simply regard such loss in negative terms—for the claimant and the historian—is to miss its fundamental basis in one of the most profound transformations in nineteenth-century America: the long, frustrating, and at times painful process by which millions of stateless people became documented citizens.[4]

Understanding freedom as a condition to be managed by the federal administrative state offers a new perspective on emancipation and Reconstruction. The historical literature on the field is immense. Much of it, though, still operates within a liberal framework that showcases individuals and communities striving for the mythical ideal of freedom, often quite far removed from matters of state policy.[5] The freedom paradigm has remained such an enduring framework because the very unattainability of the ideal has allowed scholars a useful way to cast the evolving political contests of Reconstruction and beyond. Thus, widespread political mobilization among Black Americans advanced an expansive vision of freedom and civil rights that ran headlong into reactionary forces promoting more constrictive views of freedom. In recent years, historians have begun to question the freedom paradigm's utility. Instead of focusing on the contested meaning of freedom, they have reversed the valence to ask how freedom was or was not made meaningful. The distance between legal rights on paper, even on the pages of the U.S. Constitution, and the enforcement of those rights depended on the matter of state capacity, whether men and women were included in a state powerful enough to protect all those who belonged.[6]

During the war and postwar occupation, freedpeople felt their newfound status most immediately when in proximity to the U.S. Army and the Bureau of Refugees, Freedmen, and Abandoned Lands, commonly known as the Freedmen's Bureau. To the three million or more Black Southerners who remained in a condition of bondage when the war closed in 1865, rights depended on recognition and enforcement from such federal representatives, much as during the war itself. Despite the obvious power imbalances, this was not a one-sided affair. Rather, formerly enslaved men and women intervened in the federal state every bit as much as the state intervened in their lives. And more. Hundreds of thousands of ex-slaves, including William Baltimore, had for years put themselves in the embattled custody of nearby federal soldiers, at once testing the state's capacity and willingness to enter into what one historian aptly calls a "mutually beneficial alliance." Freedpeople exchanged labor and loyalty for protection. This dynamic alliance, animated as it was by shared interests, formed the essential foundation of citizenship for thousands of Black Southerners.[7] Forged in the cauldron of military necessity, the alliance with federal soldiers was imperfectly maintained by the creation of the Freedmen's Bureau in March 1865. Tasked with incorporating Southern freedpeople into the new free labor economy, the bureau's agents negotiated labor contracts, mediated disputes with employers, sold abandoned and confiscated lands, and helped secure rations, medical care, and education for former slaves. With outposts peppered across the postwar South, the Freedmen's Bureau, where sufficiently staffed and inclined, was often the final bastion for the realization of freedpeople's rights, albeit an already divested collection of rights organized around contractual free market principles.[8]

When Black Southerners congregated behind Union lines, they did not simply enter into an already existing relationship with the central state; they were building a new one. As many scholars have shown, before the Civil War the federal government generally had only minimal contact with ordinary Americans. National citizenship was a product of the war, not a prelude to it, as many citizens had previously derived various civic rights from states, localities, and public associations.[9] The refugee camps that coalesced during the war have thus emerged in recent scholarship as critical sites for the creation of national citizenship and even the construction of the central state. Against older theories of top-down state building, the latest scholarship provocatively uses refugee camps to show that freedpeople used their positions as the Union's indispensable collaborators to make demands on federal actors and, in the process, build the central state "from the inside out." In their determined pursuit to be a rights-bearing people within a powerful nation-state they helped save, formerly enslaved men and women upended long-standing assumptions about what the federal government could and ought to do.[10]

Because the alliance's foundational reciprocity depended on a proximate relationship with federal soldiers, agents, and officials, the swift demobilization of the occupying federal army and the Freedmen's Bureau by the early 1870s shattered its very bedrock.[11] Accordingly, studies exploring freedpeople's state-centered politics abruptly end with the end of the Freedmen's Bureau, giving way to more familiar stories of temporary Black political advancement and, in the days of disempowerment and disenfranchisement, stories of protest and community building. Part of the reason for the expiration date on statist histories of freedpeople is the sudden dearth of documentation, one of the defining characteristics of the federal government's intervention in the South.[12] But the deeper explanation is the assumption that their wartime foothold in the central state had in fact ended, and with it, any immediate hopes for inclusion in a state that guaranteed citizenship rights and meaningful freedom to freedpeople and their descendants. Not until the New Deal, the argument goes, did Black Americans begin to recapture state recognition.

The relationship between freedpeople and the federal government did not end with the demise of the Freedmen's Bureau. But it did change. And the way it changed, the way emancipation was managed every day for the next seven decades, depended on the continued political exertion of tens of thousands of formerly enslaved men and women rendered no longer as allies but as claimants.

The Freedmen's Bureau has long been regarded as a pivotal, if ambiguous, agency in the history of emancipation.[13] In his 1903 classic, *The Souls of Black Folk*, W. E. B. Du Bois devoted his chapter on "the dawn of Freedom" to the career of the Freedmen's Bureau. To Du Bois, the bureau was "one of the most singular and interesting of the attempts made by a nation to grapple with vast problems of race and social condition." Indeed, the bureau was itself a "new government" created to "assume charge of the emancipated Negro as the ward of the nation," a new government replete with a constitution, commissioners, courts, schools, hospitals, and agents in nearly every ex-Confederate state to oversee lands and laborers alike. Du Bois recognized the internal limitations of the bureau, being as it was a "full-fledged government of men," but also acknowledged the monumental task before it and the vicious opposition arrayed against it from all quarters of American society, which virtually ensured that the bureau's work of "social regeneration was in large part doomed to failure." Opponents argued that the bureau's extraordinary powers were unconstitutional, especially in times of peace, and that the very existence of such an agency threatened the general welfare of all Americans by stoking the fires of racial hostilities. As Du Bois mourned the passing of the bureau and the legacies of its unfinished work, he imagined an alternative future for the Freedmen's Bureau, one in which the bureau was able to be made permanent instead of provisional, and that instead of feebly holding up "Negro suffrage as a final answer to all present perplexities," it instead could be made "a great school of prospective citizenship."[14]

By the time the bureau began winding down operations as early as 1867, the broad range of its original functions had severely contracted. As detailed in chapter 1, the bureau's remaining agents found themselves relegated to facilitating the military claims of Black soldiers and their families, particularly their applications for back wages, bounties, and pensions. Freedpeople with and without claims to make were anxiously aware of the bureau's diminution. Once a potential vehicle to deliver collective justice, above all the widely promised redistribution of land, the Freedmen's Bureau became for them a harbinger of a new order in which individuals gained recognition as individuals with specific, well-bounded claims to lodge. In some cases, men and women who performed various tasks for the Union army were able to secure their unpaid wages. In other cases, freedpeople applied for compensation for property confiscated by the Union army. But by and large, the vast majority of claimants were those who had served in the U.S. Colored Troops or who had a close familial connection to a deceased veteran that entitled them to benefits. Of the roughly 180,000 USCT, some 144,000 came from the slave states soon to be under the administration of the Freedmen's Bureau. Hundreds of thousands of individual claims can all be traced back to that initial collection of Black soldiers who secured a spot in the federal welfare state for themselves and their posterity. "It was a lucky day when de Yankees got me," recalled William Baltimore in the 1930s. "Ef they hadn't I don't know what'd become of me."[15]

The collective mobilization of Black claimants to secure military benefits confounded the individualized nature of the claims-making process and remains the most underappreciated achievement of freedpeople in the days of Reconstruction.[16] Unpaid enlistment bounties came first. Together, countless groups of comrades, families, and neighbors collaborated on each other's applications, marshaling the support of various government officials, philanthropists, private claims agents, even former enslavers to expedite their claims for long-delayed bounties. This seemingly straightforward task hinged on verifying the identities of previously undocumented subjects in a previously unregulated space. The endeavor proved so complicated for the modernizing central state, and freedpeople themselves so persistent, that the processing of bounty payments outlived the Freedmen's Bureau. When the bureau finally closed in 1872, Congress created a new agency specifically to continue the work of settling unpaid bounties. Although the Freedmen's Branch has long since escaped the attention of scholars, for thousands of formerly enslaved men and women it served as a vestige of national authority and Black citizenship rights amid the Southern federal declension of the 1870s. The ongoing mobilization of freedpeople throughout the South influenced both the size of the federal footprint and the depth of its intervention in the lives of its claimants. The remarkable, untold story of the Freedmen's Branch is the subject of chapter 2.

As freedpeople struggled to secure their bounty claims, many also began applying for federal military pensions. Unlike the Freedmen's Bureau and Freedmen's Branch, which were primarily confined to the former slave states and its formerly enslaved clientele, the Pension Bureau operated nationally for all Union veterans, white and Black, and largely irrespective of past slave status, except in cases involving heirs. Previously enslaved men and women had immense difficulties attaining pensions. If the comparative lack of eligible claimants in the South meant that the region would always be underrepresented on the pension rolls, the unique challenges facing ex-slave claimants ensured an abundance of administrative issues. Chapter 3 explores the formative role freedwomen played in the building of the Southern Division of the Pension Bureau by pressing their claims for survivor's pensions. At the heart of their story is the matter of dependency. Freedwomen were emancipated into a gendered hierarchy that placed them below, and dependent on, their fathers and husbands and sons.[17] Earning a bounty or pension as a dependent effectively erased their wartime contributions. Harriet Tubman herself spent nearly thirty-five years pursuing a pension for her work as a scout, nurse, and spy, and when she finally received a pension in 1890, it was as the widow of Nelson Davis.[18] As with their white counterparts in the North, freedwomen whose menfolk died in the war needed to prove they had been dependent on the deceased for support, and thus not on their enslavers. This fraught rhetorical maneuver challenged the most ingrained cultural assumptions about antebellum slavery, eliciting a nationwide debate.

Though long regarded as the antithesis of independent citizenship, dependency and disability were the twin pillars of the federal pension system. In this peculiar administrative space, only disabled and dependent Unionists could lay claim to the most immediate material signifier of national citizenship, ironically at a time when women, nonwhites, and disabled people were broadly excluded from its ranks. If freedwomen were forced to negotiate the tensions of dependency and autonomy, the pension system forced formerly enslaved veterans to present a carefully curated narrative of their suffering, one that eliminated any hint of preenlistment ailments. Until 1890, the single pension track for Union veterans required proof of a distinct service origin for a present disability. The sheer complexity of the bureaucratic strictures reinvigorated the documentary struggles that defined their earlier bounty claims while also precipitating new forms of collective struggle. Chapter 4 demonstrates that the high stakes of Civil War memory registered not simply in the cultural sphere but also in the administrative arena, especially in the claims of thousands of Black veterans. Claimants took to the extreme one variant of the racial progress sermons so ubiquitous in the 1880s, that remembering the sorrows and hardships of slavery only served to debase and discourage the race. Thousands of freedmen were incentivized by bureau policy to portray themselves as perfectly healthy in the days of slavery but afflicted ever since the Yankees came; their material well-being, and that of their families, thus called for drawing a bright red line between slavery and freedom—writing the former out of the stories of the latter and establishing an antislavery foundation for the new nation-state by absolving it of compensating for past wrongs.[19]

Claims-making among freedpeople persisted through the years of Reconstruction and well into the age of formal disenfranchisement and segregation. By 1884, over thirty-one thousand veterans and heirs of the USCT had applied for a pension, less than 4 percent of total pension applicants. About eleven thousand were admitted to the rolls.[20] In other words, only one in three Black claimants could hope for admission, though with no guarantee of remaining enrolled. But all could expect years of frustration, as could countless other former fellow slaves brought in to testify on a claimant's behalf. These figures improved little until the watershed Disability Act of 1890, which inaugurated a new pension track for eligible Union veterans claiming disability outside of wartime service.[21] The new program opened the door for tens of thousands of Black claimants. Although they no longer needed to carefully situate their disabilities within their military service, they confronted Pension Bureau medical examining boards staffed by local physicians deputized to evaluate a claimant's exact degree of ratable disability. Chapter 5 considers the medical examination as a site of political struggle between formerly enslaved claimants and the civilian surrogates of the federal government. In so doing, the chapter not only challenges the near absence of disability and disabled persons in scholarship on the aftermath of the Civil War by foregrounding disability's prominence in public life. It also shows that the very production of disability as a category was an intimately contested process between federal administrators, physicians, and the claimants themselves, none more so than that class of people who had so recently emerged from the commodifying clutches of the slave market. In the medical examination room, the denial of Black pain was not only routinized but also incentivized and bureaucratized, registering in smaller disability ratings and fewer Black claimants on the pension rolls.[22]

Every pension application from a former slave came freighted with the heavy heritage of emancipation. In the 1890s, as thousands of Black claimants overwhelmed the bureau's Southern Division, a massive grassroots movement among Black Southerners pushed for an expansion of the pension rolls even further to include all freedpeople, as a class, who had yet to be compensated for their years of involuntary servitude. The ex-slave pension movement electrified the South and the nation throughout the 1890s and into the next century. As shown in chapter 6, the movement to pension all former slaves was a class struggle that drew deeply from the biracial Populist movement sweeping the country, which itself relied extensively on the dexterous political mobilization of Black Southerners. The movement to pension all former slaves outlived the Populist insurgency. Whereas the latter was attacked and coopted by the Democratic establishment, the former had to contend with a coordinated assault by the federal administrative state led by none other than officials of the Pension Bureau. Under the guise of protecting unsuspecting freedpeople from fraudulent agents, the bureau simultaneously discredited the movement and protected its vested interest in policing a limited welfare state.[23] As the leaders of the ex-slave pension movement struggled against the state and one another, the sectional reunification prompted by the War with Spain in 1898 generated enthusiasm in many quarters for the inclusion of ex-Confederate veterans and heirs on the federal pension rolls by virtue of their Civil War "service." Some of those same proponents advocated universal ex-slave pensions as well, though for reasons far different from those given by freedpeople themselves. In the end, the federal administrative state defeated all efforts to expand the rolls based on competing popular notions of historical responsibility, restitution, and redistribution.

Administering Freedom argues that the promise of emancipation was not simply crushed in the early years of Reconstruction but rather was forcibly pushed through the sieve of the federal administrative state, which itself grew in large measure as a way to manage the expectations of freedpeople and delimit the boundaries of freedom in the new liberal order. Here, the plaintiff-like status of the claimant served to atomize collective efforts, and technical questions about eligibility served to diffuse and displace radical demands about the general welfare. But for freedpeople, their wartime labors had given them a collective purchase on inclusionary citizenship, such that even individualized pension claims were widely regarded in more communal terms.[24]

This book covers the broad swath of time from the Civil War to the New Deal, and therefore also encompasses the Gilded Age and Progressive Era, those years after Reconstruction long regarded as the "nadir" of the Black experience in America.[25] While the magnitude of state-sanctioned violence against Black Southerners in these decades is impossible to deny, historians have begun to challenge certain implications of the nadir thesis, namely, that the intensity of racist repression caused Black Americans to turn inward, self-segregating politically, socially, and culturally as advised by Booker T. Washington. The scholarship has similarly moved beyond the threadbare dialectic of accommodation and resistance. For some scholars, stories of migration, emigration, separatism, and pan-Africanism offer stunning rebukes to the assumed inertia of Black activism in the nadir.[26] Others have shown how Black Americans challenged the capacity of the state to respond to the Klan violence, sexual assaults, lynchings, and massacres that punctuated Black life for many decades after the war. Countless testimonies reveal not only the impact of racist violence on Black communities but also important political strategies of defiance and survival.[27] Scholars are thus increasingly attuned to the myriad forms Black political activism took in the age of disenfranchisement, most notably in labor organizing, journalistic crusades, and institution-building on both local and national scales.[28] For example, founded in 1890, the Afro-American League, and later Afro-American Council, featured the most prominent Black leaders of the era and constituted the first civil rights organization in the nation's history. Although such groups were often unsuccessful in their legal challenges to the Jim Crow juggernaut, their establishment two decades before the creation of the NAACP in 1909 demonstrates for some historians evidence of a "long civil rights movement" and for others a distinct period of Black protest to be appreciated on its own terms, not as a mere antecedent to the civil rights movement of the mid-twentieth century.[29]

One of the most promising avenues of recent scholarship has been uncovering Black activism in legal forums, most notably in Southern courtrooms. As litigants, Black men and women filed hundreds of civil suits against white Southerners throughout the age of Jim Crow. Many of their claims stemmed from disputes stretching back to the days of slavery and were not infrequently lodged against their former enslavers. This emerging body of scholarship not only showcases conflicting visions of slavery and freedom dragged before the courts, and not only the continuing relevance of enslavement decades after emancipation, but also the central role of the law in the political struggles of former slaves and their descendants. Black Southerners, both men and women, proved exceptionally agile in negotiating the power structure of the legal system, articulating in the process notions of property, contract, and restitution refined since the antebellum period. As these historians convincingly argue, the civil suits of Black Southerners reorient our understanding of Black life and politics in the era of disenfranchisement by showing modes of engagement outside the electoral arena, which for years has encouraged a durable mythology of Black political dormancy from the end of Reconstruction to the mid-twentieth century.[30]

Administering Freedom contributes to this emerging literature on the legal history of freedpeople by focusing not on judicial law but on administrative law, how administrative agencies internally elaborate on—and construct— statutory meaning.[31] It explores how tens of thousands of freedpeople encountered, confronted, and shaped federal administrative agencies at a time of unprecedented expansion and increasing autonomy. By redirecting the focus beyond voting booths and courtrooms, into what some legal scholars call an ordinary law context, it also contributes a sense of democratic accretion to the story of citizenship rights in the post-Reconstruction era.[32] If, as many historians argue, gains in the Black freedom struggle have come through state intervention, it is vital to understand how thousands of Black men and women intervened in the state, persistently and continuously, every day since the Civil War. At stake is more than simply an administrative history of emancipation; it is a history of how emancipation was administered—and how the emancipated themselves contested it for as long as they lived.

To begin to appreciate this history, *Administering Freedom* investigates the often subtle and submerged but nonetheless deeply significant administrative politics of thousands of ordinary freedpeople as they used their unique position as long-standing federal claimants to refashion their political identities as entitled, rights-bearing citizens. Like William Baltimore building a cotton scraper from spare parts or fashioning a needle threader without the gift of sight, lodging a claim for bounty or pension required considerable ingenuity and perseverance on the part of formerly enslaved claimants, as well as reliable aid from comrades and allies who, in Baltimore's words, could make all the difference between "hard times" and "setting pretty for de rest of my life." Through their efforts to earn federal benefits, individually and in concert, they not only maintained their wartime foothold in the federal government but also used it to withstand the forces of reaction. Freedpeople's success in navigating the federal administrative state to secure the fruits of citizenship may well have been their most impressive achievement in an era of disaffection and defeat.

But their story also offers a prescient warning about the narrowing aperture of freedom. Baltimore's passing remark about being free after the war but not having "mules and money to live on" invoked—seventy years after the fact—the failure of the federal government to fulfill its promise of establishing Black families on arable land confiscated from their erstwhile enslavers. The hopeful landowners in the post-Confederate South had seen the writing on the wall back in 1866 when the Freedmen's Bureau closed its Land Division and relocated its officials to the newly created Claims Division. After that, its relief provisioning tapered and its functions devolved to local authorities, who largely discarded any such obligations to the ex-slave population. The bureau devoted its final days to facilitating claims for a select class of freedpeople amid a sea of dispossessed former slaves clinging to the wartime alliance by any means necessary. As entitlement programs, bounties and pensions designated groups of citizens as eligible for public benefits; the beneficiaries themselves turned entitlements into rights, in turn generating new expectations of state capacity. "The pension is given as a right," complained one critic in 1884, "not as an act of charity."[33] The Pension Bureau enshrined selective legal entitlements as the centerpiece of the new federal administrative state, a form of what scholars call "civil citizenship," based in notions of property and contract, as opposed to "social citizenship," which maintains all citizens, by virtue of their citizenship, are entitled to social provisions from the state. Because of their explicit selectivity, entitlements such as Union pensions were inherently exclusionary, conceived and defended as a deliberate rejection of egalitarian programs based in social citizenship. Programmatic rights thus displaced universal welfare.[34]

The Pension Bureau occupied an anomalous place for Black claimants in the segregated age of *Plessy v. Ferguson*. Like the Constitution in the eyes of Justice John Marshall Harlan, the Pension Bureau was colorblind. Virtually all legislation relating to federal pensions was crafted without mention of race. When "colored claimants" were mentioned, as with legislation addressing the issue of proving "lawful marriage" among enslaved couples, it was almost always to apply greater liberality to the special cases arising from their prior status, at least in theory. Black claimants applied for federal benefits on a basis of statutory equality with their white analogues in the North. The

Pension Bureau also employed dozens of Black Americans beginning in the early 1880s, providing a unique opportunity for advancement for aspiring clerks, accountants, attorneys, and physicians of the Black professional class. Not only were the doors of the Pension Bureau open to Black employees and claimants, there was no internal segregation within the institution, no "Colored Division," as it were, only a Southern Division, which also handled the claims of white Union regiments drawn from Southern states. Yet the inegalitarian outcomes for Black claimants are undeniable. Scholars have identified a range of factors that produced racial disparities within the statutorily race-neutral Pension Bureau, from poverty and illiteracy to racist examining boards. *Administering Freedom* elaborates on these issues while grounding them historically in the evolving relationship between former slaves and the federal government.[35]

But more importantly, *Administering Freedom* pushes beyond the parsing of predictable racial disparities within the Pension Bureau to comprehend the emerging federal welfare state as a fundamentally exclusionary program. The basic issue, in other words, was not that the bureau needed racially prescribed policies and practices to close the racial disparity gaps but that the institution itself militated against universality. From its earliest days, the Civil War bounty and pension system was bewilderingly convoluted, decentralized, privatized, and means-tested; it spawned a massive rent-seeking industry and encouraged the stigmatization of its recipients as unworthy or fraudulent, all of which guaranteed that the most exploited in society would be the most exploited at the hands of the state. The Pension Bureau was at once an emblem of Union citizenship and an enduring antidemocratic triumph of the reconstructed nation-state undergirded by the commodification of disability and dependency. For select freedpeople, a pension was an inheritance of betrayal, a token of more radical, universal demands stripped and filtered until the general welfare was rendered into a tenuous contractual obligation with limited liability. Though a lifeline to thousands of emancipated families, and pursued tenaciously for decades, highly conditional federal benefits were a pale substitute for the promises of their embattled yet reciprocal wartime alliance.

What follows is a statist history of emancipation and Reconstruction as experienced by tens of thousands of ordinary freedpeople. It is a history with a large cast of characters but without a single protagonist. It is a history of the Freedmen's Bureau, the Freedmen's Branch, and the Pension Bureau, told not simply from the top, and not simply from the bottom, but in a fraught dialogue where administrators challenged claimants and claimants challenged administrators. It is a history of atomization in the face of collective struggle, and collective struggle in the face of atomization. It is a history of how former slaves acquired the status of documented and rights-bearing citizens, of how the enslaved seized freedom and how "freedom" seized them. It is a history as yet untold but one that, in the end, we may already be familiar with because it is a history that remains with us.

CHAPTER ONE

What Is Left of the Bureau

This story begins with an ending. The year 1872 saw the termination of the Freedmen's Bureau, a remarkable federal welfare agency, the first of its kind, designed to usher the newly emancipated into the free labor system while devoting special resources and attention to those who fell behind. Its closure came as no surprise. One only had to look at the increasingly halfhearted attempts to defend the temporary agency and the bipartisan assaults upon it to anticipate its eventual collapse. Or one could view the bureau not from the halls of national power but rather from its embattled outposts scattered across the post-Confederate South, once bastions of federal authority buttressed by the U.S. Army, now dwindling in number, personnel, and potency as the months dragged on. From every angle, and from all sorts of onlookers, the Freedmen's Bureau awaited a fate largely "foredoomed to failure," in the words of W. E. B. Du Bois.[1] The death of the Freedmen's Bureau forecasted another ending. Though the formal end of Reconstruction would not arrive until 1877, it, too, already appeared certain by the early years of the 1870s as the dual demobilizations of the Freedmen's Bureau and the U.S. Army sped the ambitious federal project toward an inauspicious conclusion. With the two institutions of Reconstruction gone, the Democratic insurgency began to retake state governments.

To generations of historians, the brief and captivating life of the Freedmen's Bureau has functioned as a prism of Reconstruction, embodying all of its promises and perils. In many ways out of place in the nineteenth century, the bureau chartered a great experiment in social welfare, Black citizenship, and an activist federal government. Historical appraisals of the Freedmen's Bureau have shifted considerably in the last several decades. At the birth of the historical profession in the early twentieth century, the Dunning School portrayed Reconstruction as an utter failure, not because the project fell short but because it was attempted at all. Dunningites spun Reconstruction as a fanatical attempt to artificially elevate an inferior race to political and social equality, with disastrous results.[2] Beginning in the 1960s, fully one hundred years after the bureau's inception, and more than fifty years after Du Bois's opening shot against the prevailing demonization of Reconstruction, historians reversed course and criticized the bureau for its complicity in reinstating forms of exploitation against the newly freed.[3] Despite recognizing its early radical potential—especially its authority to redistribute land to former slaves—many historians who have focused on its ignominious role in forcing the emancipated back on their former owners' estates, and thereafter enforcing the ensuing unfavorable labor contracts, came to see the agency as fundamentally conservative and paternalistic, bent on social control, and working at cross-purposes to the aims and aspirations of freedpeople. A third shift began some two decades ago. Although these scholars remain attentive to the many shortcomings and limitations of the bureau, they have tempered their judgments by acknowledging the significant role the agency played in the lives of those freedpeople who engaged it and the spectrum of possibilities it represented to agents and freedpeople alike. Long criticized as an instrument for controlling freedpeople, the Freedmen's Bureau is now widely regarded as an imperfect federal institution of many minds and motives but above all decisively lacking the muscle to enforce a more transformative program.[4]

The recent scholarly emphasis on state capacity provides a useful way to approach the Freedmen's Bureau, especially when one considers the bureau's final, attenuated days. Indeed, for all the attention the Freedmen's Bureau has rightly garnered, comparatively little of it extends beyond 1867, as the defeated agency largely consigned itself to the settlement of claims, a seemingly unremarkable task. We have therefore missed a vital part of the story of emancipation and, indeed, the very struggle for Black citizenship waged by the formerly enslaved themselves, for the way in which the bureau closed had important implications for the parameters of citizenship in the new nation-state. Unanticipated by its architects and long underappreciated, freedpeople saw in the Freedmen's Bureau a channel, albeit an increasingly narrow one, in which to press their claims for federal benefits when redistributive land reform was no longer a possibility. They did so by the tens of thousands. And in so doing, they not only prolonged their engagement with the nearest arm of the federal government but also began to fashion new political identities for themselves as documented citizens.[5]

A New Lease on Freedom

What the Freedmen's Bureau could expect to encounter in 1865 the U.S. Army had been, in some measure, confronting since the earliest days of the war, when enslaved men and women absconded their slave labor camps and made the perilous journey to the camps of the U.S. Army. These new arrivals occupied an ambiguous status, not quite enslaved, not quite free. A condition of statelessness greeted their emergence from bondage. Thousands of Black refugees thus endeavored for belonging, not only in their communities, among kith and kin, but within a powerful state that could protect them and they could protect in turn, what historian Chandra Manning calls a "mutually beneficial alliance," one "predicated upon membership reciprocity, and interdependence." Their actions forced the issue of their emancipation well before most political leaders comfortably endorsed it. In fact, historians are only beginning to rightly credit freedpeople themselves for necessitating a change in federal policy regarding their status, for making their return under the Fugitive Slave Act of 1850 not only legally untenable but strategically detrimental to the Union war effort. Congress responded in turn by passing two Confiscation Acts, in August 1861 and July 1862, the first prohibiting the return of enslaved people previously set to work behind Confederate lines, and the second nullifying the property rights of any disloyal enslaver.[6]

The intricacies of these two acts seem to have had little register with enslaved people plotting escape. Instead, these prime movers of emancipation listened to widely circulating rumors regarding the receptivity of particular Union army encampments. By the end of the war, nearly five hundred thousand self-emancipated people risked their lives to put themselves before Union authority, where they acquired the legalistic, morally objectionable status of "contrabands." Approximately 200,000 ex-slave refugees weathered the war in the Upper South, 50,000 in the Southeast, 100,000 in southern Louisiana, and 125,000 in the Mississippi Valley. These areas came under Union control during the course of the rebellion, in large part because of the density of the enslaved population. And these lands would supply, by enlistment or impressment, the vast majority of Black soldiers to the Union, staging, in the decades to follow, the most prominent struggles for Black citizenship.[7]

Whether they entered a more stable refugee camp in the east or found a more provisional encampment in the dynamic western theater, Black refugees could expect to be put to work. In fact, critical support for the earliest refugee camps owed in large part to the federal government's recognition of the potential usefulness of its self-emancipated inhabitants. The Mississippi Valley, with its seven hundred thousand enslaved people, quickly emerged as a critical region for the management of Black refugees. Early in the war, they began entering Union lines in such numbers that the War Department appointed a general superintendent of contrabands in November 1862, Chaplain John Eaton of Ohio. Awestruck by the sheer number of freedom-seeking refugees, which he likened to "the arrivals of cities," the chaplain reckoned they had no "Moses to lead, nor plan in their exodus." Though ignorant of

Black workers at the quartermaster's wharf. Union forces took control of Alexandria in late May 1861. Soon thereafter, hundreds of Black Virginians fled to the city. Many began performing military-adjacent labor for the U.S. Army, as depicted in this image of Black workers along the waterfront, not far from the city's once-prominent slave markets. (Library of Congress Prints and Photographs Division, LC-B8184-440)

their sophisticated and purposefully covert communication networks, Eaton nevertheless came to appreciate how these refugees from slavery "felt that their interests were identical with the objects of our armies." From the first, they proved able and willing to provide "information for the guidance of campaigns," as well as "laborers for the various staff departments," men "worthy of a soldier's pay and honor."[8]

Overseeing an area funneling from southern Illinois to southern Arkansas, Eaton appointed David O. McCord medical director in December 1863 and, together with an inspector of freedmen, soon organized an agency known as the Mississippi Freedmen's Department. A direct precursor to the Freedmen's Bureau—it would fold seamlessly into the latter's Mississippi office in the summer of 1865—the Mississippi Freedmen's Department worked to provide medical assistance, shelter, clothing, food, and education to the Black refugees in its charge. In the dozens of refugee camps throughout the Mississippi Valley, freedpeople set to work harvesting, cooking, cleaning, chopping, hauling, building, and gravedigging. Instead of wages, they more frequently received permission to remain in the camps. "Not a cent of money," Eaton proudly reported, "has ever been drawn from Government, for the Freedmen, on any account." Their labor paid for itself. The point merited constant repetition in reports and speeches. After all, even the most ardent supporters of the rights of freedpeople, including the Radical Charles Sumner, had to assure a skeptical public that "the freedom that has been conferred must be rendered useful, or at least saved from being a burden." The national government, in other words, granted the formerly enslaved the freedom to support themselves.[9]

When Vicksburg fell in July 1863, the Union gained control of the Mississippi Valley. It precipitated a new attitude and purpose regarding the Black population inside and outside of the region's refugee camps, including the ones that had already formed nearby the Gibraltar of the Confederacy immediately after its surrender. The Emancipation Proclamation, issued on the first of January that year, had lifted any remaining prohibitions against enrolling formerly enslaved men into the U.S. Army, but it was only with the newly won control of the Mississippi that the valley's Union commanders could begin organizing and enlisting Black troops in earnest. Just months before, one official recalled how "it was the uniform practice in the country to execute summarily all able-bodied negroes who were taken attempting to make their escape to our lines." Nearly two dozen such men were reportedly murdered that summer within forty miles of Natchez. Ever present, the danger abated somewhat with Union control of the valley, and thereafter the region's refugee camps became effective recruiting stations for the U.S. Colored Troops (USCT). General Lorenzo Thomas, who had arrived in March, instructed his officers to mobilize able-bodied Black men into the ranks. Some 237 agents fanned out across the land, with special authorizations to enter slave labor camps and homesteads and spread news of the president's proclamation to the newly freed. These agents enlisted thousands of ex-slaves into the U.S. Colored Troops, about twenty-one thousand by the end of 1863. Not infrequently were the ranks filled by threats and the forcible conscription of freedmen reluctant to leave their families to suffer retribution from enslavers or otherwise suffer themselves in military service. General Thomas became an imposing agent of emancipation, traveling throughout the theater delivering speeches to potential Black recruits, urging them to submit to the army of liberation.[10]

Yet it was not only able-bodied Black men that the U.S. forces mobilized. They sought to mobilize the entire valley against the enslavers' rebellion. This involved not only the massive military recruitment campaigns throughout the summer and fall, and the simmering resistance among the as-yet enslaved still on their slave labor camps, but also the strategic dispersal of encamped refugees to the abandoned or confiscated lands in the Cotton Kingdom. These once venerable "plantations" were to be leased out to Northern capitalists and aspiring planters who then had the responsibility of providing food, clothing, and wages to their ex-slave employees. The army would then dispatch a team of commissioners to supervise the operations. This plan theoretically relieved the government of the mass of refugees. It enabled freedpeople "to support themselves" while providing a "useful service" to the war effort, in the eyes of Edwin Stanton, the secretary of war. Thomas agreed. He devised his own scheme not only to employ men in "our Armies as laborers and teamsters," if not soldiers, but also to have "the women and children placed on the abandoned plantations to till the ground." Women, children, and nonfighting men thus found themselves conscripted into the Union's grand military strategy, integral as they were to not only occupying the land but making it profitable to help finance the war.[11]

Refugee camp superintendents sought a docile workforce. Writing from Vicksburg in late July 1863, one surgeon reported on the refugees remaining in his charge. "They are the families of soldiers and others, and consist of women, children, and worn out old men," he noted, the vast majority being children "who suffer very much from exposure and want of proper protection." From his brief time in the slave South, the surgeon had heard of how "the most successful and wealthy planters, allow no old persons to be entirely idle, but keep them occupied at such light work as may be suitable to their years of strength." This applied to children and mothers just as it did to the elderly, whom planters regarded as "still able, during the short periods of their existence, to do light work of some kind." These parables had a seductively pragmatic appeal and found a receptive audience with federal officials charged with managing the labor of ex-slave refugees. Northern-born superintendents and physicians often eagerly adopted the conceits of the old enslavers, evaluating health in relation to one's laboring potential.[12]

Lorenzo Thomas hoped to outsource the army's refugee problem. To that end, he relocated nondrafted refugees of all ages and abilities to plantations throughout the Mississippi Valley, at times in reckless violation of the Second Confiscation Act's prohibition of returning the self-emancipated to rebel enslavers. Thomas also adopted a labor program similar to those already underway in Union-occupied areas of Virginia, South Carolina, and nearby Louisiana under the command of General Benjamin Butler and General

Nathaniel P. Banks. With the contract lease system, nondrafted freedmen and able-bodied freedwomen would be put to work for wages on government-leased plantations after signing contracts with their new employers. These new employers could sometimes be their old enslavers if those employers happened to be "loyal" and happened to operate a plantation in a parish or county exempted from the Emancipation Proclamation. The entire contract lease system grew from recommendations made by enslavers themselves to Butler and Banks. It allowed both Unionist enslavers and Northern lessees to maintain productivity and control while averting any revolutionary change to the antebellum labor system. As if designed for abuse, the contract lease system only added to the confusion, frustration, and exploitation of Black refugees who frequently registered complaints about a return to slavery, or worse. After widespread agitation by freedpeople, Stanton dispatched an investigator who reported that the leasing arrangements, when coupled with excessive policing and mobility restriction, indeed betrayed a "tendency to establish a system of serfdom." Yet so far as it pulled Black workers from the miserable "contraband depots" and pushed them onto the plantations, it had this investigator's qualified approval.[13]

In September 1863, Thomas issued Special Order No. 63, which established a system of wages to be used when employing Black refugees on government-leased plantations. It suggested only seven dollars per month for male workers and five dollars for women. Part of the order also levied a 10-percent tax on wages over six dollars per month which went toward "providing for the sick and otherwise dependent" in the lessee's workforce. "It was thought," remarked Eaton, "that the negroes would submit to its collection with reluctance." But "the negro soon saw in it his first recognition by Government; and although it appeared in the form of a burden, responded to it with alacrity," and "freely acknowledged that they ought to assist in bearing the burthen of the poor." Eaton marveled at the untaught "public spirit of the freedmen." Thousands reportedly found in Thomas's new system "the first assurance of any power protecting their right to make a bargain and hold the white man to its fulfillment." Historian Steven Hahn and others have shown how the communal-mindedness of freedpeople had deep roots in the days of bondage and would continue to define Black political struggles in the days to come. For the time being, however, the bare livelihoods of the wartime refugees were still very much in doubt.[14]

After Vicksburg's fall, the Western Sanitary Commission (WSC) extended its activities to the relief of refugees. The WSC was a benevolent association committed to mitigating the health crises of Union troops. The commission's agents regularly toured the region, reported on conditions, lobbied Washington, and coordinated relief efforts with various Northern philanthropic organizations. Despite having once regarded the Black refugee crisis as "incidental" to its original mission of aiding soldiers, the WSC nevertheless "felt itself called to devote a portion of its labors to the relief of forty thousand freedmen" found along the Mississippi River, the men, women, and children "dying of exposure, hardship, and disease" in and around Eaton's camps and throughout the towns abutting the river. In Helena, Arkansas, the commission's president, James E. Yeatman, found that "the able-bodied had been worked very hard" by military commanders and "many of them never received any compensation," in part because their new Union taskmasters had taken "no account of their names or labor." The same dire state of affairs "under an arbitrary military rule" could be found up and down the Mississippi. The WSC reported shameful accounts of neglect, mismanagement, and coerced, unpaid labor. "They do not realize that they are free men," explained Yeatman after questioning "thousands" of the "poorly paid, poorly fed, and not doctored." "They say that they are told they are [free men], but then they are taken and hired out by men who treat them, so far as providing for them is concerned, far worse than their 'secesh' masters did." Moreover, by conscripting the able-bodied men for service, the military left "their wives and children, for a time, unprovided for." Though Yeatman conceded the exigencies of the moment, he nevertheless maintained that the government must devise a new plan to better "exercise a wholesome guardianship over these new-born children of freedom," to "guide, direct and protect them . . . to make them realize that they are freemen," and to vindicate the free labor system in the process.[15]

Secretary of the Treasury Salmon P. Chase read Yeatman's report on the widespread abuses of the contract lease system and intervened to assume control of the valley's abandoned lands, wresting some measure of authority from Lorenzo Thomas and the War Department. Chase decided to implement a new program, one devised by Yeatman himself. The new arrangement introduced important regulatory changes to the existing contract lease system. In addition to recommending the leasing of parceled plantations directly to freedmen, the program authorized the creation of "infirmary farms" or "home farms."[16] As Yeatman's collaborating Treasury agent, William P. Mellen, explained, the infirmary farms were "designed as places of temporary labor for those who are not otherwise employed, and for the labor of such as cannot be serviceable to ordinary planters; also for children, and the aged and infirm, without other homes." Anyone looking to hire a laborer from an infirmary farm would be required to apply to the proper superintendent to oversee the contract. The program also required superintendents to ensure that employers provided sufficient food and shelter and that the superintendents "register" and "grade" each laborer on the farm "according to their ability."[17]

Although the centrifugal forces of military policy and the leasing system significantly emptied the refugee camps of the Mississippi Valley, the camps remained focal points for freedom-seeking refugees. Meanwhile, the Treasury Department officially assumed control from the War Department over the affairs of Black workers in the region. A directive issued by Chase in July 1864 revised Thomas's starvation-wage system, offering significantly higher wages graded according to Yeatman's proposal. Under the new Treasury rubric, the monthly allowances for men were twenty-five, twenty, and fifteen dollars, for grades one to three, respectively, and for women, eighteen, fourteen, and ten dollars. As for those people too sick, old, or otherwise "unfit for regular labor," their exact contributions fell to the discretion of the superintendents. Chase's directive constituted the federal government's first foray into standardizing payment schemes based on working ability. Without enforcement mechanisms, however, the wages established by the Treasury could be no more than recommendations, and planter-lessees regularly ignored them, reaching instead their own agreements with freedpeople. In stark contrast to the "public spirit" Eaton noted among the refugees, their new employers balked at the payment and provisioning of Black workers, and frequently evaded their responsibilities to the disabled and dependent they so regrettably found under their charge.[18]

To defend the leased plantations of the valley, General Thomas raised two regiments of Black soldiers, the Ninth and Seventh Louisiana Volunteers, in October and November 1863. Soon rechristened the Sixty-Third and Sixty-Fourth USCT, the regiments had orders to protect the infirmary and home farms. The Black men composing these two regiments "were of a lower physique than that which is acceptable in the regular army," according to Eaton, but still deemed physically competent for garrison duties and resisting attacks from the rebel guerrilla bands. The so-named colored invalid corps incorporated the Treasury's contraband superintendents into the command of the regiments, giving the new contract leasing program a sense of unity, independence, and power. As commander of the Sixty-Third, Eaton later recalled with pride the humble service of these men. Though "debarred by physical incapacity from the more heroic campaigns endured by their brothers," they nonetheless gave their full measure of devotion to the cause.[19]

By the spring of 1864, the Treasury lost its grip on the leasing program. Part of the reason stemmed from jurisdictional disputes between the two executive departments vying for control. Conflicting authority generated an embarrassing and costly amount of confusion. One inspector called the administrative turf wars over freedpeople's affairs "a most absurd state of things," and he believed "the chances would be better if the whole thing were under one system of management, than to have it beating about, as it is to-day, between the Treasury and the War Departments." Eaton and Thomas soon regained control from the Treasury. Although the Treasury maintained the assignment of leasing abandoned slave labor camps, oversight of Black workers and refugees reverted to the military. After all, only the military had the power to physically compel compliance. Eaton thus argued that the only proper home for care of freedpeople belonged with the War Department. "These people, like whites in and around the army," he explained to Medical Director McCord, "must be under martial law. The War Department, under these circumstances, alone can administer and execute justice." Eaton foresaw the enduring need of freedpeople to have a well-defended garrison nearby, serving also as a hospital, dispensary, and rationing and supply center, as only the military could provide. And he endorsed the widely circulating idea of an "Emancipation Bureau," housed in the War Department, "to meet the necessity."[20]

The administrative struggle between the Treasury and War Departments hardly resolved itself by the spring of 1864, when Thomas Eliot of Massachusetts introduced a bill providing for such a bureau. Lawmakers fought over the new agency's proper home. The status of the "Emancipation Bureau" as either a civil or a military agency mattered a great deal, for it would set the parameters for the bureau's authority, power, and longevity. On the one side, Eliot argued, along with Eaton and other military leaders, that the existing labor arrangements now overseen entirely by the army ought to continue after the end of hostilities. The bill accordingly contained no explicit provisions for distributing land to freedpeople when it passed the House in March 1864. On the other side, Charles Sumner led the Radical Republicans' efforts in the Senate to place the new bureau under the auspices of the Treasury, thereby facilitating the Radicals' postwar goal of expanding Black land-ownership through a widespread redistribution of the Treasury's confiscated lands and, at the very least, ensuring that the bureau might have a more permanent character as a decidedly civil agency. In advocating for this measure, Sumner divided freedpeople into two main categories of laborers, military and agricultural. "The first class is already provided for," he argued, referring to the nearly one hundred thousand Black soldiers already enlisted by the summer of 1864. These men were "all naturally and logically under the charge of the War Department; nor do they need the superintendence of the proposed bureau. The act of Congress equalizing their condition in the Army of the United States is better for them than any bureau." And to that "other larger class, consisting in the main of women and children and farm laborers, who must find employment on the abandoned lands," they must likewise "come under the charge of the Department which has charge of the abandoned lands." Their well-being, and indeed the promise of emancipation, Sumner argued, depended on their secure connection to the land now temporarily held by the Treasury.[21]

The Radicals lost. On March 3, 1865, in the waning days of the rebellion, Congress established the Bureau of Refugees, Freedmen, and Abandoned Lands as a temporary agency within the War Department. But the passage of the Freedmen's Bureau Act did not end the jurisdictional tug of war between the two departments. It would instead return to the fore when, in just three years' time, the bureau's activities devolved to the payment of claims to Black veterans and heirs in the former slave states. By then, the hopes, promises, and potential for the redistribution of land under the stewardship of the Freedmen's Bureau were all but extinguished. Even in the midst of such revolutionary upheaval and radical potential, these reversals could have been anticipated. The bureau's charter authorized the division of abandoned or confiscated lands to freedpeople and "loyal refugees," meaning whites, and allowed them to rent from the government "not more than forty acres of such land" for three years, after which "the occupants of any parcels so assigned may purchase the land and receive such title thereto as the United States can convey." As implied by the ambiguous language in the final clause, the government's titles to its wartime possessions were anything but legally unassailable. Just as importantly, because the Freedmen's Bureau was designed to be a self-supporting agency—its operations funded by its own profits—in the end its most viable source of revenue was the rental and sale of its landholdings. Alongside conservative traits inherited from its wartime predecessors, the Freedmen's Bureau seemed from its inception an imperfect vehicle to realize the full promise of emancipation.[22]

The Freedmen's Bureau initially operated under a one-year charter. Its short tenure betrayed a monumental task, one that had vexed, stymied, and countermanded the antislavery cause for generations, that of orchestrating the transition from slavery to freedom. Freedmen's Bureau officials held varied responsibilities, from administering material aid through medical treatment and rations to mediating labor contracts and creating and staffing schools. To its officials in outposts across the South also fell the task of reporting on daily "outrages" perpetrated against freedpeople, often pleading for military assistance, often waiting in vain. Over time the bureau would exasperate and disappoint freedpeople as often as it would serve and empower. Perpetually understaffed, the poorly coordinated administrative structure and overlapping or ill-defined jurisdiction also hampered the bureau's functioning. All of these factors ensured that the agency would execute its duties idiosyncratically at best across the 750,000 square miles of the occupied South, frustrating the ambitions of its agents and officials, including its commissioner, Oliver Otis Howard, but most of all its "clients." Nevertheless, the creation of the Freedmen's Bureau marked a significant departure in the story of American citizenship, initiating as it did a more direct relationship between the U.S. government and its citizens, made all the more striking by the fact that the agency's principal beneficiaries had been enslaved just months prior—and in March 1865, many still were. For those freedpeople who enjoyed proximity to these custodians of freedom, the once imaginary connection to a distant ruler or government collapsed and coalesced in the Freedmen's Bureau official, embodying if not essentially becoming "the government."[23]

As implied by its official title, the Bureau of Refugees, Freedmen, and Abandoned Lands would provide relief to all needy Southerners devastated by the war, white and Black alike. But its public face quickly became tied to former slaves, and for that reason increasingly stigmatized and harassed. For example, from October 1865 to October 1866, a year marred by widespread crop failures, the Freedmen's Bureau distributed over 683,000 rations in the state of Georgia alone, with roughly 178,000 going to white "refugees" and 505,000 to freedpeople. Critics worried about some of these rations finding their way to undeserving mouths, above all to a growing class of disaffected freedpeople entirely dependent on the government for subsistence. In an annual report to Congress, the bureau's assistant commissioner for the state, Davis Tillson, would take pains to deny the ubiquitous charge that the bureau provided food to able-bodied freedmen who simply refused to work. Many of the bureau's defenders made clear that they supported the agency precisely because it aided white people as well as Black. As one congressman noted, by March 1868 the bureau had already issued over a quarter of its eighteen million rations to destitute whites. Seldom did critics target white refugees when attacking what they regarded as an unconstitutional abridgment of white rule in the postwar South. Conjuring as it did issues of dependency, racial equality, and government spending, the Freedmen's Bureau would prove a lightning rod of political controversy, symbolizing for many the entire project of Reconstruction writ small.[24]

The task before the Freedmen's Bureau was immense, and its authority broad. Despite the assumed Republican control of the bureau's fate during Congressional Reconstruction, the agency would forever suffer from a chronic lack of manpower, which stemmed in part from a lack of funding, and that from a lack of will among lawmakers. Despite its large presence in the popular mind, few critics truly regarded the bureau as formidable. For their part, the bureau's agents felt its limitations whenever they found themselves overworked, understaffed, beset, or simply confused. Many regrettably grew inimical to the very idea of their agency. The freedpeople who sought the bureau's aid also keenly felt its lack of enforcement capabilities. At the end of 1865, with President Andrew Johnson still in control of the Reconstruction project, the Freedmen's Bureau had a mere 799 officers, agents, and clerks across the former Confederacy and border states. It would increase to its peak employment by the end of 1868 under the phase of Congressional Reconstruction but still only boasted some 900 men, 348 of whom were clerks. By 1869, only 158 bureau employees remained. Over its entire lifespan, some 2,441 men served in the Freedmen's Bureau, and its agents increasingly relied on civil magistrates as ex officio bureau agents. Mississippi had only a dozen agents operating in 1866, and Alabama never had more than twenty agents working at any given time. William Tecumseh Sherman, never one to mince words, had warned O. O. Howard in May 1865 that the commissioner did not have the "power to fulfill one-tenth of the expectations of those who framed the Bureau."[25]

Restoration and Removal

From the Mississippi Valley to the Upper South to the Sea Islands, refugee camps at the time of Confederate surrender sheltered many thousands of freedpeople. Some even arrived after the war. Folks who had remained on their labor camps for the duration of the conflict thereafter found it safe to venture to cities and towns or encampments, seeking to reunite with lost, and perhaps long-lost, family members. Unable to find work, or waiting for special dispensation from the government, the denizens of places such as Camp Nelson, Kentucky; Roanoke Island, North Carolina; and Taylor's Farm in Virginia depended on provisions and protection from bureau officials and accordingly embedded themselves within the federal encampments. Among them were hundreds of wives and relatives of men who enlisted in the U.S.

Colored Troops, which recruited heavily from refugee camps and whose officers pledged government support to their families. They now waited on promises just as much as provisions.[26]

During the war, Black soldiers separated from their loved ones, especially those in the loyal slaveholding states, worried constantly about the threat of reenslavement. "Colored men who enlisted in the service here," protested an army officer from Missouri, "left their wives and families, with the assurance, that their reenslavement was impossible. Civil officers are now returning them, to their owners." In Vicksburg, one of Eaton's subordinates reported how "colored soldiers have complained most bitterly about the way they have been treated, by their wives being taken away from them and sent they knew not to what camp or plantation." He found it ethically imperative "to provide homes for the families of their men; since, when enlisting them, they promised them protection." Freedwomen themselves did not shy from invoking the implied contract of their husbands' enlistment. In late 1866, a group of nineteen freedwomen still living at Taylor's Farm near Norfolk wrote to the editor of the *New York Tribune*, Horace Greeley. As soldiers' wives of the Thirty-Eighth USCT, they explained how, when their husbands enlisted, they left behind "their relatives and friends to be 'cared for' by our beneficent Government." Now they feared that their husbands had been fighting expressly so "that the white man's government should be preserved." What else could they make of the scenes before them, with estates rapidly returning to unreconstructed rebels when "the families of those who fell in the great struggle for human rights are now being made homeless?" From positions of vulnerability, freedwomen leveraged their status as Black soldiers' wives to demand federal protection.[27]

Though the Thirteenth Amendment abolished slavery in December 1865, the issue of freedpeople's citizenship remained undefined until the Fourteenth Amendment in 1868. That ambiguity would play an important role in freedpeople's struggles for land, labor, and justice. No longer enslaved, hundreds of thousands of freedpeople could find themselves as effectively stateless persons lacking a discrete, defensible legal personality, not unlike their former status as wartime refugees. Those with the strongest claims for national citizenship, formerly enslaved soldiers and their wives, wasted no time in pressuring officials for land of their own, the surest—and most foundational—hope for autonomy. Members of one Black regiment in the lower Mississippi Valley pooled together their earnings, some $50,000, and applied to purchase "four or five of the largest plantations on the Mississippi," reported Thomas Conway, the bureau's assistant commissioner for Louisiana. Conway noted that many other regiments were "making similar arrangements." He was in "constant receipt of communications from companies and squads of these soldiers" inquiring about purchasing land. "This interest in the soil is general with these soldiers," Conway noted. "At the expiration of their terms of service they all want small farms." Among the more sympathetic of the bureau's ten assistant commissioners, Conway argued forcefully that Black soldiers could, and should, "purchase every inch of confiscated and abandoned land in the hands of the Government in this State." Thaddeus Stevens, the Radical Republican and fearless champion of Black rights, proposed a wholesale confiscation of the slave labor camps of some seventy thousand "arch-traitors," who together held about 394 million acres of land, about forty million of which he hoped to distribute to freedpeople by giving every adult freedman forty acres. The remaining 354 million acres could be parceled into farms and sold, with the proceeds helping to finance Union pensions.[28]

The government's lands in Louisiana were among the nearly nine hundred thousand acres actually under the bureau's control in the spring of 1865, enough to provide homesteads to twenty-three thousand families. The timing of Confederate surrender and the creation of the Freedmen's Bureau inspired widely ramifying rumors of land redistribution, particularly in areas of long-standing Union occupation. To the chagrin of Everard Green Baker, in October 1865 the enslaved men and women on his Mississippi labor camp refused to sign contracts. "They expect the government to furnish them with land stock &c &c next year," sneered Baker, "& consequently will not agree to hire for next year." Refugee camps became rumor mills, grinding out expectations of massive land redistribution to the loyal freedpeople. Northern whites attached to the camps frequently advocated land redistribution, as did some commissioned white officers of Black units. Among the latter, George Hepworth, upon witnessing scores of Black refugees "crowding within our lines," receiving "three-quarters of a ration per day," with children "dying in frightful numbers" and the people generally without work or hope and "living in the most unhealthy localities," argued that the "best thing to do was to enlist all the able-bodied men, confiscate every plantation in the department, and, dividing land up into twenty-acre lots, give each black family one such lot, and let them try the experiment of free labor for themselves." Black soldiers, who made up better than one-third of the occupying force, some eighty-five thousand servicemen, were the rumor's most enthusiastic circulators. Officials often noted that, with Black regiments stationed nearby, a "majority of the colored population" in the states of Mississippi, Tennessee, and Alabama "positively believed that the government would take the plantations, with their old masters who had been in rebel service, cut them up into forty acre parcels, and give them to the colored people." This official, Clinton B. Fisk, when marching to the Gulf, had witnessed his own troops spread word "that we were to give them the plantations and make them the lords of the soil hereafter." Planters, for their part, made similar complaints about Black soldiers, blaming the irrepressible rumors of land redistribution to be the reason for freedpeople's reluctance to enter into labor contracts.[29]

Yet even sympathetic officials of the Freedmen's Bureau predisposed to favor land redistribution found themselves compelled to dispossess freedpeople from their old wartime camps, encouraging if not coercing them into labor contracts with planters. President Johnson pardoned ex-rebels en masse in his Amnesty Proclamation of May 29, 1865, save for those great planters with $20,000 or more in taxable property. In so doing, he effectively restored their legal title to all confiscated property except, that is, their human chattel. When Commissioner Howard issued a directive stipulating that such amnesty did not apply to the landholdings of the Freedmen's Bureau, Johnson ordered Howard to reverse his earlier policy and begin denationalizing the bureau's lands. In September, Howard's Circular No. 15 performed the coup de grâce, voiding most of the federal government's claims to these lands and halting any further efforts by bureau commissioners and agents from selling these lands to freedpeople. In the case of Taylor's Farm, the return of the "old Rebel" brought certain demands and predictable resentments. The recently pardoned Confederate major William E. Taylor promptly ordered all the men who had served in the Union army off his land by November 1, 1866. According to the wives of men still in service, about one hundred such families faced eviction. They included women such as Jane R. Stageman. With her husband serving in Texas, Stageman had arrived at Taylor's Farm in May 1864 after an agent of the Freedmen's Bureau relocated her "there to remain and be cared for until the return of her said husband." She had not received any rations in over a year.[30]

The women of Taylor's Farm were not alone. Faced with dispossession and eviction, encamped freedpeople across the South mobilized themselves and sought allies wherever they could. They turned to Freedmen's Bureau officials, Northern missionaries, freedmen's aid society representatives, and Union army field commanders. In mid-1865, a group of soldiers from the Thirty-Sixth USCT begged to Howard to protect their families at Roanoke Island, North Carolina. Richard Ethridge, William Benson, and others had been promised "that our wifes and family's should receive rations from goverment. The rations for our wifes and family's have been (and are now cut down) to one half the regular ration. Consequently three or fours days out of every ten days, thee have nothing to eat." When they appealed to the superintendent at Roanoke Island, they found someone "who says that he is no part of a Abolitionist"—a man who "takes no notice of their actual suffering." Moreover, the colony was home to a substantial number of discharged soldiers carrying wounds and afflictions from the war. These men, the petitioners complained, "cannot get any rations and are not able to work, some soldiers are sick in Hospitals that have never been paid a cent and their familys are suffering." The men of the Thirty-Sixth asked for a change in bureau personnel, hoping to effect a change of policy and a change of heart.[31]

One delegation of Black men from Camp Nelson petitioned President Johnson in late 1865 to keep a military presence and martial law in the commonwealth. Exempted from the Emancipation Proclamation by virtue of having retained its civil status, in the months before the ratification of the Thirteenth Amendment, Kentucky occupied "the only Spot within all the bounds of these United States, where the People of colour Have No rights *whatever* Either in Law or in fact—and w[h]ere the Strong arm of Millitary Power no longer to curb" the enmity of Kentucky's ruling class, the petitioners warned. They reminded Johnson of the thousands of Black soldiers Kentucky gave to the Union. Should the federal government "give up the State to the control of her civil authorities there is not one of these Soldiers who will Not Suffer all the grinding oppression of her most inhuman laws," either themselves or "their wives their children and their mothers." For their part, supportive bureau officials would never fail to report on those destitute freedpeople who had relatives in the U.S. Colored Troops. Doing so raised the stakes of government action. Yet the effectiveness of the bureau, as always, hinged on the capacity of its agents, the resources they were able to deploy, and their ability to make their case to the agency's leadership. For instance, bureau agent R. E. Farwell wrote to his superior, Clinton B. Fisk, about the situation at Camp Nelson, which he described as filled with "people just emerged from bondage and nine out of ten represented by Father Husband Son or Brother in the army (and many of them away in Texas) almost all women & children no home no employmt." The reference to soldiers' families was no idle remark by the agent; instead, he intended it to arouse state attention to the plight of Camp Nelson's loyal denizens.[32]

Yet, as with their claims to confiscated lands, freedpeople's "rights" to refugee camps never attained a legally defensible status, undermined as they were at every turn by Johnson's arbitrary proclamations and Howard's dutiful if reluctant executions. Camp Nelson itself would be shut down in late 1865 by

Assistant Commissioner Fisk, a hatchet man when it came to shuttering refugee camps. His strategy had a siege-like simplicity: cut the food supply and the people will disperse. In other cases, natural disasters worked against freedpeople's efforts to maintain standing. For example, the spring of 1865 witnessed a devastating flood that threatened the encampments along the Mississippi River, including the long-standing refugee camp at Helena, Arkansas, located as it was "on the very margin of the river," noted the *Freedmen's Bulletin*. Still, it took a local ordinance passed in August 1865 as well as a public auction to clear out the remaining property. By year's end, the camp at Helena had evaporated along with the floodwaters. Except, that is, for the orphan asylum. The asylum was slated to be dismantled with the rest of the camp. Members of the Fifty-Sixth USCT who had been garrisoned in Helena combined their military savings and purchased thirty acres of land outside the city on which to rebuild the asylum.[33]

While most refugee camps disbanded in the months bookending Confederate surrender, in several instances large Black communities fought to maintain possession of their land well into 1867, thus making some of the bureau's first and final actions ones of forcible dispossession and relocation.[34] Protesting their impeding removal, in late 1865, Joseph Tillett and fifteen other freedmen of Roanoke Island wrote to the assistant commissioner of the bureau, pleading that "if driven to the necessity of leaving their old home, around which cluster many pleasant recollections," they "would be able to earn but a poor living." Their petition was to no avail. In the spring of 1866, Freedmen's Bureau officials began taking measures to break up the colony of freedpeople at Roanoke Island as well as the nearby Trent River colony, where about three thousand freedpeople similarly held onto what any observer would have regarded as their homes, having "built themselves huts or small houses, and mostly support[ing] themselves by thier [sic] own labor in and about New Berne." They lived and labored on land that would soon return to the heirs of a rebel officer killed in the war.[35]

With no alternatives to pursue, bureau officials dismantled the Roanoke and Trent River camps and relocated disabled and dependent freedpeople to what were called poor farms, temporary arrangements "conducted on the same plan as such charitable institutions are at the north." The inspector general reasoned that by "removing the destitute, these camps are broken up, and many will be induced to seek homes among their friends, or for themselves elsewhere." He voiced an emerging consensus when he complained that "the aggregation of the Freedmen in camps or colonies, especially when supported by the Govt, tends to promote idleness and a want of self reliance, and to engender clanishness and keep up an unnecessary distinction between the two races of *American* citizens." Indeed, the head of the bureau in North Carolina had issued an order in November 1865 that any individual who was offered work and refused it only to later seek rations would be arrested and punished. In the fall of 1867, the bureau ordered the dispersal of the freedpeople still occupying some "restored" plantations in Roanoke. After holding a public meeting in December, Tillett—this time with over sixty-five other freedmen—signed a petition to the officer in charge of removal. It reflected a sober assessment of the situation facing the occupying freedpeople. If only the bureau agents could show just "a little leniency" and extend the removal deadline so as not to kick the freedpeople out in the dead of winter, they sadly promised "to vacate every foot of said lands." Such palpable resignation came only after months of life-or-death struggle.[36]

Though halting and chaotic, the restoration of confiscated lands, dismantling of the remaining refugee camps, and dispersal of congregated freedpeople back to the plantations actually resulted in a radical simplification of the Southern landscape. Since the earliest days of the rebellion, wartime conditions generated a raft of communal living and laboring arrangements, with groups operating semiautonomously as in the Sea Islands or variously supervised by federal authorities as elsewhere across the South. One could find all manner of leased plantations, home farms, infirmary farms, and so forth, as well as refugee camps full of freedpeople expecting outright land redistribution. Some freedpeople had even come to call these places "citizen camps." Overlapping possessory titles, claims, promises, and hearsay abounded. But as the final refugee camps disbanded, their unembedded expatriates entered the flattened world of agrocapitalist relations, a contracted realm of employers and employees, planters and laborers, landowners and landless renters. Instead of inaugurating the year of Jubilee, January 1, 1866, saw thousands of freedpeople reluctantly signing labor contracts with white landowners, narrowing the field of economic struggle to skirmishes over wages, shares, and contractual obligations.[37]

Discriminating Relief

With the bureau set to expire after its first year, Republicans in Congress secured passage of its renewal. To the shock of many, Johnson vetoed the second Freedmen's Bureau bill and released a scathing diatribe attacking the agency. Melding together fiscal conservatism and racially charged antistatism, Johnson argued that the Freedmen's Bureau was a patronage-driven engine of dependency for feckless freedpeople, an unconstitutional military holdover in the post-surrender South. Although the bureau was "effective for the protection of freedmen and refugees during the actual continuance of hostilities and of African servitude," Johnson now denounced its renewal for endeavoring to establish "a permanent branch of the public administration, with its powers greatly enlarged." Never before had Congress "deemed itself authorized to expend the public money for the rent or purchase of homes for the thousands, not to say millions, of the white race who are honestly toiling from day to day for their subsistence," blathered Johnson, apparently unaware that the Homestead Act of 1862 did just that for some 1.6 million white settler-colonizers in the "publicly owned" indigenous lands of the trans-Mississippi West. Yet the government could certainly not be justified in doing so for the newly freed in the post-slavery South. Or much of anything. "A system for the support of indigent persons in the United States was never contemplated by the authors of the Constitution," Johnson snarled, "nor can any good reason be advanced why, as a permanent establishment, it should be founded for one class or color of our people more than another." As the prodigal stepson of the planter class, Andrew Johnson seamlessly folded anti-Black racism into antistatism—an enduring recipe for justifying American austerity.[38]

Not ready to fold themselves, Radicals in Congress passed the second Freedmen's Bureau Act over Johnson's veto in July 1866, extending the agency's life for an additional two years, and, the previous month, had also secured passage of the Southern Homestead Act, which attempted to offer Black Southerners what their white counterparts in the American West enjoyed but which ultimately floundered, delivering little to the few Black families who had the capital to pursue land claims. The renewal of the Freedmen's Bureau, though, had important consequences. It differed in several ways from the original authorizing legislation. First, it added the qualifier of loyalty to whom it would serve, stipulating that its "supervision and care . . . shall extend to all loyal refugees and freedmen." It also expanded relief and medical provisions, allowed for the retention of military officers as their regiments demobilized, authorized the payment of salaries to civilian employees of the bureau, and provided extensive regulations designed to protect and compensate freedpeople whose lands had been restored to ex-Confederates by Johnson's proclamation.[39]

Administering relief, rations, and medical care to destitute Southerners proved to be one of the most challenging responsibilities facing the Freedmen's Bureau, ironically worsened by its other responsibility of helping to disband the refugee camps. Such encampments and hospitals had been the primary sites where military officials distributed wartime relief. In anticipation of the twentieth-century "associational state," as formulated by historian Brian Balogh, the national government worked in tandem with private agencies and interest groups to deliver aid to freedpeople, including the Western Sanitary Commission, the U.S. Sanitary Commission, the American Missionary Association (AMA), and the short-lived composite group orchestrated by Commissioner Howard himself known as the Freedmen's Aid Union Commission. The AMA enjoyed a particularly close relationship with the Freedmen's Bureau. At the national level, Howard coordinated with the AMA's head, George Whipple, a personal friend of Howard's. At the local level, many field officers of the bureau enjoyed long-standing, cooperative relationships with AMA superintendents. But in certain circumstances, particularly during the closing of refugee camps, its representatives served as outspoken advocates for Black families cast aside by both planters and bureau agents. At Camp Nelson, for example, freedpeople often called upon Reverend Abisha Scofield of the AMA to intervene on their behalf. Although the AMA continued to coordinate the distribution of relief to dependent freedpeople after the war, the association diverted most of its resources and attention to education.[40]

The bureau itself would follow suit before long. But for the time being, it still bore the responsibility for supporting destitute Southerners, despite trying at all hazards to pass the burden onto freedpeople themselves by encouraging employment contracts, familial support, and, failing these, private charity. "It is not the intention of the Government," Howard quipped, "that the Bureau shall supersede the various benevolent organizations in the work of administering relief. This must still be afforded by the benevolence of the people through their voluntary societies." As the leader of the first federal welfare agency, Howard made quite clear, from the outset, his preference for private charity above all other forms of assistance. Indeed, the commissioner and others feared that a guaranteed system of government relief would undermine the compulsion necessary in a free labor system. One could not truly be free unless entirely thrown upon one's own resources. Howard urged his agents to apply "great discrimination" when it came to administering relief, careful to avoid implying the existence of a skeletal national relief system. In agreement, the bureau's assistant commissioner for Virginia explained, "While I would care, to the utmost extent, for the helpless, I would allow others to feel the spur of necessity, if it be needed to make them self reliant, industrious and provident."[41] Bureau officials accordingly preferred to relocate thousands of freedpeople to the homes of relatives and prospective caretakers or to areas of higher labor demand than to allow them to remain and remain dependent on the government. In an effort to "relieve the government of the support of the indigent," the Freedmen's Bureau transported over twenty-nine thousand freedpeople by March 1869, including roughly 14,600 men, 9,000 women, and 5,700 children. Often these relocation routes—south from Virginia, and west from Georgia, toward the Mississippi Valley—retread the paths of enslaved people in the era of the domestic slave trade, which had its own appetite for able-bodied workers.[42]

At bureau outposts in every ex-slave state, relief lines routinely featured men and women with variously impaired capacities for self-support, including many sick, elderly, orphaned, and disabled. Bureau officials struggled to come up with a working definition of dependency to be applied uniformly across the South. Yet it would always remain elusive and idiosyncratic, governed by the particular perspectives of military officers, bureau agents, and bureau physicians, and local labor market conditions. Although conscientious bureau officials would occasionally acknowledge external forces of dependency such as epidemics or crop failures that caused dependency even among the able-bodied, they increasingly framed these as temporary setbacks rather than systemic problems. As such, they began locating dependency in one's unwillingness to perform labor. As Howard himself affirmed, while the bureau "shall provide for the aged, infirm, and the sick, let us encourage, or if necessary compel, the able-bodied to labor for their own support." This "wholesome compulsion," he later commented, might redound to eventual independence. When pressed with issues of dependency and relief, bureau officials formalized the idea of health as the ability to perform manual labor, washing its slave-market pedigree in the cloudy bath waters of free labor ideology.[43]

Disabled and dependent freedpeople threatened, both materially and ideologically, the Republican Party's program for reconstructing the slave South on the basis of free labor. This project presumed legions of autonomous, able-bodied freedmen would use their unshackled labor power to win gainful employment and economic self-sufficiency for themselves and their families. As historian Jim Downs has shown, Republicans fixated on "the healing power of labor" to at once revitalize Black workers demoralized by bondage, counter long-standing racist attacks, and legitimize the Reconstruction project. Yet their single-minded focus blinded them to the ways in which a wage labor system, especially one instituted in a war-torn region, incubated dependency. Those able to work found no opportunities; those unable to work found a motley system of public and private relief, relocation, and institutionalization. In

Freedmen's Bureau issuing rations. The Freedmen's Bureau provided hundreds of thousands of rations to destitute Southerners but applied "great discrimination," in the words of Commissioner O. O. Howard. This September 1866 sketch in *Frank Leslie's Illustrated Newspaper* depicts the Richmond, Virginia, office of the Freedmen's Bureau just days before the enactment of Howard's Circular No. 10, which virtually ended the bureau's relief-provisioning practices. (Library of Congress Prints and Photographs Division, LC-USZ62-37861)

North Carolina, freedpeople "besieged from morning till night" the bureau's field offices. They arrived in wagons and carts, and "some coming many miles on foot," such that any rations received barely lasted the journey home. Freedpeople soon encountered officials who quickly assessed their physical capacities, determined as they were "that no able-bodied man or woman should receive supplies, except such as were known to be industrious, and to be entirely destitute." With scarce resources at the bureau's disposal, the notion of protecting freedpeople shifted to protecting the government "from imposition" while also attempting "to relieve the really deserving"—in effect, those whose labor was less exploitable.[44]

Across the postwar South, observers reported on planters' assessments of the new order. Around New Orleans in the spring of 1866, one congressman heard candid talk of a "willingness to submit to the principles of the emancipation proclamation" if permitted "an organized system of negro labor which they would control for themselves." The system these former enslavers imagined had two tracks, bifurcated by ability. They argued that because the government "had freed the negroes . . . [it] should be made to take care of the cripples and those who were not able to work, while they could regulate and control the labor of the able-bodied." In fact, the congressman reported they had such confidence in this arrangement—essentially wage slavery for the able-bodied—that they believed it would prove itself superior to the old system of slavery. Planters frequently complained to bureau officials about having to deal with sick and destitute freedpeople. As one Georgia planter put it in a letter to the head of the bureau in Georgia, Davis Tillson, "My Freedmen while slaves have always done well, & I had no trouble, now they do as they will & I cannot control their action." He was especially aggrieved over "a blind man whom I have taken care of for 27 years," and asked incredulously, "What shall I do with him??" The exasperated planter wanted permission to send his disabled ex-slaves away, preferably to Atlanta. But bureau officials, who had so aggressively worked to break up congregations of freedpeople in cities and camps, flatly refused these requests to transport dependent freedpeople to where they would be without familial or institutional care. "The laws of your own State," Tillson responded, "and the orders of the Bureau require you to provide for your worn out, old, and decrepid [*sic*] slaves until the State makes some other provisions to take care of its poor." Tillson offered to send any unwanted able-bodied freedpeople wherever they had secure employment waiting but demanded the ex-enslaver support his former slaves in the case no public relief agency be available.[45]

Freedmen's Bureau officials often viewed systems of relief as temporary embarrassments, an inappropriate undertaking for the federal government and one ill-suited to the cold majesty of a free labor system. Should relief be necessary, it ought to come from local authorities or private associations, they argued, ironically bringing the first federal welfare agency in the United States in line with a centuries' old tradition concerning the obligation of local communities to their "own" poor. Yet the public welfare infrastructure in mid-nineteenth-century America was underdeveloped at all levels, and virtually nonexistent in the antebellum South, owing chiefly to the planters' political control and the intentional paucity of public goods. The obliteration of the slave system also severed the traditional "obligations" of enslavers to provide for their laborers, thereby offering "a relief to their former owners." Since the war's end, bureau officials had pressured civil governments in the South to make provisions for incapacitated former slaves. In May 1866, Howard issued Circular No. 4, wherein he reasoned that "if the county officers or overseers of the poor will adopt the proper measures, the industrial and government farms, which are now so much complained of, can be dispensed with."[46] That August, in Circular No. 10, Howard forced the issue, ordering rations to freedpeople and white refugees to be discontinued by October 1, 1866, except for those residents of bureau hospitals and asylums. Local authorities, in turn, would be notified that care for these individuals now lay in their hands.[47]

Inaction by local civil authorities, widespread crop failures, and a flood of letters and petitions from starving Southerners forced a change to the bureau's policies. In late March 1867, Congress empowered Secretary of War Stanton to spend whatever was reasonably necessary "to prevent starvation and extreme want to any and all classes of destitute or helpless persons in those Southern and Southwestern States where failure of the crops and other causes have occasioned widespread destitution." He authorized the Freedmen's Bureau to conduct this relief program, with the funds already allocated to it. Howard, who set aside $500,000 for the purpose, ordered his assistant commissioners to "enter upon the work of distribution of these supplies," cautioning them as before to "use the utmost care that none but the very destitute received them." For their part, local agents should collaborate with civil authorities to determine exactly how many destitute lay in their jurisdiction. Rations for the famine crisis of 1867 peaked in the month of June at just over five hundred thousand. Though greater than the two hundred thousand or so rations seen the previous October, they still fell far below the 1.4 million rations for the months of June 1866 and June 1865. The decline in rations reflected, in large measure, the bureau's mission of forcing local and state authorities to assume care of the indigent. Billed as an "emergency" measure, famine relief further underscored the temporariness of federal welfare intervention.[48]

Several states, including South Carolina and Mississippi, enacted their own relief measures, though mainly to get rid of nettlesome bureau officials. But rather than incorporating freedpeople into the existing welfare programs for indigent whites, most states created separate systems for Black people funded by taxes leveled solely against the Black community rather than all taxpayers. Moreover, Southern states instituted relief systems as appendages of vagrancy, pauperism, and apprenticeship laws. When local relief systems worked at all in the postbellum South, then, it was in service of subordinating the Black poor and working poor. One bureau agent, writing from Meridian, Mississippi, noted that despite the tax levied for the care of freedpeople in the surrounding counties, most of the "sick old and infirm freedmen" in his district "are provided for by other relitives [sic]." Those who were not, for what-ever reason, applied to the agent "for admitance [sic] into the freedmans Hospital," having been "informed by late employers to go to the Bureau for relief." Freedpeople had already been taxed to prevent this very situation. In fact, the agent felt "certain that the freedmen of this District have paid suffi-cient to support all there [sic] destitute sick."[49]

The spring of 1867 brought not only famine to the already devastated South but a broad reorganization of the federal presence in the region. Re-sponding to widespread abuses of freedpeople countenanced by the Johnson administration, congressional Republicans wanted to bring the uncoopera-tive civil governments under martial law. On March 2, 1867, nearly two years to the day after the creation of the Freedmen's Bureau, Congress passed over Johnson's veto of the Military Reconstruction Act, which divided ten states of the post-Confederate South into five military districts each led by an army commander. The immediate goal of Military Reconstruction was to quell violence against freedpeople, especially around elections, and restore civil au-thority by forcing Southern states to draft appropriate constitutions that guaranteed Black suffrage. Although bureau officials certainly welcomed the military assistance, in practice the measure subordinated the authority of the Freedmen's Bureau by placing its assistant commissioners under the new district commanders—commanders appointed by President Johnson. As Howard's biographer, William McFeely, has astutely noted, the same army that had, in 1865, functioned as a de facto government for freedpeople now absorbed and sublimated an agency specially designated for them. With much of his authority cut out from under him, Howard had no choice but to acquiesce to his agency's impending obsolescence. "I simply conformed to the new law," he admitted, but "it was all the while my steady and avowed purpose, as soon as practicable, to close out one after another the original Bureau divisions"—lands, supplies, courts, and medical establishments. In this, at least, Howard's objectives coincided with those of the district com-manders. Although Military Reconstruction increased the number of U.S. Army outposts in the South, the number of soldiers steadily decreased over 1867, setting in motion the widespread demobilization of occupying forces and an accelerated transition to civil authorities.[50]

Within a year of the Military Reconstruction Act, another famine struck the South. In early January 1868, Howard reported to General Ulysses S. Grant on the cases of destitution flowing into his office across the Southern states. Crop failures, falling cotton prices, and other calamities ensured "that there will be great suffering from want of food in portions of Louisiana,

Mississippi, South Carolina, and in limited sections of other states before the close of the present winter." Despite his long-standing efforts to withdraw relief measures, Howard reluctantly admitted "that relief in some shape must be furnished to prevent the anarchy that many apprehend." Once again, great "care and discrimination" fell upon its recipients. If the bureau offered rations indiscriminately, warned one official in Florida, "nearly all the Freedmen in my dist. would claim that they were entitled to them, and would spend more time trying to prove that . . . than the Rations would be worth." To address the issue and discourage sensibilities of entitlement, in 1868 the bureau implemented a relief system wherein its officials would distribute rations and other relief provisions to planters, not freedpeople. In so doing, the Freedmen's Bureau could not only prevent starvation but also reinforce what it considered the proper relationship of dependence, (Black) employees on (white) employers. Former enslavers thus became nodes of federal relief— and needy freedpeople once again partly dependent on their former enslavers for their livelihoods.[51]

The human forces behind famine, unemployment, and poverty did not diminish over 1868, though the bureau's inclination to ameliorate it certainly did. In the late summer, freedpeople in southern Mississippi experienced "a good deal of sickness" and, when they appealed to their local agent, found that "no means are offered by the Government for the relief of the sick." As the agent noted, "nearly all are without money, and they or thier [sic] families suffer in silence until almost or quite to[o] late for remedy." In his report to the state's assistant commissioner, he explained, "Many cases of sickness have been reported to me, but it is not in the power of this office to furnish any relief." Some six hundred miles away, freedpeople in Aiken, South Carolina, found themselves in a similar situation in the fall of 1868, reliant as they were on charity. Despite his repeated efforts to compel the civil authorities of Barnwell County to "provide for some of the most destitute in this town," the agent there had "but little hope that they can do much if anything for them." The next month, he reported that "nothing has been done by the county officers to provide for the support of the poor" and predicted that "financial embarrassments of the new State Government prevent any effectual method of relief being adopted."[52]

The Freedmen's Bureau contributed mightily to the development of a dual welfare system. With relief distributed only after "careful discrimination" of eligibility, the bureau means-tested its provisioning. As the bureau was a subordinate agency within the War Department whose tenure was temporary and whose funding and political support always tenuous, bureau officials were disposed to collaborate with local civil authorities for distribution of resources in the short term and pressed for their total assumption of poor relief in the long term. In the end, bureau officials relegated themselves to distributing rations in bulk to planters, thereby reinforcing the economic dependency of freedpeople on their employers, a relation grounded in the broader failure of land reform. Finally, as a vestige of federal military authority primarily—but not exclusively—designed to assist freedpeople, Southern whites stigmatized Black recipients of relief as undeserving objects of special privileges from a bloated and corrupt federal government, decrying their inability to control their able-bodied workers. For all its trailblazing potential as the first national welfare agency, the Freedmen's Bureau wound up federalizing traditional poor relief by delegating it to the states and localities—relieving, in the end, the national government of its erstwhile wards.[53]

The Enlistment Bounty Scheme

Despite the undeniable precarity of the relationship, freedpeople understood the value of proximity to representatives of the Freedmen's Bureau no less than that of the U.S. Army. Both institutions proved critical not only to freedpeople's material needs but also to their conceptions of citizenship—rooted not in some distant legislative body or charter but rather in the presence of an agent on the ground, someone who could potentially hear their claims and enforce their rights. The demobilization wave of the late 1860s removed federal figures from the equation and thus profoundly disrupted freedpeople's vernacular rehearsal of a reciprocal citizenship. In late 1868, rumors of the bureau's imminent demise circulated among freedpeople across the South as states began meeting congressional requirements for readmission established under the Military Reconstruction Act of 1867, and hence no longer subject to the bureau's admittedly anemic authority. Ex-slaves in Huntsville, Texas, for instance, began "meeting together in great anxiety and asking each other if there is not something that they can do to induce the government to have it continue its protection of them through the 'Bureau' agency a year or two longer." Their bureau agent, assistant surgeon G. W. Hatch, commented on how "they seem perfectly hopeless of their ever being able to secure anything even approaching justice." In Mississippi, hundreds of freedpeople who heard "that there will be no Bureau after Christmas" crowded the office of their bureau agent, imploring "where they shall go to get Justice." From New Bern, North Carolina, ex-slave Jacob Grimes spoke for his fellow "Sitizens" when he beseeched Howard to "let the Freedmen Bureau Remain in Craven Co."

for one more year, as it "Has been Great Help to our poor old People. We do not see How we can get a long well with out it." The Freedmen's Bureau had always been an embattled institution in the South, yet the withdrawal of the army and the conspicuous removal of bureau outposts sounded a new rallying cry for white Southerners agitating for home rule. In the midst of the bureau's retreat, freedpeople collectively agonized over their place in the new order without state allies, however vestigial they might be.[54]

As early as 1867, Howard began recommending that Congress allow the Freedmen's Bureau to discontinue its work in the South, save for its educational endeavors and its settlement of freedpeople's bounty and pension claims. "It may seem hazardous to withdraw this bureau agency so soon," wrote Howard in his annual report to Congress; "it may appear like surrendering the freed people to the direction of those who have not shown themselves particularly friendly to their interests." However, he assured Congress that "this recommendation is based on the belief that each of the several States where the bureau exists or has existed will be completely reconstructed by next July." With civil authority restored, policymakers saw no justification for the continued presence of a "wartime" agency such as the Freedmen's Bureau. (Had Sumner and the Radicals prevailed back in 1865 and established the bureau within the Treasury, a different political outcome might well have materialized.) Alas, on July 25, 1868, just after readmitting Arkansas, North Carolina, South Carolina, Louisiana, Georgia, Alabama, and Florida, Congress ordered the bureau to end its work and withdraw from the South. By that time, the bureau had reportedly distributed over twenty million rations and treated nearly half a million freedpeople in its hospitals. Over the next twelve months, Howard reduced the number of bureau employees to 157 individuals. By April 1869, the bureau was relegated to operating hospitals and orphan asylums in Vicksburg, Richmond, and Washington, D.C. It was with a whimper, then, that the Freedmen's Bureau ended.[55]

Or so it seemed. There remained a large contingent of freedpeople outside of the residual confines of the agency's hospitals, asylums, and schools who would continue the work of the Freedmen's Bureau well into the 1870s. Of course the great mission of the bureau would endure as a touchstone for an alternative, more democratic future, as imagined by Du Bois and others. But even as a practical matter, the Freedmen's Bureau still had much work to do as it began shuttering its divisions. In fact, an entirely new division was created in 1866 by Howard, one that would itself live on in an entirely new agency after 1872, the Claims Division. As members of the U.S. Colored Troops began mustering out in 1866, many having never received any pay during their service, they began pressing their claims with officials of the Freedmen's Bureau. In addition to the payment of monthly wages, ex-slave veterans pushed for the enlistment bounties promised to them, up to $300. Thousands of freedpeople hoped the government could at least make good on the promises of bounty and back pay fulfillment. Doing so required a telling reorientation. When Howard created the Claims Division of the Freedmen's Bureau in March 1866, he instructed the bureau official formerly in charge of the Land Division to act instead as a claims agent, signaling a reorganization of personnel and purpose, as if one commitment came at the zero-sum cost of another. Nevertheless, after the creation of the new division, word circulated quickly in the Black press and among Black communities that the Freedmen's Bureau was ready to distribute $20 million in bounties to Black soldiers and their heirs.[56]

From the start, issues of race and, even more so, status confounded the payment of Black troops. In 1864, when Radical Republicans in Congress pushed for the equalization of pay between white and Black soldiers, some had in mind only those who were free at the time of enlistment, and some only those who were free at the start of the war. Indeed, whether a recruiting officer happened to mark an enrolled soldier as "free on or before April 19, 1861," on the muster roll would become of critical importance down the road.[57] Across the wartime South, enlistees heard all manner of promises during their recruitment, assured that they would enjoy "the pay, rations, and clothing, our other soldiers receive," according to one recruitment poster addressed "to the Free Colored Men of Charleston." Its commander, Major Martin R. Delany, the highest-ranking Black officer during the war, guaranteed enlisted men that "quarters, fuel, and medical attendance are always provided by the government, without deduction from the soldier's pay. If a soldier should become disabled in the line of his duties," Delany added, "the laws provide for him a pension." Though addressed to the city's "free colored men," most Black refugees would have considered themselves free long before legally endowed with freedom. Enlistment would prove it so.[58]

Federal policies regarding payment for Black troops generated intense conflict at the federal level; it registered more viscerally, however, with the Black soldiers who understandably viewed matters of equal pay as central to their sacrifice and vision of postwar citizenship. Legislative efforts to redress the pay inequities resulted in a staggeringly complicated payment system to Black soldiers. Between 1861 and 1872, Congress enacted nearly sixty laws regulating bounty payments to Union soldiers, white and Black, free and enslaved, while the War Department issued over forty general orders addressing the same. Complicating the matter even further was the issue of timing of enlistment and, furthermore, the loyalty of the enlistee's enslaver and thus whether he had some claim on the bounty. The Militia Act, issued alongside the Confiscation Act on July 17, 1862, authorized Black enlistment and established unequal pay between white and Black enlistees, thirteen and ten dollars, respectively, though Black soldiers were deducted an additional three dollars for clothing. The matter of bounty payments to Black soldiers proceeded sporadically and inconsistently until the Act of February 24, 1864. This act established a distinction between free Black and enslaved enlistees regarding bounties: free Black men who enlisted were entitled to $100, whereas enslaved men who enlisted would see their bounty payments redirected to their former enslavers, provided the latter remained "loyal" to the Union. As the provost marshal reasoned, "in lieu of bounty to the slave it gave him his freedom, while his master, if loyal, received a compensation for the loss of his services." The formulation equating freedom itself with a bounty paid to another would be the definitive rebuke to claims made by former slaves on the national government for decades to come.[59]

A series of bounty laws and decisions in 1864 and 1865 continued to grapple with the issue of bounties to formerly enslaved soldiers. The Military Appropriations Act of June 15, 1864 finally equalized wages between white troops and all Black troops, regardless of enslaved or free status, but approved bounty and back payments only to Black soldiers who had been free before the opening of the rebellion on April 19, 1861. Radical Republicans in Congress denounced what they called "the miserable delusion of the 19th of April provision," arguing that all regiments composed of emancipated Black men ought to receive back pay dating to their enlistment. Weeks later, a law passed on July 4, 1864, authorized an enlistment bounty of $100 per year for up to three years for "every volunteer." Attorney General Edward Bates later seized on the statute's omission of race to interpret the measure as equalizing bounties for free Black soldiers enlisting thereafter. The War Department went a step further and ordered commanders of Black regiments to reassess which of their soldiers were free on April 19, 1861, and to revise their bounty credits accordingly. But this liberality still left the great mass of Black soldiers—who were legally enslaved on April 19, 1861—unaffected. In October 1865, the new attorney general, James Speed, virtually abrogated the April 19 provision altogether by drawing on the principles of the Second Confiscation Act of 1862, which dissolved the property claims of disloyal enslavers. In his meditative opinion, Speed reasoned that "the obligations of the slaves to the Government are direct and binding," and treasonous enslavers forever severed their once federally sanctioned right to human bondage, such that "slaves fleeing the rebellion became free." Whether by self-emancipation or presidential proclamation, former bondsmen who enlisted did so, and could only have done so, as free men, notwithstanding their status at some prior date.[60]

Elegant in its simplicity, unwavering in its universality, Speed's opinion roused Congress to pass a series of half-measures in the summer of 1866. First, on June 15, Congress resolved that where neither "slave" nor "free" appeared on the muster rolls, the presumption would be "free at the time of his enlistment," until proven otherwise. On July 26, Congress removed "at the time of his enlistment" from the earlier presumption clause. Two days later, in the appropriations bill of July 28, 1866, Congress promised to "each and every soldier who enlisted into the army of the United States" an additional bounty of $100, contingent only on their date of enlistment, length of service, and the size of bounty they received or would receive (not more than $100). Speed's successor regarded the language of the July 28 act to be "comprehensive," applying to all volunteers without regard to race or status, entitling those ex-slaves to the supplemental bounty. Immediately following the attorney general's opinion in November 1866, word had spread that "all colored troops who were slaves at enlistment are entitled to the extra bounty." Of course, granting modest additional bounties under qualified circumstances fell pitifully short of the capaciousness of Speed's earlier opinion and added yet another layer of complexity to an already bewilderingly complex bounty payment system.[61]

Yet the bounty laws for Black soldiers were not merely complex; they were internally confused and inconsistently applied. Conflicting interpretations of these laws collided in the dozens of opinions, memos, and practices by attorneys general, Treasury officials, officials in the War Department, and Freedmen's Bureau agents on the ground, not to mention private claims agents and attorneys—all of whom communicated extensively with freedpeople attempting to make sense of the system themselves.[62] To some, no doubt, this hypertechnocratic payment schedule ensured fairness to the various enlistees, careful as it was not to commit the grievous mistake of "giving" a Black solider freedom along with an inappropriately high bounty. But from the perspective of formerly enslaved veterans and heirs impatiently awaiting their payment, the entire bounty payment scheme functioned arbitrarily and unjustly.[63]

The result was not only frustrating but costly. Freedpeople bore the full weight of congressional lassitude and bureaucratic incapacity. Many Black soldiers protested their uncompensated wartime service, especially at war's end. "Numbers of colored soldiers have never received any bounty whatever," observed one former USCT officer to the *Army and Navy Journal*. "There are thousands who have set their hopes on obtaining some reward for their service," he noted, "and obtaining it in sufficient time to benefit themselves in the forth-coming planting season." The officer feared that, if settled at all, the bounties would be returned too late to benefit the veterans looking to purchase land of their own, "willing and anxious" as they were to do so. The bureau had sent around relief commissions to distribute food and supplies, to be sure, but no "better relief could be afforded them than by a prompt settlement of the claims of the discharged soldiers." Had freedpeople received their bounty payments in a timelier manner, many would have had a better chance at landownership in a credit-scarce region, especially before being compelled to sign sharecropping contracts at the beginning of the year before planting season. After all, save for the most radical advocates for land reform, most policymakers still expected freedpeople to have to purchase the lands held by the government; bounty payments would have provided thousands of families the means to do so. Many refugee camp denizens thus held out not only to avoid contracts but also in anticipation of their payments.[64]

Because refugee camps so often were homes of Black soldiers and their families, they became important political sites of claims-making after Confederate surrender. From the start, Freedmen's Bureau officials were instructed to identify those individuals who might have claims against the government. For example, federal surgeons in charge of hospitals and other relief establishments had instructions to report the names of "any patient or patients under their charge who have been soldiers, or of any relative of a soldier, or discharged soldier," and include "any information that may be useful in bringing together the surviving members of the family, or in establishing claims for Pensions, Back Pay, Bounty, &c." In turn, many bureau agents solicited help from leaders in the Black community, as did the agent at Helena when he asked James Milo Alexander, a prominent Black politician and community leader in Phillips County, to report to him "the number of colored soldiers within your knowledge who have been disabled or are destitute, who now need or may soon need government aid." As the authority of the Freedmen's Bureau waned, its responsibilities narrowed and its remaining agents found their time increasingly consumed with the claims of Black soldiers and their kin.[65]

So, too, did Northern missionaries. Men and women who had once shouldered a variety of responsibilities on behalf of freedpeople during the war found themselves relegated to administering their claims against the federal government. Abisha Scofield, the active member of the American Missionary Association at the much-beleaguered Camp Nelson, seen earlier, had been working in earnest on freedpeople's claims as early as October 1865. It was, he sighed, a task that "now occupies considerable of my time—many of them suffer great wrong from their white oppressors. Officers and citizens together conspire to cheat and plunder them." One freedwoman, a widow named Sarah White, attempted to certify her claims before a judge and justice of the peace only to be threatened with jail if she did not leave the county. Though entitled to bounty, back pay, and pension, White left without getting her papers certified. Similar issues befell other applicants under Scofield's charge, including Ellen Woodson and Lydia Weathers, both of whom failed to have their papers certified or witnesses sworn in by the civil authorities. "These cases are quite frequent," reported the missionary. According to the U.S. Sanitary Commission, Camp Nelson had over two hundred unpaid claims, and more claimants were pouring in from the countryside. Many claimants were wrongfully told by the civil authorities "they must go to their old houses" in order to begin processing their claims. But many refused to leave the protection of the camp, protesting they would "rather lose their money than their lives."[66]

As Camp Nelson cleared out, Scofield became the primary claims agent, struggling to process freedpeople's applications at the threat of violence and imprisonment. By May 1866, he managed to secure 250 claims valued at over $2,000 and still had over one hundred additional claims nearly completed. Later that month, after Scofield was "cut off at Washington," the secretary of the AMA lobbied on his behalf, asking for his reinstatement as a claims agent so he can "*finish* the work at hand," having already "saved thousands of dollars to the widows & orphans of Soldiers." Assistant Commissioner Fisk eventually acquiesced. But the number of claims exceeded Scofield's ability to process them alone. Following a series of autumnal attacks on the camp—and on Scofield in particular—by a posse of armed invaders determined to break up the "nest" of freedpeople, the missionary was forced to discontinue his work in December 1866. By the spring of 1869, dozens of discharged Black soldiers had returned to Camp Nelson and, at a large meeting on April 12, elected their own post clerk, one Isaac W. Newton, an educator commissioned by the AMA and the Western Freedmen's Aid Commission, and charged him with the responsibility of "looking after their Claims." Newton wrote to the chief of the Claims Division, explaining how there were still claimants who "have, as yet, never received their full Bounty, Pension &c, & some who have *not yet received anything*." Though undeniably crucial, freedpeople's alliances with the federal government during the period of occupation were often mediated by third parties who likewise saw the state working at cross-purposes to the interests of freedpeople.[67]

Until the spring of 1867, claimants in the post-slavery South could employ a bureau agent or a private claims attorney to file their application through the second auditor's office in the U.S. Treasury. After confirming service details with the War Department, the auditor would draft a certificate for the amount of payment owed the claimant. Before March 29, 1867, a check or draft or money order would be sent to the claimant's agent or attorney, whereupon the latter would take a cut largely at their own discretion and give the rest to the claimant. Such a practice in the eyes of administrators invited the abuse of Black claimants, many of whom were only semiliterate. In fact, evidence of fraud provoked the secretary of war to temporarily suspend payments to Black claimants in the South for fear the money would wind up in the pockets of unscrupulous agents. Congress then passed the joint resolution of March 29, 1867, marking a pivotal shift in bounty payment policy. It stipulated that the second auditor of the Treasury issue certificates and payments in bulk to Commissioner Howard, who would then forward the appropriate amounts to disbursing officers across the South. Claimants, for their part, needed to appear before these disbursing officers to verify their identity, sign their voucher, and from there report to the local bank where the disbursing officer deposited their money. Bureau officials touted the Act of March 1867 as a "blessing" for freedpeople, a tightly scaled suit of bureaucratic armor against fraudulent agents. Black claimants themselves, however, understandably found the entire process byzantine, inefficient, and, given their dire circumstances, inhumane. Designed to prevent fraud, it primarily prevented a speedy delivery of bounties and, in short order, would inspire a national scandal involving Commissioner Howard; his chief disbursing officer, George W. Balloch; and several other high-ranking Treasury officials plausibly accused of underpaying Black claimants, recording them as fully paid, and relocating the funds to private accounts.[68]

Administrative Appeals

Ironically, as the Freedmen's Bureau began downsizing, it took on this outsized responsibility of serving as claims facilitators. The role severely tested the limits of the state's ability to reach a class of previously undocumented citizens across a previously unregulated landscape. Freedpeople flocked to wherever bureau agents remained, overwhelming their offices with demands for payment. Occasionally, bureau agents came to them. Having mustered in so many Black soldiers, Arkansas, for instance, was especially laden with unpaid claims. In the spring of 1868, many Black Arkansans likely encountered bureau agent Sebastian Geisreiter, who traveled some 225 miles across the state, visiting plantations and facilitating claims. Part of his mission was to locate individuals whose claims had been "settled" and were ready for payment. Freedpeople learned from Geisreiter that they could expect a special agent on June 6 to pay out those claims. The news generated "considerable excitement" among those about to be paid but a different kind of excitement "among the rest who cannot understand why others should get their pay first." Freedpeople pursuing their claims had mixed emotions: confusion, anticipation, anxiety, consternation, anger. They kept up "a constant run" at bureau offices "concerning their respective claims." A great many were "disappointed and greatly displeased because their claims had not been heard from, or the amount allowed being smaller than they were told it would be." More often than not, the discrepancy owed to mustering in as "not free" on April 19, 1861, thus entitling them only to the "additional" and not the "original" bounty.[69]

Despite their frustrations with the government, freedpeople could clearly sense when they found an ally like Geisreiter. With hundreds of claims unsettled, and more coming to his office each day, Geisreiter himself resented how "the settlement of these accounts seems to be extraordinarily prolonged." By the summer of 1868, he and other agents in the state were making headway. One agent remarked that the "few Freedmen [who] have had their bounties paid here, express themselves highly delighted, and seem well satisfied," adding that the "money spent by the Freedmen will give quite an impetus to this Town." The money "seems to have a good effect upon the Freedmen," commented another agent, "and is of great service to many of them as most of them need money now, to aid in buying provisions and keep them from getting into debt to their employers." In Little Rock, another agent reported how bounty payments to Black veterans were enabling "a great many of them to prosecute their crops and is a great relief to them, at this period, when it is almost impossible to obtain any credit whatever." After the crop failures of 1867, when freedpeople "got little or nothing for their labor," bounty payments saved many Black families from ruin.[70]

Formerly enslaved claimants repeatedly used the failure of land reform to underscore their need for financial assistance from the federal government. Writing to Howard in February 1869, Samuel Clark, a Mississippi sharecropper, explained how, under his arrangement, "the owner who furnishes everything continues to get nearly all the crops." Clark resolved "to furnish myself this year if I can only get my Bounty in time." James Davis spoke for many freedpeople enduring the new order when he complained to Howard, "We ar[e] all hear in the South without horse or Land." It had been "hard [to] get a long with out this money," and, with a certain dream still fresh in his mind, Davis planned to use his bounty money to buy a farm and a mule himself. Andrew Montgomery also found himself "greatly in need of a horse or mule to plow, without a plow the crop must be shorter." He was anxious to "make a crop of Cotton" and sent hurried letters to multiple bureau officials. The bureau received many such letters in the springtime, when expectant claimants imagined using the money to advance a crop or buy provisions or even hire a team of workers themselves.[71]

When relief finally came, many Black families proved especially enterprising with their bounty money. In Tennessee, for example, bureau agents frequently commented on the economic activities of Black bounty recipients. In Pulaski, despite "a large number of the late Colored Troops who have not as yet received their Bounty," commented the bureau agent, "their money is coming in slowly." He found them "learning very rapidly to use economy, most of them purchasing land, homes &c and preparing to work for themselves." Freedpeople had an earnest desire "to invest their money in land some thing they know can not be taken from them." In some instances, the bureau received requests from entire groups of Black veterans who proposed to use their bounty money to buy entire plantations, some endeavoring to form cooperatives. In Mississippi, 260 such freedpeople arranged to buy the A. K. Farrar farm, over ten thousand acres, at ten dollars per acre. Together these veterans formed a joint stock company to collect subscriptions, which they began doing in early 1868. Unfortunately, the bureau's mistrust of the company directors led Howard to abandon his earlier support for the company. Juxtaposed with broad-scale land redistribution, collective arrangements funded by bounty payments could appear quite modest, to be sure, but nevertheless reflected a novel approach to individuated bounty payments— and which nevertheless aimed at breaking the stranglehold of debt relations that was the base alloy of the sharecropping regime.[72]

The long delays, suspended payments, and procedural opacity that characterized the bureau's bounty payment system fatally hamstrung many freedpeople's efforts to purchase land in the critical years after the war. Defended by officials as "required by justice to the colored soldier and the public treasury," freedpeople rejected any such rationalizations for the bureau's evident torpor. They remained frustrated, incredulous as to why their claims had not yet been paid, especially in light of their obvious hardships. "I stand in need of my money very much indeed at this present time," wrote one freedman in Charleston, "and I cannot see the reason why it is not settled by this time." Two days later, a fellow Charlestonian likewise wrote to Howard, confiding in the commissioner that he also stands "in need of my money very much I cannot see the reason why it is not settled for it is going on three years now." Another simply said that "if we cant get our money from the government we must sufer [sic]." To those freedpeople sadly accustomed to broken promises from the national government, delayed payments and inscrutable responses from officials were more than mere inconveniences. They were betrayals, indicative of the larger abandonment of the promise of emancipation.[73]

Beyond lodging individual complaints, freedpeople worked collectively to leverage their entitlement and discontent to provoke bureaucratic action. Their missives told of their honest attempts to acquire land and employment while arguing that delays in their payments prevented any opportunities for advancement. In the spring of 1868, scores of formerly enslaved veterans in Charleston wrote letters to Howard regarding the status of their claims. Frank Mitchell, who had put in his claim over twelve months prior and had "not heard anything of it yet," told Howard he was "in great need of this money as I am out of employment at present and have nothing to support me." Alfred Hunter had a claim delayed over two years, and though he was told it was settled, he had not yet been able to claim it. "Please give an order to that effect," he requested Howard, "so that I may receive my money. I am in great need of it. I can not support my family and can not go on with planting a Crop because my Crop from last year has failed. . . . Times is very hard and cant get on without it." Likewise, if Joseph Cann had received his bounty money two years before when he put in his claim, he would have been able to "buy a small peice [sic] of Land and turn to and work and support my self or I would sett up a little shop but it seem very hard to get my bounty and I cannot see the reason why it is not settle yet." He, too, asked Howard to personally "interced[e] in my behalf as soon as possible."[74]

In their epistolary appeals to bureau officials, freedpeople—men and women alike—invoked a vision of citizenship premised on loyalty, valor, and ongoing sacrifice. The spring of 1868 found ex-slave Edmund Midgett "in very distressed circumstances." It had been three years since he put in his claim, with later claimants already having been paid. In poor health and with a needy family, he begged the commissioner to intercede. If Howard only knew "how destitute I am at the present time you would Pity me from your heart I was a good soldier when I was in the War and There is not a Stain on my Character hard service in the field broken down my health so for God sake see into my case as soon as possible." In North Carolina, Noah Harney expected a bounty of "two or three Hundred Dollars," as did his comrades who had already been paid. Like Howard himself, Harney had lost his right arm in the service, "thereby being disabled from hard work." Freedwomen also took pains to emphasize their physical suffering and inability to labor for their own support. "I am very unwell," Mary Lewis told Howard in March 1869, "& unable to work." Maria Beal's husband and son both died, "leaving me in my old age unable to do any work," and as she had "no reliable person to intercede" for her, she asked Howard how to proceed in her son's claim. In thousands of letters to bureau officials, freedpeople made heartrending appeals for intervention on a broader and yet more intimate scale.[75]

Freedpeople's letters had a personalized effect, as if some unspoken bond existed between themselves and the official, thereby humanizing a distant and impersonal, if not entirely imagined, relationship. "I would have not wrote," explained one freedman, inquiring after his bounty, "but Is waited so long & have not hear[d] anything of it Began to think you have almost forgotten me." Another freedman thought he "could get information from you as you have Bin Such A friend to us colored People in times that has Past." In their letters to Howard, freedpeople adopted the role of the dutiful and beleaguered ward of the commissioner. They spoke of friendship and trust—"I feel you are a friend to my race," beseeched one freedwoman—as much as they did hardship and suffering, no small amount of the latter being caused by what they perceived as the "delay and nonattention" given to the claims of freedpeople. In so doing, ex-slaves attempted to preserve their wartime relationship with federal officials, inventing an indirect means to substitute for the loss of a more direct one in the days of encampment and occupation. To meet their needs, formerly enslaved men and women turned to comparatively powerful state actors to plead for attention and favors, turning dependence, in the words of historian Gregory Downs, "from a personal condition into a political style." Against a prevailing concept of contractual freedom bestowed upon the enslaved, thousands of freedpeople rhetorically positioned themselves as worthy dependents to powerful patrons, contributing to a vernacular citizenship premised on rights and reciprocity.[76]

Freedpeople recognized that wartime service offered a singular avenue to press their claims during the battles of Reconstruction, when Black men, as enfranchised citizens, constituted the backbone of the Republican Party in the South. From the earliest days of Reconstruction, and especially during the Republican mobilizations of 1867, Democratic planters and politicians—self-described cooperationists—used a mixture of paternalistic incentives and veiled threats to stylize themselves, in explicit contrast to the meddling Yankee carpetbaggers, as the only true "friends" of Black Southerners, convincingly enough to cause some worry in Northern Republican ranks about the party's ability to maintain Black Southerners' allegiance. In this light, freedpeople's deeply personalized letters not only melded citizenship with partisanship but also reaffirmed to those allies who needed reaffirming that they vociferously rejected the disingenuous entreaties of Democratic operatives. Writing to Henry Page, the disbursing officer of Arkansas, Mingo Jeffries called himself a "poor Friend of the Govt & U.S." and asked whether Page himself was "a friend of a poor Republican who stood under the Flag." After other men in his company received their bounty payments, William Pace, a disabled veteran writing from a sheriff's office in Little Rock, begged Howard that "being a criple [*sic*] I much need the money." But his claim was not the only issue he felt compelled to bring to Howard's attention. It was just a month away from the 1868 election, and Pace informed the commissioner, "As I know you are a cold [colored] Soldiers Friend," that "our cold [colored] Brothers are being killed in this state by the K.K.K. every day and they say they will kill us all if we do vote for Grant, but give us arms and we will take care of ourselves. . . . We will not vote with Reb." A former slave in Charleston similarly assured Howard that he was "head and ears a supporter for the republicans," even as he felt exasperated over his inability to learn anything about the status of his claim. These were at once calls for help as well as strategic poses to curry favor with the Freedmen's Bureau commissioner, to reiterate one's political allegiance in a most hostile environment.[77]

As the avenues of advancement constricted with the decline of the Freedmen's Bureau, formerly enslaved men and women acted collectively. Rumors echoed about the bounty process, about receptive agents, potential delays, and of some men and companies getting paid long before others, and with inscrutably differing amounts. Prospective claimants banded together and insisted that bureau officials attend to the claims of dozens of individuals. Sometimes veterans would write on behalf of entire companies whose bounty and back payments had been hitherto neglected. In Natchez, veterans of one company had awaited their payments for years. The bureau agent wrote on their behalf to the second auditor of the Treasury, notifying him not only that "none of the members of this Co have as yet received bounty" but also that "they are making enquiry daily at this office." Writing from Charleston in the spring of 1868, George Hooker asked Howard about the status of his claim, as well as the claims of several of his comrades in the same company of the Thirty-Fifth USCT. As Black veterans and heirs in the emancipated South sensed they had no time to waste, news about payments traveled rapidly among them. For example, after one claims agent in Tennessee finally managed to secure two Black veterans their bounties, the news quickly ramified. Since then, the agent commented, "I have had very near a hundred applications."[78]

Unpaid claimants refused to lift their foothold in the federal state even as its most conspicuous agency retreated from the South. Keeping their feet planted required exceptional creativity, resilience, and coordination. Many negotiated with bureau headquarters or arranged with the most trustworthy literate person they could find, men such as one H. B. Putnam from Greenville, Mississippi. "Having been on duty with the Col^d Troops for near two years," wrote Putnam on the eve of 1869, "they are continually asking me to write for them, to make enquiries about their claims, and now that our place is not to have any Ag^t of Bureau, I am willing to be the medium of communication between your office & them." In areas absent any meaningful bureau presence, and there were increasingly many of these, freedpeople took it upon themselves to organize and command attention. This was especially true of parts of southwestern Louisiana, south-central Alabama, and southern Georgia. In isolated Palatka, Florida, freedpeople found themselves over sixty miles from the nearest bureau outpost. Not only did Joshua Hagerman and his fellow Black veterans lack a proximate bureau agent, they also well-nigh lacked any outside support whatsoever. As Hagerman explained to the Claims Division in late June 1869, "the colored men in this County have no friend who will do him Justice all our offices here are filled with such men who are deathly oppose[d] to us." He and several other discharged soldiers in the area who had yet to receive their bounty appealed to one E. G. Francis, "the only colored man here in Palatka who are able to use a pen & he does all he can for us all." Francis performed his labor free of charge, functioning as the de facto claims agent for these men.[79]

For their part, as widows, mothers, daughters, and sisters, freedwomen often proved the most vocal and persistent would-be claimants, ever increasing as the bureau's presence diminished. "I am poor & needy," wrote Fannie Little, "& while so many others have received their claims, I am sanguin[e] of getting the amount due my Father, by your prompt attention." "I have got two children and times are so hard that I hardly can get a long," confessed another freedwoman to Howard, "and if I could get the money it would be a great healp [sic] to me." She wanted desperately to know whether she would ever receive her claim, so that she "may know what to depend on, for if there is no chance of my ever getting it I must try some way to get a long with my children though I know not what to do, for I am afrade [sic] we shall suffer." In Arkansas, Maria Scott, daughter of a deceased soldier, appeared at the disbursing agent's office in Little Rock on a near-daily basis for four years. The bureau official complained to her attorney how "she calls frequently, and I want to do all I can to have her paid and get rid of her." In his reply, her attorney—whom Scott had also pressured into writing multiple letters to Washington—advised the bureau agent to remind the freedwoman that "she is dealing with a Govt & must exercise patience." Such condescension could be found in many interactions freedpeople had with private claims agents in the South. But even more than that, the exchange reveals a fundamental tension in how the two parties thought of what kind of "Govt" the freedwoman was liberated into— what, in other words, citizenship meant in a modern nation-state. To the agent and the attorney, a kind of disinterested proceduralism prevailed, guided by technical expertise and specialized bureaucratic channels. But to Maria Scott, and indeed thousands of her fellow would-be claimants, the hard lessons of enslavement and war taught her to view power in personal terms, and to negotiate with personalized appeals.[80]

The administrative realm of military benefits afforded freedwomen an expanded political role. Historian Elsa Barkley Brown and others have shown how Black women, though disenfranchised, played a central role in Southern Republican politics, in large part because they regarded the vote in collective terms, as the property of the whole family.[81] Still, in pursuing and negotiating military benefits, they acted as full-fledged political actors every bit as entitled and effective as their male counterparts. They, too, spoke of sacrifice, loyalty, and suffering, and they summoned patrons and allies. Despite reinforcing the gender hierarchy and the doctrine of dependency, military claims offered a singular space for freedwomen to practice politics and perform the rituals of citizenship in the post-slavery South. To many, this performance was a feat of physical endurance. Jane Griffith was fortunate enough to receive her claim certificate in April 1867, yet no one told her where she might exchange it for cash. Several times over the next year and a half, she would walk thirty miles from her home in Maryland to Washington, each time expecting payment. "I am very needy," she finally confessed to Howard in November, and "I have been told you are the colored people's friend, and I hope you will see to my claim for me, and aid me in getting before the inclement winter sets in as I have been in constant expectation of getting my claim and could not make but poor provision for the winter." Griffith's story represents something more than a misunderstanding or miscommunication, something more than political naïveté or delusion. Instead, her pilgrimages to the nation's capital in hopes of receiving her long-awaited payment speak to an enduring commitment to a personalized relationship with a powerful ally. The agonizing limitations of the Freedmen's Bureau scarcely limited the ingenuity or determination of the erstwhile enslaved. On the contrary, they inspired a more limitless bureaucratic politics.[82]

IN *THE SOULS OF BLACK FOLK*, W. E. B. Du Bois offered a mixed assessment of the Freedmen's Bureau. Writing in 1903, Du Bois had to defend not only its record but the very idea of such an agency dedicated in principle to the welfare and dignity of Black Americans. As it was in the 1860s, so it remained in the early 1900s that the "bitterest" foes of the bureau "were those who attacked not so much its conduct or policy under the law as the necessity for any such institution at all." At freedom's dawn the bureau faced a monumental task. And although he mourned "the passing of a great human institution before its work is done," Du Bois felt keenly the bureau's many failures, foremost among them its tendency to lock freedpeople into paternalistic arrangements with white employer-landlords that militated against self-reliance. But the bureau's ultimate failure was its inability to follow through on "its implied promises to furnish the freedmen with land." Those who managed to become landowners in the decade following emancipation, Du Bois argued, did so largely by virtue of their own thrift. Many an ex-slave with capital earned it, he added, by dint of his "labor in the army, and his pay and bounty as a soldier." Though an insufficient program, the bureau's Claim Division "put needed capital in the hands of practical paupers," by distributing millions of dollars to its Black claimants.[83]

For freedpeople, the Freedmen's Bureau tragically failed to deliver collective justice. The dream of land reform turned out to be just that, and the hopes of a broad-based landowning class of Black farmers in the South evaporated, leaving behind the precarious peonage of the tenant and sharecropping system. As the bureau entered its final phase in 1868, it commenced a rearguard maneuver of maintaining schools and hospitals and facilitating bounty and other claims. Bureau field offices began shuttering, as refugee camps had years before. The nearly thirty bureau posts in Arkansas all closed by 1869, leaving one claims agent in Helena until 1871. Georgia's reduction was even starker. It had sixty-five field offices until the end of 1868, after which it had one claims agent operating out of Savannah. Meanwhile, the liberal rights bestowed by the passage of the Reconstruction amendments were rendered ineffectual by the unwillingness or incapacity of the federal government to enforce them against the well-heeled forces of reaction. The same might have been the case with the back payments, bounties, and pensions owed to formerly enslaved veterans and their heirs had it not been for their persistence. Given the retrenchment of the Freedmen's Bureau, the general abandonment of the Reconstruction project, and the bewildering complexity of the payment system, the continued commitment to processing the bounty claims of Black soldiers and survivors was anything but guaranteed. Rather, it was only through the widespread engagement and concerted agitation of freedpeople that the Freedmen's Bureau was forced to maintain its commitment to this last measure of hope.

More than simply bearing witness to suffering, freedpeople's letters and appeals had the power to affect change in distant Washington. And not only for themselves as individual applicants in receipt of federal benefits. Despite the atomizing bureaucratic scaffolding of bounty payments made to individuals for individual service, unpaid claimants in the post-slavery South mobilized collectively, wrote joint letters and petitions, circulated rumors of federal action, and drew attention to entire companies of veterans and widows awaiting payment. Securing claims involved not just individuals, then, but comrades, families, and communities; and the process called upon not only government officials, but missionaries, private agents, judges, and even former enslavers who variously administered and lent not just veracity but officiality to their claims. Engagement with the federal administrative state by way of military claims brought tens of thousands of former slaves into the documentary gaze of the federal government for the first time. Fitting undocumented identities and relationships into bureaucratic rubrics was the deeply fraught means by which many thousands of ex-slaves earned the fruits of citizenship. In ways unimagined by the agency's architects, freedpeople's unpaid claims offered them a platform to meaningfully engage the federal government via the Freedmen's Bureau even as it withdrew from the demobilized South, creating an inverse relationship between need and ability to meet it, and eventually precipitating a new agency long since lost to history but one that remained the most enduring vestige of the wartime state.

CHAPTER TWO

The Unfinished Freedmen's Branch

The Freedmen's Branch grew out of failure. Established in June 1872, the new agency assumed the old work of the Freedmen's Bureau, relegated as it was in its final years to the management of hospitals and schools and the settlement of claims for bounties, back payments, and pensions in the emancipated South. The ostensibly minor task of settling claims consumed the working hours of dozens of agents in the bureau's final days. Given the potentially radical founding directive of the Freedmen's Bureau and its multivalent operations, the contracting sphere of bureau activity in the early 1870s has understandably led many to believe that Southern freedpeople's engagement with the federal state ended when the bureau ended. The persistent military claims lodged by freedmen and freedwomen, before and after the bureau's fall, have thus been all too easily overlooked, just as the agency created solely to continue this unfinished work has received virtually no scholarly attention at all.[1]

Yet for tens of thousands of freedpeople, the Freedmen's Branch was of immense importance to their livelihoods and was widely recognized as the vestigial connection to federal power. In the seven years of the agency's existence, from 1872 to 1879, officials in the Freedmen's Branch handled thousands of as-yet-unpaid claims for bounties owed to Black veterans and their heirs. Freedpeople anxiously wrote to branch officials or visited the agency's field offices, sometimes traveling considerable distances, other times demanding that representatives be sent to them. Their claims continued to vex federal administrators, and in the absence of agents scattered throughout the countryside, freedpeople continued to marshal private agents and patrons to settle their claims. From the perspective of formerly enslaved claimants, their ongoing struggles with federal officials of this long-forgotten agency were important battles for citizenship rights, and indeed became some of their most enduring political achievements in the era of Reconstruction. Yet the citizenship rights for which they fought differed considerably from those they had envisioned and pursued during the war years.

To be sure, the federal bureaucracy may seem a strange place to look for freedpeople's struggle for citizenship rights during the years following Southern occupation. In an unprecedented age of Black men's enfranchisement, electioneering, and officeholding, along with the endowment of legal capacities to bring suit in courts of law, the conventional arenas of political power have long captured scholarly attention. But a strict electoral focus comes at the cost of understanding how ordinary freedpeople encountered, and perhaps even influenced, that other great achievement of the Union's victory in the Civil War, the building of the central state. Though government at all levels teemed with activity in the post-Reconstruction years when much political power was deliberately decentralized, the federal government nevertheless saw a dramatic expansion of its administrative capacities. One of the key features of state building in the late nineteenth century involved concerted regulatory intervention in people's lives, be it in the workplace, in streetcars, in matrimony, or in Native American reservations in the trans-Mississippi West.[2] Such intervention both required and produced a flurry of standardized documentation to make the populace more legible to the state. Emerging as they were from their legal status as chattel within a private property regime, freedpeople were by and large undocumented. To secure federal benefits, as thousands would, they would need to cut through the documentary opacity of their prewar lives, making themselves legible to the central government. Understanding how such freedpeople pursued claims for federal military benefits through the Freedmen's Branch—how, that is, they confronted the means by which their claims were facilitated, administered, and legitimated—reveals a great deal about what freedpeople made of their new and beleaguered relationship to the modernizing federal administrative state.

All Things Being Equal

In his last report to Congress on the operations of the Freedmen's Bureau in October 1871, Commissioner O. O. Howard offered a dispirited summation of the agency's final days. With inquiries continuing to pour in from Black claimants in the emancipated South, the defeated commissioner could only reply with "words of advice and encouragement," giving "such aid as could be rendered by counsel alone." White Southerners celebrated, at long last, "the abolition of what remains of the institution," and along with it the extinguishment of "another vile political feature" of Reconstruction. Yet Howard recommended, and the Southern papers duly noted, that the "unfinished business" of bounty payments to colored troops be transferred to the army's Pay Department. This would have placed claims from the U.S. Colored Troops (USCT) on the same footing as those from other soldiers to expedite the process, replacing the system established by the joint resolution of March 29, 1867, which had required the Freedmen's Bureau to be the sole agency for paying claims. The proposed relocation would have bypassed many onerous require-ments frequently criticized by freedpeople and would have resulted in a quicker settlement of the remaining claims. (In just three months, from June to August 1865, the Pay Department made final payment to some eight hun-dred thousand white Union soldiers.) Against Howard's sensible recommen-dation, the secretary of war established a new agency under the Adjutant General's Office to complete the bureau's unfinished work—work so unfin-ished, in fact, that many observers continued to call the new agency by its old name up until 1879, when the Freedmen's Bureau can be said to have died a second death.[3]

Confusion marked the transition months following the closure of the bureau and the institutionalizing of the Freedmen's Branch. By April 1872, the bureau had settled over seventy thousand claims and disbursed over $15 million to Black claimants, those veterans of the USCT and their eligible heirs. Twenty thousand claims had been rejected, and many claims needed settlement. But the bureau had stopped recording bounty and back payment claims as of mid-March 1872. Nearly five thousand unpaid claims, amounting to nearly $750,000, were transferred to the Freedmen's Branch, some of them ready for payment since 1867. Moreover, some claimants marked as paid had not actually received their dues, suggesting either poor recordkeeping or worse. "Having been informed that the Freedman's Bureau is now closed," freedwoman Louisa Thornton had her agent inquire after her deceased hus-band's bounty and back payment claim, which she calculated at $350. That same day, another agent in New Orleans wrote on behalf of "some twenty Colored Bounty Claimants" who were "at a loss to know whether they are ever going to get their Bounty or not." Still another agent complained that freedpeople pestered him daily with questions about their claims and could give them "no satisfactory answer." From bottom to top, then, the Freedmen's Branch began in disarray.[4]

The newly established Freedmen's Branch came under the charge of Thomas M. Vincent, the assistant adjutant general. Vincent struggled to make sense of which claims had been paid, which ones were pending, and which ones had not been processed at all. He relayed to the secretary of war how "the books and files of the different offices" had been "promiscuously intermingled, the desks full of papers belonging to the files, and the files themselves in general disorder"; solders' discharge papers, necessary docu-ments to begin a claim, "had been placed on the files and in various places, seemingly at the then present convenience of the persons having them in charge, without being recorded in the books of the office, and, consequently, without any means by which they could be referred to." Nearly five thousand unpaid claims had "fallen to the office as unfinished business." If only the business could be "conducted anew, in all its parts, the new regulations . . . would enable the Adjutant-General to dispose of all cases as rapidly as settled by the accounting-officers of the Treasury, thus preventing an accumulation of unpaid claims." Alas, Vincent fully expected "some delay as to future payments, and, consequently, clamor on the part of claimants. This clamor will," he predicted, "be incited by agents, who, by their attempts at fraud on the claimants, have increased the caution necessary to full protection." Managerial misgivings aside, on September 5, 1872, Vincent sent around a circular to his nine disbursing officers with instructions for the "discovery, identification, and payment of claimants." The *re-established* business, known as the Freedmen's Branch," had begun.[5]

As the rearguard of the Freedmen's Bureau, the branch occupied fewer spaces in the postbellum South. The branch's headquarters sat in Washington, where James McMillan served as the chief disbursing officer until July 1877. At its peak, he oversaw thirteen disbursing field offices, some of which occupied places previously untouched by the Freedmen's Bureau. Established branch locations could be found at Fort Monroe, Virginia; Fort Johnston and Fort Macon, North Carolina; Charleston and Columbia, South Carolina; Savannah, Georgia; Louisville, Kentucky; Memphis and Nashville, Tennessee; Natchez and Vicksburg, Mississippi; New Orleans, Louisiana; St. Louis, Missouri; and Fort Leavenworth, Kansas. Dozens of temporary locations would be informally assigned to meet the needs of areas with fewer claimants. Disbursing officers had orders to circulate within their districts to visit groups of rural claimants pressing for an agent to settle their claims. To those Black claimants nearly out of reach, the Freedmen's Branch suffered from the same lack of manpower and presence that had hampered the erstwhile bureau: the difficulties with reaching claimants, identifying them, receiving them in the field office, and paying them. And yet, despite the explicit continuities between the two agencies, the story of the Freedmen's Branch was much more than a reenactment of the bureau's final days. Indeed, wrapped up in thousands of settlement struggles were the sorts of untiring efforts that paved inroads into the federal administrative state at a time when the political exclusion of Black Southerners was fast becoming the order of the day.[6]

Freedpeople's engagement with the federal administrative state was always embedded in larger partisan struggles. The reformation of the late bureau thus drew predictable criticism from the Southern white press. Many articles noted the new agency and its locations in various Southern cities, sometimes framing it as a mere "Bid for the Colored Vote," as did one Nashville paper, or an extension of Howard's "crime ring." By 1872, Democrats had begun recovering majorities in state legislatures and rolling back the gains of Reconstruction and Black officeholding. Those freedpeople with claims to make mobilized in ways that paralleled their feats of political organizing in the early years of Reconstruction, most notably with groups such as the Union League. In Yorktown, Virginia, for instance, when a local claims agent illegally retained part of Nancy Gordon's bounty money, other freedpeople with similar complaints called a meeting and "elected" a well-respected ally "as their agent to attend to their claims" and presented him "with a copy of the proceedings of their meeting." This man, one John Armstead, surprised them when, in response, he cautioned "that they had undertaken something that they knew nothing about, that they could not appoint or Elect any person for that business," that all he could do was direct them to the proper authorities. His answer did not satisfy his claimant-constituents, who promptly called a second meeting, where they further enjoined Armstead to lobby the War Department on their behalf to send a trustworthy agent to prosecute their claims. "I am troubled a great deal by them," Armstead confessed to the former head of the bureau's Claims Division. Freedpeople called upon him "both day and night, *from all parts of the country.*" Claims agents preferred to deal with disgruntled Black claimants on an individual, patron-client basis. Horizontal linkages, those between claimants or groups of claimants, doubly threatened the vertical hierarchies of these dyadic relationships. In a pattern that unfolded time and again, whenever groups of freedpeople exerted collective pressure on the facilitators of their claims, the latter wrote urgently for state intervention.[7]

In the summer of 1872, freedpeople in dozens of sites across the South, urban and rural, brought the government's attention to their unpaid claims. Many allies desired appointments as claims agents, given the position's importance to the Black community; they accordingly wrote to branch officials after receiving the blessing of their would-be constituents. Others simply felt bound by the urgency and persistence of freedpeople's agitation. One writer confessed he had received "so many inquiries that I am compelled to write" and asked the branch when it would send an agent to Little Rock. In Memphis, one employee of the Freedmen's Bank complained to the adjutant general of having "no agents here that seem to take any interest in the old claims." At Vicksburg, "numerous colored claimants have been anxiously waiting the arrival of a disbursing officer," for it had "been some weeks since the 'Freedmen's Bureau' ceased Bounty payments." Fifty miles northwest of Vicksburg, around Lake Providence, Louisiana, large numbers of Black claimants similarly appealed for attention to their neglected claims. And so, as the Freedmen's Branch began establishing disbursing offices at key locations in the South, Black claimants did not simply wait for the federal state to come to them. Instead, they collectively organized for its arrival and even its character in the hopes of safeguarding a swift payment of their claims.[8]

The chaotic state of freedpeople's claims thwarted any hope for quick settlement. Though some had indeed received full payment under the stewardship of the late bureau, many more had submitted claims through the bureau that were still in process when the agency closed; others received no payment but were recorded as having been paid; others received only a partial payment; others still had not managed to submit a claim at all and would do so the first time through the Freedmen's Branch. Many formerly enslaved claimants were told, as early as late 1869, to wait to file their claims until Congress finally moved to equalize bounties to veterans of the U.S. Colored Troops regardless of enslaved or free status at the time of enlistment. In a report on April 15, 1872, Secretary of War William W. Belknap found that of the 178,975 USCT, 144,426 had been enslaved at some point prior to enlistment. He estimated 105,179 colored soldiers enlisted before July 18, 1864, of whom 84,144 were recently enslaved, but only 21,037 actually appeared as "slaves" on the regimental rolls. Enslaved men who had enlisted after July 18, 1864, were already entitled to the same bounties as enlisted freemen, and where neither "slave" nor "free" appeared on the rolls, as was apparently the case for some 63,107 (recently enslaved but officially unrecorded) Black men who enlisted before July 18, 1864, the law held in favor of freedom. "It is suggested," wrote Belknap, "that all colored soldiers should be placed on the same footing as regards bounty, without regard to their civil status prior to enlistment. This view is one that has long been entertained by this Department." Radical Republicans in Congress, including Henry Wilson and Charles Sumner, had entertained the view for even longer and introduced at various times resolutions to equalize bounty payments to Black soldiers regardless of status. Doing so in 1872, however, would require additional payments to be made, reopening old cases, generating new ones, and complicating those already in process.[9]

When Arkansas's representatives returned to Congress in 1868, among them was the former Union cavalry officer who led the final charge for the equalization of bounties to Black soldiers. Thomas Boles had just resigned from his position as judge on the fourth circuit and had also served in the state's Union League—two roles that brought him face-to-face with the trials and travails of

Black veterans pursuing their bounties. At Republican meetings and conventions across the state, Boles distinguished himself as a steadfast Union man with an indefatigable hatred of the planter elite. His economic populism, appetite for confrontation, and genuine commitment to racial justice endeared him to his Black constituents. "Give my Love to Thomas Boles," wrote former Arkansas slave Abraham Daniels to Freedmen's Branch officials in Washington. Daniels, who had yet to receive his bounty after all his comrades had been paid, clearly sensed Boles would carry his interests to Washington. And Boles most certainly would. When he first took his seat in 1868, Congressman Boles immediately introduced legislation for equalizing bounties. In response to statutory ambiguity and prevarication among his colleagues, he wrote expressly to the second auditor of the Treasury, E. B. French, asking point blank "what legislation is necessary to secure to colored troops enlisted as 'slaves' the same bounty granted to others not so enlisted?" After French's reply, Boles introduced yet another bill to that effect. It also met defeat.[10]

Nevertheless, Boles's efforts garnered national attention. The *Soldier's Friend*, a popular veteran's newspaper in New York, had long supported the causes of white Union veterans. In February 1870, it turned to the overlooked Black veteran. "See yonder," imagined one editorial, "a man with dark skin knocks at the door of the Second Auditor and asks for bounty. . . . Mr. French stands at the door and says to him: 'My good sir, you were a slave in 1861. I am, on that account, prohibited from paying you a bounty.'" It would appear, noted the *Soldier's Friend*, "in looking at our laws, one would suppose that this was yet a land of slavery." The editor asked rhetorically whether there were men in Congress who would grant suffrage to a Black man and yet deny "him bounty because he *was* a slave? Hon. Thomas Boles, of Arkansas, proposes to test this matter. He has introduced in Congress a bill which proposes to do justice to his constituents, and all others who with black hands sent a loyal bullet to a disloyal heart." Two years later, in May 1872, just a month after Belknap's report to Congress on the number of enslaved soldiers denied full bounty, the Committee on Military Affairs blocked Boles's motion to reconsider the bill amending bounty laws. When Boles perhaps naively suggested that he did not "think this will cause a great deal of debate," the committee's chairman countered that it "is evidently a bill that will cause debate" and insisted that the matter be left for another day. Boles reluctantly agreed, but not before affirming that he was "willing to agree to anything that will result in giving bounties to these men. If this is due to them, it is certainly a matter of justice that they ought to have it now; they ought to have had it years ago." A date was fixed for the coming spring, 1873.[11]

On March 3, 1873, his last day in Congress, Boles gave the defining speech of his career, marked by his characteristic moral clarity and indignation. "The case of these soldiers is about this: the soldier who enlisted while he was in law a slave is denied bounty if he was so marked on the rolls. It does seem to me," Boles argued, "that if any one class of our soldiers deserve more at our hands than any other, it is that class which this bill is intended to benefit." The iconoclastic former Union officer from a seceded state thus turned the familiar argument on its head. Whereas most federal officials had worked from the premise that nominal freedom was a sufficient substitute for an ex-slave's bounty, and that any additional money would have been excessive, Boles insisted that full bounty ought to be the starting point for discussions about compensatory justice for ex-slave veterans. "They not only served the country faithfully and well," he insisted, "but they risked, and many of them laid down their lives in the defense of free government, even before they had any legal assurances that that free government would be shared by them after the victory should be won." The trials of Black soldiers, families, and refugees during the war gave ample testimony to their fidelity.

Moreover, thousands of formerly enslaved veterans, Boles continued, were beginning to ask questions upon seeing their comrades receive higher bounties. And "when they ask for the bounty that has been paid their colored comrades who enlisted long after they did," he explained, "they are told by the officers of the Department that the word 'slave' is marked on the roll opposite their names, and that under the laws governing the Department they cannot be paid any bounty." Above and beyond the confusion, frustration, and anger felt by those veterans upon seeing the wide discrepancies in bounty and back payments among their comrades, those who had no entitlements to further bounty sums at all felt especially injured and betrayed. "Of course they cannot understand" the discrepancy that befell those ex-slaves who enlisted prior to July 1864. Their indignation was entirely reasonable. Boles ended with a prescient warning. If Congress failed to pass the equalization measure at hand "we will hear of it hereafter, for these colored soldiers know what their rights are and will hold us responsible if we fail or refuse to award them their equal rights before the law as soldiers as well as citizens."[12]

On that long-awaited day, March 3, 1873, Congress finally equalized bounty payments for USCT veterans regardless of prior enslaved or free status. It held that "all colored persons who enlisted in the army during the late war, and who are now prohibited from receiving bounty and pension on account of being borne on the rolls of their regiments as 'slaves,' shall be placed on the same footing as to bounty and pension, as though they had not been slaves at the date of their enlistment." At once, the legal detainment of extra bounty money for "slave" enlistees collapsed, and a new bureaucratic challenge inaugurated.[13]

The measure came on the heels of a much larger bill, aptly named the Consolidation Act of 1873, which aggregated, reformed, and standardized the increasingly complicated array of federal military benefits, above all federal pensions.[14] Together with bounty equalization, the acts contributed to the larger project of nation-state building after the Civil War, whereby different forms of subjecthood would be erased and collapsed within the emerging framework of civil citizenship. As legal historian Laura Edwards notes, the Reconstruction amendments were "structured around the presumption that slavery could be removed from the legal order without changing much of anything else." Though removing as it did a civil disability imposed on certain enlistees with a once-enslaved status, the wording of the bounty equalization act—"as though they had not been slaves"—unintentionally evoked efforts to expunge the claims of ex-slaves along with the slave past. This was the dark implication of statutory equality in the age of emancipation: conjuring a fictitious level playing field whereon emancipated and nominally enfranchised Black Southerners, with all their paper rights, were thrown upon their own devices in the free labor economy, free to succeed or fail by their own merits. The language of "equality" featured in the bounty equalization act anticipated the infamous *Civil Rights Cases* a decade later, when the Supreme Court invalidated federal oversight of civil rights abuses and declared it time that the freedman "takes the rank of a mere citizen and ceases to be the special favorite of the laws." Such a formulation also limited the policy imagination of administrators grappling with the ongoing relevancy of the slave system in the post-slavery South and, just as importantly, undercut any compensatory claims lodged by freedpeople at the government precisely by virtue of having been enslaved. It would, in short, be a telling precedent with widely ramifying implications.[15]

Subsequent decisions reinterpreted the bounty equalization measure as even less universal—a capstone for some but a millstone for others. It came not from any court of law or representative body but instead from the federal bureaucracy. Soon after the bill's passage, E. B. French of the Treasury Department decided that the bounties conferred by the Act of March 3, 1873 applied only to formerly enslaved veterans themselves, not their heirs, whom he judged entitled only to the soldier's initial bounty sum, not the recent "gratuity." Incredulous, Thomas Vincent appealed to the second comptroller of the Treasury to overrule French's decision. Vincent pointedly asked "whether existing regulations contemplate the exclusion of the heirs . . . from the benefits of the bounty." The official concurred with French's strict interpretation, maintaining that the act indeed excluded the heirs, who were after all unnamed in the text of the remedial statute. The revisionist ruling by accounting officials went largely unnoticed by policymakers and unreported in the press. But where it registered the most was exactly where one might expect, and exactly where it was intended, in the individual claims of widows, mothers, fathers, and children of formerly enslaved soldiers. For years after the ruling, heirs expecting higher bounty payments rightly felt confused and mistreated, cheated out of additional funds Congress granted. It was a blow as petty and pitiless as it was invisible and unaccountable.[16]

Happier news of bounty equalization spread throughout the nation, with considerable traction in the South and the nation's capital. Black newspapers from Washington to Charleston to Fort Smith, Arkansas, reprinted the March 1873 act in full. Claims agents specializing in bounties and back payments to Black soldiers and heirs redoubled on advertising their services, informing their potential clients of the new legislation while promising them a speedy execution of their claims. And prospective claimants, for their part, began pressing branch officials for the additional bounties now owed to as many as twenty-one thousand Black men denoted as "slaves," or their surviving heirs, who enlisted before July 1864, further adding to the agency's workload. "There are several colored soldiers in this community who hold full discharges from federal service in the late war," reported one claims agent in South Carolina. "They are anxious to secure the bounty by late act of Congress, and ask me to attend to it for them." The *National Republican* recalled the time when bounties to enlisted freedmen were diverted to putatively loyal enslavers during the war. The tables were now turned, the editor exclaimed. Compensation "has now been renewed in favor of the slaves instead of the masters." An estimated $2.5 million would be necessary to equalize bounties. But, the paper warned, if Congress did not appropriate the necessary funds, "the business of paying colored claimants will be paralyzed."[17]

Savings and Trust

Funding, of course, had been a constant issue for the Freedmen's Bureau, and the Freedmen's Branch was no different. In fact, a knot of financial scandals inherited from the bureau nearly derailed its successor before it even began. They variously involved Commissioner Howard, Howard University, and the Freedmen's Savings and Trust Company. But it was the behavior of George W.

Balloch, the chief disbursing officer of the Freedmen's Bureau until 1871, that was at the heart of the matter. In the fall of that year, the Treasury Department noticed that nearly $280,000 was missing from Balloch's deposits with the Treasury. Balloch had apparently used $250,000 of those funds to purchase bonds, the interest of which he then used to pay Black claimants their bounties. He retained one-fifth of these bonds in his own private accounts. It was alleged by many investigators that since at least 1868, Balloch acquired these extra funds by having marked soldiers who were "slaves" at the time of enlistment as receiving a full bounty while only sending them the partial bounty and pocketing the balance, an opportunity for corruption made possible by the excessively convoluted bounty payment system. After a lengthy congressional investigation amounting to a 550-page report, it was determined that the disbursing officer's activities were of dubious legality and suspicious enough to warrant his termination in 1871. It was also determined that Howard was innocent of Balloch's wrongdoing; Congress later exonerated Howard and thanked him for his service with a glowing resolution. But it did little to negate the inglorious, ignoble end to the public life of the Freedmen's Bureau.[18]

When Thomas Vincent reopened the bureau's files, he reopened the scandal as well. Nine Treasury Department clerks set to work exclusively on investigating Balloch's old accounts. Vincent regularly reported on newly uncovered discrepancies in his annual reports of Congress. In his 1875 report, for instance, Vincent revealed that over $130,000 could not be accounted for. The exact details of the case, however, mattered less to the public than the general perception of bureau malfeasance. And such a perception decidedly contributed to the overall impression of the Freedmen's Bureau as a corrupt agency. "The Canting, Hypocritical, Meek-and-Lowly Freedman's Bureau Exposed—A Shocking Exhibit of Thieving," ran the headline of one representative article in the *Memphis Daily Appeal*. Another, from Jackson, Mississippi, crowed that "the Bureau agencies throughout the South were nothing but contrivances of extortion and plunder." Many in the Southern press spun the story as a fraud against freedpeople, in the guise of wanting only their protection. Long accosted by its critics—especially Southern Democrats— the interminable scandals surrounding the Freedmen's Bureau lent immense credibility to the view that the agency was nothing more than an intrusive vehicle of federal corruption.[19]

The Freedmen's Bureau appeared radioactive in the nation's media. It poisoned everything it touched, including the ill-fated Freedmen's Savings and Trust Company, better known as the Freedmen's Bank, chartered on the same day as the bureau, March 3, 1865. Though officially a private venture, it was the first ever savings bank created by the federal government and, as W. E. B. Du Bois noted, "morally and practically, the Freedmen's Bank was part of the Freedmen's Bureau." Dozens of branches throughout the South served as the depositories for funds owed to Black claimants in the former slave states, who would take their signed vouchers from a disbursing officer to a cashier at their local Freedmen's Bank for payment. In fact, cashiers were instructed to work closely with Black bounty claimants whenever possible. The bank's trustees imagined a didactic function for the Freedmen's Bank, to provide the means by which thousands of Black families, so recently emerged from slavery, would learn the important lessons of thrift and self-discipline, necessary traits for success in the free market system. Working, saving, and purchasing— these were the only proper means by which former slaves could acquire land of their own, argued the bank's founder, John W. Alvord, the former Freedmen's Bureau superintendent of education.[20]

Yet the Freedmen's Bank ultimately worked against freedpeople's economic security. During the war, Black soldiers frequently pooled together their resources in the hopes of purchasing tracts of land. Seeing this, white commanders instituted several small military banks for Black regiments. In South Carolina, General Rufus Saxton established the Military Savings Bank at Beaufort, while General Benjamin Butler founded another in Norfolk, Virginia. And in New Orleans, General Nathaniel Banks, a strong supporter of the contract lease system in the Mississippi Valley, founded the Free Labor Bank. The martial pedigrees of these institutions undoubtedly encouraged the trust of Black soldiers, who favored such banks with their deposits, which appeared to be fully backed and secured by no less an authority than the federal government. By the end of the war, an estimated $200,000 in unclaimed funds still belonged to deceased Black soldiers. These funds would serve as the seed capital for the Freedmen's Bank, and its branches would soon swell thanks largely to the ongoing deposits of Black veterans and heirs. Within ten years, over seventy-five thousand depositors placed their savings (and trust) in the Freemen's Bank, amounting to more than $75 million.

Though boasting a board of trustees stocked with prominent abolitionists, most board members abdicated management responsibilities immediately. Alvord, for his part, did worse than nothing, bringing aboard the former journalist-turned-war-profiteer Henry Cooke in 1867, whereafter the bank predictably started engaging in speculation. Henry, together with his more famous brother Jay, head of the First National Bank in Washington, used the deposits of the Freedmen's Bank to invest in railroad bonds. Though profitable for the short term—allowing the bank to operate thirty-two branches in the South—the high-risk speculation backfired. The economic crash of 1873, caused in large part by Jay Cooke and Company, dealt a mortal blow to the former savings bank. When it officially closed by congressional order on June 20, 1874, over sixty thousand depositors lost their savings. The federal government could have saved the Freedmen's Bank but chose not to, nor did it bother to prosecute the trustees. Half of the depositors received around eighteen dollars each as compensation. Needless to say, it was a devastating loss to freedpeople and undermined their trust in the federal government. Some depositors spent the next three decades petitioning Congress for reimbursement.[21]

Though the Freedmen's Bureau and the Freedmen's Bank ended by the early 1870s, the controversies their mismanagement engendered were undying. The twin embarrassments of the bounty fund and savings bank debacles featured prominently in the 1876 Democratic campaign manual, wherein Democratic candidates and operatives were instructed to make political hay out of the "shameless frauds upon the Negro." Attacking these two prominent Republican endeavors proved to be an effective political strategy. They would remain highly charged symbols, touchstones for the broader Democratic indictment of the Reconstruction project. Both the bureau and the bank, after all, represented federal efforts to secure the civil and economic rights of a special class of people, the formerly enslaved. Beyond the "demoralizing" dependency this inculcated in freedpeople, the Democrats argued, it simultaneously engendered corruption and drained the Treasury.[22]

Doctrines of Discovery

Through seemingly endless scandals and injustices, freedpeople in the South continued pursuing their claims. But the risk to freedpeople, according to federal policymakers and administrators, came not from federal policymakers and administrators but rather from private claims agents and attorneys in the South intent on bilking many claimants of their full bounties. Congress passed a resolution on March 29, 1867, to address the matter. The act made the Freedmen's Bureau the sole agency for paying claimants and set fixed fees claims attorneys could charge their clients in exchange for sending their claims to the Treasury for settlement. By contrast, Union veterans and heirs encountered a more straightforward system. For Northern regiments, the Treasury forwarded settled bounty claims to the paymaster general, who in turn would forward them to paymasters stationed in designated cities; the latter would send one check to the relevant attorney and another check directly to claimant. But the March 1867 resolution installed an intermediary for Black claimants in the former slave states, requiring "the officers and agents of the Freedmen's Bureau, to facilitate, as far as possible, the discovery, identification, and payment of the claimants."[23]

The Freedmen's Branch inherited these three tasks outlined by the 1867 resolution. Although branch officials were not legally authorized to act as claims agents—that is, to prepare the claims and send them to the second auditor, as bureau agents had—they retained responsibility for the second half of the process. In other words, after claimants submitted their applications directly to the second auditor of the Treasury, branch officials needed to not only locate those with settled claims wherever they may reside but also arrange for them to visit the disbursing office with their discharge certificates and two credible witnesses to prove their identity.[24] As its administrators soon learned, the very act of reaching claimants who were previously undocumented, and living in a previously unregulated region, would prove to be an extraordinarily difficult task, and ex-slave claimants, for their part, would have to learn how to make themselves reachable—and readable—to the state.[25]

When the Freedmen's Bureau was still around, freedpeople took advantage of the more numerous outposts and officers. They regularly overwhelmed claims offices in the bureau's final days. In the year ending September 1867, for example, over 245 Black claimants in North Carolina received some $35,000 from the bureau office at New Bern. But during that time, no fewer than seven thousand claimants had appeared, pressing the agent, Andrew Coats, on the status of their applications. Like so many of his counterparts, Coats found the identification of claimants extremely challenging. Often claimants would show up at his office without paperwork and inquire about their claims. Sometimes enterprising freedmen and freedwomen would assume another's identity, most often a deceased comrade or relative, and men like Coats found it "a difficult matter to guard against false personation." Federal officials had long suspected ex-slaves to have a propensity for lying out of self-interest or self-protection, a trait many sympathetic Northerners attributed to "the old effects of slavery." To protect the government, claimants were required to attach a joint affidavit of two "reputable" individuals of long acquaintance, signed before an officer of the state. On rare occasions, freedmen previously working for the bureau and with extensive knowledge of the area served as professional witnesses for those in their community. For instance, Thornton Johnson, a freedman employed in the bureau's Natchez office, sufficiently earned the confidence of the local bureau agent who in turn requested that Johnson serve as an identifier of applicants. As the agent put it to a superior, Johnson "is able to identify a majority of the claimants for bounties, and is entirely trust-worthy." In most cases, however, two credible witnesses were required. Bu-reau agents eventually settled on a shorthand way to determine the credibility of witnesses, requiring "affidavits of two persons *who write their names*." This method effectively functioned as a literacy test for witnesses.[26]

Though the processing of their claims always felt painfully slow, the greater, but by no means sufficient, presence of the Freedmen's Bureau made it comparatively easier for claimants to follow through on their applications. Bureau officials, after all, had authorization to act as claims agents for freed-people and forward and receive their claims, unlike branch officials, who only had authority to pay out settled claims. In consequence of their more limited roles, branch officials repeatedly told claimants, especially in the agency's early years, that they should address letters "directly to the Second Auditor; the Freedmen's Bureau having been abolished and there being now no officer of the Government authorized to act as the agent of claimants." This proved especially puzzling—and galling—to those with claims still pending in the late bureau. Writing from Nashville in September 1872, one attorney with some three hundred unpaid claims explained to the adjutant general that "the Claimants are left here without any means of assisting any knowledge of thire [*sic*] Claims." They now had a "worse a chance than ever" of seeing their money. The man, and doubtless his three hundred clients, waited impatiently for a disbursing officer to arrive. In New Orleans, a large contingent of Black soldiers' wives collectively demanded the adjutant general appoint a claims agent in the city. Meanwhile, in western Kentucky, dozens of Black veterans—"good worthy citizens" who had never received their bounties filed through the late bureau—began spreading rumors that Democratic claims agents had "deceived" and swin-dled them out of their "hard & perilous earnings." They accordingly sought out a local Republican Party committee chairman to appeal to the adjutant general on their behalf. Though a partisan explanation proved convincing to many claimants, ultimately their dissatisfaction owed less to malicious Demo-cratic operatives than to the bipartisan settlement on bureaucratic incapacity.[27]

Freedpeople's petitions for bureaucratic attention emerged across the de-mobilized South. In late March 1874, a group of freedpeople representing themselves as "citizens of the State of North Carolina" sent a petition to Con-gress, which was referred to the Committee on Military Affairs. The petition-ers, led by Robert Coleman of the Thirty-Seventh USCT, protested that when they applied for their bounties their discharge certificates were placed in the hands of a former Freedmen's Bureau agent in Raleigh who in turn disbursed their bounty payments. But the petitioners believed "that a portion of the aforesaid Bounties to which they were justly entitled have been withheld," and, owing to the bounty equalization act of March 1873, they wanted their additional bounties as well. Most of the petitioners received between $100 and $150, except for one, who received $300. This was evidently their source of confusion and the impetus for questioning their bounties. The petitioners asked for "the proper relief" and explained that they were "in very humble circumstances." Given the closure of the Freedmen's Bureau, the petitioners implored that they "have not means to prosecute their claims in any other manner than by petition." Even at its lowest ebb, the Freedmen's Bureau had far more personnel in the field than the Freedmen's Branch, which only employed approximately three dozen individuals in regional offices. Though distance always beleaguered both agencies, Black claimants would struggle even more so under the tenure of the Freedmen's Branch, owing to the undersized and undermanned character of the organization and exacerbated by the ossifying geopolitical restrictions on Black mobility in the sharecropping South.[28]

How claims themselves moved through the administrative state was anything but straightforward. The process began with branch officials notifying claimants of their applications' approval by the Treasury (and confirmation by the War Department); then claimants themselves would appear before the branch official with two witnesses and the proper paperwork; after branch officials verified their identity, claimants would take their signed vouchers to a designated bank for a cash payout. Administrators tellingly referred to the initial steps of this process as the "discovery" of claimants. In a real sense, it indeed marked the first time the national government endeavored to document the intimate lives of ordinary citizens, marking in turn a new departure in the relationship of citizens to their government. As historian Sarah Igo has argued, the data-collecting capacities of the American state lagged far behind its industrializing peers in the late nineteenth century. The establishment of "paper identities" as a mode of governance began in states and localities with the halting implementation of birth certificates during the Progressive Era, but would not centralize until the New Deal, when the Social Security Board assigned nine-digit identification numbers to its citizen-beneficiaries. The documentary dearth that preceded it was especially felt in the rural South, where three out of four Southerners lived at the turn of the century. Decades prior, all branch officials involved in the discovery of claimants could readily testify to the extreme difficulty of locating individuals on the payroll rosters, many of whom had moved far from their points of enlistment, well away from their old residences, and sometimes completely out of state.[29]

Establishing contact, coordinating an appearance before a disbursing officer, and confirming a claimant's identity constituted the three basic stages of retrieving a bounty claim through the Freedmen's Branch. First, consider the matter of contacting claimants. The most common means by which branch officials attempted to notify claimants of pending or approved claims was through the mail. But it often proved of limited value. "The addresses of claimants as set down in the list of claimants," complained one branch official in the lower Mississippi Valley, "is altogether unreliable owing to their constantly changing names & localities. Four out of five of the notices sent are returned through the Post uncalled." The disbursing officer at Nashville successfully identified and paid not one in thirty, believing "that the parties do not know of a Disbursing Office being established here, and another is that most of them are living on farms, more or less remote from the city." He listened approvingly to the local postmaster, who pontificated on the "roving propensities" of freedpeople that made it "very unlikely" they could be reached by post. In addition to vainly flooding local post offices with letters addressed to claimants, branch officials also placed advertisements in prominent city newspapers, especially Black newspapers and those associated with the Republican Party, such as the *New Orleans Republican*, Baton Rouge's *Grand Era*, and the *Intelligencer* of Monroe, Louisiana. Typical advertisements told all Black soldiers and sailors who had received notice of a Treasury certificate in their favor to send their names, addresses, and regiment and company to the adjutant general himself in Washington, D.C., who would see their claims fulfilled without further expense or delay. The branch's strategy garnered some positive results. Many claimants wrote to branch officials that they had seen their names in newspaper advertisements for bounties.[30]

Similarly, many disbursing officers printed names of claimants owed bounty money on large, vibrant posters in well-trafficked areas, and to fairly good effect. One particularly active solicitor was J. K. Hyer, the disbursing officer stationed in South Carolina. Groups of Black veterans from across the state began appearing at his door. By the start of 1874, so many had done so that Hyer wrote to Thomas Vincent, asking "what advice and instructions" he should give to the "several parties in this section of the state" who "claim bounty under the Act of March 3, 1873." Two days later, Hyer devised a plan. He would print the names of all unpaid bounty claimants on posters and have them "sent to every post office in the state"—all 330 of them—"and posted in the most conspicuous place, so that claimants, who may, since they presented their claims, have moved to another part of the state, be more likely reached and disbursements made." He believed that in doing so the government would finally learn the whereabouts of these remaining claimants, be they dead or alive. In the spring, Hyer's plan began yielding returns, in large part owing to the proactivity of networks of Black veterans. Dozens of unpaid Black claimants presented themselves or their cases to the federal official. George Washington, an ex-slave who had enlisted in the Thirty-Third USCT at Beaufort, found his name on one of Hyer's posters. At first surprised and "impressed it is my-self" there on the list, Washington wrote to the branch official several times over the spring inquiring after the debt owed him by the government. The same story replayed itself dozens of times in cases of ex-slave veterans such as Henry Windham, Samuel Coleman, and Joseph Smith. All wanted instructions. Some, including Smith, wanted to know whether he had to travel clear to Hyer's office in Columbia or whether the officer would ever come to Charleston and pay his and comrades' claims.[31]

Urban claimants enjoyed an immense advantage over rural ones. According to census records, at this time roughly a third of USCT veterans lived in Southern towns with more than eight thousand people, and a quarter lived in cities of more than twenty-five thousand. But even those who lived in the countryside cultivated support networks with old comrades, friends, and kin from antebellum days. As historian Anthony Kaye has shown, neighborhoods remained the locus of different relations in the postbellum plantation South, but freedom enlarged those neighborhoods and reordered them on the basis of family units and labor relations. Branch officials who had the most luck locating claimants succeeded precisely because they tapped into long-standing Black social networks, both formal and informal. The disbursing officer overseeing Arkansas and Tennessee, for instance, distributed lists of approved claimants to Black ministers, asking for them to be read and posted after each service. It was "rather out of place," commented one observer of the practice in Little Rock, "but nevertheless causing a pleasant sensation." Virginia's disbursing officer likewise reached out to Black ministers. He also came to learn the most valuable information about the whereabouts of his unpaid claimants by other claimants, those who had come to his office at Fort Monroe. He therefore planned to canvass the cities in his district, "taking a list of names and endeavoring by inquiry to ascertain where claimants reside." Doing so, he predicted, would "awaken inquiries among the colored population of the two cities, materially assisting in quickening payments." As time wore on, it seemed more and more Black claimants for unpaid bounties learned of their claims secondhand, from fellow soldiers and neighbors, third parties with a more familiar knowledge of the social land-scape than the functionaries of the central state.[32]

Defying Distance

Because the U.S. Army had a robust wartime presence in the lower Missis-sippi Valley, recruiting intensely from the enslaved population, the region teemed with unpaid claims of Black soldiers and their surviving heirs. They would all hear from George Gibson, the branch's disbursing officer for the valley headquartered at Memphis. Gibson was among the more competent disbursing officers, fastidious in his duties and capable of managing a large volume of claims. One such agent who dealt frequently with Gibson was none other than Thomas Boles. Having left Congress after securing bounty equalization for ex-slave soldiers, Boles returned to Arkansas to practice law. Naturally, he assisted his former constituents in securing their additional bounties made possible by bounty equalization. Many freedpeople came to Boles for help, and he was all too happy to oblige. Boles handled the claims of ex-slaves with dispatch and sensitivity and wrote earnestly to branch officials on their behalf. In one instance, Boles explained to Gibson that an elderly cli-ent of his, Delia Webb, would have "some difficulty in getting two witnesses to accompany her there, without considerable trouble and expense. If I should be in Little Rock at the time," he asked, "would that obviate the necessity of bringing the two witnesses required?" Gibson agreed, and Boles personally traveled with Webb more than seventy miles to Little Rock, where he helped her draw her money.[33]

When a freedman or freedwoman wrote to a disbursing officer, the latter could be sure that the claimant lived at a distance and needed accommoda-tion. Henry Jones, for example, was working as a foreman on a plantation in Bayou Lafourche eight miles outside Donaldsonville, Louisiana, and thus nearly ninety miles from the disbursing office at New Orleans. In a letter to the chief disbursing officer in Washington, Jones explained the prohibitive expense of traveling with two witnesses to the branch office, which he esti-mated would "cost me more than $25.00 beside the loss that my absent would cause to my employer." He asked instead for the money to be delivered to the postmaster at Donaldsonville. In Bolivar County, Mississippi, a large group of Black claimants were notified that the "money due them" was finally available—though at the branch office in Vicksburg, a distance of some three hundred miles. Enlisting the support of a local law firm, the men complained that they "cannot possibly go so far from home," and that they did "not possess sufficient money to defray the expenses of self and witnesses." They instead asked whether the money could be forwarded to their attorney, a practice specifically prohibited by the resolution of March 29, 1867. On occasion, branch officials made the case for postal delivery to the claimants themselves. The same disbursing officer at Vicksburg intervened in the case of Rose Bolin, the mother of a deceased soldier. He explained to the adjutant general how "on account of her great age & bodily infirmities, [she] requests that her money be sent to her at Canton," nearer her Mississippi home. "The Post Master at Canton is a friend of mine," assured the officer; "he knows the woman and is a man of high standing in that community." Despite exceptions made in special circumstances, branch officials long resisted calls to allow for payment by post to all claimants, fearing it would invite fraud. They needed to see the claimants in person.[34]

Having so many unpaid claimants in various known and unknown locations made it difficult to contact claimants by post to arrange for their arrival. For instance, one claims attorney wrote in exasperation to Gibson in late April 1873. He had been trying to get Harriet Johnson her money since 1868. After Gibson invited Johnson and her witnesses to his office in Memphis, her attorney shot back that it was "out of the question to send her and two members of the company for it would cost her 75 dollar[s], which would be nearly half of claim." Johnson, he relayed bitterly to Gibson, "has come to the conclusion that the *fuss* the U.S. makes to protect colored people do them more harm than good," and asked, "Cant [*sic*] you appoint some one here" to pay out the money? The fuss Harriet Johnson and other ex-slave claimants complained about stemmed from the mandate to pay claimants directly. Whereas administrators regarded the measure as necessary to protect Black claimants, the claimants themselves almost universally saw it as purposefully cumbersome, as if designed to frustrate people enough to the point of abandoning their claims altogether. In Helena, Arkansas, a group of Black veterans and heirs from the Sixty-Third USCT collectively hired a private attorney to prosecute their unpaid claims, for which they had "waited long & patiently." But upon learning they would be "required to go to Memphis to receive their pay," they felt "the U.S. government had about as well keep it." Before it did, however, they pressed upon their attorney to offer two proposals to the secretary of war. First, the former slaves "authorized" the War Department to send a special officer for payment—and volunteered to cover his expenses as well. Or, if the department instead planned to nominate an existing official at Helena to facilitate their claims, these men had their preferences and insisted upon nominating their own representative.[35]

Black soldiers mustered out at Little Rock. Soldiers of the U.S. Colored Troops began to muster out in early 1866, as illustrated in this jubilant scene in Little Rock, Arkansas, rendered for *Harper's Weekly*. Black soldiers left service without their expected bounty payments and, along with their surviving heirs, would struggle for years with officials of the Freedmen's Branch to receive their pay. (Library of Congress Prints and Photographs Division, LC-USZC4-2042)

Such constraints on mobility characterized the political economy of the postbellum South, in which most Black claimants found themselves in relations of precarious dependency with their employers. If Black veterans and their families fared somewhat better than their nonmilitary counterparts in acquiring enough cash or credit to purchase their own plots of land, then those still pursuing their claims in the 1870s were likely locked into tenancy or sharecropping arrangements. Such men and women in correspondence with branch officials in the late summer and fall were emphatic about their inability to leave their workplaces for any amount of time. For example, when Gibson informed Maria White of her son's bounty money ready for payment at his office, she declined. She told Gibson through her agent that she "is farming and would loose [*sic*] considerable on her crop and her witnesses are also farming and would have to be paid a very high price to justify them to go." Even if she were "to have good health good luck and good success she would [still] come back in debt." The money she could expect at Gibson's office "would not pay expence [sic] time and hire of witnesses at this time to go after it." Her agent nonetheless encouraged her to go, but White refused. She shot back that it was unreasonable to leave her field to pursue "uncertaintys [sic]." Though skeptical about whether she would be able to attain the bounty due her, Maria White knew exactly what she was owed, and it far exceeded the $150.41 on the books. Her husband enlisted in late August 1864, she told her agent, after the bounty equalization measure of July 4, 1864, and therefore "should receive 300 $bounty." Though the agent may have been unfamiliar with bounty laws, his client was not. And in the end, she was "unable to think that $150.41 closes her accounts." The interaction with the formerly enslaved woman—so versed in her rights, so prudent, assertive, and tethered to her humble plot of land—evidently made an impact on the agent. Concluding his letter to Gibson, the agent complained, "We say we make no distinction on account of race or coller [sic] yet it is less trouble to get five claims of white widows than one for a colored widow." Mere statutory equality could not, it seemed, remedy the condition of ex-slave claimants.[36]

A matrix of legal and economic mechanisms immobilized Black Southerners in the postbellum era. Vagrancy laws were central to the Black Codes enacted by Southern states under presidential Reconstruction to bind Black workers to their employers, while enticement laws prevented employers in need of labor from interfering in the proprietary relationship of fellow planters and their laborers. Black workers caught wandering in search of employment could expect to be arrested, jailed, and convicted. Many in turn were swept into the vortex of the convict lease system that emerged as a highly profitable substitute for slavery. Where white planters saw vagrancy, indolence, and rebelliousness, freedpeople saw a necessary tool to improve one's employment arrangements, to reconstruct kinship relations lost in slavery, or simply to explore in ways they had not been able to before in the days of slavery. The ability to move freely, then, became a highly contested right of Black Southerners' newfound freedom, and they tested it as needed in the Southern labor market. As historian William Cohen has detailed, freedpeople not only circulated about the region in search of higher wages and better contracts in their quest for autonomy but also took advantage of so-called labor agents who arose to shuttle Black workers long distances to future employers, a task once performed by the Freedmen's Bureau to shore up the free labor system by relocating would-be dependents to areas in need of laborers. The ongoing creation of a dynamic, geographically mobile Black workforce at once attested to the relative bargaining power afforded Black workers by high demands for labor as well as the more powerful countervailing forces of racism and exploitation that forced those same workers into unremunerative, highly vulnerable occupations.[37]

In the depressed economy of the South, white onlookers regarded the Freedmen's Branch with a kind of agitated ambiguity. Many bristled at the sight of Black claimants funneling into disbursing offices, rejoicing at times over their long-awaited bounties. Such was especially the case in cities home to branch offices, above all Memphis. There, the local paper frequently reported on George Gibson's activities, where he traveled to pay off claims, and how much money he expected to distribute. Following the bounty equalization for ex-slaves in the spring of 1873, the *Memphis Daily Appeal* noted how in the past month Gibson "paid out about fifteen thousand dollars to darkies" and estimated that he still had over $100,000 to deliver. The Appeal could only look on with a barely concealed indignation at the "comic scenes" that were "daily enacted in the Major's office by the darkies who come to receive the money so long looked for," many "unable to restrain their rapturous joy when they find themselves the owner of an amount of cash such as they never expected to possess in their lives."[38]

By the same token, many white Memphians traced a broad silver lining around the disbursing offices of the Freedmen's Branch. They surmised that these Black claimants would, after all, have to spend their earnings, thereby injecting cash into the Southern economy made all the worse by the economic meltdown of 1873. The material conditions of the South deteriorated precipitously during the economic crisis, when Northern banks called in Southern loans and Southern agricultural markets withered, bringing acute hardships to small farmers in particular. In the early 1870s, Southern states agonized over how to pay off their debts and placed much of the blame on the Republican project to reconstruct the South. Indeed, Democratic promises to combat fiscal irresponsibility and high taxation were integral to the rise of the so-called Redeemers, who sought to return the South to "responsible government," barely coded language for anti-Black and anti-labor governance. The retreat from Reconstruction, therefore, moved simultaneously with the enforcement of austerity. But in a more immediate sense, with the economic contraction causing widespread dislocation and unemployment, particularly in areas where wage labor dominated, white critics of the Freedmen's Branch seemed to welcome the influx of cash, even if it temporarily passed through the hands of Black workers. If these Black claimants were draining the federal Treasury, in other words, that blood would at least be transfused in the rising city of Memphis. "Over four thousand dollars were distributed during the past week," commented the *Appeal* in May 1873, "which doubtless quickly found its way into the coffers of the retail merchants of the city." Scores of settled claims were arriving daily, with thousands of dollars to distribute, all of "which will prove advantageous to the money market." White spectators desperate for the indirect economic stimulus of bounty payments began to lose patience with the perceived inactivity of Black claimants. Here was Gibson, they observed, ready to hand out free money, "but the colored folks appear to be too busy now with their cotton crop to come into the city, prove their identity, and receive the amounts allowed them by the department at Washington."[39]

It was not only their crops that kept Black claimants in the Mississippi Valley from their bounties. The Freedmen's Branch regularly ceased operations in the region during the sickly months of summer, when epidemics threatened officials and claimants alike. During the early summer of 1873, a purported cholera outbreak in Memphis discouraged Black claimants from venturing in from the hinterlands. By July, however, they "made up their minds and arrived at the conclusion that cholera has entirely disappeared from the city" and began boarding the "several lines of railroad which centralize in Memphis." Despite popular beliefs in Black immunity to a range of endemic diseases prevalent in the South, officials and onlookers rarely presumed that claimants would risk exposure with a trip to a disbursing office. As one agent speaking for more than a dozen rural Mississippi claimants put it in January 1877, "They prefer not to travel 200 miles for their money loose time out of their crops & run the risk of catching some disease which may end their existence." That same month, claimants in Woodville, Mississippi, decided to sell their claims at a considerable discount to collection agencies, who would in turn pursue the claims, "rather than run the risk of fever by going to Natchez."[40]

Black claimants in the rural South were keenly aware of how distance undermined their claims-making ability. Despite its high number of claimants, at any given time in the lower Mississippi Valley, there were only ever two disbursing officers for three locations—Natchez, New Orleans, and Vicksburg. Letters from Black claimants constantly implored the branch officials to come to towns and hamlets closer to communities of claimants, or in the very least to have the disbursing officers notify them of their travel plans. In February 1873, for example, Phebe Harrison wanted to know when G. G. Hunt would leave his post at New Orleans and come to his second post at Natchez, much nearer to herself and fellow claimants. "The expense of the trip to New Orleans and, above all, the difficulty, if not impossibility, of obtaining competent witnesses *there* to establish my identity," she explained, "will compel me to wait here until a disbursing officer arrives." Years later, Elizabeth Matthews wrote directly to the chief disbursing officer in Washington, explaining the utter impracticality of a sojourn to New Orleans to collect her money. Not only did Matthews have a young child with her, but the trip "would cost me some money that I could hardly be able to borrow, having been obliged to expend the little I had during my last confinement [pregnancy]."[41]

In response to the petitions and appeals from Black claimants such as Phebe Harrison and Elizabeth Matthews, Freedmen's Branch officials in Washington repeatedly authorized their disbursing officers to circulate about their districts, writing to claimants and advertising their whereabouts. Three days after the bounty equalization act, Adjutant General E. D. Townsend wrote to the disbursing officer at New Orleans, A. K. Arnold, and instructed him to travel seventy miles outside of town to Donaldsonville and arrange to pay Black claimants residing in the surrounding parishes. He advised Arnold to notify each claimant by letter of when and where to appear and gave specific dates for when he ought to remain in Donaldsonville. "In fixing the date for the appearance of claimants for payment," he explained, "you should allow a reasonable length of time"—generally two to three weeks—"for the receipt of the notification, taking into consideration the fact that as a general rule colored persons do not visit the Post Office often." In a few months, Arnold would again be pressed by claimants to return to Donaldsonville, and again was reauthorized to do so. Many officials soon realized they would need to travel far and wide to reach unpaid claimants dispersed across the countryside. In April 1873, another officer requested authorization to visit such Louisiana locales as Waterproof, St. Joseph, and Bayou Sara, having found that rural claimants in his district "are not sufficiently known away from their places of abode to establish their identity." Distance, then, both reflected and exacerbated a host of bureaucratic obstacles for the settlement of freedpeople's claims. It reflected the inadequate capacity of the federal administrative state and its inability to account for the political-economic constraints of the post-slavery South. And it exacerbated the dilemmas of claimant identification.[42]

Identity Politics

When Black claimants arrived at a Freedmen's Branch field office, they stepped into a vestibule of the modernizing administrative state. The task they confronted under its new documentary regime, that of "proving" their identity, included verifying their war records and their intimate relationships and corroborating that proof with two reliable witnesses. Every disbursing officer of the Freedmen's Branch agreed "that in the business of identification by far the greatest difficulty is experienced." The strict accounting of the past required for an unambiguous claim often eluded federal officials. Freedpeople's extraordinary lives were also largely extralegal before emancipation, and therefore bureaucratically indeterminate, frequently forcing the administrative state to make uncomfortable allowances and concessions. And for freedpeople, "proving themselves" also required yielding to the antebellum order in unforeseen and unwelcome ways. For instance, plausible identifying documents included bills of sale as well as slave passes, the latter characterized by one scholar as an "embryonic form of the modern ID." Although all such forms of antebellum identification had served their functions for the ruling and business class, they remained privately issued and idiosyncratic. The centralized documentation of citizens would not be a currency of statecraft until the early twentieth century. Freedpeople's engagement with the Freedmen's Branch anticipated these difficulties many decades before.[43]

The undocumented nature of Black claimants' prewar lives wreaked havoc on their postwar claims. When former slave Shadrick Smith wrote to G. G. Hunt in Natchez, asking about the $300 in bounty money he believed was owed to him, the official sent two routine replies detailing instructions on how to proceed. Over a year later, in June 1874, Smith confessed he was still "at a loss to know what to do in this matter." The floodwaters of the Mississippi spring had finally retreated and he was pressed into service, rendering him "without means, and very busy just know [*sic*] with my crop." He promised Hunt he could "furnish any evidence you might want to substantiate my claim as there is parties living here who were in the army with me." But making the trip to Hunt's office in Natchez, and with these witnesses no less, would have been impossible. Such evident frustration percolated in every unpaid bounty claim. But as well, Smith's promise to provide "any evidence" suggests an impending disconnect between the vernacular and the official, the former being of little use to the federal state. Those applicants visiting the disbursing office at New Orleans would have heard the federal agent stationed there bemoan, as he did in 1872, that his clientele, "being ignorant and illiterate as a rule, have no idea of what an affidavit of identification should be. They bring all kinds of documents which are of no use whatever." Every bounty application therefore functioned as a bureaucratic literacy test. The problem, however, had less to do with the alleged ignorance of claimants than their (very understandable) unfamiliarity with rarefied legal documents such as an affidavit of identification and the nagging unattainability of modern standards of documentary public evidence in the postbellum South.[44]

The Civil War helped precipitate a more direct relationship between the national government and individual citizens. And official identification facilitated that relationship. But the connection was especially fraught in the emancipated South, where previously enslaved claimants haltingly emerged from the documentary opacity of their prewar lives—indeed, from a system of enslavement predicated on the destruction of their lives, lineages, and relationships in service of labor exploitation. To be sure, most freedpeople welcomed federal involvement in their lives, insofar as it furthered the reciprocal relationships many had cultivated since the earliest days of the war when they sought protection and offered service behind Union lines. But when their wartime foothold slipped to a toehold after the demobilization waves of the early 1870s, rendering their claims-making through the Freedmen's Branch a singular channel to the federal state, thousands of freedpeople found their intimate lives and relationships exposed, probed, and demeaned. Thus, while state legibility clearly had its material benefits, it also invited intense scrutiny, loss of privacy, and threats to dignity.[45]

In theory, Black veterans had some conventional markers of identification, including regimental rolls and discharge certificates. From their official military records, the Adjutant General's Office of the War Department created so-called confidential lists. These forms stipulated for every USCT soldier his name, rank, company, regiment, commanding officer, date of enlistment, enlisting officer, date of discharge (or death), distinguishing marks or military engagements, place of birth, former enslavers, and the names of one or more comrades who enlisted at about the same time and place; they also left room for editorializing remarks, especially regarding any "peculiar fact or event connected with the soldier's history."[46] Records of wartime injury or illness were especially important, as were any scars or other physical features that doubled as unique markers of identity. True to its name, the information extracted from the official records was to be kept "*strictly confidential*," used only by Freedmen's Branch officials, who received the confidential lists upon settlement of claims from the second auditor. When Black claimants appeared before branch officials to collect their payments, they could expect a battery of questions drawn from the confidential lists, filling in the blanks of service record matrices. Safeguarding the details of a claimant's official record was essential to proving his or her identity. Thomas Vincent praised the system of confidential list-verification as the ultimate check on fraud. Individuals who may have successfully "obtained settlement of claims upon fraudulent applications" were routinely thwarted when they presented themselves to disbursing officers who interrogated them with the official record.[47]

Branch officials applied intense scrutiny when determining claimants' identities. For a people so long denied legal personality and any independent recognition by the state, it is tempting to see these examinations as an opportunity for freedpeople to "tell their story," a kind of symbolic victory, and a moral endowment for posterity. But doing so tends to romanticize what was a decidedly unromantic situation. In reality, these meetings were less open-ended interviews for self-affirmation than they were highly constrained and high-stakes interrogations with a year's worth of income on the line. Moreover, these meetings were often years in the making, and claimants had often devoted considerable time and resources to even make it to that point. Tense feelings of anxiety, vexation, and inadequacy no doubt gripped many of the claimants as they appeared before disbursing officers. The details of their lives, records, and relationships needed careful recitation to meet standards of proof that always seemed to dangle out of reach. Any discrepancy between their testimony and the official record not only jeopardized their claim but might just as well trigger a fraud investigation, leading to hefty fines or imprisonment, and always widely publicized ridicule in the white press. Such were the risks of the early welfare state in the South.[48]

Yet from an early date it became clear to disbursing officers and freedpeople alike that the confidential lists had severe limitations in practice. In Memphis, George Gibson found the lists regrettably unreliable for determining vital statistics such as age, height, and complexion. "Few, very few claimants know how old they were when they entered the service," Gibson noted, "or even measure the same now as the feet [and] inches given," and "in regard to color, the nice distinctions between mulatto, light brown, brown, dark brown and black seem to have been almost lost sight of." Claimants also educated Gibson as to how "the Recruiting officers simply jotted down what he thought would be appropriate." Likewise, in April 1873, the branch official in New Orleans, G. G. Hunt, complained that their "knowledge of the dates of enlistment, of muster in and of muster out and by whom, age, occupation, height place of nativity &c is often found to be erroneous." Owing to inaccurate, sporadic, or otherwise deficient recordkeeping, the full military record of claimants, from names and companies to hospitalization and treatment records, frequently confounded or contradicted claimants' honest recollections.[49]

The disconnect was even more pronounced in cases involving heirs. Gibson's successor, H. S. Hawkins, found that although soldiers were sometimes "ready enough in answers to questions suggested by information given in Confidential Lists," the lists were "frequently of no assistance in the examination of heirs of deceased soldiers. The examinations in such cases are long, tedious, and often unsatisfactory, causing payment to be suspended and subjecting claimants to additional expense for travel &c." On occasion, the second auditor supplemented the lists with information regarding soldiers' wives, including maiden name and time and place of the wedding ceremony, though in general a dearth of heirship information persisted and consequently undermined the claims of widows ignorant of the military history of the deceased. Furthermore, Hawkins remarked, no information whatsoever was supplied "in cases where the father, mother, brother, sister or child is the claimant, and then I experience great difficulty." And all such challenges of identification "perceptibly increases as the date of soldier's death becomes more remote." In their face-to-face interrogations of prospective bounty claim- ants, field office examiners frequently heard heirs confess something to the effect of "we never saw him after he left us," as in the case of ex-slave Melvin Gillens's parents. Others felt their chances at a loved one's bounty slip away with each unsatisfactory answer. When did Frederick Alexander enlist? the officer at Natchez asked his widow, Kitty, in February 1874.

"When they took Port Hudson," she replied.

Who enlisted Frederick into service?

"He ran away."

When and where did he muster into service? pressed the official.

Kitty could not say for sure, but she assumed Port Hudson, Louisiana. Nor could she tell the examiner her late husband's regiment, company, or com- manding officer. She could, however, identify Frederick's personal history (born in Richmond, Virginia) and his physical description (five feet, nine or ten inches, "brown or yellow" complexion) and his enslaver (James A. Stewart). But she knew little of her husband's service. "He left me near Wood- ville," she plaintively recalled, "and the next I heard he was dead & had been dead six months." She heard rumors he had died of pneumonia at Port Hud- son but could not say when exactly, or how for sure.[50]

To their credit, many disbursing officers did not generally view these testi- monial deficiencies narrowly, faulting, as it were, the individual claimants. Instead, they more frequently invoked broader explanatory forces—perhaps they had to, given the sheer volume of such cases presented to them on a daily basis. Some accounted for the relative ignorance of heirs, for example, by considering how, "in the majority of cases," the soldiers had likely "left their homes clandestinely to enter the military services of the government, enlist- ing at points more or less remote therefrom and that their means of commu- nication therewith were infrequent and uncertain." Most of the witnesses for these heirs were thus comrades of the deceased who themselves struggled to establish their identities and, before that, struggled to make themselves discoverable, owing, surmised one branch official, to their being "migratory plantation hands without fixed places of abode and with whom it would be impossible to communicate should occasion require." To some disbursing officers, it was clear that they ought to make payments as close to their claimants' homes as possible, thereby increasing the likelihood applicants might "establish their identity by credible persons in their neighborhood, residents of the localities and of a class that are not likely to remove therefrom after the making of each crop."[51]

A range of other unforeseen factors worked to undermine the integrity of the confidential lists. In areas with high claimant activity, especially in Tennessee and in the vicinity of New Orleans, designing men somehow obtained lists of entire USCT regiments and companies awaiting settlement, together with the names of officers, records of deaths, desertions, and discharges. It encouraged a precocious form of identity theft. "Any of the bounty agents, if so disposed," commented the Memphis branch official, "could so drill a negro upon the military record of any company as to enable him to give nearly all the information contained in the Confidential Lists." Some branch officials believed such a situation was ironically brought about by having publicly advertised so vigorously for unpaid Black claimants to come forward, while others believed some government official must have been selling the lists to private claims agents. Vicksburg became infamous for its alleged criminal ring of bounty sharpers. There, the disbursing officer found that several persons "had large bound volumes, containing, as to thousands of claimants, all the information that appears on the face of a *Soldier's Discharge*," as well as "the names of the witnesses who identified the claimants, his place of residence if living, and the names of his heirs if dead." The official warned the adjutant general that the "business had been reduced to a system by the old Bounty and Pension Agents." Whereas this officer was overly confident that "not one negro in ten thousand, however well crammed, can answer the questions suggested by the lists if he did not perform the service," many of his peers complained that the confidential lists were thus rendered wholly "inadequate for our protection." The threats posed to the federal government by organized bounty claim hustlers incited, on the one hand, greater governmental secrecy and criminal prosecution of alleged fraudulent behavior and, on the other, heightened suspicion of Black claimants' testimony.[52]

If such risks fell upon all formerly enslaved claimants, freedwomen bore a greater share of the burden. According to federal policy, widows enjoyed pride of place when it came to heirship, followed by children, mothers, and fathers, in that order. Thus for a mother to secure the claim of her deceased son, she had to prove that the soldier in question was in fact her biological son, that her son was in fact deceased, that the son was in fact unmarried (or that his wife deserted him), and, finally, that the son was in fact childless. Should the deceased soldier have no mother, the soldier's full brothers and sisters would be considered the legal heirs. Retroactively proving what legal scholar Margaret Burnham calls "an impossible marriage" between two enslaved people often proved one of the biggest challenges to any claim to bounty, back pay, or pension, for it also came with prerequisites of cohabitation and fidelity. In 1864, formerly enslaved widows applying for federal military benefits needed to establish a two-year term of cohabitation as a "married" couple with the deceased soldier, but in 1866 Congress modified the law by dropping the time requirement. Over the next two decades, Congress would continually pass new legislation to determine what constituted a "slave marriage" and how that might be legitimated by the state.[53]

Determining a lawful marriage mattered a great deal to a great many interested parties connected to the deceased veteran. Conflict arose when two or more people laid claim as rightful heirs. In Vicksburg, Cordelia Dorsey applied for bounty and pension as the widow of a deceased soldier, only to find that the soldier's mother had already filed a claim. Dorsey asked Commissioner Howard who exactly was entitled to the claim, and promised him she had "ample proof that he was my husband," even that "his mother dose [sic] not deny the fact." When Isaac Cook, the father of a deceased solider in Charleston, learned that an unknown person had applied for his son's claim, he protested, "I am his own legitimate father, his mother is dead, he never was married and never had a woman ever as a lover he was in fact but a boy & left no children." To buttress his claim, Cook deployed a vocabulary the federal official might understand, asserting that he could "furnish the affidavits of this whole community—that I am the only one that can make any claim whatever." Such cases of overlapping claims were not uncommon in the postslavery South. More than a few sensational, death-defying cases arose as a result. In one reported instance, a freedman named Benjamin Hall convinced one Maria Jackson that her husband, Montague Jackson, had died. Hall had allegedly seen him die and even attended his burial, and now he offered his assistance to Maria to help retrieve her husband's bounty. After swearing an oath, Maria received the money and dutifully gave the majority of it to Hall. But March 1869 saw the return of Montague Jackson, who appeared in person at the disbursing office at Natchez, whereupon the federal official had Hall arrested and Jackson's stolen bounty money returned. These rare incidents, along with the more common cases of overlapping claims, belie popular and sentimentalized notions of a homogeneous Black community naturally united in common interest. Instead, such conflicts were endemic to any and every assortment of individuals pursuing self-interest in ways that cut across boundaries of family, community, and race.[54]

Unlike the Freedmen's Branch, its predecessor had taken an active role in officiating marriages among former slaves, many of whom had already performed the rituals of matrimony in the days of slavery. Formerly enslaved couples needed to abide by prevailing norms in white society to gain official sanction from the state. Sermons on conjugal fidelity and reciprocity emanated from bureau officials, aid workers, and missionaries. Regularizing marital relations among former slaves, and bestowing upon their unions legal rights, effectively coerced formerly enslaved couples to conform to the postwar labor systems. Yet if establishing new rules for binding marriages among ex-slaves was one thing, retroactively labeling a slave relationship a marriage was another altogether, especially when material resources were at stake. With so many ex-slave widows lodging claims for military benefits via the Freedmen's Bureau, the federal government developed a set of procedures and questions to investigate the validity of intimate relations. It came not from a minister, congressman, or judge but from an accountant. In May 1870, the second auditor of the Treasury, E. B. French, wrote to Commissioner Howard regarding the "question of heirship" under slave customs, where a "man may have 'taken up' with half a dozen women in as many years, and each woman with as many men." Because such a situation prevented any settlement of marriage relations or paternity, the auditor requested the commissioner "direct a careful and thorough investigation of the facts, with a view of discovering where the parties were born, their ages, where they resided up to the time of enlistment of the soldier, and the names of *all* the masters to whom they may have belonged." French asked that the bureau's claims agents follow a similar course of examination with the claims of fathers and mothers as well as brothers and sisters, each of whom also had to establish their eligibility as heirs by proving they, too, either enjoyed a recognized marriage relation or were "the issue resulting from honest cohabitation." French's letter to Howard was reprinted dozens of times and circulated down the ranks of the Freedmen's Bureau. In 1872, Thomas Vincent circulated the letter to disbursing officers of the newly minted Freedmen's Branch, who followed a similar course of proving slave relations.[55]

Former enslavers presented themselves as the key to demystifying the erstwhile relations of their human chattel. In mid-1875, Joseph Carter, a planter in northwest Mississippi, came across a letter between George Gibson and his former slave Sally Carter, showing the latter was owed $213.50 on account of her deceased son. "Owing to lapse of time and the scattered condition of the Col^d Troops," explained the former enslaver, "she will find a good deal of trouble to make the particular proof mentioned in your note," that is, securing two of her son's comrades who could testify to her being the mother of the deceased. Carter therefore wished to know whether his word, "being the owners of Her and family at the time of emancipation . . . will not be sufficient for the purpose" of identification. It would "save a great deal of trouble and expense, as she cannot at this season of the year spare time from Home. Besides she is needy," and her former enslaver professed to have no interest in the case "outside of good will to Her." As in every bounty case involving an ex-slaveholder, the subjective question of the Mississippi planter's supposed benevolence mattered less than his assumed role as an authentic and trustworthy identifier of his former chattel for the federal government.[56]

Officials eventually concluded that the most reliable way to confirm Black people's intimate relations was to ask their former enslavers. Indeed, for most Freedmen's Branch officials, credibility seemed to hinge on not only whiteness but property. Knowing this, freedpeople strove, whenever possible, to get propertied white folks to testify on their behalf. This often proved a difficult task. Many complained that "it is impossible to get any white persons to identify them, unless they pay them from ten to twenty five dollars." Small wonder that, according to one official, "the affidavits presented will show 100 colored persons as witnesses to one white." Thousands of former slaves nevertheless continued to garner support for their claims late into the 1870s, and from an astounding array of individuals, from private claims agents and attorneys to employers and former enslavers, even former wartime captors. One employer, for instance, wrote how "two of the men in my employ have at various times represented to me that they were entitled to money from the Government for services or bounties," and thus inquired after their claims. A planter outside Tupelo, Mississippi, wrote to Gibson at Memphis. He asked about any benefit owed to Lucinda Gates, the mother of one of his tenants, whose other son died in the war. Another patron, Calvin Jones, likewise addressed Gibson on "behalf of an infirm, old, colored woman who claims the pay and bounty awarded in behalf of her son, a soldier in the Union Army in the late war." Dennis Jones had perished before receiving any pay or bounty, which his mother, Charlotte Jones, now claimed. The patron assured the branch official that he had no interest in the claim and that "what I have done has been from motives of kindness and charity to an old woman, who was my servant all her life until emancipated." Freedpeople's claims sure seemed to attract an interesting assortment of disinterested parties.[57]

Former enslavers saw freedpeople's claims as an opportunity to extend their wardship as intercessors for the federal administrative state. Their involvement at the claimant's behest—or, without it, their meddling—became a staple feature of freedpeople's claims-making. Struggling to validate one's own relationships before a branch official was dispiriting enough, but to only secure its legitimacy and the subsequent bounty after the intervention of one's former enslaver would have rendered the entire ordeal even more insulting. Consider the case of Frances Dalby, who grappled with James Curry, disbursing officer at Fort Monroe, to prove that she was indeed the mother of deceased soldier Henry Dalby. She begged that Curry allow her to prove her motherhood. "I am willing to fill up any papers you may order me," Dalby declared, "& have it proven before a magistrate & the clerk of the court or I will get a respectable col[ored] man to go with me before you & he will swear that I am the mother of Henry Dalby & that it is well known by many that I am." Referring back to her earlier failed interrogation, where, among other things, she gave the wrong age for her son, she explained to Curry, "I could not answer your questions properly because I am an ignorant woman." She ended her plea by way of an apology, fearing, "I am afraid you will tire of me but I do not know what else to do." From his post at Fort Monroe, Curry shot back an unkind letter to the adjutant general, calling her "the most ignorant dull and stupid claimant who has yet appeared at this office," while noting in passing that "for these misfortunes she cannot be held accountable, being born & raised on the Eastern Shore of Virginia." In fact, it was bringing a bit of the eastern shore to Curry that eventually secured Francs Dalby's claim. On the freedwoman's last visit to his office in the spring of 1874, she was accompanied by her former enslaver, James B. Dalby, whom Curry requested into his office to settle matters. And he did. The old enslaver convinced Curry that Frances was Henry's mother and assured him that, of course, he had no interest in the case "further than seeing an old and worthy steward of his family receive her money & getting safely to her home with the same."[58]

Though the patron-client relationships were expressly hierarchical, they freely employed a discourse of friendship. Enslavers-turned-employers stylized themselves as the beneficent guardians of a people to whom they could no longer lay legal claim. It was in this spirit of the obliging benefactor that one former enslaver, B. L. Hatch, wrote to Gibson regarding three claims of individuals in his employ. On February 18, 1864, three of Hatch's captives—Adam, Ruffin, and James—bolted from his slave labor camp to join the Union army. All three men died or went missing within a year of the war's conclusion. Now Hatch employed their widows, who, for their part, decided they needed his assistance in retrieving their bounties. Hatch's ensuing letter to Gibson was a self-portrait of magnanimity. He harbored no malice toward those bedmates of traitors. The occasion might have even recalled to his mind with dark satisfaction a warning he might have given to the three men about leaving to join the Yankees. E. H. Dabney expressed this same sentiment with a flourish in March 1877. He wanted to know about a father and his two sons who ran off and enlisted, the father and one of the sons killed at the battle of Milliken's Bend in 1863. The other son who survived, and the heirs of the two who did not, received only $40 in bounty. "I am sure a good deal of money is due them," Dabney wrote. "The colored people are perfectly at sea . . . & it behooves us all to see them right." Time and again, postbellum patrons underscored the destitute circumstances of freedpeople, true objects of charity, they argued, whose deprivation owed entirely to the interference of the federal government in their affairs—that is, to emancipation. It could be righted with a cash payout to their humble clients.[59]

In the eyes of Freedmen's Branch officials, former enslavers brought with them not only the credibility of whiteness and property but also intimacy. The more personalized knowledge proffered by ex-enslavers was undeniably biased, self-serving, and superficial, if not altogether false. Whatever information former enslavers could supply, however, clearly outweighed the testimonies of Black claimants themselves or even that of highly regarded leaders from the Black community. The official transcript of their lives that registered in the federal administrative state was thus mediated in unwelcome but financially advantageous ways by the very men who had so recently waged a war against its authority, and who now reveled in their new role as authentic and authoritative interlocutors for "their people." It was a grand irony, then, that former enslavers were so habitually afforded the chance to midwife freedpeople's war claims against the national government.[60]

Paying Off

By 1876, the branch's kinetic energy dissipated. The number of unpaid claimants had diminished, and the remaining cases appeared to be of exceptional complexity and scattered at "remote and inconvenient points." The previous two years had seen a number of consolidations and closures of Freedmen's Branch field offices. The office at Memphis absorbed the office at Nashville, and Fort Monroe absorbed Fort Macon in 1874. The offices at Fort Johnston and Columbia were both discontinued. In mid-1875, the Fort Monroe and Charleston offices closed as well, and Fort Leavenworth merged with St. Louis. By 1876, St. Louis lost its field office too, and Nashville, which had previously reopened at the bidding of unpaid Black claimants, again closed its office. Meanwhile, those at Natchez and Vicksburg transferred to New Orleans. New Orleans, Memphis, and Louisville were the only Freedmen's Branch disbursing offices left outside the Washington headquarters. Increasingly, the War Department and postmaster general collaborated to issue payment by postal order to claimants. But as eager as administrators were to close the books on the program, Black claimants insisted that the work remained unfinished.[61]

In the spring of 1876, dozens of Black claimants representing themselves as the "Colored Citizens of Arkansas" sent a remarkable petition to Congress. In it, they asked for the repeal of the current bounty payment system to Black soldiers, along with "the enactment of such laws as will place the colored soldiers on the same footing as to the manner of payment of Bounties as white soldiers." Invoking the language of the bounty equalization measure enacted three years prior, these claimants insisted on procedural equality as well in the hopes of a more equitable outcome. They complained that the payment of bounties through the late Freedmen's Bureau failed for lack of appropriations from Congress and that the subsequent transfer of its duties to the adjutant general and the Freedmen's Branch unduly burdened claimants. The petitioners found "the disbursements of money due us as soldiers of the late war through the Disbursing Officers of the Adjt Generals Office are very slow, uncertain and extremely expensive to us," and therefore prayed that Congress "repeal all laws affecting the *manner* in which the money due shall be paid and that we be paid as are white ex soldiers." The petition garnered nearly ninety signatures. It reached the office of Senator Powell Clayton, a member of the Committee on Military Affairs and the former Radical Republican governor of Arkansas.[62]

The petition supported Senate Bill 637. The measure provided that all remaining payments to USCT veterans and heirs be processed and paid by the same officers then in charge of payments to white soldiers and heirs, that is, through the accounting officers of the Treasury Department and Pay Department (the latter housed within the Department of War). Those same officers, however, would not pay Black claimants in person but rather would forward their checks or drafts to the Black claimants' respective postmasters, who would in turn shoulder the responsibility of identifying the claimants and delivering their check or draft. Thomas Vincent opposed such a plan for Black claimants, believing such an arrangement had already been considered and rejected by the second auditor back in April 1872. As French had explained, before the Freedmen's Branch even began its work, "the difficulty of reaching by mail, persons generally so illiterate and obscure, seldom resident near a post-office, and so little likely to be known to a postmaster," as well as "the chaotic character of the social and domestic relations of the colored race while in a state of slavery," made it "an extremely difficult and delicate matter to decide between several contesting parties." Moreover, "the irregularities permitted in respect to marriage; the long separation of near relatives in many cases, and the general credulity with which the race is apt to listen to the proposals of a *sharper*," made it necessary for the War Department, not the Treasury and not the postmasters, to investigate and secure bounty claims. French maintained the necessity of "some kind of organization that can deal directly with the claimants themselves." The official negative stance of the second auditor as well as the Freedmen's Branch on the proposed legislation in 1876, according to Vincent, was "the result of *actual experience*, and deemed necessary for the protection not only of the public interests, but of the interests of the claimants, who, from lack of education and ordinary business habits, were exposed to the wiles of claim-agents and others."[63]

Weighing in on the matter, the adjutant general, E. D. Townsend, dismissed the petitioners' appeal and launched into a breathtaking apologetics for virtually every policy and practice of the Freedmen's Branch. It was unreasonable to entrust Southern postmasters with the task of identifying and delivering payment to Black claimants, he scolded, for they were "under no legal accountability" and otherwise lacked experience in the matter of identification of claimants. Such a task instead demanded "the strictest possible attention" and an unwavering adherence to the confidential lists. In Townsend's view, the branch was a "perfect" system, such that "it has been found unnecessary to change or modify it in any essential particular." The disbursing arrangement of the Freedmen's Branch protected the government as well as claimants as no other arrangement could. "Complaints have been exceptionally rare," he argued, and any grievances that did reach his office were inspired by dishonest claims agents riling up otherwise content Black claimants. Townsend went so far as to allege that many of the names on the petition were forged and likely "procured through such deceptive influences as to disentitle the petition to consideration." Finally, it was important to add that these petitioners fell in the district of George Gibson, whose reputation for fairness and efficiency earned widespread praise. (To his credit, in response to the petition, Gibson made special tours of Arkansas with the object of settling the payments of the petitioners.) With such established forces arrayed against the bill—including its tepid dismissal by Senator Blanche K. Bruce of Mississippi, the first Black senator to serve a full term—the bill went down in defeat in June 1876. The duties of discovering, identifying, and paying Black claimants would remain with the Freedmen's Branch.[64]

And claimants themselves would remain frustrated. They continued to agitate and inquire about their unpaid claims throughout the late 1870s. Black claimants also used their letters to draw attention to their ongoing hardships in the postbellum South. "Will you *please* be so kind as to write and let me know when I can get my money for I am *suffering*," Edmond Smith implored Gibson. "I am in *real want*. I have no clothing nor provisions for myself and my family merchants are holding back and will not let us have the necessaries of life and I don't see what I am to do, please let me hear from you at once." As long as they were speaking to federal officials—many of whom, including Gibson, were former army commanders—freedpeople felt as though they had the ear of power, representatives who at least made a pretense of justice and protection. The constant, often self-righteous evocations of these same two prerogatives by federal officials defending the Freedmen's Branch perhaps encouraged freedpeople to redeploy the same in their pleas for payment. This tactic worked better in the days of the Freedmen's Bureau; under the charge of the bureau's successor, the disbursing officers of the Freedmen's Branch had not only fewer functions and fewer staff but also a restricted presence. Some of the most desperate letters were therefore written to the second auditor himself. "Mr. E. B. French," wrote Rachel Baptiste from Carrollton, Louisiana, "as you are the second auditor from what i can understand and the sorce [*sic*] for me to find out any true report about my claim i ask you to please let me know how my claim stand, and wetter [whether] it has bin [*sic*] settle or not . . . for the claim agent keep telling me to come and when i go then he puts me of[f] from time to time so i was told to write to you myself." Similarly, in the case of Edward Proctor, since French first replied to the former slave's letter, he had "heard nothing from my claim for bounty money due me, and am in ill health & suffering from my wound [received] at the fight at Millikens bend and destitute & really not able to provide for the necessaries of life and beg you to take immediate action on my claim."[65]

There was a world of difference between the letters received from suffering claimants and the triumphant tone of the branch's defenders. Reports to Congress conveyed the sense that all was going according to plan, that claimants were being paid in the safest, most efficient way possible. Meanwhile, the executive branch zealously pursued "the severe punishment of all persons" attempting fraud. Even though the branch only distributed about $291,000 in the year ending June 1876, "the disbursing-officers have been uniformly industrious and persistent in their efforts to discover the claimants and effect payment of their claims." But what still vexed bureaucrats and policymakers was that initial batch of claims inherited from the Freedmen's Bureau, still unsettled and in disarray. So, too, did the dominant scandal from the bureau's final days reemerge from political dormancy. In December 1875, former chief disbursing officer George Balloch was on trial once again for allegedly embezzling $110,000 from the Freedmen's Bureau. A special resolution was introduced in the House authorizing speedy investigation and payment of claimants who, under Balloch's charge, had still not received any payment despite having settlement vouchers issued. Democratic newspapers relished the impending demise of the agency, still mistakenly referred to by the name of its predecessor. "The work of winding up the affairs of the Freedmen's Bureau," noted one editorial in 1877, was making "slow progress," but at least "the expenses of the concern are decreasing accordingly."[66]

A long-awaited concession brought the affairs of the Freedmen's Branch to its administrative terminus. With even fewer officials working for the agency, its lead administrators finally relented and arranged with the postmaster general to send all remaining bounty payments by postal order. Over $34,000 in claims were disbursed through the mail in the twelve months preceding October 1877, an increase of almost 75 percent. Under this plan—similar to the one proposed in the recently rejected Senate Bill 637—postmasters across the South were furnished with the confidential lists to establish the identities of claimants, along with "special instructions enjoining the exercise of extreme care in guarding against fraud or imposition." Fraud evidently happened in only two or three cases, and even then, the money was soon secured. In October 1878, the branch had only 1,188 unpaid claims on hand, amounting to just under $140,000. In the meantime, Congress had ordered the Freedmen's Branch to be closed by January 1, 1879. "There can be no doubt," wrote Vincent, "that the work will remain unfinished" on that day. He recommended, therefore, that following the branch's closure, the business of processing all remaining USCT claims be transferred to the paymaster general, that same officer who had been in charge of processing the bounty claims of white soldiers. The Black Arkansas veterans—and no doubt many other Black claimants in the post-slavery South—finally got their wish, though without the satisfaction of being the ones credited with provoking the administrative change.[67]

The Freedmen's Branch closed on March 3, 1879. It had been fourteen years to the day after the creation of the Freedmen's Bureau. Two months later, the branch's records transferred to the Pay Department. "The great object sought," assured the paymaster general, Benjamin Alvord, "has been the payment of moneys due (not a mere check) to the identical colored soldier or his heirs, for experience had shown that they were peculiarly liable to imposition and fraud." In other words, lawful claimants, with their identity established, shall receive their accorded pay through cash or a post office money order instead of a check or a draft. Alvord placed Paymaster A. B. Carey in charge of the 997 claims inherited from the late Freedmen's Branch, amounting to over $100,000. Carey had already had extensive experience "with the payment of like dues to white soldiers paid on Treasury certificates" and immediately began settling the inherited claims in the same manner.[68]

THE FREEDMEN'S BRANCH grew out of failure. And although it managed to pay thousands of claimants, it ended in failure too. From the first, the Pay Department proved itself vastly more efficient at paying the claims of Black soldiers and heirs, especially given the alleged difficulty of those claims that eluded settlement by both the Freedmen's Bureau and its successor. It did so by utilizing the Southern postmasters in a manner that more closely resembled the system of payment enjoyed by white claimants. By September 1881, the department reported only 305 of these old claims left, and within twelve months, all but seventy-three claims were paid. The expense to the Pay Department in securing these payments, moreover, was roughly 1 percent of the total paid out in claims—a negligible overhead, especially compared with the operational costs of the Freedmen's Branch. In his 1882 report to Congress, the paymaster general justifiably noted the satisfactory progress of his department, especially the satisfaction "to the claimants, who, in every instance, receive their money in actual cash without the intervention of an agent or attorney." By September 1885, all of the old claims had been paid. In his final report to Congress, he affirmed, once and for all, that "the repeal of the law requiring a payment in person to colored claimants, and placing them on the same footing as other claimants, has greatly expedited the payment of these claims, at a saving of expense to the Government and without loss to the claimants."[69]

But the claimants had indeed lost. And as freedpeople they had lost even more. Though seldom acknowledged, the narrow focus on claimants and claim fulfillment came to stand in for broad-based, redistributive reforms in the post–Civil War South. Broken promises accordingly suffused their letters to federal administrations. In March 1874, Solomon Daugherty, who described himself as "a poor old man, 65 Years of age, crippled with Rheumatism married and a Father of nine Children, Grand Father of 7 Grand Children," wrote to the secretary of war. Daugherty not only asked that his long-awaited bounty claim be investigated but also reminded the secretary of his entitlement to a $100 state bounty, $300 additional bounty, and "162 akres [*sic*] of Congress Land." Daugherty was "the only Support for all this Children and Grand Children and it would be a great help to me, if I would get my right dues from the U. S. Government, who is willing to pay every Cent due to a Soldier" and protect the "future wellfare [*sic*] of a poor colored family." He beseeched the powerful government official to "consider all the above mentioned Circumstances" of his life, believing that if he did so he would "not hesitate to help a poor colored man, who served during the War for the Benefitt [*sic*] of this Country and his poor Family to their just Rights." Daugherty spoke for many freedpeople when, under evident duress, he asked federal administrators for a more capacious and humane understanding of the rights of freedpeople. His unpaid bounty simply gave him the standing to do so. They asked for more than bounties, for nothing less than a redefinition of justice, a consideration of a people's collective claim rather than the narrow statutory fulfillment of individual claimants. In this light, the very formulation of individual claimants—culled from the great mass of freedpeople—was itself a grave injustice.[70]

If the Freedmen's Bureau had functioned in large measure to control class conflict among Black workers in the South by defusing agitation for land redistribution by forcing them into contractual arrangements with landlords and employers, then the Freedmen's Branch managed expectations in part by deflecting requests for broader and more imaginative redress. The federal government had the capacity to settle the claims of Black veterans and heirs as quickly and equitably as it did white claimants in the North. It chose not to. Just as well, instead of simply abandoning any remaining unpaid claims in the year 1872, the new agency avoided the threat of concerted repercussions by enrobing every claim in red tape and manufacturing the threat posed by alleged fraudulent activity, thereby sapping the energy and attention of the clients and critics of the bounty payment system and ultimately passing the administrative burden onto the ex-slave claimants themselves. In so doing, branch administrators resisted any and all efforts at reforming a "perfect" system. In letter after letter, and visit after visit to federal officers, formerly enslaved men and women articulated much more than a cold balancing of ledgers. In fact, the actual conditions freedpeople conveyed to branch officials were wildly out of bounds with what those officials had authorization to address. Exactly what administrators had to regard as extraneous to the business at hand, however, was the very substance of freedpeople's vision of citizenship, of securing the welfare and livelihoods of a long-suffering people.

And so the Freedmen's Branch did more than simply continue one function of the Freedmen's Bureau. It also set a precedent for federal endeavors in welfare that were at once invasive in their means and limited in their benefits, an insidious way to discourage participation in a program whose outright abolition was too politically unfeasible. In these respects, then, the Freedmen's Branch was not a failure. Worse: it performed its role perfectly.[71]

CHAPTER THREE

Reconstructing the Pension Bureau

It was a matter of life and death for countless freedpeople. But earning a federal pension would require far more of Black claimants than their previous struggles for bounties, and for far longer. Their pension claims necessarily dragged issues of slavery, the Civil War, and emancipation into the public light well into the twentieth century, defining their primary engagement with the federal government for decades. Though much less than what newly freed men and women had hoped for in 1865, receiving a recurring stipend based on loyalty and service more nearly approximated the sort of compact they had envisioned at the dawn of freedom, a citizenship based on reciprocity and protecting the general welfare of its citizens. Unlike the Freedmen's Bureau and its successor, the Freedmen's Branch, the U.S. Pension Bureau was not explicitly designed for ex-slaves and their descendants. In fact, from the perspective of policymakers, they were closer to an afterthought in the pension system. The only "special class" to which it attended were Union veterans and their surviving heirs, regardless of race and regardless of region. Furthermore, unlike the two freedmen's agencies, the Pension Bureau would not suffer for lack of funding. By the turn of the century, the cost of federal military pensions regularly consumed more than one-third of the nation's budget, and although it would always generate considerable opposition, the size of the pension program nevertheless increased unabated. As the Pension Bureau reemerged and then expanded in the emancipated South, it remained to be seen whether freedpeople could make this more permanent agency their own.

More so than any other federal agency in the decades after the Civil War, the Pension Bureau symbolized the possibilities and limitations of the reconstructed nation-state. It became emblematic of what a powerful state could do. From its humble beginnings in the early republic, the Pension Bureau grew beyond prediction in the last four decades of the nineteenth century as it compensated with increasing generosity loyal Union veterans and surviving family members. Many observers assumed without a second thought that the beneficiaries were white Northern men and their widows, and scholars since the late nineteenth century have generally followed suit, implying that white Northern claimants were the sole clientele of the Pension Bureau or at least the only claimants worthy of sustained attention.[1] White families obviously constituted the vast majority of pensioners. But it is with that other class of claimants—formerly enslaved Southerners, overlooked by their race and region and slighted by the public memory of the Civil War—that one gains a deeper purchase on the newly consolidated federal administrative state and, with it, the construction of a Black administrative politics. And within that group, it was formerly enslaved women, as widows and mothers, who played an oversized and underappreciated role in negotiating the meaning of dependency and challenging the limitations of the new liberal order.[2]

Loyalty and Its Discontents

The first national pension law trailed behind the Declaration of Independence. Passed on August 26, 1776, it promised to every soldier in the Continental army half pay for life should his service render him incapable of earning a support. Yet the law left it up to the states to determine and execute such payments. The Continental Congress passed additional measures over the course of the war, divided along lines of rank, with commissioned officers promised greater benefits than rank-and-file soldiers. The national pension law passed by Congress on August 24, 1780, similarly drew upon the hierarchical logic of rank-based compensation, extending benefits to widows and orphans, but only to those of deceased officers. Many states bitterly protested the exorbitant costs and seemingly unrepublican nature of such social provisioning to special classes of citizens. At bottom, the rationale behind the nation's first military pension system was indeed rather cynical. It was designed not so much to protect veterans and their families but rather to encourage enlistments and retain soldiers.[3]

The first consolidation of the patchwork pension system from the Revolutionary era began in 1789. At that point, there were fewer than 1,500 Revolutionary War veterans on the general pension list. In 1790, Congress offered to pay the pensions left unpaid (or "in arrears") by the states. Although some individual states continued to offer payments to pensioners, the authority to pension veterans and heirs soon came under the charge of the secretary of war. Congress, however, continued to play an active role in soliciting the secretary for admissions of worthy individuals to the rolls. As the political scientist Laura Jensen has argued, during this time the national legislature functioned in ways that would soon be characteristic of a centralized administrative state. Pensions were key to the transformation.[4] Formalized procedures for pension applicants were set by the act of February 28, 1793, which stipulated that applicants for invalid pensions needed to present themselves before a local federal district judge or three-man commission designated by the judge, bringing all evidence of "decisive disability" owing to "the effect of known wounds, received while in the actual line of his duty." The judge would then authorize a commission of two physicians to determine the degree to which the alleged disability "prevents the claimant from obtaining his livelihood, by labor." The claimant also needed to acquire testimony from "three reputable freeholders" regarding the nature of his disability and its impact on the claimant's livelihood, as well as two other witnesses who could speak to the continuance of his disability. The judge would then transmit the evidence directly to the secretary of war, who would then verify the application with the official records and present the case to Congress for final approval. These procedures changed substantially over the course of the nineteenth century. They became more standardized, bureaucratic, and state-like, with more authority centralized in an ever-expanding administrative apparatus operating with increasing independence from Congress.[5]

The military pension program of antebellum America developed within a context of increasing industrialization and sectionalization, with the primary axis running between the industrial core of the Northeast and the agrarian empire of the Mississippi Valley. The Northeast favored tariffs to protect its manufacturers from the more industrialized Great Britain, whereas the South, which relied on the export of raw materials such as cotton, opposed tariffs. Tariffs funded the military pension system, thereby ensuring an uneven distribution of tariff revenue to the more populous North and linking the pensioned class to the projects of the northeastern industrial elite. And there would always be a class of pensioners in American politics to require tariffs. The provisioning of Revolutionary War veterans and widows, for instance, continued for over a century, from 1776 to 1878. At first, pension laws benefited officers and privates whose service had left them disabled; after March 1818, however, all surviving veterans of the Revolution—roughly 20,500 individuals—could now claim a service pension if they passed a means test for indigency. Much of this liberality on the part of Congress may be attributed to a large credit balance in the Treasury owing to the War of 1812. In the heady days of Jacksonian America, service pensions to Revolutionary veterans were allowed regardless of income beginning in 1832, and in 1836 widows of all such veterans (irrespective of rank) were allowed pensions. In the century following national independence, a regular system of army and navy pensions for "peacetime" service also grew. Yet the Seminole Wars and the U.S.-Mexican War enlarged the army and navy and generated new pension systems for regular servicemen and volunteers alike. These war-specific pension systems generally followed the same pattern set by the Revolutionary system: granting qualified pensions to disabled veterans followed by their qualified extension to widows and finally extending service pensions to all surviving veterans, often several decades after the war's end.[6]

For pensioners of old wars residing in the Southern states, this history ended abruptly in 1861. The commissioner of the Pension Bureau, Joseph H. Barrett, recommended to Congress that when a state seceded, its pensioners forfeited their claims. Congress agreed, and the commissioner ordered thousands of Southerners to be dropped from the rolls. Throughout the remainder of the rebellion, Congress attached provisions to the various pension laws affirming the basic requirement of loyalty to the Union for pensioners of wars old and ongoing—true to the original meaning of the word *pension*: a regular sum paid for past services or to maintain allegiance. Accordingly, on February 4, 1862, Congress passed an act prohibiting pension payments not only to rebel soldiers but also to anyone "who had in any manner encouraged the rebels or manifested a sympathy with their cause." This affected not only the leadership class of the Confederate Congress but also those pensioners in the middle states of Missouri, Kentucky, Maryland, and Delaware, whose loyalties came under intense scrutiny. Upon the close of the war, the pension agencies in the former Confederacy were gradually restored and folded back into the general pension administration. Pension agencies in Virginia, Tennessee, Arkansas, and Louisiana even reopened before Confederate surrender, and hence well before the readmission of those states to Congress, making the Pension Bureau the bellwether of reunification. Commissioner Barrett accordingly appointed new agents at Richmond, Nashville, Knoxville, Little Rock, and New Orleans to facilitate pension applications. "These agencies," noted Barrett, "have been reopened as fast as there seemed to be a local requirement." Others followed, such that by 1872 every ex-Confederate state saw its federal pension system in operation once again. Ironically, then, the full reestablishment of the Pension Bureau in the South coincided with the demobilization of the U.S. Army and the termination of the Freedmen's Bureau.[7]

Reconstructing the Southern pension agencies required the Pension Bureau to commission physicians to serve as medical examiners. After a veteran submitted his application for a military pension and after the bureau verified the application, the bureau would order the claimant to appear before an examiner or examining board. These federally deputized "surgeons" would provide part of the medical evidence necessary to prove the existence and degree of disability in a pension claimant. It was a crucial stage in the claims-making process. It is important to note that there were very few federal surgeons operating in the South in the first decade after the war. In 1865, ten could be found in Tennessee, three in Virginia, two in Louisiana (both in New Orleans), one in North Carolina, and one in Arkansas, all of which had high numbers of Black bounty claimants and thus high numbers of potential Black pensioners. All other ex-Confederate states would have to wait a number of years before hosting appointed surgeons. By 1868, three additional Southern states—Alabama, Georgia, and South Carolina—had commissioned surgeons. The number of surgeons roughly corresponded to the number of actual veteran pensioners in these areas. In 1866, for instance, Tennessee had 594 pensioners in 1866, Louisiana 184, and Arkansas a mere 120. These low figures might be attributed to the extended service of some U.S. Colored Troops (USCT), whose three-year enlistments ended in 1867 at the earliest, but also to the extraordinary difficulty of applying for a pension. In any event, the number of Black veterans on the rolls would take decades to accumulate.[8]

Southern pension activity in the wake of the Civil War fell into two broad categories: restoring loyal white veterans of previous wars to the pension rolls and admitting new Union pensioners, both Black and white. For claimants to be readmitted, the bureau required the claimant to "satisfactorily establish his or her loyalty to the government throughout the rebellion," after which point the claimant was also entitled to the balance accrued since its suspension in 1861. Proving unbroken fidelity to the Union drew deeply from the philosophical wellspring of loyalty oaths in the early days of Reconstruction. Attaining presidential amnesty, however, proved far easier for white Southerners than admission or readmission to the more discriminating federal pension rolls. For years after the war, even those men who deserted the rebel army to join the Union forces could not prove loyalty throughout the war and hence were barred from receiving a federal pension. Most infuriating to ex-Confederates, however, was their continued exclusion from the pension rolls of previous wars wherein they had rendered faithful service to the United States. The Southern press reported bitterly on the expulsion of veterans from the War of 1812 to the U.S.-Mexican War, simply because they had followed their state out of the Union. From the first, therefore, loyalty was an essential component of the federal pension system and, indeed, of the broader formulation of citizenship in the Civil War era.[9]

Southern freedpeople knew the issue of loyalty would be different for them.[10] They intuitively understood their faithful wartime service to the federal armies endowed them with a worthy claim to citizenship, particularly when contrasted with the undisguised treachery of their enslavers. And they heard as much promised to them, having sat through more than a few pedantic lectures by Northern commanders and missionaries during wartime occupation. In one of General Clinton B. Fisk's sixteen sermons to freedpeople, for example, Fisk counseled former slaves of what they might expect from their former enslavers—sore feelings, grievances over the loss of wealth which "melted away like wax before the fire," and the death of sons and relatives on the battlefield. The "government will grant no pensions in their cases," assured Fisk, "because they fought not under its flag." Fisk did not promise pensions to his audience of former slaves, though undoubtedly some would earn them. Instead he merely affirmed the matter of loyalty at the heart of the federal pension program. Formerly enslaved claimants would cleave to the argument of loyalty and service until the last pensioner perished. Although no ex-Confederate would ever receive a federal pension by virtue of service to the Confederacy, the threat of such provisioning always loomed, especially when the federal government came under Democratic control.[11]

The pension issue lodged itself at the center of debates over the course of Reconstruction and the limits of national citizenship. "The Federal Government has magnanimously thrown over the rebel soldier the mantle of oblivion for the past," noted the governor of Mississippi in October 1865, "but no pension from its coffers awaits him or his family." "Whether it was right or wrong to call the soldier to arms," he added, "it cannot be wrong to make such provisions for them as will relieve them and their families from want and suffering." The governor thus appealed for a state pension system to mirror the federal pension system. The number of state-run pension systems for rebel soldiers and their families grew after Republicans lost control of state legislatures and, with it, budgetary control. However, it would not be until after the fall of Reconstruction that Democratic state legislators could harness the material prosperity of the New South and the sentimentalities of the Lost Cause to fully institute pension programs for Confederate families. In 1883, for instance, the *Southwestern Christian Advocate*, a prominent Black newspaper in New Orleans, looked with disgust upon Georgia's Confederate pension system, the most robust and comprehensive state program at that time in the South. After detailing the various rates of pensions and the $25,000 annual cost, the paper complained that the taxes of Georgia freedmen were going to "support these Confederate soldiers, whose shattered frames testify of the part they played in the task of seeking to perpetuate Negro slavery in this country." Four years later, South Carolina expanded its own Confederate pension system, passing the measure by a vote of 32 to 2 in the state senate. The two votes in opposition belonged to the only remaining Black Americans in the chamber.[12]

Such schemes to build Confederate pension systems had long been fore-casted. A year after the war, a Republican official canvassing the South sensed there would be little chance defeated rebels "would help pay our debt or pension our soldiers for whipping them," while another reported that ex-rebels "talk very freely in regard to an effort being made by their members, when once in Congress, to get pay for all the negroes they have lost, or that have been freed under the President's proclamation," and how they planned "to give the disabled soldiers of the south the benefits of the pension act."[13] Bluster or bluntness, Republicans capitalized on such remarks. Senator Oliver P. Morton of Indiana, a tireless waver of the bloody shirt, spoke at length in a campaign event for Ulysses S. Grant about the Democratic threats to the republic "in the attempt to restore the rebels unconditionally to the full enjoyment of political rights." For once state governments fell to their control, Democratic success would inevitably bring about the compensation of enslavers for their emancipated "property," the assumption of the rebel war debt, and the pensioning of rebel soldiers. "Is it to be supposed for one moment," asked Morton, "that rebels when restored to power in the national government, will levy taxes and vote money to pension Union soldiers, their widows and orphans, while their own are unprovided for and left in poverty?" So pervasive were these concerns, and from such an early date, that Republicans enshrined them in the Fourteenth Amendment, submitted to the states for ratification in June 1866. The long-since-overlooked fourth section of the amendment held that "debts incurred for payment of pensions and bounties for services in suppressing insurrection or rebellion, shall not be questioned." In the same stroke, the amendment invalidated all so-called Confederate debts and prohibited their assumption by the federal government.[14]

Of course, the ratification of the Fourteenth Amendment in July 1868 did not end the periodic interrogation of the Union pension system. Fears of Democrats seizing control of Congress and thereafter incorporating ex-rebels onto the national pension rolls continued to electrify the Republican populace, none more so than Black Southerners fighting to maintain their place in state legislatures.[15] Frederick Douglass's paper, the *New National Era*, ran frequent editorials on the implications of a Democratic victory. In May 1871, it reprinted a recent speech by the great abolitionist and labor activist Wendell Phillips to the Reform League of Boston. Warning of a Democratic resurgence, Phillips predicted they would thereafter repudiate the Fourteenth and Fifteenth Amendments and refuse "to pay the pensions of our soldiers until the Southern debt is recognized and the Confederate soldiers are pensioned." In turn, "thousands of millions they would appropriate to pension rebel soldiers, pay for rebels' slaves, and for damages to rebel property."[16] Southern Republican newspapers joined in the defense. Mocking their opponents' accusations of political incompetence, the Little Rock *Morning Republican* suggested that to qualify for the Democrats' brand of "enlightened statesmanship," Republicans would have to return "the slaves they held before the war, and with the slaves, control of the seceding States and representation in the halls of Congress." They would have to strike "the name of every crippled and disabled soldier of the Federal army from the pension roll," substitute "the names of those who were disabled in the Confederate army," and assume "the debts incurred by the State in aid of the Confederacy." Well before the Supreme Court's unraveling of the Fourteenth Amendment, then, reactionary forces already threatened its proscriptions on rebel debts and pensions.[17]

Although Black claimants made up only a small fraction of the pension rolls in the early years after the war, the Black press praised the growth of the Pension Bureau and the increasingly liberal allowances it granted to Union veterans and widows. The *New National Era* frequently referred to Union pensions as the "Democratic national debt." In the early 1870s, as the Democrats returned to power, the *Era* reminded its readers of the tens of millions of dollars paid in pensions to disabled veterans and dependent widows thanks to "the luxury of the last national Democratic administration," that of James Buchanan, who failed to prevent secession and war. Though proud to care for those who sacrificed for the Union, the paper nevertheless bemoaned the "steady drain upon the tax-payers, year by year, for interest, pensions, and the army and navy, to keep Democratic rebels in subjection." The pension issue was thus inseparable from national political contests. But for Black Americans, it was not simply a partisan issue over federal spending. Rather, Black leaders such as Douglass kept alive the root cause of the pension issue, the "Democratic rebellion," and thereby not only waved the bloody shirt but tied federal pensions to the wartime promise of emancipation.[18]

The issue of pensioning rebel soldiers reached fever pitch in 1872, provoked in large part by the Liberal Republican Party. Composed of former abolitionists, free soilers, and reformers, the Liberal Republicans emerged in the early years of Reconstruction and steadily gained traction. In May 1872, the party made the fateful decision to nominate the eccentric, polarizing editor of the *New York Tribune*, Horace Greeley, as its presidential candidate to challenge Grant in the November election. Though not initially central to their ideology, opposition to Grant's alleged corruption drew many former radicals into the Liberal Republican ranks, including Charles Sumner. After Greeley's nomination, the "Southern question," or how the next administration ought to handle

Reconstruction, emerged as the defining issue of the upstart party. Greeley and his followers called for an end to federal intervention and the patronage system in all its guises. This meant, above all, removing special protections for freedpeople, whom the former abolitionist now criticized in ways indistinguishable from most Democrats. The platform also called for removing any remaining political disabilities placed on former rebels, including restrictions on voting and officeholding. Five years after he contributed to Jefferson Davis's bail bond, Greeley urged Americans to return the South to self-government and "clasp hands across the bloody chasm" by forgetting the bitter memories of war, emancipation, and Reconstruction.[19]

Greeley's campaign was a vindication to Democrats and their increasingly mainstream views on freedpeople and Reconstruction. The staunchly pro-Grant *New National Era* ridiculed the Greeley campaign and forewarned the country of the consequences of a Liberal Republican victory. In his fawning appeasement of the white Democratic South, Greeley would no doubt offer to "pay the rebel debt, compensate rebel slave-masters, pension rebel soldiers, and practically restore slavery," predicted the editor in September 1872. Though Greeley was roundly defeated—and died a few weeks after the election—the danger of federal pensions for rebels continued to haunt observers wary of the amnesia enveloping much of white America. The Liberal Republican assault on Reconstruction, moreover, hastened the end of the project by undercutting it both ideologically and materially. Republicans who had once supported efforts to remake the South were easily cowed into disinvesting and dismantling their work, abandoning the hope of a strong electoral base of Black Republicanism.[20]

At the dusk of Reconstruction, in the fall of 1877, one newspaper in Mississippi happily noted the ultimatum Democrats could now offer the country: pension all "veterans" or pension none. Either course would "do more to conquer the rebellious feelings . . . than is in the power of the federal guns." A government that is "kind and just," it continued, must "remember its crippled soldiers, whether they wore the blue or the grey, and their widows and orphans alike; it is only a malignant government that repels fealty that can discriminate. It is the part of statesmanship to soothe, not irritate, the sores of the late war." Bills to pension ex-rebels would continually resurface over the next several decades as the bureaucratic expression of the Lost Cause. It began soon after the official end of Reconstruction. On March 9, 1878, Congress passed a bill restoring to the rolls all surviving veterans and heirs of the War of 1812 who had been dropped because of disloyalty during the Civil War. It was reasoned that, given their advanced age during the latter war, they likely undertook no active role in the rebellion. Though several bills teased the boundaries of loyalty that defined the new federal entitlement program, Confederate soldiers and their heirs would never receive federal pensions by virtue of their service for the Confederacy. For all the reunionist overtures, there would always remain at least an administrative barrier to complete reconciliation.[21]

Collaboration and Corruption

The U.S. Pension Bureau embodied two affronts to white Southerners. First came the indignity of a federal agency embedded in the South whose sole purpose was the distribution of money to formerly enslaved veterans and heirs for their part in the late war. The very presence of Black pensioners in the South signaled to many that the war was not yet over. Next came the economic threat posed by Black workers, men and women alike, who were likewise pensioners. Enjoying a reliable income from one's pension made them less dependent on wages and thus less exploitable to their white employers. The relationship between freedpeople and the Pension Bureau thus seemed rather out of step with the bloody march of dispossession that otherwise characterized the counterrevolution in the post-occupation South.[22]

When formerly enslaved veterans and heirs sought military pensions, they first turned to the Freedmen's Bureau for guidance. The Claims Division of the Freedmen's Bureau, established in March 1866, functioned as a de facto pension agency, and freedpeople frequently authorized bureau agents to serve as their lawful attorneys and handle their pension claims at the outgoing and incoming stages. As the division chief reported to Commissioner O. O. Howard in October 1870, Black claimants were constantly "invoking the assistance of the Bureau in effecting their settlement," and "letters are daily received from claimants inquiring respecting the condition of their claims." In its final days, bureau agents and allied aid workers devoted most working hours toward securing bounties and pensions for eligible freedpeople, many of whom appealed desperately for help. For example, Amos Harvey had served alongside his brother Stephen, and after the war wrote on behalf of his mother to Howard. Amos's mother already received Stephen's bounty after he died in service, but now his mother "Wants to no if She is not intitle to A Penchen as She is very old and no one to soport her now."[23]

Until June 1890, all applicants for Civil War pensions applied under what was known as the general law. Established on July 14, 1862, the general law offered pensions to Union veterans disabled in some way by military service. In a departure from the pattern of only gradually extending pensions to heirs, the act also provided for widows and orphans of soldiers who died in service, or veterans who died from war-related causes.[24] As thousands of freedpeople soon learned, the requirements seemed precisely crafted to overwhelm the humble claimant. Beyond giving their names, regiment and company, certificate of discharge, and other details of their service, as they did for bounties, pension applicants also needed to provide official evidence of service-origin disability, along with a surgeon's certificate showing the present disability of the claimant. To obtain their disability certificates, claimants needed a medical examination performed by a federally commissioned medical examiner or board. The efforts of hundreds of Black veterans around Nashville convinced a local Freedmen's Bureau official, John Lawrence, of the immense difficulties in obtaining the necessary medical evidence. "Many pension claims have been suspended in order to procure a surgeon's certificate," he reported in February 1867. Such a task was "next to impossible in colored regiments . . . owing to the fact that the surgeons of those regiments live in the North, and cannot readily be found." From an early date, therefore, freedpeople and their agents diagnosed important structural difficulties peculiar to their station. Yet it was only the leading edge of the institutional challenges to come for formerly enslaved claimants in the South.[25]

In June 1870, Congress passed a law stipulating that pension agents mail all pension vouchers quarterly to the pensioner's post office address; the pensioner would then sign the voucher and return it, whereupon the pension agent would send the pension check to the claimant. Only under special circumstances would the pensioner have to appear in person to prove his or her identity, making the payment process vastly preferable to freedpeople than retrieving their bounty claims through either of the two freedmen's agencies. Yet the Freedmen's Bureau, even in its final days, also inserted itself in the middle of this straightforward process in the guise of protecting claimants, just as it had with bounty payments. Arguing that special considerations were necessary for "colored pensioners residing in States lately in rebellion," Howard arranged with the Pension Bureau commissioner to have Freedmen's Bureau agents "induce" those Black claimants in their districts "to have their communications and checks from the Pension Office and its agencies sent to the agent of the Bureau nearest their respective places of residence" instead of their post office addresses. Howard hoped doing so would prevent "their checks and certificates from falling into the hands of interested persons, who would extort compensation for pretended services rendered the pensioners." And so, even when statutorily included in the pension process on equal footing with white claimants, Black claimants in the South were encouraged to use a specialized—and increasingly incapacitated—agency to unnecessarily mediate their claims. Those who had initiated pension applications through the Freedmen's Bureau were later told in 1872 by Thomas Vincent of the Freedmen's Branch that their "case now stands as if no claim had been made." After the abolition of the Freedmen's Bureau, there was suddenly "no office of the Government authorized to act as the agent of claimants," and claimants thus had to solicit the commissioner of pensions directly or with the aid of a private claims agent.[26]

In the 1870s, Pension Bureau commissioners regularly requested the two freedmen's agencies to forward any available information on claimants with pending pension applications who might likewise have submitted bounty claims. The Pension Bureau reciprocated by furnishing the freedmen's agencies long lists of claimants with verified addresses. In this way, federal officials from three departments—Interior, Treasury, and War—shared claimants' identities, post office addresses, and military records. Just as importantly, if any claimant was denied bounty or back payment by a disbursing officer of the Freedmen's Branch, the commissioner of pensions requested a full report naming all such individuals and the reasons for rejection. This measure was expressly done with "a view to the protection of public interests in the matter of Pensions to Colored Soldiers and their heirs," in the words of Adjutant General E. D. Townsend. Many freedpeople were apparently aware of this practice and accordingly directed administrators to their other, previously vetted claims, believing that interdepartmental collaboration could do more than just locate claimants or protect the government against fraud—that it could perhaps relieve the administrative burden placed on claimants. Crecy Jackson, for one, wrote to the second auditor in pursuit of her deceased husband's bounty. She informed him that the Pension Bureau had already sent a special agent to investigate her pension claim and file a report on its merits. Jackson told the auditor that he could see the report himself "by reference at the Pension Bureau where you can get a copy. Please attend to the same immediately," Jackson implored. However much the interdepartmental collaboration aimed at increasing efficiency, in reality it more often jeopardized the claims of Black Southerners than served them. With an interlocking cadre of administrators from two or more federal agencies hypersensitive to perceived fraudulent activity, any misstep could be misconstrued and amplified in the bureaucratic echo chamber, all but terminating one's chances of receiving federal benefits.[27]

Officials of the Pension Bureau helped stoke fears of widespread fraud among Black claimants, either among their ranks or by outside criminal organizations. One special agent for the Pension Bureau, George H. Ragsdale, became particularly obsessed with ferreting out what he perceived as criminal duplicity. In a routine letter in 1873 requesting more information on a pension applicant, he warned the Freedmen's Branch disbursing officer at Fort Monroe that nearby Norfolk "has been cursed with the largest number of successful thieving claim agents of any city I have visited in two years. And that fully one half of all bounty moneys paid to mothers and widows here has been fraudulently obtained." Echoing the threadbare warnings of the Freedmen's Bureau, officials of the Pension Bureau preached the need for "constant and vigilant supervision." Only by such measures could "the real character of many more seemingly fraudulent or unworthy applications" be "definitely ascertained."[28] Tellingly, the very first mention of Black pensioners in a commissioner's annual report to Congress came in 1870 by way of a report on fraud. News had been flooding the bureau of Black pensioners being swindled on a large scale in Tennessee and neighboring states. In his report to Congress, Commissioner Henry Van Aernam took note of a special commission appointed by the Freedmen's Bureau in late 1869 to investigate the matter.[29]

Howard had sent his team of investigators to Nashville and various other points in Tennessee and northern Alabama and Mississippi. The primary purpose was to make a "full and careful investigation" of all abuses alleged against "officers and agents of this Bureau, or other persons concerned in the payment of bounties to colored soldiers, sailors or marines." News of the commission spread, and hundreds of claimants were called to testify when the commission held proceedings nearby. In the meantime, all bounty and pension payments in the region were temporarily suspended, to the utter confusion of Black pensioners. The commission examined over 750 cases across the three states. Its investigation centered on a dozen individual agents and outfits, the most notorious being D. W. Glassie, J. B. Coons, and the firm of Moyers & Dedrick. A number of ex–Freedmen's Bureau agents were called in for testimony, facing accusations of illegally withholding claimants' bounty and pension payments. Dozens of Black claimants also appeared before the commission to recite their dealings with these agents. Many complained bitterly about having been cheated of their bounties and pensions. At the end of an exhausting series of hearings, the commission reported "an amount of systematic extortion and fraud upon the ignorant pensioners and applicants . . . unparalleled in the experience of this office." Cheating Black claimants, it turned out, was a booming industry in Tennessee.[30]

Yet little came of the investigation, save for the reopening of suspended pensions and a renewed assurance among federal officials that they needed to continue serving as intercessors on behalf of Black claimants in the South. The commission therefore recommended that the Freedmen's Bureau handle pension vouchers for Black claimants as well as their vouchers for bounty (hence Howard's subsequent instructions to "induce" Black claimants to redirect their pension vouchers to their nearest Freedmen's Bureau agent). Finally, the fraud commissioners suggested "that pensioners would be protected, and frauds detected, by the publication of all payments made to colored pensioners in some newspapers in the vicinity of each pension agent, giving the names of pensioners, amount and date of payment and name of attorney or agent through whom paid." Beyond the unwelcome publicity this practice would entail, it is likely that such a tepid reform would have actually worsened the situation, exacerbating opportunities for impersonation, as Freedmen's Branch officials learned in their own quest to discover the whereabouts of unpaid bounty claimants.[31]

For all the pledges of protecting claimants, the Pension Bureau would always be more concerned about nefarious individuals bluffing their way into a pension than they were about crooked agencies cheating Black pensioners en masse. Already by 1872, the commissioner of pensions warned of the increasing difficulty of pension adjudication owing to the passage of time and perhaps even the desperation of the claimants themselves. Pension administrators constantly grumbled that the application process did not adequately protect the government, based as it was on ex parte evidence, that is, assortments of testimonies and sworn statements submitted in a claimant's favor, taken independently and without cross-examination. Commissioner James Baker argued that such conditions afforded "no security to the Government against dishonest claims." He and others longed for the day when the pension process would be meaningfully reformed. Injustice to the government was always the driving concern. And in the demobilized South, with so many vulnerable claimants, and so many deceitful agents purportedly lurking about, the Pension Bureau seemed the very embodiment of the federal government's soft underbelly.[32]

The Southern Division

Black Southerners cast about for trustworthy claims agents and attorneys to help assemble and submit the initial paperwork to the Pension Bureau, after which it flowed through several bureaucratic channels, each performing a specialized task. The Mail Division received the claim, and on the same day of its receipt, forwarded it to the Records Division. From there the claim went to one of the adjudicating divisions: Eastern, Middle, Western, or Southern. At its proper adjudicating division, the application would be placed before an examiner to determine whether the declaration for a pension and the accompanying evidence on its face merited further investigation. If an examiner deemed a claim meritorious, he would submit a request for official army records, arrange for affidavits of the applicants and two or more witnesses, and for veterans' claims, send an order for the applicant to appear before the closest medical examiner or examining board. After receiving the legal and medical evidence, the examiner would submit the case with his decision to the chief of their adjudicating division. The chief of said division would review the case and the examiner's conclusions and forward the claim to the Board of Review. From there it would go, naturally, to the Board of Re-Review. When the chiefs of both review boards concurred, the approved claim would be sent to the medical referee of the Medical Division, who would affix the size of the pension based on degree of disability. Finally, the approved and affixed claim would return to the chief of the Board of Review for a final stamp of approval, and from there to the Certificate Division. Rejected cases would be returned to their original adjudicating division for further action. The Pension Bureau therefore developed a highly sophisticated and specialized system for processing claims. And the claims that arrived with the greatest administrative difficulties—those of the formerly enslaved— ricocheted through it all.[33]

The Southern Division organized in 1879, coinciding with the termination of the Freedmen's Branch. Although its exact jurisdiction changed somewhat over the 1870s and 1880s, the Southern Division generally oversaw Union claims arising from nearly all of the former slave states as well as all claims of the U.S. Colored Troops. Headquartered in Washington with the other adjudicating divisions, the Southern Division had only one pension payment agency, located at Knoxville, Tennessee, making it the effective seat of the division. The very creation of the Southern Division came in the wake of an effort under the order of President Rutherford B. Hayes to consolidate pension agencies across the nation. In May 1877, Hayes reduced the fifty-eight pension-paying agencies nationwide to eighteen. The five agencies across North Carolina, Tennessee, Virginia, and West Virginia thus merged into the agency at Knoxville, and the three in Arkansas, Louisiana, and Mississippi into the agency at New Orleans. Then, on May 17, 1879, Hayes ordered the pension agency at New Orleans to be closed and consolidated with Knoxville. By July 1882, the Southern Division had 68 employees, and within six months there were 138, over 100 of whom were examiners.[34]

Pension Office building under construction. This photograph shows Black workers constructing the Pension Office building in November 1883. Itself a monumental testament to Union veterans and their families, the building served as the headquarters of the U.S. Pension Bureau after its completion in 1887. (Library of Congress Prints and Photographs Division, LC-USZ62-56364)

Former slaves had to overcome the formidable obstacles of documentation and legibility, for pensions no less than bounties and back payments. Universal birth registration was years in the future, and virtually all of the existing prewar documentary information regarding families and other vital statistics had fallen under the remit of the enslaver. "When I was born it was slavery times," Abram Haywood explained to a Pension Bureau examiner nearly fifty years after he joined the Union army, "and the churches kept no records of the birth of children, my old parent was ignored being a slave, and the church at that time really did belong to our master and if they had any record of the birth of their slaves it was with them, and we as slaves knew nothing of it." Haywood confessed to "relying and depending solely on what my former master told me, as he is the only record I know." Officials of the two freedmen's agencies came to begrudgingly accept this and frequently sought out former enslavers for the record. Time and again in the late 1860s and

1870s, formerly enslaved claimants convinced former enslavers to write to federal officials on their behalf, aware that their authoritative testimony would factor as significantly into pension claims as it did with bounties.[35]

In the first official report of the Southern Division, in August 1883, the division's chief, L. E. Dickey, explained to the commissioner of pensions the unique difficulties his office faced, especially when "compared with that of examiners in other divisions." The records of the U.S. Colored Troops, he complained, "are very meager," and "call after call must be made, in most cases, to obtain the testimony necessary to make up for the lack of an official record." His examiners found it "exceedingly difficult" to gather satisfactory evidence in order to meet the standard burdens of proof. Often the service record and medical record requests for the USCT were unable to be procured by the War Department or, when found, were incomplete or inaccurate, especially when it came to hospitalization records. Dickey estimated that "in not more than one in six of the claims filed since June 30, 1880, can a record of the disability alleged be found." Matters would improve little as the years went on, until June 1890 when the Disability Act provided an escape hatch by removing the burdensome service-origin requirement. In the end, the first chief of the Southern Division praised his bureaucratically beset examiners in the way most other division heads praised theirs, for their understanding and fairness.[36]

Freedpeople rarely accorded such praise to examiners of the Southern Division. Highly suspicious of pension applications from former slaves, functionaries in the Southern Division routinely called for special investigations to be conducted against claimants whose applications raised any number of red flags. One scholar has estimated that half of all Black Southern claimants could expect a special examination, compared with only a quarter of their white counterparts in the South. There were qualitative differences as well. Whereas Black claimants often endured invasive and protracted special examinations, white claimants usually encountered only cursory ones, if at all. These special examiners were sent out into the field, they relentlessly cross-examined witnesses, judged their "reputations," and forced them to submit depositions. They might as well have done so with a color swatch in hand, as white claimants regularly earned "good" to "excellent" ratings from examiners while Black claimants "fair" to "poor." Poverty likewise impacted perceptions of trustworthiness. Impoverishment was long considered a moral as well as an economic condition, especially in the nineteenth century, and visible markers of impoverishment thus signaled immorality and dishonesty to many special examiners. For example, one examiner remarked of one former slave that he "is a colored laborer who lives from hand to mouth. His reputation for truth is not good." At the same time, truthfulness for Black claimants and witnesses was often directly related to how "ignorant" they were deemed to be. One Pension Bureau official backhandedly praised one claimant's "reputation for truth, as well as for general honesty and faithfulness," for he was "as simple minded as a child, utterly incapable of attempting any sort of imposition or imposture." Too much ignorance, however, could hamper verification of crucial details of a claimant's history. With such interlocking cultural and bureaucratic assumptions at work, formerly enslaved applicants had little room to maneuver.[37]

Although legally on equal footing with their freeborn counterparts thanks to the equalization act of March 3, 1873, formerly enslaved claimants faced exceptional challenges in their bids for federal military pensions. Bureau officials harbored deep suspicions of the veracity of their claims, animated by a racial dissonance that prejudiced both the well-spoken and the unlettered. For a variety of reasons, then, the number of applications from Southern freedpeople remained relatively meager in the days of Reconstruction. In turn, the Southern Division grew more slowly than other geographical divisions, each of which boasted longer pension rolls and several pension agencies to pay out claims. The Black press caustically noted the gulf between white and Black beneficiaries. "We had twenty-two regiment[s] of colored men in the State," charged the *Semi-Weekly Louisianian* of New Orleans in 1871, "and only three regiments of Union white men, and yet the pension list of this State exhibits a role of white names to the extent of three to one over the colored." Incredulous, the paper searched for a cause. "We do not believe that the claim agents are to blame," it reasoned, betraying a strong faith in the hive of private brokers in the city, and "we know the Pension Agent is not to blame." After all, the pension agent at New Orleans was Robert H. Isabelle, a free-born Black American, a former lieutenant of the Louisiana Native Guards, and a prominent delegate to the Louisiana constitutional convention in 1867–68. The Louisiana paper affirmed that Isabelle "will do all in his power for those who may give him a call." And indeed he did, until Hayes closed his agency and consolidated all Southern Division claims in the agency at Knoxville.[38]

So the agents were not to blame. But somehow the *Louisianian* felt "equally certain that the government is not to blame." Instead, the mouthpiece of the Black Delta laid the blame "wholly at the door of those who at once refuse a benefit they are entitled to." Prospective claimants had allegedly shirked their responsibility to apply for a pension, heirs especially. The paper surmised that perhaps, to some, it looked too much "like living on the dead to take the money their deceased relatives earned in the army." But it need not be. The editor reminded his audience that soldiers had always "availed themselves of the assistance of the State, not because they in every case needed assistance, but for the purpose of encouraging those who did need it." To refuse to apply for the federal benefits to which one was entitled not only left their people deprived but also set about "consigning to oblivion the names of those who fought for the salvation of the country and the future support of their families." To Black onlookers, the stakes were therefore quite high. Material aid was only the most immediate concern, but matters of state, citizenship, and posterity held even wider significance. Rejecting the federal government's offer signaled an abandonment of an alliance forged in the days of rebellion, however increasingly one-sided and maddeningly bureaucratized that alliance became.[39]

Retroactive Recognition

The anemic pension rolls of the Southern Division hardly went unnoticed among Black claimants and their allies. Many speculated as to why so few eligible Black pensioners submitted and secured their claims. Soon lawmakers began to question the curious state of affairs. In March 1876, the House of Representatives passed a resolution calling upon the commissioner of pensions to provide information regarding the number of Black claimants in the state of Mississippi as well as the number of claims allowed, the number in adjudication, the number awaiting or under investigation, and the number of agents at work on these cases. The author of the resolution was one Guilford Wiley Wells, an Arkansas Republican and former lieutenant colonial in the Union army from upstate New York who after the war, and prior to his one term in Congress, opened up a law practice in Holly Springs. Like Congressman Thomas Boles with bounty claims, Wells's law practice exposed him to disaffected Black claimants in Arkansas struggling to receive their pensions. Together, their commands in the Union army and their affiliation with the Republican Party solidified their credentials as valuable allies for freedpeople. And the measure introduced by Wells certainly bore the imprint of the old wartime alliance. Three weeks after passage of the resolution came the official report on Black pensioners in Mississippi.[40]

In his report on March 23, 1876, Pension Commissioner Charles R. Gill offered a stunning snapshot of the injustices done to Black claimants in Mississippi. As of that date, only twenty-one Black veterans had been allowed a pension, with nineteen more pending—a total of forty applications out of roughly a dozen USCT regiments mustered from the state. Many of the pending applications were incomplete. They lacked officer's affidavits or proof of service-origin disability or evidence of medical treatment since discharge. As was true in most other Southern states, the majority of Black claimants in the early years of the reconstructed Pension Bureau appeared as widows, minors, and dependent relatives. Whereas only forty Black veterans from Mississippi had applied for an invalid pension by 1876, surviving heirs had sent 735 applications. Only 164 had been allowed, 37 were rejected outright, and fully 534 were still pending. By the year of the report, Black Mississippi veterans had a 50 percent chance at admittance to the pension rolls, while their widows and dependents—twenty of whom applied for every veteran—were rejected 20 percent of the time and required further information three-quarters of the time. The evidence in the report elicited little reaction from the commissioner, who plainly recited the proofs required to establish each claim. His findings implied that the sparely populated rolls from Mississippi owed in large part to the inability of Black claimants to meet the high burdens of proof required by law, but he quickly justified such burdens in light of the "frauds and attempts at fraud perpetuated by agents and attorneys" against "colored persons in the Southern States." The commissioner found that "special investigation is necessary in nearly every case for the protection of the government." Given the "doubtful character of the evidence furnished," adjudicating the claims of Black Southerners ex parte in distant Washington was insufficient, if not "utterly impossible." What the government needed, argued the commissioner, was to send special examiners to "the vicinage of the claimant and witnesses." But the bureau currently detailed only one employee in the whole state for that purpose, and he was charged with investigating some two dozen cases a month. It was lack of funding for these very necessary investigations that caused the delay. That, explained the commissioner, was the real injustice.[41]

It was one thing for the head of the Pension Bureau to bloodlessly itemize the required proofs to seated congressmen, but it was another altogether to present them to a recently widowed ex-slave. After Susan Sledge submitted her application for a widow's pension—her husband went missing in action at the Fort Pillow massacre in 1864—her claim came back to her in February 1869 through a Freedmen's Bureau agent at Vicksburg. The agent explained to Sledge that her application needed additional evidence and proceeded to intone the necessary bureaucratic rites. First, her declaration for a pension needed to take place before a court of record. Second, she needed to furnish evidence of her marriage, from the day and year to the place and officiator. "If you have no marriage certificate and there is no church, nor any public or private record of your marriage," continued the agent, "you will have to make oath to the fact." And if the minister's testimony was unable to be procured for whatever reason, then affidavits of two eyewitnesses were required. Third, the Pension Bureau needed proof of her two children's ages, presumably to determine whether they could have been fathered by the claimant's husband. For this, Sledge needed baptismal records or, barring that, the affidavits of two witnesses to their birth. Her application further required "the affidavit of [a] regular practicing physician (where professional standing must be certified to by the officer administering the oath) setting forth that after a careful examination of the children he verily believes their ages to be as stated giving name and age of each." Finally, she had to furnish an affidavit of the commanding officer of her husband's company, setting for when and how he died and that it "was in the performance of his duty." It would take Sledge another ten years to earn her pension. Her case, meanwhile, languished among the 534 pending widows' claims presented to Congress in 1876.[42]

The case of Susan Sledge, and indeed of the whole state of Mississippi at the nation's centennial, not only lays bare the profound difficulties facing Black claimants in the emancipated South; it also suggests that the reconstruction of the Pension Bureau depended largely on the "dependents," especially Black mothers and widows. Indeed, it would be many years before veteran applicants would outpace their womenfolk in submitting applications for federal benefits. The preponderance of pending applications from dependents also illustrates the incapacity of the federal administrative state in its emerging stages in the South, how ill-equipped it was, conceptually and administratively, to handle the fraught cases of freedwomen whose lives, more than any other class of claimant, seemed to defy and confound bureaucratic expectations.

These expectations revolved around the gravitational pull of lawful heirship. Heirship was central to the Pension Bureau's image as a generous system of welfare to reward the patriotic sacrifice of not only soldiers but their families. The July 1862 act that laid the groundwork for the Civil War pensions system made explicit provisions for the soldier's legal widow. If the soldier left no widow, the pension next went to his legitimate orphaned children under sixteen years of age. In each case, the size of the pension was to be comparable to what "the husband or father would have been entitled to had he been totally disabled." If the deceased soldier was unmarried and childless, the pension reverted to his mother, who "was dependent upon him for sup-

USCT soldier and family. The pension system operated on gendered notions of familial dependency. Determining legitimate, and thus pensionable, heirship among formerly enslaved couples proved one of the most vexing challenges for claimants and officials alike. (Library of Congress Prints and Photographs Division, LC-DIG-ppmsca-36454)

port, in whole or in part." Absent all of these relatives, the act finally granted the soldier's pension to his orphaned minor sister or sisters. Later measures would insert dependent fathers next in line after dependent mothers, and orphaned brothers after orphaned sisters. Policymakers and administrators praised the Pension Bureau for its ever-expanding liberality regarding families of veterans. "Former laws," boasted the secretary of the interior in 1867, "made no provision for relatives in the ascending or collateral lines." Now such provisions were made.[43]

The new latticework of dependency reflected and reinforced prevailing gender hierarchies in nineteenth-century America. Men provide as husbands and fathers; their wives and children were dependent on them, as were elderly or widowed parents. The pension system took this logic one step further, anticipating workingmen's compensation statutes around the turn of the century, as detailed by legal scholar John Fabian Witt. In the bureau's formulation, a widow's pension substituted for the lost wages of the husband, making the widow still dependent on her husband's earnings in the form of a pension. Widows' pensions were explicitly equal to veterans' pensions accorded for total disability. Total disability was therefore functionally equivalent to death. Should a widow remarry, she would enter into a new relation of dependency and thus forfeit her claim to a widow's pension. To avoid this, many widows apparently chose not to remarry but simply "take up" with another man so as to retain their pensionable status. For this very reason, some critics accused the bureau of encouraging illicit relations among widows, incentivizing them to live in sin. To others, and to bureau officials especially, the practice simply meant that greater scrutiny needed to be applied to widows' claims. It brought the federal government into the intimate relations of families like never before as it sanctioned proper forms of marriage and kinship by rewarding those applicants with pensions and disciplining those applicants who violated those norms. Predictably, the disciplinary gaze of the Pension Bureau fell hardest on Black women claiming pensions.[44]

If the loyalty of the formerly enslaved was taken for granted in their war claims, the legitimacy of their professed relationships was anything but. It first came to the attention of the federal government during the earliest days of wartime occupation when military and civil leaders inserted themselves into communities of freedpeople to lecture them on proper marital relations. These officials and reformers universally regarded marriage and the family as the bedrock of American citizenship. Sorting out legitimate Black marriages and families from the tangle of enslaved relations was "among the most delicate which came up for decision before the constituted authorities," according to one observer in Port Royal, South Carolina, in the spring of 1863. On the one hand, abolitionists blamed the immoral practices of enslavers for forced marriages, concubinage, and infidelity, decrying those "who parceled out wives as he parceled out blows or tasks in the field." But on the other hand, they expressly warned that "God will not wink at adultery and fornication among you now." Abolitionists tried their best to reckon with the sexual dynamics of the old order while holding out hope that, with strict Yankee tutelage, freedpeople could finally enter the world of good spouses, good parents, and good citizens. In addition to the compulsions of the enslavers, some Northerners suggested that their putative sexual improprieties were partly a matter of public shame, or the lack thereof. "Public opinion did not compel them to virtuous courses under the old slave system," the logic went, implying that it certainly ought to in the new one. And when a freedwoman's pension application triggered a special investigation, things could get very compulsive and very public indeed.[45]

The efforts of freedwomen to secure federal benefits immediately provoked questions over the nature of domestic relations under slavery as well as their continuity into the post-slavery era. Freedpeople heard from missionaries and evangelizing federal officials alike that forming families was essential not only in the eyes of God but in the laws of man. "When you were slaves you 'took up' with each other," presumed General Clinton Fisk, "and were not taught what a bad thing it is to break God's law of marriage. But now you can only be sorry for the past, and begin life anew, and on a pure foundation." He insisted those "who have been and are now living together as husband and wife, and have had children born to you, should be married according to law, as soon as possible. This will give you the civil rights of married persons, and will make your children the legal heirs to your property." For such reasons of legal recognition, and reasons all their own, many formerly enslaved couples rushed to sanctify their unions after the war—and especially after passage of the Black Codes, which in many states made cohabitation and childrearing among unmarried couples a punishable offense.[46]

Pensions for dependents hinged on the legitimacy of marital and familial ties. Although Black applicants followed the same hierarchy of pension eligibility, because marriage among the enslaved was fundamentally an extralegal practice, requiring marriage certificates or any official documentation of slave unions before the war would have been tantamount to prohibiting pensions for ex-slave widows and heirs. This, in fact, was the shameful state of affairs until mid-1866, owing to the Act of July 14, 1862, which required legal marriage for Union widowhood. The Fort Pillow Massacre of Black soldiers in April 1864 prompted Connecticut senator Lafayette S. Foster to introduce an amendment to a bill in June of that year to include the widows and children of deceased Black veterans in the general law pension system. In place of requiring state documents, the measure would have required only two credible witnesses to prove two years of cohabitation and habitual recognition of the parties as married. It made no distinction as to enslaved or free status; instead, it offered an escape hatch for couples living in states that would not have authorized their marriage—that is, the slave states. As Foster argued, it would thereby place the heirs of Black soldiers on a level with those of white soldiers, correcting an injustice inflicted on so many surviving Black families. But the remedial measure provoked strong opposition, leading to the formation of a reconciliation committee composed of three senators and three representatives. The committee agreed to the measure, but not before adding an exclusionary clause providing that the recipients of pensions for deceased Black veterans were "free persons." Such a proviso effectively excluded the very class of claimants the bill's author intended to reach, and ironically would have even excluded the vast majority of widows and heirs of the Sixth U.S. Colored Heavy Artillery, organized in the state of Alabama (which had enslaved 99 percent of its Black population in 1860) and later engaged at Fort Pillow. The bill passed both houses on July 4, 1864.[47]

Formerly enslaved widows would have to wait another two years before attaining pension eligibility. In June 1866, Congress passed two measures addressing the ambiguities of slave unions and conferring conditional inclusion. The first, on June 6, invoked the original spirit of Foster's 1864 amendment by erasing the "free person" proviso of the July 1864 act. It bestowed discretionary authority on the couples themselves in determining the bonds of marriage. It likewise granted discretionary authority to the Pension Bureau, stipulating that widows of deceased Black soldiers and sailors were "entitled to receive the pensions, bounty, and back pay provided by law without other evidence of marriage than proof, satisfactory to the Commissioner of Pensions, that the parties had habitually recognized each other as man and wife, and lived together as such." This legitimacy would in turn be conferred on the children of such unions. The act was amended several days later by a resolution on June 15, which added the element of the couple having been "joined in marriage by some ceremony deemed by them obligatory, followed by their living together as husband and wife up to the time of enlistment."[48] With such conditions met, formerly enslaved widows could claim legal (and pensionable) widowhood. Previously denied the right to marry, freedpeople's unions were thus accorded retroactive legitimacy—rights, in the words of historian Giuliana Perrone, "that granted ex post facto legal pasts to former slaves." The latter-day deference to the couples' ceremonial discretion and communal acknowledgment owed much to the efforts of former slaves during those two intervening years from 1864 to 1866, when they pushed federal officials to recognize their antebellum unions. As historian Tera Hunter has argued, they "made their presence known and felt within Union lines as kinfolk, not simply as indiscriminate individuals seeking protection and relief."[49]

Democrats reacted with hostility to the special legislation and newly won latitude afforded to Black claimants. Their reactions mixed equal parts revulsion, anger, and resentment for loosening the eligibility requirements for a seemingly unworthy class. One Northern paper, for example, decried the resurgence of the polygamy issue in Congress. "The wooden horse in which the dreaded foe entered unperceived the halls of Congress," it warned, was not via "Brigham Young's Patriarchate" in faraway Mormon Utah but rather through "an amendment to the Pension Laws, giving the widows of colored soldiers and sailors a right to pension" and the reconsideration given to "what constituted the wife of a negro." Southern senators, who reputedly had "much experience in the matter," offered little satisfactory guidance as to the marital habits of Black Southerners in the days of slavery. A considerable number believed that enslaved men "had a good many wives," and therefore if marriage for Black claimants was merely proof of cohabitation, "there might be a half-dozen wives claiming pension." The editor complained as well of the allegedly higher burden of proof faced by white widows to prove marriage above and beyond mere cohabitation. Coming shortly after the Civil Rights Act of 1866, the editor joined the cacophony of opposition, sneering that "the negro gets 'equal rights, and a little more.'"[50]

Awash in the turbulent waters of national prudery, federal officials steeled themselves for countless high-stakes contests of legitimation with a beleaguered but determined base of widowed claimants. Bureau officials seized upon any discrepancy between the oral testimony of a prospective claimant and the official service records to purify the pension rolls, or at least purge them of polygamists. Of course there were occasional incidents of impersonation and obvious efforts to fraudulently obtain a pension. But such sporadic cases were amplified at all levels of the administrative state, giving them an outsized quality in the public and administration. Emma Johnson, whose pension had been suspended in 1869 for having been processed by the corrupt agency of Moyers & Dedrick, claimed to be the widow of one Henry Johnson of the Fiftieth USCT. Yet upon examination by a Freedmen's Bureau agent, Johnson produced seemingly contradictory testimony regarding her marriage ceremony, claiming to have been married both in Vicksburg and on her captor's slave labor camp in Tensas Parish. Her two witnesses, named as former fellow slaves, also gave incongruous testimony, signaling to the Freedmen's Bureau agent that Emma Johnson had made a false claim upon the government. In another case, not officially ending an unofficial marriage resulted in a freedwoman forfeiting her pension. Louisa Taylor was considered married to a deceased soldier. They had escaped their enslaver's labor camp together in 1863; he made his way to Vicksburg to enlist while she remained in Natchez. There she married another man "under the flag" by an army chaplain and later obtained a marriage license from the Freedmen's Bureau. Taylor's official marriage therefore disqualified her from a widow's pension to her first husband.[51]

The two acts of June 1866 may have granted retroactive legitimacy to slave unions under certain conditions, but such an endowment was less like an accomplished state than a state of war, remapping as it did the battlegrounds of violation from dismissive exclusion to derogatory inclusion. In other words, the extralegal nature of slave marriages worked in tandem with the federal government's searching recognition of legitimate unions to virtually guarantee extensive and invasive intrusions into the most intimate spheres of Black family life. And it made freedwomen the most targeted claimants for investigation by special examiners of the Southern Division and the bureau as a whole.

Specialization and Interrogation

In 1881, the Pension Bureau officially established a Division of Special Examinations. It came as an early reform effort of Commissioner William W. Dudley, who wanted to bring greater transparency, standardization, and oversight to special investigations. The new division, he hoped, would address the many deficiencies of the old system, including those dramatized by the 1876 report on Black claimants in Mississippi. In the past, the bureau's special examiners were dispatched by the commissioner when he suspected fraudulent activity. They gathered evidence largely in secret. But beginning in July 1881, the special examiner "now works up his case on the ground, brings all witnesses face to face with the claimant or his attorney, and frequently establishes a meritorious claim when the claimant would have failed" to do so left to their own devices. The commissioner praised the reform as a way to protect poor and vulnerable claimants of limited means.[52]

In 1882, the Pension Bureau also began circulating a guidebook for its special examiners, with later editions to follow. Dudley delegated its authorship to Calvin B. Walker, his deputy commissioner, who put into writing the "unwritten code" that had been practiced in the adjudication of claims. The treatise contained, among virtually every subject relating to pension claims, explicit recommendations for handling the claims of Black heirs. Because documentary evidence was so lacking in the post-slavery South, bureau officials reluctantly conceded a reliance on personal recollection and communal consensus, with all the imprecision those modes of knowledge entailed. Alongside the circumstances of illiteracy, poverty, and postwar upheaval in the South, bureau officials challenged the retrieval of reliable information. As such, the guidebook stipulated that "wherever it is possible, the former owners or members of owners' family, and the fellow-slaves of both the soldier and the claimant, should be carefully examined." As in claims for bounties through the two freedmen's agencies, the special examiners of the Pension Bureau would often call upon ex-enslavers to determine the validity of slave marriages and the paternity of ex-slave children. It was best practice.[53]

The guidebook also alerted examiners of ostensibly widespread tactics among Black women who sought to profit from fraudulent claims. It cautioned, for instance, "that colored claimants (widows) adopt for the time being, while they are working up their claims through an attorney, children not their own." The examiner should therefore take special care to personally view all the children in a pending pension claim, not only to estimate their probable age but also to note their skin color. To that end, the bureau granted special examiners license to try their hand as amateur race scientists in assessing children's pigmentation to determine "whether they are the children of the soldier and the claimant." Finally, the guidebook warned special examiners that, on occasion, Black claimants will have no relation whatsoever to the soldier in question, but instead have been swept up in the schemes of private claims agents who earn a living on their fees. These warnings were strictly confined to the treatise's section on Black claimants; it expressed no such concerns about white widows in the North. The official publications produced and distributed by the Pension Bureau precisely for the training of its inquisitorial vanguard were thus marbled with cynicism and incredulity, debasing the authenticity and legitimacy of ex-slave relations, even the adoption of orphans.[54]

In the teeth of procedural antagonism, formerly enslaved mothers and widows pressed forward, writing directly to an array of federal officials inquiring about their pension claims, often tapping individuals of means and standing in the white community to advocate on their behalf. For many years, freedpeople would turn to their former enslavers out of necessity to help them authenticate their claims for bounties and pensions. There was an unmistakable irony to the endeavor, for it underscored that their place as rights-bearing claimants in the reconstructed federal state owed in no small part to the assistance of the defeated enslaver class, who now acted as brokers of freedpeople's authenticity. Still, for many former slaves, guided by practicality if not necessity, securing such distinguished testimony was their best hope to earn the fruits of citizenship otherwise under serious assault in the unoccupied South. Though application requirements for bounties and pensions overlapped, all parties involved recognized an important difference between the lump sum of a bounty payment and a recurring stipend, the latter being more desirable for its promise of ongoing support and security. White employers recognized this as well and seem to have been far greater advocates when helping elderly claimants secure their dependent pensions than working-age men and women in their employ. Advocating for elderly dependents gave them the platform on which to perform sentimentality or responsibility for longtime family "servants," and perhaps even served as a genuine psychological liniment after having cut off any financial support. But employers often viewed the prospect of testifying for Black workers with greater ambiguity. A federally backed living wage for their employees or tenants may undermine their ability to control them. Or, by the same token, it might render them indebted to their patrons.[55]

Pension applications sometimes conjured disturbing stories out from the antebellum shadows. In 1869, a group of unpaid freedwomen claimants in Missouri urged one James Overton to write to the head of the Claims Division of the Freedmen's Bureau. He agreed. In his letter, Overton notified the official that freedpeople were beginning to suspect they were being cheated out of their benefits. But his letter brought another incident to light as well. He took it upon himself to advocate for "a very needy old colored woman who lost one son in the Federal army and has two other[s] still in it." He wanted to know whether there was any chance she might receive a bounty and pension for her deceased son. The woman had never married, Overton explained, "but gave birth to several children all, I believe by *white men* or a white *man*, who is still living." He feared that the boy's white father—"an intolerable Rebel"—would attempt to secure the bounty and pension instead of his mother, whom the father would likely declare dead. He worried, too, that the woman would be denied a pension altogether because of the illegitimacy of her children. In any event, it seemed to the freedwoman's advocate "very hard that an ignorant old negro should under such circumstances be deprived of the benefits of that which was due to her deceased boy," especially with her so "in need of the necessaries of life." Her situation was sadly common. "There are several cases of this kind here, as no doubt there are, in most (formerly) slave districts," noted Overton. He thought it only right that "Congress ought to amend the laws so as to apply to such cases." But Congress never did. Somehow even the granting of positive rights and the removal of civil disabilities—the juridical acrobatics of retroactive legitimacy—were not adroit enough to reach the victims of slavery's sexual economy.[56]

The Pension Bureau rewarded legitimacy, not equity. And Congress approved. The only exceptions Congress granted for formerly enslaved pension claimants came in the two laws of June 1866, which substituted cohabitation and mutual recognition for the marriage license denied to enslaved people. Such couples therefore had to live together until enlistment, but marital fidelity was required for both parties and, after the husband's death, for as long as the widow hoped to receive her pension. Rumors that a widowed pensioner was living with another man might be enough to surrender the pension claim. This happened in the case of one North Carolina freedwoman in Craven County who, "on the point of starvation" according to the local justice of the peace, "was unjustly stoped [sic] from getting her Pension through a villinous [sic] detective from the Pension Office who reported she was remarried, which was not only false but maliciously so." With relatively broad statutory latitude, bureau officials exercised considerable discretion in determining the parameters of pension eligibility, and indeed the very functioning of the Pension Bureau. And in the fall of 1875, nearly ten years after Congress said its last word on the subject, the commissioner of pensions rendered a decision on the matter of extramarital cohabitation among Black claimants.[57]

The case involved one Martha Hodges, the widow of a USCT soldier who had begun cohabitating with another man after her husband's death. Commissioner Henry M. Atkinson maintained Hodges's entitlement to a widow's pension despite her living with another man. In the days of slavery, he reasoned, "the marriage of slaves was not recognized by the local laws of the South, and, therefore, after their emancipation Congress passed a law that the right to a pension might be conferred upon any colored woman that had lived with a soldier up to the date of his enlistment and death as his wife." During Reconstruction, however, all Southern states had codified laws regulating the institution of marriage, and "no marriage is legal that does not conform to the law." Simple cohabitation and mutual recognition, in other words, were no longer considered an equivalent to marriage when and where marriage was a legal option. Thus, while Martha Hodges was indeed living with another man, they both denied they were married and were regarded by the state as unmarried. And so Hodges had no legal claim on her housemate for support; she was not legally his dependent. The commissioner's ruling in 1875 was a humane one. It parlayed the strictures of the marriage requirement into a means to protect Black American widows against charges of "remarriage," affording them more dignity and autonomy in the process.[58]

Yet this leniency did not last long. In response to allegedly widespread activity, Congress passed a law in August 1882 stipulating that a widowed pensioner who cohabitates with another man in an open and adulterous manner loses her claim to a pension, whether or not they were married. Although the law was race-neutral, historian Brandi Brimmer has argued that it marked a new chapter in the morality policing of Black women who claimed pensions— and provoked from them vigorous refutations of sexual misconduct and countervailing assertions of their respectability. Public conflicts over the sexual propriety of Black women claiming Union widowhood at once tested the class solidarities of Black communities and defined their new relationship with the federal government.[59] The Washington *Bee* was one of many Black newspapers that likewise objected to the bureau's policy and practice regarding widows losing pensions upon remarriage, and did so from its characteristically middle-class perspective. "Women earnestly desiring marriage are induced to live lasciviously in order to keep up their pensions," argued one editorial. "They are afraid to forsake the apparent and visible income." The 1882 law against cohabitation was not enough to induce those women to leave their partners. In making its case, the Black newspaper did not so much strike out against the morality policing of the Pension Bureau as it did against the unintended consequences of the bureau's welfare restrictions—namely, incentivizing pensioned widows to cohabitate rather than remarry. All of the Union's "fatherless and husbandless should be provided for," countered the *Bee*. "The country owes them protection." Though couched in upholding respectability, such arguments from the emerging Black professional class nevertheless imagined a more capacious and empowering system of federal benefits.[60]

For decades after the war, freedwomen presented thorny claims to officials at all levels, from the clerks and special examiners of the Southern Division all the way to the pension commissioner and the secretary of the interior. The Department of the Interior frequently intervened to rule on complex pension cases not easily comprehended by established protocols in the Pension Bureau. From 1887 to 1930, the department published twenty-two volumes of decisions it rendered on pension cases on appeal from an adverse ruling by the commissioner of pensions. As the assistant secretary of the interior explained in the inaugural volume, the goal of the series was to establish "a line of consistent precedents in departmental rulings." In this way, as legal scholar Jerry Mashaw has argued, the Department of the Interior and the Pension Bureau joined other federal departments and bureaus in constructing "internal precedent," much of it in the face of statutory silence or vacuity. Tellingly, in all of those five-hundred-plus-page volumes, nearly every pension case featuring a formerly enslaved claimant involved matters of marriage and heirship, with freedwomen as the leading plaintiffs.[61]

For instance, in November 1881, Secretary of the Interior Samuel J. Kirkwood, formerly the wartime governor of Iowa, ruled on the claim of one Frances Parker. Her case involved two men: John Parker and Solomon Saunders. A special investigation revealed that she and Parker had lived together and raised several children in Virginia. After Parker was sold out of state in

1857, she later took up with Saunders in 1863 and together lived as husband and wife. But Parker came back to Virginia with his regiment in early 1864, found Frances, and "claimed her as his wife." Frances Parker went to live with her first husband in his regimental quarters for a brief time until she returned again to Saunders. John Parker died that year, and Frances Parker began collecting a widow's pension from John Parker's service, all the while living with Saunders and marrying him by official ceremony in 1872. When this came to light, Frances Parker was dropped from the pension rolls, but so, too, was the claim of her children with John Parker, "for reason that they were not legitimate." It became clear that the act of August 1882, which terminated the widow's claim upon evidence of cohabitation or "immorality," made no provision for the claims of legitimate minors from the previous union. In his ruling, Secretary Kirkwood upheld the rejection of Frances Parker's claim as a widow but allowed for the minors' claim. Her children with John Parker were legitimate, as was her union with him at the time, and they remained the rightful heirs to his claim after their mother forfeited her right to the money. Thus was established the bureau precedent that in certain cases, remarriage of a pensioned widow resulted in the pension reverting to the veteran's minor children conceived legitimately before remarriage.[62]

Historian Dylan Penningroth has suggested that Black people's relationship with each other shaped their experiences of enslavement and freedom every bit as much as their struggles with whites. In this light, pursuing a pension meant more than grappling with federal officials and navigating the federal bureaucracy. Resource scarcity—in this case, pensions—also engendered competition with relatives, community members, and the occasional imposter. In spite of the invasive scrutiny and public voyeurism within and without the Black community, freedwomen pursued pensions well into the twentieth century, reifying in the process all of the conflicts, controversies, and legacies of slave unions. Their choice to claim Union widowhood and pursue pensions through a cultural and bureaucratic minefield underscores the necessity of federal aid in the lives of working-class Black women. Braving all the indignities and behavioral strictures that accompanied federal beneficence, freedwomen fashioned for themselves an important if embattled identity not only as mothers and wives of loyal soldiers but as rights-bearing citizens. Their activism, coupled with the fraught, indefinite complexity of their claims, forced the hand of the federal government, necessitating an ever-increasing apparatus of agents and special examiners from multiple departments to administer their claims. State building, in other words, was one by-product of their struggles.[63]

Unbounded Dependency

Freedwomen's claims to bounties and pensions provoked extensive commentary on the murkiness of slave relations and their translation into the state-sanctioned realm of proper family ties. For many observers, how former slaves organized their families augured how well they would conform to the boundaries of citizenship. In the nineteenth century, the household acquired a new cultural significance, understood as a haven from external market relations where the only proper forms of dependency could take root, children upon parents and women upon men. Under this cultural and legal rubric, able-bodied white men had the most natural claim to citizenship.[64] Widows could thus lay claim to the lost earnings of their husbands, and widowed mothers to the lost earnings of their sons. In order to be eligible for a mother's pension, the claimant needed to prove not simply the "legitimacy" of her marriage and children but moreover that she had been dependent on her son's wages and, by the same token, that the son had materially contributed to her support. The Consolidation Act of 1873 set out two main criteria for determining both sides of the contributory-dependency equation: a mother would be eligible first if, at the date of her son's death, the mother "had no other adequate means of support than the ordinary proceeds of her own manual labor and the contributions of said son or of any other persons not legally bound to aid in her support" and second "if, by actual contributions or in any other way, the son had recognized his obligations to aid in support of said mother." In short, contributions from a son to a mother therefore needed to be substantive and mutually recognized. Ideally, the gesture would be public, with an audience to verify that the mother declared her need and the son responded that the money in his hands was intended for her support and should be understood as such by all present as he handed it over. It was the stuff of bureaucratic fantasy.[65]

Even for white mothers, the burden of proof was a senselessly difficult one to meet, particularly for mothers of young soldiers who relied more on their parents than the other way around.[66] When applied to the seekers of Black Union motherhood and fatherhood, however, the laws of dependency proved to be one of the most nettlesome challenges facing policymakers and the Pension Bureau. As Black mothers forced the issue with their persistent applications, they further disrupted established understandings of nothing less than the very meanings of enslavement and freedom. If chattel slavery was premised on all enslaved peoples being dependent on their captors for "support," how, then, could dependency be adequately demonstrated among (formerly) enslaved family members? Could an enslaved mother ever be said to "depend" on her enslaved son, and what would such a dependency look like? In other words, could lateral ties of dependency exist within a space defined by the vertical ties between enslaver and enslaved? If not, then all formerly enslaved mothers would fail to meet the eligibility requirements; if, instead, such ties of dependency were possible independent of the enslaver, should evidence of such ties be required in every case? Ex-slave claimants had been schooling federal officials for some time on the existence, durability, and nonconformity of Black families under slavery. Would they now convince federal administrators that the rudiments of familial dependency, so integral to citizenship, had actually existed during slavery?

In the mid-1870s, federal administrators began to apply a more liberal reading to the 1873 dependency statute in the claims of formerly enslaved mothers. In 1875, Secretary of the Interior Zachariah Chandler decided in the case of ex-slave Mary Bryant that her condition of dependence on her enslaver did not disqualify her from her right to a mother's pension. Repeating the familiar equalization mantra, Chandler held "that the freedmen are to be treated, in pension matters, as though they had never been slaves." Whatever state laws may have existed to compel enslavers to support their enslaved men, women, and children, he argued, no longer hold any validity and should be "ignored." All the Pension Bureau should seek to determine is whether the "soldier actually contributed to, and such contribution was necessary for, the parents' *comfortable* support." Any financial support a soldier or future soldier managed to render his parents, therefore, was deemed constitutive of a dependent relationship, whether or not that support was the claimant's only means.[67] This support was necessarily financial, meaning it came in one of three ways: from hiring out their time, independent production, or military pay. The former two practices varied considerably across the slave South but were sufficiently widespread to allow thousands of bondspeople to earn cash and retain property. Enslaved laborers in urban areas took advantage of the demand for a flexible workforce, while those in rural areas where the task system of labor dominated were often able to tend to their own gardens or raise their own livestock for sale in the local market. At all events, despite being legally considered property themselves, many ex-slave claimants testified to a surprising internal economy, and thus a system of interdependent relations operating on a different social register from the enslaver-enslaved dynamic.[68]

For years, federal administrators seemed to appreciate the prevalence of economic activity among the enslaved enough to abide the requirements of showing material support from enslaved child to enslaved parent. Yet such recognition in some cases proved too burdensome. Enslavers restricted access to time and land at will, and the communal acknowledgment of slave property, much like slave marriages, was ultimately extralegal and thus vulnerable to confiscation by the enslaver or the occupying Union army. More lenient (and realistic) approaches to the dependency of enslaved mothers came in the early 1880s. The 1882 edition of the Pension Bureau's treatise on practice devoted an entire section to dependency claims for Black claimants. Following Chandler's 1875 ruling, the bureau instructed examiners that enslaved status did not "work the forfeiture" of a mother's claim, nor did the inability of an enlisted son to send money to his mother during the war have any "important bearing." When handling such claims, the bureau cautioned, there indeed "must be some evidence of contributions or a recognition of obligation to aid in the support of a mother on the part of her adult son at some period of time prior to his death, but in such cases great liberality in regard to the amount of proof should be practiced." And so, through the combination of administrative rulings and the gradual accretion of bureau practice, accepting the relative dependency of two enslaved family members and looking for any reasonable show of support became the working interpretation of the pension dependency statutes. As one pension attorney later commented, the equities in these claims "are so strong that, even if we had not the practice of the Pension Office to warrant us, we should feel justified in appealing to the *discretion* allowed you in such matters."[69]

Yet discretion could be an administratively volatile concept. In the absence of congressional legislation, the bureau's internal rulings and practices were subject to the agendas of the appointed commissioners, who were inescapably politicized "apolitical" actors. While working to institute his own guidelines in the early 1880s, Commissioner Dudley had also pushed for an official amendment to the statutes governing dependency pensions to put the practices on a more secure legal footing.[70] His successor would soon prove the necessity of such a precautionary endeavor. John C. Black received his appointment from Grover Cleveland, the first Democrat in the White House since the Civil War. Black was decidedly unsympathetic toward formerly enslaved claimants, and those mothers pursuing claims under his tenure met with frustration and failure. Commissioner Black reversed the vector of liberality, making it bureau policy to deny pensions to formerly enslaved mothers on the grounds that they were not dependent on their enslaved sons but rather on their enslavers, unwriting in the process a decade of internal law.

In the summer of 1886, one of Black's rejection letters was leaked to the press, provoking a surprising outburst of sympathy for a formerly enslaved mother, known to the public as the mother of Arnold C. Shaw of the Seventeenth USCT. "This claim for a pension," noted Black, "has been rejected on the ground that as the claimant was a slave at the time of the soldier's death, she was not dependent upon him for support at that time." Newspapers across the country seized upon Black's "heartless ruling." They objected not only to the baseness of denying a pension to an old woman who had four sons in the Union army, one who "was shot to death in defending the old flag," but also to its apparent antagonism to the Emancipation Proclamation, released on January 1, 1863. Shaw had enlisted in August 1863, explained the *St. Louis Post-Dispatch*, when "there were no slaves in the Southern States, unless Gen. Black proposes to override the emancipation proclamation of President Lincoln." Even the *St. Louis Globe-Democrat* joined in. "The emancipation proclamation had gone into effect on January 1, 1863," it quipped, "but Mr. Black hadn't heard about that little incident. Black's ignorance, malevolence and mendacity constitute a trinity of qualifications which make him one of the most useful officials of the Administration."[71]

Despite properly placed sympathies, the press seems to have overlooked that the proclamation did not apply to the entire South, only to those areas still in active rebellion. It exempted the four upper South states of Missouri, Kentucky, Maryland, and Delaware, as well as thirteen parishes in southeast Louisiana, the western counties of Virginia (soon to be West Virginia), and the entire state of Tennessee, where Shaw's regiment was organized in late 1863. Those areas, under Union control, legally retained whatever was left of the slave system—and years later would generate some of the most fraught dependent-pension claims. Or, perhaps, the press conflated previous wartime acts prohibiting the return of self-emancipated men and women who made it to Union lines, along with promises that the families of enlisted men were likewise declared free. In any event, the technical intricacies of the two Confiscation Acts and the Emancipation Proclamation mattered less in the public mind than the latter's memorialization as the watershed of wartime abolition, the point of no return.[72]

Commissioner Black had other methods for handling mothers' claims arising from the rebel-controlled areas that were in fact encompassed by the Emancipation Proclamation. Two years after the Shaw case, Black rejected the claim of Emily Williams, mother of William Jones. In April 1873, one month after the bounty equalization act, Williams had submitted her claim for bounty, writing directly to the second auditor of the Treasury, pleading that "all the son I hade [*sic*] in the world to help me died in the army. . . . I am now 90 years of age har[d]ly can get up when I am Down." Six months later, she filed her pension application. A lengthy investigation followed, conducted by E. A. Barringer, the bureau's special examiner deployed in New Orleans. Williams, who had never married, testified that she and her son had lived on the slave labor camp of their mistress, Eliza Richardson, and they both left the estate during the war when the Union army marched through central Louisiana as part of General Nathaniel Banks's Red River campaign. She fled to New Orleans along with "many other people." Her son, however, decided to enlist, and she never saw him again. Military records indicate that he died of measles in July 1864 at Fort St. Philip, Louisiana. "Nothing was ever said by my son about supporting me or contributing to my support," Williams let slip, inadvertently undermining one of the central criteria for dependency. And although "my mistress supported and took care of me on the plantation up to the time I left" for New Orleans, she affirmed, "after I left the plantation I supported my self." Another witness corroborated her story, as did her former mistress, who confirmed that she supported Williams until the time she left the labor camp around the spring of 1864.

However, the examiner concluded that the mother and son remained on Eliza Richardson's plantation "for a period of 15 or 16 months after they became free," which he dated to January 1, 1863. In those months between the proclamation and their escape and her son's enlistment, her son allegedly "neither contributed nor expressed any liability or contract to support the mother." For his part, Black reasoned that because the part of Louisiana in which they were living, Rapides Parish, was freed by the proclamation, the son, William Jones, was therefore under legal obligations to support his mother— even though he was a minor. The mother therefore needed to prove dependency on her son, which she failed to do. Black's reasoning held that mothers such as Emily Williams went from being dependent on their enslavers to being dependent on their menfolk overnight. And proving dependency with actual material contributions during and immediately after wartime emancipation was an insurmountable feat for many. To Commissioner Black, that was precisely the point.[73]

The uneven attrition of wartime emancipation produced a seemingly endless variety of such cases, far more than federal administrators anticipated. Consider the case of Elizabeth Small, who had the misfortune to file her papers for a mother's pension a year and a half into Black's tenure, September 1886. She and her son, Henry Small, had both been enslaved in Talbott County, Maryland, before he enlisted in the Second USCT, dying about two months later in November 1863. Before a special examiner in Baltimore on

February 8, 1889, Small admitted, "I cannot say that I depended upon him [Henry] to any extent during his life-time, because we were all slaves and supported by our master. My son was not in a position, on that account, to aid me and did not do anything for me up to his enlistment, and I received no money from him after." Yet she claimed a pension "on the ground that, if my son Henry was living, he would help me." She told the examiner of how she and her husband and her whole family "remained with our old slave master until the Christmas of 1865, when the war closed." Her husband then worked as a farm hand in their old neighborhood up to his death. That was about eleven years before her application for a pension. And throughout that time, the widow Small "depended upon the charity of my relatives," until she first learned of her entitlement through Isaiah Turner, a Black claims agent, who encouraged her to apply. Commissioner Black rejected her application for a pension later that spring on the narrow grounds that no dependency was demonstrated to exist between the formerly enslaved mother and son, that the son was over twenty-one years of age at the time of enlistment, and that he sent none of his earnings from the army to his mother. Though the Emancipation Proclamation exempted Maryland, its citizens passed a new constitution abolishing slavery on October 13, 1864, nearly a year after her son's death. She remained, in Black's jaundiced view, dependent not on her deceased son but on her former enslaver.[74]

So firmly engrained was the idea that the enslaved were intrinsically dependent on their enslavers that evidence of the reverse was unimaginable. Nancy Dixon had been pursuing a mother's pension since 1870. Her enslaver, one Howard Stringfellow, fled his own slave labor camp in northern Virginia when the war broke out, leaving Dixon under the care of her son, Richard. She swore in an affidavit for the bureau that Stringfellow had "never done anything more for me since the year 1860." In fact, when he returned at one point during the war, he "was sick and *I took care of him*, feeding and nursing him with my own means," with produce and proceeds from her and her son's own garden plot on the estate. Once Richard enlisted, he began sending wages to his mother. In fact, a witness testified that Richard left his mother "all of the produce of his garden and cornfield for her support." Throughout the 1870s and early 1880s, Nancy Dixon's claim was continually rejected on the grounds that she was not dependent on her son but rather remained under the "care custody and control" of her variously absentee and invalid captor. "It is true that I remained on the place until 1865," Dixon explained in July 1886, "but I was *not supported by my master*. He was a sickly man and not able to support himself." It was enough to convince the special examiner assigned to her case, who recommended her admission to Commissioner Black in August 1886. But Black rejected her claim nonetheless. In response to the rejection, Dixon's agents managed to submit a private pension bill before the House Committee on Invalid Pensions to grant her a special pension, as had dozens of other claimants excluded from the pension rolls. The committee, however, reported adversely, maintaining that Dixon failed to prove that Richard was her sole means of support.[75]

On March 27, 1889, James Tanner replaced Black as pension commissioner, to the literal relief of millions. Appointed by President Benjamin Harrison—who had campaigned vigorously on the welfare of Union veterans—Corporal Tanner, as he was affectionately known, had lost both of his legs below the knee and had been the stenographer at Lincoln's deathbed, a popular spokesman on the Republican lecture circuit, and generally one of the most admired and celebrated figures of the Gilded Age. He entered office with the express intention of liberalizing the Pension Bureau and reversing the course established by his predecessor. Tanner immediately began reviewing the claims rejected under Black's administration. Within two weeks of taking office, Tanner circulated a decision on the matter of dependency among formerly enslaved mothers and sons—a decision that affected Elizabeth Small's case as well as hundreds of others. The new commissioner held that "although the son may not by direct acts have recognized his obligations to aid in the support of his mother, if the mother and son were slaves on one plantation, or owned by one master it will be held that the son's labor was a contribution to the common maintenance of all, and in this sense was a contribution to the support of his mother." Slave labor was, then, an inexorable contribution to the enslaved community and all its members.[76]

Tanner's decision reflected a more capacious understanding of enslavement, one that recognized slavery as not only a system of social relations but more fundamentally a system of labor exploitation. Doing so radically reworked notions of dependency in bondage, as mothers such as Nancy Dixon had tried to do on an individual basis. Because enslavers depended on all their captives' laboring power collectively to maintain their estates, in turn all enslaved peoples contributed to each other's support. That only a very small portion of their labor-created wealth found its way back to their cabins and dinner plates should not obscure the fact that without their labor their enslavers were nothing. In contrast to other forms of welfare, pensions were long regarded (and still are) as contributory in nature, that is, based on prior contributions from recipients. Tanner's decision gave enslaved mothers the discursive space to claim not only contributions from their sons but also the contributions they themselves made while enslaved.

It was not long before Tanner's decision made headlines. "The new commissioner of pensions," carped the *Atlanta Constitution*, "will distinguish himself, if there is any virtue in extreme rulings." The paper estimated that the commissioner's decision would open the rolls to twenty thousand new Black pensioners. In previous years, John C. Black had kept them at bay, as "the democratic commissioner decided that the mother was not dependent upon her son because both were slaves." But such "reasoning did not strike Corporal Tanner," "the most radical of republicans." The *Constitution*—which functioned as a mouthpiece for the New South and its promotion of business, industry, prosperity, and Black subordination—nevertheless found easy consolation in the regional justice wrought from the racial injustice of Tanner's decision. The paper sardonically noted "his 20,000 new pensioners will draw just that much money southward. The sum expended in the payment of their pensions will be an unjust burden upon the country at large, but in the long run it will be utilized in building up the south. Perhaps," the editor concluded, "when the commissioner thinks it over, he will not be so well satisfied with his ruling."[77]

He was, as were others. Empowered by the new commissioner's decision, Elizabeth Small instructed her attorneys to file an appeal that same month, in April 1889. In a letter to the secretary of the interior, they argued that talk of her son obtaining his legal majority (twenty-one years) was irrelevant because he was enslaved, and "under the laws in force" his enslaver remained "entitled to his service and labor." But while rendering service, he was obviously "contributing directly to the support of his mother also a slave to the same master: This must be apparent to any logical mind, and the question as to whether he was eighteen years old, or thirty five does not enter into the case." Second, although they admitted that her son never sent home wages from his two months' service before his death, they reminded the secretary that Henry Small was discharged from the hospital sick, "unfit for military or any other service. He never recovered, and finally died." He thus never had any opportunity to aid in his mother's support. For all intents and purposes, after he enlisted "the Government took the place of his master for three years and demanded and received his entire time and service." Small and her attorneys ended their appeal by asking whether Congress, when placing freedpeople "on the same footing" with their white counterparts, "intended to require of claimants impossibilities." Operating on liberal assumptions of equality, lawmakers and administrators threatened to use the facts of enslavement against emancipated claimants, setting an unrealistic, even impossible, standard for the attainment of federal benefits. Offering material contributions to one's enslaved mother while dying in a faraway regimental hospital was certainly an impossibility. Small thus requested "a decision conforming to the spirit rather than the strict letter of the law."[78]

Elizabeth Small would not get the equity and discretion she had wanted. In another dispiriting rejection, the Department of the Interior overruled Tanner's decision and upheld Black's earlier removal of Small from the pension rolls. The rejection was authored by Assistant Secretary of the Interior Cyrus Bussey, a brigadier general and former aide-de-camp to Samuel Kirkwood. Bussey affirmed the rejection on June 13, 1889, in a long, breathless decision. To Bussey, the matter hinged on a strict interpretation of the statute requiring the deceased son's actual contributions to be the sole means of support for a mother. It left no room for discretion, argued Bussey, who found Tanner's decision that all enslaved people, by virtue of their labor, contributed to the maintenance of all on a given slave labor camp to be "too obscure for definition, and too remote from every possibility of proof, to be accepted as a ground for pension within the meaning of the Statute." An enslaved person's labor was neither a direct nor even an indirect contribution to the enslaved community on a given estate, he decided, but rather "belonged to the master who claimed it, exacted it, and lived on it." The enslaver thus not only stole the labor of the enslaved but so mystified its origins as to have it effectively sprout from his account books. What's more, according to Bussey, no familial dependency could meaningfully exist between enslaved individuals until the abolition of slavery. The son, Bussey scoffed, "had nothing to contribute or tender; he had nothing out of all his toil, even for himself, but a bare and gross subsistence while he was a slave." What this case—and others like it—needed, according to the career sidekick, was a reminder that laws were meant to be interpreted by the letter, that administrative bodies were not meant to legislate, and that rough legal equality was to prevail over matters of historical equity and redress. "The law," he continued, "makes no discrimination between races, whether white and free, or black and slave, in defining pensionable dependence." Formerly enslaved people such as Elizabeth Small were thus fully entitled to all the joys and hazards of freedom, before which they lacked any legal personality.[79]

News of Bussey's ruling ramified throughout the nation. Excerpts from the decision, alongside Small's appeal, appeared in the *New York Herald* and the New Orleans *Daily Picayune* under headlines such as "Refusing to Pension a Colored Woman Because Her Son Was a Slave." Reactions were negative, if emotionally muted. Yet all understood the gravity of the decision which, in the words of the *Herald*, "practically decides many other cases."[80] For countless formerly enslaved mothers, news of the ruling must have left them stunned and disheartened. On top of their efforts to obtain bounties and back payments, many had been in decades-long struggles for pensions, consuming an immense amount of time, energy, and resources. They endured the invasive scrutiny leveled at their claims—tremendous blows to their privacy and dignity. Yet the tragedy of it all was something more than an aggregate of individual injustices. By a strict construction of ostensibly status-blind, egalitarian statutes, federal administrators such as Cyrus Bussey, John Black, and scores of others ensured that the toil of countless former slaves went fully unrequited. The new liberal order was indeed based on such an important denial.

AS PENSION CLAIMANTS, Black mothers had to negotiate several layers of dependency. As enslaved laborers, they were presumed dependent on their enslavers, as wives they were regarded as dependent on their husbands, and as mothers they were dependent on their sons, but only under certain conditions. Freedwomen were in turn compelled to argue for their entitlements not from positions of independence but rather from its ascriptive opposite. It was an extraordinarily precarious position. Formerly enslaved mothers lost much of their wartime foothold in the federal government in the two decades after emancipation. But in those critical years, they along with thousands of other formerly enslaved veterans, widows, fathers, and children proved relentless and resourceful in their quests for military pensions. As they had in their struggles for back payment and bounties, formerly enslaved heirs solicited assistance from the two freedmen's agencies as well as private claims agents and men and women of standing in the community. They even conscripted their former enslavers into the process, aware of the deference federal officials so eagerly bestowed on them to lend legitimacy to their claims. When the established channels failed to satisfy, they wrote directly to those in charge at the highest levels of government.

The full impact of their efforts to gain federal benefits is difficult to quantify. In 1885, Commissioner Black offered Congress a tabulated report on the number of pension claims filed since the beginning of the war. Veterans of the USCT still had not surpassed their womenfolk in applying for pensions, having filed some 12,635 claims, but only 3,780 were admitted to the pension rolls. This was but a small fraction of a total of the nearly 540,000 veteran applications with over 290,000 admissions. Their widows had greater success, filing 11,470 claims, though less than half (4,963) were admitted; mothers filed 3,543 claims but only 883 were admitted. In the twelve months surrounding Bussey's 1889 ruling on the Elizabeth Small case, only 277 mothers applied for a pension and only 140 were admitted.[81]

What these grim figures belie, however, are the intense struggles waged by all formerly enslaved claimants and their outsized consequences. Unsuccessful claims often consumed far more administrative resources and attention than did successful ones. Consider the amount of administrative energy devoted to denying Emily Williams, Nancy Dixon, and Elizabeth Small a twelve-dollar monthly stipend. Clearly, freedwomen, as widows and mothers, forced issues which the administrative state would have rather not dealt with—indeed, issues that it proved incapable of dealing with. Their mobilization not only accelerated the reconstruction of the Pension Bureau in the postbellum South but reached the highest echelons of executive authority in the nation, demanding that commissioners and even cabinet-level secretaries redefine statutory definitions of dependency and marriage to adequately redress their claims. Passed over for the franchise by the Fifteenth Amendment and excluded from the formal electoral arena, freedwomen were some of the most surprisingly formidable actors in the emerging federal administrative state. However much administrators likened formerly enslaved claimants to individuated, atomized applicants, freedwomen knew that securing federal pensions was fundamentally a communal endeavor, particularly when matters of dependency were involved. No one pursued a pension alone. When their menfolk made their own claims, freedwomen once again proved themselves a force to be reckoned with, provoking time and again a national confrontation with how Americans ought to regard slavery, dependency, and freedom.

Receiving a pension was a matter of life and death. As one formerly enslaved parent put it in 1883, "This pension claim is the only hope I have."[82] But appreciating the struggles and successes of formerly enslaved claimants in the pension system should not obscure the very need to seek a pension in the first place to simply survive in the post–Civil War South. What should also be transparent is why the pension system was so deeply invested in the gendered hierarchies of the family. For all the liberalizing efforts of some administrators working within the system, the family remained the locus of proper relations of dependency not only in a cultural sense but in a material one as well. By design, the redistributive powers of the Pension Bureau only went so far. Limitations of race and status always ensured unequal treatment for former slaves. But on an even deeper level, the Pension Bureau operated on the unstated premise that redistributive policies must begin and end at the family unit. Once made the target of selective entitlements, the process of determining legitimate family relations invited a heap of conservative sensibilities and racial prejudices into the equation. Viewing the much-celebrated generosity of the Pension Bureau from the vantage of the post-slavery South, in the ever-lengthening shadow of more ambitious, equitable, and humane visions of land and wealth redistribution, federal pensions to highly scrutinized individuals were but proverbial crumbs, a sop to more radical promises.

CHAPTER FOUR

Of War and Theft

If the reconstruction of the Pension Bureau in the South proceeded slowly, as it did so, it exposed at every turn the intensely fraught challenges faced by formerly enslaved men and women as they made their claims in a federal bureaucracy maladjusted to accommodate them. As widows and mothers, freedwomen proved unexpectedly persistent in their efforts to secure bounties and pensions, forcing the bureau to make discretionary exceptions when it became clear that enforcing statutory equality was tantamount to excluding the vast majority of formerly enslaved heirs from their entitlements. Their cases provoked issues that had been central to the functioning of antebellum slavery, from the denial of family and marriage to the value of enslaved labor and the perverse dialectic of ownership and dependency. Because the pension claims of heirs were fundamentally about family ties and relationships, their cases offer incomparable windows into the intimate lives of millions of Black Americans otherwise rendered unknowable by lack of literacy and documentation. As such, historians have overwhelmingly relied on the claims of widows in their efforts to piece together stories of slavery and emancipation. In their own ways, however, Black veterans' pensions have much to reveal about the mechanics of the burgeoning federal welfare state.

In addition to the familiar paperwork establishing one's identity and service record, the ordeal of the medical examination represented a critical juncture in the pursuit of a so-called invalid pension for thousands of formerly enslaved men. For the first twenty-five years after the Civil War, all applicants needed to prove a service origin for a soldier's disability or death in order to receive a pension. Because claimants needed to trace their alleged disabilities to their time in the Union army, evidence that they had somehow entered service in ill-health could disqualify their claims. Knowing this, Black claimants walked a discursive tightrope in narrating their stories of suffering to federal officials who, for their part, brought a cartload of assumptions about slavery and the enslaved to bear on their interactions with Black veterans. Furthermore, these interpersonal struggles were embedded within a broader cultural landscape laden with contested memories of slavery, the Civil War, Reconstruction, and the all-consuming discourse of racial progress.

Body Counts

For decades, the law under which Union veterans and heirs applied for a pension awarded them on the basis of service-related injuries, afflictions, and deaths. The diseases and deprivations that plagued military encampments from the early days of the war ensured that soldiers encountered more camp diseases than combat injuries. Camp conditions inspired a massive mobilization of scientific knowledge to promote the health of the nation's soldiers. In April 1861, Henry W. Bellows and other prominent civic leaders of New York City created the U.S. Sanitary Commission, a philanthropic group that assumed many public health–related functions for the federal army, a private agency doing work "for the public good." Though it generated great enthusiasm from the start, its actions remained limited until the spring of 1862, when it overcame the War Department's reluctance to grant access to Union lines. Thereafter the Sanitary Commission sent agents throughout the wartime South to collect data on conditions and procedures, administer medicine, distribute supplies, and make (often unsolicited) recommendations to military officers and surgeons. Women were its foot soldiers. They not only were found in Union camps as nurses and caretakers but also shouldered nearly all of the organizing efforts on the home front. Doctors and staffers were stationed throughout all theaters of the war and among white and Black troops alike.[1] The authority granted to the Sanitary Commission allowed highly motivated physicians to test hypotheses, sharpen their medical knowledge, and put it to practical use alleviating human suffering. Yet this was not the commission's stated mission, with white or Black troops. Rather, the Sanitary Commission's official history proclaimed that its "ultimate end is neither humanity nor charity. It is to economize for the National service the life and strength of the National solider." With its unromantic goal of economizing the health of the soldier, the Sanitary Commission labored to establish a new, modern citizenship based on efficiency and scientific professionalism.[2]

Beyond improving camp conditions and laying the groundwork for postbellum public health initiatives, perhaps the most important and lasting contribution of the Sanitary Commission was to help forge the theoretical commodification of citizens as a foundational justification of the modern nation-state. Promoting efficiency and discipline over the trappings of humanitarian sentiment, the Sanitary Commission reminded the American public that "the death of every soldier is a considerable pecuniary loss to the country." Indeed, the value of a deceased soldier's life could be not only mourned but, more importantly, quantified. When one considered the price of his enlistment, his pay, rations, bounty, and pension to his lawful widow and heirs—on top of his absence as a productive member of the postwar society—the cost of each soldier "is certainly not less than one thousand dollars." Of course, the commission was careful to note, "men are not among the commodities we buy and sell," despite having been so before in the slave South; nevertheless, if each of the Union war dead "was worth as much to the country as the average South Carolina field hand to his owner," then the Sanitary Commission was saving the Treasury hundreds of thousands of dollars each year. The organization's interest in cultivating a self-image as scientific, professional, and objective helps explain its hard-nosed, objectifying logic. But the ease with which the Sanitary Commission compared the value of the soldier to the value of the enslaved was especially revealing, coming as it did during the war of emancipation. South Carolinian enslavers were indeed losing field hands precisely because of the war; the commission implied that the federal government ought not make the same mistake with its own men. What the commission overlooked, however, was that many of those Carolina field hands, in fact, would subtract from both ledgers at once when they died in blue uniforms.[3]

Though illness was a common companion to all soldiers, the men of the U.S. Colored Troops (USCT) endured more afflictions than their white counterparts. Leaders of the Sanitary Commission proved among those most invested in discovering the root cause of higher disease rates among Black troops, whether it be environmental, behavioral, or racial. Embarking on such a quest, Dr. Benjamin Woodward made a tour through the USCT camps in Arkansas in August and September 1865, many months after the Mississippi Valley came under Union control. He traveled from Cairo to Vicksburg, passing the refugee camps established by John Eaton, from which so many Black soldiers were drawn. Woodward circulated a questionnaire among the regimental surgeons of the USCT as well as others deemed to have expertise on the issue of racial distinctiveness, asking for scientific commentary "as to the Physiological Status of the Negro as compared with white soldiers." Shocking cases of neglect by white army doctors quickly surfaced, leading the physician-inspector to conclude that "if Negroes are to be used as soldiers more care must be used." Some had refused to treat Black soldiers, claiming that "they cannot diagnose in the negro." But Woodward argued that if only Black soldiers were "closely watched and promptly treated there would be no more deaths than in White Regts. Negro responds readily to remedial agents, and the same treatment and doses are effectual as with whites." Woodward was among many sanitary workers and regimental surgeons who seriously questioned the popular view that Black and white people had fundamentally different physiological makeups and thus required fundamentally different diagnoses and treatments, an opinion held by many theorists but evidently not followed by many Southern medical practitioners.[4]

In the same spirit of scientific inquiry, Dr. Ira Russell, another agent of the Sanitary Commission and Woodward's eastern colleague, investigated the Hospital L'Ouverture in Alexandria, Virginia. Named after the famed Haitian revolutionary—and abutting the former slave pen of Price & Birch—Toussaint's namesake was constructed in 1863 and opened its doors in 1864 for Black troops and refugees. Although Russell largely concurred with Woodward's findings of essential sameness between white and Black subjects "under the same conditions," he regarded his Black subjects as very poor estimators of the relative importance of their symptoms, owing, he surmised, to an immunological naïveté among a people lacking resources and bodily autonomy, leading them to unwittingly place greater weight on the trivial while overlooking the grave. Russell essentially argued that white doctors treating Black patients had to treat them as children, taking their testimony with a grain of salt. The examining physician had to make a thorough investigation, forming his own opinions by "taking into account the rational and physical signs." Russell, who claimed to have performed over eight hundred autopsies on Black and white soldiers, thus explicitly advocated for the privileging of Black bodies over Black testimonies. It was an enduring formulation, one that Black veterans would confront time and again in their medical examinations before pension boards in the postbellum South.[5]

The leaders of the Sanitary Commission endeavored with an infectious ambition to make use of the preponderance of somatic data they had collected. They wanted to produce definitive, quantifiable knowledge for future use, and to that end inaugurated a massive study of the physical attributes of the nation's white soldiers. And in the summer of 1864, the newly appointed head of the organization's Statistical Bureau, Benjamin A. Gould, directed the incorporation of Black soldiers into the study as well, and amended the form previously used by the investigators of white soldiers to better suit the measuring of Black subjects. "*This* field is exclusively ours," exclaimed Elisha Harris, who led the Sanitary Commission's Medical Bureau. The anatomical measurement of Black soldiers for comparison with whites began in the final months of the war and continued for months after. Gould and his team of investigators deployed an apparatus called the andrometer (from the Greek, "man" and "measure") along with an assortment of other devices to calculate distances, weights, and volumes—the full battery of calculations that defined the physical limits of man. Although examiners asked a handful of basic questions about the subject's birthplace, ancestry, marital status, and so forth, by and large the quantitative data were paramount. Objectivity required strict objectification.[6]

Gould published his findings in 1869, inspiring other statistical studies looking to strip away the contextual wrappings that obscured the great anatomical truths. His finished work showcased dozens of matrixes populated by data from roughly 10,000 white soldiers and 2,100 Black soldiers. The subjects had exhibited varying levels of compliance during the ordeal. Some resolutely refused to be measured, or to strip naked, or to give accurate information. Perhaps for many Black soldiers the process was too strikingly reminiscent of the slave markets, where buyers would inspect, prod, measure, and assess enslaved people at will. Even still, as historian Leslie Schwalm has suggested, the examinations by Gould's team jeopardized much more than one's dignity in the moment; the entire project hoped to scientifically establish that racial differences were in fact real, embodied, and measurable. This point was underscored in 1875, when the federal government released its own anthropometric study compiled by J. H. Baxter. This collection of data was gathered through the work of the provost marshal during and immediately after the war. It boasted data from over one million recruits. But overall, the evidence of the Gould and Baxter studies proved inconclusive, and its authors and editors generally avoided drawing any biologically deterministic conclusions based on their findings. They merely presented the facts. Yet the inconclusiveness hardly deterred future statisticians, actuaries, and professional racists from using the data to serve their own ends, which they would do well into the twentieth century.[7]

Measurements of the living were, of course, not the only body counts in the Civil War era. General mortality statistics garnered from the War Department would be deployed in a range of forums to praise the hardiness of native-born white soldiers while at the same time asserting their corporeal supremacy over foreign-born and Black troops. In December 1866, the widely read *Army and Navy Journal* printed an editorial that made extravagant claims about the "superior endurance of the white soldier" based on a handful of raw, decontextualized figures from the provost marshal's office. The editorial reported that of the 184,331 Union men who died of disease during the war, 158,120 were white (of about 2.5 million enlistees) and 26,211 were Black (of about 180,000 enlistees). In other words, one in sixteen white men died of disease compared with one in seven Black men. And for every five white men who died of disease, three died in battle or of battle wounds, whereas for

Black troops the ratio was eight to one. From these figures, the editor naturally concluded that "the present physical condition of the white man is doubly better fitted than that of the negro to endure the hardships of military service." Seldom did any observer pay any regard to the wartime context that was so patently undeniable to Sanitary Commission field workers and others confronting the unnecessary suffering of ex-slaves behind Union lines— seldom as well did they ever credit the testimony of Black soldiers themselves. In the war-weary culture of postbellum America, such humanized considerations proved less attractive than the comprehendible, anthologized data culled from the physical mass of humanity.[8]

Medical examinations conducted by the Pension Bureau drew on these prior statistical undertakings, though not in ways one might expect. They did not, for instance, encourage the development of separate medical examination forms or procedures or policies for Black claimants owing to popular beliefs in biological difference. Instead, the activities of the Sanitary Commission, the various statistical reports on the nation's soldiers, and the innumerable forthcoming medical examinations conducted by the Pension Bureau signaled the nation-state's newfound interest in the data drawn from its citizens, reflecting the modern allure of transforming social and political questions into biological and economic ones. These official, state-sanctioned projects underwrote the new authority of the state as an arbiter of knowledge acquired through putatively unbiased technologies. The objective statistics would demonstrate the central state's capacity not only to know its citizens—to make its soldiery, if not its entire population, legible—but also to establish the normal and the average and, by the same token, the abnormal and the deviant. Finally, these racialized wartime projects demonstrate how emancipation ironically gave the federal government an opportunity to appropriate the bodies of formerly enslaved men, deploying the resultant data to lay theoretical groundwork for abandoning freedpeople to their fate. These projects of comprehensive statistical compilation, then, sought to extinguish the red-hot promises of radical social transformation with the cold resignation of biological destiny.[9]

Sound at the Start

Ironically, despite the widespread acknowledgment that Black soldiers suffered disproportionately from diseases incurred during service, as veterans they struggled to prove it on an individual basis. For many, the dearth of documentation interlaced with prejudice against Black claimants worked to undermine their bids for pensions under the general law. The locus of these struggles was the medical examination. In front of an individual or board of deputized federal physicians, claimants would briefly explain their disabilities and narrate how and when they were acquired. Following the claimant's preface would be a thorough examination, with each body part evaluated for its laboring potential. A final disability rating on a scale of eighteenths would suggest to the Pension Bureau headquarters an appropriately sized pension. Though seemingly mundane, these examinations brought two discrete narratives into conflict over the legitimation and recognition of suffering.[10]

Pension applications from Black soldiers and heirs began trickling in as soon as the war ended, aided as they were by Freedmen's Bureau agents. Many early claimants bore physical markers of injuries incurred during military service. Most readily apparent were, of course, gunshot wounds. Consider the actions of Carolina Haines, Isaac Jenkins, and Mingo Singleton, all comrades in the Thirty-Third USCT, the famed South Carolina regiment commanded by the practicing abolitionist Thomas Wentworth Higginson and attended to by the intrepid Black nurse Susie King Taylor. After mustering out in late January 1866, each of these men lodged pension claims on account of gunshot wounds received during the late war—Jenkins applied that same month, Singleton applied in July 1867, and Haines in October 1868. All received pensions, though often not for several months.[11] By 1882, in fact, only sixty-five veterans of the Thirty-Third had applied, and only twenty were admitted to the rolls. The remaining forty-five invalid cases were pending, and featured veterans claiming ailments of inexact temporal origin, most commonly rheumatism, heart disease, lung disease, and intestinal complaints.[12]

Unlike with the claims of Black mothers and widows, the Pension Bureau made no official exceptions when it came to the invalid claims of Black veterans. They were assumed to be as self-autonomous as their white analogues in the North. This assumption revealed itself in the bureau's 1882 handbook, not only in its absence of special consideration for formerly enslaved applicants but also in its stated affinity for officially documented medical evidence at three key stages: the claimant's prewar life, his wartime service, and the postwar continuance of his service-origin disability. "Almost every claimant can furnish some testimony showing prior soundness," the guidebook reasoned. Only one witness is necessary for this proof, that is, "if he is the family physician of the claimant," and provided he is able to establish the claimant's prewar health with specificity. If not, lay testimony would be collected with extreme care and skepticism. Medical evidence was also required for the next stage, proving service origin, ideally coming from the surgeon who treated the claimant during service. Given the poor wartime recordkeeping, however, the bureau often settled for testimony from one officer or two comrades. At this stage, the handbook frankly admitted, "There is no established rule on the subject, the circumstances surrounding these cases rendering it impracticable to adopt one." Yet the bureau's hierarchy of credibility nevertheless clearly favored documentary evidence from medical officials and clearly devalued lay testimony from seemingly ignorant or interested parties at all stages of the process.[13]

To cordon off their wartime suffering, Black veterans needed to retroactively prove they were healthy and fit for military service upon enlistment. White veterans, of course, needed to do so as well, but for those emerging from bondage the requirement was infinitely more challenging. In American political culture, generations of abolitionist activism engendered sensational understandings of the deprivations of slavery; and on a material register, the physical conditions of enslavement and self-emancipation in a war zone made ill-health at enlistment a reasonable assumption. Few cultural artifacts better encapsulated this phenomenon than the widely popular article printed in *Harper's Weekly* on July 4, 1863. Under the heading "A Typical Negro," the article featured a triptych of three lithographs of a former slave named in the article as "Gordon." The images were based on three cartes de visite—calling cards, or small, photographic portraits—originally taken by photographers in Baton Rouge the previous April. The centerpiece is the iconic image of Gordon, seated, with his hand on his waist as he makes a quarter-turn over his left shoulder to the viewer, whose eyes are inescapably drawn to his back, embossed with scars and welts like a topographical map of slavery's cruelest terrain. The image is captioned "Gordon under Medical Inspection." Two smaller portraits flank it, depicting "Gordon as He Entered Our Lines," sitting cross-legged on a stool in tattered clothing, and "Gordon in His Uniform as a U.S. Soldier," standing straight and proud, hands gripping the end of an upright musket barrel, eyes confidently locked with the viewer's. The message from the triptych alone was clear: this was a war of emancipation, and through enlistment in the army of liberation, Black men can overcome their brutal pasts and prove their manhood. The blue uniform had healing powers, spiritual and corporeal.[14]

This was a redemption narrative. But not one without deep currents of ambivalence. The article relayed the story of Gordon escaping his Mississippi slave labor camp, chased for days through the swamps by bloodhounds, before making it to Union lines near Baton Rouge. In the army, Gordon served

A TYPICAL NEGRO.

We publish herewith three portraits, from photographs by M'Pherson and Oliver, of the negro Gordon, who escaped from his master in Mississippi, and came into our lines at Baton Rouge in March last. One of these portraits represents the man as he entered our lines, with clothes torn and covered with mud and dirt from his long race through the swamps and bayous, chased as he had been for days and nights by his master with several neighbors and a pack of blood-hounds; another shows him as he underwent the surgical examination previous to being mustered into the service—his back furrowed and scarred with the traces of a whipping administered on Christmas-day last; and the third represents him in United States uniform, bearing the musket and prepared for duty.

This negro displayed unusual intelligence and energy. In order to foil the scent of the blood-hounds who were chasing him he took from his plantation onions, which he carried in his pockets. After crossing each creek or swamp he rubbed his body freely with these onions, and thus, no doubt, frequently threw the dogs off the scent.

At one time in Louisiana he served our troops as guide, and on one expedition was unfortunately taken prisoner by the rebels, who, infuriated beyond measure, tied him up and beat him, leaving him for dead. He came to life, however, and once more made his escape to our lines.

By way of illustrating the degree of brutality which slavery has developed among the whites in the section of country from which this negro came, we append the following extract from a letter in the New York *Times*, recounting what was told by the refugees from Mrs. Gillespie's estate on the Black River:

The treatment of the slaves, they say, has been growing worse and worse for the last six or seven years. Flogging with a leather strap on the naked body is common; also paddling the body with a hand-saw until the skin is a mass of blisters, and then breaking the blisters with the teeth of the saw. They have "very often" seen slaves stretched out upon the ground with hands and feet held down by fellow-slaves, or lashed to stakes driven into the ground for "bucking." Handfuls of dry corn-husks are then lighted, and the burning embers are whipped off with a stick so as to fall in showers of live sparks upon the naked back. This is continued until the victim is covered with blisters. If in his writhing of torture the slave gets his hand free to brush off the fire, the burning brand is applied to them.

Another method of punishment, which is inflicted for the higher order of crimes, such as running away, or other refractory conduct, is to dig a hole in the ground large enough for the slave to squat or lie down in. The victim is then stripped naked and placed in the hole, and a covering of green withes laid over the opening. Upon this a quick fire is built, and the live embers sifted through upon the naked flesh of the slave, until his body is blistered and swollen almost to bursting. With just enough of life to enable him to crawl, the slave is then allowed to recover from his wounds if he can, or to end his sufferings by death.

"Charley Sloo" and "Overton," two hands, were both murdered by these cruel tortures. "Sloo" was whipped to death, dying under the infliction, or soon after punishment. "Overton" was laid naked upon his face and burned as above described, so that the cords of his legs and the

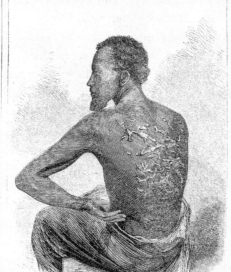

GORDON AS HE ENTERED OUR LINES.

GORDON UNDER MEDICAL INSPECTION.

GORDON IN HIS UNIFORM AS A U. S. SOLDIER.

"Gordon" as refugee and soldier. The iconic scarred back of "Gordon" as it appeared in the July 4, 1863, issue of *Harper's Weekly*. The accompanying narrative, though, confounds the linear trajectory of the slave-turned-soldier redemption story. (Library of Congress Prints and Photographs Division, LC-DIG-ds-05099)

as a scout and a guide. On one mission in Louisiana, he was captured by rebels, "who, infuriated beyond measure, tied him up and beat him, leaving him for dead. He came to life, however, and once again made it to our lines." Gordon's reported story alone, therefore, gave lie to the simple trajectory of progress emblazoned in the three images—indeed, a hypothetical fourth image, perhaps "Gordon as He Re-Entered Our Lines," was needed, suggesting in turn a decidedly less triumphant and linear liberation narrative. Historians have since raised doubts about the veracity of the story and the origins of the photos themselves, suggesting that "Gordon" may have been a composite figure based in part on the actual freedman photographed, a Louisiana runaway known only as "Peter." Widespread circulation of the cartes de visite and the July 4th edition of *Harper's* attracted the attention of surgeons from several different Union regiments claiming to have examined the very man, noting in the same breath the frequency of such scarring among the refugees. Yet the facts of the story, as it were, matter less than their social resonance and political function in mid-1863. In addition to provoking sympathy for the plight of Black Southerners, the article also sought to convince readers of the death-defying fidelity of Black men, their devotion and utility to the Union cause.[15]

The man with the scourged back came to be an indisputably powerful symbol. Yet thousands of Black pension claimants might well have interpreted the images and accompanying narrative quite differently than intended. For example, the disputed history and identity of the subject, even among regimental surgeons who supposedly examined the man, would have registered more intimately with them, striking a more disquieting note as they struggled to prove their own histories and identities before a different set of surgeons. Despite the uplifting arc of the triptych, the vaunted healing power of the uniform was in the end simply a cloak, one that camouflaged potential ailments lurking beneath. Yet not all ailments were of equal import. Fear of contagion among former slaves was ubiquitous, from cities to refugee camps to Black regimental quarters. In fact, as historian Jim Downs has argued, contagious diseases such as smallpox were the overwhelming concern precisely because of the potential to cross the color line; when seemingly contained within a given Black population, smallpox was often discussed as the natural consequence of emancipation. Detecting such diseases from raw, ex-slave recruits before they spread to white soldiers was the primary objective. But because scar tissue was neither contagious nor necessarily disabling, uncovering it could be safely confined to the realms of symbolism, propaganda, and culture, as the case of "Gordon" illustrates. In a final irony, if anything, such scars, when noted by the examining surgeon, would help to verify the identity of claimants in their future applications for federal benefits, serving as a morbid kind of dorsal fingerprinting.[16]

Enlistment examinations among Black recruits in the South varied widely in their thoroughness. But in their postbellum testimonials, Black veterans routinely assured pension board surgeons that they underwent a thorough examination at enlistment, recounting how they were stripped naked and examined and declared fit for service. In 1886, John Jones recalled being "thoroughly stripped naked" at his enlistment and affirmed that before the war he "never had any sickness of any kind," that he was a "sound and able bodied man in every way." Lazarus Fields of the Thirty-Third USCT likewise remembered being "stripped and examined by the doctors to see as to my soundness." He passed, but he commented how "a number of the men were rejected and sent home. These were given an 'exempt paper.'" Some rejected recruits could still qualify for the kind of noncombat labor that nonetheless often dominated the wartime experiences of Black soldiers. Stephen Tillman, for one, served as a witness for Samuel Preston of the Ninety-Third when Preston applied for a pension. Tillman himself never soldiered. But he remembered that Preston was examined right before him and passed the examination, and that he tried to do the same "but the surgeon would not have me." Denied by the medical examiner, Tillman was still "taken as a recruit" for labor and "followed the regiment off & on & saw it at various times & places." He joined thousands of other freedmen and freedwomen drawn from plantations and refugee camps who performed every variety of labor for Union armies.[17]

The sheer varieties of wartime labor engendered widespread confusion after surrender when it came time for payments and military benefits. Dozens of unpaid, nonenlisted Black laborers confronted the commission sent by the Freedmen's Bureau to Tennessee in 1869–70 to investigate fraudulent claims. Ann Barrow, case number 20, worked as a washerwoman at a hospital for eighteen months but received no pay. Cato Hines, case number 23, worked for fourteen months on a fortification laying stone with the promise of wages but soon began hearing "much complaint that government would not pay." Meredith Woodfolk, case number 46, was a cook for a company of Ohio cavalry. Grandison Puryear, case number 53, claimed he was owed $270 for digging graves for the quartermaster's department. Harriet Ensley, case number 60, worked in a government hospital for two and a half years and was owed eleven months' pay. The presence of the federal commission in Tennessee brought dozens of these forgotten laborers out of the woodwork. The task of the commissioners, as one dissembling claims agent put it, was to distinguish the hundreds of legitimate claims from those leveled by men and women "who, like flies about a kitchen, swarmed about hospitals to find something to eat without working for it. . . . They were always in the way, and would steal everything they could lay their hands on, carrying it off, and sell it to citizens, and buy whisky, smuggle it to the soldiers, &c., and now claim pay for having been supported by the government." The cynicism animating such uncharitable remarks contributed mightily to the broader cultural project of erasing the wartime service of Black refugees, divorcing their labors from their claims to recompense, and reifying the sanctity of the explicitly endorsed contract.[18]

Enlisted soldiers, even those strictly relegated to military labor, at least had greater security in their postwar claims for remuneration. But they still struggled to retroactively certify that they passed their enlistment examinations— indeed, that they even had one at all. At this crucial stage in the pension process, formerly enslaved men had to rely heavily on each other's testimony. Together, though in separate testimonies, they vouched for having seen each other thoroughly examined at the recruiting station and as well having been pronounced fit for military service. Take the case of David Higgins and his comrades of the One Hundred Fourth. Higgins needed their testimony on the matter of his enlistment at Charleston, for his certificate of discharge, issued on October 12, 1865, listed a "deformity of right ankle-joint which existed before enlistment," making him ineligible to claim a pension for such an injury incurred during service. But his comrades knew he "was a sound man before the war," Higgins explained many years later in 1889, and he called on them to substantiate his testimony. On cue, Frank Gaillard remembered how he and Higgins were together "stripped naked and examined in the Old Guard House on Broad St." in occupied Charleston. Daniel Drayton, for his part, also remembered that Higgins "was stripped and examined like I was, for I heard all the recruits say that they had been examined." Higgins had "walked like a sound man and was not crippled." Gaillard and Drayton also testified to witnessing firsthand the injury Higgins suffered in service—the accident on Hilton Head Island in the fall of 1865 that left him with a broken ankle and laid him up in the regimental hospital and which ultimately resulted in his discharge. Higgins might well have had some deformity in his ankle, though not one that appreciably inhibited his mobility, the same ankle he broke during service as his comrades testified. The pension system failed to comprehend the simple explanation of reinjury, regarding the initial ailment as a preexisting condition, latent and permanently unpensionable.[19]

Given the strictures of the pension process, so much had to be left unsaid in these interviews. The Guard House in Charleston, where all of these men underwent enlistment examinations, had been at the heart of one of the largest slave-trading markets in North America. Its captors and kidnappers were among the shrillest advocates for reopening the Atlantic slave trade. And the Guard House itself—"with its grated windows, its iron bars being an appropriate design of double-edged swords and spears," as Northern war correspondent Charles Coffin observed—had served as a holding pen for the enslaved before they went up for auction at the markets nearby. When Union forces seized Charleston in February 1865, advertisements for slave auctions still littered the buildings in the trading district on Broad and Chalmers. How did Higgins and his men make sense of this experience, of submitting to an undignified if not invasive public examination by a federal recruiting officer in an old slave jail and in the immediate shadow of the old slave markets? Perhaps some of his comrades had been sold there, as some members of his regiment, composed chiefly of former slaves, most definitely were. By the same measure, what better place to unravel the old regime? Union occupation meant that "the guard-house doors were wide open," Coffin mused. "The jailor had lost his occupation" and "the last slave had been immured within its walls." All the while, the very presence of Black soldiers guarding the Guard House and occupying the city was "the deepest humiliation" to the haughty whites of Charleston. A pension examination conducted years later—by local Charlestonians, no less—was no place for these Black troops to reminisce about the pride they must have felt when they occupied the city, administered passes to its citizens-turned-subjects, policed their behavior and speech, and turned that venerable old slave jail into a prison for unruly rebels.[20]

In their testimonies, formerly enslaved veterans often went beyond a simple assertion of fitness at enlistment, choosing instead to leave as little doubt as possible that they entered the army in the best of health. They accordingly had to invert the narratives of suffering displayed in the Independence Day issue of *Harper's Weekly*, turning the centerpiece into an unmistakably healthy figure under medical inspection. And this they did time and again. Richard Dargan, a comrade of Higgins's, went so far as to declare, "I never had any sickness of any kind prior to my service and never had any physical threat to me," the latter perhaps a cloaked reference to violence inflicted by a former overseer or enslaver. The exaggerated quality to these appeals owed to a knowing pragmatism on the part of claimants. After all, such declarations served well the service-origin requirement for general law pensions. But they also involved a delicate performance on the part of ex-slave claimants who were conscripted into playing a distinctive role in the "public transcript" of the Lost Cause.[21] By their having to dismiss, ignore, or erase the suffering experienced in the days of slavery, at least before the official eyes of the state, an image of slavery as a beneficent institution unsettlingly and inescapably emerges in the files of their pension claims. Hardships, deprivations, and lasting injuries were hallmarks not of enslavement but of the abolition war.[22]

After establishing service origin, Black claimants also strained to prove that their wartime afflictions continued to affect them in the present. Bureau practice, as affirmed in its 1882 guidebook, held that "the question of continuance is one of great importance." But because so much time had passed since contraction of illnesses and injuries, the degree of disability was liable to have changed, sometimes significantly so. As such, "not only the fact of continuance must be shown, but also the degree of disability from time to time during the whole period since discharge." For this, the bureau required sworn affidavits from neighbors or, better yet, physicians who had treated the claimant since discharge. Both parties had to be able to substantiate the claimant's condition with the greatest specificity. General remarks about a claimant's suffering were considered "wholly worthless for the purpose of rating." At every turn, the bureau required official and well-supported testimony. Claimants who fell short could expect an agonizingly protracted application process, and often a dreaded special examination. Benjamin Smith, for example, failed to obtain the necessary statements from physicians who had treated him since discharge and from others who could corroborate his story of incurring kidney and bladder disease during the war. In 1884, nearly twenty years after the fact, Smith pointed out what should have been obvious to even the casual observer, that "so many persons have died or moved away" that he "has experienced great difficulty in procuring the information already obtained and humbly prays that some determination may be arrived at in his case."[23]

As seen earlier, ex-slave claimants who had pursued bounty claims knew how difficult it was to secure acceptable testimony. In their claims for invalid pensions, though, ex-slaves not only needed witnesses to identify them and relations, they also needed witnesses to share intimate knowledge of the claimant's condition—to recite, in other words, when exactly comrade Benjamin Smith began complaining about kidney pain, the extent of the pain, and how that pain affected his physical ability. Testimony from Northern officers and surgeons eluded many Black claimants, whose claims suffered as a result. They sent so many protests to the Southern Division that the office in turn created a record of the names and addresses of all USCT officers and regimental surgeons and provided prospective claimants with the same. This was done to both assist the claimants and lighten the workload of the office. Yet the division also kept an annotated record of the character of public notaries and justices of the peace as well as "every physician whose credibility has been inquired into in the course of the examination of any claim." Claimants who happened to use such individuals would find their claims earmarked for special investigation.[24]

Although formerly enslaved claimants had long been compelled to seek out their former enslavers in their claims for military benefits, the latter played the most ambiguous role in their claims for pensions. Former slaves sought pensions at all hazards, even if it meant casting themselves in Lost Cause–inflected dramas of plantation harmony. And former enslavers had certain incentives to help them do so. Substantiating the requisite story of prewar soundness, ex-enslavers could at once demonstrate a seigneurial benevolence as well as vindicate the idea that the war of abolition was a tragic mistake and a humanitarian disaster. Consider the case of Thomas Robinson, once enslaved by Peter Sparkman of the South Carolina Lowcountry. Robinson sought a pension for an injury to his eyes while serving in the Twenty-First USCT. A special examiner tracked down two relatives of the deceased enslaver, Jesse and George Sparkman, both of whom gladly testified to Robinson's health before enlistment, emphasizing how Robinson "was a sound healthy man, and free from any physical disability whatever." In his final report on the Robinson case, the special examiner reflected on being thoroughly convinced by the "testimony of the surviving members of the 'Sparkman' family embodied in this examination." Robinson won his pension. James Childs likewise met his old enslavers on the new stage of the Pension Bureau. Childs's pension agent called in the son of his former captor, who subsequently testified to the former slave being "a strong healthy young fellow before the war." In fact, "he was one of the strongest hands on the plantation."[25]

In the eyes of bureau examiners, there was no more credible source to authenticate the prewar health of ex-slave soldiers than their former enslavers. Who, after all, were more literally invested in their laboring health? These ex-enslavers thereby conjured up the power relations of slavery in their new role as mediators of the federal government. Yet their sworn testimonies required surprisingly little adaptation to conform to the new order. As Charlotte Munson began applying for a bounty and a pension, investigators pulled her former enslaver, one Thomas Dabney, to validate her relationship to her deceased husband. He had claimed ownership of the Munsons and their two children before the war. They had been married on his slave labor camp and were recognized by all as husband and wife. And although Dabney had "no personal knowledge of his service in the army," he told his interviewer that "Squire Munson was a healthy able bodied man & free from disease when he went off to the Federal Army." Dabney even made the remarkable assertion that had he "sold him at the time he went off he would have valued him as a sound man & would have warranted him as such." Perhaps Dabney tipped his hand, betraying a regret for having not sold Munson when he had the chance, and before the went off to join the Forty-Ninth USCT. But more likely Dabney used the language of slave sales to certify his assessment of Munson's prewar health. His valuation proved convincing to the federal officials administering the case. Between the vernacular assessments of the slave labor camp and the technocratic linguistics of the Pension Bureau stood the lingua franca of the slave market.[26]

Alongside former enslavers, former slave doctors played a conspicuous role in the pension process. For instance, though the comrades and neighbors of ex-slave Aaron Ancrum testified that he had been "in perfect health and soundness of body, & had always been well & healthy until he enlisted," after his application met rejection in 1871 on the ground of prior disability, Ancrum solicited the testimony of his former slave doctor, Charles Witsell, who also served as his enslaver's family physician. Witsell had known Ancrum since 1854. He was "well acquainted with him" and reported that the ex-slave claimant "was in good bodily health at the time of the breaking out of the war, having no illness or disability at the time the said Ancrum was taken from his plantation by Col Montgomery of the United States forces in 1863." Not only did Witsell's testimony afford the rhetorical space to reimagine the beneficence of slavery, at least on this particular South Carolina slave labor camp, it also allowed him to deny the freedman the agency of choosing to join the Union army. In the end, however, the former slave doctor's testimony was not enough. The bureau's examiners believed Ancrum brought his rheumatism into the army, a preexisting condition, and he therefore died without receiving a pension. Yet his widow, Sallie Ancrum, decided to petition the House Committee on Invalid Pensions for relief, which Congress granted in a private bill in June 1886.[27]

Only under special circumstances was evidence of a soldier's prewar illness tolerated in a pension claim under the general law, and often this came at the insistence of bureau agents themselves. In her bid for a bounty and pension as the widow of Andrew Jackson, Crecy Jackson underwent a special investigation by the Pension Bureau agent George H. Ragsdale in the mid-1870s. The official military record listed the soldier as having died in May 1864 at Lake Providence, Louisiana. He had grown up not too far away, and the special examiner turned to several of Jackson's former fellow slaves for more information on the soldier's health. Richard Stephens, who had lived on an adjoining labor camp, recalled that "Jackson was subject to attacks of Pneumonia for years before his enlistment. That he exposed himself a great deal working after night & at other undue seasons in order to make a little something for himself, after he had put in the required time for his master." To his recollection, "this disease appeared in his chest & he would complain of pains in his breast and this would end in a cough." Other former fellow slaves concurred, remembering Jackson as "a weakly man," one who "often became sick at the stomach and threw up." He had "some kind of internal disease," perhaps "liver disease," "but would not give up but worked right along." He was one of many Black soldiers who had passed the medical examination at enlistment without official objection.[28]

Jackson died shortly after having entered service in December 1863, of illnesses he was rumored to have had in the days of slavery. Writing to the commissioner of pensions, the special examiner reported that Crecy Jackson was "able to furnish the most satisfactory evidence on all points involved in a widows claim except the origin of soldiers fatal disease, after enlistment." Moreover, Ragsdale noted, Jackson "was not at any time more than 50 miles from home, so there was no change of climate," which would have been considered an important factor in weakening his constitution. The examiner urged that an exception to the service-origin requirement be made in this case, as Jackson did not enter the Union army willingly. "He was taken into the army against his will," explained Ragsdale, who went on to explain how recruitment in the lower Mississippi Valley often involved officers who "went out into the country around Vicksburg and pressed every darkey they could find until their companies were full." Although most Black recruits were drawn from the refugee camps that formed near Union lines, others were indeed impressed directly from the slave labor camps, enraging the enslavers who had thought their own professed loyalty to the Union would secure their human property. "It seems hardly fair," he argued, "to deny this claimant a pension under the circumstances. She is old, broken down, and without any means of support. She is receiving help now on the strength of her claim and if this fails she will be deserted." Ragsdale noted that Jackson had not yet received her husband's bounty and wages and requested that the commissioner approve her claim and intercede on her behalf with the second auditor of the Treasury, the official tasked with issuing bounty and back payments. Less than a week after the depositions in her case in March 1877, Jackson also wrote to the second auditor, informing him of the concluded investigation. "This matter has bin delayed some considerable time," she added. She requested him to address her case immediately, as "I am in great need and distress by so doing you will confer a great favor on your friend."[29]

Crecy Jackson's talk of favors and friendship was no idle remark, even when made to a stranger one thousand miles away in Washington. It invoked relationships enslaved men and women painstakingly made with the national government during the late war. These alliances were founded upon the labors that Black men and women performed in the wartime South in service of the Union army, labor that was not always contracted and not always requited. Still, their alliance with flesh-and-blood proxies of federal power was, for freedpeople, the essential foundation of citizenship, sealed with the mortar of loyalty and labor. One testifier in Crecy Jackson's case, for instance, assured the Pension Bureau that Jackson "was Loyal to the United States government during the war, and that she in no way aided or abetted the rebellion in the United States, and that she was ready and willing at any time to aid and assist the government of the United States, if in her power to do so." Jackson's loyalty to the Union was not in doubt as she pursued her widow's pension, but such declarations of fidelity served their purposes. As in their claims for bounties and back payments, freedpeople who emphasized their embattled but unwavering support for the federal government hoped to gain the favor and trust of its officials. They served to identify their claims as singularly worthy in a land choked with rebels still hostile to federal power.[30]

The Southern Claims Commission

The connection between wartime loyalty and citizenship frayed by the 1870s. The Fourteenth Amendment, rightly celebrated for its establishment of birthright citizenship, also undercut freedpeople's working understanding of citizenship based on demonstrated acts of labor and fidelity to the Union. The extension of amnesty and pardon to former rebels by President Andrew Johnson was premised on affirmations of postwar loyalty at the expense of demonstrable wartime disloyalty. Through an official policy of amnesia, the federal government lifted virtually all of the legal disabilities it had imposed on ex-Confederates in the earliest days of Reconstruction. Yet there remained important venues where wartime loyalty still mattered, and Black Southerners would prove especially adept at exploiting those opportunities. Alongside the Pension Bureau, the Southern Claims Commission (SCC) served as a critical venue through which demonstrably loyal citizens could apply for redress. Created by Congress in 1871 after significant debate, the SCC was a temporary federal agency whose immediate purpose was to award compensation to loyal Southerners, Black and white, who could satisfactorily prove material damages by the Union army during the late war. But the very issue of who qualified as a loyal, property-owning Southerner—and thus who had standing—beleaguered the commission from the start.[31]

The SCC featured three commissioners appointed by President Ulysses S. Grant and a host of special commissioners stationed across the South. These local commissioners conducted interviews with claimants and their witnesses according to the standardized questionnaires. They then decided on the merits of each case and submitted their recommendations to Congress for final approval. All told, Southerners filed over twenty-two thousand claims, of which about five thousand were allowed. The commissioners did not anticipate that nearly five hundred freedpeople would also lodge claims with the agency. The fundamental irony for federal policymakers was understanding how a people legally considered to be property themselves could also own property, all manner of property except, that is, themselves. The claims commissioners—all of whom were white, Northern Republicans—carried south with them a wealth of ignorance and misassumptions about Southern slavery and the enslaved. And the learning curve was steep. The cases before the commissioners from Black Southerners forced them to reimagine the liberal tenets of property ownership similar to the ways in which Pension Bureau officials had to adapt many standardized practices to better accommodate the circumstances of freedpeople. Whereas many white Northerners believed only they could properly instruct freedpeople to value the private property foundations of the free labor system, ex-slave claimants quickly taught the SCC their own valuation of private property, by communal consensus rather than title deed.[32]

The largely unforeseen claims of ex-slaves should not have come as a surprise to any careful observer of Black administrative politics in the post–Civil War South. As those five hundred freedpeople began submitting their claims with the SCC from 1871 to 1880, many had already had extensive experience with federal claims, from the Freedmen's Bureau and Freedmen's Branch to the U.S. Pension Bureau. Nevertheless, the commissioners scrambled to adjust their standardized inquiries in order to accommodate the special cases presented by former slaves. Despite not enjoying the status of citizens during the war years, their loyalty to the Union cause was by and large taken as a given during their hearings. For their part, many ex-slaves took the establishment of birthright citizenship to its logical conclusion, retroactively assigning on the official commission forms their (estimated) date of birth synonymously with their tenure of citizenship. For example, Pompey Lewis was enslaved until the end of the war but "avers that he is a citizen of the United States, and has been since A. D. 1805." White Southern claimants, by contrast, underwent considerable questioning to determine the extent of their loyalty or disloyalty in the rebellion. Whereas such an inquisition proved universally unnecessary for freedpeople, they nevertheless found creative ways to emphasize their wartime fidelity to the Union while drawing attention to their endless array of underappreciated labors and as-yet uncompensated offerings on the nation's behalf.[33]

In their claims through the SCC, former slaves in Union-occupied areas during the war recounted in detail their first contact with their deliverers. Several themes emerge from their testimonies. First, ex-slave claimants recalled their long-standing, covert desire to have the Yankees displace their enslavers. They even extrapolated how all their fellow slaves were "anxious for the Yankee Army to come in hopes of gaining our freedom," in the words

Refugees and laborers in Yorktown. Formerly enslaved men and women performed incalculable labors for the Union army as part of their reciprocal wartime alliance, including laundering and wood splitting, as shown in this 1862 photograph taken outside Yorktown, Virginia. (Library of Congress Prints and Photographs Division, LC-DIG-ds-05120)

of ex-slave James Smith. One formerly enslaved South Carolinian from Georgetown named Alonzo Jackson assured his special commissioner of his loyalty to the Union. "I wanted to be free—and wanted my race to be free," he explained in his 1874 claim, and "I knew this could not be if the rebels had a government of their own." Jackson felt before, during, and after the war that "the Union people were the best friends of the colored people." He recalled that he "always rejoiced over Union victories," but only could talk "with a few white men at Georgetown and with such colored men as I could trust, in favor of the Union. . . . I knew my life would be taken if it was known how I really felt about the war." One of Jackson's witnesses confirmed his sympathies, noting that although he never said "anything about the war to any white man," because "colored people in those days could not say what they thought always," Jackson nevertheless "was known by all the colored people to be in favor of the Yankees."[34]

Although Jackson submitted a claim for two mules, a double-barrel shotgun, and twenty 600-pound casks of rice, the story of how the Yankees acquired his property spoke volumes about his encounter with the liberating army. And so, in addition to detailing their expressed wishes for a Union victory, Jackson's claim illustrates a second characteristic of ex-slave claims through the SCC: their narratives intentionally showcased stories of service to Yankee soldiers even as they recited the property lost to them. All the while, they placed an unmistakable emphasis on befriending agents of the federal government. As Jackson exclaimed, "I did what I could for the Yankees and wanted to do more! I was always ready and willing to do what I could even at the risk of my own life." About one month after the Union army reached Georgetown, Jackson began delivering rice and other provisions to the army on a flatboat along the Black River. He remembered how "the rebels came very near catching me, they fired at me, and I heard them threaten me—They said they would 'kill me for taking provisions to the yankees.'" On one of his freighting expeditions several months later, Jackson and his partner saw three white men approach the boat cautiously. "As soon as the 3 white men saw we were colored men," he remembered, they approached Jackson and told him they had been prisoners at the rebel stockade in nearby Florence and had recently escaped. They pleaded with Jackson for succor and shelter. Jackson was glad to help. The soldiers made him no promises, nor had he ever "received anything for any service rendered to any Union soldiers." Yet they showed their gratitude. So, too, did two other escapees several weeks later, when Jackson spotted them running away in a swamp. He called out to these two men that there was no danger, and as they approached they asked Jackson if he "was a friend to them." Jackson, who by this point had essentially become a Southern conductor on the Underground Railroad for Fugitive Yankees, laughed that he "was as good a friend as ever they had in their lives!"[35]

Boson and Nancy Johnson of Liberty County, Georgia, also had occasion to harbor a Union runaway from a Confederate prison. As rebel search parties hunted him, the Johnsons hid him in their quarters for a day before secreting him off to Union lines. Nancy recognized this man when he returned to the labor camp one January day with a cadre of Union soldiers to scavenge. The man told her that he would try "to keep them from burning my house but he couldn't keep them from taking everything we had." The men had been "starved & naked almost" as they ransacked the quarters for provisions, taking the Johnsons' food, cookware, clothing, and cloth, before also commandeering their horses, hogs, and chickens. "They said that they didn't believe what I had belonged to me," Johnson later recalled, but she swore to them that it did. Aside from demonstrating the predominant Northern attitudes toward slave property ownership, Nancy Johnson's story illustrates how compulsion formed a third crucial element to the property claims of former slaves through the SCC. Though compelled to surrender their property—often in a forceful or cruel manner—their testimonies rarely betrayed outright feelings of bitterness at having to enter the world of freedom stripped of their hard-won possessions. Far more likely were expressions of understanding and sorrow, a strategic posture they had learned when seeking federal compensation. One ex-slave claimant from Alabama explained that he had waited to put in his claim "because I was willing to let that go to help the United States Government that much for what they done for me." What this strongly implied, however, was that by the early 1870s the government had stopped doing things for him; now he wanted to wrest from it all he was owed, and much more than the $340 he begrudgingly received.[36]

Fourth, ex-slave claims frequently recounted promises of compensation for confiscated property, often coupled with an invitation to join or follow along with the army. Nancy Johnson begged one of the Union officers to leave them with something, fearing that her family would starve. The soldier assured Nancy—as so many others had—that "we ought not to care what they took for we would get it all back again," and invited her family to "come & go along with us." Enslaved men of military age often had no choice in the matter and were forcibly conscripted. Many women, children, and other dependents were consequently swept up in the military's man-eating undertow. Johnson's own fourteen-year-old son, Henry, had been out in a nearby swamp at the time of the raid watching the wagons of provisions when soldiers took the wagons and the boy. Nancy "never saw him anymore." Had she sought to retrieve Henry, she feared her enslaver or his sons would kill him. After Union soldiers stole his horse, David Harvey in nearby Beaufort County was also offered the chance to "go along with them." But Harvey refused, explaining that he could not leave his family. Samuel Fuller was similarly told he "could go stay with them and they would give me food, but I was afraid I could not walk so far," having "not entirely recovered from a broken leg." The soldiers instructed Fuller that he should not "take offense at what they did, that it would be all made good to me and I would be free." The ex-slave later assured the commissioners he "did not feel angry towards any of them." When Napoleon Prince confronted that same party from General William T. Sherman's army, he was not even asked to join. Instead they forced him into their company as a cook. "I told them I did not want to go," Prince later recalled, "but they said if I said so again they would shoot me, so I consented to go and did so at once, as soon as they had taken my property I went with them." He worked for about eight months at the promised monthly wage of ten dollars, equivalent in theory to a Black soldier's pay, and traveled as far as Raleigh before he "ran away because they did not pay me anything."[37]

Though the Southern Claims Commission offered Black Southerners who had not officially joined the Union army an opportunity for redress, there were many claimants who had in fact enlisted, as the above stories of forced conscription attest. The claims of these men therefore involved both property confiscation and military service. These claimants often took care to note overlapping and as-yet uncompensated claims to federal officials. For example, William Drayton of the Thirty-Fourth USCT opened his claim by noting his three-year service record and that his "discharge papers are in Washington with the Second Auditor of the Treasury for the purpose of proving my claim for Bounty." Together with his former fellow slave Edward Brown, who later applied for a pension, Drayton escaped to Union-occupied Beaufort in 1863 with the soon-to-be-confiscated mules. By the time Drayton testified before the SCC, he had already applied for a pension.[38] In another case, a former slave's payment for confiscated property was suspended indefinitely precisely because of his enlistment. After fleeing Memphis, Robert Houston set about chopping wood on an island in the Mississippi that had been occupied by Union forces. It held mostly refugee women and children from nearby labor camps. Federal officials there had issued rations to those who could not work and put to work those who could. Houston had amassed nearly 150 cords by the time a Union steamer arrived to take most of the wood, and any available men, south to Helena. "When called upon I went into the Union Service very willingly," Houston remembered, "having by this time learnt something of the principles & object of the war." Meanwhile an officer gave him a receipt for the wood. Houston enlisted after disembarking in Helena, though he apparently was not permitted to be paid for the wood and was told that he "must wait till mustered out & take it with Bounty money." But following his discharge Houston made so many "unsuccessful attempts for pay till finally the receipt was worne out and lost."[39]

Though submitted on an individual basis, freedpeople's claims through the SCC relied extensively on eyewitness testimony. They were fundamentally communal endeavors for freedpeople, whose property rights in the days of enslavement rested largely on social consensus. Their close living quarters before the war further ensured property taken from their home would be witnessed by neighbors who would later be called upon to re-create the circumstances before the claims commission. As such, ex-slave claimants regularly appeared in each other's claims through the commission, testifying to the same act from multiple angles. This communal, multiperspectival nature of narration therefore represents a fifth characteristic of ex-slave claims. The aforementioned Samuel Fuller, reluctant to travel with his broken leg, served as a witness for Napoleon Prince, who himself was present to witness the confiscation of Fuller's property before his conscription. Both men also testified for Essex Dargan, who likewise testified for Fuller.[40] Freedpeople thereby turned the theoretically linear claims into sophisticated evidentiary webs. Evidence suggests the special commissioners judged favorably testimony from manifestly intelligent, hardworking claimants and witnesses. But as a rule for federal benefits, the best confirmation for ex-slave claimants came not from their former fellow slaves but from their former enslavers, and they accordingly appeared throughout the SCC cases of Black Southerners. Thus David Harvey's former enslaver served as the best witness to "his good character, his superior ability & industry," and ultimately the fact that Harvey's claim was indeed legitimate. Alexander Dudley, for his part, called on two former enslavers to testify on his behalf, Christopher W. Dudley and Joel L. Easterling, the latter having claimed ownership of the claimant's wife, Mary Alexander. Both men vouched for the couple's character.[41]

Col. C. W. Dudley, as he liked to be known, was not only Alexander's former enslaver. He was also his claims attorney. In fact, Dudley was the preeminent claims attorney in South Carolina, specializing in the cases of Black claimants. Despite his title, Dudley held no military or civil office in the so-called Confederacy, and he opposed secession while in the South Carolina legislature. After the war, as he jockeyed for political office, he earned a spot in the 1865 constitutional convention for his state after assuring President Johnson that he did not even need a pardon "because I never yet felt myself to be a criminal—never having '*voluntarily*' lifted a finger to aid in this unholy war." With half his enslaved wealth abolished in 1865, Dudley later sensed an opportunity when the SCC organized in 1871. Writing directly to the commissioners in April, he explained that although, "strictly speaking, the negro was not a 'citizen,' according to Southern doctrine," the commissioners should not presume "that Congress intended to provide for the white man only, & used the word 'citizen' for that purpose." Fearing their potential exclusion— and the loss of professional income, to be sure—Dudley argued that during the rebellion "the coloured people actually did the most" on behalf of the Union.[42]

Though the Northern commissioners may have been unable to comprehend ex-slaves bringing for claims for lost property, to Dudley it came as no surprise. To the contrary, he felt himself eminently qualified to school the Northern commissioners on the true nature of Southern slavery. As Dudley explained, "any industrious slave, always was allowed opportunities of making something for himself, in a small way. . . . Many of them acquired a little property, very little, to be sure, but of vast importance, to *'them'*. They are claiming but little, they are poor—very poor—& would all sacrifice every thing they have, for the Republican party," Dudley assured the commissioners. That month Dudley received instructions from the commission to help "make the work of the Special Comr. easier." He accordingly began to *"'hunt' the negroes up*, & told them of the glad news, & revived their hopes about getting for them, what they had long supposed to be forever lost." Dudley and other former enslavers routinely argued that they had the best interests of the freedpeople at heart. In this instance, at least, it was an undeniable irony that a former enslaver would serve as facilitating agent of federal authority in the postbellum South on behalf of his chattel-turned-claimants.[43]

By the mid-1870s, Dudley's vigorous solicitation raised suspicions. A local Black politician accused Dudley of using his position as a claims attorney to electioneer for office against him, "persuading them to make claims for property they never owned." Dudley, of course, denied it. Instead, he presented himself as the only friend freedpeople had in making their claims in his county. "When I first opened an office here, to prepare these claims," he protested, "none of us could undertake to say, whether or not, any of them would be paid." In the first place, they had not enough money to pay the special commissioner to hear their claims. "Looking at the poverty of these people, I proposed to the claimants, one & all, that I would do all the work, & charge them nothing, unless they rec'd something." His frantic letter to the commissioners braided defensiveness and self-righteousness. "They are grateful for my services in their behalf," he sputtered, "& would do any thing but *'vote'* for me, for they think their interest lies in voting for a colored man." For all its self-regard, Dudley's letter to the SCC underscores the fact that these administrative claims for redress were inescapably partisan. Onlookers who witnessed large sums of money changing hands between former slaves and sharp-tongued white agents feared the possibility of foul play and political corruption.[44]

Anxieties surrounding Black mobilization, white manipulation, and federal intervention saturated South Carolina politics during the 1870s. From 1867 until the Democratic coup of 1876, the South Carolina legislature had a Black majority. Conservatives vehemently opposed a house of such composition in large part because its Black members had made significant inroads with working-class constituencies that cut across racial lines. Opponents bristled at the specter of Black and white workers controlling public affairs and redistributing wealth to the mudsills. Charges of corruption came laced with denunciations of "Negro rule." With tensions high, violence erupted in late 1870 between disgruntled ex-Confederates (who had organized two years earlier as the Ku Klux Klan) and the nearly all-Black state militia. News of the outbreak shocked Northern Republicans, who pushed through Congress the Ku Klux Klan Act of 1871, in many ways a final show of force—the last measure of Northern devotion to federal intervention in Reconstruction. Alarmed by the growing nationwide organizing and unrest among the working classes, however, Northern Republicans came to see the benefits of restoring order and the imagined harmony of interests between labor and capital. In this light, South Carolina freedmen metamorphosed into dangerous radicals who would rather plunder the state treasury through special legislation and favors from their equally corrupt politicians than earn their bread through hard work. By 1876, even moderate Northern Republicans were calling for the state to be "redeemed" by the self-styled reform party of Wade Hampton and his Red Shirts, who would purge the state of Republicans and their working-class Black constituents. An emerging consensus between corporatist Republicans and racist Democrats thus combined to discredit and destroy South Carolina's fledgling attempt at biracial democracy and reestablish, in the words of W. E. B. Du Bois, "the domination of property in Southern politics."[45]

It was in this hostile context foreshadowing the downfall of the Reconstruction government of South Carolina that former slaves submitted their lost-property claims with federal officials. Their claims frequently suffered from the assumption that they eschewed hard work, preferring handouts instead. Accordingly, claimants took pains to emphasize past labors, their productivity, their thrift, and their honesty, as well as their unthreatening distaste for politics. The SCC offered select freedpeople not only the opportunity for limited compensation but also a platform to remind its officials of the invaluable services they rendered to save the Union, not for the sake of posterity but for the needs of the present. One special commissioner, Virgil Hillyer, remarked that there "is no class of Southern Claimants who suffered so much in proportion to their means, by the Union army as the colored people. Through their toil and many other hardships," he reflected, "they had gotten together some of [the] comforts of life." Hillyer bemoaned the fact that Black Southerners "had been led, almost instinctually, to believe the Union army for which they had been so long praying were and would be their best friends," and that in turn they were the very first to be made "to contribute to the wants of their *'best friends,'*" only to have Union soldiers plunder all they had. It seemed unjust to them, though they dared not express it. In their claims, freedpeople skillfully articulated their material sacrifices to the Union army, careful to balance feelings of pain and loss with affirmations of loyalty and service, aware that fixating only on damages incurred from the war for emancipation could inadvertently contribute to the pernicious mythmaking of the Lost Cause.[46]

The claims of former slaves filed through the SCC thus required considerable navigational skills, resourcefulness, and determination. By the time special investigators fanned out across the South, many claimants had been waiting nearly a decade for some reimbursement for confiscated property. Their claims had to withstand a slew of questions and laborious scrutiny. In the very same case that Virgil Hillyer movingly recommended for approval, the head commissioners confessed to Congress that "as in all claims of colored claimants we were doubtful & suspicious." And special investigations regularly showed "that much less property was taken than is charged & some of it entirely worthless to the army."[47] Despite freedpeople's best efforts—or perhaps because of them—in the end the commissioners of the SCC held their claims every bit as suspect as other federal administrators regarded their claims for bounty and pension. All such federal claims were premised on compensating loyal claimants for precisely the amount owed them by the federal government, by way of property loss or loss of laboring potential. All claims registered in an environment laden with racially inflected antifraud bias. And all claims were regularly downgraded, discredited, or dismissed altogether. Yet, as involved as these investigations through the Southern Claims Commission were, they rarely matched the demanding complexity of freedpeople's claims for federal pensions, nor would they require decades of vigilant claims-making on behalf of pensioners. Nor, it should be said, would the Southern Claims Commission bring nearly as many former slaves into contact with the reconstructed federal government as the U.S. Pension Bureau.

Claiming the Bounty Fund

The 1870s was the decade of settling accounts. But by its close, few were settled in favor of freedpeople. Democratic newspapers routinely complained about the Republicans paying every bounty claim presented to them, knowing full well that "large numbers of these 'truly loyal' claims are grossly fraudulent." In that way, "millions of dollars have been paid out in the past years on account of these claims," fumed one editorial, "but we never hear any anxiety expressed by the Republican organs about the tremendous raid on the Treasury therein involved." As the Freedmen's Branch prepared to close in 1878, it had disbursed nearly $11 million to Black veterans and heirs. Yet administrators soon learned of a sizable fund of unpaid bounty claims to Black soldiers and heirs. Since 1872, over $350,000 had been returned to the Treasury after administrators failed to locate the lawful heirs of deceased Black claimants. "Parties are continually applying for the money," wrote the second auditor, E. B. French, and the greatest care needed to be taken to guard against fraudulent claims. In 1879, the public took notice of the unclaimed bounty funds, and soon the question of what to do with the money generated a vigorous debate among Black Americans.[48]

In early May 1879, Nashville hosted one of the era's great national "colored conventions." Over the course of three days, leading Black politicians, ministers, and activists gathered with an "unusually large assemblage" of participants to discuss the most pressing issues of the day. The proceedings opened with a brief address by former Louisiana governor P. B. S. Pinchback, followed by another from John R. Lynch, the dynamic ex-slave from Mississippi who had recently lost his House seat. The central theme of the convention was the uplift of the race. With the rights of the freedman trampled at every turn by violence and intimidation, the ballot box remained a foremost field of struggle. Yet two other issues dominated the convention: the ongoing agitation by Black Southerners for migration and the urgency of establishing a free and compulsory system of public schools for children of all races. The Committee on Migration asked Congress for an appropriation of $500,000 to aid in the great exodus of Black folks from the Egypt of the lower Mississippi Valley. Meanwhile, the convention approved the report of the Committee on Education and Labor, which promised to send a memorial to Congress asking for the $300,000 in unclaimed bounties "to be used in establishing and maintaining an Industrial and Technical School for colored youth in the unoccupied buildings" at Harpers Ferry, a site many regarded as the birthplace of the abolition war.[49]

These two projects dominated the publicity surrounding the conference. Some agreed that a national industrial school for young Black men should be constructed, "where in colored boys from all sections of the country can be instructed in some useful trade," but suggested the nation's capital as an alternative location to Harpers Ferry. Another commentator, writing in the *Weekly Louisianian*, argued that the "money belongs to these soldiers and sailors, but if they cannot be found—and it now seems that they cannot—it should be distributed in such a manner as to benefit the greatest number of the class to which these brave soldiers and sailors belonged in the Southern States." Rumors had begun circulating that, instead of building the industrial school at Harpers Ferry or Washington, a group of congressmen were already conspiring to have the Treasury turn over the money to Howard University. The writer considered it a "nefarious scheme" to remedy the "broken fortunes" of the university, which had been mired in scandal throughout the 1870s. He argued that "Howard university has no better claim to this fund than a private individual" and proposed that the bounty money ought to be devoted "to the relief of the poor colored emigrants who are accumulating upon the shores of the Mississippi."[50]

Emigrationism bitterly divided Black leaders. As Steven Hahn has observed, its strongest advocates hailed from cotton-growing regions that saw extensive political mobilization during the early years of Reconstruction, and extensive terrorism after it, areas such as the Black Belt and the delta counties of Mississippi and Arkansas. Black leaders without roots in these locales generally lacked the emigrationist sensibility, and some, most notably Frederick Douglass, were actively hostile to the very thought of Black workers quitting the South—and the Republican Party along with it. The convention-goers saw the situation much differently than the increasingly disconnected Black abolitionists of the old guard. In its official report, the Committee on Education and Labor enumerated the wealth produced in the previous twelve months by Black agricultural workers and explained that "the first want of the colored laborer, whether he shall remain at the South, or shall emigrate to the West, is to become a land-holder to his own home." Those content to hire their labor annually "without an effort to obtain land, not only impedes his own material progress, but is a heavy weight upon the uplifting of his race." Nearly twenty-five thousand Black Southerners struck out for Kansas in 1879–80. The many thousands not yet gone, yet who openly expressed desire to do so, remained constricted by the very impoverishment and landowner intimidation that excited their desire to migrate in the first place.[51]

But the long-percolating threat of the Black Exodus elicited a frenzied reaction in the halls of political power. Congress felt compelled to create a committee to investigate and hear testimony on the causes of the impending migration. And Mississippi, a state particularly threatened by the prospective removal of Black workers en masse, held a special convention at Vicksburg in May 1879 to address the matter. Unlike the simultaneously Black-led convention in Nashville, the Mississippi Valley Labor Convention, as it was called, joined together prominent white planters and leading Black politicians, including Senator Blanche K. Bruce and former Senator Hiram Revels, members of the Black elite who, by virtue of their propertied status, were disposed to accommodate and improve rather than agitate and move. The goal of the convention's white organizers was to pass a resolution dismissing political oppression as the driving force behind removal, and instead promise to devise a more equitable system of labor and credit between planters and tenants. Moderates of all stripes applauded the ideal of industrial cooperation as the solution to the bone-deep disaffection of freedpeople in the cotton South.[52]

The hollow bargain struck at the Vicksburg convention included the creation of technical schools. Senator Bruce, a vocal critic of emigration, emerged from the Vicksburg arrangement to synthesize the racial dialectic of migration versus improvement and proposed to use the unclaimed bounty fund to do so. In December 1879, he introduced in the Senate a bill to appropriate the USCT bounty fund—now estimated at $510,000—to sustain nearly two dozen Black schools and universities in fifteen states, including prominent institutions such as Atlanta University, Fiske University, and Howard University. Bruce introduced the bill at the same time two Southern Democratic colleagues submitted bills of their own, calling for $2 million to indemnify Black depositors of their losses through the Freedmen's Bank—what one newspaper mocked as "that swindling concern, the Freedman's Saving and Fraud Company." The press closely followed Bruce's bill and its counterpart in the House as it came before the Committee on Education and Labor. In late January 1880, fifteen Black schools sent representatives to the House committee to lobby on its behalf, and the committee members appeared ready to recommend the measure.[53] Yet the committee reported adversely on the bill after Secretary of the Treasury John Sherman informed its members that the bounty fund was significantly smaller than assumed, just above $200,000, and dropping by the day. Ironically, the publicity surrounding the unclaimed bounty fund seems to have alerted many Black claimants to the possibility that they had not received their bounties, and they scrambled to do so. Whatever was actually left in the fund—the second auditor now estimated only $45,000—was "being constantly drawn upon by claimants."[54]

In the end, the ordeal of the unclaimed bounty fund revealed more than the unwillingness of the federal government to support Black educational initiatives or emigration. It demonstrated, on the one hand, the communal sensibilities of many Black Southerners who proposed projects to uplift the race using money they rightly argued belonged to them as collective heirs of the U.S. Colored Troops, while at the same time exposing significant cleavages in Black politics. On the other hand, it underscored the contractual logic that governed the postbellum order, which explicitly refused to recognize collective claims of the sort proposed in Bruce's bill. The unclaimed bounty fund was instead regarded as an aggregate of individual claims owed to individual claimants; any money left over would be returned to its rightful place, the U.S. Treasury, to be disbursed by the representatives of the people at large.[55]

Revealing Origins

If the remaining bounty fund was finite, the payment of pensions was seemingly infinite. In January 1879, Congress passed its most consequential pension bill to date, dramatically reversing the declining rates of original applications. Known as the Arrears Act, the measure remitted any limitations to benefits on filing a pension under the general law. Now when a veteran's pension was awarded, the claimant could expect accrued pension payments dating from his discharge, with regular payments thereafter; for widows who may have filed for a pension years after the death of their husbands, their pension payments likewise backdated to their husband's death. The payment of arrears was a boon for pensioners. Veteran's groups such as the Grand Army of the Republic had long pushed for such a measure, while many white Southerners, Democrats, and fiscal conservatives vehemently protested it. They predictably complained that it would bleed the Treasury and create "pensioners out of sound and undeserving men," as critic Edward V. Smalley put it in 1884. "Any one looking at our national affairs from an outside point of view," he grumbled, "would naturally suppose that as our civil war ended nearly eighteen years ago, the accounts must long since have been adjusted, the sick and wounded provided for, and the books closed." And the number of pensioners might indeed naturally have shrunk with "the inroads of mortality, and steadily diminish year by year," were it not for a Congress so eager to flex its generosity by "widening the range of pensionable classes."[56]

The Arrears Act of 1879 met a very different reception in the Black press. "Justice at Last," proclaimed one editorial in the *Weekly Louisianian*. While "under the pressure of public sentiment in the interest of a long suffering but patient class," Congress finally "passed a bill to pay arrearage of pensions." In fact, the paper found that "colored people have a greater interest in this measure than ordinary bills that receive executive sanction," for they were often the least equipped to file an application in the first place. Even the Southern white press took note of the Arrears Act, and of course its potential for an influx of money in the South. In the spring of 1880, the *Daily Constitution* of Atlanta learned that there were "a large number of disabled colored men in Georgia who lost their usefulness while members of the federal army during the late war." Although they were "entitled to pensions from the government and many to arrears of pensions, amounting in some cases to several thousand dollars," many from Georgia had not yet applied. In fact, according to a Pension Bureau official in Washington, "the fewest possible applications have been received from Georgia, although several thousand colored persons entitled to pensions must be residing in the state." The editorial ended by suggesting that someone with knowledge of the pension application system "might perform a worthy charity by aiding these colored men to get their share of the largess which the government is distributing to nearly a million men in the north."[57]

Black Southerners would always receive but a small share of the federal government's pensionary largesse. The first separate classification of USCT pension claims, as opposed to the undifferentiated rolls of the Southern Division, came by way of Commissioner William W. Dudley's 1882 report to Congress. Since the close of the war, some 22,615 total USCT claimants had applied for a pension, with 8,381 admitted. Another 11,390 of their claims were still pending. Black veterans accounted for 8,308 of these applications, with 2,612 admitted and another 5,696 pending; meanwhile, their widows had sent in 8,629 applications, with 3,706 admitted and 4,923 pending; another 2,333 applications had come from minors (1,386 admitted, 947 pending) and 3,345 from other dependents such as mothers and fathers (with 677 admitted and 2,668 pending). Though modest compared with the raw figures of the other geographical divisions, USCT claims constituted a majority of Union claims handled by the Southern Division, which at the end of June 1883 reported a total of 10,710 Union invalid and dependent pensions on the rolls, some three-quarters of whom were Black.[58]

Knowingly or otherwise, many former slaves who had served in nonmilitary roles during the war deemed themselves worthy of a pension. Ex-slave John Anderson of North Carolina, for instance, alleged service in the Fortieth USCT when in fact he was only hired as a cook. Ex-slave Henry Johnson of Virginia likewise found employment as a laborer and teamster for the Tenth USCT and claimed a military pension on those grounds, even though he, too, had "rendered no military service during his lifetime." Martin Howard of Alabama collected over $1,200 by alleging wounds in service despite never having served. Yet to even make such an attempt, these freedmen had to bring forth ailments and disabilities that could plausibly be tied to military service, whether on the open battlefield or in the bacteriological battlefields of the Union camps. The daily violence and deprivations of enslavement and its aftermath blurred the neat divisions of the war years and afforded claimants such an opportunity to chance a pension and hazard ending up on the bureau's so-called fraud register. Lodging false claims indeed entailed considerable risk, often criminal prosecution. But for those in dire situations, it may have been riskier to not even try.[59]

Enterprising freedpeople found creative ways to exploit the ambiguous divisions at the heart of the pension system, especially the porous boundary between enslavement and war. Try as they might, they could never entirely extricate their slave pasts from the process. Take the case of Horace Brown. Born on a Combahee River slave labor camp, Brown was later sold at a public auction in Charleston, not far from where he would later join the Union army. But before that day, more sales would follow. In fact, he been sold so many times before the war—and acquired so many different surnames—he had forgotten which one he had given to the recruiting officer. He suffered a gunshot wound at the Battle of Honey Hill and was thereafter transferred to a hospital in Beaufort, where a surgeon amputated his right leg. He convalesced alongside an officer in the famed Fifty-Fourth Massachusetts. After five months of treatment, he was discharged from service, though later he lost the disability certificate to prove it. Brown claimed to have submitted his application for a pension through the Freedmen's Bureau but had never received confirmation.

Struggling to support his family in Georgetown and "dependent on the charity of old comrades," according to a special examiner, Brown resubmitted his pension application in August 1883. He traveled all the way to Washington, D.C., where he enlisted the services of one Walter D. Plowden, a Black pension agent Brown first met in Beaufort. During the war, Plowden had served as a scout and spy for Major-General David Hunter—service Congress would later recognize with a $1,000 reward in March 1869. Plowden had also established a thriving claims agency in Washington, specializing in the claims of Black veterans and widows. In 1886, a bill to pension Plowden was introduced by Congressman Robert Smalls, the widely celebrated former slave who in 1862 commandeered a Confederate ship and delivered it to the Union navy outside Charleston harbor. A few years before the bill, however, Plowden had been disbarred from practicing as a claims agent for the Pension Bureau for allegedly soliciting illegal fees and withholding pension money.[60]

Plowden's disbarment undermined the veracity of the pension claims he facilitated. But he would continue to be a part of Horace Brown's case, and even served as a witness to his military service in Beaufort. His client needed allies. One examiner believed Brown to be an "imposter" given his association with Plowden, whom he smeared as "a notorious colored pension 'crook.'" The examiner even suggested the possibility of bringing criminal proceedings against Plowden and Brown alike. On top of his tainted application, the fundamental trouble of Brown's case was that he did not appear on the rolls of his supposed regiment, the Thirty-Third USCT. None of his aliases or slave-market surnames did either. Moreover, special examiners assigned to the case struggled to locate former enslavers or fellow slaves who could testify to his identity. This made his amputation—ordinarily a very easy case to prove—extraordinarily vexing. As one investigator put it in his letter to the notorious pension commissioner John C. Black, he "kept this case over four months in the hope of establishing [the] claimant's identity so that he might get justice, if he really lost his leg as alleged." After the investigator's report reached the Board of Review in August 1887, Brown's application was promptly rejected for lack of proof.[61]

Brown's case attracted the attention of former senator Samuel C. Pomeroy, who in 1889 asked an investigator to look into the claim. The investigator, Dr. J. E. Carpenter, interviewed Brown in his office and "questioned him as to his history from the time he left his last master, until the alleged injury was received." Carpenter "was impressed with the truthfulness of his story," particularly of his guard duty at Morris Island and Hilton Head before the battle that cost him his right leg. There, Brown had been ordered to guard a rebel prisoner, one Major McDowell Carrington, whom, being a current resident of Washington, Carpenter decided to call in for questioning. Carrington indeed remembered Brown and corroborated his story, leading the investigator to believe that Brown's identity should be easy to establish. But beyond that, he explained to Pomeroy in the tone of a last-ditch effort, "Brown's leg is off, and the amputation is such as could only be performed by a skillful Surgeon." He was plainly an impoverished freedman who would not have been able to afford a proper surgery outside of military service. "If the leg was not lost as alleged," Carpenter concluded, "the Claimant has concocted a marvelous story such as his education, or rather his want of education, and general history would seem to render him quite incapable of." The investigator's logic was equal parts ingenious and demeaning. And it proved unsuccessful. Horace Brown, alias Horace Magruder, alias Horace Haywood, never received a pension.[62]

Although most Black veterans never faced such extreme circumstances, their own struggles to establish a service origin for their disabilities were challenging enough. After proving their health at enlistment, Black veterans also needed to offer a convincing narrative of how their wartime service resulted in a lasting illness or disability. More often than not, these were not heroic stories of battlefield bravery but rather stories of miserable environments, hard labor, and reckless commands. The task at hand required them, in their medical examinations, to erase any preconditions inherited from servitude and direct all focus to the years of military service. No bright line naturally separated the two, so they had to inscribe it themselves. But how could one attribute strictly to military service something as temporally inexact as heart disease, or rheumatism, or general debility? George Bragg of the Ninety-Second USCT was among the thousands of ex-slave veterans who confronted such a dilemma. He told medical examiners of how, in January 1864, he was transported with his comrades from Berwick Bay, Louisiana, to New Orleans. Placed in open cars, "many of the men froze their feet because of the great storm and very severe cold weather. I suffered greatly in my feet and legs from the cold," Bragg remembered. Some men even died from the trip. Others died from the exposure to cold that awaited them at Port Hudson. Before their service was over, the men of the Ninety-Second would build a bridge over the Red River at Alexandria, Louisiana (to provide a retreat for Nathaniel Banks's army), and construct the fortification at the Mississippi River town of Morganza.

Throughout all of these tasks, Bragg recalled feeling heart palpitations for the first time. Then his legs began to swell and stiffen. Frequently he was excused from duty. Two regimental doctors treated him several times during service. But because their treatments were unrecorded and their testimony unattained, Bragg's story remained unverified. After discharge, he made several visits to Charity Hospital in New Orleans to receive a more exact diagnosis. "This disease," he told the board of surgeons, "frequently troubled me at other times and places subsequent thereto while in service. It has followed me since discharge and [is] now so bad as to totally disable me from all excitement or hard work." At Charity Hospital, the doctors diagnosed the former slave with heart disease and rheumatism, two of the most commonly pensioned afflictions. In August 1889, a board of surgeons approved his pension claim, noting that "the existing condition and the history of this claimant" made it "probable that the disability was incurred in the service as he claims." But positive ratings by examining boards still had to earn the approval of the bureau's legal and medical reviewers, who were less convinced of the probability suggested by the examiners. In Bragg's case, despite the board's approval, the reviewers in Washington refused his admission to the pension rolls. The origins of Bragg's present afflictions remained unverified at the alleged time of contraction.[63]

Both before and during the war, freedpeople confronted a range of environmental hazards that negatively impacted their bodily health. But distinguishing medically between prewar and wartime ailments evoked considerable ambiguity. In their postwar claims, former enslaved veterans frequently attributed their disabling illnesses to general service-related causes such as exposure, excessive labor, or improper diet, all of which they undoubtedly experienced as bondsmen at some point in their lives.[64] But greater specificity in naming diseases helped anchor their claims in service, particularly when so named by regimental surgeons. Take the case of Stephen Hurt. Although Hurt saw little combat alongside George Bragg in the Ninety-Second, his service record was shot through with bodily trauma. Hurt believed he contracted malarial poisoning and sunstroke in the spring of 1864 at Port Hudson, when he started experiencing bowel troubles along with "chills and fever from change of climate and living on army diet." From 1864 into 1865, during his time at Morganza, he had two attacks of what he considered typhoid fever and, in August 1865, claimed to have been "sun-struck while on guard duty." Yet no physician was ever able to diagnose Hurt with precision. He knew he had shortness of breath and that this impaired his ability to plow and split rails after the war, but beyond that, he admitted, "I do not know what was the matter with me." Hurt was able to secure multiple eyewitnesses to testify to his prewar soundness and wartime sickness but, like so many other Black veterans in the South, failed to obtain the vaunted testimony from commissioned officers or regimental surgeons, the vast majority of whom came from— and returned to—the distant North.[65]

Providing eyewitness testimony of a sick or injured comrade was one thing, but to do so twenty or more years after the fact and, furthermore, to provide details precise enough for a retroactive medical diagnosis strained the memories of all but the clairvoyant. Washington Jones pursued a claim that underscores the frustrations of state recognition premised on airtight recollections of past traumas. In his claim, he cited both a physical ailment (frostbite) and a neurological ailment (neuralgia), tracing both to the exposure he endured around Morgan City, Louisiana. Jones stated early in his case that one Dr. Blackwood of the Eighty-First USCT had treated him for neuralgia while in service, commenting that he "was seldom healed in the army" and that "of course it has been increasing ever since." After his application met rejection on the basis of no official record of service-origin, Jones marshaled two former comrades, Mitchell Tucker and Thomas McGruder, to testify on his behalf. A special examiner interrogated him accordingly. "By whom do you expect to establish the origin of the neuralgia of the head?" asked the examiner.

"Dr. Blackwood knew this," Jones answered, with some confidence.

"By whom can you prove the existence of varicose veins in the army?"

"No one," Jones replied, but "Tucker and McGruder will know I had pains in my legs."

"Tucker and McGruder do not know you had any trouble with your legs," countered the examiner, having referred to their depositions taken earlier.

Feeling himself cornered, Jones conceded that his comrades "knew I was sick but that is all I suppose."[66]

Jones then learned that his two witnesses indeed had not actually remembered hearing him complain of his legs in service; he would not take the same chance with his next witness, his comrade Edward Alexander. Before he testified, Jones slipped him a scrap of paper listing the complaints he had in service and asked Alexander to make an affidavit for him, which Alexander did. He took the paper to a clerk of the court near Magnolia Plantation in West Feliciana Parish and signed it. Months passed. Over the course of his investigation, Jones changed the alleged injury to his legs. Initially it was frostbite (until roughly 1891), then for years it was varicose veins, and finally (around 1899) frostbite once again. A special examiner questioned him on these discrepancies in May 1899. "Well, I suppose it is all about the same thing—the result of marching and frozen feet," explained Jones. Whatever it was exactly, it happened "on the march from New Iberia to Franklin it was dark and snowy and . . . we laid down in the woods like logs together and when we awoke the snow had done covered us up. Then is when I first took my attack of pain in my feet. Later it went to my head, back and shoulders." Jones was understandably exasperated that his pension hinged on a precise diagnosis of an affliction he incurred a quarter-century prior. "I don't know what you may call that," he admitted, but "I have felt the pain of this neuralgia every day ever since my discharge but some days it has been worse than others." Consciously or otherwise, by changing his self-diagnosis, Jones sought plausibility without undermining his own credibility. A special examiner found him "rather brighter mentally than the average of his race and social status in this section," but, perhaps for that reason, he "also impressed me as being rather unreliable."[67]

The pension case of Washington Jones dramatizes the high stakes of wartime memory, and the lengths to which freedpeople had to go in order to achieve federal recognition for their wartime suffering. Where administrators might see a cunning manipulator, a malingerer, or an imposter looking for undeserved federal support, the reality was that Jones had suffered immensely in a war that desperately needed his support and the support of his comrades, and that he believed his inability to self-diagnose and retrieve detailed if not omniscient testimony from his fellow soldiers and officers should not bar him from the federal benefits to which he felt entitled.

As Jones and thousands of other ex-slave claimants pursued their pensions in the final two decades of the nineteenth century, they confronted a hostile cultural landscape that at once erased the contributions of Black men and women to the Union war effort and glorified the propaganda of the Lost Cause. In 1885, the *Southwestern Christian Advocate* feared that the heroic role Black Americans played during the enslavers' rebellion was being scrubbed from the nation's memory at the twenty-year anniversary of the war's end. "There are thousands of Negroes all over the country," the paper reminded its readers, "who draw their pension and enjoy their bounty thereof which was purchased for them by the blood and suffering of Negro heroes and patriots who fell for the National cause and for freedom." They not only won "freedom for themselves" but also ensured their posterity could "gather in freedom and citizenship, the abundant and imperishable fruit of their planting." The editor asked that when patriots celebrate Memorial Day and scatter flowers over the graves of the Union dead, the graves of Black soldiers be not forgotten.[68]

Historian Kathleen Ann Clark has argued that public acts of commemoration by Black Americans were vital to the legitimation of their citizenship. Although revisiting the war before a special examiner of the Pension Bureau was appreciably different from celebratory public fêtes, both were important forums of debate over the meaning of freedom, the uses of the slave past, and the destiny of the race. History itself was a staple of Black oratory in the 1880s and 1890s, just as personal histories were for pension applicants. But Black leaders were divided over how to remember the dark days of slavery—or whether to remember them at all. In his 1885 address at Harpers Ferry, the Black minister Alexander Crummell offered a meditation on the critical importance of forgetting. Unlike his friend and sometime rival Frederick Douglass, who relentlessly advocated for remembering slavery and the war that destroyed it, Crummell warned that nothing was "more hurtful for any people than a habit such as this. For to dwell upon repulsive things, to hang upon that which is dark, direful, and saddening, tends, first of all, to morbidity and degeneracy. Accustom this race to constant reminiscence of its degradation," Crummell exhorted, and all hope of progress will be dashed upon the rocks of an undying feeling of "servitude and inferiority." "We can, indeed, get inspiration and instruction in the *yesterdays* of existence," he concluded, "but we cannot healthily live in them."[69]

In recounting their personal histories, Black pension applicants most certainly had to emphasize the hardships and degradations they endured, and they could elaborate on their accomplishments during the war, though at the same time they had to carefully redirect attention away from the sufferings of their preenlistment lives if they hoped to earn a pension. Federal policies, in fact, forced Black claimants into the most extreme rhetorical positions when it came to the history of slavery, a discursive space perhaps articulated best by African Methodist Episcopal Church leader Theophilus Gould Steward, who even surpassed Crummell in the theology of forgetting. In one address to his Brooklyn congregation in 1876, Steward went so far as to argue that "slave history is not history." It "is something to be ashamed of, rather than proud of, hence it has not power to unite but great power to divide." For Black veterans in the emancipated South, the contests over the meanings of history and the promises of progress were far from a theoretical exercise. Their claims, and indeed their livelihoods, depended on silencing much of their slave pasts. Any lasting marks from the violence or deprivations of slavery threatened to upend their claims to the benefits of Union citizenship.[70]

In Service and Servitude

While a veteran's "previous condition of servitude" would not in and of itself preclude his chances at a federal pension, the actual conditions of that servitude might. For nearly three decades after the Civil War, the policies and practices of the Pension Bureau all but necessitated that formerly enslaved veterans testify to enjoying perfect health in the days of slavery. Honoring an ex-slave's military service required a break with his enslaved past—a tacit forfeiture of claims arising from antebellum suffering. Thus, unlike the act of applying for recompense through the Southern Claims Commission, when formerly enslaved veterans applied for a pension from the federal government, they almost never discussed their experiences of physical suffering in slavery, only mentioning instead their place of birth, their enslavers, any relevant connections to former fellow slaves, and then, most importantly, when they left for Union lines and how healthy they were at enlistment. Under the general law of 1862, talk of slavery's lasting marks was a huge liability to be avoided at all costs. Yet when special examiners forced the matter, Black veterans were made to confront the bright line being drawn between slavery and freedom, the boundary delimiting the new liberal order in emancipated America.

Former Louisiana slave Robert Green tried desperately to insulate his military service from his past servitude. In the final month of the rebellion, April 1865, the spring-thawed Mississippi swelled toward the peninsular Union encampment at Morganza. Before Green lay a long gangplank leading up to the *White Cloud*, originally a Confederate provisioning ship that had been captured in 1863 by the Union navy. Beside him stood his comrades of the Eighty-Fourth USCT with orders to evacuate the fort's cannons onto to the ship. Six of them wheeled one up, but it soon became unmanageable. One man lost his grip, then the rest. The weight of the cannon fell upon the hand-spike Green was using to guide it, throwing him violently to the dock. Witnesses thought he had been killed. Word of his death quickly found its way to the commanding officer of another Black regiment garrisoned at the fort, Colonel H. N. Frisbie. His comrades carried him away unconscious on a stretcher to the military hospital, where two regimental surgeons would treat him over the coming months. Green survived the incident but was left with fractured ribs, a broken wrist, and deep cuts across his head. He could only perform light duty for the remainder of his service. But having never fully recovered from his injuries, he could only perform light work for the rest of his life. He first applied for a pension in June 1880. "Nearly all the time since discharge," he explained years later, "I have suffered from the disabilities incurred as above set forth and have been confined to light work not remunerative and I could not at no time gain employment at my usual occupation." Even when he managed to find work, he "could not have kept it as I have not been physically able to do the work. I am a poor crippled old man knocked about from pillar to post for whatever any one will give me . . . all because I am a physical wreck caused by the disability incurred in service and in line of duty."[71]

Like all pensioners, Green called upon his former comrades to testify to his health in the service. To that end, Henry McKinney and Andrew Jackson both swore that he was in "sound physical health and strength" when he enlisted, "free from injury." In a series of affidavits between 1882 and 1883, Green told and retold his story. In December 1884, the Pension Bureau requested that he locate more witnesses, which he would do over the next two years. McKinney reappeared, but he disclosed contradictory testimony. In January 1887, he testified that he was present and saw Green sustain the "injury to left wrist broken injury to the left side and some ribs broken," but two months later he changed his story, admitting he had not witnessed the accident personally, only saw him shortly afterward. Apparently, Green had come to McKinney three years earlier, around the time of the bureau's request for additional witnesses in December 1884. He asked McKinney to be his witness, even though he knew little of Green's injury. "I never knew anything about him breaking any ribs," McKinney claimed in March 1887. Nor did Green tell him explicitly how he hurt his arm. "All I know about him being injured," he claimed, "is by seeing him with his arm in a sling and hearing that he was crippled" from the accident. McKinney's testimony shed enough doubt on Green's story to have the Pension Bureau appoint a special examiner to re-work the case.[72]

The task of the special examination was to determine Robert Green's health at enlistment, which required delving into his life as an enslaved man. Green was born in 1825 in Maryland and was sold in a Louisiana slave market before the war. Around 1855, he was purchased by Franklin A. Hudson, owner of Blythewood Plantation in Iberville Parish, whose enslaved laborers pro-duced sugar and bricks. According to Hudson's journal, when Green arrived at Blythewood (which he always called "Blightwood"), he would have en-countered a system marked by brutal productivity, frequent runaways, insub-ordinate overseers, and relatively high mortality. The special examiner set about to interrogate the Hudson family as well as any former fellow slaves who would have known Green. And although Franklin Hudson, his immedi-ate family, and two of his overseers were dead, the examiner eventually man-aged to track down a number of Green's former fellow slaves, including Flora Hudson, Eliza Johnson, and William Lloyd.[73]

Together, Green's former fellow slaves would present seemingly incongru-ous evidence, undermining the service-origin claim Green had so laboriously tried to build. Flora Hudson, who was charged with tending to Green upon his arrival at the slave labor camp in 1855, remembered an incident where he "got in a fight with his wife, Louisa in the quarters one night. They were rais-ing such a fuss, that we were all standing around there watching them when the overseer ran in and struck Bob over the head." Green was knocked uncon-scious for some time, and when he came to, his head bore a massive lump he carried for several weeks. Eliza Johnson, for her part, recalled a separate inci-dent that happened two years before Green ran away to the Union army, when he "was struck on the wrist by the overseer and after that a lump formed on his wrist and staid there till the time he ran away." When pressed by the special examiner to remember any injury to Green's ribs while enslaved, Johnson could not recall. But William Lloyd could. As he would have it, about two years before Green ran away, they were building a cabin together. Green evidently fell and fractured his ribs. A doctor was sent for, and the pa-tient convalesced for some two weeks. About a year after that, Lloyd remem-bered that Green "got into some trouble with the overseer. And was struck over the arm," thereby corroborating Johnson's story. So there it was: evidence of antebellum injuries to Green's wrist, ribs, and head, years before his calam-ity under the *White Cloud*.[74]

The special examiner confronted Green with these narratives that seemed to discredit his own wartime accounts. The examiner read him their depositions. Evidently perturbed, Green began systematically disavowing the testimony of his former fellow slaves. "The witnesses who testify that I was disabled before the war are just mistaken," he claimed. It was untrue "that my master or anyone else ever broke my arm or injured my head," or that "[I was] injured in any manner whatever before or since the war," he argued. But with an abundance of stories from the days of slavery arrayed against him by his former fellow slaves, Green could not afford to deny having ever been assaulted. "Of course I got lots of beatings from the overseer," he finally admitted, adding defiantly that he "wouldn't stand any foolishness so it was always a fight or a foot-race and if I didn't get to the woods I got a beating, but I was never injured as they say." Thus Green did not—and could not—disclaim all instances of violence and suffering in slavery. But what he unequivocally denied was lasting injury or disability. Like other former slaves applying for a pension, he asserted perfect health at the enlistment examination. Against federal officials who sought an antebellum explanation for his present condition of disability, Green struggled to embody the marks of wartime service while acknowledging but cordoning off those of servitude.[75]

Robert Green understood what he had to argue to make himself eligible for a pension. Above and beyond not pensioning injuries from the days of slavery, Green knew all too well that bureau officials would not even pension reinjuries. The multiple special examiners appointed to his case throughout the 1880s all dismissed the testimony of his former comrades as being of "doubtful reputation." In doing so, the examiners privileged the stories of injury in slavery told by other former slaves. Green, they argued, was forever marked by the violence of slavery. And the federal government, reconstituted on an antislavery, free labor foundation, was not to be held accountable for the wounds of slavery.

After years of trial and rejection, Green denounced the special examiner the Pension Bureau appointed to his case. He accused him of spending three years "attempting to get up evidence to defeat my claim." And the Pension Bureau itself, he argued, must have had full knowledge that the examiner "was acting under some secrete [*sic*] instruction to defeat negro claims in the south—which seemed to be in pursuance of a general policy of no more negro pensions," a campaign inaugurated by the Democratic commissioner John C. Black. Green believed he could prove the special examiner falsified the evidence in his case as well as in the cases of his comrades and fellow would-be pensioners. He repeatedly called into question the examiner's loyalty, calling him a liar, a conspirator, and a rebel. "Here is ten years spent in trying to determine whether I was injured in the service. It would seem that time enough had been spent to determine this fact. My case is held back because of a rebel policy on a rebel's testimony manipulated by a willing fool who . . . would not hesitate to make up any evidence to suit his secrete [*sic*] orders." Despite myriad insults and rejections, Green kept pursuing his pension into the 1890s. So, too, did his much-maligned comrades of the Eighty-Fourth and their families.[76]

Tens of thousands of pension cases involving former slaves represented national reconciliation struggles writ small. Two parties clashed over how the Civil War and its true cause ought to be remembered. But here, unlike virtually anywhere else, the roles were paradoxically reversed. Through the Pension Bureau, the federal state avoided reckoning with slavery precisely by acknowledging the lasting marks of it, thereby absolving itself from compensating its survivors. Just as the federal government would not compensate the slaveholders for losing their chattel, nor would it compensate the enslaved for incurring disabilities while in bondage. If "remembering" slavery's wounds in these pension cases was a way to write it off the nation's moral and economic ledgers, former slaves ironically had to silence their experiences of slavery in order to achieve a measure of recognition for their suffering.

AS THE 1880S CLOSED, so too did many opportunities for Southern freedpeople in the dwindling embers of Reconstruction. The resurgence of the Democratic Party on national, regional, and local scales—aided and abetted by the Republican Party's acquiescence to interests of the propertied class—paved the way for the widespread disenfranchisement of Black Americans by the turn of the century.[77] Black Southerners were to be increasingly relegated to electoral insignificance. On the eve of the long night of disempowerment, Bishop William Henry Heard of the African Methodist Episcopal Church, himself a former slave, reflected on the "unfavorable" condition of the Black man in America in 1889: "He is a man without being allowed to enjoy manhood; a citizen without enjoying citizenship; law-abiding without being protected; a taxpayer without representation." All levels of government "demand of him allegiance but do not guarantee him protection of life, or property. His true condition is that of a weaker in the hands of a stronger." Indicative to Bishop Heard and others of this woeful state of affairs was that "colored soldiers have more difficulty today in establishing a pension plan than any other class." Although the Pension Bureau remained one of the few arenas that offered statutory equality regardless of race, freedpeople faced extraordinary difficulties in their quests for pensions. In the year when Bishop Heard made his remarks, veterans of the USCT filed 4,026 applications, but only 810 received admission. Together with their widows, mothers, fathers, and children, Black claimants that year filed 6,035 applications, with pensions awarded to only 1,217.[78]

By mid-1889, veterans and surviving heirs of the U.S. Colored Troops had filed nearly forty-seven thousand original pension claims, with over fifteen thousand admitted to the rolls. Thousands more claims were pending.[79] Each claim, successful or otherwise, took extraordinary effort. The cumulative effect was nothing short of formidable, as claims administrators routinely attested. These Black veterans and survivors were subjected to much higher rates of special examination, owing to a range of mitigating factors unforeseen by the bureau's legislative architects and executive managers. These cases required greater attention and additional evidence, witnesses, and investigations. To win their pension cases for themselves and their posterity, veterans not only had to meet the high evidentiary threshold for proving a service origin of an ongoing affliction but also had to craft a convincing narrative about their wartime suffering. Before claims agents and special examiners of the Pension Bureau, ex-slave claimants told stories of dangerous environments, exposure, hard labor, hunger, and material deprivation, all the while careful to draw a firm line between those very same conditions they undoubtedly experienced at one point or another while in bondage or while fleeing it. As with their claims to confiscated property filed through the Southern Claims Commission, ex-slave pensioners could seek redress only under the strictest of parameters. The War of the Rebellion, as many historians now argue, did more than simply reunite the country; it remade it. A fundamental component of that remaking was a severance with the slave past—a dismissal of any and all damage claims arising from the enslavers' regime.

CHAPTER FIVE

Some Measure of Justice

The Civil War's casualty lists grew after 1865. Hundreds of thousands of soldiers carried wounds, ailments, and other traumas into their postwar lives, making recovery and reconstruction not only national tasks but intimate ones as well, as millions of ordinary Americans encountered and endured disability like never before. The task for many was finding a way to honor republican sacrifice without sacrificing republican honor, and with it the ideals of manly independence and productivity. Few veterans could dodge the prevailing Gilded Age antagonism toward disabled persons. Even those onlookers who maintained that "worthy" veterans deserved the nation's material support still worried about the consequences of a swelling welfare state subsidizing the potentially fraudulent, lazy, and unworthy. In the decades after the war, unforeseen armies of disabled Union veterans and dependents mobilized to lobby for passage of increasingly liberal bounty and pension legislation. Efforts to eliminate distinctions between ranks, lower eligibility requirements, increase rates of pensions, and broaden categories of disability consumed the labors of policymakers in Washington, particularly Republicans beholden to the soldier vote. But despite its centrality to the history of the Civil War and Reconstruction, disability has only recently begun to garner the scholarly attention it deserves.[1]

Then as now, disability was not a neutral, physiological condition existing only in a biological realm. On the social register, it was a political field of open contestation, subject to extensive and intensive struggle between lawmakers, bureaucrats, physicians, and the general public, including those with impairments themselves. The federal administrative state labored to define disability in the years following the war. Owing to its vast operations, the U.S. Pension Bureau became the chief architectural firm in this project. Proceeding from the general assumption was that disabled people would fare poorly in competing with nondisabled people in the labor market, the bureau defined disability with the market in mind, though without requiring pensioners to be out of it. The question thus became how much a specific impairment inhibited one's theoretical wage-earning potential. To determine this, the Pension Bureau deputized hundreds, then thousands of physicians across the United States to conduct medical examinations on Union veterans to assess their precise level of inability to perform manual labor. Those who fell short of "total disability" received a proportional rating, theoretically equivalent to wages lost by the perceived loss of functionality. The subjectivity of medical perception stymied any and all efforts to enforce uniformity in disability ratings across examining boards, and all the while the number of examining boards relentlessly grew over the years. In hundreds of thousands of medical examinations, surgeons struggled against claimants to not simply diagnose a disability but also to rate it, that is, to quantify and commodify it, affixing a number so the Pension Bureau may affix a price.

If disability as a category of analysis has only recently begun to factor into histories of the Civil War and Reconstruction, the experiences of disabled freedmen remain conspicuously marginalized. Proving a wartime origin for the same postwar ailment was a burdensome endeavor for ex-slave claimants, and for many insurmountable. The Disability Act of June 27, 1890 opened the door for tens of thousands of Southern freedpeople to seek federal pensions by creating a parallel pension track for postwar disabilities regardless of origin. Yet the annulment of the service-origin requirement fundamentally shifted the focus away from the wartime experiences of Black veterans and made their bids for pensions more immediate, more individuated, and in the eyes of many critics, more suspect and contemptible. No longer did Black Union veterans have to carefully narrate their stories of wartime suffering and postwar continuity—though many still did. Instead, they needed only to demonstrate their current inability to work as well as they could if they were able-bodied. The experiences of formerly enslaved men in the post-Confederate South were a world apart from those of their white analogues in the North. Whereas all veteran applicants faced some degree of antagonism or discrimination from a suspicious public, only ex-slaves faced the prospect or reality of meeting a former enslaver or slave doctor as they undressed in the examining room, face-to-face with the unwelcome new figures of federal authority.[2]

Rating Disability

The Civil War crushed the enslavers' regime and created a new nation-state sustained by a new legal order. At the conceptual foundation of the modern liberal state lay the self-owning, rights-bearing individual capable of self-government, which accorded full personhood and citizenship to able-bodied white men. In the Civil War era, when the very concept of citizenship was in flux, disability provided a convenient way to separate those worthy of citizenship from those deemed unworthy, on the grounds of a compromised self-ownership. Attributing an inborn "disability" to Black Americans, women, and immigrants saddled these groups with the onus of being regarded as unfit and therefore proper subjects for discrimination. Consequently, as historian Douglas Baynton has persuasively shown, struggles for equal rights often began with vigorous assertions that one was not disabled, physically or morally, and therefore not properly assigned to an inferior status—a status that may, as such arguments imply, be properly assigned to others.[3]

From 1882 to the 1920s, disability functioned as the primary vehicle for immigration restriction, a state project Baynton regards as "the least ambiguous expression of this growing aversion to disability." Medical inspectors of the Immigration Bureau wielded the power to screen out those immigrants deemed to have "defects." Ostensible "hereditary defects," in fact, served as a shorthand for the much more abstract category of race. Thus in the hands of the inspectors, race itself came to be understood as a general tendency toward defectiveness, a proxy for a group's unfitness to successfully compete in the race for life. "It was not this imagined category" of race, Baynton suggests, "that finally held promise or danger, but rather the actual fit or defective individuals who composed it." The low-born were likely more prominent among certain racial groups and therefore less likely to attain independence and more likely to contaminate the nation. And so, examinations by immigration officials identified undesirable immigrants as "likely to become a public charge," a label coined in 1891 to certify a perceived inability to support oneself.[4]

All of these same issues of disability and public dependency animated the medical examinations of pensioners. But the dynamics were notably inverted. The Pension Bureau excluded from the rolls the physically and mentally fit, those who could not prove themselves "ratably disabled," and rewarded those claimants who presented the greatest disabilities with the highest stipends. Contrary to the exclusionary politics of the Immigration Bureau, then, the Pension Bureau generated an inclusionary one, provoking in turn a new set of challenges for its participants who already held claim to national inclusion by way of their birthright citizenship.

Disability remained an important cultural signifier of personhood even for the American-born in the age of birthright citizenship. Throughout the nineteenth century, a wide swath of the lay and educated white public deemed Blackness itself a disability, for reasons biological or environmental. Disability discourse had flourished on both sides of the slavery debate in the antebellum era. Abolitionists argued that the very condition of bondage was a disabling force and praised the healing powers of free labor. For their part, proslavery spokesmen argued that Black people were inherently dependent and unfit for freedom; they would suffer widespread disability and perhaps even extinction if set free from white tutelage. Anti-Black theorists, many of them with medical degrees, redoubled their wager after emancipation. They drew on evolutionary theory and medical science to modernize biological racism and fasten on it the badge of scientific expertise. Medical journals, scientific magazines, and insurance pamphlets were all littered with articles detailing the "effects of freedom" on the minds and bodies of Black Americans. As one representative physician, John Fullenwider Miller, put it in 1896, the second decade of freedom had "brought a beautiful harvest of mental and physical degeneration and he is now becoming a martyr to an heredity thus established." Talk of Black extinction naturally followed the latest mortality statistics, reenergized whenever an epidemic such as smallpox seemed hesitant to cross the color line, as it did to many wishful white observers during the Civil War. Put simply, postbellum medical science was decidedly arrayed against the Black lives widely deemed unfit for freedom.[5]

Marbling scientific and political judgment, the Darwinian notion of fitness signaled an individual's capacity for survival in the "natural" environment of free market capitalism. As such, perceived physical disabilities among Black Americans as a whole both encouraged and reflected the imposition of legal disabilities on newly enfranchised freedmen in the wake of Reconstruction, effectively excluding them from the body politic. Cutting into this exclusionary palisade lay the narrow but inclusionary politics of the Pension Bureau. In one of the most arresting paradoxes of the history of emancipation, for tens of thousands of formerly enslaved claimants, their citizenship rights in the form of federal pensions depended on proving they were, in an individual sense, disabled and unfit for productive society. These men and women thus faced a vexing dilemma, one that far surpassed the situation faced by their white comrades in the North. According to historian David Roediger, conceding dependency for white veterans afforded them an "emancipation from whiteness," an ideological severance of their presumed fitness for independence, in turn seeding a radical new potential for solidarity with other marginalized groups, above all former slaves. Yet disabled Black veterans likewise conceded dependency (though presumably did not attain a corresponding "emancipation from Blackness," whatever that would mean). Racial metaphysics aside, as freedpeople conceded dependency they did so in the literal faces of people who had suspected their intrinsic disability all along.[6]

Former slaves therefore braved a racially charged discourse on disability when seeking federal relief through the Pension Bureau. Undeterred, they applied for pensions and for increases in their rates to such an extent after passage of the Disability Act of 1890 that they forced the bureau to address the demand. The bureau appointed more medical examiners and built up the clerical and adjudicating staff of the Southern Division. Of the roughly 180,000 U.S. Colored Troops (USCT) who served during the Civil War, over one hundred thousand veterans have some pension activity associated with their names, whether they themselves applied or their widow, or their dependents, or some combination of the three. Though fewer than the gross number of white applicants, the proportion of Black pension applicants to Black servicemen eclipsed rates of application and increase among white claimants. Their struggles for disability pensions under the 1890 law also marked a significant break from their decades-long contests for bounties and general law pensions. Black Southerners accordingly adapted their strategies to meet the new challenges engendered by the new law. Appreciating the ongoing efforts of formerly enslaved pension applicants is therefore crucial to understanding Black administrative politics in the age of disenfranchisement.[7]

The entire pension scheme reflected the expertise-driven ideology of one of the most influential benevolent associations in the Civil War era, the U.S. Sanitary Commission. In addition to its work in field hospitals and camps, and its anthropometric studies of Union soldiers, the Sanitary Commission drafted a blueprint for how society ought to manage the war's aftermath. Its leaders predicted that the care of those who survived the war would be a grave "trial to the order, industry, and security of society" and "a burden to its already strained resources." In August 1862, the commission's president, Henry W. Bellows, wrote to an agent, Stephen Perkins, with instructions to tour the invalid hospitals of Europe and report on the pension systems offered to veterans. Bellows wanted a policy generous enough to reach all affected veterans but one that would also shield itself from abuse and political interference, fearing that politicians would make political capital out of public sympathy through appeals to "demoralizing sentimentality." "The utmost endeavor," Bellows insisted, should be taken "to promote the healthy absorption of the invalid class into the homes, and into the ordinary industry of the country." Without strict rules in place for the distribution of federal pensions, Bellows worried the system would create a general disposition to treat pensioners as exempt from the "ordinary rules of life."[8]

With these goals in mind, the agent toured France, Prussia, Austria, and Italy and submitted his proposal to the Sanitary Commission board in April 1864. Some of these military pension systems, he discovered, were a "mere pittance," barely enough on which to survive, and pensions should at least afford a subsistence, a living wage, to its recipients. And unlike in other countries, where pensions were sharply graded by military rank, Perkins's proposal maintained that pensions should be based on the severity of the war-related injuries or illnesses themselves. He believed three categories of rating were appropriate: a maximum-rate pension would subsidize disabilities equal to the loss of two limbs, a medium rate for the equivalent to the loss of one limb, and a minimum rate for all other injuries. Widows and orphans of those who died from wounds ought to be entitled to half the maximum rate. Perkins also recommended the establishment of soldiers' homes—or, as he called them, "invalid industrial villages"—for unmarried veterans, wherein residents would be assigned various forms of agricultural and manual labor suited to their capabilities and "paid wages according to the value of their labor."[9]

In December 1865, Bellows issued a final report on the recommendations of the Sanitary Commission for provisioning veterans and their dependents. Conveniently enough, Americans had what Bellows called "a spirit above dependence." They relied not on government charity but rather on a vast familial and communal network of support. In fact, the "disposition to provide in larger and expensive ways for sick and disabled soldiers, in public asylums, has almost entirely ceased," Bellows declared with undisguised pride. Pensions, however, were debts due to the soldier and his dependents. They had a "moral right to claim" pensions. A pension was not an act of charity or welfare or relief but an entitlement owing to past contributions, in this case military service. The existing pension laws in the United States were not only more generous than those of Europe, he suggested, but were in the end "a great mercy." Pensioners could collect their stipends while living at home and performing any light and remunerative work they could manage in the labor market. There was no need for soldiers' homes and, not incidentally, no need to restructure the economy. In place of national caretaking institutions, Bellows envisioned a provisioning system to preserve the dignity, autonomy, and productivity of claimants by grading the monetary loss owing to one's precisely classified disability.[10]

The Sanitary Commission's solution to the problem of disabled veterans was thus pro-market and anti-institutional. Yet legislating such a program required considerable administrative capacity—and a National Home for Disabled Volunteer Soldiers arose nonetheless, with branches throughout the North.[11] And where the Sanitary Commission recommended three general grades, Congress instead passed dozens of bills fixing rates of pension for specific disabilities and classes of disability. The more complicated the rating system, the more managers it required, reflecting what anthropologist David

Graeber has called "the Iron Law of Liberalism." On July 4, 1864, Congress established fixed rates for loss of both hands, loss of sight of both eyes, and loss of both feet. Increasingly Congress began adding more fixed rates for more specific disabilities. The Act of March 3, 1865, passed in the final weeks of the war alongside the first Freedmen's Bureau bill, entitled veterans who lost one hand and one foot to twenty dollars per month. With the Act of June 6, 1866, the loss of sight of one eye, with the sight of the other having been lost before enlistment, entitled one to twenty-five dollars per month. More detailed disabilities followed, including loss of a leg at hip joint, loss of an arm at shoulder joint, and loss of an arm at or above elbow, or a leg at or above knee. Fixed rates were relatively unambiguous and easily assessed. A missing body part represented a permanent, specific loss of functionality in an individual. This functionality ought to be supplemented with a standardized monthly payment. Such logic easily snowballed. By the early 1890s, there would be more than 119 fixed rates of pay under the general law.[12]

All ratings were designed to correspond to a theoretical inability to perform manual labor to earn a support, regardless of the claimant's actual occupation, wealth, or income. "The gauge of a pensioner's disability," as one critic complained, "is always his unfitness to do manual work. The pension laws go upon the idea that every soldier is a day laborer. No account is made of the ability of the man to work at his trade or profession." The Pension Bureau, in other words, abstracted working capacity from the specific claimant's actual occupation. The pension system thus required means-testing not of a financial sort, one's wages or salary, that is, but a physical one, what might be called physical means-testing. Under this rubric sat the broad categories of fixed and unfixed disabilities. The Act of June 6, 1866 created three general grades of disability ratings for unfixed disabilities. It allowed for twenty-five dollars monthly for first-grade disabilities that made a veteran "so permanently and totally disabled as to render them utterly helpless," or "nearly so as to require the constant personal aid and attendance of another person." It granted twenty dollars for second-grade disabilities that rendered one "incapacitated for performing any manual labor," and fifteen dollars for third-grade disabilities "equivalent to loss of a hand or a foot." The Act of June 8, 1872 increased these rates, as did many subsequent acts throughout the 1870s and 1880s. Despite the implicit confidence underlying the taxonomy of disability ratings, administrators and examiners might very well have suspected that disability itself was an unstable and malleable category. The three grades for "unfixed" disabilities always bedeviled Pension Bureau administrators. As one commissioner remarked not ten years after the war, the bureau's "method of rating disabilities is attended with great confusion and uncertainty, and is open to grave objections." And yet it was the sandy foundation upon which the federal state's largest civil agency rested.[13]

Congress granted the Pension Bureau commissioner the discretionary authority to appoint civilian physicians to serve as federal surgeons but left no exact criteria as to qualifications, numbers, or locations. Administrators well knew that so much depended on the determinations made by the appointed surgeons who, after all, were the primary point of contact between claimants and the larger pension administration. Commissioners stressed the importance of hiring the physicians of the "highest order of professional qualification" to serve as examiners. Their credentialed expertise not only ensured greater uniformity and fairness to applicants but, more importantly, protected the government against fraud. To that end, administrators circulated dozens of explanatory pamphlets and treatises to discipline examining surgeons in their ratings. Guidance they needed, for the pension process mandated a string of examinations for every claimant: original, renewal, increase, biennial, and special. Since 1859, pensioners required an examination every two years to determine the continuance of the alleged disability. "As we recede from the war of the rebellion," warned Commissioner James H. Baker in 1871, "many disabilities, in their nature temporary, are disappearing by recuperative energies, and the pensioner, reluctant to lose his gratuity, oftentimes tries to fortify himself by evidence, which only consumes the time and labor of the office to no purpose."[14]

Within half a decade after the close of the war, commissioners had already initiated two major reforms as a concerted effort to exert greater control over the examining process. First, Commissioner Henry Van Aernam, a former (and future) Republican congressman, sought to professionalize the medical review process of the bureau. A physician himself, Van Aernam appointed a handful of reviewers with medical training, including a medical referee, general examining surgeon, and two special examining surgeons, to serve at the bureau's headquarters in Washington. The team proved so vital that within a couple years, it institutionalized into a Medical Division and was formally announced in the bureau's 1871 annual report. Two years after that, Congress passed the Consolidation Act and officially authorized the creation of the bureau's already-existing Medical Division. (As would often be the case with the Pension Bureau, its own administrative practices and protocols and rulings— its internal law—would gestate in the wide legislative latitude given to the agency.) Organized around the office of the medical referee, the Medical Division had final say over the accuracy of the reports from examining surgeons and hence the disability rating and corresponding size of the pension. The division worked to balance control over the professional behavior of examining surgeons—already numbering over 1,300—while also maintaining their independence. The second major reform was the gradual institutionalization of examining boards to replace individual examining surgeons. By 1882, Congress intervened and required all Pension Bureau medical examinations to be done before boards of three surgeons, unless "impracticable" for the claimant. But the matter of how to staff these boards was, again, left to the discretion of the commissioner. Betraying an awareness of criticism from disaffected Democrats, many commissioners, being political appointees themselves, sought to balance the boards politically.[15]

Medical reviewers in the central office had few means to corroborate the examining board reports, knowing only what the surgeons chose to transmit. Critics inside and outside the bureau diagnosed endemic inconsistency, confusion, and corruption in the examining board system.[16] Commissioners, for their part, had long complained about the fee-based system upon which examinations were conducted. In 1871, Baker observed that the $1.50 fee for an examination, split among three examiners, hardly attracted the reputable sort of medical professional the pension process demanded. "The surgeons must leave their daily practice," he explained, "go to a specified place, strip and thoroughly examine the applicant, make a written diagnosis of the case, report it to the pension agent and to this Bureau, and enter the same upon the journal they are required to keep. All this is to be done for the pittance of 50 cents to each surgeon." Given such an important task, Baker called the system "absurd" and unprofessional. It remained so after Congress boldly raised the fee to two dollars in 1873. Baker's successor, H. M. Atkinson, suspected that even with increased fees for increased medical talent, "local prejudices and influences would operate to render it almost an impossibility to secure perfectly fair examinations in all cases. A surgeon dependent upon a community for his practice," argued the commissioner, "is dependent upon the opinion of his neighbors."[17]

Pension commissioners harnessed reform efforts to a larger movement in nineteenth-century America to substitute fees for salaries as a federal official's lawful income. Legal scholar Nicholas Parrillo has called this effort the "salary revolution in American government." Salaries worked to standardize the delivery of federal services. Moreover, by removing "facilitative payments," salaries reduced profit-seeking corruption by severing officials' conduct from their income. Customer-oriented exchange, in other words, would give way to the claims-making and fulfillment processes more befitting a modern state.

Together with his reformist medical referee, Dr. Thomas B. Hood, Commissioner John A. Bentley devised a scheme to replace the semiprivate, fee-based compensation system of examining surgeons with a system of salaried, full-time federal surgeons appointed to specific districts. Surgeons would be "ordered from place to place within the district, and to be changed about from one district to another as the emergencies of the service might require." In each district, the surgeon and accompanying clerk would "constitute a commission on behalf of the Government to make the required medical examinations in any case, and to receive the parol[e] testimony offered in its support; and to that end the claimant, with his principal witnesses, should appear before them and submit themselves to cross-examination on behalf of the government." In his annual message to Congress in 1879, Bentley contrasted the ex parte system with the adversarial legal system of the civilized world, that of "open public proceedings, [and] bringing parties and witnesses face to face that they may be interrogated."[18]

Bentley's plan, dubbed the Sixty Surgeon Pension Bill, thus attempted to reform the medical examination process through stronger civil service organization with an internal juridical component required for every case. Its stakes were heightened by the deluge of pension applications following recent passage of the Arrears Act of 1879. Yet the measure met with defeat in early 1881, just before Bentley left office. It would remain one of the most ambitious proposals to reform the Pension Bureau, and the bureau's most prominent critics would continue advocating for such reforms to better protect the government for years to come. As political scientist Theda Skocpol has suggested, such a plan, if implemented, almost certainly would have resulted in a more restrictive pension system and fewer admittances to the rolls. Though this would likely have been the case for Northern white claimants who enjoyed greater leverage with their neighborhood practitioners on the local examining board, formerly enslaved claimants would have benefited immensely from such a reform.[19]

Because Bentley's plan was never enacted, the issues resulting from the decentralized, public-private partnership for medical examinations continued in full force. The working independence of examining boards combined with the lack of systematic oversight proved especially embarrassing and intractable. The bureau's Medical Referee needed some way "to fix uniform rates and decide on obscure questions in medicine," policing their application across the nation's examining boards. In July 1881, Bentley's successor, William W. Dudley, increased the Medical Division's staff but left the fee-based, semiprivate system of examining surgeons unchanged. By the next year, moreover, in response to congressional legislation and the increased demand for medical examinations, the Pension Bureau had deputized over 244 boards across the country, with another eighty pending. Assured that "some of the best medical men in the country are now borne on the roster of examining surgeons," a newfound confidence in the Medical Division grew, at least among the bureau's managerial class. Dudley himself boasted in 1883 that "in no branch of the office have such rapid strides of improvement been observed as in the Medical Department."[20]

These examining boards made up of neighborhood physicians were the gatekeepers of the Pension Bureau. Despite any belabored managerial conceits of standardized practice, the examining boards wielded considerable discretion as the key intercessors between individual claimants and the larger apparatus of the Pension Bureau. The number of examining surgeons grew rapidly in the earliest years after the war and hovered between 1,400 and 1,500 surgeons in the 1870s. Yet few examining boards could be found in the Deep South until the passage of the all-important Disability Act. For example, in 1875, when very few eligible Southerners lodged claims to veterans' pensions, Arkansas had only five medical examiners, spread across five towns, and performed a total of fifty-four examinations that year. Neighboring Louisiana had only one medical examiner, George Kellogg, stationed at New Orleans, who performed sixty-three examinations. All that was about to change. In 1883, Dudley's goal had been to establish four hundred boards of surgeons, believing that number sufficient to handle all the necessary physical examinations. By 1900, there were over 1,500 examining boards across the country. Around the turn of the century, some 139 examining boards could be found in the former Confederacy: nine boards in Alabama, twenty-four in Arkansas, seven in Florida, nine in Georgia, five in Louisiana, seven in Mississippi, fourteen in North Carolina, four in South Carolina, forty-one in Tennessee, thirteen in Texas, and six in Virginia. The dramatic rise in Southern examining boards owed to the passage of the Disability Act. In many ways, it was one of the act's greatest unintended consequences.[21]

The New Law

In the late 1880s, Union veterans collectively pushed for the lowering of eligibility requirements and an increase in the rates of pension. The vehicle of their collective will, the Grand Army of the Republic (GAR), had organized hundreds of thousands of Union veterans into arguably the most powerful congressional lobby in late-nineteenth-century America. GAR posts could be found across the nation. Black veterans were nominally included, with the national GAR platform prohibiting segregated posts, but Black veterans nonetheless could face stinging discrimination. This was especially true in the Deep South, where GAR groups were already embattled and comradeship between white and Black veterans sorely tested. Regardless, all Union veterans benefited from the overt political organizing of the GAR, the fruits of which were borne in the Disability Act of June 1890, its crowning achievement several years in the making.[22]

Grover Cleveland was the first Democrat, and nonveteran, in the White House since the end of the war, and his presidency galvanized opposition among Union veterans. A devoted enemy of federal spending, and above all pension legislation, Cleveland exercised his veto power with alarming frequency while his appointed commissioner of pensions, John C. Black, set about reexamining cases and cutting "unworthy" claimants from the rolls in a series of highly publicized purges. The sum and substance of Cleveland's anti-pension ideology reflected a bone-deep aversion to welfare, patronage, taxes, tariffs, and federal spending. With civil service reform sweeping the nation, Cleveland stylized himself as the reformer's candidate, and indeed peeled away from the fold many reform-minded Republicans wary of the ostensible corruption engendered by unchecked Republican power. The issue of federal military pensions became a litmus test for political loyalties in the mid-1880s. No longer would both Democratic and Republican Party platforms agree on the "just claim" veterans had upon their fellow citizens and the nation. For Democrats after 1884, the federal pension scheme had gone too far, and, in the post-Reconstruction landscape of political culture, the Pension Bureau supplanted the late Freedmen's Bureau as the embodiment of all the evils engendered by federal overreach.[23]

Grover Cleveland was an anti-pension ideologue of breathtaking proportions. He seized on any opportunity to not only reject pension bills but also pontificate on the dangers of excessive federal spending. Even "private" pension bills for individual claimants brought before Congress, usually rubber-stamped, met Cleveland's spirited opposition.[24] Consider the case of Mary Norman, the widow of Turner Norman, a veteran of the Thirty-Fifth USCT. The soldier had suffered a wound at the battle of Olustee, Florida, giving him partial deafness and a fractured jawbone that never healed. According to her 1884 affidavit, her husband "was entitle[d] to a Pension and would Receive it, but he died before it was allowed," and argued "that she is Entitled to the same." Norman assured officials she was a "hard working woman when she is able," but now was so poor and sick she was unable to work. She asked only for "the same Rights and Justice as the other Poor widow[s] of Decease[d] soldiers." Yet her husband had died of drowning while attempting to cross the Roanoke River in North Carolina, technically rendering Norman ineligible for a widow's pension. But she ingeniously argued that his death should be regarded as the extended result of his war-related wounds. A healthy man could have heard warnings shouted from the shore and could have saved himself before the boat sank. The Pension Bureau rejected Mary Norman's pension on the grounds that her husband's death was not directly traceable to his military service. Desperate, she succeeded in getting her representative to sponsor a private bill granting her a pension, one of the hundreds of pension bills vetoed by Cleveland. In his June 1886 veto message to the House Committee on Invalid Pensions, the president questioned how Turner Norman "could have saved his life if he had heard the warning" and concluded that Mary Norman's was "not a proper case for the granting of a pension." The House committee disagreed. "It will not require a stretch of the imagination," they countered, "to see that a man who has suffered for years with a wound in the head would not be able in the time of peril and danger to act with the same degree of promptness and effectiveness as a person not so disabled." Though, strictly speaking, Cleveland's objections hewed closely "to the rulings of the Pension Office," the committee argued that "the equity and justice of this case are with the widow, who is now poor and destitute," and recommended passage of the bill.[25]

Though Cleveland took a rather obscene interest in rejecting private pension bills, he dedicated his greatest energy toward defeating what was called the Dependent Pension Act. A predecessor to the Disability Act of 1890, the original bill would have provided a twelve-dollar monthly pension for total inability to earn subsistence by manual labor to all veterans with at least three months of service. Critics of the bill protested that the size of pensions ought to be proportionate to the claimant's disability—in other words, that it ought to be subject to the sort of physical means-testing that was then applied under the general law system. Passing the House and Senate, it met Cleveland's veto on February 11, 1887. Cleveland's accompanying message quickly secured a place in the anti-pension canon. In it, he bitterly attacked the "evil" bill as a drain on the Treasury and an insult to patriotic sacrifice. The indefinite wording of the law opened the rolls to any veteran who could plausibly claim any disability that incapacitated them "for the performance of labor in such a degree as to render them unable to earn a support." With the effective universalizing of disability claims, "a wide field of inquiry would be opened for the establishment of facts largely within the knowledge of the claimants alone, and there can be no doubt that the race after the pensions offered by this bill would not only stimulate weakness and pretended incapacity for labor but also put a further premium on dishonesty and mendacity." In short, the bill threatened to create an unholy army of thieving, vampiric paupers, drinking from the open veins of the Treasury.[26]

Following Cleveland's assault on the pension bill, veterans mobilized to overthrow the Democrats and made the 1888 election a national referendum on the pension question. Benjamin Harrison's victory in that contest owed in large part to the support he garnered from the GAR and wider veteran community. In return, Harrison appointed James B. Tanner head of the Pension Bureau. Tanner immediately earned notoriety for generous administrative rulings and for proposing that Congress increase rates of pension. He likewise lent his support to the bill that would become the Disability Act. In control of the House and Senate, Republicans in the "Billion Dollar Congress" passed the Disability Act on June 27, 1890. It created a parallel pension system, commonly known as the new law, that operated alongside the general law of July 14, 1862. Under the new law, Union pension eligibility was not restricted to war-related ailments. Much of the language was drawn directly from the 1887 bill. For example, it defined a pensionable disability as one that "incapacitates them from the performance of manual labor in such a degree as to render them unable to earn a support." Yet in a significant revision of its parent bill, the Disability Act allowed for gradations of disability, from minor to total, as opposed to the flat twelve-dollar rate of the 1887 bill. As critics feared, removing the service-origin requirement of the general law significantly lowered the threshold for entry and allowed virtually any veteran with at least ninety days of service to apply. The number of pensioners on the rolls nearly doubled to over 966,000 claimants within three years of the law's passage. Pension expenditures soared to $157 million in the year 1893, consuming more than 40 percent of the federal budget. By the turn of the century, three-quarters of all surviving Union veterans drew a pension, and by 1915, an astonishing 93 percent. In that year, the federal government's $5 billion in expenditures on pensions surpassed what it had spent to prosecute the Civil War itself.[27]

For all its acclaimed liberality then and since, the Disability Act simultaneously heightened the scrutiny of medical examinations and displaced stories of wartime suffering. Through its sheer volume of applicants, the new law inaugurated the most ambitious federal project of biomedical data collection on its citizens to date: heights, weights, and ages; eye, hair, and skin colors; rates of pulse and respiration; and so on. And these were only the "objective conditions" called for in the bureau's standardized forms. Claimants also found every inch of their bodies assessed for impairments, each receiving its own rating out of eighteen. Their reports, tucked securely in each claimant's case file, were readily accessible for reevaluation at will. Unsatisfactory reports frequently required correction. Thus in 1915, a full half century after the Civil War, the pension commissioner called on an examining board to give greater details on the ailments of the formerly enslaved veteran Abram Haywood, who had first applied for a pension in 1889. "Give condition of muscles, tendons, and joints," the commissioner instructed, "describe fully and in detail all objective symptoms of rheumatism and disease of heart. Is the heart normal in size, location and function?" he inquired. "Do you find cardiac murmurs? Does soldier appear to be well nourished? State condition of lungs and kidneys. Rate separately every disability found. Show clearly the degree of disability for the performance of manual labor due to the pensioned causes alone." To the managerial class of the Pension Bureau, the barrage of measurements to determine the worth of one's disability required not only medical expertise but the most scrupulous of bureaucratic safeguards.[28]

A tidal wave of public opposition swelled in response to the Disability Act. In the weeks surrounding its passage, for example, the staunchly anti-pension *New York Times* argued that instead of saving veterans from poverty, the bill would actually "offer a large premium for professional pauperism, and the number of the unworthy who will receive its benefits will be so large that they will throw discredit upon all who share with them." Other critics complained of "the pollution of the pension roll" with all of the "unworthy" veterans unscathed by war, and that the new law was "socialism of an extreme and dangerous type." Social Darwinists were especially aggrieved, arguing that welfare or charity should come only from private charitable institutions, if at all. Because many Gilded Age Americans saw poverty as an individual moral problem, and not a result of greater social and economic forces, the dependent individual could rightly be held in contempt. One critic writing in the *North American Review* reminded readers of General O. O. Howard's advice to veterans, that "as much real patriotism may be displayed by refraining in times of peace from inflicting unnecessary burdens on the country as by coming to her defense in time of war."[29]

The Black press, however, celebrated the passage of the Disability Act for embracing the thousands of Black veterans and heirs struggling to obtain their pensions under the old system. Black editors from Washington to New Orleans instructed their readers on the parameters and procedures of the new law. Many claims agents and attorneys took to advertising in those same papers, sensing an untapped and potentially lucrative market in new Black pensioners. Tanner himself, upon leaving office, opened a claims agency in the capital and regularly solicited in the city's most prominent Black newspaper, the *Bee*.[30] Yet in Washington, as elsewhere, it was Black attorneys— men and women alike—who proved especially adept at acquiring such new claimants. With the burdensome threshold of the general finally breached, a massive rent-seeking industry arose to facilitate Black pension claims under the Disability Act.[31]

Medical Testimony

Navigating the two pension systems could prove difficult, especially for freedpeople in the rural South with limited literacy and resources. Some, such as John Floyd, were directed to the new law when they sought compensation for a wartime affliction. While he was with the Thirty-Third USCT in South Carolina, Floyd had contracted pleurisy from exposure near Beaufort, and for a month thereafter he was unable to do any duty. He was treated in camp by assistant surgeon John Milton Hawks, a "radical anti-slavery man" according to the regiment's head surgeon. Floyd left the army with rheumatism, selftreating as he could. In seeking a general law pension in the 1890s, he solicited testimony from his former regimental surgeon. Yet Hawks had forgotten that he treated Floyd at Beaufort, and Hawks was likewise perplexed by Floyd's decision to pursue a general law pension case after the passage of the new law. "You probably know about the Act of 27 June 1890," Hawks wrote to Floyd. "Under that law you can get a pension if you need it now, for total disability, you get $12. a month," and "you do not need to prove that you were disabled or sick in the service." Though recognizing Floyd's apparent need for a pension, Hawks was unwilling to file an affidavit testifying to having treated Floyd in the service, thereby undercutting Floyd's bid for a general law pension. In all likelihood, despite the warm familiarity of his letter, Hawks probably did not remember having treated Floyd so long ago, and the new pension system provided Hawks an excuse to abandon the rigors of proving service origin. But his former patient in turn had to abandon the potentially higher rates of the general law.[32]

Such cases notwithstanding, many formerly enslaved veterans were able to successfully gain the support and advocacy of Southern white physicians in their bids for a pension. James Richardson of the One Hundred Thirty-Sixth USCT, for instance, enjoyed such a relationship with a physician by the name of E. S. Porter. Richardson first came to Porter around 1880, when he complained of rheumatism and coughing up blood. In his 1897 affidavit, Porter certified that he has "known James Richardson for 14 or 15 years & have been his family physician for the same length of time," treating him when "he is down as long as 3 weeks at a time from hemorrhage of the lungs." Porter explained how "rheumatism stiffens him up very badly. At times he is not able to go about at all." The examining board had found no ratable disability in Richardson's respiratory or intestinal systems before he brought Porter into the process. But with Porter's help, Richardson began receiving a pension the following year.[33]

While some Black veterans leaned heavily on a single physician of long acquaintance in their bid for a disability pension, others alternated between two or more as they sought more favorable assessments. Richard Anderson, for example, solicited help from two physicians in Louisiana, variously asking for affidavits to support his pending disability claim. Anderson told the examining board he was "not able to perform hard manual labor regularly," and although he managed to "do so at times," his "foot causes considerable trouble" and he would "sometimes experience pain of a shooting character" in his leg. His condition severely inhibited his work as a blacksmith and wheelwright. In his medical testimony on Anderson's behalf, Jefferson gave a full account of Anderson's physical ailments, from chronic rheumatism to sciatica to heart palpitations. "In short," declared Jefferson, "he is a 'physical wreck' and is not able to earn a support at manual labor." After years of rejection, Anderson had another physician, T. N. Brian, testify. Brian, who had just started working as Anderson's family physician, seemed to hold little back in his affidavits. Anderson is "not worth any thing as manual laborer," Brian claimed; "the old man is so stiff he is unable to do any work at all he can't do a man's work at any thing nor can he work even one hour." Brian's gendered description of the former slave's working ability proved to be an effective and frequently deployed tactic among the physician-advocates of Southern Black claimants. Whether or not individual racial bias played into such easy associations, the routine classification of freedmen as physically deteriorating aligned with dominant currents in American professional medicine, that Black men and women freed from white control suffered immense bodily and mental affliction. Earning a pension, then, required toeing the line of this racist fantasy.[34]

Relatively little is known about the health and healthcare practices of ordinary Black Southerners in the final three decades of the nineteenth century. Much of this owes to the fact that for white doctors the number of Black patients dropped precipitously after abolition.[35] Thomas P. Bailey of the South Carolina Lowcountry, for one, refused to see any Black patients in his postwar practice. Others agreed to administer care to dozens of sharecroppers, signing year-to-year contracts. Alternatively, many Black Southerners pooled their resources into benevolent associations whose leadership would then contract with various physicians on behalf of its members. Yet many former slaves could not afford to hire physicians, or there were not any in their vicinity, or they simply did not believe those physicians did any good, as they often commented to examining boards curious about the claimant's lack of postwar medical evidence. Thus Edward Brown "often wanted to employ a physician, but was too poor to do so," and at any rate "none lived within many miles." In any event, if and when they did manage to receive care, freedpeople could by and large expect the same kind of condescension and suspicion they experienced in the days of slavery.[36]

In this racially charged medical terrain, formerly enslaved claimants demonstrated a keen sense of how to negotiate for the right medical testimony. Not only did individual claimants garner support from multiple physicians, but in many instances, pension documents reveal group efforts among former slaves using the same physician. In addition to his work for Richard Anderson, for instance, Dr. Jefferson treated many other members of the Ninety-Third. Veterans of the One Hundred Fourth in South Carolina relied heavily on two local physicians in particular. Freedpeople were thus able to take advantage of the adversarial nature of the pension process by garnering support from practicing physicians known among their comrades to be reliable and successful advocates for their disability claims. On occasion, this brought them into contact with enterprising practitioners similarly looking to exploit the pension process. In Vicksburg, for example, a physician by the name of Carter J. Hill kept a close watch on Black claimants leaving their pension board medical examinations with low ratings. Hill would contact these disappointed claimants, offering to privately examine them and fill out an affidavit testifying to their total disability, all for the reasonable fee of $2.50. Regardless of whether they turned to such figures, it is abundantly clear that formerly enslaved claimants in the South seldom let the judgment of a medical examining board stand unchallenged, electing instead to offer their own estimation of disability supported by testimony from physicians more or less of their choosing.[37]

In addition to seeking more favorable medical testimony, Black veterans also persistently applied for increases in their pension rates. Although applications for increase were common among white claimants as well, the ability of former slaves to officially challenge a medical diagnosis—and to have that dissent registered with the federal government, sometimes to direct material benefit—marked a tremendous departure from the days of slavery, when

Black men and women enjoyed little bodily autonomy. Through pension attorneys, freedpeople filed declarations for increase to both general law and new law claims. Washington Moore, a formerly enslaved veteran of the Ninety-Third, began drawing an eight-dollar pension under the Disability Act, yet he believed he merited a higher rating, suffering as he was from rheumatism and heart palpitations. To that end, Moore first asked his comrades' regular physician, the aforementioned Dr. Jefferson, for an affidavit in 1894. To Moore's delight, Jefferson agreed with his conclusion, finding his "muscular system debilitated generally" and adding that he was also "a sufferer from chronic rheumatism in the joints of the long bones on both sides." Explaining that Moore was unable "to do any manual labor at wages that will afford him a support," the physician's evaluation convinced the examining board and the bureau administrators and earned the claimant a slight increase in his pension. But Moore was still unsatisfied and continued pressing for an even greater increase throughout the rest of the 1890s and into the next century.[38]

If most Black applicants could expect an unfavorable rating from the bureau's medical examiners, then the bureau could expect pushback. Take the case of William Wallace, who applied for an increase to his eight-dollar pension in December 1898. Wallace requested "that he be favored with another medical examination with the view of determining his right to $12 per month, the full rate allowed under the Act of June 27, 1890, for the reason that he is now totally unable to do any manual labor." Isaiah Taylor likewise considered himself "entitled to a re-rating" and argued through his own claims agent that "the rate originally allowed him was too low and not commensurate with the extent of his disability, nor in proportion to the rate allowed to others for similar and equivalent [disabilities]." Taylor's brief reference to other pension claimants underscores an important component of the administrative politics of Black pension claimants in the post-slavery South. It suggests that in addition to frequently using the same pension agent or consulting physician, Black claimants also shared their ratings and experiences of medical examinations with other pensioners, discussing successful tactics and strategies, alerting each other to unfair and unequal treatment. In doing so, they not only took examiners to task on the issue of inconsistency but also parlayed that inconsistency to their advantage.[39]

Working Ability

Freedpeople's collective struggles for adequate relief suffused the daily institutional functioning of the Pension Bureau in the post-slavery South. Within a year of the Disability Act, the Southern Division reported receiving nearly 119,000 claims, no longer disaggregating USCT claims from those of white Unionists. Together with 186,000 pending claims, the division had nearly 306,000 claims on hand on July 1, 1891. Under the new law, 29,238 veterans had submitted original claims to the division, along with 17,295 widows; nearly 15,000 veterans and 6,500 widows submitted "additional" claims under the new law, that is, claims with supplemental evidence, a total of nearly 68,000 claims. The division also reported over forty-three thousand claims for increase. Although the Disability Act presented Black Southerners with a wider avenue to pursue their claims, as suggested by these figures, certain modes of engagement had narrowed. Under the Disability Act, the very idea of work took on a new meaning, becoming at once more abstracted and more embodied.[40]

In the late nineteenth century, the American medical profession helped construct an enduring medicalization of disability that turned a social and political problem into an individual and biological one. The bureau's physical means-testing further contributed to the medicalization of disability by requiring claimants to present their own bodily impairments as the source of their economic hardships in a faultless political economy. They did not do so alone. In assembling outside physicians and demanding reratings, freedpeople insisted upon their own understandings of disability and how their ailments impacted their ability to perform manual labor despite a strong work ethic. And although they were long accustomed to having their laboring capacities intensely monitored and scrutinized as enslaved workers, never before was the terrain of struggle so strictly limited to their very bodies—and, importantly, only the bodies of male applicants.[41]

Decades before pension board examinations, talk of able-bodiedness and "soundness" pervaded the South, from the slave labor camps and slave markets to the courtrooms. Enslavers and managers rated their chattels "by the hand," meaning how fully they could perform standard fieldwork. Those imagined to fall short of full capacity would be rated anywhere from a half to a quarter hand. Enslavers typically exempted from field labor those men and women with significant bodily impairments, deploying them elsewhere on the estate. Some, for example, were tasked with care of kin or with miscellaneous jobs. Willie Wallace of Pine Bluff remembered how his father's disability prevented him from field labor and was instead ordered to "bring the children out to the field to be suckled." Fellow Arkansas slave Frank Fikes, whose foot had been impaired since birth, spent his adolescence tending to the other enslaved children. "I could not get around like the other children, so my work was to nurse all of the time. Sometimes, as fast as I got one baby to sleep I would have to nurse another to sleep." (Although he admitted it was relatively easy work compared with what his able-bodied peers were put to, Fikes commented that there were likely one hundred families on his captor's estate, "and nearly every family had a baby, so I had a big job after all.") Just as the practices of Southern slavery blurred conventional gendered divisions of labor, so too were functions of disablement similarly bound to the political economy of slavery. Rather than a flattened binary of disabled or able-bodied, then, enslaved men and women found any working ability they had to be carefully exploited by the enslaver class.[42]

In everyday struggles on the slave labor camps, enslaved people with physical impairments knew how to manipulate them to their advantage. After dislocating his knee as a child, James Lindsay Smith was considered crippled and given the menial task of scaring crows away from the crops. Wishing for a break one lonely Sabbath, he first thought he "would feign sickness; then I said to myself, that will not do, for they will give me something that will physic [treat] me to death." So Smith "devised another scheme," deciding upon self-injury. He struck his foot against a stone and "made out that I had broken my leg again." Smith lay in his bedroom, pretending "that I was in so much pain that I could not raise myself," and won the sympathetic attention of his mistress. Then his eternally suspicious enslaver arrived and ordered another enslaved worker to "bring him the rawhide." But his mistress, convinced by Smith's wails, put a halt to the threats of whipping and fieldwork until Smith's reinjured leg improved. For two weeks, he remained in bed, during which time the murder had departed.[43]

Being physically unfit sometimes gave some enslaved men and women a measure of autonomy not extended to more able-bodied enslaved people. Calvin West remembered his father's leg being "crippled" with rheumatism. This apparently permitted the elder West the freedom to move about the slave labor camps and markets of eastern Arkansas, for an able-bodied enslaved man would have been quickly profiled as a potential runaway. The elder West, however, posed no such threat. And he was more "useful" selling goods in the marketplace than performing small tasks around the grounds of the estate. And so, every Sunday he would "load up a small cart wid cider and ginger cakes and go sell it out." Despite the occasional harassment by slave patrols and suspicious planters, West was an active participant in what historians call "the slaves' economy."[44]

Disability was everywhere in the slave South, hidden in plain sight. Yet precisely because of its ubiquity and fluidity, its near-seamless folding into the political economy of slavery, disability defied easy classification. The prominent Savannah doctor Juriah Harriss complained as late as 1858 that physicians were constantly called upon to provide medical testimony on enslaved people bought and sold in the market, and the lack of a uniform system for determining soundness was an embarrassment to the profession. He attempted therefore to create a standard guide for use in slave markets and Southern courtrooms. In a series of articles, Harriss differentiated exhaustively between soundness and health. Whereas health referred to well-being, soundness signified an unimpaired ability to labor. One could be healthy but unsound (as with an amputated leg) or unhealthy but sound (as with a benign tumor). Harriss cited rheumatism and asthma as examples of two widespread conditions of "chronic or constitutional character" that rendered the body unsound. When applied to the enslaved, unsoundness meant, more precisely, that the condition *"incapacitates the negro for the performance of the usual duties of his calling, viz: hard labor."* It was this understanding of soundness, of health as an abstracted ability to perform equally abstract manual labor, that became the dominant paradigm in medical examinations for the Pension Bureau.[45]

As historians Walter Johnson and Ariela Gross have revealed, medical professionals were staple figures in the antebellum slave markets and courthouses, where men such as Juriah Harriss offered their services in the diagnosing and "warranting" of an enslaved person's health. "Slave masters and litigants wished that slaves' bodies were easy to read," writes Gross, "that all defects and characteristics could be plain and apparent on the surface." But "slaves' bodies contained hidden mysteries," and the enslaved themselves were liable to conceal or manipulate. Increasingly, the courts believed that only medical expertise could solve the problem of "the unknowable slave body." Buyers, too, hired medical examiners or adopted diagnostic tactics in the midst of a sale. They forced enslaved people into motion, at once evaluating their motor skills and imagining their physical performance in the cotton field or gin house. Those who survived slavery, including John Brown of Georgia, recalled how he and his fellow enslaved men and women for sale were made "to show themselves off; dance, jump, walk, leap, squat, tumble, and twist about, that the buyer may see they have no stiff joints, or other physical defect." Physicians privileged physicality over testimony, relying upon the demystifying powers of the medical gaze to cut through the dissembling tendencies of Black subjects.[46]

The connective tissue between the slave market investigators and the Pension Bureau examining boards was unbroken. Black claimants as well became fluent in the technocratic language of soundness, readily invoking the different metrics for quantifying disability in their depositions and affidavits. When

August Burke made his bid for a pension, his fellow former slaves of Beaufort enslaver Randolph Sams were called upon to rate him. One former fellow slave believed Burke's "disabilities have kept him from doing more than 1/3 manual labor," while the other commented "I think he has done 1/2 the work of an able man since discharge." When another ex-slave claimant, Arthur Kelly, alleged failing eyesight and rheumatism, his former fellow slave rated Kelly as "1/2 hand in the field," as would another who testified on his behalf, contrasting Kelly's stout, healthy condition before entering the army with his present condition. Now the claimant was not "capable of doing a man's work," and his fellow freedman rated him as a "1/2 hand." The bureau's medical examinations relied heavily on gendered notions of labor, conceptually flattening a wide range of different tasks into a question of how well a man could perform hard manual labor in field or factory. Robert Green claimed that his injuries "greatly interfered" with his "ability to make a living by manual work," barely eking out a subsistence as the "head of the trash gang and over the women when making hay." Like the witnesses for Arthur Kelly, Green emphasized how his disabilities emasculated him, relegating him to not only a poorly compensated plantation job but also one typically held by women and other dependents.[47]

Claimants and their allies thus made direct connections between physical inability to perform labor and subsequent inability to make a living, bypassing the most common criticism against white claimants in the North, that many were of the managerial class and hence did not rely on any sort of physical labor.[48] But in the post–Civil War South, even able-bodied freedpeople had a tenuous income—indeed, a tenuous existence. Any physical impairments could have dire consequences for themselves and their families. Former slaves typically emphasized as much as they could about how their disabilities kept them from earning a subsistence, per the language of the Disability Act itself, which required the claimant to prove, in cases of total disability, incapacitation for manual labor to the extent that the claimant is rendered "unable to earn a support." Charles Ballard and Adam Finely assured the bureau that their comrade Richard Dargan "was a man who always endeavored to make a living" but that his advanced age and disabilities forced him to quit. Now "he is entirely dependent on his pension money for a living." So, too, with Sampson Cuthbert, who struggled to survive on his small farm in Beaufort. Men who had worked alongside Cuthbert in slavery and freedom believed his disability rendered him not "half as strong a man as he used to be," and that he could barely perform "more than one fourth of the work that a strong man can do." Initially unsuccessful, Cuthbert acquainted himself with a white physician in 1893, who later made an affidavit on his behalf, explaining how "the claimant is a farmer by occupation, but in consequence of disabilities . . . he has been obliged to suspend all forms of labor within the past year and depends solely upon his wife & friends for a livelihood while undergoing medical treatment."[49]

The Pension Bureau reinforced a gender hierarchy by associating men with work and disability, and women with widowhood, motherhood, and dependency. Unlike the veterans' disability-centered system, for widows' pensions the task was to prove dependency, a reliance on the wages of others. Just as talk of laboring abilities filled veterans' pensions, the claims of widows were saturated with notions of sexual propriety and respectability. Thus while they did not undergo physical examinations as their husbands did, Black widows were indeed subject to a state policing of their bodies through their most intimate of associations. After an 1882 law made remarriage or cohabitation a disqualification for widow's pensions, policing could take the form of bureau officials intruding into their homes, seeking proof of infidelity or immorality.[50]

And yet, above and beyond meeting the requirements of proper Union widowhood, many Black widows surprisingly did in fact confront the same challenge as their late husbands, that of proving physical disability. In navigating the state's gendered regime, many formerly enslaved women pursued, expanded, and even changed the disabilities of their deceased husbands in order to secure a higher rate of pension for themselves. For example, to receive her widow's pension, Sallie Ancrum had to prove, before both the Pension Bureau and the House Committee on Invalid Pensions, that her deceased husband enlisted as a sound man, contracted ailments during the war, and was unjustly denied a pension. Harriet Butler confronted a similar problem. Her husband, George Butler of the Ninety-Second, claimed to have contracted "blood poison" at Port Hudson, Louisiana, around April 1864. The affliction broke down his constitution, resulting in acute rheumatism, general debility, and diseases of the stomach, liver, and lungs. He frequently coughed up blood. Butler's application for a general law pension failed, as did his claim for a pension under the new law. After multiple appearances before medical examiners, Butler finally managed to convince the board that he was ratably disabled, and he began receiving eight dollars per month in September 1892. He filed a claim for increase in October of that year. Six years later—one and a half years after Butler's death—his claim was rejected.[51]

For Harriet Butler to receive a widow's pension, she had to prove legal widowhood as well as dependency. The Pension Bureau deployed a special examiner to verify her marriage to George Butler, that they had not divorced, and that she had not remarried or "taken up" since his passing. The special examiner had a difficult time establishing her eligibility. Yet as Harriet Butler made her case, she continued to press her deceased husband's disability claim as well. Veterans who died while drawing a pension from the Disability Act of 1890 conferred upon widowed applicants the standard rate of eight dollars. When Butler pushed for a bureau acknowledgment of total disability, she was hoping to earn years of back pay when her late husband was denied his petitions for increase. In April 1896, a month after the bureau rejected her deceased husband's petition for increase, she filed an appeal. In it, she argued that "the medical and other testimony on file clearly shows that the claimant was wholly and totally incapacitated for the performance of any manual labor." The Board of Pension Appeals rejected her claim on March 1, 1898, citing the 2/18 rating given to George Butler during his last and final board examination. The ruling also dismissed the medical testimony of his physician, who at Harriet's request had submitted an affidavit stating that he treated the claimant for various ailments in the winters of 1890 to 1893. Butler relied on the medical evaluation of her husband's physician against that of the board. The Pension Bureau, however, privileged the findings of the board. With the help of her pension attorney, Butler made a second appeal on April 1, again citing the existence of compelling medical evidence of bodily disability beyond the board's findings.[52]

Although Butler was unsuccessful in securing a higher disability rating for her deceased husband, her efforts speak volumes about the trials faced by formerly enslaved women as they navigated the pension system. Applicants such as Harriet Butler faced challenges that were at once relational and bodily. First, she needed testimony from as many witnesses as possible to corroborate her account of faithful marriage that began between two enslaved people on different slave labor camps in Livingston Parish. Second, she needed to claim dependency. Harriet had been dependent on her husband, she argued, but now was "entirely dependent upon her own personal exertions for her support." (For women at the time, being self-dependent did not translate to independence but rather even greater dependency.) And finally, like so many veteran applicants, she relied on pension attorneys and outside physicians to help make a claim for a higher disability rating.[53]

Sometimes, as in the case of Harriet Butler, the task was to prove the deceased husband had been given an unfair rating by the federal examining board. Other times, widows attempted to shift their pensions from the eight-dollar rate of the new law system to the twelve-dollar rate of the general law.[54]

Sarah Higgins was one who thus worked to recast her husband's death in a more remunerative light. Her husband, David Higgins, had officially died of heart failure in February 1897. He had been drawing a general law pension for an injury to his leg sustained in service—not heart disease. Two physicians had treated Higgins near the end of his life. One of them, she alleged, had promised to give her a medical affidavit stating that the affliction of the veteran's foot ultimately produced the heart disease that killed him. Yet the physician refused to testify on her behalf, likely unwilling to claim that an injury to the leg could directly cause heart failure. Still, Higgins argued in her appeal that the physician did after all believe that the leg injury caused his death. Though bureau officials regarded such cases as fraudulent, even criminal, there are more important lessons to draw from the ordeal. Like their husbands, Black widows were not passive receptors of federal diagnosis. Although spared from medical examinations, many labored to continue their husbands' efforts for higher and more equitable disability ratings. The singular persistence demonstrated by ex-slave widows in waging their two-fronted contests changed the size and shape of the Pension Bureau in the South, necessitating more resources and staff to adjudicate their claims.[55]

The pension system created by the Disability Act effectively functioned as workmen's compensation at a time when a vast array of institutions began experimenting with a new body of jurisprudence known as accident law. As legal historian John Fabian Witt has argued, the hazards of industrialization generated a profound crisis for free labor ideologues. Risk could no longer be shouldered entirely by "freely" contracted employees who jeopardized their lives and the livelihoods of their families. Workers were increasingly seen as entitled to safe workplaces, and any damages that befell them were to be properly compensated.[56] The seat of such legal reform was decidedly in the urban North, particularly the Northeast, which boasted the highest levels of industrialization, leaving Black Southerners outside the boundaries of tort law. Injured Black workers turned when they could to the Pension Bureau— even before the Disability Act. Here the story of Tyler Sewall is instructive. His case emerged during a lengthy congressional investigation into the alleged mismanagement and fraudulent activity of the Pension Bureau in 1881. Sewall suffered a wound in his arm while serving in the First USCT and applied for a pension in late July 1874 on account of having lost the arm due to mortification of the wound. Yet a special examiner discovered that Sewall had his afflicted arm torn off by a threshing machine at his work. Had Sewall retained his arm with its clearly evidenced wartime wound, he might have secured a pension, but having lost that same arm to a workplace accident a decade after the war, and before the new law of 1890, he never received compensation. Nor, for that matter, did his widow.[57]

Although Tyler Sewall was repeatedly disparaged as ignorant in the bureau official's congressional testimony, his attempt to earn a federal pension actually showed considerable ingenuity, a hallmark of Black administrative politics in the emancipated South. No doubt, countless applicants exaggerated their incapacities verbally and physically. Some, like Sewall, adapted a postwar injury to a wartime one. Others impersonated soldiers, or claimed to have served themselves, presenting plausible wartime injuries and ailments—or making them by turning a case of scrofula into a gunshot wound, for instance. Others falsely testified (alongside other witnesses) that an applicant was the mother of a deceased soldier or, in other cases, that a widow had not remarried. Scores of Black claimants living in the vicinity of Baton Rouge were swept into criminal prosecution after the bureau discovered their pension attorney, one Amos L. Wheeler, had routinely forged the signature of a local notary public in order to expedite their claims. Others were likely complicit in working with claims agents to fabricate affidavits testifying to a veteran's death from war-related injuries. The tactics were as innumerable as they were illegal. But to confine our attention merely to the bare allegations of fraud would be to forsake entirely the politics behind such decisions, from the solidarities they relied on to the exigencies that drove many to take such a chance in the first place.[58]

Most of the stories showcasing freedpeople's daring efforts first passed through the legal waystation of the Pension Bureau. For years after the war, the bureau deployed investigators from the Special Service Division to examine suspicious and potentially fraudulent claims. Positive findings in most cases simply resulted in the termination of pending applications or claimants being dropped from the rolls and their stipends reimbursed to the Treasury. In others, such as those involving perjury, the Pension Bureau submitted cases to the Justice Department for criminal prosecution. Perjury convictions could result in fines of up to $2,000 and up to five years of imprisonment. In 1881, Commissioner Dudley created the Division of Special Examinations "to aid in prosecuting offenders against the pension law," thereafter increasing the size and capacity of the division and hence the number of investigations and cases dispatched for criminal prosecution. By the next year, the division specially examined nearly 1,900 claims and forwarded 176 for prosecution; in 1884, it made nearly 7,500 investigations with over 275 sent to the Justice Department. But if Dudley's foray into professionalizing the special examination process blazed a bureaucratic trail, his successor, John C. Black, paved it into a superhighway. Black's administration investigated over thirty-one thousand claims in 1887 alone, an explicit show of force meant to inspire, in his words, "a wholesome regard for the power of the Government."[59]

But left unsaid in dozens of self-congratulatory reports from division chiefs and commissioners was this fundamental irony: charging hundreds of individual pensioners and applicants and attorneys with fraud was an effective way to at once distract from accusations of unfairness or mismanagement and to shore up the legitimacy of the pension system itself. In this light, the antifraud efforts of the 1880s were a training ground for confronting the unprecedented movement in the 1890s to universalize pensions to freedpeople.

Abnormality and Abjection

Applying for a pension entailed considerable risk for Black claimants too desperate to reject it. Yet all of the larger structural forces of political economy that rendered people desperate were explicitly stripped away by the bureau's process of physical means-testing. References to labor arrangements or markets, for instance, had to be kept purposefully vague, focusing instead on how one's specific, individuated disability hindered their physical power to labor as normal. Disabled persons in the late nineteenth century struggled against an emerging concept of normality. The concept had emerged in the professional realm around midcentury to replace classical notions of the ideal with notions of the average garnered from the new science of statistics. The celebrated anthropometric studies of the U.S. Sanitary Commission after the war drew a battery of measurements from thousands of soldiers, white and Black, native-born and foreign, in one of the earliest endeavors to establish the parameters of the "normal" body. Normality grew into a powerful concept medically and culturally. It was applied to nearly every aspect of life in the age of industrialization. Medical textbooks bearing titles such as *The Human Mechanism* (1906) propagated the modern idea that the body behaved mechanistically, obedient to factory-like physiological laws. The very image of the machine, with interchangeable parts and interchangeable workers, had considerable salience in the functionalist culture of Gilded Age America, permeating cities, factories, and bodies alike.[60]

By the turn of the century, new biomedical technologies enabled scientists and physicians to measure bodies and bodily functions with greater precision, in turn constructing the biomedical standard of the normal body. Under the newly minted paradigm of normality, disability was regarded not as unnatural but instead as a deviation from an able-bodied norm, marking the objectively substandard as worthy of exclusion. The Pension Bureau adopted and enforced this view of disability as an individual deficit from a fixed bodily norm. In so doing, the bureau's examining surgeons helped establish what scholars of disability call the medical model, which locates disability in the bodies of individuals, a medical problem the individual must overcome. By so medicalizing disability, the larger forces of political economy that render someone with impairments disabled were, and are, deliberately hidden.[61]

Far from a fixed definition deployed consistently by the modern state, however, millions of ground-level negotiations defined and produced disability. Though the Pension Bureau established uniform rubrics of disability, it depended on the accuracy of the examinations performed by thousands of physicians throughout the nation. These examinations were thus profound sites of negotiation over what constituted disability; contests, in effect, between the medical model and the socioeconomic model. Formerly enslaved claimants readily grasped the bodily politics of medical examinations. They sought to influence the medical board's disability rating with testimonials from outside physicians and neighbors and their own accounts of how their afflictions impaired their ability to perform manual labor, and with astounding frequency, they challenged board ratings with applications for increase.[62]

Just as the medical profession aided the Pension Bureau in establishing and enforcing the parameters of disability, so too did the bureau help establish the authority of the medical profession. Indeed, the bureau worked to enshrine medical orthodoxy in the United States at a time of intense competition between several schools of medical thought and practice, especially between the regulars, or orthodox practitioners, and the homeopaths, increasingly known as unorthodox practitioners. Differences between the two sectarian groups were somewhat exaggerated, but their respective members perceived vast and irreconcilable differences in training, treatment, and philosophy. By the early 1870s, regulars began to oust homeopaths from their positions on state medical licensing boards and national medical organizations such as the American Medical Association. Yet the forces of unorthodoxy remained, and even grew, such that their mere presence invoked a challenge to the regulars' aspirational monopoly on medical authority. Commissioner Henry Van Aernam, himself a regular physician, dismissed a number of homeopathic practitioners from service as medical examiners of the Pension Bureau. In March 1871, the *New National Era* took note of Van Aernam's removal of two surgeons, "not because they are bad surgeons and pathologists, not because they cannot tell whether a man is sick or wounded, or shamming illness and simulating injuries, but because they 'do not belong to the school of medicine recognized by this bureau.'" Decrying what the *Era* deemed "medical bigotry," the editors argued that because "pension surgeons do not administer medicine, and as their qualifications are those of education and general knowledge, the removal of these two surgeons was unjustifiable." The Black press joined other voices in calling for a more ecumenical approach to staffing pension boards.[63]

Such an approach indeed prevailed after Van Aernam left office. His successor took care to note in his annual reports to Congress how "greater than ordinary care has been exercised to secure men of broad views, liberal education, and thorough professional acquirements, without regard to theories or schools." By the 1870s, as detailed by medical historian Paul Starr, the orthodox and homeopathic practitioners had fought each other to a draw, and the two sides began working out an uneasy compromise that allowed both groups to thrive independently by restricting state medical licensing to professionally educated physicians such as themselves. As states began to more closely regulate medical practice in the 1880s, the Pension Bureau continued prescribing rules and regulations for their own examiners, who, of course, only served as federal surgeons part-time. Ironically, the popularity of unorthodox physicians grew with their embattled, outsider status; once peaceably ensconced in the halls of medical power, they quickly lost the good will of the public. By the first decade of the twentieth century, they lost numbers and clout, uncharitably regarded by many as relics of a prescientific past. Meanwhile, regular physicians and their allied researchers devised striking new biomedical technologies, rendering their methods even more authoritative. Brandishing stethoscopes, laryngoscopes, and an assortment of other diagnostic tools, the orthodox prided themselves on their newfound arsenal of medical objectivity. The myriad measurements that went into defining a man and identifying his abnormalities brought a new kind of precision to the medical profession that contemporary critics found hard to doubt and easy to celebrate.[64]

The elaborate disability ratings system, with all its bureaucratic checks and balances, its cascade of explanatory treatises and handbooks, never enjoyed the unquestioned authority its administrators hoped it would achieve. Subjectivity was the lifeblood of the ostensibly objective arrangement of disability ratings. Predictably, the demand for medical examinations skyrocketed after the passage of the Disability Act, as did the intractable problems endemic to the examination system. As the commissioner noted in 1891, the bureau ordered over 603,000 medical examinations in the past year, but just over 475,000 were performed by the overworked examining boards. All the while, the bureau demanded "more complete descriptions than has been heretofore required." Of those 603,000 examinations ordered, nearly one-quarter (132,816) were called for by the Southern Division, showing disproportionately high activity among the largely Black pensioner class. This activity did not result in disproportionately high admittance to the rolls, however. Only 70,460 of those claims were forwarded to the board of review after a medical examination, and of those submitted claims, fewer than forty-six thousand were admitted; the rest were either rejected or turned over for special examination, a roughly 35 percent success rate. Many more would-be pensioners still awaited their first appearance before an examining board.[65]

Commissioners struggled to rein in the centrifugal forces of the sprawling, semiprivate medical examination system. Although no plans matched the boldness of Commissioner Bentley's proposals in the mid-1870s, many sought to exert greater oversight over the examining boards. In 1896, for example, one commissioner suggested sending a contingent of experts from the Medical Division in Washington "to visit and instruct the 1,285 boards throughout the country." In place of this prodigious, if not impossible, task and others like it, the bureau settled on circulating ever more detailed instructions to its boards. This paltry remedy failed in pathetic fashion. Henry Clay Evans of Tennessee, one of the most influential pension commissioners to hold the office (1897–1902), complained that despite the instructions furnished to the highly competent boards, the surgeons simply "read and understand their instructions differently." In his 1898 annual report to Congress, Evans cited a notorious case study that had been recently conducted by the bureau. An individual pensioner in the North was sent before four different examining boards within a forty-eight-hour period. The reports, all thoroughly detailed and all unanimously agreed upon by the board members, revealed the same applicant entitled to four different rates of pension: zero, eight, seventeen, and twenty-four dollars. Hence the common complaint of inconsistency between boards. "It is beyond the power of this Bureau," Evans concluded, "to cause uniform ratings for like disabilities, though the very greatest care is exercised by the Bureau and skilled men employed to examine papers as reported by the 4,600 physicians employed throughout the country." The commissioner, widely admired for being the "watchdog" of the Treasury, thus partly conceded that the Pension Bureau was indeed an unwieldy beast threatening to drain the federal coffers one arbitrary rating at a time.[66]

The decentralized, semiprivatized examining boards left this most critical stage of the pension process susceptible to local influence. Evidence suggests that many veterans complained of unsatisfactory treatment at the hands of the bureau's gatekeepers. Some claimants accused boards of general incompetence. Others complained of inconsistency or political or personal bias. One critic, speaking of Northerners' experiences, complained that board members frequently "use their positions, not only for political purposes, but to reward friends and to punish enemies." The failure of the Pension Bureau to standardize the medical examination process is telling. It not only underscores a certain subjectivity to medical perception and the socially constructed nature of disability but also calls attention to the contested nature of these physical examinations. While many claimants could level accusations of unfairness at bureau officials, only freedpeople ever felt compelled to accuse their local examining board members of being former enslavers.[67]

Though often submerged in seemingly mundane bureaucratic struggles, deep-seated resentments occasionally erupted in pension cases involving former slaves. Richard Dargan of South Carolina had such a case. Decades earlier, in March 1865, when General William T. Sherman's army marched through Sumter County, Dargan escaped his slave labor camp and joined the One Hundred Fourth USCT. Shortly after enlistment, he developed eye troubles and general debility. Failing to prove their origin in service, Dargan seized on the new law, which afforded him an eight-dollar pension beginning in July 1890. Throughout the decade, he would pursue both his general law claim and an increase in his new law rate. Testimony from physicians, neighbors, and comrades supported Dargan, but his claim met with a severe blow when he was suspected of having syphilis. This was problematic for Dargan because every pension applicant had to prove that their disabilities could not be attributed to "vicious habits." Admission to the rolls presented federal administrators with what they considered a weapon to punish claimants with certain so-called vices, including alcoholism, venereal diseases, and in the case of widows, infidelity. For thousands of Black claimants, then, it was not enough to satisfy the bare corporeal requirements for disability; they also had to prove sobriety, that their ailments were not the result of reckless or vicious habits. The onus proved burdensome to many Black claimants so recently accorded bodily autonomy and little else. Vice-related disabilities were deemed unworthy of federal aid, and indeed negated all other worthy and unrelated disabilities that same claimant might also present.[68]

The targeted assault on claimants such as Richard Dargan revealed a combination of forces. First, Pension Bureau officials laid heavy suspicion of all such habits on Black claimants, the belief being that only enslavement prevented members of the race from engaging in morally destructive behavior.

Thomas P. Bailey, the South Carolina physician seen earlier excluding freed Black families from his private medical practice, was also a public health official in Georgetown. "Before the war," he wrote, syphilis "among the blacks was almost unknown and now we see it in its varied forms." "If this race as a laboring class is to be fostered and preserved," he continued, sounding much like an official of the late U.S. Sanitary Commission, "this subject is replete with interest to the statistician and sanitarian apart from the claims of humanity." Another physician, J. M. Barrier, concurred, finding that the whites of Louisiana had successfully "defined the social and political status of the negro, but there is still a more serious phase of the 'negro problem' which confronts us, namely, the sanitary condition of the race." Many physicians in the last decades of the nineteenth century decried the increase of communicable diseases among Black Americans, especially smallpox and tuberculosis. Conceding that much of the reason for disease in the Black community could be traced to derelict landlords who encouraged drunkenness, many insisted on a physician-centered, paternalistic control of Black neighborhoods. "What he is physically," concluded Barrier, "must come from the white man." The salience of such scientific racist dogma encouraged the possibility of such diagnoses by the bureau's examining boards, which would have found much professional support in their presumption of communicable diseases such as syphilis among Black claimants from Black-majority locales in the South. And more than a few Southern public health officials moonlighted as medical examiners.[69]

If the broader, arid landscape of scientific racism set a hostile scene, the reelection of the anti-pension Democrat Grover Cleveland to the White House returned a pivotal figure to the drama. Chief executives could exercise considerable sway over Pension Bureau policy if they had the political will. And Cleveland most certainly did. "The lessons of paternalism ought to be unlearned," declared Cleveland in his second inaugural, "and the better lesson taught that while the people should patriotically and cheerfully support their Government its functions do not include the support of the people." In his triumphant restoration to the presidency, ending the interregnum of the pensioners' president, Benjamin Harrison, Cleveland brought his axe to grind, appointing William Lochren as his pension commissioner. Under Cleveland's orders, Lochren directed bureau officials to begin reexamining claims and claimants with the express intent of lowering ratings or purging from the rolls altogether based on a newly discovered "unworthiness." The Black press saw it coming. Just days after Lochren took office, the *Bee* warned its readers that the new commissioner's dragnet policy "will be to make a clean sweep of all

Pension Bureau special examiners. Special examiners of the Pension Bureau investigated pension cases suspected of fraudulent activity. Democratic commissioners rigorously deployed special examiners to purge the pension rolls; Black claimants found themselves subjected to disproportionately high rates of special examination. (Library of Congress Prints and Photographs Division, LC-DIG-cwpbh-03423)

the officials of the Pension Office who have any voice in determining action upon pension cases or construction of pension laws."[70]

Within two months, Lochren appointed a special force of twenty investigators to reexamine all pension cases granted under the Disability Act of 1890, especially those whose disability ratings had been increased due to an October 1890 order by his liberal predecessor, Green B. Raum, which allowed for separate, minor disabilities to be aggregated into a larger disability rating. Lochren ordered instead that all disabilities should be now considered for their cumulative effect on one's laboring potential.[71] Lochren also gleefully introduced what he called "credibility inquiries," designed not only to determine what witnesses "really know or remember about the matters stated in their affidavits" but also to establish the very fact that they exist at all. "Without the restraint of special examination investigations," the commissioner warned, "fraud would flourish and the dishonest practitioner and dishonest

claimant would lead by far in the successful establishment of pension claims."
In the first year of Lochren's tenure, his Law Division conducted over forty
thousand investigations and sent over five hundred cases to the Justice Department for prosecution. But the *Bee* estimated that when all was said and
done, at least 150,000 claimants would have their pensions severely reduced
or discontinued altogether owing to the new commissioner's so-called merit
work. Black Southerners, whose pension claims seemed to preternaturally invite special investigations, found themselves disproportionately subjected to
removal from the rolls. Dargan was among them. Writing to Lochren in late
1895, Special Examiner E. D. Gallion, who had dutifully performed the credibility inquiries in Sumter County, recommended the rejection of Dargan's
pending general law claim and possibly his removal from the new law rolls on
the grounds of vicious habits—a recommendation that Gallion confessed he
was sorry to have to make, as Dargan seemed "to be a good old man and
truthful" and he doubted the octogenarian would "survive a great while" longer. Lochren swiftly dropped the former slave on January 11, 1896.[72]

But Dargan refused to be refused. He kept reappearing before the Charleston board, insisting on a fair assessment of his disabilities. Frustrated by his
repeated rejections, he enlisted the help of a claims agent and began addressing letters to both the commissioner of pensions and the secretary of the interior. In a series of razor-edged letters, Dargan called attention to the injustice
inflicted by what he considered a rogue examining board. The ex-slave denounced the board physicians as "descendants of former slave holders." These
men, he argued, were "against me and universally against the old veterans
hereabouts." One he called a "full fledged democrat and former slave owner . . .
who can not possibly do Justice, particularly to negro soldiers for their part in
the last war." Another examiner was a man whom Dargan and his comrades
had petitioned for years to be removed from the board. His continued membership "on the present board after the numerous complaints made by us
against him," Dargan charged, "is an outrage against *Justice.*" And the final
board member, for his part, "is quite arrogant and threatens to have any pensioner who kicks against the present board dropped from the roll and as I am
still against the board why I can not trust his report of my condition to be
truly made." Unintimidated by threats and rejections, Dargan declared himself "always ready to kick against such a board." He denied the objectivity of
their medical opinion, tying the board's diagnoses to a vicious political agenda,
and vowed to never willingly accept such treatment. What might have begun
as an immediate, limited grievance escalated into an incisive, wide-ranging
critique that begged to be reckoned with.[73]

Richard Dargan articulated as clear a connection as anyone could between the structure of the Pension Bureau and what would later be called institutional racism. Whereas the bureau's white critics complained of friendly (and thus corrupting) alliances between Northern examining boards and their claimants, the vast majority of Black Southerners could expect the very opposite. Both sets of experiences sprung from the bureau's policy of deputizing neighborhood practitioners. But the way to reform the examination process was not through somehow incorporating racial considerations. It required instead, as Dargan's testimony implied, a basic appreciation of the larger social forces at play in the post-slavery South, or, in more practical terms, the centralization of the examining process by replacing local civil physicians in places such as Charleston with salaried federal surgeons. And even so, such reforms could only proceed so far. Aware of the bureau's fatal flaws, and powerless to restructure the federal administration, Dargan insisted the bureau allow him to appear before a different board—one in Georgetown, South Carolina—where he believed he would have a fairer examination. "I do not see any reason why . . . we [are] not permitted to appear before any examining surgeon appointed for the purpose without regard to locality," he wrote, questioning the rationale for restricting claimants to particular examining boards, a restriction often lifted for white petitioners.[74] Although the gateways to the bureau were many, for Black claimants they were not interchangeable. Where one lived determined precisely where one could be examined, for better or worse. If Black claimants were "not permitted to request" a new medical examination, then "are we [also] not permitted to ask information in relation to our rights under the law?" he demanded. Incredulous and embittered, Dargan was also far from alone. "I am only one [of] many complainants who are dissatisfied," complained Dargan, for the current system ensured that "we are inslaved to the will of the clerks in the department rather than the liberality of the law."[75]

Dargan continued to agitate. In his barbed missives to high-ranking executives, he vigorously maintained that the actions of the Charleston board of surgeons were systemic, indicative of a larger, more pernicious spirit drawn deeply from slavery and infiltrating the new order. Other formerly enslaved veterans felt the same. Together they registered complaints, signed petitions, and wrote appeals. They spoke of fraud, conspiracy, and reenslavement. And so, as a pension claimant, Dargan did more than make bids for a twelve-dollar monthly pension; he also became the spokesman for a community of people who were being wronged and mistreated, a people who had something profound to say about justice. Dargan's story demonstrates with full force that although former slaves cultivated an understanding of freedom as attached to the state, they were not passive receptors of federal power. Their coerced compliance with the rules of the Pension Bureau convinced them that the bureau must operate with the fairness that they believed the law intended, rather than the arbitrariness of leaving vital state functions in the deeply compromised care of former enslavers and slave doctors. No one had a better or more visceral sense of arbitrary power than former slaves. And no one else was better able to diagnose it in the new federal administrative state.[76]

Black Professionals

Because of the great latitude given to the bureau's medical examiners— and because of the position's prestige and affiliation with the federal government—a generation of Black physicians fought for inclusion on pension boards. Their presence on the boards not only symbolized Black achievement and the rise of a Black professional class but also promised to help facilitate the claims of hundreds of Black applicants who might otherwise have been greeted with hostility and rejection. Though the Black press paid close attention to appointments and dismissals from local pension examining boards, they were particularly invested in the efforts of Black physicians to gain such high-profile positions. For example, one of the most renowned and respected Black physicians of his day, Alexander T. Augusta, became a medical examiner for a pension board in Washington, D.C. Having ably served during the late war as a surgeon for the Seventh USCT, Augusta ran the Lincoln Hospital in Savannah before relocating to Washington, where he opened his own practice and joined the staff at both the newly formed Howard University Medical School and the Freedmen's Hospital. Commissioner Van Aernam had dismissed Augusta, though his successor, James H. Baker, reinstated him. "The new Commissioner of Pensions has done a wise as well as a just thing restoring Dr. A. T. AUGUSTA," proclaimed the *New National Era* in June 1871, "as he was undoubtedly removed by VAN AERNAM for being guilty of a skin not colored like his own." With its vibrant Black community, thriving Black press, and symbolic importance as the nation's capital, Washington proved to be a hotbed of political activism. The city's examining boards, before which appeared hundreds of Black veterans, were thus widely regarded as important positions of authority.[77]

Pension examining boards in the South were occasionally dramatic distillations of emancipation's transformative history. In 1893, A. W. McKinney of Alabama recounted a story that later appeared in the preeminent Black New

Orleans newspaper, the *Southwestern Christian Advocate*. McKinney's subject was the "intellectual status of the Negro." It attempted, as did an infinite number of public lectures at the time, to address the question of how far the race had come since the end of slavery. He noted that in his own city of Huntsville, a graduate from Meharrey, one of the earliest Black medical schools, "holds the position of pension examiner under the appointment of the United States government. On the same board is his former owner." McKinney relayed how one day a question arose as to how to spell a particular ailment. "The colored physician readily spelled it; whereupon, his old master remarked: 'B., this is mighty strange! I used to own you; now, you are teaching me to spell, and excelling me in my own profession.'" For McKinney, the episode proved the intellectual capabilities of Black Americans freed from the intellectual shackles of bondage. Whereas the phenomenon of a former slave serving on the same examining board as his former enslaver may have been exceedingly rare, there were notable examples of a handful of former slaves attaining that position, though not nearly as often as their former enslavers.[78]

The struggles for inclusion on examining boards were inescapably partisan. The late 1890s soon witnessed the greatest number of Black physicians appointed as examining surgeons. That year, the *Bee* reprinted an article from a Mississippi newspaper enthusiastic about the recent seating of a Black surgeon on the pension board at Yazoo City. The appointment of twenty-five-year-old Lloyd Tevis Miller, the first medical director of the city's Black hospital, owed in part to the efforts of ex-slave and former two-time congressman John R. Lynch, who had recently opened a legal practice in Washington and lobbied for Miller's appointment.[79] Two years later, in August 1899, Black Republicans in Jackson held a convention to denounce the patronage schemes of their white Republican allies. The chief resentment involved an incident whereby Republican managers secured the appointment of "three Democratic physicians" to serve on an examining board, passing over a Black Republican applicant. The convention also raised more familiar, spectacular, and violent issues that had come to punctuate Black life in the Jim Crow era, above all lynching—the Democratic encouragement of it and the white Republican indifference to it. "If the Republican leaders insist upon abandoning the principles of the party," noted one Black correspondent, "the colored voters will insist upon abandoning them." Thus to the Black Republicans gathered at Jackson that summer, lynching was considered alongside other meaningful issues of federal appointments and political betrayal.[80]

In the summer of 1902, the appointment of Black physicians to several examining boards in South Carolina ignited a virulent protest and an administrative crisis. It was provoked by the U.S. district attorney for the state, John G. Capers, a native South Carolinian and Democrat-turned-Republican. When delegated with the responsibility of naming appointments to the pension boards at Columbia and Greenville, Capers identified one Democrat and two Republicans—one Black, one white—for each of the medical boards. But in Greenville, noted one Black newspaper, "the white physicians would not serve with the colored doctor." As such, there threatened to be no examining board at Greenville. The Pension Bureau therefore requested that Capers "withdraw the name of the colored doctor and in its place recommend a white man. He declined to do it," however, "stating that the appointment was in no wise a social one, and as long as he felt satisfied that the colored physician recommended by him was a man of character and capacity he would not withdraw his recommendation." Greenville remained without an examining board for nearly a year, until Capers named another suitable board location at Spartanburg and, again, nominated one Black and one white Republican physician. The *Colored American* applauded how Capers "resisted all pressure which has been brought to bear upon him to exercise his influence in having competent colored men removed from the service."[81]

In addition to occupying highly visible and politically charged positions on examining boards, Black Americans also secured a modest toehold in the Pension Bureau itself as salaried employees. Black workers first appeared on the roster of bureau employees in 1881, under the tenure of Commissioner Dudley. By the time he left office three years later, the forty Black employees had grown to nearly 120. Dudley received jubilant praise from the Black press, particularly from the Washington newspapers that paid close attention to Black advancement. In a widely endorsed remark, the *Bee* plainly stated that there was only "one department under the government, where colored men are treated like human beings, and that is the Pension Office, under Col. W. W. Dudley." He had proven himself "a practical and good friend to our race," offering "a good square chance in the race for life." Aside from a handful of cases, however, whites held the most coveted positions in the Pension Bureau throughout the late nineteenth century. Instead of division chiefs, assistant chiefs, medical referees, medical examiners, principal examiners, or special examiners, Black workers most frequently occupied the roles of clerks or copyists in the major adjudicating divisions, and laborers or messengers in the Superintendent's Division, where the majority of Black workers found employ. With around two thousand employees in the last decade of the nineteenth century, the number of Black workers in the Pension Bureau scarcely exceeded 5 percent.[82]

Nevertheless, for the growing Black professional class, the Pension Bureau represented a singular avenue of public-sector advancement in the age of electoral disempowerment. Prominent among the Pension Bureau's Black employees was none other than Charles R. Douglass, son of the famous abolitionist, who held a clerkship in the Southern Division. He would almost certainly have agreed that "the colored citizen gets a better show in the pension department than in any other department of the government," as the editor of a Black paper in North Carolina commented in 1897. Part of their success lay in the bureau's hiring practices, which favored Union veterans, including veterans of the U.S. Colored Troops. Moreover, the bureau's Black employees secured their positions only after "passing competitive examinations through the civil service commission," thereby demonstrating their qualifications for the job beyond bare partisan considerations. But partisanship still played a role with each presidential cycle. Outspoken Black Democrats, for their part, might have fared especially well in securing lucrative positions in the bureau, including men such as Edward A. Clark of Missouri, who owed his position to not only his "excellent reputation" but his political allies in the National Negro Democratic League, or a Black editor in Cairo, whose clerkship in the bureau came after his paper putatively convinced one hundred Black Illinoisans to vote the Democratic ticket in 1884. Partisan affiliations in no way diminished the commendation heaped upon these success stories by the Black press. Indeed, their appointments came at a time when the political allegiances of the dwindling Black electorate were in flux—and soon to be rendered moot. By attaining positions of rank in the bureau, they earned not only comfortable salaries but high esteem among many in the Black community as cross-partisan exemplars of the race's professional class.[83]

By far the most conspicuous Black officeholder in the bureau was Henry Clay Bruce. Appointed by Dudley in 1882 with the advocacy of his brother, Senator Blanche K. Bruce of Mississippi, Henry Clay Bruce would become one of the longest-serving Black officials in the Pension Bureau. Newspapers proudly noted his steady rise through the bureau as the ex-slave secured promotion after promotion. In 1895, Bruce released his autobiography, *The New Man: Twenty-Nine Years a Slave, Twenty-Nine Years a Free Man*. Bruce's narrative epitomized the emerging genre of slave narratives published after slavery that decidedly broke from the heroic antislavery tradition of their antebellum counterparts. Accordingly, Bruce sought "to present an impartial and unprejudiced view of that system," namely, that "all masters were not cruel, and that all slaves were not maltreated. There were brutal masters and there were mean, trifling lazy slaves." He considered his own experiences as an enslaved

Henry Clay Bruce. Former slave Henry Clay Bruce began working as a clerk
for the Pension Bureau in 1882. In 1895, he published his autobiography,
The New Man, a striving account of slavery and freedom widely praised for its
"balanced" portrayal of the peculiar institution and its candid look inside
the federal agency. (Documenting the American South, University Library,
The University of North Carolina at Chapel Hill)

man in Virginia, Mississippi, and Missouri to be relatively humane, and resented the cultural domination that the militant slave archetype had on a Black man's self-respect—the notion that only a rebellious enslaved man, one who ran away, one who joined the Union army, could claim dignity. Bruce wanted to show the moral courage it took to acknowledge their own helpless condition and, instead of giving in to either violent resistance or abject servility, quietly endure as industrious, trustworthy, and reliable wards, in short, to "so live and act as to win the confidence of their masters, which could only be done by faithful service and an upright life." Though Bruce gained his freedom at age twenty-nine—thanks to the efforts of thousands of militant bondspeople—he proudly served masters his whole life.[84]

What brought such notoriety to Bruce's narrative, and indeed what set it apart from similar moralizing treatises of the Booker T. Washington variety, was its candid look inside the Pension Bureau and its managerial class. Though Bruce recalled with unapologetic pride his own appointment in 1882 and promotions in 1886 and 1889, he broke ranks with the Black press, which used the appointment and promotion figures of Black employees as a metric for judging commissioners. Bruce instead assessed commissioners based on their perceived efficiency and fairness, their fidelity to merit and rules above all else. Many Black readers were surprised—shocked, even—to learn that Bruce held John C. Black in the highest regard. Bruce believed the Cleveland appointee held that office "with more dignity, ability, and impartiality, than any of those under whom I have served." First, Commissioner Black earned special accolades from Bruce for his disciplinarian approach to the daily operations of the agency. The clerk relished how Black enforced strict rules regarding attendance, going so far as to require a written pass to leave one's desk, and how he delivered swift reprimands to discourage tardiness or truancy. In a distant second were promotions under Black's tenure, which Bruce regarded as "based upon merit solely, and with respect to Colored men it was eminently so; for they were Republicans and had no special claims upon a Democratic administration." Bruce persuaded himself that more Black employees were promoted under Black's administration than any other for precisely that reason. Even if that were true, it was undeniable that the total number of Black employees at the Pension Bureau dropped by about one-third under Black's tenure. Bruce ignored this inconvenient fact. But it was not lost on the Black press. In a review of Bruce's book, the *Bee* shot back that while "Black was no doubt kind and good to Mr. Bruce" on an individual basis, "there were others and especially republicans who were dismissed and reduced because they were republicans. There were very few negroes, if any,

[who] benefited under Gen. Black's administration." But Bruce believed himself one of them.[85]

Bruce published his autobiography under the tenure of Commissioner Lochren, the hatchet man President Cleveland used to fell the mighty pension rolls. Yet even this hallmark undertaking of Lochren's administration received no notice in Bruce's narrative, which instead relegated Bruce's focus to personal interactions and the management of bureau personnel. On that score, Bruce explained how Lochren demoted twenty Black employees, including the author himself. Yet Bruce assured his readers that it "was a political matter purely, and did not reflect upon my efficiency as a clerk." True to form, Bruce did not complain, and despite his demotion confessed that he had "never received more respect and kindness under any administration" and that Black employees as a whole were "fairly treated." For their part, prominent Black newspapers such as the *Bee* and the *Colored American* generally criticized efforts by administrators to restrict admissions or curb the pension rolls, and this generally involved attacks on the Democratic Party. But they saved their most pointed criticisms for hiring practices that discriminated against Black employees, often under Republican-appointed commissioners.[86]

Despite their differences of opinion, Henry Clay Bruce and his critics at the *Bee* both operated on the relatively narrow grounds of Black professional advancement. *The New Man* began as a sprawling, didactic freedom narrative intended for the millions who survived slavery and ended with a granular assessment of bureaucratic personalities and a guide to aspiring clerks in the federal government's vast bureaucratic machine. "One of the first lessons a new appointee should learn, and I might say the most important one," Bruce concluded, "is entire and complete subordination, for without this he cannot succeed. He must make up his mind to lay aside what he calls his manly instincts and personal independence, and resolve to submissively obey all order of his superiors without a murmur." Recycling his own advice on how to endure slavery, Bruce advised the young clerk "that he must so act as to win the respect and confidence of his superiors in office, and to so live as to hold them."[87]

The vision of freedom presented in *The New Man* had nothing to do with liberation, racial or otherwise, or even a conservative, Washingtonian adherence to thrift and trade-based labor as a seemingly apolitical maneuver for economic self-sufficiency. Instead, freedom to Henry Clay Bruce meant a slightly less fettered chance for individual upward mobility—an assimilationist and elitist struggle for "social standing and influence." This he did as an enslaved man, rising to the rank of foreman on a cotton plantation, and this he did as a federal bureaucrat, promoted up to the rank of a Class Two clerk. One could advance only by associating with the better classes of people. Bruce even dabbled in blood quantum metaphysics to justify his class position, confessing at the outset his "deep conviction" that humanity was "divided into two great classes." Everywhere he looked he saw "certain characteristics of good blood," not "divided into white blood and black blood" but rather "divided into inferior and superior, regardless of the color of the individual in whose veins it flows." Bruce's love for the aristocracy, and bitter hatred for the poor, especially poor whites, was hardly lost on his readers. The *Washington Post*, for instance, applauded *The New Man* for not depicting "the old Southern proprietor class as monsters and tyrants—quite the contrary—or pretend[ing] that all the virtue, kindness, worth, and loyalty of that section was to be found in the Negroes." Bruce was not "a professional colored man," noted the *Post* with a sense of relief, just a professional. The great mass of Black workers, with their excessive fondness for racial agitators, would do well to ponder the wisdom of Bruce's fifty-eight-year career path.[88]

THE VARIETY OF ENCOUNTERS with the Pension Bureau exposed the class fissures among Black Americans in the late nineteenth century. All of the preoccupations of Black respectability politics, in the end, seemed distant from those of Richard Dargan, and indeed many thousands of other formerly enslaved claimants struggling not only with their impairments but with their disabilities and quantified disability ratings at the hands of the Pension Bureau. When Grover Cleveland returned to office in 1893, not three years after the passage of the Disability Act, the Pension Bureau's Southern Division annually distributed around $7 million in pensions to roughly forty-five thousand claimants on the general law and new law rolls. Despite the waves of rejections, reductions, and purges, by the final year of the nineteenth century, the rolls of the Southern Division had over sixty thousand claimants. Another ninety-four thousand claims were still pending. It is impossible to tell how many Richard Dargans were among those tens of thousands of pensioners or would-be pensioners, how many endured silently, mobilized collectively, or appealed directly to the nation's highest executives. If the bureau's managerial class were more or less aware of the subjective nature of medical examinations, no class of applicant felt that subjectivity more viscerally than those who had known it their entire working lives. No class of applicant had had their "worth" determined so strictly by reference to their laboring potential. When Black claimants fought back in simultaneously institutional and insubordinate ways for some measure of justice, they grasped for not merely a higher stipend but, just as importantly, the right to bodily autonomy and security.[89]

The dramatic changes in pension policies and procedures in the first three decades after Appomattox precipitated nationwide debates over the proper role of the federal government in providing for its citizens who had sacrificed on its behalf. In the popular imagination, this was the white Union veteran, his widow, and his orphans. Heated battles over how (or whether) the federal government should distribute benefits consumed a growing portion of law-makers' time and energy and made great demands upon a government far more inclined to subsidize railroad and other corporate interests than even limited welfare provisions. Though the Pension Bureau itself never escaped notice, its Black pensioners often did. Out of hundreds of pieces of public pension legislation passed by dozens of Congresses during this period, only a handful included any mention of Black claimants. The struggles of Black claimants within the Pension Bureau demonstrate that racially restrictive leg-islation was not a precondition for consistently unequal outcomes for Black claimants. Rather, substantive injustice was built into the very structure of the pension administration, nowhere more tangibly than the point of friction between claimants and medical examiners. Although many Black claimants succeeded in wresting moderate stipends from the ordeal, and although those entitlements gave many the very means of survival, every claimant had envisioned and expected more. By the turn of the twentieth century, new grassroots movements arose to elaborate on the limited welfare program of federal military pensions—movements that would challenge and retrench the federal administrative state like never before.

CHAPTER SIX

Pensions for All

It was said there was neither North nor South in the Pension Bureau. It knew only loyalty. This axiom was no less true in the 1890s than it had been at the time the Union pension system began. Legions of loyal Southerners from seceded states gave lie to the sectionalist charge commonly leveled against the bureau, none more so than the growing contingency of Black Southerners who lodged their pension claims at extraordinary rates, isolated in many areas as the lone federal beneficiaries.[1] Yet the flurry of pension activity in the South following the Disability Act of June 1890 developed alongside a welter of other movements challenging the boundaries of the reconstructed federal state. Indeed, in the decades straddling the turn of the century, the very idea of the state's responsibility for past damages came to the forefront of national politics in ways seldom approached before or since. In this new paradigm, the memory of the Civil War and emancipation was more than just a commemorative act of collective identity; it was also the starting point for larger political movements demanding a more expansive welfare state, democratic representation, and reparations for slavery.

Three seemingly oppositional currents electrified the South. First, widespread agrarian unrest spawned a Populist insurgency, opening new channels of biracial political arrangements to wield power on behalf of the producing classes. In the hands of Black Populists operating within their long-cultivated networks, the movement advanced toward social democracy in a visionary redux of Reconstruction before meeting a similar fate by the mid-1890s. Second, those same years witnessed a massive mobilization of Black Southerners on behalf of pensions for all former slaves, regardless of military service, by virtue of their uncompensated years of enslaved labor. Their case for reparations thus turned the logic of the federal pension system on its head. The ex-slave pension movement overlapped geographically and organizationally with the Black Populist insurgency. Members of the ex-slave pension movement faced public hostility but from a different sort of opponent, not Democratic Party operatives but federal administrators. Leaders of the movement routinely invoked the Pension Bureau as a model, and in the end it would be the Pension Bureau that led the coordinated government assault against it. Third, at the turn of the century, white Southerners, many with Populist pedigrees, endeavored to add former Confederates to the federal pension rolls, specifically owing to their service in the Civil War. Many of those Confederate pension advocates began arguing as well for federal pensions to all "loyal" freedpeople, but for reasons far different from those articulated by the formerly enslaved pension advocates. All three movements struggled over the redistribution of wealth and power. They depended on mobilizing the poor and powerless but also on mobilizing a radical new vision of the shared burdens of historic responsibility and a government dedicated to both repairing and securing the general welfare of its citizens.

Veterans of the Plantation

Three days before President Benjamin Harrison signed into law the Disability Act of June 27, 1890, a congressman from Nebraska introduced a pension proposal of his own. Unlike under the Disability Act, which offered modest monthly pensions to qualified Union families, the beneficiaries of William J. Connell's bill were to be all former bondspeople. Acknowledging the economic precarity of the increasingly elderly freed population, the bill awarded them bounties and stipends strictly according to age. Those ex-slaves who were under sixty at the time of the bill's passage were to receive a $100 lump sum and eight dollars per month; those under seventy were to receive a $300 bounty and twelve dollars per month; and those seventy or older, $500 and fifteen dollars per month. The bill said nothing of the enslavers' complicity or culpability, nor did it allow them any compensation in the matter. It instead directly implicated the federal government in recognizing and maintaining the institution of chattel slavery. Connell's proposal was nevertheless a remarkable piece of legislation for its time. Aside from a few individual cases, talk of indemnity around emancipation had historically centered on the former enslavers, whose loss of human property required immediate redress, or "reparations," as it was unironically called at the time. The bill introduced on June 24, 1890, by an obscure Canadian-born congressman from Nebraska may well have been the first piece of national legislation to attempt to reverse the vector of reparations in the history of Atlantic slavery.[2]

The authorship of the bill came from a similarly unlikely source, a Democrat born to a family of enslavers in Virginia. After growing up in Selma, Alabama, he relocated out west, to Iowa, wherein he served as mayor, and later to Nebraska, wherein he operated a newspaper dedicated to the interests of the working classes. By most accounts, Walter Raleigh Vaughan seemed an improbable figurehead for the ex-slave reparations movement. Many of Vaughan's contemporaries doubted his sincerity, if not his sanity, and scholars today routinely dismiss him as a cynical opportunist, an avatar of sectional reconciliation, and a grasping paternalist who cared little for the welfare of freedpeople. The main goal of his pension scheme, the argument goes, was to divert more federal money to the South and, through membership in Vaughan's organization, to Vaughan himself.[3] But such attacks do not withstand a fair assessment of the record. After Connell introduced the legislation, commonly referred to as the "Freedmen's Pension Bill," Vaughan released a stirring manifesto in its defense. It began with an extensive historical analysis of Black slavery in the American colonies and later United States, it continued through a discussion of the Civil War that unambiguously centered the Black soldier's role in the struggle, and it concluded with a moral cataloguing of the injustices done to freedpeople by Southern planters and the federal government—a story of betrayal that indicted not abolition itself but the failure to make good on it. Throughout the work, Vaughan insisted that "liberty without compensation for the long era of slavish toil is but a mockery of justice."[4]

Little moonlight glimmered in Vaughan's history of Black Americans. To Vaughan, it was clear the practice of slavery revolved around the economic self-interest of the enslaver class, and thus racial justice could only be achieved or even approximated through class struggle. "Over the pages of more than three centuries of American history," Vaughan argued, "there has been written the curse of slavery, of which the black man was the cruel victim." To be sure, "his servitude begot that degree of watchful care which is inseparable from self-interest," wherein "the interest of the master required the creature comfort of his slave to be considered as a matter of prime importance." But the investment ended with subsistence. Feelings of benevolence or affinity were as rare as they were irrelevant to the larger system of exploitation. Instead of happy portrayals of antebellum slavery featured in countless works of saccharine revisionist drivel, then, Vaughan focused exclusively on the stolen labor at the heart of American slavery, a theft that enriched not simply individual enslavers but the entire nation, such that "no volume of money that might be poured out at the feet of the old slaves would compensate the negro race for the deep wrong they have endured." To Vaughan, slavery was indeed a "deep wrong"; it was a "heartless bondage," a "curse," a "great wrong," a "flagrant wrong," a wrong "founded in ancient error of government" and practiced "in defiance of human right" and against "the law of God and of humanity." Hardly the words of a nostalgic reunionist, much less an apologist for slavery.[5]

Vaughan's understanding of the wartime contributions of Black Southerners in many ways anticipated the arguments of W. E. B. Du Bois in his groundbreaking 1935 work *Black Reconstruction* and, at all events, far surpassed those of contemporary white historians who almost universally subscribed to Lost Cause ideology. Although Vaughan conceded, wrongly, that some enslaved people were hesitant to relinquish their support for their enslavers, he nevertheless recounted how they soon "flocked in numbers to Union encampments, beyond the facilities of army officers to equip them for military service, as Union troops advanced into the heart of the Confederacy." Time and again, Black men wishing to serve were rebuffed by federal military and civil officials who were at best "slow to accept the service of armed negroes as soldiers of the republic." But once the "rigidity against the employment of colored troops" crumbled under the weight of military necessity, once "the black people became thoroughly apprised that the advance of the Union armies carried with it freedom to the slaves they fell into a support of the Union cause with enthusiasm." In Vaughan's appraisal, the entire war pivoted on the Lincoln administration finally coming to accept Black enlistment, what ex-slaves had been urging for some time. Once it did, the government "opened a new field for the negro, and charged him with a grand importance in crippling the power of the white master, and enabling the black serf to do his part" in terminating the enslavers' rebellion.[6]

As Vaughan saw it, the war offered a rich testimony to Black ability and devotion to the repurposed federal government. He ended his plea with a series of biographical sketches of Black leaders in politics, education, and the ministry, while also praising unnamed, ordinary freedpeople in the humblest walks of life. In no conceivable way was Vaughan's indictment of the conditions many faced in "freedom" a reproach of abolition itself; instead, it was a blistering critique of the federal government's abandonment of former slaves in abolition's wake, leaving them dispossessed and in the thrall of "heartless employers." Likewise, his focus on the role of the federal government in perpetuating slavery—that government which made Black men and women "the unwilling subjects of lawful authority"—was less an exoneration of individual enslavers than a frank acknowledgment that American slavery was a national institution and a national wrong whose repair required a national effort. Finally, when Vaughan talked about sectional reconciliation it was premised not on white supremacy but rather on redistributive justice. He believed that pensioning ex-slaves would help ensure their financial independence, which he argued was a necessary precondition to resolving racial animosities in the South and the nation as a whole, making, in his words, "their conditions harmonious and conducive to the general welfare." The ballot was necessary and deserved, but on its own insufficient to realize Black freedom. "Money,"

Vaughan argued, "is the agency that will solve the negro problem. Enable the old slaves to acquire homes, to live in comfort, and they will at once acquire a respectability they have not hitherto attained" with the deck so stacked against them. Pensions would ultimately "enable an impoverished race, reduced to penury through no fault of their own, to place themselves in a position of relative independence."[7]

Vaughan's plan to "pension" former slaves invoked the federal provisioning of Union veterans and heirs through the Pension Bureau. In noting the beneficial effects that military pensions had on countless Northern families, Vaughan asked that "the nation be just to him [the freedperson] as it has been just to the soldiers of the Union"—to provide, in other words, for "the aged veteran of the plantation." Vaughan envisioned the current pension system as a theoretical model, and even stipulated in his bill that the secretary of the interior would oversee the program. Yet Vaughan also harbored the standard Democratic critique of the Pension Bureau, calling it "truly a plague spot in the affairs of Government" as currently administered, with worthless claims fulfilled and worthy claims stuck in adjudicatory limbo. For these reasons, the association of ex-slave pensions with Union pensions worried Vaughan. Some potential supporters as well balked at the nomenclature in his proposal, given how much the government was currently spending on military pensions. One senator from Kansas argued that it was the first duty of the government to look after its disabled soldiers, not to provide material aid to "able-bodied people, who are quite capable of making a living," and that "if all governments are to be held responsible for all damages resulting from the passage and execution of laws, the unfortunate tax-payer would be constrained to sell out." Vaughan shot back that it was hardly an act of justice that freedpeople should be denied pensions simply because disabled soldiers and widows were receiving pensions of their own, and, moreover, that the "laws by which a race of people were enslaved for hundreds of years certainly do not have a place by the side of statutes that have occasioned trivial injuries or losses," as the senator's glib remarks implied.[8]

The economic solution posed by Vaughan to the plight of so many Black Southerners also drew criticism from Black Americans of the professional class, as would the more general push for ex-slave reparations later in the decade. When Connell introduced the Freedmen's Pension Bill, he personally delivered a copy to the three remaining Black members of Congress to solicit their views. Together, Thomas E. Miller, Henry P. Cheatham, and John Mercer Langston all rejected the idea of ex-slave pensions, instead devoting their energies to education. Vaughan had heard it before. Back in 1883 when he proposed the idea of pensioning ex-slaves to then-senator Benjamin Harrison, he, too, suggested "the most efficient way in which the government can aid the colored people is by some provision in aid of education in the South." The lack of support from Black congressmen in the 1890s nevertheless frustrated Vaughan. He wondered whether all the millions of freedpeople who had survived years if not decades of slavery could be repaid simply "by making provision for 'knowledge and useful information' to be imparted to the 'rising generation!'" While not dismissing the importance of education, Vaughan rightly questioned its applicability to elderly ex-slaves as well as its place at the leading edge of the fight for meaningful Black freedom.[9]

Vaughan had predicted bitter opposition to his bill. And he got it, especially from "that class of capitalists who berate any act of justice which is likely to call for an assessment for taxation upon their stores of wealth." Some of the most hostile criticism directed at the proposal came from the *Atlanta Constitution*, the mouthpiece of the New South, which printed a mocking rejoinder to the bill in July 1891. "Instead of this piecemeal way of pensioning the people—taking classes and races from time to time," the editor scoffed, "why not make a neat and complete job of the whole thing by granting pensions to everybody?" Aggravated by the growing classes of Union pensioners to the North, and perhaps within the Black South, the editor jeered that "with pensions for everybody, there will no longer be any financial problem to bother us." Of course, there are always those "ready to sound a discordant note," those who asked, for instance, "where would the money come from?" Vaughan would do well to accept this enlarged pension plan, concluded the editor, for it stood "as good a chance of becoming a law as his ex-slave pension bill."[10]

Despite the caustic reaction from many white Southerners, Vaughan's plea on behalf of freedpeople spoke directly to regional and class interests in ways readily acknowledged by the mass of Black Southerners. From Arkansas, S. P. Havis, a former slave and editor of the *Pine Bluff Republican*, wrote to Vaughan in July 1890 and commended him on his principled cause. He noted that "news of such a measure pensioning ex-slaves has spread among them like wildfire, and they are now watching with eager eyes, and listening with attentive ears, to see who their friends are, whether democrats or republicans." For his part, Havis believed that "southern congressmen should support the bill for another reason beside[s] justice," namely, that "nine-tenths of the money will come south, and as most all of the merchants and land owners in the south are whites, of course it will circulate amongst them." Any measure designed to materially benefit freedpeople, the vast majority of whom could be found in the South, would necessarily bring greater wealth to the South as a whole. The Freedmen's Pension Bill thus promised to inject cash into an economically depressed agricultural region, drilled ever deeper into debt by declining cotton prices. Yet it would do so strictly from the bottom up. In placing former slaves upon the new pension rolls, Vaughan argued before the House Committee on Invalid Pensions, the measure would not only be "a delayed act of justice, to a once enslaved race, but it would occasion an expenditure of treasure throughout the entire southern region that would visibly enhance the material prosperity of all classes of people within that section."[11]

For this reason, Vaughan's proposal earned considerable scorn from Republicans as well, chief among them the writers at the *Chicago Tribune*. In one editorial, the paper argued that any pensions paid to ex-slaves "must be the free act of a touched and regenerated Southern conscience, remorseful for the wrongs done the bondmen in the past." It should, in other words, be paid by the ex-enslavers themselves upon the conclusion of their own individual, personal journeys of atonement. (Put yet another way, it should not and would not happen.) The "non slaveholding North" had "not benefitted by slave labor" and was already saddled with the enormous debt of prosecuting the abolition war. "The account is square with the ex-slaves," concluded the *Tribune*, the North's hands were washed, and the ex-slave ought to be content with his having been "taught to labor," "taught Christian civilization," and taught "to speak the noble English language instead of African gibberish." Some Southern newspapers, such as the Charleston *News and Courier*, wryly observed that if millions of Black Americans had lived in the North instead, the *Tribune* would be singing a much different tune.[12]

Newspapers across the nation followed Vaughan's promotional tour with mixture of alarm, interest, and derision. In the spring of 1891, Vaughan took his campaign before large crowds of Black Americans in Chicago, which provided the occasion for the *Tribune*'s attack. One editorial in the *Inter Ocean*, a local Black newspaper, reported closely on Vaughan's address, aware that it was "strange" to hear such sentiments "coming from such a man as Mr. Vaughan," being a white Democrat with Southern heritage. Still, Vaughan seemed to have won over many Black Chicagoans. He told the audience that had it "not been for the colored man the war would be going on yet," and that while they "don't owe the white race anything; the world owes the negro race a great deal." It was a rousing speech, one that helped launch a nationwide mobilization of Black Americans across regional and party lines. "There are 9,000,000 negroes in this country," he proclaimed, "and if they stick together they can dictate to all political parties. Stand by yourselves and the nation will tremble." In marked contrast to Black politicians urging their constituents to remain loyal to the increasingly disinterested and, in the post-Reconstruction South, disintegrated Republican Party, Vaughan sought to create an independent political movement that could leverage the collective will of its members to secure the bill's passage.[13]

To accomplish this, Vaughan would rely on Black Americans' own "talent and penchant for organization in a way to advance their personal claims upon the Government." He thus encouraged the creation of Black fraternal associations throughout the United States. "The formation of a cordon of Freedmen's Pension clubs," as they soon came to be called, "would bring together a political strength and power that would be irresistible because of its ability to sway party organizations and to bring victory or defeat to friends or enemies." All such associations would come under the national banner of Vaughan's Ex-Slave Pension Club, which charged an initial membership fee of twenty-five cents followed by recurring dues of ten cents per month to help support the organization's goal of passing the ex-slave pension bill. It is difficult to judge how many members Vaughan's organization attracted nationwide, in large part owing to the formation of these pension clubs as secret societies, and more difficult still to disaggregate their own interests from those of larger movements convulsing in the South and presenting Black Southerners with promising new opportunities for biracial, working-class alliances.[14]

Black Populists

The emergence of Vaughan's pension program on the national stage drew deeply from a groundswell political movement that would threaten to upend the two-party system in ways not seen since the 1850s. With cotton prices at historic lows, pervasive agrarian unrest coalesced in the mid-1880s, giving rise to a dizzying array of collectives, alliances, and unions. With notable exceptions, most of these arrangements were racially separate or segregated, though their eventual electoral apotheosis, the Populist or People's Party, accepted Black Americans as subordinate members. The electoral task for the Populists was to peel away enough disaffected Black voters from the Republican ticket in order to win elections in the Democratic South. For a time around the party's 1892 national debut, Black and white Southerners mobilized under the Populist banner in formidable enough numbers to challenge, and in some areas break, the Democratic stranglehold on the New South. White Populists needed Black voters, while Black voters needed a partisan vehicle attentive to their needs. Far from hapless pawns or victims of white Populist machinations, however, Black Populists leveraged their teetering position to advance their own political agenda, one that foregrounded an end to the convict lease system, the passage of anti-lynching laws, and federal oversight of education and elections, in addition to higher wages and better credit for Black agrarians. So different were the expectations of Black and white Populists that historian Charles Postel suggests the emergence of two distinct Populisms astride the "racial chasm" of the New South.[15]

Though long seen as a mere appendage of the Populist movement, if not overlooked entirely, historians have come to understand that the Black Populist persuasion began independently, emerging from a dense web of Black networks that channeled political energy into the early movement.[16] Important nodes included Black benevolent and mutual aid societies, fraternal orders, and, above all, churches. As the strength of the Southern Republican Party receded with demobilization in the 1870s, remaining Black Republican voters worked with the anti-monopoly Greenback-Labor Party to challenge Democratic rule. This practice of "fusion" with the Greenbacks garnered some success in parts of Alabama, Arkansas, Louisiana, Mississippi, and Texas. The most impressive era of fusionist politics, however, came with the Readjuster movement of the late 1870s and early 1880s, which united poor white and Black farmers in their desire to redistribute the debt burden from individual producers to corporations, a class-based appeal that cut across racial divisions and partisan affiliations. Readjuster offshoots appeared more or less in every Southern state, but the most dramatic success came in Virginia. There, the Readjustment forces led by the former Confederate major general—and Democrat—William Mahone took control of the state legislature in 1879; and in 1881, the governorship. Virginia's Readjuster movement owed much of its electoral success to cooperation with restless Black Republicans who sought a politically beneficial alliance to combat the forces of Democratic reaction and Republican complacency. Although the Greenbacker and Readjustment movements soon folded to Democratic dominance, they offered a cunning blueprint for political action and foreshadowed a resurgence of Black involvement in fusionist and independent politics by the early 1890s.[17]

In the mid-1880s, Black Southerners also enthusiastically joined the Knights of Labor, participating in key labor strikes, and Black farmers formed dozens of agrarian and sharecropper associations and labor unions, including the Colored Agricultural Wheels, the Colored Farmers' Alliance (CFA), and the Cooperative Workers of America, amassing hundreds of thousands of members across the South. In the final two decades of the nineteenth century, over 90 percent of Black men found themselves landless as sharecroppers or farm hands, making these organizations pressing for higher wages and workers' rights vital to their economic interests. The CFA formed in December 1886 as the segregated wing of the Southern-based Farmers' Alliance. The CFA's founding delegates elected Richard Manning Humphrey as their spokesman. Humphrey was a white Baptist preacher well known and respected in the Black community whom the Black delegates decided would serve well as a "racial surrogate," a figure better able to espouse radical views without transgressing one's "place." By 1891, when the CFA had chapters in every Southern state, he boasted 1.2 million members, a figure that perhaps more closely approximated the group's constituency of Black sharecroppers than the number of active, dues-paying members. Still, with Humphrey at the helm, Black organizers and lecturers mobilized tens of thousands of their comrades at the grassroots—and did so largely surreptitiously, as they had in different ways for decades to avoid detection and violent backlash. Black churches and ministers were veritable switchboards of political knowledge and engagement. With their help, CFA locals spread across the Southern countryside with breathtaking rapidity. As the CFA grew, it came under attack from planters, Democrats, white Alliancemen, and, for the cruelest cut, Black Republicans.[18]

When the embattled CFA, together with other overlapping agrarian organizations, turned from economic cooperation to electoral politics in 1889–90, it formed the seedbed for a consolidated Black Populism. Many Black Southerners inside the Alliance were quick to see the necessity of independent electoral action to defeat the Democrats. They orchestrated small-scale fusion campaigns with Republican candidates and, while cautiously supporting the white Southern Alliance, sought to prevent shortsighted fusions with Democratic candidates, the more instinctual choice for white Southerners in the Alliance, historically averse as they were to the Republican brand. Beginning in St. Louis in 1889, delegates of the national white and Black Alliances met to discuss a possible consolidation of the various agrarian factions that were ominously beginning to splinter over issues of region and race. The Southern Alliance insisted on the exclusion of the CFA's Black members, and the CFA, for its part, also rejected consolidation with the white alliance for fear of cooptation and permanent subordination.

Out of equal parts animosity and practicality, the principle of racial separatism prevailed at the St. Louis convention. The next year, in Ocala, Florida, the white and Black Alliances again met separately but simultaneously. Worsening economic conditions nudged the CFA toward confederating with the white Alliances, though its members continued to cultivate a more radical social democratic vision than their white counterparts, including a single tax on landowners so steep it would prevent a land monopoly—a key policy of the radical Henry George's economic treatise *Progress and Poverty* (1879). Economic self-interest could be promoted without openly challenging racism, agreed the delegates, and upon this armistice a tenuous unity among the Alliances was achieved. As Humphrey saw it, the ensuing confederation not only guaranteed the "mutual protection, co-operation, and assistance" of all members but also "recognizes common citizenship, assures commercial equality and legal justice, and pledges each of the several organizations for the common protection of all." Humphrey went so far as to declare that the Ocala accord "will be known in future ages as the burial of race conflict, and finally of race prejudice."[19]

Leaving the South's racial order in place, however, meant the white Alliance refused to join the CFA in support of the landmark Federal Election Bill making its way through Congress. The so-called Lodge Bill guaranteed federal oversight of voting in national elections and even federal intervention if only a small number of constituents petitioned a federal judge. The bill's author, Massachusetts representative Henry Cabot Lodge, argued on the House floor on June 26, 1890, that all Americans have a vested interest in fair elections, especially at the federal level, and that the "first step . . . toward the settlement of the negro problem and toward the elevation and protection of the race is to take it out of national party politics." With President Harrison's support, the bill passed the House down party lines before a filibustered death in the Senate in February 1891. Dubbed the Force Bill by opponents, Southern Democrats easily conjured recent memories of Reconstruction and "Negro rule" in their assaults on the legislation, while the Northern public displayed its characteristic mix of apathy and animosity to the idea of again coming to the aid of "ignorant" or "corruptible" Black Southerners at the expense of the South's "better classes." News of widespread agitation among Black workers demanding higher wages only reinforced this image of Black Southerners as an unworthy lot, dependent on special legislation and vulnerable to political demagogues.[20]

Though the Massachusetts congressman was no Populist, Lodge's measure would have offered the chance of limited but vital protection against election fraud as the fledgling movement began challenging Southern Democrats at the polls in the early 1890s. The failure of the white Alliances to support the Lodge Bill forecasted a bitter defeat in the coming years. As the bill languished in early 1891, the confederated Alliance met in an unsegregated convention in Cincinnati. They discussed the looming matter of whether to form a third party. Black Alliancemen proved much more receptive to forming an independent party to challenge the racist Democratic establishment on the one hand and, on the other, a Republican Party increasingly aligned with Northern capital and industry and increasingly unmoved by the cries of Black Southerners as voters or victims. With white Alliancemen still unwilling to relinquish possible fusion with the Democratic Party, the delegates agreed to postpone the decision until the next meeting on February 22, 1892. But before that second meeting in St. Louis, the devastating conditions facing hundreds of thousands of Black cotton pickers demanded action, and the Black Alliancemen decided to test their strength and the professed unity of their white comrades. Black Alliancemen persuaded Humphrey to call for a strike of one million cotton pickers in mid-September 1891, until planters agreed to pay them one dollar per one hundred pounds of cotton picked (double the prevailing rate). Though Arkansas cotton pickers had engaged in a strike in 1886 with the support of the Knights of Labor, the scale and ambition of the 1891 strike worried many in the CFA. Dissent soon emerged in the state chapters. Most feared the strike was too risky for the individual pickers and the organization as a whole. As such, many also argued that the organization ought to continue the group's original, nonpartisan work of "educating ourselves and cooperating with the white people," in the words of Edward Richardson, the CFA superintendent of Georgia. Despite objections and admonitions from Black Alliancemen throughout the region, Humphrey proceeded with the strike as planned. He instructed his followers who refused to "pick at starvation wages" to "unite more closely and stand firmly together," and to present themselves as "men who seek peace and desire justice."[21]

Given the disaffection among certain factions in the CFA, Humphreys created a secret Cotton Pickers League composed entirely of landless Black Southerners to help organize the strike, and in the months leading up to it made an extensive tour of the cotton South to mobilize support. Texas and Georgia proved most hostile to the strike, among Black Alliancemen and white farmers alike. In Georgia, the CFA state lecturer condemned the strike as "dangerous for a thousand reasons." He advised his fellow Black Georgians to have "nothing to do with the strike," for strikes "have never done poor people any good, only those who order and lead them are benefited." The *Atlanta Constitution* surveyed dozens of Black and white farmers who opposed the strike or felt it would never come to pass in their state, in part because "the alliance hasn't the strength here in Georgia to carry out the plan proposed." For all their confidence and bluster, many whites in the cotton South were more than a little disturbed by the threatened strike and the potential power behind it. On the appointed day of the strike, September 12, the *Mobile Daily Register* complained how "easy" it was "for the negroes to organize into secret societies. They like that sort of business." Doing so put them in a position "to demand anything they may wish and to enforce their wishes through their secret society. There is nothing more dangerous to liberty than secret political societies," the *Register* warned, "and there is nothing more dangerous to the white land-owners of the South than the secret political societies of negroes which can dictate wages."[22]

The general strike hardly went as planned. Sporadic, isolated pickets occurred in South Carolina, Mississippi, Louisiana, Arkansas, and east Texas, but they were made all the more vulnerable by staggered start dates. In most places, these localized outbursts were met with a summary firing of all strikers. But in Lee County, Arkansas, across the river from Memphis, the labor organizing provoked a bloodbath. There, a Black farm worker, and likely member of the CFA, Ben Patterson, crossed the Mississippi River into the Arkansas Delta to mobilize cotton pickers. Two dozen or more were to strike on September 20, more than a week after the original date, and they were to do so on the plantation of former Confederate colonel H. P. Rodgers. Fighting erupted, and the sheriff summoned a posse of some seventy-five heavily armed and mounted men to violently break the strike. The cotton pickers counterattacked and "made a break to liberty" by fleeing to the swamps, only to be surrounded by the sheriff and his posse. When the dust settled over a week later, seven lay dead and nine fell to the lynch mob, including Patterson himself, who had been wounded during the battle in the canebrakes and escaped to a steamer before it was boarded by the mob. According to the *Arkansas Gazette*, "force was necessary, and force was used. Those ruffians drove the cotton pickers into idleness. They would neither work themselves nor permit others to work . . . for the fiat went forth that no cotton should be picked below the rate these ignorant, though temporarily all-powerful, dictators had established." Black organizers, and their white agitators, upset the racial and economic order of the New South. It was the duty of all law-abiding Southerners to uncover and suppress such insurrectionary plots.[23]

Following the disastrous cotton pickers' strike, the white Farmers' Alliance cut ties with the Colored Farmers' Alliance, and with Humphrey thoroughly discredited, the CFA dissolved as an independent organization. Yet it still sent nearly one hundred representatives to the St. Louis convention in 1892, sitting alongside some six hundred white Alliancemen. As historian Omar Ali has shown, through "measured participation" at the convention, Black Alliancemen formed coalitions with mainly Northern white Alliancemen disaffected with a Democratic Party they considered intractably resistant to reform, all while insisting that racially discriminatory policies fatally undermined the unity the movement needed to win power. The convention ended with a Black CFA member from Virginia unanimously elected assistant secretary and a call for another meeting, in Omaha, on July 4, 1892, when the Alliances would create a platform and elect a presidential candidate on the People's Party ticket. The assistant secretary, William Warwick, suggested the creation of a Black-edited newspaper to reach more voters, tapping into the grassroots networks that, despite the strike debacle, proved so influential to the development of the CFA and remained integral to the push for an independent, national political party.[24]

Though the People's Party won just over one million votes nationwide in the 1892 presidential election (to Benjamin Harrison's 5.2 million and Grover Cleveland's 5.6), it was undeniably building momentum. This was especially evident in down-ballot contests. Black Southerners played a leading role in this process from the start, when they began fielding local and state-level candidates in the months leading up to the Omaha convention. Kansas, Texas, and Louisiana in particular saw a surge of Black electioneering on behalf of the People's Party in the early 1890s. Their candidates increasingly received endorsements from anemic Republican candidates in the South. Hard-won gains were also made in Georgia and North Carolina, where Populist insurgencies managed to dislodge many deeply entrenched Democrats in the legislature and governor's office. Although racial and partisan divisions continued to threaten the unity of the People's Party, as one clear marker of the party's success in the South, worried Democratic onlookers fixed upon it the moniker of the "Negro Party," much as their fathers had done for the Republican Party of old. And indeed, one prominent Black newspaper proclaimed that "to the colored man the People's Party in Georgia is largely what the Republican Party was to him in this nation thirty years ago." And just as the Republican Party that came to see "the necessity of freeing the slave," so too has the "People's party, from the very necessities of the occasion . . . delivered the colored voter in Georgia from political bondage."[25]

The deliverance, however, was short-lived. Over the 1890s, courting Black votes in the South became even more of a political liability than it had been in the days of Reconstruction, and Democrats eagerly painted Populists as the Black Republicans of old. Before long, there were few Black votes to court at all. In 1890, the Democratic stronghold of Mississippi introduced its scheme to disenfranchise Black voters, just before the Populist revolt. Other Southern states followed suit by way of constitutional convention, constitutional amendment, or a series of targeted laws. Yet the move to disenfranchise was delayed until the collapse of the Populist insurgency—the next constitutional convention was not called until 1895, in South Carolina. In neither state did Populism seriously threaten Democratic control, least of all in the Magnolia State. As historian C. Vann Woodward observed long ago, Democrats in other Southern states "eyed the results of the Mississippi Plan enviously" but were forced to hold off on rewriting their state constitutions for fear of Populists gaining control at the conventions. As the results of many state elections in 1894 showed, the white vote was considerably split, and many regarded Black voters as having an uncomfortable degree of power to swing an election. White Populists, too, resented the growing power of their Black comrades, as well as their visibility within the party. With Republicans enforcing a lily-white policy against Black officeholding on their ticket, white Populists could ill afford to appear not only a party dominated by Black men but, worse, the party of Black domination, and so made the fateful decision to close ranks on the disenfranchisement of their most maligned and indispensable comrades. To their chagrin, white Populists did not, in the end, benefit from the removal of Black voters and organizers, but instead hastened the party's collapse by 1896 and absorption by what was soon the only operative party in the turn-of-the-century South, the Democratic Party.[26]

The extensive labor agitation and political mobilizations of the 1890s had nevertheless rattled the established order. New democratic possibilities were glimpsed by the fragile alliances forged between Black and white agrarians throughout much of the South. Their early success can perhaps best be approximated by the reactionary forces deployed against it, from not only conservative cotton belt Democrats but also Northern Republicans. It should be noted as well that the Populist tide swelled in the immediate wake of the dramatic transformation of the Civil War pension system in June 1890. Conservatives vigorously opposed the expansion of the welfare state and the creation of legislation to benefit a distinct class of citizens, especially when that class was widely regarded as unworthy. Nowhere was such a mantle fixed more ominously than on the disaffected Black worker in the South. On the eve of the Cotton Pickers' Strike of 1891, the *New York Times* sneered that "the cotton pickers are discontented with their condition and desire to improve the same, and, like many white workingmen, they think they can attain this laudable object better by not working when there is a special demand for their service than by working." Instead of labor, thrift, and submission, Black workers agitated for federal aid and even intervention in Southern affairs to ensure that their party, the People's Party, could upend the proper working order of the South and indeed the nation. In short, for many white observers, Black Populists and would-be pensioners demanded socialism of the most menacing sort.[27]

To Peaceably Assemble

Black Populism and the beginnings of the ex-slave pension movement shared more than just an overlapping chronology. They both relied extensively on semiclandestine Black associations cultivated since the days of slavery that stretched across the rural South; both experimented with biracialism, even racial surrogacy, to build a broad base of support; and both pursued a discrete program of economic and racial justice. But unlike the Populists, who were attacked at the polls and, in the case of Black Populists, in their homes and workplaces, the Black Southerners behind the ex-slave pension movement confronted an administrative phalanx organized and deployed against their grassroots, democratic movement to lobby for material redress.[28]

Following the introduction of the Freedmen's Pension Bill in 1890 and the publicity around Vaughan's manifesto, Black Southerners began organizing associations for ex-slave pensions. Much to his consternation, only some of these groups fell under Vaughan's umbrella organization. By the mid-1890s, dozens of splinter groups had organically emerged, among them the Ex-Slave Petitioners' Assembly, led by Isaac L. Walton from Madison, Arkansas; the National Industrial Council of America, under the direction of S. P. Mitchell; and the National Ex-Slave Mutual Relief, Bounty, and Pension Association, chartered in Nashville, Tennessee, and led by former Vaughan acolyte Isaiah H. Dickerson and the group's secretary, Callie D. House. All of the organizations supported the same legislation, voiced the same principles laid out by Vaughan, and adopted the same basic membership scheme as Vaughan's original club, twenty-five cents to enroll and ten cents in monthly dues. Despite their obvious unity of interests, rivalries plagued these associations from the start and significantly undermined the collective solidarity necessary to exert political pressure. The various associations fought one another on petty promotional and leadership issues, resisted efforts at consolidation, and inadvertently contributed to the fatal confusion among their constituents and would-be supporters. After the turn of the century, a number of these groups even created their own political parties, further diluting whatever political power they had left. Most of all, in the days of the Populist insurgency, the extensive but often conflicting mobilizations around the issue of ex-slave pensions drew the attention of the Pension Bureau, which in turn coordinated with other federal agencies to discredit and destroy the potentially dangerous threat arising in the Black South.[29]

Yet the first volley came from Vaughan himself. Increasingly frustrated by the centrifugal forces pulling apart the movement he initiated years prior, Vaughan scolded those who organized for ex-slave pensions outside of his organization. After consulting with Pension Bureau officials, in 1897 Vaughan circulated an open letter to newspapers warning readers that he was the sole legitimate leader of the ex-slave pension movement, that the bill was in fact copyrighted to him, and that all other groups and agents imitating his methods or impersonating his organization were fraudulent. Around the same time, he deputized as his national director and successor a Black man and freemason by the name of P. F. Hill, and relocated his base of operations from Chicago to the more properly Southern locale of Nashville, Tennessee, soon to be a hub of ex-slave pension activity. He rechristened the group the Ex-Slave National Pension Club Association. All the while, Vaughan continued to distribute his manifesto, gather signatures for petitions, and secure the introduction of his Freedmen's Pension Bill eight additional times in Congress between July 1890 and 1903. Vaughan's bill received explicit endorsements from the various ex-slave pension assemblies during conventions and in their promotional literature.[30]

None of these nearly identical bills would come to pass. Yet the federal government, primed by the Populist threat, grew alarmed at the widespread remobilizations of freedpeople and their allies across the South, and worried perhaps more about the consequences of the bill's failures than its passage. Before the end of the decade, their activities on behalf of ex-slave pensions would attract the attention of not only the Pension Bureau but the Post Office Department and the Attorney General's Office. These federal agencies operated on the assumption that the leaders of the ex-slave pension assemblies were falsely representing themselves to be federal agents and that the organizations knowingly lied about the passage and enactment of the Freedmen's Pension Bill, all while soliciting money from naive freedpeople under false pretenses and perhaps using the federal mails to advance their scheme. At the helm of the effort to investigate the matter was Commissioner Henry Clay Evans of the Pension Bureau, appointed by the Republican president William McKinley. In the spring of 1897, Evans received reports from field examiners on the various meetings of freedpeople in the several ex-slave pension assemblies in his home state of Tennessee. One had been investigating Isaiah H. Dickerson's National Ex-Slave Mutual Relief, Bounty, and Pension Association. The examiner confirmed that "a fraud . . . is being perpetrated on the ignorant negroes through Middle and West Tenn. to a very great extent." At least a half dozen or more agents were in operation, he estimated, and began working local officials to determine whether these agents had misrepresented themselves as federal employees. This, he believed, was the only way the law could intervene.[31]

Around the same time, an inspector for the Post Office investigated Vaughan's organization in Nashville. Like his Pension Bureau counterpart, the postal inspector noted that the "question of endeavoring to get Congress to grant pensions to all former slaves has been repeatedly agitated in this section as well as in other sections of the South." Yet after its national director, P. F. Hill, invited the official to examine the organization's books, the latter found nothing incriminating. "This effort on the part of the negroes may be a waste of time and money," he concluded, "a misguided and foolish move, but I fail to find any criminal intent on the part of the local managers here and recommend the case be closed." Such reports hardly slowed the federal government's campaign against the collective ex-slave pension movements. The ostensible lack of evidence, in fact, only confirmed in the minds of the federal investigators the cleverness of the grifters, careful as they were to offer vague promises while avoiding anything potentially criminal.[32]

In the early fall of 1897, Commissioner Evans turned his attention to Isaac L. Walton's Ex-Slave Petitioners' Assembly in Arkansas. Beginning in November, Evans, along with the chief of his Law Division, circulated letters to every supposed pension agent of the Ex-Slave Assembly and similar organizations. The letter recited the many complaints that the bureau had ostensibly received from Black Southerners suspicious of certain agents drumming up support for the most recent introduction of the Freedmen's Pension Bill in February 1896, Senate Bill 1978. The bureau alleged that some nominal associates of the Ex-Slave Assembly claimed, wrongly, that the bill had passed and Congress appropriated $99 million for the purpose. With threats of imprisonment and enormous fines, the chief of the Law Division advised the agents that the bill had failed and that "there is no provision of law under which an ex slave can be pensioned as such," and to therefore desist from making any misleading representations.[33]

The circular intimidated its recipients as intended. In their frantic replies, dozens of men and women denied knowledge of any wrongdoing and claimed to have never represented themselves as agents of the government. Some promised to resign. Others thanked the bureau for looking into the matter and assured the officials they were honest organizers for the Ex-Slave Petitioners' Assembly. One woman swore to the division chief that the Ex-Slave

Assembly simply "asked me to send them A few names . . . that they might ask for this [pension bill] for the benefit of the old & Cripple who was once A slave," but understood that "it is no law yet and perhaps will not be." She confessed to have "sent my mothers name & some other but when I learned that we must pay to join I did not send any more names because the old people have no money." Like this woman, some of these supposed "agents" were recognized leaders in their communities, but perhaps many more were simply individuals who had taken it upon themselves to collect names and addresses for the petitions. Black ministers found themselves frequent targets of the government's crusade, whether they were suspected organizers themselves or whether they simply knew of the operations of swindlers at work among their congregants. One Alabama paper reported that Black ministers were telling Evans that their "congregations have got the ex-slave pension fever, and they write to know the true condition of affairs." For his part, Rev. C. P. Jones told the bureau he had indeed heard about fraudulent agents in his part of Arkansas, but that was the extent of his knowledge. He pledged, "If you say that I am vilating [*sic*] the Law of the government in this matter I will stop at once," but added his belief that "the time well come when the ex slave will Be pensions."[34]

Evans thought otherwise. Wasting no time, the commissioner spent the final month of 1897 broadcasting warnings to alleged agents of organizations across the country and notifying the postmasters of areas suspected of having pension-related activity, leaving virtually no Southern state untouched. He instructed his examiners in the field to do the same, the very men charged with investigating "suspicious" pension applications from veterans, widows, and heirs. The practice of so many Pension Bureau special examiners, who were long known for their intrusiveness into Black communities and homes, likewise investigating the activities of the various ex-slave pension movements doubtless added to the confusion among Black Southerners. Moreover, when coupled with threats from a powerful federal agency, such confusion served to discourage Black political mobilization at a time of widespread agitation. For example, writing from northern Mississippi, veteran Henry Gearing told the bureau of an imposter claiming authority from the federal government to organize ex-slaves for pensions for a recently passed law. Now, he noted, "they are very much disturbed and mistrust every one that attempts to organize them. I would be very glad to get any information as to our rights to organize and petition the government in our behalf." In fact, "as a soldier myself," Gearing wanted to know whether he had even "a right to look up and assist other soldiers or there [*sic*] widows in obtaining there [*sic*] pensions."[35]

Freedpeople living in isolated parts of the rural South often did not have access to reliable information on the rules and procedures of the actual federal pension system. For some, the shadowy, peripatetic agents of the ex-slave pension movement may have brought the matter of pensions to their attention for the very first time. The two pension programs, one established and one aspirational, thus intertwined in mutually detrimental ways. For example, writing from eastern Texas, Jordan Ellis asked the Pension Bureau for a list of the ex-slaves in his area, "for some of them cant give me name of company and Regiment Because they never was taught the numbers and names." As Ellis explained, "when freedom was declared you know that they was ignorant and they wasant [sic] expecting any pensions." Another wrote to the bureau from northern Louisiana. Having heard of the introduction of the latest ex-slave pension bill, he wished "to be appointed to see after the slaves sending in their claims for bounty as there are a great many of them in my parish also in my city." There was once an agent stationed in Monroe "who used to see after the Col. soldiers of the civil war geting [sic] their pension and bounty," but he recently passed away and the position sorely needed to be filled. For decades, then, Black Southerners not only understood the importance of local agents in mediating federal claims but also insisted on filling that role themselves.[36]

At all events, the vernacular slippage between the federal pension system and the ex-slave pension movement was virtually unavoidable. Even by the late 1890s, many ex-slave veterans had original claims to make based on their military service. Many others made clear in their letters of inquiry to the Pension Bureau that they were only "veterans of the plantation" but still wondered whether they were eligible for a rumored universal pension to all ex-slaves. Others still who had served as nonenlisted laborers during the Civil War also understandably questioned whether the latest pension movement was designed to include them. Writing near Memphis, Perry Williams told the bureau of his work as a teamster during the war and explained that there was "so much ta[l]k of that Pension and the Ex slave Pension I though[t] as I am getting old I would write for information." All around west Tennessee, there were "so many club meetings goin on," he confessed he was afraid "to join in with any of them" until he knew of their lawful legitimacy.[37]

Williams's evident caution in joining an ex-slave pension assembly may have stemmed from frugality or skepticism, but his fear of doing so likely emanated from an awareness of the federal government's ongoing attack on all such ex-slave gatherings. Around 1898, the bureau's Law Division began investigating fraudulent claims in Tennessee, where a "well-organized gang of pension swindlers" was purportedly discovered to have forged over a hundred claims. The chief of the division attributed the high concentration of fraudulent activity in the state to the "23,000 refugees employed at Nashville in various civilian capacities" during the war. "The lack of knowledge possessed by these people as to the difference between an enlisted soldier and a civilian employee," complained the official, "afforded unprincipled agents an opportunity to prey upon the innocent and procure the filing of claims for the pecuniary profit." A Tennessee newspaper similarly noted that there were indeed Black veterans and widows drawing pensions; that fact alone "may lead unsophisticated ex-slaves to believe that the system may be extended to themselves, but their case is very different." The paper sensed that the Union "pension system is losing instead of gaining in popularity in this country" and that the "people have all of the burden of that kind they are going to stand, and no class other than the old soldiers will ever profit by the Government's largess."[38]

Throughout 1897–98, Evans and his examiners continued fielding messages from concerned Black Southerners wary of the federal government's anti-pension crusade. In reply, they demanded any and all information on suspected swindlers. Recipients of the bureau's threatening letters attempted to clear their names of any wrongdoing while simultaneously asserting the moral urgency of the ex-slave pension bill. In Tennessee's Shelby County, for example, J. J. Porter assured Evans he was an honest agent who had "been engaged in acting for the Ex Slave under the Vaughn [*sic*] Ex Slave Pension Movement for over one year." He spent that time working diligently and within the boundaries of the law to earn for the erstwhile slaves what they were "justly entitled to . . . for thar years of unwilling involingterry Ser[v]itude," a nod to the language of the Thirteenth amendment abolishing slavery. From Texas, R. J. Lowry told Evans that "the old 'ex-slaves,' needs a pension and all the help we can get," but decried the dishonest individuals scamming freedpeople out of their money. "You know," he sighed, "that my people have been frauded enough since the 'Emancipation' by such humbugry." Asking for "the proper information as to the 'Pension bill' for ex-slaves," Lowry pleaded with Evans to intervene. In January 1898, one woman from Texas read of Vaughan's 1890 bill in the paper of Walton's Ex-Slave Petitioners' Assembly and wanted to know whether it had been passed. There are, she wrote, "a good many ex slaves here some who are so old & helpless as to be on the mercy of the people & if it is a fraud we want to know it." Such appeals had strategic value in helping to establish one's own innocence but also had the unintended effect of reaffirming the bureau's suspicion of systematic pension fraud.[39]

Postmasters wary of Black political gatherings forwarded promotional materials to the Pension Bureau, which in turn promptly dispatched examiners into the field. Before long, undercover investigators began embedding themselves in the many ex-slave pension gatherings across the South. In January 1898, for instance, the bureau sent one examiner to Chattanooga to attend a widely advertised gathering of the Ex-Slave Association at the local courthouse. He was under explicit instructions to "procure the best available evidence to establish that" the group's leader, Isaiah Dickerson, did in fact "represent himself to be an officer of the Government of the United States." In his report, the special examiner confessed that he neither witnessed nor learned anything of the sort. No federal laws had been breached. The speakers merely urged the passage of the Freedmen's Pension Bill and encouraged enrollment to lobby for that purpose alone. "The meeting that I attended last evening," noted the examiner, "was the third meeting *this week*." As he surmised, "the word Pension in the name [of the organization] attracted many."[40]

Such congregations attracted the press as well. Black newspapers frequently noted these political gatherings, sometimes with enthusiastic approval. But while many claimed to be sympathetic in theory with ex-slave pensions, most editors ultimately concluded the entire scheme was a fraudulent attempt to steal hard-earned pennies from poor freedpeople in exchange for false hopes. From New Orleans, the *Southwestern Christian Advocate* plaintively observed, "Our people do not read Negro newspapers to the extent they should." Why else would "thousands have been defrauded by designing agents who have represented to them that they are going to secure the passage by Congress of a bill to pension all ex-slaves"? The *Advocate* joined other Black papers in condemning all ex-slave pension agitation as providing an open door for dishonest swindlers to exploit the vulnerable freedpeople. Likewise, in the fall of 1898, the *Richmond Planet* reported on two months of meetings in Suffolk, Virginia, that were "well attended by large numbers of people from the surrounding country." Each meeting grew larger. Upon reflection, the editor wondered, "Is not this whole scheme and talk of pensioning the ex-slaves, a bare-faced fraud," designed to enrich those willing to manipulate "our old fathers and mothers who have survived the abolition of slavery"? It was already "very difficult for those who fought to abolish slavery to get a pension," referring to the hard-won claims of Black veterans and heirs through the bureau, but it was impossible for "any of the ex-slaves of this country ever getting a pension by virtue of his or her ever being a slave."[41]

If Black newspapers regarded the proliferation of ex-slave pension assemblies with ambivalence, and positively denounced those responsible for defrauding freedpeople, white newspapers expressed a combination of revulsion and mockery. Large gatherings of Black Americans rarely escaped the notice of white onlookers. Turn-of-the-century gatherings to petition for ex-slave pensions were among the most commented-upon mass movements in the early years of the Jim Crow South. The *Atlanta Constitution* regularly featured editorials exposing the activities of Black pension-seekers who gathered in the hundreds in and around the city. In general, its reporters held Black ministers to be the ringleaders of the scam, inducing credulous freedpeople to contribute money and register their names and all the while preaching the "bright hopes of a government pension." Amid all the excitement gripping the poor, elderly, or disabled Black men and women at these gatherings, the *Constitution* noted that the "more intelligent class of negroes pay no attention." Such perceptions of a class divide between Black supporters and opponents of the movement were consistent across all newspaper coverage. Indeed, aside from smatterings of derision in the white press, white and Black editorials on the ex-slave pension movement were virtually indistinguishable from one another. The burgeoning Black professional classes shared with the most cynical whites the view that universal pensions for former slaves would never come to pass and, as such, were nothing but a grift of the already benighted and dispossessed.[42]

Counterinsurgency

In 1898, Republican senator William E. Mason of Illinois reintroduced the Freedmen's Pension Bill. Coming as it did at the peak of ex-slave pension activity, the bill proved to be a focal point around which disparate groups organized, surpassing even the publicity of the original Freedmen's Pension Bill in 1890. Furthermore, the so-called Mason Bill arrived in the immediate wake of the chartering of the Ex-Slave Association in Nashville, christened as "a united organization of ex-slaves and friends," whose leaders included the full text of the bill, along with the senator's portrait, on their promotional materials as well as the organization's official *Constitution and By-Laws*. Petitions circulated far and wide for the passage of the Mason Bill. They drew explicit connections to Black veterans and their as-yet-unpaid claims to both pensions and bounties. "This government," one petition held, "owes the unknown and deceased Colored Soldiers a large sum of money which is unclaimed.... Many of these soldiers have brothers, fathers, mothers and sisters among us, who are destitute and starving." The precedent had already been set "by the patriots of this country to relieve its distressed citizens," yet "millions of our deceased people, besides those who still survive, worked as slaves for the development of the great resources and wealth of this country" and had received less than nothing. It was only "just and right to grant the ex-slave a pension."[43]

Amazingly, as the petition indicated, there still remained a cache of bounty funds owed to veterans and heirs of the U.S. Colored Troops (USCT), a full twenty years after the closing of the Freedmen's Branch and almost thirty-five years after the end of the Civil War. The Senate Committee on Education and Labor explained that the funds (now in the hands of the admittedly more competent Pay Department) remained undispersed "because of the lack of properly certified claims against it." The committee identified the ambiguities of slave marriages as the main factor in unsettled accounts. "The law governing the proper adjudication of these claims," the committee continued, "requires that the heirs of the deceased soldier must prove their lawful marriage relation by record evidence, and that to be certified to by a notary public or clerk of the court in the several States." Given the virtual "impossibility of making the required proof," especially that far removed from the war, the committee deemed it "probable that by far the greater part of this amount will never be paid out to heirs of deceased colored soldiers."[44]

Yet again, news of an unclaimed USCT bounty fund emerged at a time of momentous upheaval. As was the case with the estimated $200,000 in unclaimed bounties discovered back in 1879, in the midst of the Black Exodus from the South, what to do with the $230,000 discovered in 1898 became an energizing, divisive political issue among Black Americans. "The money clearly belongs to the colored people," reported the Senate committee, "and numerous requests have been made that it be used for the benefit of their race." One such request was for the establishment of the Home for Aged and Infirm Colored Persons in Washington. This plan was spearheaded by Black leaders in the capital, who organized themselves into a corporation and solicited funds for the purchase of a tract of land. Mostly ministers, these men also included the editor of the *Bee*, the prominent Black newspaper in Washington. They sought $100,000 of the unclaimed funds for erecting the home itself, with the remainder invested for its future maintenance.[45]

The project met vigorous opposition during the Ex-Slave Association's grand convention from late November to early December 1898. The delegates elected Rev. Dudley McNairy president, who proceeded to issue a circular to the other ex-slave groups in operation nationwide, warning them of the consequences of the bill, whose passage seemed imminent. "We do not want any such compromise legislation," he exclaimed, "partly because it would be of no practical benefit to our people, but chiefly because the enactment of such a measure would block the passage of the Mason Bill for all time to come." Having fought for years "to get Congress to recognize our rights," having built a grassroots organization whose "banner has been unfurled in every State and almost every county across the entire South . . . we cannot afford to have all our efforts go for naught by sitting idly by and allowing the passage of this little compromise measure which our enemies are now trying to thrust upon us." With this rallying cry, aimed at an allegedly compromised or otherwise myopic group of established Black reformers with very different class interests than the working poor of the cotton belt, the Ex-Slave Association called upon all assemblies of the movement to make a modest donation to help defeat the bill. With the proposal's ultimate defeat, the ex-slave pension movement dodged a potentially fatal blow. And its organizing efforts continued with the spirited vigor of having survived a near-death experience.[46]

Lobbying efforts for the Mason Bill brought renewed federal scrutiny on the ex-slave movements. Far-flung and seemingly spontaneous rallies worried federal officials, who sensed a potentially massive galvanization of disgruntled Black Southerners. Once again, letters from concerned Black Southerners kindled these growing fears. One Alabaman informed Evans that his "people are greatly excited over the Ex Slave Pension question there is some so call[ed] Leader of the Colored Race who are going about establishing associations among them . . . to pass the Mason bill." From North Carolina, a minister confessed to Evans that agents infiltrated his congregation, "telling my members that their [*sic*] is a bill passed giving them a[n] ex slave pension." Though informed to the contrary by the minister, the flock remained true believers. Another Black minister nearby, Rev. T. Parker, had formed his own ex-slave club and appealed to Evans for information on the Mason Bill. As was so often the case, the reverend had heard highly charged rumors "that there is something for us." Rarely was it ever left at that. Letters from Black Southerners made the necessity of federal assistance quite clear. "If there ever was a time that Southern ex-slaves needed anything now is the time, we need it," urged Parker, as "our county price [for cotton] is low here for what we make to live upon and we are getting old unable to work as we has in the past."[47]

Up and down the seaboard South, through the Black Belt to Texas, up to Tennessee and Kentucky, letters flooded the Pension Bureau. With such excitement percolating across the South, in early 1899 Commissioner Evans warned the Republican chair of the Senate Committee on Pensions, Jacob Gallinger, of the latest in the series of ex-slave pension bills. Though Evans supposed it was never "thought of seriously, or intended in any way to give them pensions, it was published all over the south and has afforded occupation for many bad men to take advantage of the poor and ignorant negroes." Associations cropped up everywhere, so it seemed, creating, in Evans's view, "a fine field ... for bad men to operate in." Evans, together with the Post Office and other federal agencies, deployed another cadre of special examiners into the South, targeting two hubs of organizing, the Arkansas-based Ex-Slave Petitioners' Assembly and its Tennessee counterpart, the Ex-Slave Association. Before the end of the year, Evans would gleefully forward to Gallinger the fraud orders issued by the Post Office against several of the ex-slave pension organizations.[48]

One such fraud order targeted Isaac Walton, who had formed the Ex-Slave Petitioners' Assembly in his hometown of Madison in 1897 and thereafter secured incorporated status from the Arkansas secretary of state. Walton solicited membership in the usual manner with the usual fees, and circulated a newspaper fittingly called the *Ex-Slave Assembly*. Within a few years, Walton's organization had 12,381 members on the books. Most could be found in the states of Louisiana (3,857), Florida (3,116), Georgia (1,328), and South Carolina (1,194), according to William L. Reid, the Post Office official who had been sent to Little Rock to investigate the matter. Reid's report in May 1899 underscored the sense of urgency animating federal officials. "The movement is setting the negroes wild, robbing them of their money and making anarchists of them," he cried. Walton and his so-called agents were conducting a "wholesale robbery of the colored people" and were "doing much to break down his race, fill his people with insane ideas and make them 'rainbow chasers' of the most idiotic character." To Reid, the entire scheme was designed to enrich Walton. If the government should choose to let such a fraudulent operation continue—to acquiesce to a growing and potentially revolutionary population of dispossessed Black Southerners—Reid predicted "it will not be many years until the Government will have some very serious questions to settle in connection with the control of the race." In short, Reid implied in no uncertain terms that destroying the ex-slave pension movement was a necessary measure of race control, to stave off nothing less than a race war.[49]

Inspector Reid's all-consuming desire to prosecute Walton met resistance from the U.S. attorney at Little Rock, who suggested to the inspector that the very publication of Walton's paper fulfilled the promises of lobbying for an ex-slave pension program. Walton's Ex-Slave Assembly had therefore violated no laws. Nevertheless on June 17, 1899, the Post Office threatened Walton

REV. I. L. WALTON,
Advocator of the Ex-Slave Pension and Chief Commissioner of the N. I. C.

Isaac L. Walton. Isaac L. Walton led the Ex-Slave Petitioners' Assembly in
Madison, Arkansas. Repeatedly harassed and threatened by the Pension
Bureau and Post Office, Walton proved himself a resilient organizer for
ex-slave pensions and, in the early years of the twentieth century, sought to
merge all ex-slave pension organizations into the National Industrial Council.
(*Washington Bee*, January 31, 1903)

with a fraud order and gave him until July 1 to prove his innocence. To that
end, he employed an attorney long associated with the Ex-Slave Assembly,
Walter Gorman, to address the Post Office. Gorman defended his client well,
assuring the officials that Walton had committed no illegal acts to warrant a
fraud charge and the stoppage of his mail privileges. He explained how the
original charter members of the Ex-Slave Petitioners' Assembly conceived of
the idea to create a fund to build support for ex-slave pensions and turned to

Walton, a man of stature in the community, to lead the organization. His newspaper was the central focus in the fraud order, with the government claiming that it falsely represented the imminent passage of an ex-slave pension bill. Gorman refuted these charges. After all, Walton had gone so far as to reprint official documentation from Congress noting the bill's failure. But in the end, Gorman's defense was not enough. In the fraud order issued on August 12, the Post Office maintained that "Walton well knew that no pension would be granted to ex-slaves by this Government" and that he was "holding out expectations which it is known cannot be realized." Gorman shot back, asking about the government's seemingly prophetic powers. Though he himself did not personally feel "that such a result will ever be realized," if such a precedent of censorship were established, Gorman demanded, "what would become of 'the right to petition'"? People would first have to solicit the attorney general's opinion as to whether a potential piece of legislation has a likelihood of passage and only thereafter deign to petition on the likely measure's behalf. Use of the mail connected the nodes of Black organizing across the rural South, allowing for greater cohesion and unity of message. The Post Office's fraud order was thus only superficially about preventing crime through the mails. Its most basic function was to undercut political organizing among Black Southerners. Such organizing had threatened to upend the established order with the Black Populist insurgency of the early 1890s, and now with the ubiquitous movement for ex-slave pensions.[50]

Commissioner Evans's annual report of 1899 addressed the highly publicized struggle against the ex-slave pension movement. Despite the federal government's best efforts, organizing efforts continued apace, from the formation of assemblies to the collecting of monthly dues and the issuance of membership certificates "resembling more or less a pension certificate." Each reintroduction of the Freedmen's Pension Bill only encouraged the growth of this "industry" and its dishonest exploiters. And letters from disconcerted freedpeople continued to inundate his office. "I have taken the responsibility of saying, in reply to these inquiries," Evans scoffed, "that there is absolutely no prospect or possibility of any bill of that nature ever becoming a law, and that the slave was granted his pension when he was presented with his freedom." It was an astonishing admission for the commissioner of the Pension Bureau. In addition to ignoring the thousands of formerly enslaved men of the USCT and heirs already on the pension rolls, Evans's remark construed freedom itself as a gift bestowed upon a people once held in bondage who made no contributions whatever to the abolition war and, moreover, that the gift of freedom was itself a kind of monetary award, doled out on a regular basis in return for their years of suffering and service. Perhaps, too, he considered the value erased by abolition, an estimated $5 billion, converted into imaginary "pensions" whose monthly deductibles four million freedpeople would never meet in the remainder of their lives.[51]

The implications were arresting. Vaughan and the other reparations advocates had a very different understanding of slavery, emancipation, and freedom and hence a different understanding of historic responsibility and justice. They argued that generations of involuntary servitude—the theft of lives and labor—and heroic contributions during the war entitled those who survived slavery not only to a "grand recognition" but also to actual material compensation. The earliest advocates for reparative justice, including Thaddeus Stevens and countless freedmen and freedwomen, demanded a broad redistribution of land confiscated from rebel planters. Some three decades after those hopes were crushed, reparations advocates turned instead to pensions, the only institutionalized program of restitution conceivable within the established liberal framework. Vaughan held pensions to be necessary but insufficient, only "a slight recompense to emancipated freedmen" and "a measure of recognition of the inhumanity practiced by the government." For his part, Commissioner Evans articulated what had become a standard liberal rejoinder to radical claims on the government, one born in the crucible of federal intervention in the post–Civil War South. Liberal Republicans such as Edwin L. Godkin, editor of the *Nation*, accepted the Reconstruction amendments at face value and in turn argued that freedpeople were emancipated into the world of self-ownership and individualism, or as Godkin put it, "on the dusty and rugged highway of competition." The success of their race, the *Nation's* editor surmised in 1867, "depends almost entirely on the negro himself." Once a useful cudgel to attack slavery, the increasingly threadbare panacea of self-ownership became the essence of freedom in the post-slavery republic.[52]

William Graham Sumner, the Yale sociologist and orthodox Social Darwinist, captured this transformation in his acclaimed 1883 work *What Social Classes Owe Each Other*. Anticipating Evans by nearly twenty years, Sumner explained how Black Americans, "once slaves in the United States, used to be assured care, medicine, and support; but they spent their efforts, and other men took the products. They have been set free," however, and freedom, properly understood, meant that "they now work and hold their own products, and are assured of nothing but what they earn." With abolition, freedpeople "lost claims," above all the assurance of basic necessities. "Will any one say that the black men have not gained? Will any one deny that individual black men may seem worse off?" Sumner asked with his characteristic conceit. "If any one thinks that there are or ought to be somewhere in society guarantees that no man shall suffer hardship, let him understand that there can be no such guarantees, unless other men give them—that is, unless we go back to slavery, and make one man's effort conduce to another man's welfare." To Sumner, slavery was welfare and welfare slavery. As the head of the Pension Bureau, Evans could only follow Sumner's conclusions so far. But they both agreed that freedpeople had swapped claims on their enslavers for a claimless condition of self-ownership, and all the glorious dangers of freedom that came with the trade.[53]

The government's fight against ex-slaves securing any "additional" pensions continued. After Walton's outfit, the next target of the summer of 1899 was the considerably larger Ex-Slave Association, most closely associated with the figures of Isaiah Dickerson and Callie House. In this matter, Evans worked closely with Harrison J. Barrett, the acting assistant attorney general for the Post Office Department. As with the Ex-Slave Petitioners' Assembly, the line of attack centered on the use of federal mails to supposedly scam "poor and ignorant" freedpeople. Postmasters across the South were put on alert and dutifully forwarded Dickerson's materials to Barrett. "The evidence presented to this Department," the latter reported to Evans, "clearly showed the scheme and operations of this concern to be fraudulent, although ostensibly designed to aid and benefit ex-slaves or their descendants." Barrett issued a fraud order against the Ex-Slave Association in September 1899, effectively cutting off the delivery of all mails to and from the organization. The order singled out the organization's leadership—Dickerson, McNairy, House, Rev. N. Smith, and Rev. R. Head—and stopped their mails used for official capacity. How to distinguish their official capacities from their personal ones was never articulated or, for that matter, respected.[54]

Throughout the fall, Dickerson and House waged a desperate struggle against Barrett, at once defending their organization and pleading their cause. Dickerson assured Barrett that his association's sole "object is to unite our Race especially the Exslave and friends in petitioning the Congress of the United States for the passage of Some measure by the Congress of the United States for the Relief of the Suffering Ex-Slaves who are bent up with Rheumatism from the hard ship of Slavery." These aging men and women were "unable to perform manuel [*sic*] Labor to Support them," so the Ex-Slave Association sought to both "look out for the welfare of our Race in general care for Sick & disable members and Politically Advise our membership voters to vote for measures that will be of Benefit to Our Race." It had nothing to do with the "wicked Hearted men" who falsely presented themselves as agents of the association. Needless to say, Barrett remained unmoved and unconvinced and pitilessly recited the fraud order. For her part, House offered a more expansive, thoughtful, and compelling case for the legitimacy of the group. "I do stoutly deny the charges made against the Ex Slave Mutual Relief Bounty & Pension Association," she began, and explained its two main objects, first that of "organizing our selves together as a Race of people who feels that they have been wronged," and second, to petition Congress to pass the Mason Bill, or a similar measure, as an "indemnity" for years of stolen labor, leaving in its wake "old decrepit men and women who are bent up with Rheumatism from the exposure they under gone in the dark days of Slavery." Contrary to the austerity-laden dogma of Gilded Age liberals, House argued that "if the Government had a right to free us she had a right to make some provision for us as she did not make it soon after our Emancipation she ought to make it now."[55]

But House's stirring rebuke failed to move the administrative counterinsurgents. Barrett circulated his latest batch of fraud orders to postmasters across the South who forwarded them to the press. Editors, and no doubt many of their readers, breathed a collective sigh of relief at the long-awaited prosecution of the ex-slave pension movements. The *Atlanta Constitution*, for example, celebrated the fraud order, designed as it was to finally "put a stop to the systematic robbery of ignorant colored people by a gang of schemers." In Charleston, South Carolina, another paper expressed gratitude at the federal government's activism. It bewailed how all of the warnings from the white press actually served to encourage freedpeople to join the movement. Stopping the mails was a necessary first step toward the dissolution of the movement and the criminal prosecution of its leaders. In so doing, the federal government "would perform a signal service to the wards that it took unto itself some years ago and to whom it does not always extend that tender parental care which their ignorance and helplessness merit." Crushing the fraudulent pension movement among former slaves, in other words, would help make up for the wrongs done to freedpeople after the war.[56]

The Black press likewise applauded the federal government's crusade against the movement. With evident embarrassment, the Baltimore *Afro-American* told its readers of how "ignorant" and "credulous colored people" were "duped" out of thousands of dollars by the scheme's promoters. The editor laid considerable blame at the feet of Black ministers, who were "induced to preach to their congregations the bright hopes of a Government pension." But such madness only worked on the lower classes of freedpeople.

"Many of the intelligent colored people have declined to go into the scheme," the *Afro-American* concluded, and have rightly "denounced it as another Freedman's Bank swindle." For its part, the *Colored American* complained that in spite of "the widespread warnings of the press, both white and colored, there are still some people foolish enough to pay over their hard cash to sundry confidence sharks who run up and down the country pretending that Congress is about to grant pensions to ex slaves." The paper sounded a note of mournful resignation, admitting that "no such thing will be done in this or any other generation" for the formerly enslaved.[57]

The Vanishing Horizon

As a cause and consequence of increased public hostility, the various ex-slave organizations began denouncing imposters as well. Doing so could possibly help to fortify their own embattled legitimacy as well as their organization's sole authority to command the ex-slave pension movement. The Ex-Slave Association was the most outspoken in discrediting competing organizations as fraudulent. In one circular from late 1899, the group warned its audience not to "be deceived by bogus calls issued by men who are not even members of the National Ex-Slave Mutual Relief, Bounty and Pension Association," adding, disingenuously, that theirs "is the only chartered Ex-Slave movement working solely for the welfare of our race, and all others are frauds and suprious [sic] and are being operated for personal benefit and not for the good of our race." It called out by name P. F. Hill and D. B. Garrett, ranking officers of Vaughan's old organization. But Garrett, who had been the former "national chancellor" of the Ex-Slave Association, would not be the only defector marked by his erstwhile comrades. The circular also targeted one Rev. R. D. Campbell of Little Rock, who had been elected as a delegate to Washington by the Ex-Slave Association at the convention back in November 1898 before a falling out with the group's leadership, who now denied that Campbell was ever a member of the organization.[58]

The Ex-Slave Association was clearly on the defensive. In an effort to avoid confusion and federal harassment, Dickerson's organization rebranded itself as the Ex Slave Mutual Relief, Benevolent and Aid Association, dropping the words "bounty" and "pension" from the original. An attorney for the Ex-Slave Association took depositions from leaders of various state chapters of the group in the hopes of clarifying the nature of their organization, the promises the association made in terms of securing an ex-slave pension, and how it disposed of funds from membership fees. To circumvent the mail stoppage, the group began using a private express company which, according to the postmaster at Nashville, brought nearly a dozen letters a day to the association's managers. All the while, Callie House continued writing letters of protest to Harrison J. Barrett. "I have Lectured to both white and Colored People on this movement," she explained in an effort to demonstrate her sincerity and transparency, "and I have always stated clearly and distinctly that the Bill was not a law but we wanted to Petition to Congress to Pass the Mason bill or some others." Though duly elected, the organization was not hers; rather, it belonged "to the People and not to the officers." Against the charge that the Ex-Slave Association had done nothing to actually lobby for the passage of legislation, House cited the efforts of Rev. McNairy, sent by the group to Washington back in 1898 for that very purpose.[59]

Throughout the year 1900, leaders of the Ex-Slave Association penned scathing letters to Barrett and Evans. Their letters were remarkably consistent in explaining the purposes and operations of the group, full of pain and anger and rectitude. In March, National Secretary N. Smith reminded Barrett that the Ex-Slave Association was "a Benevolent Institution; we take care of our sick, bury our dead and look after the general interest of our race." In this respect, the local branches of the organization were similar in function to hundreds of other Black fraternal and benevolent associations across the South, wherein members pooled resources for distribution in times of need. Without any meaningful public welfare system, these local, grassroots organizations were essential for Black solidarity and indeed survival in the days of Jim Crow. What made the Ex-Slave Association different, besides its national character, was its additional function of petitioning the federal government "to pension the ex-slaves Men and Women by the thousand, old and decrepit, bent up with Rheumatism from exposure." The latter description is repeated time and again in the group's literature, a stock phrase to promote the group's interests. It not only underscored the dire conditions endured by aging freedpeople but also drew a connection to the most commonly cited ailment among Union pensioners at the time.[60]

The ex-slave pension movement fell back on the ropes as the twentieth century dawned. The latest version of the Freedmen's Pension Bill had been introduced in December 1899 by Alabama senator Edmund Pettus, who was not only a former officer in the Confederate army but a former Grand Dragon of the Ku Klux Klan. Pettus introduced the measure by request and made his disapproval of it known. In the month after the bill's reappearance, Gallinger released a lengthy adverse report intended as a deathblow to the movement, the last word on the last bill. Such measures, repeatedly introduced, have "given an opportunity for dishonest people to impose upon the ignorant and credulous freedmen and their children of the South in a way that will surprise the people of this country when they know the facts," Gallinger crowed. And so he gave them "the facts," from the movement's origins with Walter Vaughan right down to the fraud orders imposed on the two most public-facing organizations of the movement. He reproduced letters from Evans and even cited several letters written by Black Southerners complaining of certain designing men roving around their communities impersonating federal officials. The committee indefinitely postponed the bill.[61]

But it would not, in the end, be the final word on the matter, or even the final ex-slave pension bill introduced in Congress. Yet the committee and its administrative allies had indeed dealt the movement a serious blow, particularly its most notorious wing, the Ex-Slave Association, whose leadership by 1901 was harried, deceased, or, in the case of Dickerson, under indictment. The organization itself relocated from Nashville to Petersburg, Virginia. "I am glad to say," boasted the postmaster at Nashville in one of his many sycophantic letters to Barrett, "that from your efforts, the ex-slave Pension scheme in Nashville, and I think in the South, has been busted all to pieces." He forwarded to the Post Office clippings from various newspapers reporting on Dickerson's trial, conviction, and imprisonment in Atlanta. One such editorial, appearing in the *Nashville Banner*, described how "branches of this association have been established in almost every little hamlet and village throughout the South and it was growing to such proportions that there is no telling where it would have stopped had it not been for the action of the Attorney-General of the Postoffice [*sic*] Department." With the ringleader Dickerson behind bars, "the chances are the whole scheme will die a natural death." Yet Dickerson's fraud conviction was overturned the next month in the Georgia State Supreme Court. And Callie House, who had been implicated in Dickerson's first conviction, remained at large.[62]

In spite of the relentless federal assault on the movements and its leaders, and in spite of an almost universally hostile press, the embattled ex-slave pension movement continued apace in the early years of the new century. Long practiced in clandestine meetings, local chapters increased their efforts in the wake of the fraud orders. To the dismay of officials and onlookers, they continued sending petitions to the White House urging executive support of pensions for former slaves.[63] New figures emerged, including a new president of the Ex-Slave Association, one J. B. Mullins, who, with a touch of self-aggrandizing hyperbole, remarked in a letter to President William McKinley in March 1901 that his "mission here is somewhat of the nature of Moses' to

Pharaoh." Mullins distanced himself from the old leadership, including the disgraced ex-president and, in so doing, attempted to reaffirm the association's legitimacy and necessity. Having been elected at the Montgomery Convention in late October 1900, Mullins tactfully declared himself agnostic as to "whether the former officers acted in good faith toward the members of the association or not," though he (also tactfully) conceded "there must have been some bad conduct on their part, to warrant the action of the Department." Speaking for the convention-goers, Mullins relayed that they generally regarded the government as warranted in targeting the group's former officers but not in stopping the mails for the organization.

Their grievances, though, reverberated far beyond the abridgment of the group's right to free speech. Its members, according to Mullins, also insisted "the right of franchise be restored them in sections where it has been taken from them by unconstitutional legislatures" and that "they desire equal protection of the law, equal rights." Finally, Mullins reminded McKinley that his people "have always been loyal to the flag of this country, and have no idea of revolting." In an otherwise dutifully obsequious letter, this parting assurance left a chilling note in the air. Who said anything about revolting? If, as had evidently been the case, all of these secret meetings were still pulsing in the South, perhaps the state did not have such a firm finger on the movement's circulatory system after all. If, moreover, the full weight of the state's civil authority was not enough to stop the restless schemes, what plans might lay ahead for these disenfranchised citizens driven to desperation? If, in the end, a handful of schemers could so easily bilk Black Southerners out of their savings for the mere hope of a pension, what else could they convince Black Southerners to do?[64]

Though the early years of the twentieth century found the Ex-Slave Association on the defensive, other such movements made proactive efforts at consolidation. The former head of the Ex-Slave Petitioners' Assembly, Isaac Walton, himself charged with fraud orders in 1899 and 1901, agreed to merge his organization with S. P. Mitchell's National Industrial Council of America. The new group was officially incorporated in Washington in February 1902 as the National Industrial Council of America, though the exact nomenclature varied somewhat in the press, perhaps in confusion with other separate but similarly named groups. In any event, Walton and Mitchell's National Industrial Council launched itself as a new political vehicle for Black advancement with a set of demands beyond a bill for ex-slave pensions. Indeed, its original platform included no mention of lobbying for such legislation, instead favoring the promotion of civil rights, an antilynching law, and protests against disenfranchisement and racial discrimination in public transportation and accommodation.[65]

To advance these interests, in the spring of 1902, the National Industrial Council allied with a new political party formed by none other than Walter Vaughan, whose own National Ex-Slave Pension Club Association effectively disbanded in 1899 before the federal onslaughts began. (In the interim, Vaughan had continued to lobby for the ex-slave pension bill both in person and through his latest newspaper, the *New-Eagle*.) Known as Vaughan's Justice Party, the collaboration signaled Vaughan's long-standing animosity toward the two existing political parties that he felt had done the South a collective injustice by refusing to pension ex-slaves. The Black press remained dubious of Vaughan's motives and his strategy, as it had during the days of the People's Party. "Why not," asked the *Colored American*, "engraft a 'justice' policy in the platform of some of the existing parties that have a show to win?" At the inaugural convention of the National Industrial Council in April 1902, Vaughan took the stage to once again make his case for ex-slave pensions, decrying "the woes of the needy ex-slaves and the injustice of paying $150,000,000 out to veterans, without doing something for the southern blacks." Another article in the *Colored American* reported how Vaughan "has concluded that existing parties will never do justice to the South, and has determined to make his bill a national issue," the passage of which he believed "will restore harmony between the white and colored people of the South." In a move reminiscent of the days of the Populist insurgency, the convention passed a resolution to field candidates in any contest where neither incumbent nor challenger from the regular parties pledged support of the Ex-Slave Pension Bill.[66]

When the National Industrial Council reconvened at several points in January 1903 under the direction of Walton, a renewed sense of possibility and hope was in the air. Even the usually skeptical Washington *Bee* ran a sympathetic, front-page editorial about the assembly, calling Walton "a great organizer" and "a man of remarkable push and influence among his people." Another leader of the organization, Rev. Smith Frampton of South Carolina, remarked that although he remained a Republican, the purpose of the council was to "look after the interests of the ex-slave and freedmen" in ways that the current Republican Party clearly had not. Another advocate, one John Wesley Gaines of Tennessee, drew a contrast in the distribution of federal pensions, complaining that "the East receives so much more in pensions than the South." Why shouldn't the former slave receive a pension, he asked. Everyone knew "that it was their labor that opened up this great section." Moreover, Gaines argued, "by adopting this method of caring for the old people, the discrimination between the East and the South will disappear in a great measure and more of the pension money will go South." By 1900, there still remained an estimated two million people who had been born into slavery, roughly 20 percent of the Black population. But time, of course, was running out.[67]

The grand idea of the January conventions was to merge the council, which claimed 175,000 members, with its rival, the Ex-Slave Association, then led by Isaiah Dickerson and (unofficially) Callie House, which claimed some 600,000. Days of negotiation followed, with Mitchell and Walton pressing hard for joining the movements. Despite the obvious advantages to consolidating with the like-minded organization, itself the product of successful mergers—and despite, in the end, holding out the possibility of a united front that could lend considerable legitimacy, consistency, and political power to the ex-slave pension movement—the leaders of the Ex-Slave Association rejected the offer. With the most disciplined and dynamic branch of the movement divided from the largest and most visible, the Ex-Slave Association's refusal rang like a death knell over the struggle for ex-slave pensions.[68]

As the Ex-Slave Association drowned in legal troubles, Mitchell and Walton solicited support from numerous congressmen and were even reported to have met with President Theodore Roosevelt, wielding, as they claimed, 320,000 Black votes. Walton soon secured the sponsorship of Senator Mark Hanna, a Republican from Ohio, who in February 1903 introduced what would predictably become known as the Hanna Bill, a successor to the 1898 Mason Bill. It was destined to be the last great measure introduced by the early ex-slave pension movement. Coverage of the bill was exhaustive. The response from the Black press varied from cautious support to frenzied criticism. One editorial from Houston, reprinted in the *Bee*, hailed the senator as being "among the host of good men in this country who believe in giving every man his just dues. The Negroes who served 244 years as slaves in this country had much to do with the general welfare and prosperity of these United States and there is no good reason why he should not get pensioned."[69]

Yet negative coverage far outstripped appeals to the morality of pensionary reparations. The fundamental concern once again involved the bill's unintentional encouragement of fraudulent agents. The *Southwest Christian Advocate* professed itself "only too glad to see every one of the aged ex-slaves pensioned" but curdled at the practices of the movement's grifters. For its part, the *Colored American* "urge[d] our people throughout the South to beware of the aggitation [*sic*] now progressing over the proposition to pension the aged ex-slaves of their section." Others speculated that Hanna's introduction of the measure was a calculated move to win the support of Black Southerners in his upcoming presidential bid, betraying the Ohioan's shamelessness in taking "advantage of any movement which may grow out of this scheme to bamboozle ignorant Negroes of the South." The day after the Hanna Bill's introduction, word had already spread to rural Louisiana, and the new commissioner of pensions, Eugene F. Ware, was receiving inquiries relating to its passage.[70]

White newspapers, especially the *Atlanta Constitution*, served up so many breathless reports on the bill its editors went hoarse with contempt. One article hypothesized that Hanna may have been oblivious to the prior charges of fraud that hobbled the various ex-slave movements. After all, he had introduced it by request, and so the senator was probably indifferent to its fate. Yet he may have had other reasons for endorsing the bill. As he was a rising star in the Republican Party, the *Constitution* argued that his sponsorship came after hearing—incorrectly—of Roosevelt's support of the ex-slave pension bill. In any event, given Hanna's public stature, his introduction of the bill invited gangs of swindlers to descend upon the uneducated freedpeople of the South yet again, tricking them out of their earnings and confusing them as to who their true friends were.[71]

The *Constitution* was unrelenting in its denunciation of Hanna's bill. It reprinted excerpts from dozens of other newspapers across the partisan divide that likewise questioned or condemned the legislation. The *Washington Post, Washington Star, Pittsburg Gazette, Pittsburg Dispatch, Baltimore Herald,* and *Philadelphia Record* all joined in the chorus, the latter remarking, "Forty acres and a mule in reconstruction times was nothing in comparison with the Hanna bill to bestow government pensions on the emancipated slaves. In either case the doom of the poor negro is to be cruelly duped." The *Constitution* was forced to conclude that Senator Hanna owed it as a "duty" to "these misguided, credulous colored folk ... to withdraw this unfortunate measure." But beyond that, "it is the duty of the white people of the country to do everything in their power to see that the surviving ex-slaves are protected from the fraudulent designs of such negroes as Vaughn [*sic*] and other schemers living easy on this fake."[72] Hanna withdrew the bill that summer. He cited the widespread agitation sparked by the bill's introduction and repudiated the bill's hijacking by fraudulent parties, all the while pleading ignorance of the negative Senate committee report released three years prior by Gallinger. And thus the man considered by many the "personification of the republican party" made his ignominious exit from the struggle for ex-slave pensions. It was altogether fitting.[73]

The ex-slave pension movement was a carnival for the white press. But more than that, it served an indispensable function in the national political digestive system. Former slaves and their descendants were overwhelmingly laborers and tenant farmers who were burdened with debt and increasingly disillusioned with the Republican Party. For white Republicans, then, attacking the ex-slave pension movement was a proxy battle for the corporatist assault on labor organizing more generally. Moreover, as the party most responsible for the dramatic expansion of the federal budget over Union pensions, crushing a notorious grassroots effort for yet another expansion of the welfare state was good political self-defense, demonstrating at once fiscal responsibility and faithful stewardship of a well-guarded system of entitlements. It was in this spirit that Evans wrote to the commander-in-chief of the Grand Army of the Republic, warning the group of Black agitators infiltrating its outposts and rousing "false hopes concerning a supposedly overdue restitution of 'Freedmen's Bureau funds,' or reparation for historical wrongs, to be followed by inevitable disappointment, and probably distrust of the dominant race and of the Government." Comfortable as they were resting on the laurels of the Great Emancipator, Republicans seldom feared any remaining Black voters switching allegiances to the openly white supremacist Democratic Party. By the second decade of the twentieth century, all such electoral considerations became moot as Black disenfranchisement subsumed the entire South.[74]

For white Democrats, Southerners in particular, the cathartic criticism of the ex-slave pension movement was even more useful. The entire movement was seen as a raft of fraudulent practices, orchestrated by Black people against Black people, and sometimes sponsored by white Republican cynics representing themselves to be the true friends of the ex-slave when they simply cared about his vote. One such detractor sneered that "if the money must be spent, why the south will not object to having it scattered through this section. Many of the old slaves are dependent on their former masters, and these masters, pension or no pension, will continue this labor of genuine kindness and charity." Another, Congressman David De Armond of Missouri, found it "sobering to think of the old negroes in their cabins in the south giving up their small earnings until the time came when they could turn for relief to their natural protectors—the white people of the south."[75]

From sensational stories of imposters to moralizing condemnations of the movement as a whole, the white press of the post-Confederate South reveled in attacking the organizational efforts of ex-slaves. It was a pincushion for every barb of white pathos. "While the newspapers east and west are discussing a few sporadic cases of lawlessness in the south"—the lynching epidemic, that is—"in which guilty colored men are victims," the *Constitution* instead "would direct their attention to other outrages upon the race, more infamous in that they are practiced upon the trusting and confiding, who are duped and led astray." These designing agents exploited the natural "secretiveness" of their victims, just as their Populist counterparts had done years before in the bloody days of labor organizing. "Do not let your employer know" was the cardinal rule, thereby setting worker against owner, neighbor against neighbor, Black against white, in a most perverse and unnatural reordering of society. The popular reactions to the ex-slave movement managed to be at once patronizing and self-absolving, signaling that ex-slaves were a vulnerable class that did not warrant federal patronage and, ironically, that organizing to create political change was so threatening because such change was not possible.[76]

To Bind the Nation

While many bystanders ruthlessly criticized the ex-slave pension movement, opposition to the idea of ex-slave pensions was not universal, even in the Democratic South. The movement was partly coopted by promoters of the Lost Cause. After the introduction of the Hanna Bill, for example, a meeting of the United Confederate Veterans in Birmingham passed a resolution supporting the measure. Their rationale for supporting ex-slave pensions turned the movement's own justifications inside out, seizing upon the idea that emancipation itself had been a mistake. The Alabama ex-Confederates held that "the slaves were in no way responsible for the bringing on of the war between the States, and they were highly eulogized for their fidelity to their masters while they were fighting in the field." Those who did not join the rebel army, the group noted, "peaceably cultivated the plantations of their masters." For many white Southern advocates of the Lost Cause, it was but a short leap from pensioning the blameless ex-slaves to pensioning the blameless ex-rebels. By the turn of the century, then, the pension issue had thus spun far beyond the parameters of the Disability Act, and indeed far beyond the confines of the Pension Bureau, as proponents of ex-slave and ex-Confederate pensions would pirouette on the national stage for many years to come.[77]

The first white supporters for universal ex-slave pensions could be found among the Populists. As with Walter Vaughan—who, though a nominal Democrat, was steeped in Populist politics in Nebraska and a vocal spokesman for labor—white Populists who advocated ex-slave pensions did so out of a sense of justice, for reasons of region, race, and class. Pensioning freedpeople was a common Populist rejoinder to calls from the haughty Democratic establishment to compensate former enslavers for their loss of human capital. As the *Times-Picayune* of New Orleans griped, "forty acres and a mule never came to the freedman through the government's colored bureau, and pensions for ex-slaves will never come to them as a reward for being forced to freedom. It is a fact, though, that many ex-slaveholders need pensions, which they will not get." Thomas L. Nugent, a two-time Populist candidate for the governorship of Texas in the early 1890s, once had an argument with a wealthy gentleman who similarly argued that "if the slave-holders had been paid for their slaves it would have been nothing but justice." Although Nugent himself came from a family of enslavers in Louisiana, and indeed served in the Confederate army, he shot back that, "having had the services of the slaves for several generations for nothing, justice rather demanded that the slaves, rather than their owners, ought to have been paid." For likeminded Populists, a Confederate pedigree served to insulate such genuinely held opinions from charges of race treason.[78]

At the same time, however, legislation such as the Hanna Bill gave enterprising ex-rebels with no Populist politics—or labor solidarities—an opportunity to showcase their Lost Cause apologetics to the nation. Support for the federal pensioning of freedpeople could at once underscore the marginality of slavery to the outbreak of the war, the steadfast loyalty of the enslaved to their enslavers, and the performative benevolence of enslavers compared with the cruelty of Yankee-imposed freedom. It was in this sprit that the Nashville-based *Confederate Veteran*, the official organ of the United Confederate Veterans and the United Daughters of the Confederacy, often featured appeals for federal ex-slave pensions. In one editorial from 1903, a Georgia woman announced her support for the Hanna Bill, crying, "We all want to see the old slaves pensioned—not for policy's sake, but for humanity's sake; not for the negro vote, but for the suffering around us." The Georgian could not understand "how a people who were so hysterical over slavery can be so callous now." The misery of the former slaves, consigned as they were to far-away Southern hovels, no longer seemed to trouble the minds of Harriet Beecher Stowe's children.[79]

Similar motives underwrote the calls for Southern states to include on their state pension rolls what historian Kevin Levin has termed "camp slaves," or enslaved men forced to follow their captors into the Confederate encampments. Only gradually did states create modest pension systems for Confederate veterans and widows, and only gradually were camp slaves tentatively added to the rolls, though in explicitly inferior positions. Mississippi became the first to do so, adding camp slaves to its state pension program in 1888, on the eve of disenfranchisement. The *Confederate Veteran* took the lead in calling for the inclusion of camp slaves on the remaining Confederate state rolls in the 1890s, priding itself on being "the first and only paper in the United States to come out boldly and advocate honestly the pensioning of our old slaves." Yet no state would join this other "Mississippi Plan" until the 1920s: Tennessee in 1921, South Carolina in 1923, and Virginia in 1924. In 1927, North Carolina became the fifth and final ex-Confederate state to open the rolls to camp slaves. Unlike the federal pension for USCT veterans and heirs, and unlike proposals for universal ex-slave pensions, state pensions for Confederate camp slaves were deliberately designed to reinforce the racial hierarchy of Jim Crow by forcing eligible freedmen desperate for money to perform abject subservience and loyalty to their old enslavers and the Old South. In the end, some 2,800 ex-slaves were granted Confederate pensions for their service as camp slaves, those "ignorant, yet faithful" servants "quick to leave the old plantation to go to the front to bear the burdens of the master, forage for him, and nurse him while sick or wounded," as the *Confederate Veteran* rhapsodized. In peace and war, "the negro slave delighted in serving his white folks." Black Southerners were never impressed with the Confederate cause, only by it. Among the many things stolen from them by their captors was the opportunity to escape to the Union army, enlist as soldiers, and live out their days on a more substantial and dignified Union pension.[80]

State pension programs in the former Confederacy developed sporadically and without significant funding. They were, in effect, custodial tributes to the living monuments of the Lost Cause. Federal pensions were always the prize. Comparatively generous, they necessarily invoked a claim on the nation-state, a recompense for patriotic sacrifice, whether in the War of the Rebellion or, as proponents of reparations argued, the war that was American slavery. The cultural and economic chasm between the federal military pension behemoth and the fourteen state programs for Confederate pensions was an incontrovertible and inescapable barrier to full sectional reconciliation, even as the nation reunited politically. White Southerners resented bearing the tariff burden to finance the federal pension system—though not nearly as much as Black Southerners resented their taxes to fund Confederate state pensions—and sought a way to remedy the economic imbalance by opening the rolls to rebels.[81]

Such a scheme found a professional advocate in the first scholar of the Pension Bureau, William Henry Glasson. Though tinged with standard Democratic hostility toward the federal agency, Professor Glasson's two studies—*History of Military Pension Legislation in the United States* (1900) and *Federal Military Pensions in the United States* (1918)—would shape scholarly attitudes toward the bureau for decades. Glasson also dedicated several articles in support of federal pensions for Confederate veterans and their heirs. The "extravagance and waste of the federal pension system has worked especial hardship" on the South, Glasson argued, which had "its own burdens to bear." He asked his readers, was "this position of financial disadvantage to be accepted by the South as the necessary consequence of an unsuccessful attempt at secession? Is it part of the fortune of war?" Glasson of course thought otherwise. He suggested federal pensions to ex-Confederates would go a long way toward unburdening the South—an act that "may be regarded in some sense as due reparation for an injustice done."[82]

The idea of federally pensioning ex-Confederates alongside Union veterans had been around for some time when Glasson made his proposal. It could be traced back as far as the failed Horace Greeley campaign for the presidency in 1872, and continuing through the mid-1880s, when Southern congressmen successfully restored U.S.-Mexican War veterans to the federal rolls in spite of their later service to the Confederacy. But universal Civil War pensions still eluded them. In September 1898, the *Confederate Veteran* published a stunningly perverse argument linking the Emancipation Proclamation to the necessity of Confederate pensions beyond the simple demand for compensation. According to John N. Lyle of Waco, Texas, because Lincoln's proclamation was issued as a military necessity to preserve the Union, the South "was made to contribute about four million slaves . . . to its salvation" and, by virtue of this contribution, the "South has exhibited as much, if not more, regard for the integrity of the Union than the States of the North." Such a counterfactual rendered the rebellious enslavers as the true saviors of the Union and liberators of the enslaved—all at the mere cost of removing any trace of violence or coercion from the history of the Civil War. Lyle made his case, ironically, in front of the Patrick Cleburne Camp of the United Confederate Veterans, named after the Confederate general who had proposed the enlistment of enslaved men as soldiers in 1864, eliciting a barrage of condemnation from the Confederate government, for which the perpetuation of slavery was its sine qua non.[83]

Ultimately, though, it was a speech delivered by President William McKinley that reignited political interest in adding ex-Confederates to the federal pension rolls. The occasion for McKinley's brief address on December 14, 1898, was to celebrate the recently signed peace treaty between the United

States and Spain, ending the late war. Scholars have long understood the Spanish-American War to be a flashpoint in the history of sectional reconciliation, when Northern and Southern whites could unite in common cause against Spanish "barbarism." As historian Greg Grandin has written, "The War of 1898 was alchemic. It transformed the 'Lost Cause' of the Confederacy—the preservation of slavery—into humanity's cause for world freedom." McKinley thus proudly proclaimed that "sectional lines no longer mar the map of the United States" and that "the Union is once more the common altar of our love and loyalty, our devotion and sacrifice." Every soldier fallen in the late War with Spain deserved the nation's care, as did his widow and his memory. Indeed, the nation's cemeteries, McKinley suggested, were proof of the nation's patriotism. "Every soldier's grave made during our unfortunate Civil War," waxed the president, "is a tribute to American valor." And then, to deafening applause and cheering, McKinley pledged to forever put aside sectional differences by offering to help care for the graves of rebel soldiers. The speech resonated with white Southerners who felt the sting of every neglected, dishonored Confederate graveyard. But the speech was especially significant because it was delivered by a Republican president in the South, in Georgia's state assembly.[84]

McKinley's speech reanimated the ex-rebel pension scheme. After quoting several incriminating blocks of McKinley's speech, the Black editor of the *Richmond Planet* concluded that although he did not outright "recommend the pensioning of the ex Confederates, . . . he will no doubt be asked to do it. This will be a test of the kind friendship manifested. It will be practical legislation against that of the sentimental kind." Plenty of romanticized paeans to the Lost Cause suffused the national landscape, serving as the coin of the cultural realm for much of the long post-Reconstruction era. But to invite exrebels onto the federal pension rolls, in many ways the last bastion of Unionist loyalty, would legislate away the War of the Rebellion. The *Bee*, for its part, ran numerous editorials in December 1898 attacking McKinley. It ridiculed his Southern tour, in which the president so vainly appealed to "the vanity of the southern people." But "stretching flowers over the graves of ex-confederates" would "not unite the sections," just as McKinley's "appointment of southern brigadiers did not bring him votes." Likewise, T. Thomas Fortune, the influential civil rights leader and editor of the *New York Age*, berated the president at a mass meeting of the National Racial Protective Association in Washington, held to protest McKinley's refusal to intervene against lynching. Fortune demanded that if the Republican Party wanted to "unload the colored voters," voters deserved to know whether the federal government actually intended to care for Confederate graves, and thereafter the widows, orphans, and veterans of the Confederacy. To Fortune and many other Black onlookers, the revolting prospect of pensioning ex-rebels was folded into the greater betrayal of the Republican Party.[85]

Their fears prove justified. As many in the Black press predicted, care of the Confederate dead easily slipped into care of Confederate living. One month after McKinley's speech, Senator Marion Butler of North Carolina, once the leading Populist in the state, introduced an amendment to a general pension bill that would make ex-Confederate soldiers and their heirs eligible for admission to the federal pension rolls by virtue of their service during the Civil War. Butler argued that the measure would ensure "that in the future the Government shall make no distinction in the matter of pensions between the citizens of the different States." Technically it already made no such distinction, recognizing only the past loyalty or disloyalty of individuals within those states, North and South alike. On the Senate floor, Butler relitigated secession and war in a speech so heroically ahistorical it might have caused even the "Unionist" Confederate John Lyle to raise an eyebrow. Butler spun an account wherein there was not a single "rebel" in the whole state of North Carolina, and indeed "that not a single Southern soldier was a traitor or rebel against this Government"—in fact "there was no rebel army." Secession was entirely legal and peaceable and the war itself was an act of Union aggression and Confederate self-defense. And the South should no longer be considered a "conquered territory" when it comes to federal provisioning.[86]

Although Butler was forced to withdraw the amendment soon after its introduction, his initiative, coming as it did on the heels of McKinley's speech, ignited a firestorm in the Black press. The strongest reaction came in the pages of the *Bee*, a tireless opponent of pensions for all ex-slaves and all ex-rebels alike. Deploring the senator's "disgusting and false" argument that "those who took up arms against the Union were not rebels but were patriots," the editor exclaimed that they had in fact "rebelled against the government which they had sworn to serve and honor. They rebelled against every sentiment of loyalty to the Union and openly declared their right and duty to dismember it." As for their oft-repeated postwar loyalty, Black Americans knew better. When the defeated Confederates "were asked to return to the Union, they scornfully refused to do so and by pelf and plunder sought to strengthen their hands with the sinews of war. They were not only rebels then, but they are rebels now." One can imagine the editor taking a cue from Commissioner Evans, dismissing the matter with the argument that the ex-rebel was granted his pension when he was permitted to leave the battle-field with his life spared.[87]

Yet white Southerners, even Confederate veterans, were divided on the issue. Some had advocated their inclusion on the federal rolls for decades and enthusiastically supported Butler's measure. Others were insulted, aggrieved by the apparent threat to their masculinity. They staunchly opposed the Butler amendment. The Confederate camp at Vicksburg thought the idea "humiliating," as did one in Arkansas, which wanted "no special favors of the government." Most of these critics seem to have been wealthier veterans, of the political and economic class that opposed any such redistributive legislation. Other petitioners, however, spoke in favor of Butler's amendment, and the senator read them aloud to enter them into the record. Within a few months of Butler's speech, more camps spoke out in favor of the amendment. Some had even switched positions entirely. Having previously passed a resolution critical of federal ex-Confederate pensions, the camp at Dalton, Georgia, reversed course, endorsing the amendment and forwarding a letter of praise to Butler. They now regarded the measure as "a vindication of the Confederal cause," and a way to balance the ledgers of thirty-five years of "paying their part of the pensions for the Union soldiers," a concrete measure to "cement the whole country, eliminating sectional lines," which would at last "prove to the world that we are a united people."[88]

The U.S. Pension Bureau thus occupied a rather ambiguous, ironic place at the turn of the century. On the one hand, to most Northerners and to Black Southerners, it was a unifying force for the nation, so long as certain populations were excluded; on the other hand, for much of the white South, the bureau could cease to be divisive only if it treated all states, and, more precisely, all sides of the conflict, equally. In the early twentieth century, some conciliatory Northern commentators stressed how the Pension Bureau already functioned as a unifying force. They insisted that Southern Unionists were every bit as much a part of it as their Northern counterparts. Such anti-sectionalist appeals likewise buttressed the agency's status quo against any further enlargements of the federal pension program, whether to ex-rebels or ex-slaves. One such appeal came from the pen of Thomas A. Broadus, a long-time employee of the bureau. In an article from 1901 titled "The South and the Pension Bureau," Broadus suggested that the agency was a "unifier" and relied heavily on Lost Cause ideology to build his case. The Civil War, he conceded, "was a terrible debate between sincere debaters," and the process of "reconstruction" only began after the end of Southern occupation. Broadus ran through the history of the Union pension system, noting how "successive acts removed limitations, opened wider doors, increased benefits, and constantly liberalized the system," while at the same time maintaining a firm line on the matter of loyalty. But it would be wrong to assume the South was not benefiting from the federal largesse. Broadus reminded his Southern readers most pensioners of the "old wars" prior to the War of the Rebellion had been restored, and Southern veterans of the recent Spanish-American War, unborn at the time of Appomattox, had flocked to the regular U.S. Army and afterward were now well represented on the rolls.

But above all, Broadus cited the Southern Division as the great reconciler. He praised its treatment of Black veterans and survivors. It was a challenging feat for the division. Special examiners, "sent to investigate a case, had to wade through revoltingly muddy waters of fact and detail to ascertain the truth." Meanwhile, their former enslavers remained benevolently involved in the process. They were "still found for witnesses," these men and women "who once ruled over great plantations and are now very poor and very feeble, but glad to leap back in memory over the years of shabby-genteel existence to their proud days of opulence and power, and recall the incident when 'our Jane was married to Colonel Duval's Sam, with consent of owners.'" (Broadus's Pension Bureau, it seemed, reconciled not only North and South but the oxymoron of bureaucratic sentimentalism.) The past was the past, Broadus noted wistfully. But a glorious future lay ahead for the United States and its binding conquests abroad.[89]

Black Americans refused to abide the persistent and increasingly brazen efforts to somehow allow ex-Confederates on rolls of the Southern Division. Those fighting at the same time for universal ex-slave pensions to remedy two and a half centuries of injustice drew a profound contrast between their own push for inclusion and that of their old captors and sworn enemies of the Union. In late 1901, a longtime Black political leader in Arkansas, M. M. Murray, submitted a plea for ex-slave pensions to the *Colored American* in Washington. His appeal invoked the much-tested patience and patriotism of Black Southerners but braided it with the matter of ex-Confederate pensions and government welfare more generally. "Does not the Negro stand to-day as a foundation stone or monument to this proud American Government?" Murray beseeched his readers. "Do you not know that a number of the Southern States have enacted laws pensioning the old incapacitated ex-Confederate soldiers, but refused to appropriate a copper cent for the old incapacitated ex-slave?" Thousands of veterans of the U.S.-Mexican War who joined the rebel army were drawing pensions to supplement their physical inability "to earn support." But what of the half million freedpeople still living who were every bit as disabled? When the federal government allowed pensions to men who served a mere ninety days but denied pensions to men and women who labored their entire lives to build the country—and were as well "incapacitated from hard labor to earn support"—it affixed "a dark star in the crown of our America," surrendering any lingering nostrums of equal protection under the law.[90]

IN THE END, the grassroots ex-slave pension movement and the episodic attempts to federally pension ex-Confederates both met defeat. They rose and fell simultaneously, intersecting in surprising ways from the 1890s into the second decade of the twentieth century. The fifty-year anniversaries of Civil War battles punctuated legislative efforts to take the final step to full reconciliation and enroll ex-rebels in the federal pension system. The Baltimore *Afro-American* joined many in complaining that "pensions for the soldiers that fought against the Union" had become the rallying point for the Democratic Party in 1913. The sought-after "prestige through the [federal] pensioning of Confederate soldiers" was part of their nationwide propaganda campaign against Black Americans, an idea that "took deep root at the reunion, held Gettysburg." White America, it seemed, needed constant reminding that allowing "Confederates pensions would be a complete reversal of the present scheme of allowing pensions [to] Union soldiers."[91]

Meanwhile, the besieged Ex-Slave Association, now officially led by Callie House, doggedly struggled not only to organize for reparations but merely to survive as an organization. Working with the Black attorney Cornelius Jones, House filed suit against the federal government in July 1915. Their legal case centered on the so-called cotton tax, which had been applied to confiscated cotton from Confederate slave labor camps during the Civil War. Taxed from 1862 to 1868, the fund reached over $68 million. Jones and House argued that this money should not be redistributed to the respective planters or used to fund state Confederate pension programs, as many Southern senators wanted, but instead redistributed to the surviving freedpeople. Here was a literal debt owed to workers who produced wealth. In response to Jones's argument— which he carefully calibrated on the narrow matters of taxation and property rights, avoiding grander talk of historic injustice—the Treasury Department insisted that the funds from the cotton tax belonged to the federal government, and that if freedpeople "had any claim it would be against their masters." In so doing, it immunized the government against reparations claims. And indeed it was on the grounds of government immunity that the case, and the early ex-slave pension movement, was defeated. But freedpeople and their children continued writing to the Pension Bureau about the matter of pensioning ex-slaves. Some even cited the remaining cotton fund. The reparations ideal articulated by the ex-slave pension movement had more staying power than the organizations that gave it a more cohesive form and direction.[92]

In the shadow of the Populist insurgency, the tumultuous coexistence of the ex-rebel agitation and the ex-slave pension movement sketch out a future history that might have been. Though both efforts suffered attack for different reasons, their assailants generally shared a political ideology hostile to universal welfare and resolutely devoted to policing an elaborate system that distributed limited benefits to a particular class of citizens. As such, they sought not to create empowered citizens bound together in collective solidarity but rather atomized (and stigmatized) subjects bearing an individual, contractual relationship with the liberal state. Against two very different interest groups vying for federal benefits, Pension Bureau administrators, with the aid of its professional and ruling classes, shielded their agency against the expansion of rights, entitlements, and welfare. Their technocratic utopia may have mitigated suffering on a certain scale, but it was also premised upon limited, contractual mitigation alone. Those suffering without specific claims to lodge might as well suffer in silence, for their conditions lay beyond the power or purview of the administrative state.

Freedpeople hoped for better, for a more responsive, accessible, accountable, and compassionate government. "It is a wonderful thing to live," reflected M. M. Murray, "and whenever any government decides that it is not responsible for all of its citizens in a certain degree, it has failed to learn to live."[93]

Conclusion

In 1904, only months after the demolition of the ex-slave pension movement, rumors circulated of plans to abolish the U.S. Pension Bureau as well. Such talk swirled around the reelection campaign of President Theodore Roosevelt, whose nomination was secured after the death of his primary challenger, Senator Mark Hanna, less than one year after the latter disavowed support for universal ex-slave pensions. The Black press worried that the reelected president would remove the Pension Bureau from the Department of the Interior and place it fully under the control of the adjutant general in the War Department, the office that once oversaw the Freedmen's Branch. Yet Roosevelt did not relocate or consolidate or abolish the Pension Bureau. Instead, he inaugurated a new, final pension program. It came by way of Order No. 78, issued on April 13, 1904, and taking effect on March 15. It broadened the terms of the Disability Act so as to offer the first age-and-service pension in the nation's history.[1]

Old age was now regarded as an infirmity. All veterans who had served at least ninety days and reached the age of sixty-two were entitled to a fixed-rate pension that increased every three years until the veteran reached seventy, when he could expect a twelve-dollar monthly stipend for the remainder of his life. Such rates were offered regardless of income, wealth, or disability and, as such, applied to virtually every Union veteran, removing much stigma from the pensioner class. The following year, 1905, saw the high-water mark of the pension rolls. Congress wrote the executive order into statute law on February 6, 1907. The press had indeed predicted a "rush for pensions" in its wake, but such widespread fears of an "unknown army" of prospective pensioners in the end proved groundless, as most of those enrolled under the service law simply transferred from the rolls of the Disability Act of 1890 to take advantage of the higher rates (and liberate themselves from medical examinations, no doubt). From February 1907 to June 1909, the Pension Bureau issued nearly 445,000 certificates under the 1907 service law, but fewer than 4 percent were from first-time claimants. Still, longtime critics of the bureau who had fought the uphill battle against federal welfare expansion continued to grit their teeth at these final acts of deathbed generosity.[2]

With only two major requirements, the service law was the most universal pension program to date. Yet it rested on a set of assumptions that scanned more readily with the citizens of the industrialized North than the newly doc-umented citizens of the agrarian South. Without birth certificates or state or church registries, freedmen struggled to prove their exact age.[3] If their birth-date was unknown, in many cases it would simply remain unknowable, and ex-slave claimants would still require a physician's examination to approxi-mate their age. Thus when former slave Solomon Johnson applied for a pen-sion under the service law less than three weeks after it came into effect, the commissioner of pensions returned his rejected application, explaining that "the best obtainable evidence of the date of your birth is required by this Bureau." Then followed a set of proofs needed to verify his age. "If there is a public record of your birth," wrote the commissioner, "you should forward a verified copy of it. If there is no such record, and there is a baptismal record, a verified copy of the baptismal record should be forwarded. If there is no baptis-mal record, and there is a family record showing the date of your birth, a verified copy of the family record should be forwarded." That family rec-ord, a Bible most often, needed its authenticity verified by a magistrate. "If you are unable to furnish any of the evidence indicated," the note concluded, "you should state that fact, and the reasons why you are unable to furnish it, under oath." In reply, Johnson plainly stated that he "was born a slave and that there was no record of his birth [as] far as known. All he knows of his birth and age is from the information from his master and mistress who told him he was born on the 2nd or 3d day of March, 1834." Having Johnson's date of birth on his enlistment and discharge records in the War Department did not seem to help. After all, with wartime enlistees, exact age mattered less than the sound-ness of a potential recruit.[4]

And so, as Solomon Johnson and many other ex-slaves learned, the near-universal service law of 1907 could still bedevil the previously undocumented. Many, in fact, found themselves locked in the lower rates of the Disability Act with its burdensome requirements for regular medical examinations. In Charleston, for instance, the first decade of the twentieth century found Dan-iel Drayton suffering from a host of ailments, from blindness to paralysis, such that he easily met the threshold for the highest rates under the Disability Act. Yet as a septuagenarian, he would have received more under the service law, and therefore ventured his application. Without satisfactory proof of his age, though, the bureau rejected his claim, and like Johnson, Drayton recited the vernacular account of his alleged birth date, that "he was often told, by his mother, that he was born in 1832 but . . . can not remember the month of the year," and that his enslaver's wife had long ago told him as "far as she can rec-ollect, that I am only a few years younger as [*sic*] she is, and she says she is seventy eight." The only written record was the plantation book that had been destroyed by fire in the war.[5]

By necessity, then, for many ex-slave claimants, the simplest fields of inquiry, one's birthdate, often evoked personal stories of slavery and wartime emancipation—fraught, indeterminate, unmappable stories that could not fulfill the strictures of the administrative state. Robert Roddy confessed to his inability to furnish his birthdate, there being "no church or public record," nor any "family record of his birth as his parents & himself were slaves." He likewise never heard of "a Bible or family record" being used by his family's enslavers. What he did know, however, was that when he was brought to Louisiana from "South Carolina in 1846 by the negro traders," he had been sold as a sixteen-year-old. Unscrupulous as the traders invariably were, "repackaging" their human products to the point where they were not simply selling enslaved people but making them, moments of sale punctured the memorial fabric of many enslaved men and women. Roddy thus remembered his age "from that year to the present time." From Big House Bibles and dusty plantation journals to the records of slave sales, the instruments-turned-artifacts of the old enslavers' regime continued to infiltrate, and indeed substantiate, freedom's paperwork.[6]

In ways unanticipated, freedpeople's documentary struggles for pensions continued well into the twentieth century. Such a case is enshrined in the classic 1944 autobiography *Black Boy*, by Richard Wright. In one heartrending sequence, Wright narrates his grandfather's fifty-year feud with the War Department, which had denied him a disability pension on grounds of mistaken identity, a clerical error that enlisted him as Richard Vinson instead of Richard Wilson. "In letter after letter," Wright recalled, "Grandpa would recount events and conversations. . . . He would name persons long dead, citing their ages and descriptions, reconstructing the battles in which he had fought, naming towns, rivers, creeks, roads, cities, villages, citing the names and numbers of regiments and companies with which he had fought, giving the exact day and the exact hour of the day of certain occurrences, and send it all to the War Department in Washington." Whenever a "businesslike envelope" came back from Washington in reply, Wright's grandfather would hand it over for him to read, only ever to learn that his claim "had not been substantiated" and his pension application consequently rejected. Cursing under his breath, his grandfather would take the letter to his comrades in the neighborhood, asking them to read it as well. So constant was this trial, even in the 1920s, that the young autobiographer himself began to dream of one day receiving an apologetic letter from the federal government verifying at last his grandfather's claim, commending his service to the country, and begging his forgiveness. But no such letter ever came. And his grandfather died brooding and bitter, his Kafkaesque bureaucratic ordeals having fully convinced him that the Civil War was in fact unfinished and would soon start again.[7]

As slavery's final survivors struggled for relief, the dynamic and transformative history of the Pension Bureau began to ossify and erode. As the pension rolls tapered, the pension issue lost its power as one of the most notorious and intractable problems of the seemingly eternal Civil War. Aside from a few pieces of legislation increasing rates of payment to veterans, widows, army nurses, and caretakers, no new pension programs were created in the bureau's final years. By 1930, fewer than forty-nine thousand Union veterans remained on the rolls, eclipsed by more than 167,000 widows and minor children. On July 21, 1930, nearly one hundred years after the creation of the Pension Bureau, President Herbert Hoover signed Executive Order 5398, creating the Veterans' Administration by consolidating the Pension Bureau with the Veterans' Bureau and the National Home for Disabled Volunteer Soldiers. It officially ended the Pension Bureau.[8]

IN ITS FINAL DECADES, the Pension Bureau had practically functioned as an old-age national pension system for Union families. It would not be until 1935, with the passage of the Social Security Act, that a long-term program for universal old age assistance would be implemented at the federal level.[9] The federal government now expressed a renewed if limited sense of moral responsibility to the welfare of its citizens, including Black Americans, the kind of broad-based commitment that had been painfully dormant since the fitful end of Reconstruction. At the same time, the various social policies of the New Deal sounded an ambiguous note regarding racial and economic disparities. On the one hand, some have argued that any discriminatory features were soon eclipsed by the New Deal–inspired civil rights movement thirty years later. On the other hand, the institutionalization of New Deal social policy also seemed to institutionalize existing racial disparities in the United States. Central to the latter perspective is the contention that the Social Security Act of 1935 deliberately excluded Black Americans at a critical juncture in the history of federal relief. Southern lawmakers in Congress, the argument goes, spearheaded these exclusionary efforts, determined as they were to uphold the racial caste system of Jim Crow amid the inclusionary thrust of the New Deal.[10]

Much like their attitudes toward Reconstruction-era endeavors, white Southerners consistently bristled at any perceived federal interference in state affairs, particularly when done to protect Black Americans. But, much like the suite of federal pension legislation in the preceding seventy years, the language of the Social Security Act was facially race-neutral. It was agricultural and domestic workers, as a class, who found themselves excluded from certain parts of the act, in addition to a host of other workers, from the self-employed and the day laborer to professionals such as doctors, lawyers, and ministers, as well as employees of the government at the federal, state, and local levels. The statutory exclusion, in other words, was based entirely on one's occupation irrespective of race. Approximately twenty million Americans—half the workforce—were excluded from the old age insurance program, of whom fifteen million were white. Given the size of their class, agricultural and domestic workers received the most attention from policymakers and scholars. According to the Census Bureau, the roughly 11.5 million white agricultural and domestic workers constituted 74 percent of all excluded workers, while the 3.6 million Black Americans in those occupations amounted to only 23 percent. It appears that if race was the primary motivation for exclusion, the Social Security Act was poorly tailored to that end, recklessly shutting three times as many whites out of its old-age insurance provisions. From another vantage, however, the 3.6 million excluded Black Americans made up about 65 percent all Black workers, a significant majority of the Black working class who, even after the Great Migration of the early twentieth century, still remained largely tethered to the rural South. Yet it seems rather questionable that 11.5 million white workers could be simply written off by their white representatives as collateral damage in the quest to exclude 3.6 million Black Americans. A better explanation for the exclusion involves the interplay of class, politics, welfare, and the modernizing administrative state.[11]

The debate over the exclusion of agricultural and domestic workers from certain benefits involved a wide array of bureaucrats and policymakers. It began with the earliest proposals for social welfare developed by the staff of the Franklin D. Roosevelt administration. In June 1934, Roosevelt ordered the creation of the Committee on Economy Security (CES), led by Secretary of Labor Frances Perkins. The foundational directive of the CES was to establish a comprehensive program for ensuring the welfare of the unemployed, poor, and elderly, creating a safety net for the nation's "dependents." Those joining Perkins included Secretary of the Treasury Henry Morgenthau Jr., Secretary of Agriculture Henry Wallace, and the director of the Federal Emergency Relief Administration, Harry L. Hopkins. Roosevelt charged the cabinet-level committee with designing a program whose funds were to be derived "by [worker] contribution rather than by an increase in general taxation." The CES favored a business-friendly policy in line with the prevailing technocratic ideology of the day best articulated by the so-called Wisconsin School, a group of policy experts from the University of Wisconsin. So oriented to corporate interests were the committee leaders, in fact, that businesses saw no need to even bother lobbying. Operating under the cabinet-member executives of the CES was its executive director, Edwin Witte (of the University of Wisconsin), under whom came the technical board led by one Arthur Altmeyer, and finally an assemblage of other experts, academics, and bureaucrats from other federal agencies, all of whom influenced the final product of the CES, a bill for a national welfare program to be introduced during the next legislative session.[12]

While the experts busied themselves with designing a sensibly discriminatory system of welfare, two other welfare bills, long since forgotten, spawned mass movements across the country. Unlike the future Social Security Act of 1935, the Lundeen Bill and the Townsend Bill called explicitly for a redistribution of the nation's wealth in order to provide for its workers. The Townsend Bill levied a 2 percent tax on all financial transactions, deposited into a fund that paid a flat $200 per month to every U.S. citizen over age sixty, stipulating that the entire monthly sum needed to be spent within thirty days, thereby guaranteeing the money's immediate injection into the economy. The Populist-inspired Townsend Bill explicitly sought to empty the coffers of eastern banks and the hoarders of great wealth. Its supporters included the roughly twenty-five million individuals who signed petitions for its passage. "Why," they asked, "should a small percent of the people of this great America possess over 90% of all of the wealth, which the two past generations have produced?" Yet the radicalism of the Townsend Bill was outstripped by the Lundeen Bill, which proposed a truly universal, national unemployment insurance program funded by increased taxes on the income and wealth of the rich. Within the concise, two-page bill sat a muscular antidiscrimination clause mandating that unemployment benefits "shall be extended to all workers, whether they be industrial, agricultural, domestic, office, or professional workers, and to farmers, without discrimination because of age, sex, race, color, religious or political opinion or affiliation." Petitions for the Lundeen Bill garnered millions of signatures. It likewise earned the enthusiastic endorsement of dozens of labor unions, including the American Federation of Labor, as well as fraternal organizations, veterans' associations, and groups affiliated with the Communist Party.[13]

Against the threats posed by mass mobilizations of Townsend and Lundeen supporters, the CES devised an omnibus bill composed of eleven titles authorizing seven distinct welfare programs. Title I created an Old Age Assistance program (OAA), offering federal subsidies to state-run public assistance programs set up to offer immediate cash payments to poor, elderly people. (It would later inspire Medicaid in 1965.) Title II instituted Old Age Insurance (OAI), wherein workers and employers contributed a fixed amount from their paychecks in return for future retirement benefits. It later became known as "Social Security" and was the only fully nationalized program in the 1935 act. Title III established a federally funded and mandated but state-administered insurance program for Unemployment Insurance (UI). Other state-run programs introduced by the act included Aid to Dependent Children, later renamed Aid to Families with Dependent Children.[14]

The Social Security Act exposed and widened the jagged fault line in the American welfare state between "insurance" and "welfare." The OAI program, for example, equated insurance and old age pensions with an independent, deserving, morally responsible citizenry to whom the government owed a legitimate obligation—they had, after all, contributed to their own insurance funds—whereas the OAA program and other immediate and temporary assistance efforts of the Social Security Act signaled welfare, relief, and charity to undeserving and dependent subjects. The former enjoyed maturation, the latter stigmatization. In this "two-track welfare state," the upper track operated for empowered, rights-holding citizens, whereas the lower track means-tested vulnerable and unworthy dependents, disproportionately women, racial minorities, and people with disabilities.[15]

Only a universal, federally funded and administered program such as the one proposed in the Townsend Bill or, better still, the Lundeen Bill could have challenged the deepening racial hierarchy in the federal welfare state. Moreover, all evidence suggests that these two bills enjoyed the support of the vast majority of the American public, and the near unanimous support of organized labor. Their universalized proposals were clear, easily graspable, and defensible and would have been easily administered as well, all while communicating an unmistakable message about the value of workers and the centrality of their labor to citizenship—not unlike the foundation of the reciprocal alliances forged by freedpeople with the Union army during the war, exchanging labor for protection. But unlike these radical redistributive measures, the Social Security Act was born and raised not in the streets, fields, factories, and houses of the nation, or even in the Jim-Crowed halls of representative power, but in a policy laboratory. Cooked up by a cadre of experts and academics, the Social Security Act had no obvious popular support and did not seem to need any. Its elaborate series of programs operating at multiple levels of government obscured any easy comprehension among the lay public. It neither received nor required the public's endorsement. And that was precisely the point.[16]

The Social Security Act was passed in large measure to stave off the challenges posed by more radical welfare measures. It was thus not a "compromise bill" per se, with a give-and-take between two or more opposing sides, but rather a bill fundamentally compromised from the start. There remains a live historical debate as to how, and why, the exclusion of agricultural and domestic workers entered into the final bill. Pinpointing its origins has had important implications for many scholars seeking to understand how federal welfare policies institutionalized racial discrimination and contributed to the racial wealth gap. Southern Democratic representatives have long been identified as the most culpable group responsible for inserting the exclusions into the measure. It was in Congress, after all, that agricultural and domestic workers were made ineligible for two forms of insurance, the nationalized Old Age Insurance or Social Security (OAI of Title II) and the hybrid federal-state program of Unemployment Insurance (UI of Title III). In the 1930s, Southern Democrats, members of Roosevelt's own party, controlled both the House and Senate and likewise occupied key leadership positions on important committees, including the House Ways and Means Committee and the Senate Finance Committee. They accordingly wielded considerable power in Congress and, the argument goes, used that power to ensure that a federal welfare state would be a Jim Crow one.[17]

Two interrelated explanations have emerged to explain the motivations of Southern Democrats, one racial and one paternalistic. The racial explanation centers on the existential necessity of protecting Jim Crow, whereas the paternalistic explanation maintains that the control of the planter class through a racially undergirded—though not exclusively race-based—system of sharecropping and tenancy militated against an "external" system of benefits to workers. Both explanations assume a "solid South" united against any and all forms of welfare, particularly to Black Americans. Yet in 1935, the South encompassed, as it always had, a diverse array of interests tied not only to racialized systems of labor but also to regional and local demographics, political ideologies, and competing modes of production. Though most white representatives shared a general belief in white supremacy, the slogan could mean vastly different things to different people, depending on their class position; such an explanation therefore has little purchase on the complexities of creating a permanent federal welfare state. No Southern consensus existed. Moreover, some of the New Deal's strongest critics and supporters could be found among the ranks of Southern representatives.[18]

Despite potentially having a personal economic interest in excluding their own domestic and agricultural workers from the benefits of federal pensions, insurance, and assistance, Southern representatives were surprisingly passive on the issue of exclusion, as historian Mary Poole has revealed. Unlike the deluge of letters and petitions they received in support of the Lundeen Bill and the Townsend Bill, they received only a handful of letters complaining about the prospective inclusion of agricultural workers under UI and OAI. Moreover, conflicting interests arose between plantation owners and the business community in the urban South, wherein the latter would have certainly benefited from an infusion of federal funds into the hands of ordinary Southerners, Black and white alike, dependent as they were on the buying power of the working classes. Instead of viewing the bill as an opportunity to further exploit destitute Black and white workers or to discriminate against the former, most Southern representatives objected that the bill was discriminatory against the South as a region, an accusation consistently leveled against the Pension Bureau for decades. Southern agricultural workers would face higher taxes on manufactured goods levied to support UI and OAI while never hoping to benefit from those programs. As many Southern representatives, including Senator Hugo Black, pointed out, a state administration of these programs would only exacerbate the disparities between wealthier classes and states and poorer ones, leading some Southern representatives to call for a nationally administered and funded program to operate irrespective of state and county lines.[19]

Hearings in the House Ways and Means Committee began in January 1935 and continued through mid-February. By the time the bill was reported out of committee in April, two important changes had been made to the original CES proposal: agricultural and domestic workers were excluded from the two insurance programs (UI and OAI), and a key clause was stricken from the state-run assistance program (OAA), that which required all recipients be accorded equitably sized grants. The change made to insurance eligibility came by way of key members of the CES staff. First, when reporting before the House Ways and Means Committee, Edwin Witte off-handedly suggested that Congress may in the future deem it "wise" to exclude certain populations from OAI, especially farm workers. Later, before the Senate Finance Committee, he appeared strikingly nonchalant about the entire matter, admitting that despite the CES originally recommending "that you include the entire employed population," whether the committee wishes "to follow our recommendation or not or whether you wish to make certain exemptions, is, of course, entirely up to the Congress." Then, on February 5, 1935, Secretary of the Treasury Henry Morgenthau Jr. dwelled at length on the "administrative burdens in the bill," wondering aloud how the Bureau of Internal Revenue would be able to collect the contributory taxes of millions of casual laborers not governed by yearlong contracts with employers. Though other industrialized Western nations, including Great Britain, overcame similar issues when administering their own social welfare programs, Morgenthau expressed much trepidation over the feat, calling the challenges of including such workers "extremely formidable" and "insuperable" and potentially jeopardizing to the whole program. He thus recommended that the bill start small and that "after the system has been in operation for some years, more inclusive coverage may prove to be entirely practicable; but we should like to see the system launched in such a fashion that its administrative as well as its financial provisions contribute directly to the assurance of its success." When pressed by a committee member whether agricultural and domestic workers specifically were the ones Morgenthau had in mind when he expressed doubts to the committee about the bill's "feasibility of practical administration," Morgenthau simply replied "yes." Seven million people, he was told, incorrectly.[20]

Morgenthau's testimony blindsided the congressional committee and others present at the hearing. Perkins recalled how her staff was "startled to have Secretary Morgenthau make an appearance with a carefully prepared formal memorandum in which he apologized to his fellow members of the Committee on Economic Security." Evidently troubled that "it would be a difficult problem to collect payments from scattered farm and domestic workers often one to a household or farm, and from the large numbers of employees working in establishments with only a few employees," Morgenthau, as Perkins recounted, "begged to recommend that farm laborers, domestic servants, and establishments employing less than ten people be omitted from the coverage of the act." Having favored universal coverage, Perkins called Morgenthau's move a "blow" to the program. With the House committee sufficiently "impressed by the size of the project and the amount of money involved," they simply assented to "Secretary Morgenthau's proposal of limitation," Perkins later concluded. Morgenthau's testimony, more than any other factor, proved decisive in the decision to bar agricultural and domestic workers, fifteen million people, from the benefits of UI and OAI.[21]

Though still far from a unified bloc, Southern representatives were collectively more concerned with a particular clause in Title I of the Social Security Act, the OAA program. In this hybrid federal-state welfare system, the operative issue was the original bill's stipulation that federal funds would be withheld from states that failed to ensure "a reasonable subsistence compatible with decency and health" in a nondiscriminatory fashion. Southerners insisted in no uncertain terms that the open-ended language in this clause allowed for potential federal interference in the racial caste system, dangling the threat of withholding funds if standards for Black Southerners were not upheld. As CES director Edwin Witte reported, Southern members took the lead in excising the reasonable subsistence clause from the House bill because they "feared that someone in Washington would dictate how much of a pension they should pay to the negroes." More than a mere relief measure, the Social Security Act threatened to "serve as an entering wedge for federal interference with the handling of the Negro question in the South." Perhaps Southern representatives tapped into the recent memory of Black Southerners' engagement with the Pension Bureau, or the deeper memory of the Freedmen's Branch and Freedmen's Bureau, all of which similarly functioned to place federal administrators and federal dollars in between Black workers and their aggrieved employers. At all events, the only way to prevent federal interference was to strike the reasonable subsistence clause and tilt the program's discretionary power in favor of the states, to insulate the Jim Crow welfare state.[22]

George E. Haynes understood as much. A leading Black member of the Federal Council of Churches, and the executive secretary of its Department of Race Relations, Haynes testified on February 7 to the House committee, vigorously protesting the discriminatory potential of the OAA and indeed the Social Security Act as a whole. He offered extensive evidence on the long history of federal funds deployed by the states to racially discriminatory ends with particular attention to the New Deal relief programs enacted just a few months prior. "The welfare of the Negro population," he reminded Congress, "is bound up with the welfare of the whole people," and accordingly he urged the inclusion of a nondiscriminatory clause to ensure greater equity whether administered by federal or state officials. "We do not believe that this protection against racial discrimination," Haynes concluded, "should be left to the will or discretion of any administrator."[23]

Another testifier, this time a spokesman for the NAACP, Charles H. Houston, similarly harbored grave concerns over the discriminatory features of the bill. After all, three out of every five Black workers faced exclusion under its parameters. His organization therefore opposed the Social Security Act and urged its defeat, for "the more it is studied ... the more holes appeared, until from a Negro's point of view it looks like a sieve with the holes just big enough for the majority of Negroes to fall through." The NAACP favored instead a "strictly Federal old-age-assistance program either with direct benefits or with Federal grants in aid to the States, and such guaranties against discrimination which will insure that every American citizen shall receive his fair and equal share of the benefits according to his individual need." In this regard, Houston argued, Black Americans would most certainly get fairer treatment from a system fully funded and administered at the national level.[24]

Surprisingly, a sizable portion of the Southern Democrats in Congress also spoke out on behalf of greater federal control over OAA. In fact, one scholar has found that of the two dozen representatives who defended increased federal funding for the OAA, fifteen were Southerners. Recognizing the economic distress of the South, and the fact that fewer than 20 percent of the nation's population of sixty-five-year-olds could be found there, these representatives felt that the Social Security Act stood to discriminate against the South as a region. As a matching-funds program, the pervasive fear of many representatives and administrators, and Roosevelt himself, was that the South would be unable to meet federal allotments. And when the South faced discrimination as a region, those in the most vulnerable class position, Black workers, stood to suffer the most.[25]

Finding matching funds in Southern state budgets for the OAA program dredged up one of the darkest ironies in the history of American social welfare. As it happened, though Southern states did not have existing unemployment or old-age programs for the general population like some Northern states, they did have one sort of operative state pension system similar to those designated for Confederate veterans and widows. These hallowed programs, tributes to living monuments of the enslavers' rebellion, survived the economic turmoil of the early 1930s to present Southern representatives with a viable apparatus to merge with the OAA. A deal struck in confidential hearings on the Social Security Act ensured that the money paid via pensions to Confederate veterans and heirs would count toward the state's matching OAA funds. This amounted to as much as $12 million annually, which the federal government met. At once, this bargain, coupled with state discretionary control and the absence of a nondiscrimination clause, allowed Southern states to effectively increase stipends to Confederate veterans and widows while keeping grants for ordinary Southerners, and especially Black Southerners, abysmally low. It was not uncommon for OAA grant recipients to receive less than 8 percent of a typical Confederate pension. Black claimants could expect even less.[26]

And so, at this critical junction in the history of a national American welfare system, the states retained considerable control over Black lives and livelihoods. Nearly three of every four Black Americans, and some 90 percent of Black farmers, still found themselves in the South in the 1930s, a region desperately impoverished, where agricultural and domestic laborers lived and worked on a knife's edge. Nearly 40 percent of the South's farm workers were Black; in 1940, they represented more than 55 percent of the region's sharecroppers. The financial chains of indebtedness bound them to not simply the South as a region but to particular planters, perhaps the very descendants of their former enslavers, who rented out their lands and farm implements and animals, sold them seed and food, and extended credit out of every motive but altruism. The average annual income of a Black family in the rural South at that time was $565, roughly one-third of the average family income of their white counterparts. Relegated to a status of severe dependency by the forces and figures commanding the political economy, former slaves and their descendants found little respite in the newly minted national welfare system—a race-neutral, selective, decentralized welfare system that excluded large swaths of the working class.[27]

Yet for all of the exclusions baked into the Social Security Act of 1935, simply adding an antidiscrimination clause to that piece of legislation would have done little to ensure equitable treatment and even less to ensure universality. Racism indeed played a role, but only just, and is by itself an insufficient explanation for the development and implementation of the Social Security Act. Instead, racism combined administratively with capitulations to the states, hostility to working-class and poor people, and the fetishization of policy expertise to ensure geometric degrees of oppression to Black workers, men and especially women, in the economically depressed and deliberately disadvantaged rural South. The scheme was not lost on them. In 1949, the great Communist leader and activist Claudia Jones argued for the necessity of "organizing the exploited domestic workers, the majority of whom are Negro women," in part through a "legislative fight for the inclusion of domestic workers under the benefits of the Social Security Law." This meant challenging the "recurrent questions regarding 'administrative problems' of applying the law to domestic workers."[28]

LONG SEEN AS AN opening gambit, the Social Security Act of 1935 was at the same time a fitting capstone to the long history of the U.S. Pension Bureau, particularly the administration of claims for Black Union veterans, widows, and dependents. Though racially and regionally inclusive, the vast majority of its beneficiaries could be found in the Northern states. That being the case, many Black pensioners in the post–Civil War South eventually managed to secure benefits in no small part because it was a national system, administered by federal officials, thus bypassing state governments—a critical maneuver for Black claimants since the counterrevolution against Reconstruction. However, the federal apparatus was not entirely staffed by federal officials. At the crucial stage of the medical examination, for instance, claimants found civil physicians deputized as federal surgeons to perform fee-based medical examinations on persons claiming disability. Beginning in the early 1870s, commissioners and critics alike proposed to reform the semiprivatized medical examination procedure to ensure fairness to the Treasury in the case of white Northern claimants, who could often expect a more or less perfunctory exam, all while overlooking the issue of unfairness to the Black Southern claimants, who often faced forbidding scrutiny.

The very idea of medical examinations, of precisely quantifying a level of disability and calibrating it to a stipendiary scale, invoked a technocratic enterprise of staggering complexity. In the fifty years after the war, Congress passed hundreds of laws affecting rates of pay and created three separate Union pension systems. With considerable administrative latitude, the Pension Bureau grew to an unprecedented size, generating a raft of specialized divisions and subdivisions all replete with experts, examiners, and clerks who developed "expertise" on the ever-aggrandizing statutes, rules, and practices of the bureau, its own internal law. For Black claimants in the rural South, most of them formerly enslaved, the dozens of explanatory pamphlets and treatises attempting to demystify the pension process barely burned through the bureaucratic fog. Their struggles were at once personal and collective, impersonal and visceral. Black claimants who lived, worked, and worshipped together viewed their individual claims as composite parts of a collective struggle for not only citizenship rights but a citizenship entirely reimagined.

Yet for freedpeople, the selective, means-tested, technocratic barriers of the bounty system, pension system, and Social Security system undercut the idea of citizenship rights. The broadly discriminatory and essentially nonredistributive welfare systems were designed to curb democratic politics, producing not empowered citizens but beleaguered subjects, forcibly pressing a collective will through the sieve of politically stultifying bureaucratic processes.[29] That tens of thousands of formerly enslaved Black Americans were able to endure this particular administration of "freedom" is an astounding feat worthy of our utmost appreciation. And if we care to look, we might recover in the documentary wake of their struggles, lapping against the stony bureaucratic promontories of yesteryear, an incomparable guide to a more compassionate and just society.

Epilogue

"A misery got me in the chest, right here, and it been with me all through life," remarked the former slave Boston Blackwell to an interviewer in the late 1930s. Blackwell had in fact "filed for a pension on this ailment." During the Civil War, Blackwell fled his captors to join the U.S. Army near Pine Bluff, Arkansas. "It was cold, frosty weather," he recalled, and the journey took two days and nights filled with the sounds of "hounds a-howling," their haunting echoes trailing Blackwell and his freedom-seeking comrades. At last they reached "the Yankee camp," believing "all our troubles was over." Blackwell reckoned he had joined hundreds of runaway refugees and soon found himself conscripted as a driver in the Quartermaster's Department. Promises followed. "The officers told us we would all get slave pension. That just exactly what they tell." And not just a pension but a parcel of land—forty acres, in fact. "Nothing ever hatched out of that, neither."

Blackwell recalled his frontline service during one fiery battle, where he made trips to and from the nearby river to squelch the flames licking at the cotton bales that served as makeshift ramparts. He recalled swearing into the U.S. Army, and even recited from memory the pledge for his interviewer. He recalled where he stood at five-foot-six when he made that pledge some seventy years prior. He recalled his enlistment details. He even recalled his pension application number. "Always I was a watching for my slave pension to begin coming. 'Fore I left the army my captain, he told me to file." He held onto his discharge papers for decades, until "white and black folks bofe told me it ain't never coming—my slave pension—and I reckon the chilren tored up the papers." He sadly confessed that "the Govmint never took care of me like it did some soldiers. They said I was not a 'listed man; that I was a employed man, so I couldn't get no pension. But I filed, like they told me." "I give my whole time to the Govmint for many years," he exclaimed. "White and black bofe always telling me I should have a pension. I stood on the battlefield just like other soldiers. My number is in Washington. . . . Iffen you go there," he begged his interviewer, "see can you get my pension."[1]

Pain and hurt coursed through Boston Blackwell's interview. He had braved a dangerous escape in a war-torn region, helping others to make it to Union lines, where he served dutifully and, later, waited patiently for promises to materialize while working as a sharecropper on a cotton plantation until disability and old age incapacitated him. Blackwell rightly felt betrayed by the federal government, which not only failed to make good on its promises of land redistribution and economic security but similarly refused to compensate his service for the army, which Blackwell tellingly referred to not as his military pension but rather as his "slave pension," perhaps invoking—or conflating—the massive ex-slave pension movement at the turn of the century. These issues had been at the heart of the Black freedom struggle during the long Reconstruction, and it is telling that they still animated slavery's survivors seventy years hence in the midst of the Great Depression.

Blackwell's very interview comes to us as part of an ambitious effort to record the testimonies of formerly enslaved men and women still alive in the late 1930s. Operating under the Works Progress Administration (WPA), members of the Federal Writers' Project fanned out across a third of the country, including the entire post-Confederate South (except Louisiana), collecting invaluable accounts from over two thousand elderly freedpeople and their kin. Although these interviewees represented only about 2 percent of those former slaves still alive, their testimonies have nevertheless offered scholars an extraordinary documentary window, the last of its kind, into the firsthand experiences of enslavement and emancipation.[2]

Yet for decades many historians proved reluctant to use the WPA narratives, particularly historians of antebellum slavery. The perennial concern has been the passage of time. Any former slave alive in the 1930s would have been very young at the time of emancipation, and many scholars have expressed skepticism over the historicity of their stories from "slavery days," more or less discrediting their memories as inaccurate, rambling, untrustworthy, or wholly invented. Others cite the racial climate of the 1930s, and the suffocating racial etiquette overlaying the meetings themselves, wherein the federal employee taking the testimony was often, but not always, white. Moreover, the interviewees not only learned to avoid antagonizing white people but perhaps sought to curry favor with the federal representatives in their midst.[3] However, these concerns about a distorted, Depression-era portrayal of slavery rely on a misguided assumption that certain genres of historical evidence automatically meet a threshold of objectivity and are therefore less demanding of historical scrutiny or skepticism. To regard the WPA narratives as somehow tainted, and thus inadmissible, would be to miss the richly textured and multigenerational narratives they offer.[4]

At the same time, appreciating what the vernacular histories of freedpeople can reveal about their experiences of slavery and freedom—even those collected in the 1930s for the WPA, or the 1880s with the Pension Bureau, for that matter—requires close attention to the specific context in which these documents were produced. What is clear from the testimony of Boston Blackwell and others is that their Civil War–era struggles were still very much ongoing when these testimonies entered the historical record.[5] Although many WPA interviewees expressed considerable pride and relief in still drawing a "soldier's pension," for many others in the Black South, an interview with a federal official occasioned an opportune moment to invoke their long-standing struggles for a pension. In Arkansas, J. F. Boone recalled that his father fought in the war and that "they were supposed to give him a pension, but he never did get it. They wrote to us once or twice and asked for his number and things like that, but they never did do nothing." George Greene remembered losing his father's discharge papers, remarking that if he still had them, he would be "drawin' pension." Greene even made a special trip to where his father had mustered out, but he could not find the papers anywhere. And Omelia Thomas relayed how her brother tried several times, unsuccessfully, to get her father's pension. "They made away with the papers somehow," she sighed, "and we never did get nothin.'" Enoch Beel remembered his father drawing a pension until his dying day, but only later in life. Moreover, despite being told he would "get a bounty," his father "never got a red cent. He come back broke as he went off." Asked why, Beel explained that his father was "turned loose soon as he could and mustered out and lef[t] them right now," with "no time" to ask any questions. Beel himself, while working on a farm in Helena, had lost a leg, which "cost bout all I ever had cumlated," was living with his sister, and was receiving eight dollars per month in welfare.[6]

As Beel's case illustrates, in the 1930s, intergenerational efforts for relief involved the struggle not only for a long overdue "soldier's pension" but also for the various welfare and insurance provisions afforded by the Social Security Act. Nannie Eaves of Kentucky, for example, told of how her father escaped his slave labor camp during the war and enlisted in the Union Army. Interestingly, though she was "now drawing a pension from Uncle Sam," she remarked that if her father had not enlisted, she would be just like those other Black folks "now on de Government," that is, on welfare. On the one hand, Eaves's comment thus underscored the growing cultural divide between welfare and pensions, relief and insurance, unworthy and worthy, as well as a generational divide between freedpeople and those born after abolition. On the other hand, it spoke to a material gulf between the size of hybridized federal-state relief benefits (particularly to Black Southerners) and federal military pensions to Union veterans and heirs. Other interviewees, including Lizzie Barnett, confessed to relying on old age assistance for bare survival.[7]

The hardships percolating in the WPA narratives have sometimes encouraged an especially flattened portrayal of the interviewees. Here, as elsewhere, freedpeople were not simply adopting a posture of victimhood, gathering an audience to bear witness to their suffering as they recorded their "voices" for posterity—a favorite conceit among scholars, who often like to imagine themselves the intended recipients and stewards and, most outrageously, even the "givers" of those voices. Interpreting ex-slave narratives through a modern liberal lens patronizes them and distorts their actions and aspirations. Whether engaging a New Deal employee or applying for a bounty or pension, freedpeople could ill-afford to be content with the presentist cultural token of "validation" that ostensibly comes from having others "see" them and "hear" them. Every testifier knew that speaking truth to power only went so far and that testimony, by itself, however righteous, was not in the least empowering. Their testimonies therefore always had both a broader political purpose, to use their claims-making ability to advance their understanding of citizenship as a relationship of mutual benefit, and an immediate practical purpose, to offer the *right sort* of testimony for the government representatives standing before them—and very much between them and their livelihoods.[8]

Boston Blackwell tried as much, begging the interviewer to see after his pension application, and taking care to repeat his name and application number. Others literally prayed for a pension in their interviews. Some respondents could barely contain their anger at years of mistreatment, forgivably misdirected though it may have been. In South Carolina, Sabe Rutledge incredulously asked his interviewer to tell him how to get his social security payments. "You can't tell me bout this pension?" he exclaimed. "Look like to me somebody trying to smother something. Letters come. Cards come," all with instructions to send money and expect "two hundred a month." Rutledge needed useful information and felt that the withholding of it was a deliberate scheme to confuse, mystify, and exasperate. Other respondents similarly felt they were being cheated by arbitrary bureaucrats—fearing that the government would decide someone else "needs it worser than us does"—and still others cried that "us all gwine to be daed [*sic*] 'fo it even come out."[9]

For all their agonies and discouragements, freedpeople and their descendants remained committed to their fundamental belief that they were fully entitled to government reciprocity as part of the bargain they had struck during the war. Whether as contractually defined bounties and pensions for military service or as universal ex-slave pensions or as relief to the needy and elderly, formerly enslaved men and women insisted on their entitlements owing to their incalculable contributions to the nation. Indeed, even as late as the 1930s, many still held out hope for an ex-slave pension, associating it with the retracted promise of forty acres and a mule. One Arkansas freedman wondered why the government was sending around workers for the Federal Writers' Project at all, thinking it was somehow related to an effort, at long last, to enroll all living ex-slaves in a pension program he remembered from the turn of the century. "Are they goin' to give the old slaves a pension?" he wondered. If not, then why do "they want to ask all these questions for then?" Another Arkansas freedman, who was currently drawing welfare from the state, noted, "If there's any chance for me to git a slave's pension, I wish they would send it to me." A freedwoman nearby recalled with evident sadness how, decades before, "they made like they was goin' to give old slave folks a pension. They ain't gimme none yit," she commented; "I'm just livin' on the mercy of the people. . . . I wish I could git a pension. It would help keep me up till I died." The much-celebrated Social Security Act, with its restrictive and state-run discriminatory programs, offered little mercy. "They won't even as much as give me nothin' on the relief," she explained. "They say these grandchildren ought to keep me up. I have to depend on them and they can't hardly keep up theirselves."[10]

Each struggle for a pension, then, was at once a struggle for their own well-being and that of their posterity, each a testament to how, without the assurance of general welfare—without the right to live—one is not free. Of all the lessons to be learned from the world-making and as-yet-unfinished history of emancipation in America, few have been more obscured than the interminable struggle against the administrative diminution of freedom waged in contest and concert by the freedom generation. Their story ends with a beginning.

Acknowledgments

Appreciating history requires, above all, an abiding devotion to contingency, the principle that things might have turned out differently had different actors made different choices in the past. So, too, with this book. At any number of points in its decade-long development it might well have been abandoned. (After all, my limited time in academia was bookended by contingent faculty positions.) That this book was not ultimately abandoned, and that it appears in its current form, owes nothing to providence and everything to those who supported me and my work against the odds—and sometimes beyond all reason.

I never knew quite how to pinpoint my earliest interest in history. Nor did the experiences of being routinely asked the question by searching students and search committees alike encourage any fruitful introspection into the matter. I know, at least, that sometime when I was an undergraduate at Miami University, my nascent interest in the past began to coalesce into a somewhat foolhardy notion that I somehow might turn it into something of a career. My adviser, Andrew Cayton, lent his inimitable encouragement by according me a sense of interest, investment, and deference far above my station. I still recall my surprise when, at my honors thesis defense, Drew suggested that we swap places in his office, me sitting behind his desk, in his very chair, while he sat alongside my other committee member, Amanda McVety, in the two chairs opposite. At some point that hour, something in me made the modest turn from dilettante to apprentice. And in 2013, when we met at a conference in St. Louis, I couldn't help but reflect on that formative moment and on all his guidance had meant to me over the years. I still do, and always will. I learned of Drew's passing only a few months before I defended my dissertation. With a heavy heart, I dedicated it to his memory, but his dedication to my earliest forays into the profession indebted me more than I can ever repay.

I entered graduate school at Washington University in St. Louis in 2010, in the churning wake of the global financial crash, utterly oblivious to what else I could do and what else there even was. Though I still shudder at the six-year learning curve, it was made infinitely worthwhile by my close colleagues and friends; they are entirely responsible for my uncommonly mirthful views of graduate school today. My adviser, Iver Bernstein, was an inspiration to me in the truest sense. In my best moments—writing, teaching, advising—I never fail to reflect on his enduring influence. The History Department and American Culture Studies program supported me in myriad ways. A special thanks to Matt Fox-Amato, Monique Bedasse, Daniel Bornstein, Adrienne Davis, Darren Dochuk, Alexandre Dubé, Gerald Early, Douglas Flowe, Andrea Friedman, Maggie Garb, Christine Johnson, Peter Kastor, David Konig, Lerone Martin, Nancy Reynolds, Leigh Eric Schmidt, and Lori Watt. My stalwart friends enriched my life immeasurably; among the lot are Ethan Bennett, Andy Chen, Noah Cohen, Alex Eastman, Luca Foti, Brian Higgenbothem, Javiera Jaque Hidalgo, Jared Klemp, Amanda Lee, Lisa Lillie, Josh Marshack, Lauren McCoy, Ben Meiners, Gonzalo Montero, Mike O'Bryan, James Palmer, Santiago Rozo, Joel Sherman, Amanda Scott,

Erik Strobl, Melanie Walsh, and Jenny Westrick. It's easy to miss, St. Louis. And indeed not a day goes by.

It took a tenure track offer for me to leave. I owe much to the search committee at Texas Tech University that took a chance on me—Julie Willett, Jeff Mosher, Matt Johnson—for one can withstand only so many rounds on the wretched academic job market. There are more people than I can thank at Tech, but any short list must include Gretchen Adams, Jacob Baum, Paul Bjerk, Zach Brittsan, Laura Calkins, Kim Calvert-Gibson, Lucia Carminati, Amanda Chattin, John Conrad, Stefano D'Amico, Mayela Guardiola, Barbara Hahn, Justin Hart, John Howe, Erin-Marie Legacey, Miguel Levario, Rick Lutjens, Randy McBee, Daniella McCahey, Kalea McFadden, Ron Milam, Victor Moore, John William Nelson, Ben Poole, Nina Pruitt, Victoria Stambaugh, Mark Stoll, Allison Powers Useche, Richard Verrone, and Julie Zook. Special gratitude goes to my dear friend Patricia Pelley, in whose compassion and ribaldry I took refuge and joy.

During my brief sojourn at the University of California, Santa Barbara, I had the good fortune to be welcomed by an exceptional group of scholars. I would be especially remiss in not thanking Nirupama Chandrasekhar, Utathya Chattopadhyaya, Juan Cobo, Manuel Covo, Robyn Fishman, Brynna Hall, Casey Haughin, Harold Marcuse, Alice O'Connor, and Erika Rappaport for their camaraderie and support.

This book is not the product of prestigious yearlong fellowships, sabbaticals, postdocs, or invited talks, nor did it benefit from the work of any research assistant. The National Endowment for the Humanities funded this project with a summer stipend in 2019 that I used to complete my research—just in time before the COVID-19 pandemic. In addition to a start-up package from the History Department at Texas Tech, I also received a course reduction in the spring of 2020 from the Humanities Center as well as summer funding from the Alumni Center. Those modest research funds I managed to garner frequently took me to D.C. I owe many thanks to the archivists at the Library of Congress and National Archives and Records Administration, who have been instrumental to my project at all its stages and have always demonstrated extraordinary solicitude and forbearance.

Over the years, a number of collaborators have helped refine my thinking on this project. I benefited from my fellow panelists at several conferences: Abigail Cooper, Carole Emberton, and Autumn Hope McGrath; Greg Downs, Melissa Millewski, Giuliana Perrone, and Amy Murrell Taylor; Sarah Gardner, Rana Hogarth, Gretchen Long, Leslie Schwalm, and Melissa Stein; and Susan Pearson, Alaina Roberts, and Barbara Young Welke. Anthony Kaye offered me invaluable advice on researching the pension files of the U.S. Colored Troops before I knew the first thing about them. Jim Downs read an early draft of a dissertation chapter on essentially a cold call. Judith Geisberg, then editor of the *Journal of the Civil War Era*, published my first article and graciously introduced herself to me after my first conference panel. And David Waldstreicher and Van Gosse accepted a conference paper proposal from me, and later a chapter for their edited volume, and provided expert counsel all the while. No one had to join or include me in any of these endeavors; that they all did so, in one way or another, speaks to their broad generosity.

Publishing with UNC Press has long been an aspiration of mine. I am grateful for my editor, Debbie Gershenowitz, whose enthusiasm and critical support of this book has been essential beyond words. Thanks as well to my associate editor, Andrew Winters; to Dino Battista, Valerie Burton, Mary Caviness, Andreina Fernandez, Catherine Hodorowicz, Iris

Levesque, Elizabeth Orange, Lindsay Starr, and the entire team at UNC Press; and to the anonymous reviewers of the manuscript for their constructive and timely engagement.

Lasting friends and family have been and will always be there. David, June, Neil, and Laura Kretz all deserve more than a mere acknowledgment for variously putting me up and putting up with me over the years—not quite sainthood but certainly something between a peace prize and a formal apology. The Moore family—Dennis, Clorinda, Tim, Evan, and Amanda—welcomed me into the fold. Stephen Keeney has always shown an abiding interest in my work, and my days writing this book, as my days before, would have been dimmer without him. My archival trips to D.C. were made possible—and memorable (most nights)—by Luke Cumberland-Lambert, poet, novelist, and selfless comrade. Dearest thanks to Logan Cumberland-Lambert as well for her warm generosity. And then there's Irene Domingo and Max Forrester. We have shared so much together and, I like to think, have grown together as well, though reuniting with them in St. Louis or St. Paul or Pasadena always seems to take place outside the passage of time. When I first met Max just days before the start of graduate school, I could not have foreseen just how much I would come to rely on him, on his companionship and confidence, just as now I can scarcely imagine making it through those years or those thereafter without him.

And, at last, to my partner in crime, Katie Moore, whom I found in Texas newly transplanted from the East Coast, New Jersey, Boston, wherever, my coastal elite with whom I've talked endlessly about a society without classes, without need or needless suffering, with whom I've driven across the country and with whom I've fallen in love, as improbably as irrevocably, and without whom I know exactly where I would be, the last place I'd ever want to be, a place without her, which will never do and which will never be.

Notes

MC   Mother Certificate
MFD   Records of the Mississippi Freedmen's Department ("Pre-Bureau Records"),
         Office of the Assistant Commissioner, M1914, NARA
MiA   Minor Application
MiC   Minor Certificate
NARA   National Archives and Records Administration
OR   *The War of the Rebellion: A Compilation of the Official Records of the Union
         and Confederate Armies*, 128 vols. (Washington, D.C.: GPO, 1880–1901)
RBR   Records of the Board of Review, 1874–1881, RG 15
RG   Record Group
SCC   Southern Claims Commission, Records of the Third Auditor, RG 217
SHC   Southern Historical Collection
USCT   United States Colored Troops
USSC   U.S. Sanitary Commission Records
VSP   Valley of the Shadow Project, University of Virginia
WA   Widow Application
WC   Widow Certificate

Introduction

1. William Baltimore, Arkansas Narratives, vol. 2, pt. 1, 97–100, *BIS*; U.S. Census 1930, Arkansas Population schedules, T626, reel 79, NARA.

2. Scholars of the American Political Development (APD) school have sought to account for the growth of the federal government during and after the Civil War. Foundational works include Skowronek, *Building a New American State*; Bensel, *Yankee Leviathan*; Bensel, *Political Economy of American Industrialization*. While maintaining a state-centered analysis, newer APD scholarship has broadened the approach to state building, emphasizing the dynamism of public and private actors in the creation of policy. Novak, *People's Welfare*; Carpenter, *Forging of Bureaucratic Autonomy*; Clemens, "Lineages"; Novak, "Myth"; Balogh, *Government Out of Sight*; Nackenoff and Novkov, "Introduction"; Balogh, *Associational State*; Pearson, "New Birth of Regulation."

Theda Skocpol's indispensable *Protecting Soldiers and Mothers* was the first work of APD scholarship to study the Pension Bureau as a project of welfare-state building, famously deeming it a "precocious social spending regime" and "America's first Social Security System." While the presence of Black pensioners is garnering more attention, their role in the state-building project of the Pension Bureau is still too easily overlooked or dismissed owing to their marginal status on the pension rolls compared with white veterans. Many scholars therefore focus on the bureau's racial disparities rather than approaching Black pensioners as agents in building the administrative state. Skocpol, *Protecting Soldiers and Mothers*; Skocpol, "America's First Social Security System"; Shaffer, "'I Do Not Suppose'"; Goldberg, *Citizens and Paupers*, 93; Logue and Blanck, "'Benefit of the Doubt'"; Wilson, "Prejudice and Policy."

3. For many years, the pension files of the USCT were the sole purview of genealogists and military historians, and to a great extent, the records are still primarily used to tell stories outside of their contested bureaucratic origins. But historians have taken a renewed look at the pension files in the past two decades, producing exceptionally creative studies.

The pathbreaking book was Elizabeth Regosin's 2002 work *Freedom's Promise*, which used the pension files as a window into familial relations in slavery and freedom. Noralee Frankel, Brandi Brimmer, and Tera Hunter have similarly explored issues relating to formerly enslaved women as pension claimants, especially issues of marriage, sexuality, and gendered notions of respectability. Anthony Kaye's *Joining Places* also used the files to examine relational patterns within enslaved and emancipated families, broadening the scope further to reconstruct the shifting political boundaries of neighborhoods. All of these important studies rely chiefly on widows' depositions. Because the Civil War pension system had separate tracks for men (as veterans) and women (as mothers or widows), each group had different eligibility requirements. Whereas men had to prove disability, women had to prove lawful marriage and heirship. The familial matters of widows' claims frequently resulted in more intimate and richly descriptive stories of Black life. Donald Shaffer's *After the Glory* makes novel use of veterans' pensions to detail the post–Civil War struggles of Black veterans, from family and marriage to migration, politics, welfare, masculinity, and memory. Frankel, *Freedom's Women*; Regosin, *Freedom's Promise*; Kaye, *Joining Places*; Hunter, *Bound in Wedlock*; Brimmer, *Claiming Union Widowhood*; Shaffer, *After the Glory*; Regosin and Shaffer, *Voices of Emancipation*.

4. On statelessness, citizenship, and "documentary regimes," see esp. Kerber, "Stateless as the Citizen's Other"; Torpey, *Invention of the Passport*; Lawrance and Stevens, *Citizenship in Question*; Igo, *Known Citizen*, 55–98.

5. Gregory Downs has written the most persuasively on the centrality of the state, particularly the U.S. Army, to the illiberal process of emancipation. See esp. Downs, *After Appomattox*; Downs, "Force, Freedom." Works on the federal occupation of the South during the years of war and postwar surrender often acknowledge how the freedom of freedpeople depended on military force. Ash, *When the Yankees Came*; Grimsley, *Hard Hand of War*; Fitzgerald, "Emancipation and Military Pacification"; Whites and Long, *Occupied Women*; Lang, *In the Wake of War*.

6. Blight and Downs, *Beyond Freedom*, 1–7; Emberton, "Unwriting the Freedom Narrative." For exemplary works that challenge the freedom paradigm, see esp. Hahn, *Nation under Our Feet*; Glymph, *Out of the House*; Rosen, *Terror in the Heart*; Downs, *Sick from Freedom*; Kantrowitz, *More Than Freedom*; Emberton, *Beyond Redemption*; Downs and Masur, *World the Civil War Made*; Manning, *Troubled Refuge*; Reidy, *Illusions of Emancipation*; Glymph, *Women's Fight*.

7. Manning, *Troubled Refuge*, 14–15.

8. The literature on citizenship in the age of emancipation is vast, and increasingly radiating far afield from legal history. Indeed, citizenship is now appreciated not simply for its endowment of rights in the legal and electoral arenas but also for its social and cultural dimensions. Although there is broad agreement that emancipation did not automatically confer citizenship status on former slaves, considerable debate remains over what their status actually was in the years before the Fourteenth Amendment. Kaczorowski, "To Begin the Nation Anew"; Edwards, "Status without Rights"; Vorenberg, "Abraham Lincoln's 'Fellow Citizens'"; Samito, *Becoming American under Fire*; Baker and Kelly, *After Slavery*; Edwards, *Legal History*; Quigley, *Civil War*; Mathiesen, *Loyal Republic*, 118–44.

9. Kettner, *Development of American Citizenship*; Novak, "Legal Transformation"; Foner, *Second Founding*.

10. Though still in its early stages, the literature on contraband camps is growing rapidly. The most recent works, especially Chandra Manning's, emphasize the formative role played by Black refugees in developing notions of citizenship and reciprocity with flesh-and-blood state actors—what might be called the building blocks of state building at the ground level. Rose, *Rehearsal for Reconstruction*; Gerteis, *From Contraband to Freedman*; Hermann, *Pursuit of a Dream*; Berlin et al., *Slaves No More*; Click, *Time Full of Trial*; Engs, *Freedom's First Generation*; Siddali, *From Property to Person*; Downs, *Sick from Freedom*; Manning, "Working for Citizenship"; Manning, "Emancipation as State Building"; Silkenat, *Driven from Home*; Manning, *Troubled Refuge*; Taylor, *Embattled Freedom*.

11. Because this book focuses on the claims-making activities of freedpeople in the post-Confederate South, it does not address the simultaneous efforts by the federal government to subjugate Indigenous peoples in the trans-Mississippi West. Other historians have begun the necessary work of expanding the traditional parameters of Reconstruction, uniting the West and South as twin ventures in the violent consolidation of national sovereignty, a process some call "Reconstructing the West" and others the "Greater Reconstruction." West, "Reconstructing Race"; Richardson, *West from Appomattox*; Rockwell, *Indian Affairs*; Cahill, *Federal Fathers and Mothers*; Genetin-Pilawa, *Crooked Paths to Allotment*; Krauthamer, *Black Slaves, Indian Masters*; Hahn, "Slave Emancipation, Indian Peoples"; Clampitt, *Civil War and Reconstruction*; Field, *Growing Up with the Country*; Roberts, *I've Been Here*.

12. Historians of emancipation in America have relied extensively on the documentary records produced by federal officials during and after the Civil War. In 1976, under the direction of historian Ira Berlin, the Freedmen and Southern Society Project was established to uncover, transcribe, and publish tens of thousands of documents from the National Archives and Records Administration in Washington, D.C. There are currently six volumes of the projected nine-volume series titled *Freedom: A Documentary History of Emancipation, 1861–1867*. As the most influential and invaluable anthology of primary sources relating to emancipation and Reconstruction, *Freedom* puts the enslaved and formerly enslaved at the center of an extraordinarily complex process. Although that process certainly did not end when the series is slated to end, 1867, the material record relating to freedpeople does diminish abruptly with demobilization. For a cautionary note on the use of Freedmen's Bureau sources that echoes these concerns, see Downs, "Emancipating the Evidence."

13. Historical appraisals of the Freedmen's Bureau have changed dramatically since the days of the Dunning School, which regarded the agency in much the same way that contemporary white Southerners had, as an unconstitutional and unnatural federal interference in Southern society on behalf of an "unworthy" race. But by the 1960s, the scholarly indictment of the bureau turned on its head. Historians then rendered the Freedmen's Bureau a vehicle of social control, ensuring the continued subordination of freedpeople in the postemancipation South. This view was perhaps best articulated by William S. McFeely's critical 1968 biography of the bureau's commissioner, Oliver Otis Howard, tellingly titled *Yankee Stepfather*. Paternalist pretentions and a cold enforcement of the contract-labor system preoccupied many such historians—with the notable exception of Foner's *Reconstruction*—until around the turn of the twenty-first century, when historians began taking seriously freedpeople's perspectives in their interactions with bureau officials and, as well, in the bureau's very limited capacity to effect change. In a sense, historians today have finally adopted Du Bois's framing of the Freedmen's Bureau, with his acknowledgment of the

agency's historical singularity and promise alongside his warning against overestimating its capabilities. Bentley, *History of the Freedmen's Bureau*; Cox and Cox, "General O. O. Howard"; Nieman, "Andrew Johnson, the Freedmen's Bureau"; McFeely, *Yankee Stepfather*; Litwack, *Been in the Storm*; Nieman, *To Set the Law*; Cimbala, *Under the Guardianship of the Nation*; Cimbala and Miller, *Freedmen's Bureau and Reconstruction*; McPherson, "Afterward"; Oubre, *Forty Acres and a Mule*; Farmer-Kaiser, *Freedwomen and the Freedmen's Bureau*; Foner, *Reconstruction*.

14. Du Bois, *Souls of Black Folk*, 13–35.

15. Baltimore, Arkansas Narratives, 100, *BIS*. Legal historian Mary Frances Berry has argued that demobilization relieved the federal government of responsibility for sustaining the rights of Black Union soldiers. Berry, *Military Necessity*.

16. Studies of claims-making among freedpeople demonstrate how they used their newly won status to press for recognition and restitution. Issues of family, kinship, property, and loyalty constitute the central categories of analysis in these works. See esp. Regosin, *Freedom's Promise*; Penningroth, *Claims of Kinfolk*; Regosin and Shaffer, *Voices of Emancipation*; Manning, "Working for Citizenship"; Lee, *Claiming the Union*; Hunter, *Bound in Wedlock*; Brimmer, *Claiming Union Widowhood*.

17. For studies of simultaneously gendered and racialized inequality, especially in relation to the changing legal terrain of the mid-nineteenth century, see Edwards, *Gendered Strife and Confusion*; Bardaglio, *Reconstructing the Household*; Stanley, *From Bondage to Contract*; Franke, "Becoming a Citizen"; Cott, *Public Vows*; Welke, *Recasting American Liberty*; Bercaw, *Gendered Freedoms*; Rosen, *Terror in the Heart of Freedom*; Welke, *Law and the Borders*; Farmer-Kaiser, *Freedwomen and the Freedmen's Bureau*; Emberton, "'Only Murder Makes Men'"; Hunter, *Bound in Wedlock*.

18. Colonel James Montgomery, whose troops Tubman helped lead on the Combahee River raid, argued that Tubman "has a double claim on the Government. She went into the field and hospitals and cared for the sick and wounded. She saved lives. In her old age and poverty a pension of $25 per month is none too much." On February 28, 1899, a private pension bill acknowledging her role as a Union nurse increased her $8 monthly widow's stipend to $20. Clinton, *Harriet Tubman*, 191–214; *Increase of Pension for Harriet Tubman Davis*; Nelson Davis file, Co. G, 8th USCT, WA 449.592, WC 415.288, CWPF; H.R. 4982, 55th Cong., 3d Sess. (1899).

19. O'Donovan, "Writing Slavery into Freedom's Stories." See also Hahn, *Nation under Our Feet*; O'Donovan, *Becoming Free*.

20. Dudley, *ARCP* (1884), 32–33.

21. By 1889, some 46,702 USCT veterans and heirs applied for a pension, with 12,416 reportedly admitted to the rolls. These figures were determined by adding the last *cumulative* USCT original application totals in the Pension Bureau's annual report of 1885, with the *annual* USCT totals compiled each year from 1886 to 1889. Beginning in 1890, the Pension Bureau no longer distinguished between USCT claims and other claims filed in the Southern Division. Black, *ARCP* (1885), 29–30; Black, *ARCP* (1886), 26; Black, *ARCP* (1887), 43; Black, *ARCP* (1888), 50; Tanner, *ARCP* (1889), 34; United States, *Statutes at Large*, 26:182–83.

22. As David Roediger has argued in *Seizing Freedom*, disability has been significantly—and curiously—overlooked in studies of the Civil War, despite the fact that far more soldiers left the war disabled than not at all. This omission is even starker for disabled Black

veterans, who are also largely passed over by Roediger. Scarcely a handful of historical studies examine the experiences of disabled freedpeople, let alone Black veterans of the USCT. There is, however, an emerging body of scholarship on the lives of disabled white veterans in the postwar North and South. Roediger, *Seizing Freedom*, 12; Downs, "Continuation of Slavery"; Logue and Blanck, *Race, Ethnicity, and Disability*; Logue and Blanck, *Heavy Laden*, 153–92. For studies of white veterans, see Marten, *Sing Not*; Hasegawa, *Mending Broken Soldiers*; Miller, *Empty Sleeves*; Handley-Cousins, *Bodies in Blue*.

23. The historiography of the ex-slave pension movement essentially begins and ends with Mary Frances Berry's widely celebrated *My Face Is Black Is True*. It focuses on the life of Callie D. House and her efforts with the Nashville-based National Ex-Slave Mutual Relief, Bounty, and Pension Association, the largest group in the crowded field of ex-slave pension outfits.

24. Although this project uses evidence from nearly every Southern state, most bounty and pension claims from Black claimants emerge from ex-Confederate states under longstanding Union occupation, those of the greater Mississippi Valley and the Atlantic seaboard, especially coastal Georgia and South Carolina. Before the war, these areas had among the highest concentrations of enslaved peoples in the South; during the war, they held the vast majority of contraband camps and were the most active sites of recruitment in the USCT; and after surrender, they housed the field offices of the Freedmen's Bureau and Freedmen's Branch.

25. The "nadir" was first periodized from 1877 to 1901 by historian and civil rights activist Rayford Logan but later extended, by Logan himself, to World War I and subsequently to 1920 and 1940. Logan, *Negro in American Life and Thought*. See also Beatty, *Revolution Gone Backward*. For an admirable study that still cleaves to the nadir thesis, see Litwack, *Trouble in Mind*.

26. Steven Hahn has shown that the very repression deployed against Black Southerners was a reaction to their political mobilizations during the years of Reconstruction. Hahn, *Nation under Our Feet*, 413–14. In addition to Hahn's work, for studies of Black mobility in the decades following the Civil War, see Grossman, *Land of Hope*; Cohen, *At Freedom's Edge*; Barnes, *Journey of Hope*; Gregory, *Southern Diaspora*; Schwalm, *Emancipation's Diaspora*; Berlin, *Making of African America*; Jones, *Labor of Love*.

27. Williams, *Great South Carolina Ku Klux Klan Trials*; Keith, *Colfax Massacre*; Giddings, *Ida*; Waldrep, *African Americans Confront Lynching*; Rosen, *Terror*; Feimster, *Southern Horrors*; McGuire, *At the Dark End*; Williams, *They Left Great Marks on Me*; Emberton, *Beyond Redemption*.

28. See esp. Woodruff, *American Congo*; Ortiz, *Emancipation Betrayed*; Kelley, *Right to Ride*; Williams, *Torchbearers of Democracy*; Baker and Kelly, *After Slavery*; Trotter, *Workers on Arrival*; Kelley, *Hammer and Hoe*.

29. Hall, "Long Civil Rights Movement"; Cha-Jua and Lang, "'Long Movement' as Vampire"; Sullivan, *To Lift Every Voice*; Gilmore, *Defying Dixie*; Alexander, *Army of Lions*. Recently, a number of scholars have begun to view the post-Revolutionary era as the "first reconstruction," inaugurating a "first civil rights movement" in antebellum America. Waldstreicher and Gosse, *Revolutions and Reconstructions*; Gosse, *First Reconstruction*; Masur, *Until Justice Be Done*.

30. For legal histories of antebellum claims-making by Black Americans, see Morris, *Southern Slavery and the Law*; Gross, *Double Character*; Edwards, *People and Their Peace*;

Twitty, *Before Dred Scott*; Kennington, *In the Shadow*; Schweninger, *Appealing for Liberty*; Welch, *Black Litigants*; Jones, *Birthright Citizens*; de la Fuente and Gross, *Becoming Free, Becoming Black*.

For legal scholarship on the postbellum period, see Penningroth, *Claims of Kinfolk*; Milewski, *Litigating across the Color Line*; Milewski, "Taking Former Masters to Court"; Perrone, "'Back into the Days of Slavery'"; Perrone, "What, to the Law"; Perrone, *Problem of Emancipation*.

31. Carpenter, *Forging of Bureaucratic Autonomy*; Mashaw, *Creating the Administrative Constitution*; Parrillo, *Against the Profit Motive*; Tani, *States of Dependency*; Parrillo, "Jerry L. Mashaw's Creative Tension"; Tani, "Administrative Constitutionalism."

32. On "ordinary law," see Metzger, "Ordinary Administrative Law"; Metzger, "Administrative Constitutionalism."

33. Smalley, "United States Pension Office," 430.

34. Jensen, *Patriots, Settlers*, 11, 40, 221; Fraser and Gordon, "Contract versus Charity"; Goldberg, *Citizens and Paupers*, 1–27.

35. This is not a comparative study of the experiences of Black and white claimants. In fact, my work suggests that a singular focus on racial disparities in the emerging welfare state engenders mistaken conclusions about the source of inequalities. Even if Black and white pension claimants, for example, had the same rates of acceptance—if, in other words, there was no group-level racial disparity—the fundamental selectivity of the welfare program would remain, along with the broader social injustice it reinscribed. Reed and Chowkwanyun, "Race, Class, Crisis," 167–68.

Chapter One

1. Du Bois, *Souls of Black Folk*, 25.

2. The earliest monograph on the Freedmen's Bureau, written under the influence of the Dunning School, portrays the bureau as a divisive political machine run by carpetbaggers. George Bentley's 1955 monograph on the Freedmen's Bureau struck a more sympathetic note, although he ultimately concluded that the bureau "sought too much for the Negro too soon—and not so much for his own sake as for the benefit of a faction of a party bent on the economic and political exploitation of the states where the Negro lived." Peirce, *Freedmen's Bureau*; Bentley, *History of the Freedmen's Bureau*, 214. For a useful appraisal of the Dunning School, see Smith and Lowery, *Dunning School*.

3. Du Bois, "Reconstruction and Its Benefits"; Du Bois, *Black Reconstruction*.

4. Cox and Cox, "General O. O. Howard"; McFeely, *Yankee Stepfather*; Nieman, *To Set the Law*; Cimbala, *Under the Guardianship*; Cimbala and Miller, *Freedmen's Bureau and Reconstruction*; Oubre, *Forty Acres and a Mule*; Farmer-Kaiser, *Freedwomen and the Freedmen's Bureau*.

5. On the role of state capacity and its misinterpretation as ideology, see esp. Downs and Masur, *World the Civil War Made*, 9–10, 18n5.

6. Vorenberg, "Abraham Lincoln's 'Fellow Citizens,'" 151; Blight and Downs, *Beyond Freedom*, 1–7. On the "mutually beneficial alliance" freedpeople cultivated with Union army officials, see Chandra Manning's brilliant and comprehensive study of refugee camps. Manning, *Troubled Refuge*, 14, 218. For other valuable studies on the "contraband" issue, see Siddali, *From Property to Person*; Gerteis, *From Contraband to Freedman*; Taylor, *Embattled Freedom*.

7. FSSP, ser. 1, vol. 2, pp. 77–78; Berlin et al., *Slaves No More*.

8. [Eaton,] *Report of the General Superintendent*, 4. On federal emancipation policy and practice in the Mississippi Valley, see esp. Teters, *Practical Liberators*.

9. [Eaton,] *Report of the General Superintendent*, 8; Sumner, *Bridge from Slavery to Freedom*, 1, HL; Schmidt, *Free to Work*.

10. Gerteis, *From Contraband to Freedman*, 119–33; Oakes, *Freedom National*, 370–86; Testimony of Captain J. H. Matthews, March 10, 1866, in *Report of the Joint Committee on Reconstruction*, pt. 3, p. 143; *OR*, ser. 3, 3:100–101; FSSP, ser. 2, vol. 1, p. 117.

11. Edwin Stanton to Lorenzo Thomas, March 25, 1863, Letters Received by the Adjutant General, RG 94, NARA; Lorenzo Thomas to Edwin Stanton, April 1, 12, 1863, Letters Sent by the Adjutant General, RG 94, NARA; Gerteis, *From Contraband to Freedman*, 122–23; Taylor, *Embattled Freedom*, 109–16.

12. Surgeon James Bryan to Hon. E. M. Stanton, July 27, 1863, in FSSP, ser. 1, vol. 3, doc. 170, pp. 715–18; Downs, *Sick from Freedom*, 42–64; Foster, "Limitations."

13. "Testimony of General Wadsworth," in file no. 5: New Orleans and Mississippi, reel 200, p. 72, AFIC; Powell, *New Masters*, 84–86; Manning, *Troubled Refuge*, 140–46.

14. Special Orders, No. 63, in Moore, *Rebellion Record*, 7:512; [Eaton,] *Report of the General Superintendent*, 20–21; Hahn, *Nation under Our Feet*; O'Donovan, "Writing Slavery into Freedom's Story."

15. Forman, *Western Sanitary Commission*, 110, 113–14; Yeatman, *Report on the Condition of the Freedmen*, 7–8, 16.

16. Gerteis, *From Contraband to Freedman*, 135–38, 155–56; Manning, *Troubled Refuge*, 141–42; Taylor, *Embattled Freedom*, 113; Bentley, *History of the Freedmen's Bureau*, 23; Eaton, *Grant, Lincoln, and the Freedmen*, 107–10; [Eaton,] *Report of the General Superintendent*, 69; Yeatman, *Report on the Condition of the Freedmen*, 7; Yeatman, *Suggestions of a Plan of Organization*, 4.

17. Mellen, *Report Relative to Leasing*, 8–9, African American Pamphlet Collection, LOC; George M. Peal to T. V. Dayton, March 25, 1865, Letters Received, reel 5, MFD; John Eaton to D. O. McCord, February 6, 1864, Letters Sent, reel 5, MFD; Order No. 11 by Gen. L. Thomas, March 19, 1864, Letters Sent, reel 5, MFD.

18. Regulations of the Secretary of the Treasury, July 29, 1864, enclosed in Wm. P. Mellen to Hon. Wm. P. Fessenden, February 6, 1865, in FSSP, ser. 1, vol. 3, doc. 119, pp. 539–43; A. W. Harlan to Maj. W. G. Sargent, February 5, 1864, in FSSP, ser. 1, vol. 3, doc. 193, pp. 786–89; Powell, *New Masters*, 86; Manning, *Troubled Refuge*, 142.

19. Eaton, *Grant, Lincoln, and the Freedmen*, 106–12; Gerteis, *From Contraband to Freedman*, 125–26; Handley-Cousins, *Bodies in Blue*, 28–31.

20. "Testimony of General Wadsworth," in file 5, New Orleans and Mississippi, reel 200, p. 72, AFIC; John Eaton to D. O. McCord, February 6, 1864, Letters Sent, reel 5, MFD; Gerteis, *From Contraband to Freedman*, 147–81. The idea to create an "Emancipation Bureau" was first proposed by the exploratory American Freedmen's Inquiry Commission, created by Congress in March 1863 to broadly investigate the conditions of freedpeople and recommend provisioning for their future. Frankel, *States of Inquiry*, 204–33.

21. Sumner, *Bridge from Slavery to Freedom*, 5–6, HL; Gerteis, *From Contraband to Freedman*, 185–92; Cox, "Promise of Land for the Freedmen"; Lieberman, "Freedmen's Bureau and the Politics."

22. United States, *Statutes at Large*, 13:507–9.

23. Manning, *Troubled Refuge*, 262–78; Cimbala and Miller, *Freedmen's Bureau and Reconstruction*, xv; Du Bois, *Souls of Black Folk*, 20–21.

24. United States, *Statutes at Large*, 13:507–9; *Laws in Relation to Freedmen*, 57; *Congressional Globe*, 40th Cong., 2d Sess. (1868), pp. 1814–15; Bentley, *History of the Freedmen's Bureau*, 140.

25. W. T. Sherman to O. O. Howard, May 17, 1865, quoted in McFeely, *Yankee Stepfather*, 18; Summers, *Ordeal of the Reunion*, 56; Farmer-Kaiser, *Freedwomen and the Freedmen's Bureau*, 19–20; Bentley, *History of the Freedmen's Bureau*, 136.

26. Howard, *Statement of Br. Maj. Gen. O. O. Howard*, 3–4, HL; Williams, *To Help Me*, 139–70.

27. Captain John Gould to Hon. E. M. Stanton, January 21, 1864, in FSSP, ser. 2, vol. 1, doc. 93, pp. 247–48; A. D. Mitchell to John Eaton, in Eaton, *Extracts from Reports of Superintendents*, 20–23; "Letters from the Wives of Colored Soldiers," *New York Times*, November 7, 1866, enclosed in W. E. Taylor to Major Genl. O. O. Howard, November 12, 1866, in FSSP, ser. 3, vol. 2, doc. 81A, pp. 319–21.

28. Conway, *Freedmen of Louisiana*, 34–35, HL; Manning, *Troubled Refuge*, 252–56; Nieman, *To Set the Law*; Vorenberg, *Final Freedom*; Blair and Younger, *Lincoln's Proclamation*; Edwards, *Legal History of the Civil War*; Du Bois, *Black Reconstruction*, 197–98; Jaynes, *Branches without Roots*, 10; Roediger, *Seizing Freedom*, 63; Egerton, *Wars of Reconstruction*, 93–133.

29. Entries on October 22, 1865, January 13, 1866, Everard Green Baker Papers, SHC; E. G. Baker to Messrs Irby, Ellis and Mosely, October 22, 1865, in FSSP, ser. 2, vol. 1, doc. 325, pp. 747–49; Hepworth, *Whip, Hoe, and Sword*, 25–26; Testimony of Clinton B. Fisk, January 30, 1866, in *Report of the Joint Committee on Reconstruction*, pt. 3, pp. 30–31; Hahn, "'Extravagant Expectations' of Freedom."

30. W. E. Taylor to Major Genl. O. O. Howard, November 12, 1866, in FSSP, ser. 3, vol. 2, doc. 81A, doc. 81B, pp. 319–21, 321–25; Hahn, *Nation without Borders*, 302–309; Downs, *After Appomattox*, 69–70; Mathiesen, *Loyal Republic*, 127–31.

31. Richard Etheridge and William Benson to O. O. Howard, [May or June 1865], Letters Received, reel 16, M843, BRFAL; Click, *Time Full of Trial*.

32. Chas. A. Roxborough et al. to Mr. President, [June 1865], in Bergeron, *Papers of Andrew Johnson* 8:204–5; R. E. Farwell to Brig. Genl. C. B. Fisk, October 20, 1865, in FSSP, ser. 3, vol. 1, doc. 172B, pp. 654–56; Taylor, *Embattled Freedom*, 222.

33. *Freedmen's Bulletin* quoted in Taylor, *Embattled Freedom*, 223, 231, 235–36.

34. Manning, *Troubled Refuge*; Taylor, *Embattled Freedom*; FSSP, ser. 3, vol. 2, pp. 51–52.

35. Joseph Tillett et al. to the Assistant Commissioner, Bureau Refugees, Freedmen & Aband Lands, State of N.C., December 4, 1865, in FSSP, ser. 3, vol. 2, doc. 84, pp. 335–36; F. D. Sewall to Major Genl. O. O. Howard, May 14, 1866, in FSSP, ser. 3, vol. 2, doc. 254, pp. 756–59.

36. F. D. Sewall to Major Genl. O. O. Howard, May 14, 1866, in FSSP, ser. 3, vol. 2, doc. 254, p. 758; Col. E. Whittlesey, Circular, No. 4, November 10, 1865, in FSSP, ser. 3, vol. 1, doc. 175, pp. 666–68; George Baum et al. to Col. Charles Benzoni, December 1867, Letters Received, reel 11, M843, BRFAL; Click, *Time Full of Trial*, 177–90, 226–27; Downs, *Declarations of Dependence*, 63–69.

37. Edward F. OBrien to Lieut. S. N. Clark, October 13, 1865, in FSSP, ser. 3, vol. 1, doc. 171, pp. 648–51; Rose, *Rehearsal for Reconstruction*, 346–408; Franke, *Repair*, 19–80; Col. H. N.

Frisbie to Capt. Hemenway, October 19, 1865, in FSSP, ser. 3, vol. 1, doc. 173, pp. 663–65; Abbott, "Free Land, Free Labor"; Hahn, "'Extravagant Expectations' of Freedom," 153–58; Manning, *Troubled Refuge*, 269–78. On state projects of "radical simplification," see Scott, *Seeing Like a State*.

38. *Veto Message*, 168–73; Foner, *Reconstruction*, 246–49; Egerton, *Wars of Reconstruction*, 121–28; Abel and Cox, "Andrew Johnson."

39. United States, *Statutes at Large*, 14:173–77; Foner, *Reconstruction*, 246; Lanza, "'One of the Most Appreciated,'" 67–92; Oubre, *Forty Acres and a Mule*.

40. Balogh, *Associational State*; Richardson, *Christian Reconstruction*; McFeely, *Yankee Stepfather*, 88–89; Taylor, *Embattled Freedom*; Abisha Scofield to Clinton B. Fisk, April 21, 1866, Letters Received, reel 11, M999, BRFAL.

41. Circular No. 2, May 19, 1865, in *Report of the Commissioner of Bureau of Refugees, Freedmen, and Abandoned Lands*, 44; Howard, *Autobiography of Oliver Otis Howard*, 2:220; Circular No. 5, May 30, 1865, in *Report of the Commissioner of Bureau of Refugees, Freedmen, and Abandoned Lands*, 45; Col. O. Brown to Maj. Genl. O. O. Howard, July 16, 1865, in FSSP, ser. 3, vol. 1, doc. 158, pp. 621–22; FSSP, ser. 3, vol. 1, pp. 611–12; FSSP, ser. 3, vol. 2, p. 714n10; Testimony of Colonel Orlando Brown, February 15, 1866, in *Report of the Joint Committee on Reconstruction*, pt. 2, p. 12.

42. Howard, "Report of the Commissioner of Bureau of Refugees, Freedmen, and Abandoned Lands" (1867), 623; Howard, "Report of the Commissioner of Bureau of Refugees, Freedmen, and Abandoned Lands" (1869), 515. For examples of bureau officials asking funds to transport needy freedpeople to distant relatives, hospitals, or asylums, see Frederick S. Tukey to Orlando Brown, January 22, 1866; Frederick S. Tukey to Orlando Brown, January 22, 1866; John P. How to W. Storer How, March 22, 1866; W. Storer How to Orlando Brown, April 22, 1866; Frederick S. Tukey to Orlando Brown, April 25, 1866; Frederick S. Tukey to Orlando Brown, April 25, 1866; Henry M. Whittelsey to Orlando Brown, May 11, 1867; Thomas P. Jackson to Cyrus Alexander, May 30, 1867, all in "Freedmen's Bureau: Public Welfare," VSP.

43. Howard, *Autobiography of Oliver Otis Howard*, 2:221; Downs, "Continuation of Slavery." On "soundness" in the antebellum South, see Fett, *Working Cures*, 15–35; Johnson, *Soul by Soul*; Gross, *Double Character*, 22–46, 122–52; Boster, *African American Slavery and Disability*, 34–54, 55–73; Barclay, *Mark of Slavery*.

44. "Summary Report of North Carolina, Colonel E. Whittlesey, Assistant Commissioner," October 15, 1865, in *Report of the Joint Committee on Reconstruction*, pt. 2, pp. 186–87; Downs, *Sick from Freedom*, 120–45. Marta Russell, the late disability rights activist and scholar, has persuasively argued that the "primary oppression of disabled persons (i.e., of people who could work in a workplace that was accommodated to their needs) is their exclusion from exploitation as wage laborers." Russell and Malhotra, "Capitalism," 2.

45. Testimony of Hon. John Covode, March 3, 1866, in *Report of the Joint Committee on Reconstruction*, pt. 4, pp. 118–19; John B Walker to Genrl. Tillson, November 17, 1865, and Brig. Genl. Davis Tillson to John B. Walker, Esq., November 20, 1865, both in FSSP, ser. 3, vol. 1, doc. 178, pp. 670–72.

46. Testimony of Colonel Orlando Brown, February 15, 1866, in *Report of the Joint Committee on Reconstruction*, pt. 2, p. 126; Circular No. 4, May 21, 1866, in *Message of President on Refugees, Freedmen, and Abandoned Lands*, 3–4.

47. Circular No. 10, August 23, 1866, in *Report of the Secretary of War*, 39th Cong., 2d Sess. (1866), 767; FSSP, ser. 3, vol. 2, pp. 721–22; J. W. Alvord to O. O. Howard, January 14, 1870, in Alvord, *Letters from the South*, 14, HL; Report of C. C. Sibley, February 29, 1868, reel 32, M798, BRFAL.

48. United States, *Statutes at Large*, 15:28; *Report of the Secretary of War*, 40th Cong., 2d Sess. (1867), 639–50; *Report of the Secretary of War*, 41st Cong., 2d Sess. (1869), 501–2; White, *Freedmen's Bureau in Louisiana*, 70–71; Lieberman, "Freedmen's Bureau," 418–19. Congress's joint resolution anticipated major disaster relief efforts of the mid-twentieth century. Dauber, *Sympathetic State*.

49. FSSP, ser. 3, vol. 1, pp. 613–14; Report of Jonathan D. Moore, June 30, 1868, reel 33, M826, BRFAL; White, *Freedmen's Bureau in Louisiana*, 166–89; Rabinowitz, *Race Relations*, 128–51.

50. Howard, *Autobiography of Oliver Otis Howard*, 2:332–33; McFeely, *Yankee Stepfather*, 291–96; Simpson, "Ulysses S. Grant and the Freedmen's Bureau," 22–24; Foner, *Reconstruction*, 271–91; Downs, *After Appomattox*, 187–92; Blair, "Use of Military Force"; Sefton, *United States Army and Reconstruction*, 260–62.

51. O. O. Howard to Ulysses S. Grant, January 2, 1868, Letters Sent, reel 4, pp. 220–21, M742, BRFAL; Bentley, *History of the Freedmen's Bureau*, 142–43; McFeely, *Yankee Stepfather*, 301; Downs, *Sick from Freedom*, 141–45. See also A. W. Harlan to Maj. W. G. Sargent, February 5, 1864, in FSSP, ser. 1, vol. 3, doc. 193, pp. 786–89.

52. Report of E. E. Platt, August 28, 1868, reel 33, M826, BRFAL; Report of William Stone, September 1, 1868, reel 36, M869, BRFAL; Report of William Stone, October 1, 1868, reel 36, M869, BRFAL.

53. Downs, *Sick from Freedom*, 120–45; Goldberg, *Citizens and Paupers*, 39–40; Cimbala, *Under the Guardianship*, 180–205; Rabinowitz, *Race Relations*, 128–51; Rabinowitz, "From Exclusion to Segregation"; Bentley, *History of the Freedmen's Bureau*, 143–44.

54. G. W. Hatch to B. F. Butler, December 7, 1868, "Condition of Freedmen in Texas," Committee on Freedmen's Affairs, 40th Cong., 1st Sess. (1867), RG 233, NARA; Jas. H. Pierce to T. D. Elliott, December 9, 1868, "Condition of Freedmen in Mississippi," Committee on Freedmen's Affairs, 40th Cong., 1st Sess. (1867), RG 233, NARA; Jacob Grimes to O. O. Howard, December 16, 1868, "Condition of Freedmen in North Carolina," Committee on Freedmen's Affairs, 40th Cong., 1st Sess. (1867), RG 233, NARA; Report of George S. Smith, September 16, 1868, reel 33, M826, BRFAL; Howell G. Flournoy to T. D. Elliot, January 9, 1868, vol. 171, Letters Sent, reel 43, M1903, BRFAL; J. L. Roberts to Thaddeus Stevens, November 15, 1867, Committee on Freedmen's Affairs, 40th Cong., 1st Sess. (1867), RG 233, NARA; Manning, *Troubled Refuge*, 263–64; Downs, *Declarations of Dependence*, 75–100; Downs, *After Appomattox*, 39–60; McFeely, *Yankee Stepfather*, 290–92; Colby, "Freedmen's Bureau," 224.

55. *Report of the Secretary of War*, 40th Cong., 2d Sess. (1867), 691–92; United States, *Statutes at Large*, 15:193; Howard, "Report of the Commissioner of Bureau of Refugees, Freedmen, and Abandoned Lands" (1870), 515; Lieberman, "Freedmen's Bureau," 417; Bentley, *History of the Freedmen's Bureau*, 209–10; Howard, *Statement of Br. Maj. Gen. O. O. Howard before the Committee on Education and Labor*, 38–39, HL.

56. *Report of the Secretary of War*, 40th Cong., 2d Sess. (1867), 621–23; *Report of the Secretary of War*, 40th Cong., 3d Sess. (1868), 1017; "Bounties to Colored Soldiers," *Baltimore Sun*, August 10, 1866; *New South*, August 25, 1866; "Bounties to Colored Soldiers," *Richmond Dispatch*, August 10, 1866; *Army and Navy Journal*, October 6, 1866, p. 114.

57. The date April 19, 1861, refers not to the bombardment of Ft. Sumter (April 12) but rather to the firing on the Massachusetts and Pennsylvania militias in the so-called Baltimore Riot.

58. Delany, "To the Free Colored Men of Charleston," in Reelin, *Life and Public Services*, 211–12, HL.

59. United States, *Statutes at Large*, 12:589; United States, *Statutes at Large*, 13:6; United States, *Statutes at Large*, 14:321; [Fry,] *Final Report Made to the Secretary of War*, 60–70; Rapp, *Complete Digest of Laws*; Raff, *War Claimant's Guide*, 144–45. See also the commentary in a leading military periodical: J. M. Broadhead, "Bounties to Colored Troops," *Army and Navy Journal*, October 21, 1865, p. 142; *Army and Navy Journal*, October 28, 1865, p. 145; *Army and Navy Journal*, November 4, 1865, p. 161.

60. United States, *Statutes at Large*, 13:126; *Commonwealth*, January 7, 1865, quoted in Belz, "Law, Politics, and Race," 212–13; United States, *Statutes at Large*, 13:379–80; Edward Bates to Abraham Lincoln, July 14, 1864, in Rapp, *Complete Digest of Laws*, 73–75; [Fry,] *Final Report Made to the Secretary of War*, 60–70; *OR*, ser. 3, vol. 5, pp. 658–60; Circular 60, August 1, 1864, in *OR*, ser. 3, vol. 4, pp. 564–65; James Speed to Hugh McColloch, October 17, 1865, in Rapp, *Complete Digest of Laws*, 77–81.

61. United States, *Statutes at Large*, 14:322–23; United States, *Statutes at Large*, 14:367–68; United States, *Statutes at Large*, 14:322–23; Henry Stanbery to Edwin M. Stanton, November 13, 1866, in Rapp, *Complete Digest of Laws*, 85–87; "Circular to Paymasters Relative to Colored Soldiers Entitled to Bounty," *National Republican*, November 22, 1866.

62. "Rules for the Presenting of Claims," *Evening Star*, December 15, 1865; E. B. French to E. B. Washburn, February 8, 1866, repr. in "Bounties to Colored Soldiers," *Chicago Tribune*, February 27, 1866; *Army and Navy Journal*, December 29, 1866, p. 294; E. B. French to Britton & Gray, December 6, 1867, Letters Received, reel 22, M1910, BRFAL; A. P. Howe to Perry Williams, August 9, 1869, Letters Sent, vol. 2, p. 359, CBCD.

63. For the Treasury's register of bounty payments to USCT veterans and heirs, maintained from July 1867 to April 1874, see the five-volume *Abstracts of Payments to Colored Troops* (APCT). The field offices of the Freedmen's Bureau also kept registers of claims, and with additional details including dates and the identifying party or parties. Reports relating to bounty claims and disbursements of each state's Claims Division can often be found in the offices of the bureau's assistant commissioners.

64. "The Bounty for Colored Discharged Soldiers," *Army and Navy Journal*, February 16, 1867, p. 410; Ransom, "Reconstructing Reconstruction."

65. Freedmen's Bureau, *Officers' Manual*, 26, 106, HL; J. Watson to James Milo Alexander, April 19, 1870, James Milo Alexander Papers, HL.

66. A. Scofield, "Facts for the People," October 14, 1865; A. Scofield to Messers Strieby and Jocelyn, October 18, 1865; J. G. Fee to Bro. Strieby, October 28, 1865, all in Sears, *Camp Nelson, Kentucky*, 276–77, 281–82, 290–91.

67. Edward P. Smith to Clinton B. Fisk, May 26, 1866; J. G. Nain to Bvt. Lt. Col. Jas. H Rice, December 2, 1866; A. Scofield to Revd. Strieby and Whipple, December 14, 1866, all in Sears, *Camp Nelson, Kentucky*, 341–42, 352–53, 354–58; Isaac W. Newton to William P. Drew, May 24, 1869, Letters Received, box 3, vol. 2, CBCD; Taylor, *Embattled Freedom*, 236–38.

68. After March 29, 1867, freedpeople could only use private claims agents to *apply* for bounty; agents were also prohibited from receiving bounty payments to return to their cli-

ents, with their fees now fixed by law. United States, *Statutes at Large*, 15:26; Raff, *War Claimant's Guide*, 156–61; "The Frauds in the Settlement of Bounties to Colored Soldiers," *New York Daily Herald*, June 30, 1868; "Modus Operandi," *Public Ledger*, April 3, 1869; "Notice to Colored Bounty Claimants," *Brownlow's Knoxville Whig*, September 4, September 11, 18, October 2, December 18, 1867; A. Coats, Report of the Operations of the Claim Division in the State of N.C. from Oct. 31st 1866 to Sept. 21st 1867, reel 37, M843, BRFAL.

69. Report of S. Geisreiter, June 1, 1868, reel 27, M979, BRFAL; Report of R. W. Barnard, October 31, 1868, reel 27, M979, BRFAL. The chief of the Claims Division, A. P. Howe, routinely sent letters of explanation to freedpeople, disabusing them of expectations for more. But by 1869, the new head of the division, William P. Drew, began anticipating "probable legislation by the present Congress removing the disqualifications as regards bounty of colored soldiers who have been slaves." A. P. Howe to Jonathan Gregory, April 6, 1868, Letters Sent, vol. 1, pp. 72–73, CBCD; A. P. Howe to Perry Williams, August 9, 1869, Letters Sent, vol. 2, p. 359, CBCD; E. B. French to Britton & Gray, December 6, 1867, Letters Received, reel 22, M1910, BRFAL; A. P. Howe to Jonathan Bow et al., July 23, 1868, Letters Sent, vol. 1, p. 70, CBCD; A. McL. Crawford to A. P. Howe, October 1, 1867, Letters Sent, reel 21, M1910, BRFAL; A. P. Howe to Ambrose Smith, June 4, 1869, Letters Sent, vol. 2, p. 225, CBCD; A. P. Howe to Richard Harrison, July 22, 1869, Letters Sent, vol. 2, p. 292, CBCD; *Bounty to Colored Soldiers*, 57–60; William P. Drew to F. C. von Schirach, December 24, 1869, Letters Received, reel 22, M1910, BRFAL; William P. Drew to Charles Garretson, August 2, 1870, Letters Received, reel 22, M1910, BRFAL; William P. Drew to Charles Garretson, April 1, 1870, Letters Received, reel 22, M1910, BRFAL.

70. Report of S. Geisreiter, July 1, 1868, reel 27, M979, BRFAL; Report of William S. McCullogh, June 30, 1868, reel 27, M979, BRFAL; Report of William McCullogh, July 31, 1868, reel 27, M979, BRFAL; Report of A. S. Dyer, June 30, 1868, reel 27, M979, BRFAL; Report of C. R. Simpson, June 1, 1868, reel 18, M999, BRFAL.

71. Samuel Clark to O. O. Howard, February 1, 1869, Letters Received, box 2, vol. 2, CBCD; James Davis to O. O. Howard, January 25, 1869, Letters Received, box 2, vol. 2, CBCD; Andrew Montgomery to O. O. Howard, March 20, 1869, Letters Received, box 3, vol. 2, CBCD; Andrew Montgomery to William P. Drew, April 1, 1869, Letters Received, box 3, vol. 2, CBCD.

72. Report of Charles R. Simpson, September 2, 1868, reel 18, M999, BRFAL; Report of C. R. Simpson, July 31, 1868, reel 18, M999, BRFAL; Oubre, *Forty Acres and a Mule*, 165–67. On the rise of sharecropping, see esp. Foner, *Reconstruction*, 402–10; Jaynes, *Branches without Roots*; Ransom and Sutch, *One Kind of Freedom*; Hahn, *Roots of Southern Populism*, 137–69; Litwack, *Trouble in Mind*, 127–38.

73. "Payment of Bounties," *Baltimore Sun*, October 1, 1866; Briston Welcome to O. O. Howard, September 10, 1868, Letters Received, box 2, vol. 1, CBCD; Renty Jefferson to O. O. Howard, September 12, 1868, Letters Received, box 1, vol. 1, CBCD; Lot Hines to O. O. Howard, September 23, 1868, Letters Received, box 1, vol. 1, CBCD.

74. Frank Mitchell to O. O. Howard, February 2, 1868, Letters Received, box 1, vol. 1, CBCD; Payment to Frank Mitchell, 3:309, APCT; Alfred Hunter to O. O. Howard, March 3, 1868, Letters Received, box 1, vol. 1, CBCD; Payment to Alfred Hunter, 2:88, APCT; Joseph Cann to O. O. Howard, April 3, 1868, Letters Received, box 1, vol. 1, CBCD; Payment to Joseph Cann, 2:94, APCT.

75. Edmund Midgett to O. O. Howard, March 27, 1868, Letters Received, box 1, vol. 1, CBCD; Edmund Midgett to O. O. Howard, May 19, 1868, Letters Received, box 1, vol. 1, CBCD; A. P. Howe to Edmund Midgett, May 22, 1868, Letters Sent, vol. 1, p. 55, CBCD; Payment to Edmund Midgett, 2:90, APCT; Noah Harney to O. O. Howard, November 3, 1868, Letters Received, box 1, vol. 1, CBCD; Mary Lewis to O. O. Howard, March 16, 1869, Letters Received, box 3, vol. 2, CBCD; Maria Beal to O. O. Howard, April 10, 1869, Letters Received, box 2, vol. 2, CBCD.

76. Edward Robinson to O. O. Howard, May 27, 1868, Letters Received, box 1, vol. 1, CBCD; Samuel Jefferson to O. O. Howard, April 6, 1869, Letters Received, box 2, vol. 2, CBCD; Louisa Toler to O. O. Howard, July 4, 1868, Letters Received, box 2, vol. 1, CBCD; William Cowans to O. O. Howard, July 30, 1868, Letters Received, box 1, vol. 1, CBCD; Downs, *Declarations of Dependence*, 1.

77. Mingo Jeffries to Henry Page, July 3, 1869, Letters Received, reel 3, M1901, BRFAL; Payment to Mingo Jeffries, 3:71, APCT; William Pace to O. O. Howard, October 8, 1868, Letters Received, box 1, vol. 1, CBCD; J. M. Johnson to O. O. Howard, February 9, 1869, Letters Received, box 2, vol. 2, CBCD; Foner, *Reconstruction*, 291–307; Hahn, *Nation under Our Feet*, 198–206; Parsons, *Ku-Klux*.

78. O. C. French to E. B. French, February 19, 1869, Letters Sent, reel 38, M1907, BRFAL; O. C. French to [George W. Balloch], February 27, 1869, Unregistered Letters Received, reel 39, M1907, BRFAL; George Hooker to O. O. Howard, March 24, 1868, Letters Received, box 1, vol. 1, CBCD; Lewis Hill to O. O. Howard, July 9, 1868, Letters Received, box 1, vol. 1, CBCD; Joseph Ramsey to J. B. Coons, November 23, 1867, Letters Received, reel 7, M1911, BRFAL. For the payment records of the Thirty-Fifth USCT, see 2:81–100, APCT.

79. H. B. Putman to O. O. Howard, December 29, 1868, Letters Received, box 3, vol. 2, CBCD; Joshua Hagerman to William P. Drew, June 24, 1869, Letters Received, box 2, vol. 2, CBCD; Joshua Hagerman to O. O. Howard, May 30, 1869, Letters Received, box 2, vol. 2, CBCD.

80. Fannie Little to O. O. Howard, June 9, 1869, Letters Received, box 3, vol. 2, CBCD; Fearabe Marks to O. O. Howard, June 8, 1869, Letters Received, box 3, vol. 2, CBCD; Henry Page to D. B. Granger, May 20, 1869, Letters Received, reel 3, M1901, BRFAL; D. B. Granger to Henry Page, May 20, 1869, Letters Received, reel 3, M1901, BRFAL; Henry Page to George Balloch, May 21, 1869, Letters Received, reel 3, M1901, BRFAL. Maria Scott finally received her payment of $348.27 in April 1870. Register of Claimants, July 1866–October 1871, reel 6, M1901, p. 140.

81. Brown, "To Catch the Vision"; Brown, "Negotiating and Transforming."

82. Jane M. Griffith to O. O. Howard, November 30, 1868, Letters Received, box 1, vol. 1, CBCD. See also Nancy A. Walden to O. O. Howard, October 28, 1867, Letters Received, box 2, vol. 1, CBCD; Sallie Howard to O. O. Howard, October 1, 1868, Letters Received, box 1, vol. 1, CBCD; Complaint of Elizabeth Richards, October 17, 1868, Letters Received, box 1, vol. 1, CBCD; Nancy Priestly to O. O. Howard, October 20, 1868, Letters Received, box 1, vol. 1, CBCD; Emily Edmundson to O. O. Howard, January 7, 1869, Letters Received, box 2, vol. 2, CBCD; Martha Tibbs to O. C. French, February 15, 1869, Letters Sent, reel 38, M1907, BRFAL; O. C. French to O. O. Howard, February 15, 1869, Letters Sent, reel 38, M1907, BRFAL; Louisa Overton to [O. O. Howard], May 24, 1869, Letters Received, box 3, vol. 2, CBCD; A. P. Howe to Louisa Overton, July 22, 1869, Letters Sent,

vol. 2, p. 291, CBCD; Sarah Neubles to O. O. Howard, July 14, 1869, Letters Received, reel 3, M1901, BRFAL; Susan James and Johanna James to Henry Page, March 11, 1870, Letters Received, reel 5, M1901, BRFAL; Johanna Jones to Henry Page, July 3, 1870, Letters Received, reel 5, M1901, BRFAL; Deliley Rowland to [O. O. Howard], December 7, 1870, Letters Received, reel 4, M1901, BRFAL.

83. Du Bois, *Souls of Black Folk*, 13–35.

Chapter Two

1. There currently exists no scholarly treatment of the Freedmen's Branch. Its operations are briefly hinted at in the final three pages of George R. Bentley's extensive study of the Freedmen's Bureau, and garnered one line in William S. McFeely's critical biography of O. O. Howard. To date, the fullest discussion of the Freedmen's Branch can be found in the descriptive pamphlet for microfilm publication M2029, produced by Reginald Washington and his team at the National Archives and Records Administration. Bentley, *History of the Freedmen's Bureau*, 212–14; McFeely, *Yankee Stepfather*, 327–28; Washington et al., "Records of the Field Offices."

2. Classic accounts of the growth of the federal government during and after the Civil War include Skowronek, *Building a New American State*; Bensel, *Yankee Leviathan*; Skocpol, *Protecting Soldiers and Mothers*; Bensel, *Political Economy of American Industrialization*. More recently, important work challenges the traditional top-down nature of the American political development school, focusing on the regulatory apparatuses of the states or offering a decentered or otherwise multifaceted approach to state building. See especially Novak, *People's Welfare*; Carpenter, *Forging of Bureaucratic Autonomy*; Rockwell, *Indian Affairs*; Pearson, *Rights of the Defenseless*. On the relationship of emancipation in the United States to state building, see esp. Manning, "Emancipation as State Building"; Novak, "Myth"; Nackenoff and Novkov, "Introduction"; Pearson, "New Birth of Regulation."

3. Howard, "Report of the Commissioner" (1871), 454; United States, *Statutes at Large*, 17:366; *Knoxville Daily Chronicle*, November 16, 1871; *Natchez Democrat*, November 30, 1871; "Another Vile Political Feature Extinguished," *Edgefield Advertiser*, July 18, 1872; "The Freedmen's Bureau," *New York Times*, November 13, 1871; *Democratic Advocate*, April 14, 1877; Munden and Beers, *Union*, 300–303.

4. E. B. French to Secretary of War, April 24, 1872, in *To Provide for Payment* 2–3; A. W. Brattle to Adjutant General, June 29, 1872, Letters Received, box 1, FBHQ; H. J. Dugan to Secretary of War, June 29, 1872, Letters Received, box 1, FBHQ; Thomas Killaly to Adjutant General, July 2, 1872, Letters Received, box 1, FBHQ.

5. Thomas M. Vincent to E. D. Townsend, October 7, 1872, in *Condition of Affairs*, 1–4; E. D. Townsend to Thomas Vincent, June 27, 1872, Letters Received, box 1, FBHQ.

6. E. D. Townsend to Thomas M. Vincent, August 8, and September 2, 1872, in *Condition of Affairs*, 6–8; Thomas M. Vincent to E. D. Townsend, October 7, 1873, in *Report of the Secretary of War*, 43d Cong., 1st Sess. (1874), 74–75.

7. "A Bid for the Colored Vote," *Nashville Union and American*, August 13, 1872; "Claims of Colored Soldiers and Sailors," *Daily State Journal*, August 14, 1872; "Claims of Colored Soldiers and Sailors," *Daily Dispatch*, August 15, 1872; "Payment of Colored Soldiers' Claims," *New Orleans Republican*, August 20, 1872; Hahn, *Nation under Our Feet*; Fitzgerald, *Union*

League Movement; John Armstead to William P. Drew, July 13, 1872, Letters Received, box 1, FBHQ; Scott, *Domination*, 61–62.

8. W. H. Pemberton to Secretary of War, July 15, 1872, Letters Received, box 1, FBHQ; N. D. Smith to Adjutant General, August 2, 1872, Letters Received, box 1, FBHQ; F. R. Wilcox to James McMillan, February 13, 1873, Letters Received, box 5, FBHQ; James M. Hanks to W. W. Belknap, July 24, 1872, Letters Received, box 1, FBHQ; John T. Rankin to Secretary of War, August 9, 1872, Letters Received, box 1, FBHQ; Zeno I. Fitzpatrick to Wm. W. Belknap, October 5, 1872, Letters Received, box 2, FBHQ.

9. William P. Drew to F. C. von Schirach, December 24, 1869, Letters Received, reel 22, M1910, BRFAL; William P. Drew to Charles Garretson, August 2, 1870, Letters Received, reel 22, M1910, BRFAL; William P. Drew to Charles Garretson, April 1, 1870, Letters Received, reel 22, M1910, BRFAL; Wm. W. Belknap to House Committee on Military Affairs, April 15, 1872, in *Bounty for Slaves*; "Bounties for Colored Soldiers," *Sun*, February 10, 1869; *New York Daily Herald*, January 29, 1870; "Bounties to Colored Soldiers," *Vicksburg Daily Times*, February 27, 1872; *Charlotte Democrat*, February 27, 1872; Belz, "Law, Politics, and Race."

10. *Morning Republican*, November 2, 1868; Abraham Daniels to [George W. Balloch], December 13, 1868, Letters Received, reel 3, M1901, BRFAL; "Speech of Hon. Thomas Boles," *Congressional Globe*, 42nd Cong., 3d Sess. (1873), Appendix, 158–59; "Carroll County Convention," *Morning Republican*, September 16, 1868; "Thomas Boles," *Morning Republican*, October 20, 1868; "Hon. Thomas Boles," *Morning Republican*, November 4, 1869; "Franklin County Republican Convention," *Morning Republican*, August 25, 1870; "The Poor Man's Friend," *Daily Arkansas Gazette*, October 2, 1870.

11. "Shall We Deal Justly With All?," *Soldier's Friend*, repr. in *Morning Republican*, February 14, 1870; Thomas Boles on H. R. 1580, May 17, 1872, in *Congressional Globe*, 42d Cong., 2d Sess. (1872), 3562.

12. "Speech of Hon. Thomas Boles," *Congressional Globe*, 42nd Cong., 3d Sess. (1873), Appendix, 158–59.

13. United States, *Statutes at Large*, 17:601.

14. United States, *Statutes at Large*, 17:566–77.

15. United States, *Statutes at Large*, 17:601; *Civil Rights Cases*, 109 U.S. 3 (1883); Edwards, *Legal History*, 124; Perrone, "'Back into the Days.'" On the Civil War's remaking of citizenship for Black Americans, see esp. Manning, "Working for Citizenship"; Baker and Kelly, *After Slavery*; Edwards, "Status without Rights"; Kantrowitz, *More Than Freedom*; Lee, *Claiming the Union*; Foner, *Second Founding*.

16. E. B. French to R. H. Isabelle, May 27, 1873, repr. in "Bounty for Colored Soldiers," *New Orleans Republican*, June 4, 1873; Thomas M. Vincent to Second Comptroller, November 28, 1873, Letters Received, box 12, FBHQ; Second Comptroller to Thomas M. Vincent, December 1, 1873, Letters Received, box 12, FBHQ; *DDI* (1900), 10:108; A. Burroughs Jr. to Secretary of War, May 24, 1876, Letters Received, box 24, FBHQ.

17. "The Bounties for the Colored Volunteer Troops," *New National Era*, April 24, 1873; "Bounties for Colored Volunteer Troops," *Herald and Tribune*, May 1, 1873; "Equalization of Bounty to Colored Troops," *New National Era*, May 15, 1873; A. J. Ransier, "To Colored Soldiers," *Missionary Record*, July 5, 1873; *Fort Smith Weekly New Era*, August 6, 1873; *New National Era*, July 17, 1873, January 22, 1874, May 15, 1874; *Hinds County Gazette*, November 11, 1874; H. G. Lucas to J. H. Counselman, June 5, 1873, Unregistered Letters Received,

Charleston, reel 1, FOFB; "Bounties to Colored Soldiers and Sailors," *National Republican*, February 26, 1874; "The Bounties for the Colored Volunteer Troops," *New National Era*, April 24, 1873; Joseph McGee to W. W. Belknap, November 23, 1874, Letters Received, Memphis, reel 25, FOFB.

18. Peirce, *Freedmen's Bureau*, 105–28; *Charges against General O. O. Howard*; Bentley, *History of the Freedmen's Bureau*, 213–14; *Answer to Resolution*, 3–5; Townsend, "Report of the Freedmen's Branch" (1876), 415–37; Howard, *Autobiography Oliver Otis Howard*, 2:451–52; *Secretary of War, Transmitting*, 1–8; Du Bois, *Souls of Black Folk*, 31–32. For a tiny fraction the press's sensational reaction to the scandal, see, for instance, "Alleged Frauds in Pay Department," *Times-Picayune*, July 1, 1868; "The Frauds in the Settlement of Bounties to Colored Soldiers," *New York Daily Herald*, June 30, 1868; "Immense Frauds," *Richmond Dispatch*, June 30, 1868; "From Washington," *Baltimore Sun*, June 29, 1868; "Alleged Discovery of Startling Bounty Frauds—Official Investigation," *Charleston Daily News*, July 1, 1868; *Greensboro Patriot*, July 2, 1868.

19. Peirce, *Freedmen's Bureau*, 127–28; *Work of Late Bureau*; "The End of It," *Memphis Daily Appeal*, July 10, 1873; "Swindlers," *Knoxville Daily Chronicle*, June 14, 1873; *Semi-Weekly Clarion*, February 2, 1872. For additional articles accusing the government of defrauding freedpeople, see "Sambo among the Sinners," *Charleston Daily News*, January 3, 1872; *Daily Phoenix*, June 14, 1873; *Daily State Journal*, June 13, 1873; "Major General O. O. Howard," *Evening Star*, July 9, 1873; "The Freedmen's Bureau," *New York Times*, July 14, 1873; *Memphis Daily Appeal*, July 14, 1873; "Frauds on the Freedmen," *Edgefield Advertiser*, July 17, 1873.

20. Du Bois, *Souls of Black Folk*, 32; Baradaran, *Color of Money*, 10–39; John W. Alvord to O. O. Howard, January 1, 1866, in *Report of Commissioners of Freedmen's Bureau*, 39th Cong., 1st Sess. (1866), 347–50; Joseph Warner to George Gibson, January 27, 1873, Letters Received, Memphis, reel 23, FOFB; *National Savings Bank*, January 1, 1868, February 1, 1868, in "National Freedmen's Savings and Trust Company," Committee on Freedmen's Affairs, 40th Cong., 1st Sess. (1867), RG 233, NARA; Washington, "Freedman's Savings and Trust Company"; Osthaus, *Freedmen, Philanthropy, and Fraud*, 27.

21. Harmon, *Negro as a Business Man*, 81; Harris, *Negro as Capitalist*, 28; Washington, "Freedman's Savings and Trust Company"; Baradaran, *Color of Money*, 23–30; Osthaus, *Freedmen, Philanthropy, and Fraud*, 2, 173–200; Levy, *Freaks of Fortune*, 104–49; Freedman's Savings and Trust Company, *Charter and By-Laws*, 8–11, LOC; D. L. Eaton to Committee on Freedmen's Affairs, July 5, 1868, in "National Freedmen's Savings and Trust Company," Committee on Freedmen's Affairs, 40th Cong., 1st Sess. (1867), RG 233, NARA; Foner, *Reconstruction*, 531–32; McFeely, *Frederick Douglass*, 307–12.

22. *Campaign Text Book*, 536–62; Perman, *Road to Redemption*, 149–77; Richardson, *Death of Reconstruction*, 122–55.

23. United States, *Statutes at Large*, 15:26.

24. Each field office disbursing officer of the Freedmen's Branch periodically received lists of claimants to be paid, along with the lump sum of their bounty payments, from the chief disbursing officer in Washington. In addition to the various markers of personal identification, these forms also stipulated the claimants' residences and the names and addresses of the agents who prosecuted their claims.

25. General Orders No. 79, August 8, 1872, in *Condition of Affairs*, 6–7; United States, *Statutes at Large*, 14:367; Circular, August 3, 1872, in *Condition of Affairs*, 5–7; Thomas M. Vincent to E. D. Townsend, October 7, 1873, in *Report of the Secretary of War*, 43d Cong.,

1st Sess. (1873), 74–75. For the bounty payments to white Union veterans, see Munden and Beers, *Union*, 300–303; United States, *Statutes at Large*, 16:54–55; J. M. Broadhead to Second Comptroller, April 28, 1869, in Rapp, *Complete Digest*, 96–97.

26. A. Coats, *Report of the Operations of the Claim Division in the State of N.C. from Oct. 31st 1866 to Sept. 21st 1867*, Reports of Claims Division, reel 37, M843, BRFAL; Nordhoff, *Freedmen of South-Carolina*, 24–25, HL; A. P. Howe to Anthony Covington, July 20, 1868, Letters Sent, vol. 1, p. 69, CBCD; A. P. Howe to Peter Overton, September 29, 1868, Letters Sent, vol. 1, p. 117, CBCD; O. C. French to Major John Tyler, February 12, 1869, Letters Sent, reel 38, M1907, BRFAL; J. H. Chapman to Sukey Young, November 22, 1869, Letters Sent, reel 58, M1907, BRFAL; William P. Drew to Henry Page, March 18, 1870, Letters Received, reel 4, M1901, BRFAL; J. H. Chapman to Rachel Guy, December 28, 1869, Letters Sent, reel 58, M1907, BRFAL. On deceit, survival, and "slave trickster tales," see esp. Levine, *Black Culture and Black Consciousness*, 102–35.

27. E. B. French to Secretary of War, April 10, 1873, Letters Received, box 6, FBHQ; James McMillan to Sidney Ann Williams, August 29, 1872, Letters Sent, vol. 1, p. 95, FBHQ; W. H. Morse to E. D. Townson [Townsend], September 9, 1872, Letters Received, box 2, FBHQ; Littleton Hughes to Adjutant General, September 28, 1872, Letters Received, box 2, FBHQ; Thomas M. Vincent to J. H. Root, October 21, 1872, Letters Sent, vol. 1, p. 311, FBHQ; Thomas M. Vincent to E. C. Huggins, October 25, 1872, Letters Sent, vol. 1, p. 337, FBHQ; A. J. Armstrong and H. Jones to E. D. Townsend, March 1, 1873, Letters Received, box 5, FBHQ; A. D. Dougherty to E. D. Townsend, May 28, 1873, Letters Received, box 7, FBHQ.

28. J. A. Logan to W. W. Belknap, March 27, 1874, Letters Received, box 15, FBHQ. For examples of claimants' difficulties in traveling to Freedmen's Bureau offices for payment, see Abraham Murah to Henry Page, September 23, 1870, Letters Received, reel 5, M1901, BRFAL; E. W. Martin and G. S. VanValkenburgh to Henry Page, September 4, 1869, Letters Received, reel 3, M1901, BRFAL; S. Geisreiter to William P. Drew, November 25, 1869, Letters Received, box 4, vol. 3, CBCD. For the constraints of the Southern political economy affecting claims under the bureau, see James O. Churchill to Henry Page, February 9, 1871, Letters Received, reel 5, M1901, BRFAL; John M. Stanton to Henry Page, January 11, 1871, Letters Received, reel 5, M1901, BRFAL. For works on the transformation of the postbellum Southern economy, see esp. FSSP, ser. 3, vols. 1–2; Glymph and Kushma, *Essays*; Wright, *Old South, New South*; Litwack, *Been in the Storm*, 336–449; Mandle, *Roots of Black Poverty*; Ransom and Sutch, *One Kind of Freedom*.

29. A. K. Arnold to E. D. Townsend, January 11, 1873, Letters Sent, New Orleans, reel 42, FOFB; G. G. Hunt to E. D. Townsend, April 15, 1873, Letters Sent, Natchez, reel 34, FOFB; G. G. Hunt to E. D. Townsend, November 7, 1872, Letters Sent, Natchez, reel 34, FOFB; Igo, *Known Citizen*, 59–60; Kazin, *War against War*, 210–11; Pearson, *Birth Certificate*.

30. Thomas M. Anderson to E. D. Townsend, May 14, 1874, Letters Sent, Vicksburg, reel 55, FOFB; R. S. La Motte to Adjutant General, October 19, 1872, Letters Received, box 3, FBHQ; A. K. Arnold to E. D. Townsend, January 11, 1873, Letters Sent, New Orleans, reel 42, FOFB; Thomas M. Vincent to A. K. Arnold, February 10, 1873, Letters Received, New Orleans, reel 42, FOFB; *Knoxville Daily Chronicle*, February 14, 1873; Special Notice, June 12, 1877, Letters Received, New Orleans, reel 46, FOFB; James McMillan, Circular, n.d. [1877], Letters Received, Memphis, reel 27, FOFB; John E. Rush to George Gibson, December 19,

1873, Letters Received, Memphis, reel 24, FOFB; Harry Harrison to E. D. Townsend, January 17, 1874, Letters Received, New Orleans, reel 43, FOFB; Sam C. Roane to George Gibson, May 5, 1874, Letters Received, Memphis, reel 25, FOFB; William Collins to George Gibson, June 15, 1874, Letters Received, Memphis, reel 25, FOFB; James Henry to G. G. Hunt, December 31, 1874, Letters Received, Natchez, reel 36, FOFB. On the U.S. Postal Service and its role in the expanding federal administrative state, see Blevins, *Paper Trails*; Carpenter, *Forging of Bureaucratic Autonomy*, 65–178.

31. J. K. Hyer to Thomas M. Vincent, January 20, 1874, Registered Letters Received, Charleston, reel 1, FOFB; J. K. Hyer to Assistant Adjutant General Thomas Vincent, January 22, 1874; J. K. Hyer to Assistant Adjutant General Thomas Vincent, February 14, 1874, both in Letters Sent, Charleston, reel 1, FOFB; George Washington to J. K. Hyer, February 25, 1874; George Washington to J. K. Hyer, March 5, 1874; George Washington to J. K. Hyer, March 17, 1874; Henry Windham to J. K. Hyer, February 27, 1874; Henry Windham to J. K. Hyer, March 5, 1874; Samuel Coleman to J. K. Hyer, March 5, 1874; Joseph Smith to J. K. Hyer, April 13, 1874, all in Registered Letters Received, Charleston, reel 1, FOFB.

32. Shaffer, *After the Glory*, 51–65; Kaye, *Joining Places*, 177–220; *Daily Arkansas Gazette*, May 16, 1876; James Curry to E. D. Townsend, May 16, 1874, Letters Sent, Fort Monroe, reel 21, FOFB; Edith Winder to James Curry, February 10, 1874, Letters Received, Fort Monroe, reel 22, FOFB; Eddie Winder to James Curry, March 1, 1874, Letters Received, Fort Monroe, reel 22, FOFB.

33. Thomas Parker to George Gibson, February 2, 1875, Letters Received, Memphis, reel 25, FOFB; Thomas Boles to George Gibson, December 14, 1875, Letters Received, Memphis, reel 26, FOFB.

34. Henry Jones to James McMillan, March 17, 1877, Letters Received, New Orleans, reel 45, FOFB; Martin & Moore to Adjutant General, July 3, 1873, Letters Received, box 8, FBHQ; United States, *Statutes at Large*, 15:26–27; Thomas M. Anderson to E. F. Townsend, January 20, 1874, Letters Received, Vicksburg, reel 55, FOFB; Major Woods to A. K. Arnold, April 12, 1877, Letters Received, New Orleans, reel 45, FOFB.

35. John S. Duffie to George Gibson, April 28, 1873, Letters Received, Memphis, reel 24, FOFB; James M. Hanks to W. W. Belknap, October 26, 1872, Letters Received, box 3, FBHQ; James M. Hanks to W. W. Belknap, July 24, 1872, Letters Received, box 1, FBHQ; B. D. Hyam to Secretary of War, October 3, 1872, Letters Received, box 2, FBHQ.

36. E. Lee to George Gibson, March 31, 1874, Letters Received, Memphis, reel 25, FOFB; United States, *Statutes at Large*, 13:379–80; Woodman, *New South, New Law*; Jaynes, *Branches without Roots*, 280–300; Jones, *Labor of Love*, 43–130.

37. The best account of Southern Black mobility in the fifty years after the Civil War remains William Cohen's 1991 study *At Freedom's Edge*. On the convict lease system, see Le-Flouria, *Chained in Silence*; Blackmon, *Slavery by Another Name*; Lichtenstein, *Twice the Work*; Oshinsky, *Worse Than Slavery*.

38. *Memphis Daily Appeal*, March 9, 1873, April 4, 1873.

39. *Memphis Daily Appeal*, May 26, 1873, March 1, 1874, July 10, 1874, April 23, 1875, May 29, 1875; Hahn, *Nation under Our Feet*, 373–74; Foner, *Reconstruction*, 512–63; Perman, *Road to Redemption*, 213–14; Summers, *Ordeal of the Reunion*, 336–50; Barreyre, "Politics of Economic Crises."

40. Thomas M. Anderson to E. D. Townsend, June 3, 1873, Letters Sent, Vicksburg, reel 55, FOFB; *Memphis Daily Appeal*, July 14, 1873; William J. Davis to G. G. Hunt, February 5,

1873, Letters Received, Natchez, reel 34, FOFB; E. D. Townsend to A. K. Arnold, August 6, 1873, Letters Received, New Orleans, reel 43, FOFB; E. D. Townsend to Thomas M. Anderson, August 6, 1873, Letters Received, Vicksburg, reel 55, FOFB; Thomas M. Vincent to A. K. Arnold, July 20, 1874, Letters Received, New Orleans, reel 43, FOFB; Thomas M. Vincent to A. K. Arnold, July 24, 1876, Letters Received, New Orleans, reel 45, FOFB; E. D. Townsend to A. K. Arnold, July 24, 1876, Letters Received, New Orleans, reel 45, FOFB; E. D. Townsend to G. G. Hunt, July 24, 1876, Letters Received, Memphis, reel 27, FOFB; James C. Harris to A. K. Arnold, January 5, 1877, Letters Received, New Orleans, reel 45, FOFB; Elder & Co. to A. K. Arnold, January 27, 1877, Letters Received, New Orleans, reel 45, FOFB. On epidemics and public health in the post–Civil War South, see esp. Humphreys, *Malaria*; Humphreys, *Yellow Fever and the South*; Warner, "Public Health in the Old South"; Ellis, *Yellow Fever*.

41. Phebe Harrison to G. G. Hunt, February 21, 1873, Letters Received, Natchez, reel 34, FOFB; Elizabeth Matthews to James McMillan, March 17, 1877, Letters Received, New Orleans, reel 45, FOFB. For claimants asking the disbursing officer to come to Natchez, see Henry Dawson to G. G. Hunt, February 12, 1876, Letters Received, Natchez, reel 36, FOFB; Grover & Whitcomb to G. G. Hunt, February 26, 1873, Letters Received, Natchez, reel 34, FOFB; and to Vicksburg, see Henry Smith to G. G. Hunt, December 17, 1875, Letters Received, Natchez, reel 36, FOFB; Robert Roddy to G. G. Hunt, February 12, 1876, Letters Received, Natchez, reel 36, FOFB; Dabney Williams to G. G. Hunt, February 19, 1876, Letters Received, Natchez, reel 36, FOFB.

42. R. S. La Motte to Adjutant General, November 5, 1873, Letters Received, box 11, FBHQ; James H. Tonking to Adjutant General, April 28, 1874, Letters Received, box 15, FBHQ; A. K. Arnold to E. D. Townsend, March 13, 1874, Letters Received, box 16, FBHQ; E. D. Townsend to A. K. Arnold, March 6, 1873, Letters Received, New Orleans, reel 42, FOFB; A. K. Arnold to Adjutant General, May 6, 1873, Letters Received, box 7, FBHQ.

43. G. G. Hunt to Adjutant General, April 15, 1873, Letters Received, box 6, FBHQ; Parenti, *Soft Cage*, 13–32. For the difficulties of registering undocumented Americans for Social Security, see McKinley and Frase, *Launching Social Security*.

44. A. K. Arnold to Adjutant General, October 16, 1872, Letters Received, box 2, FBHQ; Shadrick Smith to G. G. Hunt, March 2, 1873, Letters Received, Natchez, reel 34, FOFB; Shadrick Smith to G. G. Hunt, June 4, 1874, Letters Received, Natchez, reel 35, FOFB.

45. Edwards, *Legal History*, 152; Manning, *Troubled Refuge*; Keller, *Affairs of State*; Igo, *Known Citizen*, 1–16.

46. Clerks of the Freedmen's Bank collected similar information from depositors who opened new accounts, including the names of their former masters, family members, regiment and company, place of birth, residence, occupation, and a physical description. The circumstances of this data collection, however, differed appreciably from that of the bounty collection process, wherein Black claimants had to verify what the federal government believed it already knew about the Black claimants and buttress their testimony with two credible witnesses. Depositing one's own money, after all, lends its own credibility to self-identification, whereas retrieving funds from a specific claim required and elicited significant scrutiny. Still, it is easy to see why Freedmen's Bank officials sometimes acted as de facto claims agents for would-be bounty claimants. O'Donovan, "Mapping Freedom's Terrain," 179–82.

47. E. D. Townsend to Thomas M. Vincent, Circular of September 7, 1872, in *Condition of Affairs of the Freedmen's Bureau*, 8–9; Circular, December 18, 1874, Letters Received, Natchez, reel 36, FOFB; Thomas M. Vincent to E. D. Townsend, March 29, 1876, in *To Provide for Payment of Bounties, etc., to Colored Soldiers*, 44th Cong., 1st Sess. (1876), S. Exec. Doc. No. 46, pp. 1–5. Examinations of claimants were annotated on standardized memoranda rubrics (Form 41) similar to the confidential lists supplied by the Adjutant General's Office (Form 24). For extant memoranda of claimant examinations recorded at disbursing field offices of the Freedmen's Branch, see the records of Louisville (reels 9–16), Natchez (reel 38), New Orleans (reel 47), and Vicksburg (reel 56), all in FOFB.

48. E. F. Townsend to Charlotte Munson, April 4, 1873, Letters Sent, Vicksburg, reel 55, FOFB; Thomas M. Anderson to E. F. Townsend, May 12, 1873, Letters Received, Vicksburg, reel 55, FOFB. On the laws of slavery and denial of legal personality, see Fehrenbacher, *Slaveholding Republic*, 205–52; Morris, *Southern Slavery and the Law*; Wahl, "Legal Constraints on Slave Masters"; Fede, "Legitimized."

49. George Gibson to E. D. Townsend, April 6, 1874, Letters Received, box 15, FBHQ; G. G. Hunt to E. D. Townsend, April 15, 1873, Letters Sent, Natchez, reel 34, FOFB; George Gibson to E. D. Townsend, July 8, 1873, Letters Received, box 8, FBHQ.

50. H. S. Hawkins to Adjutant General, February 25, 1876, Letters Received, box 23, FBHQ; Alfred and Johannah Gillens, BC 534.159, Memoranda of the Result of Special Examination, February 20, 1875, Natchez, reel 38, FOFB; Kitty Alexander, BC 605.285, Memoranda of the Result of Special Examination, February 3, 1874, Natchez, reel 38, FOFB.

51. G. G. Hunt to Adjutant General, April 15, 1873, Letters Received, box 6, FBHQ; H. S. Hawkins to Adjutant General, March 1, 1876, Letters Received, box 23, FBHQ.

52. H. S. Hawkins to Adjutant General, February 25, 1876, Letters Received, box 23, FBHQ; Thomas M. Vincent to R. S. La Mott, October 25, 1872, Letters Sent, vol. 1, p. 343, FBHQ; Thomas M. Anderson to Adjutant General, December 26, 1874, Letters Received, box 19, FBHQ; George Gibson to E. D. Townsend, April 6, 1874, Letters Received, box 15, FBHQ; G. G. Hunt to Adjutant General, December 9, 1874, Letters Received, box 19, FBHQ.

53. George W. Balloch to J. B. Coons, September 7, 1867, Letters Received, reel 7, M1911, BRFAL; A. P. Howe to Elizabeth Sample, December 31, 1868, Letters Sent, vol. 1, p. 198, CBCD; Henry Page to George Balloch, March 15, 1869, Letters Received, reel 3, M1901, BRFAL; A. P. Howe to Margaret Dickson, October 13, 1868, Letters Sent, vol. 1, p. 119, CBCD; A. P. Howe to Alexander Steele, August 27, 1869, Letters Sent, vol. 2, p. 388, CBCD; Regosin and Shaffer, *Voices of Emancipation*; Hunter, *Bound in Wedlock*; Berlin and Rowland, *Families and Freedom*; Schwalm, *Hard Fight for We*; Edwards, "'Marriage Covenant'"; Burnham, "Impossible Marriage."

54. Cordelia Dorsey to O. O. Howard, November [n.d.], 1868, Letters Received, box 1, vol. 1, CBCD; Isaac Cook to O. O. Howard, September 10, 1868, Letters Received, box 1, vol. 1, CBCD; O. C. French to O. O. Howard, March 3, 1869, Letters Sent, reel 38, M1907, BRFAL; T. M. Vincent to Jesse Isaacs, August 10, 1872, Letters Sent, vol. 1, pp. 29–30, FBHQ. For conflict within the "Black community," especially as it related to matters of property and compensation, see Penningroth, *Claims of Kinfolk*, 163–92.

55. Hunter, *Bound in Wedlock*, 233–60; Stevenson, "'Us never had no big funerals'"; Farmer-Kaiser, *Freedwomen and the Freedmen's Bureau*; Litwack, *Been in the Storm*, 229–47;

Shaffer, *After the Glory*, 97–118; E. B. French to O. O. Howard, May 11, 1870, Letters Received, reel 9, M1911, BRFAL; William P. Drew to J. B. Coons, June 21, 1870, Letters Received, reel 9, M1911, BRFAL; Thomas M. Vincent to E. F. Townsend, October 22, 1872, Letters Received, Vicksburg, reel 55, FOFB.

56. Joseph Carter to George Gibson, June 14, 1875, Letters Received, Memphis, reel 26, FOFB. See also A. K. Arnold to E. D. Townsend, February 25, 1874, Letters Sent, New Orleans, reel 42, FOFB; C. C. Pool to James Curry, May 7, 1873, Letters Received, Fort Monroe, reel 21, FOFB.

57. G. G. Hunt to E. D. Townsend, November 7, 1872, Letters Sent, Natchez, reel 34, FOFB; G. G. Hunt to E. D. Townsend, November 11, 1872, Letters Sent, Natchez, reel 34, FOFB; Thomas M. Anderson to E. D. Townsend, July 17, 1873, Letters Sent, Vicksburg, reel 55, FOFB; A. K. Arnold to E. D. Townsend, August 1, 1873, Letters Sent, New Orleans, reel 42, FOFB; E. H. Rush to G. G. Hunt, May 1, 1874, Letters Received, Natchez, reel 35, FOFB; Calvin Jones to George Gibson, March 1, 1873, Letters Received, Memphis, reel 23, FOFB; E. L. Hawkins to George Gibson, January 14, 1874, Letters Received, Memphis, reel 25, FOFB; Thomas M. Anderson to E. D. Townsend, April 30, 1874, Letters Sent, Vicksburg, reel 55, FOFB; N. G. Gill to George Gibson, June 7, 1873, Letters Received, Memphis, reel 24, FOFB.

58. E. D. Townsend to E. B. French, March 25, 1874; Frances Dalby to James Curry, April 7, 1874; James Curry to E. D. Townsend, April 15, 1874, all in Letters Received, Fort Monroe, reel 22, FOFB.

59. B. L. Hatch to George Gibson, April 12, 1876, Letters Received, Memphis, reel 26, FOFB; E. H. Dabney to A. K. Arnold, March 3, 1877, Letters Received, New Orleans, reel 45, FOFB.

60. For an account of the ideology and practice of "patronalism" forged during the Civil War and extending until the Progressive Era, see Downs, *Declarations of Dependence*. On the patron-client relationship or "clientelism" as it is more commonly referred to by scholars of Latin America, see Scott, "Exploring the Meaning of Freedom"; Eisenstadt and Roniger, "Patron-Client Relations."

61. *Report of the Secretary of War*, 43d Cong., 1st Sess. (1874), 74–75; Townsend, "Annual Report of the Adjutant General on the Operations of the Freedmen's Branch," October 10, 1875, in *Report of the Secretary of War*, 44th Cong., 2d Sess. (1876), 415–37; "Colored Troops and Their Bounty," *Baltimore Sun*, April 9, 1877.

62. "Petition of Colored Citizens of Arkansas," in Committee on Military Affairs, 44th Cong., 1st Sess. (1876), box 217, RG 46; Powell Clayton to A. Taft, March 15, 1876, Letters Received, box 23, FBHQ.

63. E. B. French to Secretary of War, April 24, 1872, in *To Provide for Payment of Bounties*, 2–3.

64. *Petition of Colored Citizens*; *Congressional Record—Senate*, 44th Cong., 1st Sess. (1876), pp. 1434, 2148, 3672; George Gibson to Thomas M. Vincent, April 19, 1876, Letters Received, box 24, FBHQ; George Gibson to Thomas M. Vincent, May 10, 1876, Letters Received, box 24, FBHQ.

65. F. L. Dunn to Adjutant General, April 2, 1877, Letters Received, box 25, FBHQ; Edmond Smith to George Gibson, January 27, 1874, Letters Received, Memphis, reel 25, FOFB; Rachel Baptiste to E. B. French, July 30, 1875, Letters Received, New Orleans, reel 44,

FOFB; Edward Proctor to E. B. French, January 23, 1878, Letters Received, New Orleans, reel 46, FOFB.

66. *Report of the Secretary of War*, 44th Cong., 2d Sess. (1876), 415–16, 417–27; *Annual Report of the Secretary of War* (1877), 476; *Democratic Advocate*, April 14, 1877.

67. *Memphis Daily Appeal*, June 22, 1877; *Annual Report of the Secretary of War* (1877), 473; *Estimates from Paymaster-General*; United States, *Statutes at Large*, 20:11–12; Thomas M. Vincent to Adjutant General, January 8, 1878, Letters Received, box 28, FBHQ; E. B. French to E. D. Townsend, January 25, 1877 [1878], Letters Received, box 28, FBHQ; L. D. Allen to G. G. Hunt, August 30, 1878, Letters Received, box 29, FBHQ; "Bounties to Colored Soldiers," *Baltimore Sun*, April 8, 1878; "Bounties Due Colored Soldiers," *Evening Star*, April 8, 1878; "Washington," *Memphis Daily Appeal*, April 7, 1878; S. F. Phillips to George W. McCrary, December 30, 1878, in *Official Opinions of the Attorneys General of the United States*, 239–40.

68. *Annual Report of the Secretary of War* (1879), 417–18; Benjamin Alvord to G. G. Hunt, March 8, 1879, Letters Received, box 30, FBHQ; A. B. Carey to G. G. Hunt, March 10, 1879, Letters Received, box 30, FBHQ; United States, *Statutes at Large*, 20:403; *Vicksburg Herald*, May 19, 1881.

69. A. B. Carey to Paymaster-General of the Army, September 1, 1885, in *Annual Report of the Secretary of War* (1885), 779–94. See also *Annual Report of the Secretary of War* (1880), 529–39; *Annual Report of the Secretary of War* (1881), 537–49; *Annual Report of the Secretary of War* (1882), 489; *Annual Report of the Secretary of War* (1883), 633–48; *Annual Report of the Secretary of War* (1884), 747–58; *Annual Report of the Secretary of War* (1886), 693–706; *Annual Report of the Secretary of War* (1887), 695–711; *Annual Report of the Secretary of War* (1888), 877.

70. Solomon Daugherty to Wm. W. Belknap, March 4, 1874, Letters Received, box 14, FBHQ.

71. McFeely, *Yankee Stepfather*, 1–8, 149–65; Litwack, *Been in the Storm*, 364–86; Schmidt, "'Full-Fledged Government of Men'"; Herd and Moynihan, *Administrative Burden*.

Chapter Three

1. Glasson, *History*; Glasson, *Federal Military Pensions*; Oliver, *History*; Weber, *Bureau of Pensions*; Skocpol, *Protecting Soldiers and Mothers*; Marten, *Sing Not War*; Blanck and Millender, "Before Disability Civil Rights"; Goldberg, *Citizens and Paupers*, 93; Roediger, *Seizing Freedom*.

2. Notable exceptions include the work of Elizabeth Regosin, Brandi Brimmer, and Tera Hunter. See esp. Regosin, *Freedom's Promise*; Hunter, *Bound in Wedlock*; Brimmer, *Claiming Union Widowhood*.

3. The following discussion of pension laws in early America is based on Glasson, *History*; Glasson, *Federal Military Pensions*; Weber, *Bureau of Pensions*, 1–15; Quadagno, *Transformation of Old Age Security*, 29–47; Resch, *Suffering Soldiers*; Cox, *Boy Soldiers*, 131–58; Jensen, *Patriots, Settlers*.

4. Jensen, *Patriots, Settlers*, 7.

5. United States, *Statutes at Large*, 1:324–25; Weber, *Bureau of Pensions*, 1–15; Glasson, *Federal Military Pensions*, 19–122; Jensen, *Patriots, Settlers*, 44–122.

6. Hahn, *Nation without Borders*; Jensen, *Patriots, Settlers*, 171–221; Bensel, *Sectionalism and American Political Development*, 60; Wecter, *When Johnny Comes Marching Home*, 250.

7. Oliver, *History*, 7–8; Harlan, "Report of the Secretary of the Interior" (1865), vi; United States, *Statutes at Large*, 12:337; Barrett, "Report of the Commissioner of Pensions" (1865), 775–76; *Report of the Secretary of the Interior*, 42d Cong., 2d Sess. (1871), H. Exec. Doc. No. 1-5, p. 408; Baker, *ARCP* (1872), 39.

8. Barrett, "Report of the Commissioner of Pensions" (1865), 776–91; Barrett, "Report of the Commissioner of Pensions," in *Report of Secretary of Interior*, 39th Cong., 2d Sess. (1866), 515–36; Barrett, "Report of the Commissioner of Pensions," in *Report of Secretary of Interior*, 40th Cong., 2d Sess. (1867), 396–416; Cox, "Report of the Commissioner of Pensions," 426–47.

9. Entry on March 17, 1874, box 1, book A, pp. 59–60, DDR; *Daily Mississippian*, August 11, 1865; *North Alabamian*, February 23, 1866; Mathiesen, *Loyal Republic*, 118–44; Blair, *With Malice toward Some*; Grimsley, *Hard Hand of War*; Hyman, *Era of the Oath*.

10. Though the Confederate war machine forcibly impressed hundreds if not thousands of enslaved men, none had served as soldiers. Levine, *Confederate Emancipation*; Martinez, *Confederate Slave Impressment*; Levin, *Searching for Black Confederates*, 1–67.

11. Manning, *Troubled Refuge*; Lee, *Claiming the Union*; Manning, "Working for Citizenship"; Mathiesen, *Loyal Republic*, 87–117; Jefferson Hart to O. O. Howard, January 18, 1869, Letters Received, box 2, vol. 2, CBCD; Henry Kline [Kind] to James McMillan, July 19, 1874, Letters Received, New Orleans, reel 43, FOFB; Elbert Hildebrand, Affidavit, September 18, 1876, in Crecy Jackson file, Co. A, 66th USCT, WA 157.317, WC 177.492, CWPF; Fisk, *Plain Counsels for Freedmen*, 10–11, HL.

12. "Governor's Inaugural Address," *Daily Mississippian*, October 17, 1865; *Southwestern Christian Advocate*, November 15, 1883; "Pensions for Ex-Confederates," *Atlanta Constitution*, December 1, 1887; Address of Andrew Johnson, December 4, 1865, in *OR*, ser. 3, 5:576; "From the President's Message," *South Carolina Leader*, December 16, 1865; "Public Lands of the Southern States," *Daily News and Herald*, May 7, 1866; "Five Minutes with the Democracy," *Morning Republican*, February 2, 1870. For more on state pension systems, see Glasson, "South's Care"; Glasson, "Federal and Confederate Pensions"; Gorman, "Confederate Pensions."

13. Testimony of Hon. John Covode, March 3, 1866, in *Report of the Joint Committee on Reconstruction*, pt. 4, pp. 118–19; Testimony of A. L. Chetlain, March 14, 1866, in *Report of the Joint Committee on Reconstruction*, pt. 3, p. 150.

14. "The Issues of 1868," *Milwaukee Daily Sentinel*, January 24, 1868; "Speech of Senator Morton," *New National Era*, April 13, 1871; Sanders, "Paying for the 'Bloody Shirt,'" 139–44; U.S. Constitution, amend. 14, sec. 4.

15. On Black officeholding at the state level, see esp. Foner, *Freedom's Lawmakers*; Egerton, *Wars of Reconstruction*; Behrend, *Reconstructing Democracy*; Hahn, *Nation under Our Feet*; Du Bois, *Black Reconstruction*.

16. "Wendell Phillips's Speech," *New National Era*, May 18, 1871; "The Difference between Democracy and Republicanism," *New National Era*, May 4, 1871; "Our Taxes the Price of Democratic Treason," *New National Era*, April 20, 1871; *New National Era*, May 25, 1871; "Jeff. Davis Again at the Front," *New National Era*, June 1, 1871.

17. "'Enlightened Patriotism,'" *Morning Republican*, May 18, 1871. For the classic account of Civil War memory and sectional reconciliation, see David Blight's *Race and Reunion* but

also Caroline Janney's *Remembering the Civil War*, a study that challenges the notion that reunion entailed any meaningful "reconciliation," forgetting, or forgiving, particularly among veterans.

18. "Democracy Illustrated," *New National Era*, September 29, 1870; "Where the Money Goes," *New National Era*, August 17, 1871. See also "Reduction of Government Expenses," *New National Era*, September 8, 1870. "Keep It Always before the People," *New National Era*, September 22, 1870; *New National Era*, October 27, 1870; "Facts and Figures for the People," *New National Era*, August 10, 1871; "Pensions," *Weekly Louisianian*, June 21, 1879.

19. Foner, *Reconstruction*, 501–10; Slap, *Doom of Reconstruction*; Summers, *Ordeal of the Reunion*, 305–15; Richardson, *Death of Reconstruction*, 93–129; Blight, *Race and Reunion*, 98–139.

20. "The Old Issues," *New National Era*, August 8, 1872; "How They Are Going to Do It," *New National Era*, September 12, 1872; "Love for Traitors and Hate for Loyalists," *New National Era*, October 31, 1872; *New National Era*, March 27, 1873; "The Blue and the Gray," *Afro-American*, January 7, 1899; Egerton, *Wars of Reconstruction*, 245–83; Wang, *Trial of Democracy*.

21. *Meridian Mercury*, repr. in "Beginning to See It," *Bangor Daily Whig & Courier*, September 24, 1877; United States, *Statutes at Large*, 20:27–29; Glasson, *Federal Military Pensions*, 111; Jensen, *Patriots, Settlers*, 171–221.

22. Jaynes, *Branches without Roots*, 280–300; Shaffer, *After the Glory*, 23–66; Litwack, *Been in the Storm*, 387–449; Mandle, *Roots of Black Poverty*; Ransom and Sutch, *One Kind of Freedom*.

23. A. P. Howe to Alfred Small, October 4, 1867, Letters Sent, vol. 1, p. 4, CBCD; Wyley Green, Declaration for Invalid Pension, September 29, 1869, Letters Received, reel 22, M1910, BRFAL; Howard, "Report of the Commissioner of Bureau of Refugees, Freedmen, and Abandoned Lands" (1870), 320–22; A. McL. Crawford to J. H. Barrett, July 15, 1867, Letters Sent, reel 21, M1910, BRFAL; Isaac W. Newton to William P. Drew, May 24, 1869, Letters Received, box 3, vol. 2, CBCD; Amos Harvey to O. O. Howard, October 16, 1868, Letters Received, box 1, vol. 1, CBCD; A. P. Howe to Henry Wright, August 25, 1869, Letters Sent, vol. 2, p. 383, CBCD.

24. United States, *Statutes at Large*, 12:566–69.

25. John Lawrence, Report for the Month of February 1867, Reports Relating to Bounty Claims and Disbursements, reel 25, M999, BRFAL. On army surgeons and Black regiments, see Humphreys, *Intensely Human*; Glatthaar, *Forged in Battle*; Trudeau, *Like Men of War*; Rogers, "Letters of Dr. Seth Rogers."

26. Howard, "Report of the Commissioner of Bureau of Refugees, Freedmen, and Abandoned Lands" (1870), 316, 320–22; United States, *Statutes at Large*, 16:193–95; T. M. Vincent to Jesse Agason, August 5, 1872, Letters Sent, vol. 1, p. 21, FBHQ; T. M. Vincent to Martha Taylor, August 8, 1872, Letters Sent, vol. 1, p. 25, FBHQ; Acting Commissioner of Pensions to Adjutant General, August 8, 1872, Letters Received, box 1, FBHQ; Thomas M. Vincent to Enoch Reed, October 8, 1872, Letters Sent, vol. 1, p. 215, FBHQ; G. H. Ragsdale to James Curry, December 18, 1873, Letters Received, Fort Monroe, reel 21, FOFB; Letia Harrison to Adjutant General, July 27, 1873, Letters Received, box 9, FBHQ.

27. E. D. Townsend to G. G. Hunt, January 12, 1875, Letters Received, Natchez, reel 36, FOFB; Crecy Jackson to E. B. French, March 20, 1877, Letters Received, New Orleans, reel 45, FOFB; O. C. French to L. D. Allen, August 19, 1870, Natchez, Letters Sent, reel 39, M1907,

BRFAL; William P. Drew to Charles Garretson, October 3, 1870, Letters Received, reel 22, M1910, BRFAL; E. D. Townsend to E. H. Totten, January 12, 1875, Registered Letters Received, Savannah, reel 52, FOFB; Thomas M. Vincent to George Gibson, January 29, 1875, Letters Received, Memphis, reel 25, FOFB; Thomas M. Vincent to G. G. Hunt, January 30, 1875, Letters Received, Natchez, reel 36, FOFB; Thomas M. Vincent to A. K. Arnold, March 31, 1875, Letters Received, New Orleans, reel 44, FOFB; George Gibson to W. Y. Elliott, October 3, 1875, Letters Received, Memphis, reel 25, FOFB.

28. G. H. Ragsdale to James Curry, November 7, 1873, Letters Received, Fort Monroe, reel 21, FOFB; Krowl, "'Her Just Dues,'" 62–63; Brimmer, *Claiming Union Widowhood*; E. L. Hawkins to George Gibson, January 14, 1874, Letters Received, Memphis, reel 25, FOFB; Barrett, "Report of the Commissioner of Pensions," in *Report of Secretary of Interior, 1867*, 418.

29. Cox, *Report of the Secretary of the Interior, 1870*, xii; Van Aernam, "Report of the Commissioner of Pensions," 434.

30. Special Order No. 189, December 7, 1869, Records of the Commissioner, Selected Series, reel 7, p. 425, M742, BRFAL; "Payment of Bounties to Colored Soldiers," *National Republican*, December 20, 1869; "Payment of Bounties to Colored Soldiers," *Times-Picayune*, December 24, 1869; Christopher C. Cox to O. O. Howard, February 13, 1869, Letters Received, box 3, vol. 2, CBCD; William P. Drew to F. C. von Schirach, November 8, 1869, Letters Received, reel 22, M1910, BRFAL; Cox, *Report of the Secretary of the Interior, 1869*, vi–vii; *Hinds County Gazette*, September 15, 1869; Van Aernam, "Report of the Commissioner of Pensions," 434; Cox, *Report of the Secretary of the Interior, 1870*, xii; *Army and Navy Journal*, November 12, 1870, p. 200; *Bounty to Colored Soldiers*, 200–204.

31. *Bounty to Colored Soldiers*, 41st Cong., 35–39; Howard, "Report of the Commissioner of Bureau of Refugees, Freedmen, and Abandoned Land" (1870), 316. Following the investigation, Commissioner Van Aernam asked Howard's agents to examine every pension claim that had been suspended owing to the pending investigation. H. Van Aerman to O. O. Howard, March 18, 1870, Natchez, Registered Letters Received, reel 39, M1907, BRFAL; J. H. Chapman to William P. Drew, April 12, 1870, Vicksburg, Letters Sent, reel 58, M1907, BRFAL; J. H. Chapman to William P. Drew, May 4, 1870, Vicksburg, Letters Sent, reel 58, M1907, BRFAL; J. H. Chapman to E. Whittlesey, May 21, 1870, Vicksburg, Letters Sent, reel 58, M1907, BRFAL; J. H. Chapman to W. F. Callius, October 4, 1870, Vicksburg, Letters Sent, reel 59, M1907, BRFAL; J. H. Chapman to William P. Drew, May 3, 1870, Vicksburg, Letters Sent, reel 58, M1907, BRFAL. J. H. Chapman to William P. Drew, May 19, 1870, Vicksburg, Letters Sent, reel 58, M1907, BRFAL; J. H. Chapman to E. Whittlesey, May 21, 1870, Vicksburg, Letters Sent, reel 58, M1907, BRFAL.

32. Baker, *ARCP* (1872), 15; Baker, *ARCP* (1873), 12. In the Southern press, it was rare indeed to read an article on bounties and pensions that was not wrapped in a sensationalized exposé of criminality and corruption. Claims administrators and agents trafficked in these stories as well. J. B. Coons to William P. Carlin, September 30, 1868, Letters Received, reel 7, M1911, BRFAL; *Weekly Georgia Telegraph*, November 5, 1869; "The Colored Veteran Frauds," *South-Western*, November 17, 1869; G. H. Ragsdale to James Curry, December 18, 1873, Letters Received, Fort Monroe, reel 21, FOFB; "A Corrupt Pension Agent," *Atlanta Constitution*, November 20, 1887; "Pension Frauds," *St. Louis Post-Dispatch*, May 18, 1890.

33. Black, *ARCP* (1887), 3–5; Mashaw, "Federal Administration and Administrative Law," 1422–24; Kretz, "Southern Division," 206–7.

34. Bentley, *ARCP* (1878), 7–8; Bentley, *ARCP* (1879), 14; Dudley, *ARCP* (1881), 5–6; L. E. Dickey, "Southern Division," August 15, 1883, in Dudley, *ARCP* (1883), 52–55; Kretz, "Southern Division."

35. Claim for Abram Haywood, August 2, 1912, in Abram Haywood file, Co. B, 33d, USCT, IA 686.146, IC 498.602, CWPF; Igo, *Known Citizen*, 55–98; Pearson, *Birth Certificate*; Pearson, "'Age Ought to Be a Fact'"; Landrum, "State's Big Family Bible."

36. L. E. Dickey, "Southern Division," August 15, 1883, in Dudley, *ARCP* (1883), 53–54; D. W. Wear to John C. Black, July 5, 1887, in Black, *ARCP* (1887), 75–76.

37. N. Picard to Commissioner of Pensions, September 17, 1884, in Robert Green file, Co. K, 84th, USCT, IA 392.965, IC 669.203, CWPF; [Unsigned] to Commissioner of Pensions, November 30, 1892, in Hester Smith file, Co. H, 92nd, USCT, IA 623.999, IC 855.651, WA 640.872, WC 596.850, CWPF; Atkinson, *ARCP* (1875), 15; Logue and Blanck, "'Benefit of the Doubt'"; Shaffer, *After the Glory*, 129. For attitudes regarding race and poverty between the Civil War and the New Deal, see Bremner, *Philanthropy and Welfare*; Gordon, *Pitied but Not Entitled*; Katz, *In the Shadow*; Goldberg, *Citizens and Paupers*; Fox, *Three Worlds of Relief*; Ruswick, *Almost Worthy*.

38. "Pensions," *Semi-Weekly Louisianian*, June 18, 1871; *Official Journal of the Proceedings of the Convention*; Berry, "Negro Troops"; Hollandsworth, *Louisiana Native Guards*; Weaver, *Thank God*, 61; Redkey, *Grand Army of Black Men*, 249–54; Binning, "Carpetbaggers' Triumph"; Krousser, "Before *Plessy*, before *Brown*."

39. "Pensions," *Semi-Weekly Louisianian*, June 18, 1871.

40. *Congressional Record—Senate*, 44th Cong., 1st Sess. (1876), p. 1414; "Wells, Guilford Wiley," in *Biographical Directory of the United States Congress*; G. Wiley Wells to George Gibson, May 17, 1873, Letters Received, Memphis, reel 24, FOFB; Chas. R. Gill to M. C. Kerr, March 23, 1876, in "Report of the Commissioner of Pensions upon House Resolution of 2nd March, 1876, relative to claims for pensions of Colored Applicants residing in Mississippi," in Committee on Invalid Pensions, 44th Cong., 1st Sess. (1876), RG 233, NARA.

41. Chas. R. Gill to M. C. Kerr, March 23, 1876, in "Report of the Commissioner of Pensions upon House Resolution of 2nd March, 1876, relative to claims for pensions of Colored Applicants residing in Mississippi," Committee on Invalid Pensions, 44th Cong., 1st Sess. (1876), RG 233, NARA. For studies of Black Mississippians in Reconstruction and the nadir, see esp. Behrend, *Reconstructing Democracy*; Kaye, *Joining Places*; Bercaw, *Gendered Freedoms*; Frankel, *Freedom's Women*; McMillen, *Dark Journey*; Wayne, *Reshaping the Plantation South*; Davis, *Good and Faithful Labor*.

42. J. H. Chapman to Susan Sledge, February 1, 1869, Vicksburg, Letters Sent, reel 58, M1907, BRFAL; Susan Sledge file, Co. C, 11th USCT, WA 218.204, WC 197.674, CWPF; Christopher C. Cox to Henry Page, April 22, 1869, Letters Received, reel 3, M1901, BRFAL; J. H. Chapman to William P. Drew, January 3, 1871, Vicksburg, Letters Sent, reel 59, M1907, BRFAL.

43. United States, *Statutes at Large*, 12:566–69; United States, *Statutes at Large*, 14:56–58; United States, *Statutes at Large*, 15:235–37; Browning, *Report of the Secretary of the Interior*, 4; Cox, "Report of the Commissioner of Pensions," 453; *DDI* (1903), 13:173–75.

44. Regosin, *Freedom's Promise*, 114–50; Franke, "Becoming a Citizen"; McClintock, "Civil War Pensions"; Brimmer, *Claiming Union Widowhood*; Witt, *Accidental Republic*; Kelly, *Creating a National Home*; Jones, *Labor of Love*, 43–103; Hunter, *Bound in Wedlock*.

45. Nordhoff, *Freedmen of South-Carolina*, 23–24, HL; Fisk, *Plain Counsels for Freedmen*, 31–32, HL.

46. Fisk, *Plain Counsels for Freedmen*, 31–32, HL; *DDI* (1900), 10:441–43; *DDI* (1902), 12:447–50; Hunter, *Bound in Wedlock*, 241–46; Franke, "Becoming a Citizen," 251–309; Foner, *Reconstruction*, 199–209; Farmer-Kaiser, *Freedwomen and the Freedmen's Bureau*, 99; Ranney, *In the Wake of Slavery*, 46–47; Goring, "History of Slave Marriage"; Litwack, *Been in the Storm*, 366–71; Nieman, "Freedmen's Bureau"; Du Bois, *Black Reconstruction*, 167–80.

47. *Congressional Globe*, 38th Cong., 1st Sess. (1864), pp. 3233, 3514, 3547; United States, *Statutes at Large*, 13:389; Brimmer, *Claiming Union Widowhood*, 9, 61–66; Regosin, *Freedom's Promise*, 82–84; McClintock, "Civil War Pensions," 473–74.

48. United States, *Statutes at Large*, 14:56–58; United States, *Statutes at Large*, 14:357–58; *General Instructions to Special Examiners*, 28–29; Curtis and Webster, *Digest of the Laws*, 259; Raff, *War Claimant's Guide*, 9–10, 27–28; *Army and Navy Journal*, June 16, 1866, p. 678; *Army and Navy Journal*, July 7, 1866, p. 736; *National Republican*, June 19, 1866; *Daily Arkansas Gazette*, April 13, 1867; *DDI* (1887), 1:326–27; *DDI* (1891), 4:359–62.

49. Perrone, "'Back into the Days of Slavery,'" 130; Hunter, *Bound in Wedlock*, 193–94; Masur, *Example for All the Land*, 51–86.

50. "The One Wife Question," *Daily Cleveland Herald*, May 22, 1866; Gordon, *Mormon Question*; Postel, *Equality*.

51. *To Provide for Payment of Bounties*; *Estimates from Paymaster-General*; J. H. Chapman to William P. Drew, May 19, 1870, Vicksburg, Letters Sent, reel 58, M1907, BRFAL; John N. Wager to G. G. Hunt, March 4, 1876, Letters Received, Natchez, reel 36, FOFB. See also J. H. Chapman to William P. Drew, April 3, 1869, Letters Received, box 2, vol. 2, CBCD; William P. Drew to F. C. von Schirach, January 13, 1870, Letters Received, reel 22, M1910, BRFAL; Moses Bird file, Co. A, 99th USCT, WA 161.446, WC 158.494, MA 276.500, MC 193.144, CWPF.

52. Dudley, *ARCP* (1881), 10; Regosin, *Freedom's Promise*, 23–53.

53. Dudley, *ARCP* (1882), 26; Walker, *Treatise*, 5, HL; R. Harris to Commissioner of Pensions, July 28, 1875, Jefferson Grigsby file, Co. B, 12th USCT, WA 109.220, MA 221.911, FA no. 223.043, FC 287.137, CWPF; H.R. 9545, 51st Cong., 1st Sess. (1890); *Pension to Washington Grigsby*. By 1904, the Department of the Interior drew a distinction (first in the case of Celia Robinson) between a "moral marriage" and an illicit one, the former having been "entered into with the master's consent." In South Carolina, enslaved couples enjoying such a "moral marriage" had their union automatically ratified on December 21, 1865, when the legislature legalized marriage among Black Americans as part of the state's Black Codes; those "illicit" unions based solely upon the mutual recognition of enslaved couples thereafter required state sanction. *DDI* (1904), 14:537–42. See also *DDI* (1905), 15:503–25.

54. *General Instructions to Special Examiners*, 28–29; Mitchell, *Raising Freedom's Child*. The chief of the Southern Division put Walker's *Treatise*, together with his *Digest*, "into the hands of each examiner," deeming the two works to be "of great value, placing in convenient form, as it does, the information necessary to a thorough understanding of the office, and securing uniformity of action in the adjudication of claims." L. E. Dickey, "Southern Division," August 15, 1883, in Dudley, *ARCP* (1883), 54.

55. Henry Page to William Drew, December 27, 1869, Letters Received, reel 4, M1901, BRFAL; William Price to James McMillan, December 26, 1872, Letters Received, Memphis,

reel 23, FOFB; William Carson to O. O. Howard, September 18, 1868, Letters Received, box 1, vol. 1, CBCD; Regosin, *Freedom's Promise*, 44; Jaynes, *Branches without Roots*; Davis, *Good and Faithful Labor*; Flynn, *White Land, Black Labor*; Nieman, *From Slavery to Sharecropping*; Reidy, *From Slavery to Agrarian Capitalism*; Glymph and Kushma, *Essays*.

56. James W. Overton to [William P. Drew], January 12, 1869, Letters Received, box 3, vol. 2, CBCD. See also A. P. Howe to James W. Overton, February 9, 1869, Letters Sent, vol. 2, p. 44, CBCD. On illicit sex and sexual assault in nineteenth-century America, see esp. Rosen, *Terror*; Sommerville, *Rape and Race*; Hodes, *White Women, Black Men*; Davis, "Private Law of Race and Sex."

57. Thomas M. Vincent to E. F. Townsend, October 22, 1872, Letters Received, Vicksburg, reel 55, FOFB; Curtis and Webster, *Digest*, 284–85; *DDI* (1903), 13:173–75; Entry on January 13, 1883, box 2, book B, pp. 13–14, DDR; William L. Palmer to James Curry, November 9, 1874, Letters Received, Fort Monroe, reel 22, FOFB; Mashaw, "Federal Administration"; Mashaw, *Creating the Administrative Constitution*; Carpenter, *Forging of Bureaucratic Autonomy*.

58. *Army and Navy Journal*, September 18, 1875, p. 89; "Domestic," *North American and United States Gazette*, September 13, 1875; Atkinson, *ARCP* (1875), 10.

59. United States, *Statutes at Large*, 22:345; Brimmer, *Claiming Union Widowhood*; Regosin, *Freedom's Promise*, 79–113; Shaffer, "'I Do Not Suppose'"; McClintock, "Civil War Pensions," 456–80; Randolph and Hall, *Pension Attorney's Guide*, 74.

60. "Damaging Outgrowth of Pension Laws," *Bee*, June 30, 1888; Schwartzberg, "'Lots of Them Did That'"; Franke, "Becoming a Citizen," 291–92; Mitchell, *Righteous Propagation*, 108–40.

61. *DDI* (1887), 1:iii; Mashaw, *Creating the Administrative Constitution*, 23, 309. In 1897, Jonathan M. Reynolds, the assistant secretary of the interior, compiled excerpts from the first eight volumes of the Interior Department's *Decisions* into the *Digest of Decisions*. "It has been said that the pension law is a law sui generis," noted Reynolds in the volume's preface. "Its system is broad and complex, embracing the most abstruse propositions of legal science." He therefore intended the comprehensive *Digest* to demystify the pension process. In 1905, Eugene B. Payne produced an updated version compiled from volumes 9 through 15 of the *Decisions*. Reynolds, *Digest* (1897), vii–viii; Payne, *Digest* (1905).

62. Curtis and Webster, *Digest*, 284–85; Tanner, *ARCP* (1889), 9; John Parker file, Co. B, 5th USCT, WA 169.511, WC 160.102, MiA 207.709, MiC 197.706, CWPF. Sometimes, as in the case of Eliza Douglass, the mother of James Douglass, the heirship of a remarried widow was redirected by Congress to his dependent mother. Conducting bureau affairs in the absence of specific legislation required greater administrative coordination and was ultimately vulnerable to changes in bureau leadership. In 1889, the commissioner of pensions therefore asked Congress to amend the act of 1882, so that such cases should vest immediately with the minor in question. James Douglass file, Co. H, 5th USCT, MA 292.006, MC 245.114, CWPF; *Pension to Eliza Douglass*; *Invalid Pensions, Douglas[s], Eliza*; *Congressional Record—House*, 50th Cong., 1st Sess. (1888), p. 4910; Entry on March 13, 1883, box 2, book B, p. 18, DDR.

63. Penningroth, *Claims of Kinfolk*, 188; Brimmer, *Claiming Union Widowhood*; Hunter, *To 'Joy My Freedom*; Frankel, *Freedom's Women*; Schwalm, *Hard Fight for We*; Igo, *Known Citizen*, 175; Nackenoff and Novkov, "Introduction."

64. Franke, "Becoming a Citizen," 292–93; Stanley, *From Bondage to Contract*; Welke, *Law and the Borders of Belonging*.

65. Section 13 of the Consolidation Act drew from the acts of July 14, 1862, June 6, 1866, and July 27, 1868. It became section 4707 of the Revised Statutes, and was more frequently referred to as such. United States, *Statutes at Large*, 12:566–69; United States, *Statutes at Large*, 14:56–58; United States, *Statutes at Large*, 15:235–37; United States, *Statutes at Large*, 17:601; Sec. 4707, in *Revised Statutes of the United States* (1878), 917.

66. Dudley, *ARCP* (1882), 13.

67. Walker, *Digest*, 154; *Washington Law Reporter* 15, no. 30 (July 27, 1887): 493; Zachariah Chandler, Circular, November 5, 1875, RBR. See also "Heirs of Colored Soldiers," *Weekly Louisianian*, June 5, 1880; *Pensions for Heirs*; *Army and Navy Journal*, January 27, 1883, p. 581.

68. Edwards, *Unfree Markets*; Penningroth, *Claims of Kinfolk*, 45–78; Kaye, *Joining Places*, 114–18; Morris, *Southern Slavery and the Law*, 132–58; Schermerhorn, *Money over Mastery*; Berlin and Morgan, *Slaves' Economy*.

69. Walker, *Treatise*, 92, HL; Decision, May 4, 1889, in Elizabeth Small file, Co. F, 2d USCT, MA 344.335, MC 302.879, CWPF; Charles Neher file, Co. B, 11th USCT, MA 286.400, MC 326.984, FA 277.966, CWPF; James Hughes file, Co. F, 117th USCT, MA 307.117, CWPF; Regosin, *Freedom's Promise*, 194n43.

70. Dudley, *ARCP* (1883), 14–15; Entry on [March–April 1883], box 2, book B, pp. 19–20, DDR; Moses Moore file, Co. G, 7th USCT, FA 248.134, FC 228.010, CWPF; Curtis and Webster, *Digest*, 186–87.

71. Anderson Shaw file, Co. H, 17th USCT, MA 299.889, MC 230.285, CWPF; "The National Capital," *St. Louis Post-Dispatch*, June 29, 1886; *St. Louis Globe-Democrat*, June 30, 1886; "A Heartless Ruling," *Daily Inter Ocean*, June 30, 1886.

72. William J. Nottingham, Deposition, June 6, 1890, in Edith Winder file, Co. A, 10th USCT, WA 418.488, MA 337.608, MC 271.649, CWPF; Foner, *Fiery Trial*, 206–47; Oakes, *Freedom National*; Siddali, *From Property to Person*; Berlin et al., *Slaves No More*; Gerteis, *From Contraband to Freedman*.

73. Emily Williams to E. B. French, April 25, 1873, Letters Received, New Orleans, reel 43, FOFB; Emily Williams, Deposition, May 28, 1888; Mary Glay, Deposition, June 1, 1888; Eliza Richardson, Deposition, June 20, 1888; E. A. Barringer to John C. Black, June 26, 1888, all in Emily Williams file, Co. I, 77th USCT, MA 212.237, MC 247.115, CWPF. See also the case of Harriet Tinnan, an enslaved mother from Mississippi whose claim for her deceased son's pension was denied on the grounds of having remained on their slave labor camp after the release of the Emancipation Proclamation. Tinnan thereafter remained "in a locality where the authority of the United States had not been reestablished by force of arms," and thus still dependent on her enslaver. Outrageously, as in so many other cases of formerly enslaved mothers, the case hinged on "the legal obligation of her master to maintain and support her" as though nothing had been "affected or changed by the proclamation of emancipation." *DDI* (1897), 8:218–23.

74. Elizabeth Small, Deposition, February 8, 1889; M. B. Bailey to James Tanner, May 24, 1889, both in Elizabeth Small file, Co. F, 2d USCT, MA 344.335, MC 302.879, CWPF; H. M. Teller to W. W. Dudley, November 13, 1883, Curtis and Webster, *Digest*, 175–78; *DDI* (1890), 3:62–67.

75. Affidavit of Nancy Dixon, March 22, 1880; Affidavit of John Williams, June 6, 1880; Affidavit of John Williams, March 22, 1880; Affidavit of Nancy Dixon, July 23, 1886;

A. B. Newcomb to John C. Black, August 26, 1886, all in Richard Dixon file, Co. A, 1st USCT, MA 184.218, MC 225.663, CWPF; *Invalid Pensions, Dixon, Nancy*.

76. Marten, *America's Corporal*; James Tanner, Decision, April 10, 1889, in Elizabeth Small file, Co. F, 2d USCT, MA 344.335, MC 302.879, CWPF.

77. "Twenty Thousand New Colored Pensioners," *Atlanta Constitution*, April 17, 1889; Ayers, *Promise of the New South*; Doyle, *New Men*; Woodward, *Origins of the New South*.

78. E. H. Gelstin to Secretary of the Interior, April 16, 1889, in Elizabeth Small file, Co. F, 2d USCT, MA 344.335, MC 302.879, CWPF.

79. Cyrus Bussey to James Tanner, June 13, 1889, in Elizabeth Small file, CWPF.

80. "Refusing to Pension a Colored Woman Because Her Son Was a Slave," *New York Herald*, repr. in "General Bussey's Latest Ruling," *Daily Picayune*, July 29, 1889.

81. Black, *ARCP* (1885), 30; Tanner, *ARCP* (1889), 34.

82. General Affidavit of Moses Moore, January 12, 1883, in Moses Moore file, CWPF.

Chapter Four

1. Giesberg, *Civil War Sisterhood*; Humphreys, *Intensely Human*; Humphreys, *Marrow of Tragedy*, 103–9; U.S. Sanitary Commission, *Documents of the U.S. Sanitary Commission*, vol. 1, doc. 2; Ellis, *Leaves*; Wormeley, *Sanitary Commission*; Stillé, *History*.

2. Frederickson, *Inner Civil War*, 98–112; Schwalm, "Body of 'Truly Scientific Work'"; U.S. Sanitary Commission, *Statement of the Object and Methods of the Sanitary Commission*, 5.

3. U.S. Sanitary Commission, *Documents of the U.S. Sanitary Commission*, vol. 2, no. 69. For an incisive discussion of the parallels between military service and enslavement, see Emberton, "'Only Murder Makes Men.'"

4. Benjamin Woodward, "Notes of Trip through Arkansas," reel 1, USSC; Elisha Harris to Benjamin Collins, July 7, 1865, reel 1, USSC; Benjamin Woodward, "Notes on Helena, Arkansas," 1865, reel 2, USSC; Benjamin Woodward to Elisha Harris, September 23, 1865, reel 2, USSC; Schwalm, "Body of 'Truly Scientific Work,'" 659; Benjamin Woodward, "Request from Woodward on Physiology of Negro Soldiers, Survey," reel 1, USSC; Foster, "Limitations"; Finley, "In War's Wake." As medical historian Steven Stowe has argued, abstract biological concepts of race were of limited value in the actual treatment of afflictions. Stowe, *Doctoring the South*, 114–18, 200–17.

5. Ira Russell to Standing Committee, July 15, 1865, reel 1, USSC; "Dr. Russell's Report on Hospital L'Ouverture," reel 3, USSC. For more on Russell, see esp. Humphreys, *Intensely Human*.

6. Woodward's and Russel's qualitative findings were later assembled and discussed by Hunt, "Negro as a Soldier" (1867); Hunt, "Negro as a Soldier" (1869); Elisha Harris quoted in Schwalm, "Body of 'Truly Scientific Work,'" 655.

7. Gould, *Investigations*; Baxter, *Statistics, Medical and Anthropological*; Hoffman, *Race Traits*; Schwalm, "Body of 'Truly Scientific Work,'" 658–59; Farland, "W. E. B. DuBois"; Costa, "Measure of Man"; Humphreys, *Intensely Human*, 151–53; Haller, *Outcasts from Evolution*, 20–29.

8. *Army and Navy Journal*, December 12, 1866, p. 285; Faust, *This Republic of Suffering*; Menand, *Metaphysical Club*.

9. Frankel, *States of Inquiry*; Cassedy, *American Medicine and Statistical Thinking*; Cassedy, "Numbering the North's Medical Events"; Burnham, *Health Care in America*, 123; Scott,

Seeing Like a State; Foucault, *Security, Territory, Population*; Foucault, *Discipline and Punish*; Foucault, *History of Sexuality*.

10. Shaffer, *After the Glory*; Regosin and Shaffer, *Voices of Emancipation*; L. E. Dickey, "Southern Division," August 15, 1883, in Dudley, *ARCP* (1883), 53–54; D. W. Wear to John C. Black, July 5, 1887, in Black, *ARCP* (1887), 75–76.

11. Higginson, *Army Life*; Taylor, *Reminiscences*, 79–82; Henry C. Haines file, Co. B, 33d USCT, IA 136.393, IC 96.152, MiA 66.819, MiC 486.899, CWPF; Isaac W. Jenkins file, Co. B, 33d USCT, IA 101.138, IC 90.164, MA 707.865, CWPF; Mingo Singleton file, Co. B, 33d USCT, IA 127.027, IC 179.706, CWPF.

12. Dudley, *ARCP* (1882), 145.

13. Walker, *Treatise*, 32–35, HL.

14. "A Typical Negro," *Harper's Weekly* (July 4, 1863); Silkenat, "'Typical Negro'"; Collins, "Scourged Back"; Clark, "'Sacred Rights of the Weak'"; Wood, *Blind Memory*, 266–69; Willis and Krauthamer, *Envisioning Emancipation*, 37; Abruzzo, *Polemical Pain*, 201–5; Emberton, *Beyond Redemption*, 102–4; Fox-Amato, *Exposing Slavery*.

15. Emberton, *Beyond Redemption*, 102–4; Fox-Amato, *Exposing Slavery*, 172–75; Silkenat, "'Typical Negro.'"

16. Downs, *Sick from Freedom*, 95–119; Humphreys, *Intensely Human*, 80–103.

17. Affidavit of Jacob Forrester, April 28, 1863, FSSP, ser. 2, vol. 1, doc. 6B; John Jones, Deposition, January 18, 1886, in Eliza Jones file, Co. D, 21st, USCT, IA 230.307, IC 362.233, WA 751.484, WC 580.140, CWPF; Lazarus Fields, Deposition, August 30, 1893; Richard Fuller, Certificate of Disability for Discharge, August 13, 1864, both in Richard Fuller file, Co. B, 33d, USCT, IA 676.192, IC 515.652, CWPF; Stephen Tillman, Deposition, June 22, 1897, in Samuel Preston file, Co. K, 93d, USCT, IA 969.653, IC 919.571, WA 750.557, CWPF.

18. *Bounty to Colored Soldiers*, 2–6, 48–57.

19. David Higgins, Deposition, September 2, 1889; Frank Gilliard [Gaillard], Deposition, September 3, 1889; Daniel Drayton, Deposition, September 4, 1889, both in Sarah Higgins file, Co. A, 104th, USCT, IA 472.153, IC 452.244, WA 649.483, WC 465.695, CWPF. See also J. G. Gibbes to William Lochren, November 3, 1893, in Richard Fuller file, Co. B, 33d, USCT, IA 676.192, IC 515.652, CWPF. One Mississippi freedmen, William Coleman, told a special examiner of the Pension Bureau that his "left hip was severely injured in the service & in line of duty," but it was later discovered "that he was so injured when a youth" before enlistment. Claim of William Coleman, no. 773.384, 8:188, CCR.

20. Coffin, *Boys of '61*, 482–507; Bancroft, *Slave Trading*, 165–96.

21. Richard Dargan, Deposition, July 27, 1895, in Richard Dargan file, Co. B, 104th, USCT, IA 582.807, IC 600.682, CWPF. See also Frank Coleman, Deposition, April 11, 1901, in Lucinda Coleman file, Co. C, 104th, USCT, IA 904.269, IC 696.648, WA 926.943, WC 745.397, CWPF. For more on the concept of the "public transcript," see Scott, *Domination*.

22. Historians up to the present day have tended to elide the issue of Black suffering in the wartime and postemancipation years. Downs, *Sick from Freedom*, 6–7. Studies of violence in postemancipation America have been more consistent in portraying the continuity of hardships Black Americans experienced throughout the age of emancipation. For example, see Emberton, *Beyond Redemption*.

23. Walker, *Treatise*, 33–35, HL; Benjamin Smith, Affidavit, December 11, 1884, in Benjamin Smith file, Co. B, 33d USCT, IA 127.936, IC 346.558, WA 368.624, CWPF.

24. L. E. Dickey, "Southern Division," August 15, 1883, in Dudley, *ARCP* (1883), 54. See also Dudley, *ARCP* (1884), 12.

25. Thomas Robinson, Declaration for Original Invalid Pension, December 16, 1882; George W. Sparkman, Deposition, September 17, 1886; Jesse Sparkman, Deposition, September 15, 1886; Thomas Mitchell to Commissioner of Pensions, September 20, 1886, all in Catharine Robinson file, Co. H, 21st, USCT, IA 468.191, IC 346.240, WA 639.500, WC 453.433, CWPF; John R. Childs, Deposition, December 27, 1893, in James Childs file, Co. B, 33d, USCT, IA 666.016, IC 945.512, CWPF.

26. E. F. Townsend to Charlotte Munson, April 4, 1873, Letters Sent, Vicksburg, reel 55, FOFB; Emma and Letitia Munson file, Co. F, 49th USCT, WA 249.312, WC 188.236, MiA 228.846, MiC 181.749, CWPF.

27. Affidavit of Samuel Cunningham and John Proctor, January 27, 1869; Aaron Ancrum, Application for an Invalid Pension, December 18, 1869; Affidavit of Edward Brown and Sampson Drayton, August 3, 1871; Medical Affidavit of Charles Witsell, September 17, 1872; Affidavit of Sallie Ancrum, July 3, 1885, all in Aaron Ancrum file, Co. G, 34th USCT, IA 126.8111, WA 288.999, WC 224.448, CWPF; *Ancrum, Sallie, Invalid Pensions*; United States, *Statutes at Large*, 24:797.

28. Elbert Hildebrand, Affidavit, September 18, 1876; Richard Stephens, Deposition, March 14, 1877; Thomas Cory, Deposition, March 14, 1877; George Galloway and Nelson Robinson, Deposition, March 14, 1877, all in Crecy Jackson file, Co. A, 66th USCT, WA 157.317, WC 177.492, CWPF.

29. G. H. Ragsdale to J. A. Bentley, March 19, 1877, in Crecy Jackson file, CWPF; Crecy Jackson to E. B. French, March 20, 1877, Letters Received, New Orleans, reel 45, FOFB; Gerteis, *From Contraband to Freedman*, 119–33; Oakes, *Freedom National*, 370–86; *OR*, ser. 3, vol. 3, pp. 100–101; Teters, *Practical Liberators*; FSSP, ser. 2, vol. 1, pp. 116–22. For more on Union recruitment of freedmen in the lower Mississippi Valley, see chapter 1.

30. Manning, *Troubled Refuge*; Downs, *Declarations of Dependence*, 43–100; Elbert Hildebrand, Affidavit, September 18, 1876, in Crecy Jackson file, CWPF.

31. Mathisen, *Loyal Republic*, 118–66; Lee, *Claiming the Union*, 1–38, 90–112; Manning, *Troubled Refuge*, 283; Jones, *Birthright Citizens*; Blair, *With Malice toward Some*. For the earliest accounts of the SCC, see Klingberg, "Southern Claims Commission"; Klingberg, *Southern Claims Commission*.

32. The history of enslaved peoples both "being" and owning property is especially well articulated in Penningroth, *Claims of Kinfolk*, 6; Penningroth, "Slavery, Freedom." See also Lee, *Claiming the Union*.

33. Petition of Pompey Lewis, in Approved Claim of Lewis Pompey, no. 41494, Marlboro, South Carolina case files, SCC.

34. Alonzo Jackson, Deposition; Job Mazyck, Deposition, both in Approved Claim of Alonzo Jackson, no. 15646, Georgetown, South Carolina case files, SCC. See also George Hollon, Deposition, in Approved Claim of George Hollon, no. 15645, Georgetown, South Carolina case files, SCC; James Smith, Deposition; John Rivers, Deposition, both in Approved Claim of Pompey Smith, no. 41494, Beaufort, South Carolina case files, SCC.

35. Alonzo Jackson, Deposition, March 18, 1873, in Approved Claim of Alonzo Jackson, SCC.

36. Nancy Johnson, General Interrogatories by Special Com'r, March 22, 1873, in Approved Claim of Boson Johnson, no. 15505, Liberty, Georgia case files, SCC; Alfred Scruggs,

Deposition, Approved Claim of Alfred Scruggs, no. 2392, Madison, Alabama case files, SCC.

37. Nancy Johnson, General Interrogatories by Special Com'r, March 22, 1873, in Approved Claim of Boson Johnson, SCC; David Harvey, Deposition, in Approved Claim of David Harvey, no. 43400, Beaufort, South Carolina case files, SCC; Samuel Fuller, Deposition, May 26, 1874, in Approved Claim of Samuel Fuller, no. 41495, Marlboro, South Carolina case files, SCC; Napoleon Prince, Deposition, in Approved Claim of Napoleon Prince, no. 41499, Marlboro, South Carolina case files, SCC.

38. Approved Claim of William Drayton, no. 10096, Beaufort, South Carolina case files, SCC; William Drayton file, Co. H, 34th USCT, IA 139.413, IC 794097, CWPF; Approved Claim of Edward Brown, no. 21768, Beaufort, South Carolina case files, SCC. Edward Brown would apply for a pension as well, though not until 1889. Edward Brown file, Co. H, 34th USCT, IA 725.142, IC 1.052.082, WA 734.680, WC 544.043, CWPF.

39. John Wood, Deposition, June 9, 1873; Robert Houston, Deposition, June 6, 1873; Mingo Scott, Deposition, June 6, 1873, all in Approved Claim of Robert Houston, no. 21992, Phillips, Arkansas case files, SCC.

40. Samuel Fuller, Deposition, in Approved Claim of Napoleon Prince, SCC; Napoleon Prince, Deposition; Essex Dargan, Deposition, both in Approved Claim of Samuel Fuller, SCC. Samuel Fuller, Deposition; Napoleon Prince, Deposition, both in Approved Claim of Essex Dargan, no. 41493, Marlboro, South Carolina case files, SCC.

41. Remarks, in Approved Claim of David Harvey, SCC; T. W. Parmele, Remarks by Special Commissioner, in Approved Claim of Alonzo Jackson, SCC; Remarks, in Approved Claim of Moses M. Washington, no. 43420, Beaufort, South Carolina case files, SCC; Alexander Dudley, Deposition; Mary Alexander, Deposition; Joel L. Easterling, Deposition, all in Approved Claim of Alexander Dudley, no. 48015, Marlboro, South Carolina case files, SCC.

42. C. W. Dudley to the Commissioners of Southern Claims, April 20, 1871, quoted in Lee, *Claiming the Union*, 90; Benjamin F. Perry and C. W. Dudley to Andrew Johnson, July 31, 1865, in Bergeron, *Papers of Andrew Johnson*, 8:509–10; Bailey, Morgan, and Taylor, *Biographical Directory*, 1:430–31.

43. C. W. Dudley, Remarks, in Approved Claim of Samuel Fuller, SCC; Du Bois, *Black Reconstruction*, 424–25.

44. C. W. Dudley, Remarks, in Approved Claim of Samuel Fuller, SCC. For claims filed by Dudley with checks made payable to him, rather than the claimant, see the Marlboro County, South Carolina case files of the SCC.

45. Richardson, *Death of Reconstruction*, 83–121; Du Bois, *Black Reconstruction*, 381–430. On South Carolina during Reconstruction, see esp. Kelly, "Class"; Kelly, "Labor and Place"; Kelly, "Black Laborers"; Schwalm, *Hard Fight for We*; Saville, *Work of Reconstruction*; Holt, *Black over White*.

46. Lee, *Claiming the Union*, 106; Virgil Hillyer, Remarks, September 12, 1872, in Approved Claim of Harriet Dallas, no. 34185, Chatham, Georgia case files, SCC.

47. Summary Report, in Approved Claim of Harriet Dallas, SCC.

48. *Courier-Journal*, November 16, 1878; E. B. French, "Report of the Second Auditor" (1878), 339; Townsend, "Annual Report of the Adjutant General on the Operations of the Freedmen's Branch," October 10, 1875, in *Report of the Secretary of War*, 44th Cong., 2d Sess.

(1876), 416; E. B. French to E. D. Townsend, January 25, 1877 [1878], Letters Received, box 28, FBHQ.

49. "Report of the Committee on Education and Labor," in *Proceedings of the National Conference of Colored Men of the United States*, 66; "National Colored Convention," *Buffalo Courier*, May 9, 1879; *Evening Star*, May 9, 1879; *Baltimore Sun*, May 9, 1879.

50. Henry Johnson, "An Appeal for the Colored Race," *National Republican*, September 24, 1879; "Washington," *Weekly Louisianian*, May 10, 1879; "Colored Convention," *Union Springs Herald*, May 12, 1879.

51. Painter, *Exodusters*; Richardson, *Death of Reconstruction*, 156–82; Hahn, *Nation under Our Feet*, 320–45; Blight, *Frederick Douglass*, 601–5; McFeely, *Frederick Douglass*, 327–32; "Report of the Committee on Education and Labor," in *Proceedings of the National Conference of Colored Men of the United States*, 66–67.

52. Richardson, *Death of Reconstruction*, 168–73; Painter, *Exodusters*, 216–23; Hahn, *Nation under Our Feet*, 334; U.S. Congress, *Select Committee to Investigate the Causes of the Removal of the Negroes from the Southern States to the Northern States*.

53. Bruce's bill is reprinted in "Education of the Colored Race," *Clarion-Ledger*, January 6, 1880. See also "Education of Colored People," *Richmond Dispatch*, December 17, 1879; "Bill to Aid in Education of Colored Race," *Wilmington Morning Star*, December 9, 1879; "Education of Colored People," *Evening Star*, January 22, 1880; "Unclaimed Bounty Fund for Colored Soldiers," *National Republican*, January 23, 1880. On the indemnity bill, see "For the Benefit of the Colored Race," *Clarion-Ledger*, December 24, 1879; *New York Times*, December 29, 1879. On the activities of the school spokesmen, see "Unclaimed Bounties of Colored Soldiers," *Baltimore Sun*, January 23, 1880; *Times-Democrat*, January 23, 1880; *Wilmington Morning Star*, January 23, 1880; "The Committee on Education," *Atlanta Constitution*, January 31, 1880.

54. "Shrinkage of the Colored Bounty Fund," *Baltimore Sun*, February 6, 1880; "Unclaimed Bounties—Eight-Hour Law," *Baltimore Sun*, February 13, 1880; *New Orleans Daily Democrat*, February 13, 1880; *New York Times*, February 13, 1880; *To Distribute Certain Unclaimed Pay*.

55. After the defeat of Bruce's bill, advocates for Black educational institutions continued to petition for the reallocation of the unclaimed bounty funds. In late March 1880, one representative submitted a petition of seventy-five "colored citizens of Maryland" asking for a portion of the remaining funds to be distributed to Storrs College at Harpers Ferry. "Unclaimed Bounty," *Baltimore Sun*, March 26, 1880; *Congressional Record—House*, 46th Cong., 2d Sess. (1880), p. 1951.

56. United States, *Statutes at Large*, 20:265; Bentley, *ARCP* (1879), 4; Dudley, *ARCP* (1883), 9; Smalley, "United States Pension Office"; Glasson, *History of Military Pension Legislation*, 88–93.

57. "Justice at Last," *Weekly Louisianian*, January 25, 1879; "The Black Belt," *Daily Constitution*, May 30, 1880.

58. The 1882 report went so far as to index all pension claims by regiment and battalion, including the USCT. Dudley, *ARCP* (1882), 144–46, 156; L. E. Dickey, "Southern Division," August 15, 1883, in Dudley, *ARCP* (1883), 53. In addition to the 10,710 Union pensioners, the survivors and widows of the War of 1812 brought the total on the Southern Division's rolls to 17,189 as of June 30, 1883. Dudley, *ARCP* (1883), 85.

59. Claim of John Anderson, no. 1.290.843, 10:86, CCR; Claim of Henry Johnson, no. 1.283.024, 10:179, CCR; Claim of Martin Howard, no. 836.911, 10:111, CCR.

60. Horace Brown, Deposition, March 30, 31, 1887, in Horace Brown file, Co. D, 33d, USCT, IA 493.764, CWPF; United States, *Statutes at Large*, 15:441; *Congressional Record—House*, 49th Cong., 1st Sess. (1886), p. 594.

61. Walter D. Plowden, Deposition, March 14, 1887; Horace Brown, Deposition, March 30, 31, 1887; Isaac J. Hawkins, Deposition, March 29, 1887; Joseph R. Hawley to John C. Black, March 10, 1887; J. E. Jacobs to John C. Black, August 13, 1887; J. E. Jacobs to "General," December 20, 1887, all in Horace Brown file, CWPF; *Irregular Practices of Pension Attorneys*, 1021–27.

62. J. E. Carpenter to S. C. Pomeroy, January 28, 1890, in Horace Brown file, CWPF.

63. George Bragg, Affidavit, December 2, 1889; William O. Domcell and Jno. B. Vanderguss, Surgeon's Certificate, August 21, 1889; Charley Miller, John Sunman, Wallace Cooper, and Edward Holmes, Affidavit, July 28, 1889; George Bragg, Affidavit, December 2, 1889, all in Polly Bragg file, Co. A, 92d, USCT, IA 678.192, IC 653.239, WA 598.893, WC 414.795, CWPF.

64. Downs, *Sick from Freedom*; Weiner and Hough, *Sex, Sickness, and Slavery*; Long, *Doctoring Freedom*; Fett, *Working Cures*; Savitt, *Medicine and Slavery*.

65. Stephen Hurt, History of Claim, August 24, 1887; William A. Rothwell, Thomas Irwin, and J. C. Todford, Surgeon's Certificate, August 24, 1887; Harry Mathias, General Affidavit, February 27, 1889; Peter Hurt, General Affidavit, February 27, 1889; Gabriel Hall, Affidavit, April 6, 1865 [1889]; Lewis Terrell, Affidavit, April 28, 1887; Stephen Hurt, Inability Affidavit, May 17, 1889, all in Millie Hurt file, Co. B, 92d, USCT, IA 602.110, IC 617.223, WA 660.852, WC 770.582, CWPF.

66. Washington Jones to John C. Black, February 27, 1886; Application for Invalid Pension, October 28, 1895; Washington Jones, Deposition, September 30 and October 21, 1896; Mitchell Tucker, Deposition, October 21, 1896; Thomas W. McGruder, Deposition, October 21, 1896; Washington Jones file, Co. E, 93d, USCT, IA 556.206, IC 617.232, CWPF.

67. Edward Alexander, Deposition, February 19, 1897; James N. Clements to Commissioner of Pensions, February 23, 1897; J. P. Boushee to H. Clay Evans, October 11, 1897; Bureau of Pensions, Special Claims Division, June 30, 1898; Special Claims Division, May 18, 1899; Washington Jones, Deposition, May 29, 1899; E. C. Wiggenhorn to H. Clay Evans, May 31, 1899, all in Washington Jones file, CWPF.

68. "Scatter Flowers over Their Graves," *Southwestern Christian Advocate*, September 3, 1885. For important studies of Civil War commemoration, see Foster, *Ghosts of the Confederacy*; Silber, *Romance of Reunion*; Savage, *Standing Soldiers, Kneeling Slaves*; Blight, *Race and Reunion*; Blair, *Cities of the Dead*; Janney, *Remembering the Civil War*; Domby, *False Cause*.

69. Clark, *Defining Moments*, 2–3, 133–87; Alexander Crummell, "The Need of New Ideas and New Aims," in Crummell, *Africa and America*, 13–14; Blight, *Beyond the Battlefield*, 128–30; Blight, *Frederick Douglass's Civil War*.

70. T. G. Steward, "Colored Society," *Christian Recorder*, December 14, 1876, quoted in Clark, *Defining Moments*, 179–80; Kachun, "Before the Eyes."

71. Robert Green, Affidavit, June 21, 1880; H. N. Frisbie, Affidavit, July 3, 1882; Robert Green, Affidavit, July 27, 1882; Robert Green, Affidavit, April 2, 1883; Robert Green, Affidavit,

April 3, 1884; Robert Green, Deposition, December 3, 1888; Robert Green, Deposition, August 8, 1889; Andrew Jackson, Affidavit, July 27, 1882; Nelson Joseph and Andrew Jackson, Affidavit, April 2, 1883; Daniel Davis, Affidavit, [n.d.] 22, 1886; Henry McKinney, Affidavit, January 18, 1887; Nelson Joseph and Joseph Matthews, Affidavit, January 18, 1887; Daniel Shaw, Affidavit, January 18, 1887; Daniel Shaw, Deposition, March 2, 1887; Daniel Davis, Deposition, December 7, 1888, all in Robert Green file, Co. K, 84th, USCT, IA 392.965, IC 669.203, CWPF; Kretz, "Pensions and Protest," 432–33.

72. Henry McKinney, Affidavit, May 3, 1882; Andrew Jackson, Affidavit, July 27, 1882, both in Robert Green file, CWPF.

73. Robert Green, Affidavit, September 15, 1882; Robert Green, Deposition, May 5, 1890; W. S. Roudebush to Commissioner of Pensions, May 5, 1890, all in Robert Green file, CWPF; Entries on July 25, 26, August 27, 1856, Franklin A. Hudson Diary, SHC.

74. Flora Hyson, Deposition, April 28, 1890; Eliza Johnson, Deposition, April 28, 1890; William Lloyd, Deposition, April 28, 1890, all in Robert Green file, CWPF.

75. Robert Green, Deposition, May 5, 1890; Robert Green, Affidavit, February 19, 1891, both in Robert Green file, CWPF.

76. N. Picard to Commissioner of Pensions, September 17, 1884; W. S. Roudebush to Commissioner of Pensions, May 5, 1890; Robert Green, Affidavit, February 19, 1891, all in Robert Green file, CWPF. See also Jane Matthews file, Co. K, 84th USCT, IA 1.158.491, WA 621.190, WC 452.602, CWPF; Daniel Shaw file, Co. K, 84th USCT, IA 899.203, IC 817.602, CWPF.

77. Perman, *Pursuit of Unity*, 169–76; Painter, *Standing at Armageddon*, 216–30; Hahn, *Nation under Our Feet*, 442–51; Richardson, *Death of Reconstruction*, 209–44; Perman, *Struggle for Mastery*; Litwack, *Trouble in Mind*, 218–29, 244–62, 352–70; Ayers, *Promise of the New South*, 146–49, 289–309; McMillen, *Dark Journey*, 35–71; Woodward, *Origins of the New South*, 321–49.

78. Wm. H. Heard, "The True Condition of the Negro in America," *Christian Recorder*, October 10, 1889; Tanner, *ARCP* (1889), 34. See also Heard, *From Slavery to the Bishopric*.

79. According to the Pension Bureau's annual reports from 1885 to 1889 (the final years in which separate USCT data were reported), the total number of USCT original claims filed was 46,702, with 15,416 admitted to the rolls; USCT veterans had filed 22,873 of those original claims and accounted for 6,514 of those admitted to the rolls. Black, *ARCP* (1885), 30; Black, *ARCP* (1886), 26; Black, *ARCP* (1887), 43; Black, *ARCP* (1888), 50; Tanner, *ARCP* (1889), 34.

Chapter Five

1. For important historical studies of disability in the Civil War era and late nineteenth century, see esp. Handley-Cousins, *Bodies in Blue*; Roediger, *Seizing Freedom*; Marten, *Sing Not War*, 75–124; Rose, *No Right to Be Idle*; Logue and Blanck, *Race, Ethnicity, and Disability*; Welke, *Law*; Clarke, "'Honorable Scars'"; Grant, "Reconstructing the National Body," 285–86.

2. There are only a handful of studies that focus on Black Civil War veterans and Pension Bureau medical examinations. Virtually all of them rely on a set of data samples created under the auspices of the Center for Population Economics at the University of Chicago,

and later the Early Indicators of Later Work Levels, Disease, and Death project (http://uadata.org). Teams of researchers have recorded the vital statistics, diagnoses, disability ratings, and pension sizes for nearly forty thousand white Union soldiers and some twenty-one thousand Black Union soldiers, revealing what some consider valuable data about the life experiences of these veterans. Yet there is good reason to be skeptical of an endeavor that accepts on its face the veracity (much less the validity) of disability ratings. In unsettling ways, this project replicates the medico-bureaucratic impulse of the late nineteenth century in its grand attempt to quantify the unquantifiable, to strip away all the political struggles that produced these subjective, contested, and heavily freighted "data points"—for Black veterans in the South especially. Accordingly, I have avoided use of these data samples entirely.

3. Welke, *Law*, 3; Baynton, "Disability."

4. Baynton, *Defectives in the Land*, 6, 25–29; Baynton, "Defectives in the Land."

5. Miller, "Effects of Emancipation"; Boster, *African American Slavery and Disability*; Barclay, *Mark of Slavery*; Haller, *Outcasts from Evolution*, 40–68; Downs, *Sick from Freedom*, 102–11; Handley-Cousins, *Bodies in Blue*, 28–29; Powell, *New Masters*.

6. Although Roediger correctly notes that "the dominant race dominated the pension rolls," his analysis of disability is largely confined to a dialectic between "the freed slave and disabled [white] veteran." Roediger, *Seizing Freedom*, 77–79, 88.

7. The National Archives and Records Administration has partnered with Fold3 to digitize dozens of collections relating to the U.S. military. It has digitized the index cards of Union pension applications, grouped according to the units in which the associated veterans served (NARA microfilm T289). Over one hundred thousand index cards exist for the U.S. Colored Infantry alone. Those who cite the aforementioned data samples from the Union Army Data set (and predecessor) extrapolate from those samples different estimates of the number of white and Black applicants under each system as well as their success rates. Logue and Blanck, "'Benefit of the Doubt'"; Shaffer, *After the Glory*, 122–24, 238n39.

8. U.S. Sanitary Commission, *Documents of the U.S. Sanitary Commission*, vol. 2, doc. 67.

9. Perkins, *Report on the Pension Systems*.

10. Bellows, "Report concerning Provision Required"; Kelly, *Creating a National Home*, 22–26.

11. Historian Patrick Kelly has found that approximately eighty Black veterans resided in the National Home annually during the 1870s, living in segregated quarters. By the turn of the century, only 2.5 percent of veterans sheltered in the National Home for Disabled Volunteer Soldiers were Black. Kelly, *Creating a National Home*, 98–99; Marten, *Sing Not War*, 159–98; Shaffer, *After the Glory*, 137–42; Logue and Blanck, *Race, Ethnicity, and Disability*, 130–41; Logue and Blanck, *Heavy Laden*, 154; *Report of the Board of Managers of the National Home for Disabled Volunteer Soldiers*, 25.

12. Graeber, *Utopia of Rules*, 9; United States, *Statutes at Large*, 13:387–89; United States, *Statutes at Large*, 13:499–500; United States, *Statutes at Large*, 14:56–58; Wilson, Burdett, and Church, "How Shall the Pension List."

13. Smalley, "United States Pension Office," 430; Glasson, *Federal Military Pensions*, 130–31; United States, *Statutes at Large*, 14:56–58; United States, *Statutes at Large*, 17:335; Baker, *ARCP* (1873), 14.

14. Van Aernam, "Report of the Commissioner of Pensions," 435–41; Baker, "Report of the Commissioner of Pensions," 382, 388; United States, *Statutes at Large*, 12:566–69;

Barrett, "Report of the Commissioner of Pensions," in *Message of the President of the United States*, 791; Cox, *Report of the Secretary of the Interior, 1870*, xi; Mashaw, *Creating the Administrative Constitution*, 263–66. For guides distributed to examining surgeons, see esp. *Instructions to Examining Surgeons for Pensions* (1882) and its 1884 updated edition.

15. Mashaw, *Creating the Administrative Constitution*, 263–66; Van Aernam, "Report of the Commissioner of Pensions," 435–41; Cox, *Report of the Secretary of the Interior, 1870*, xi; Baker, "Report of the Commissioner of Pensions," in *Report of Secretary of Interior, 1871*, 388–89; United States, *Statutes at Large*, 17:601; United States, *Statutes at Large*, 22:174–76.

16. Parrillo, *Against the Profit Motive*, 145–62; Testimony of L. E. Dickey, June 5, 1880, in *Testimony Taken*, 348–50.

17. Baker, "Report of the Commissioner of Pensions," in *Report of Secretary of Interior, 1871*, 388–89; United States, *Statutes at Large*, 17:566–77; Atkinson, *ARCP* (1875), 12–14.

18. Parrillo, *Against the Profit Motive*, 1–8, 149–53; Bentley, *ARCP* (1876), 19–21; Bentley, *ARCP* (1877), 6; Bentley, *ARCP* (1878), 12; Bentley, *ARCP* (1879), 6–7; Carpenter, *Forging of Bureaucratic Autonomy*, 59–60.

19. Smalley, "United States Pension Office," 430; Skocpol, *Protecting Soldiers and Mothers*, 118–20; Goldberg, *Citizens and Paupers*, 76–101; Dearing, *Veterans in Politics*, 284.

20. Dudley, *ARCP* (1881), 5–6; N. F. Graham to Commissioner of Pensions, September 21, 1883, in Dudley, *ARCP* (1883), 37–39; United States, *Statutes at Large*, 22:174–76; Parrillo, *Against the Profit Motive*, 150.

21. Dudley, *ARCP* (1883), 24; Evans, *ARCP* (1899), 17; Warner, *ARCP* (1905), 29.

22. McConnell, *Glorious Contentment*; Shaffer, *After the Glory*, 144–45; Gannon, *Won Cause*, 28–34.

23. Bensel, *Political Economy*, 130–32; Skocpol, *Protecting Soldiers and Mothers*, 125–27; Marten, "Those Who Have Borne"; McMurry, "Political Significance"; McMurry, "Bureau of Pensions."

24. The Black press took special note of Cleveland's pension bill vetoes during his two nonconsecutive terms. "Pension Bill Vetoes," *Bee*, October 22, 1892; "Gems from Grover," *Bee*, October 22, 1892; "The Veto Messages," *Weekly Inter Ocean*, June 30, 1886; "The Press on the President's Letter," *News and Observer*, September 12, 1888; "Sickles Still Defiant," *Bee*, October 8, 1892; "For Harrison," *Bee*, November 5, 1892.

25. Affidavit of Mary Norman, September 5, 1885; Affidavit of Mary Norman, November 15, 1884, both in Turner Norman file, Co. G, 35th USCT, WA 259.615, WC 289.190, CWPF; *Norman, Mary, Invalid Pensions*, 49th Cong., 1st Sess. (1886), H. Report No. 3203; *President's Veto; Granting Pension to Mary Norman; Norman, Mary, Invalid Pensions*, 49th Cong., 1st Sess. (1886), H. Report No. 1107.

26. Glasson, *Federal Military Pensions*, 209–18; *Congressional Record—Senate*, 49th Cong., 1st Sess. (1886), pp. 4667–81; *Journal of the House of Representatives*, 49th Cong., 2d Sess. (1887), pp. 567–73.

27. Tanner, *ARCP* (1889), 9–12; Marten, *America's Corporal*, 92–158; United States, *Statutes at Large*, 26:182–83; Skocpol, *Protecting Soldiers and Mothers*, 128–30; Glasson, *Federal Military Pensions*, 273; Summers, *Ordeal of the Reunion*, 37.

28. Gaylord M. Saltzgaber to J. P. Waring, September 24, 1914, in Abram Haywood file, Co. B, 33d, USCT, IA 686.146, IC 498.602, CWPF.

29. *New York Times*, June 13, July 10, August 19, May 25, 1890; *New York Times*, May 5, 1893; Sloane, "Pensions and Socialism," 183; *New York Times*, April 16, 1894; Wilson, Burdett, and

Church, "How Shall," 426. For more on social welfare and benefits in the Gilded Age, see Ruswick, *Almost Worthy*; Goldberg, *Citizens and Paupers*, 76–101; Quadagno, *Transformation of Old Age Security*, 21–75; Trattner, *From Poor Law*, 77–103; Katz, *In the Shadow*, 68–102; Bremner, *Public Good*, 144–207.

30. On pension agents and attorneys, see esp. Marten, "Those Who Have Borne"; Blanck and Song, "Civil War Pension Attorneys"; "Political Review," *Southwestern Christian Advocate*, May 8, 1890; "Political Review," *Southwestern Christian Advocate*, July 10, 1890; "General News Items," *Southwestern Christian Advocate*, July 24, 1890; "Pensions," *Bee*, April 25, 1891, April 29, 1893, August 19, 1893.

31. "Pensions! New Law!" *Richmond Planet*, August 30, 1890, October 4, 1890; "Pension Claims," *Bee*, September 13, 1890; *Atchison Daily Globe*, April 9, 1891; "The Colored Attorneys," *Bee*, June 30, 1894; "The Trend of Sentiment: Rich People of Color," *Southwestern Christian Advocate*, January 11, 1894; "Pulies-Lester," *Bee*, November 5, 1898.

32. Because Hawks refused to offer a certificate of disability, John Floyd's General Law pension case floundered until it met final rejection in 1902. John Floyd, Claimant's Affidavit, May 22, 1891; John Floyd, Claimant's Affidavit, June 8, 1891; J. M. Hawks to John Floyd, July 21, 1891; John Floyd, Claimant's Affidavit, [n.d.] 1891; John Floyd, Invalid Pension, May 29, 1902; John Floyd, Deposition, October 14, 1903, all in Maria Floyd file, Co. A, 33d, USCT, IA 898.798, IC 697.338, WA 844.743, WC 612.242, CWPF; Seth Rogers to [Isabel Rogers], December 27, 1862, in Rogers, "Letters of Dr. Seth Rogers," 338–39; Higginson, *Army Life*; Ash, *Firebrand of Liberty*. For other claimants who struggled to navigate the two pension systems, see A. McL. Crawford to Dr. Hawks, April 16, 1867, Letters Sent, reel 21, M1910, BRFAL; A. McL. Crawford to Lorenzo Thomas, April 11, 1867, Letters Sent, reel 21, M1910, BRFAL; J. M. Hawks, Deposition, December 19, 1884, in Eliza Jones file, Co. D, 21st, USCT, IA 230.307, IC 362.233, WA 751.484, WC 580.140, CWPF; M. W. Robertson to Jno. C. Black, June 28, 1888, in Hamilton Brown file, Co. E, 21st, USCT, IA 441.549, IC 436.839, WA 563.895, CWPF; Frank E. Marble to Commissioner of Pensions, November 19, 1886, in Catharine Robinson file, Co. H, 21st, USCT, IA 468.191, IC 346.240, WA 639.500, WC 453.433, CWPF; Glatthaar, *Forged in Battle*, 231–64.

33. E. S. Porter, Physician's Affidavit, November 8, 1897, in Sarah Richardson file, Co. A, 136th, USCT, IA 715.285, IC 764.841, WA 761.825, WC 542.082, CWPF.

34. W. R. Lastrapes, Surgeon's Certificate, July 8, 1896; T. L. Jefferson, General Affidavit, December 18, 1895; T. N. Brian, Physician's Affidavit, September 11, 1900; T. N. Brian, Physician's Affidavit, March 27, 1902, all in Richard Anderson file, CWPF.

35. "Much of what we know about race and medicine in the post–Civil War South," notes historian Lynn Marie Pohl, "relates to the racial beliefs and actions of white physicians." Pohl, "African American Southerners," 179, 182–93; Stowe, *Doctoring the South*, 265; Haller, "Physician versus the Negro"; Savitt, *Race and Medicine*.

36. Samuel Preston, Inability Affidavit, December 27, 1894; Samuel Preston, Deposition, May 25, 1897, both in Samuel Preston file, CWPF; James Lursey, General Affidavit, June 14, 1888, in Jane Lursey file, Co. C, 33d, USCT, IA 643.828, IC 767.273, WA 552.234, WC 360.302, CWPF; Arthur Emory, Claimant's Affidavit, October 1, 1889, in Margaret Kelly file, Co. A, 136th, USCT, IA 724.258, IC 552.023, WA 841.495, WC 673.880, CWPF; Daniel Beckton, Claimant's Affidavit, December 10, 1887, in Daniel Beckton file, Co. F, 92d, USCT, IA 487.397, IC 663.252, CWPF; General Affidavit of Charles Nicholas and Friday Hamilton,

April 30, 1890, in Edward Brown file, Co. H, 34th USCT, IA 725.142, IC 1.052.082, WA 734.680, WC 544.043, CWPF; Brady, "Negro as a Patient."

37. Case of Carter J. Hill, 5:85, CCR.

38. T. L. Jefferson, General Affidavit, October 1, 1894; T. L. Jefferson, General Affidavit, November 25, 1895; Washington Brusaw, Declaration for Increase of Pension, November 25, 1895; Washington Brusaw, Increase of Invalid Pension, March 31, 1897; Washington Brusaw, Declaration for Increase of Pension, September 11, 1899; Washington Brusaw, Declaration for Increase of Pension, August 14, 1901; Washington Brusaw, Increase of Invalid Pension, May 20, 1902; Washington Broussan [*sic*], Application for Increase of Pension, April 13, 1907, all in Washington Moore file, Co. K, 93d, USCT, IA 923.162, IC 737.271, CWPF.

39. William Wallace, Declaration for Increase of Pension, December 3, 1898, in William Wallace file, Co. K, 93d, USCT, IA 912.022, IC 928.790, CWPF; Isaiah Taylor, Declaration for Re-Rating of an Invalid Pension, February 3, 1898, in Isaiah Taylor file, Co. K, 84th, USCT, IA 877.583, IC 748.262, CWPF.

40. F. H. Allen, "Report of Chief of Southern Division," in Raum, *ARCP* (1892), 43.

41. As Marta Russell has persuasively argued, disability was—and is—an outcome not simply of medical diagnosis or prejudice but of political economy, a socially imposed classification defined in the context of labor relations. As such, the political function of the category of disability is to single out able-bodied workers for proper exploitation while excluding those with impairments from full participation in society and the workforce. Russell and Malhotra, "Capitalism and the Disability Rights Movement"; Johnson, *River of Dark Dreams*, 151–208; Baptist, *Half Has Never Been Told*, 111–44; Rosenthal, *Accounting for Slavery*.

42. Willie Wallace, Arkansas Narratives, vol. 2, pt. 7, p. 42, *BIS*; Frank Fikes, Arkansas Narratives, vol. 2, pt. 2, p. 283, *BIS*; Boster, *African American Slavery and Disability*; Barclay, *Mark of Slavery*.

43. Smith, *Autobiography of James L. Smith*, 3, 21, 23–24.

44. Calvin West, Arkansas Narratives, vol. 2, pt. 7, p. 104, *BIS*; Edwards, *Unfree Markets*; Penningroth, *Claims of Kinfolk*; Berlin and Morgan, *Slaves' Economy*; Hahn, *Nation under Our Feet*, 24–33.

45. Fett, *Working Cures*, 15–35; Harriss, "What Constitutes Unsoundness" (emphasis in original); Boster, *African American Slavery and Disability*, 34–54, 55–73.

46. Johnson, *Soul by Soul*, 119–42; Gross, *Double Character*, 22–46, 122–52; Brown, *Slave Life in Georgia*, 117.

47. Cato Yates, Deposition, August 26, 1895; Stephen Tripp, Deposition, August 26, 1895, both in Tyra Burke file, Co. A, 33d, USCT, IA 736.326, IC 552.410, WA 757.457, WC 538.921, CWPF; Arthur Emory, Claimant's Affidavit, October 1, 1889; Major Walker, General Affidavit, October 15, 1889; Caesar Reed, General Affidavit, October 15, 1889, all in Margaret Kelly file, CWPF; Robert Green, Affidavit, April 2, 1883; Robert Green, Affidavit, April 3, 1884, both in Robert Green file, Co. K, 84th, USCT, IA 392.965, IC 669.203, CWPF.

48. Raum, *ARCP* (1892), 8; Smalley, "United States Pension Office," 430; Johnson, "'Great Injustice.'"

49. Joseph Morris and Redick Barrett, General Affidavit, August 12, 1896, in Washington Moore file, CWPF; United States, *Statutes at Large*, 26:182–83; Charles Ballard and Adam

Finley, Affidavit, November 30, 1895, in Richard Dargan file, Co. B, 104th, USCT, IA 582.807, IC 600.682, CWPF; Higginson, *Army Life*; A. P. Prioleau, Surgeon's Certificate, July 7, 1886; Sampson Cuthbert, Declaration for an Original Invalid Pension, September 6, 1890; Joseph Cuthbert, Neighbor's Affidavit, November 22, 1890; R. S. Bryant, Neighbor's Affidavit, November 22, 1890; E. M. Pinckney, Physician's Affidavit, February 21, 1895; Sampson Cuthbert, Deposition, June 25, 1902, all in Sampson Cuthbert file, Co. D, 33d, USCT, IA 920.342, IC 690.548, WA 822.951, CWPF; South Carolina State Board of Health, *Annual Report* (1882), 95; South Carolina State Board of Health, *Annual Report* (1894), 12.

50. United States, *Statutes at Large*, 22:345; Brimmer, *Claiming Union Widowhood*; Regosin, *Freedom's Promise*, 79–113.

51. Affidavit of Sallie Ancrum, July 3, 1885, in Aaron Ancrum file, Co. G, 34th USCT, IA 126.8111, WA 288.999, WC 224.448, CWPF; *Ancrum, Sallie, Invalid Pensions*; United States, *Statutes at Large*, 24:797; F. W. Wesseler, Jos. McCluss, and Thos. Hawley, Surgeon's Certificate, July 10, 1889; Joseph Jackson, General Affidavit, August 17, 1889; Ben Morgan, Deposition, February 3, 1898; Lydia Jackson, General Affidavit, March 29, 1890; George Butler, Declaration for Invalid Pension, August 4, 1890; George Butler, Invalid Pension, February 26, 1891; Charles Davis et al., Surgeon's Certificate, April 8, 1891; F. W. Wesseler, Jos. McCluss, and Thos. Hawley, Surgeon's Certificate, April 27, 1892; George Butler, Invalid Pension, August 5, 1892; W. Davis to Commissioner of Pensions, October 31, 1899, all in Harriet Butler file, Co. H, 92d, USCT, IA 700.868, IC 810.171, WA 639.434, WC 460.305, CWPF.

52. Charles Dowell to Commissioner of Pensions, September 25, 1897; R. C. Atkinson et al., Surgeon's Certificate, March 4, 1896; Harriet Butler, Appeal, Docket No. 43.474, Department of the Interior; Frederick W. Fout to Secretary of the Interior, April 1, 1898; J. F. Raub to F. D. Stephenson, September 25, 1899; W. Davis to Commissioner of Pensions, October 31, 1899, all in Harriet Butler file, CWPF.

53. Harriet Butler, General Affidavit, August 4, 1896, in Harriet Butler file, CWPF.

54. Under the Act of July 27, 1868, qualified widows were entitled to an eight-dollar pension, plus two dollars for each minor child. The Act of March 9, 1886 raised all widow's pensions to twelve dollars. United States, *Statutes at Large*, 15:235–37; United States, *Statutes at Large*, 24:5–6; Glasson, *Federal Military Pensions*, 139–42.

55. David Higgins, Declaration for an Original Invalid Pension, January 31, 1883; G. H. Kellers, Surgeon's Certificate, November 23, 1887; David Higgins, Deposition, September 2, 1889; A. C. McClenman, Surgeon's Certificate, March 26, 1890; William H. Johnson, Physician's Affidavit, January 12, 1897; City of Charleston, S.C., Department of Health, No. 158, January 3, 1898; Sarah Higgins, General Affidavit, June 7, 1898, all in Sarah Higgins file, CWPF.

56. Witt, *Accidental Republic*, 1–42.

57. Tyler Sewall file, Co. G, 1st USCT, IA 195.088, WA 557.050, CWPF; *Testimony Taken*, 221–22.

58. Claim of Washington Stump, no. 695.702, CCR, 5:176; Claim of Anderson Stallings, no. 629.725, CCR, 8:145; Claim of Samuel Jones, no. 589.564, CCR, 6:13; Claim of Jennie M. Smith, no. 505.486, CCR, 6:7; Claim of Fannie Pillow, no. 585.921, CCR, 6:32; Lucy Bowers file, Co. B, 2d, USCT, IA 103.846, IC 70.147, WA 234.494, WC 223.234, CWPF. For some of the cases involving Amos L. Wheeler, see CCR, 6:144, 147–50, 153, 174, 177–78, 247.

59. Bentley, *ARCP* (1879), 15; Dudley, *ARCP* (1881), 5–6, 12–13; Dudley, *ARCP* (1882), 19, 33; Jno. M. Welty, "Special Examination Division," September 20, 1883, in Dudley, *ARCP* (1883), 39–43; Dudley, *ARCP* (1884), 23; Black, *ARCP* (1887), 26, 45. Black also created the Law Division primarily to facilitate pension appeals, but in 1887 ordered the division handle and transmit all proposed submissions to the Justice Department from the Special Examination Division—what a future Law Division clerk would call "the half-sister of this division"—leading to considerable confusion, inaccuracy, and redundancy. James M. Ward, "Report of the Law Division, July 2, 1888, in Black, *ARCP* (1888), 95; Frank E. Anderson, "Report of Law Clerk," August 1, 1893, in Lochren, *ARCP* (1893), 16.

60. Gould, *Investigations*; Baxter, *Statistics, Medical and Anthropological*; Hough and Sedgwick, *Human Mechanism*; Trachtenberg, *Incorporation of America*, 38–69.

61. Davis, *Enforcing Normalcy*, 23–45; Warner, *Therapeutic Perspective*; Burnham, *Health Care in America*, 123; Baynton, "Disability," 35–36; Baynton, *Defectives in the Land*; Handley-Cousins, *Bodies in Blue*, 4–7.

62. Longmore and Umansky, "Disability History," 3, 13; Thomson, *Extraordinary Bodies*, 41–54.

63. Starr, *Social Transformation of American Medicine*, 93–112; "Medical Bigotry," *New National Era*, March 2, 1871.

64. Baker, "Report of the Commissioner of Pensions," in *Report of Secretary of Interior*, 42d Cong., 2d Sess. (1871), H. Exec. Doc. No. 1-5, pp. 388–89; Baker, *ARCP* (1872), 11–12; Starr, *Social Transformation of American Medicine*, 93–112.

65. Raum, *ARCP* (1891), 4–5; Thos. D. Ingrahm, "Report of Medical Referee," in Raum, *ARCP* (1891), 33–36; F. H. Allen, "Report of Chief of Southern Division," in Raum, *ARCP* (1891), 40–41; Raum, *ARCP* (1892), 20.

66. Murphy, *ARCP* (1896), 9–10; Evans, *ARCP* (1899), 17–18; Evans, *ARCP* (1898), 12; Evans, *ARCP* (1901), 70; Evans, *ARCP* (1899), 12–13; "A Tried Watch-Dog Who Will Be Retained," *Puck* (October 30, 1901). The *North American Review* frequently featured reform-minded articles criticizing the pension system. See esp. Baber, "Our Pension System," 663–64; Wilson, Burdett, and Church, "How Shall the Pension List"; Veazey et al., "Further Views."

67. Veazey, O'Neil, and Enloe, "Further Views," 628; Clark, "Some Weak Places."

68. Richard Dargan, Deposition, July 27, 1895; Richard Dargan, Invalid Pension, May 2, 1894; E. D. Gallion to William Lochren, September 30, 1895; Adam Finley, General Affidavit, September 17, 1896; Richard Dargan, Declaration for Original Invalid Pension, October 18, 1896, all in Richard Dargan file, CWPF; Kretz, "Pensions and Protest," 434–37.

69. H. M. Stuart to H. D. Fraser, September 19, 1883; B. C. Norment to Henry D. Fraser, September 26, 1883; T. P. Bailey to H. D. Fraser, September 6, 1883; L. B. Johnson to Henry D. Fraser, September 29, 1883, all in South Carolina State Board of Health, *Annual Report* (1883), 21–22, 28–29, 31–32, 37–38; Barrier, "Tuberculosis," 226–27, 233; Hunter, *To 'Joy My Freedom*, 187–218.

70. *Inaugural Address of Grover Cleveland* (1893), 4; Lochren, *ARCP* (1894), 8–10; "Pension Office Sweep," *Bee*, April 29, 1893.

71. Following the passage of the Disability Act, the Pension Bureau under President Harrison's administration made efforts to further expand benefits to disabled veterans. To that end, Commissioner Raum issued an order in October 1890, which many interpreted as

holding claimants entitled to a disability rating that was the sum total of various minor disabilities. For example, claimants could combine a 6/18 rating for rheumatism, a 2/18 rating for heart disease, and a 2/18 rating for general debility, thereby earning an aggregate pension rating of 10/18. This practice led to considerably higher pension ratings between 1890 and 1893, until the Department of the Interior revoked the order, alleging that in originally approving the order it "did not intend that small rates should be added together." Only the claimant's "chief disability" would receive a rating. Glasson, *Federal Military Pensions*, 239–40; Evans, *ARCP* (1899), 30–33.

The discrepancy between considering disabilities "all together" and aggregating all individual ratings reflected not only the definitional ambiguities of "disability" but also its inescapably political nature. Two presidential election cycles after the Department of the Interior revoked Raum's order in 1893, Congress passed a new law that resurrected the rescinded order. The Act of May 9, 1900 held that in fixing the ratings of pensioners, "each and every infirmity shall be duly considered and the aggregate of the disabilities should be rated." However, Commissioner Henry Clay Evans opposed this measure and immediately issued an order reinterpreting the act. In June 1900, Evans declared, once again, that all infirmities ought to be evaluated together. The matter of aggregating disabilities was not only confused at the matter of high policy; it also resulted in considerable inconsistency at the level of the medical examining boards. The bureau would never entirely resolve the matter. United States, *Statutes at Large*, 31:170; Evans, *ARCP* (1900), 31–32; Glasson, *Federal Military Pensions*, 246–48.

72. James R. Fritts, "Report of Chief of Special Examination Division," August 13, 1894, in Lochren, *ARCP* (1894), 34; Lochren, *ARCP* (1895), 8–10; James R. Fritts, "Report of Special Examination Division," August 29, 1895, in Lochren, *ARCP* (1895), 28; Frank E. Anderson, "Report of Law Division," August 9, 1895, in Lochren, *ARCP* (1895), 22; "Sifting the Pension List," *Bee*, June 24, 1893; "Washington Letter," *Richmond Planet*, March 10, 1894; Shaffer, *After the Glory*, 129; Richard Dargan, Deposition, July 27, 1895; Thomas Smith, Deposition, July 31, 1895; Ellen McFarland, Deposition, August 2, 1895; Simon McFarland, Deposition, September 30, 1895; E. D. Gallion to William Lochren, September 30, 1895, all in Richard Dargan file, CWPF.

73. Richard Dargan to Commissioner of Pensions, September 30, 1899; Richard Dargan to Secretary of the Interior, October 21, 1899; Richard Dargan to Secretary of the Interior, December 5, 1899; A. C. McClenman, J. N. Roberts, and J. S. Buist, Surgeon's Certificate, January 16, 1901; A. C. McClenman, J. N. Roberts, and J. S. Buist, Surgeon's Certificate, December 10, 1902; Richard Dargan, Brief for Reopening, January 13, 1904, all in Richard Dargan file, CWPF; Kretz, "Pensions and Protest," 434–37.

74. *Irregular Practices of Pension Attorneys*, 1438–39; Brown, "Some Observations," 46–49; Parrillo, *Against the Profit Motive*, 437–38n218.

75. Richard Dargan to Secretary of the Interior, December 5, 1899; Richard Dargan to Commissioner of Pensions, September 30, 1899; Richard Dargan to Secretary of the Interior, October 21, 1899, all in Richard Dargan file, CWPF.

76. On the idea of freedom as attachment to a powerful state, see esp. Downs, *Declarations of Dependence*; Downs, *After Appomattox*; Manning, "Emancipation."

77. "Another Act of Justice," *New National Era*, June 22, 1871; Masur, *Example for All the Land*; "The Southern States," *Daily Picayune*, April 1, 1893; "Dr. Noble Appointed," *Rich-*

mond Planet, September 23, 1899; *Richmond Planet*, November 4, 1899; "Dr. Charles Harrison Promoted," *Colored American*, March 30, 1901; "The Late Dr. J. G. Clayton," *Colored American*, July 4, 1903. For more on Augusta, see Long, *Doctoring Freedom*, 114–78; Humphreys, *Intensely Human*, 62–64; Downs, *Sick from Freedom*, 88–89, 117–18. On the rise of Black medical professionals after emancipation, see Long, *Doctoring Freedom*, 90–178; Ward, *Black Physicians*; Gamble, *Making a Place for Ourselves*; Hine, *Black Women in White*; Smith, *Sick and Tired*; Savitt, "Entering a White Profession."

78. A. W. McKinney, "The Present Status of the Colored Man in the South," *Southwestern Christian Advocate*, January 19, 1893. On postemancipation narratives of Black progress, see Shaffer, *After the Glory*, 169–93; Clark, *Defining Moments*, 133–87; Blight, *Race and Reunion*, 300–337; Laski, *Untimely Democracy*, 1–160.

79. "Dr. Holmes Received an Appointment," *Richmond Planet*, May 29, 1897; "Federal Appointments Given Colored Men," *Richmond Planet*, October 15, 1898; Mason and Smith, *Beaches, Blood, and Ballots*, 17; Behrend, *Reconstructing Democracy*; McMillen, *Dark Journey*.

80. "Colored Voters Kicking," *Richmond Planet*, September 2, 1899.

81. "Bitter Feeling in Greenville," *Atlanta Constitution*, July 21, 1902; "South Carolina Politics," *Colored American*, July 4, 1903.

82. *Annual Register of the Department of the Interior* (1881); *Annual Register of the Department of the Interior* (1884); *Bee*, December 30, 1882, January 13, 1883; *Southwestern Christian Advocate*, March 8, 1883; "Scraps and Notes," *Bee*, April 7, 1883; "Scraps and Notes," *Bee*, January 20, 1883.

83. *Gazette*, September 18, 1897; "Washington," *Daily Picayune*, July 12, 1887; "Slow But Sure," *Bee*, August 19, 1893; Alexander, *Army of Lions*, 129–76; Hahn, *Nation under Our Feet*, 364–411; Perman, *Struggle for Mastery*; Litwack, *Trouble in Mind*, 218–29; Krousser, *Shaping of Southern Politics*; Woodward, *Origins of the New South*, 321–49.

84. Bruce, *New Man*, xiii, 39. On Bruce's promotions, see "Our Weekly Review," *Bee*, October 30, 1886; "A Worthy Promotion," *Bee*, August 17, 1889. The authority on ex-slave autobiographies, historian William Andrews estimates that three-fourths of all postbellum slave narratives rejected the "heroic rebel-fugitive profile." Andrews, *Slave Narratives after Slavery*, xi

85. *Bee*, May 29, 1886; Bruce, *New Man*, 158; *Annual Register of the Department of the Interior* (1884); *Annual Register of the Department of the Interior* (1889); "A New Man," *Bee*, September 21, 1895.

86. Bruce, *New Man*, 168–69; *Annual Register of the Department of the Interior* (1893); *Annual Register of the Department of the Interior* (1897); "Commissioner Tanner," *Bee*, April 20, 1889; "Promotions," *Bee*, July 27, 1889; "The Pension Office," *Bee*, June 29, 1889. For critiques of the Raum administration, see *Bee*, February 22, 1890; "Our Symposium," *Southwestern Christian Advocate*, April 24, 1890.

87. Bruce, *New Man*, 171.

88. Bruce, *New Man*, iii, 38, 86, 171–72; "The Negro Bond and Free," *Washington Post*, April 14, 1895.

89. Lochren, *ARCP* (1893), 29–30, 34; Murphy, *ARCP* (1896), 30–31; Evans, *ARCP* (1897), 14–15; Evans, *ARCP* (1899), 67; Evans, *ARCP* (1900), 51; Downs, *Sick from Freedom*, 8–9.

Chapter Six

1. For the clearest statement of the bisectional aphorism, see Broadus, "South and the Pension Bureau," 206.

2. H.R. 11119, *Congressional Record—House*, 51st Cong., 1st Sess. (1890), p. 6464; Araujo, *Reparations*, 45–82, 84–88. On early reparations cases, see esp. Finkenbine, "Belinda's Petition"; Finkenbine, "Wendell Phillips."

3. Writing in 1910, the first scholar to assess the ex-slave pension movement, Dunning School historian Walter Lynwood Fleming, regarded Vaughan as "an eccentric person, probably ill-balanced mentally," but correctly argued that he was "possessed by two ideas: that the South was being robbed by the Federal pension system, and that the negroes by slavery had been robbed of proper returns for their labor." Unlike Fleming, who doubted Vaughan's sanity but not his sincerity, many historians today accept his sanity but doubt his sincerity. According to Mary Frances Berry, for instance, Vaughan "saw slavery as a benign institution that had benefited African Americans," "lamented the unfortunate destruction of the southern way of life," and had nothing but "disdain" for freedpeople. There is little evidence to substantiate these rather pejorative claims against Vaughan, and Berry herself offers none, simply implying that Vaughan's race, family, and political affiliation precluded any possibility of genuine allegiance with ex-slaves. Fleming, *Ex-Slaves Pension Frauds*, 3; Berry, *My Face*, 37. This mischaracterization is relayed without question in Ibram Kendi's *Stamped from the Beginning* (on pp. 270–71), ironically a book about the transmission of false ideas. For an important exception—notably published before Berry's 2005 work—see Farmer-Paellmann's "Excerpt from *Black Exodus*," 28–29.

4. Vaughan, *Vaughan's "Freedmen's Pension Bill,"* 107.

5. Vaughan, *Vaughan's "Freedmen's Pension Bill,"* 28–31, 36, 58.

6. Vaughan, *Vaughan's "Freedmen's Pension Bill,"* 18–21, 29–30; Du Bois, *Black Reconstruction*; Shaffer, *After the Glory*, 169–93; Blight, *Race and Reunion*, 255–337; Janney, *Remembering the Civil War*, 197–231; Smith and Lowery, *Dunning School*.

7. Vaughan, *Vaughan's "Freedmen's Pension Bill,"* 27–29, 31, 58–59, 142.

8. Vaughan, *Vaughan's "Freedmen's Pension Bill,"* 28, 151; Preston B. Plumb to W. R. Vaughan, August 27, 1883, in Vaughan, *Vaughan's "Freedmen's Pension Bill,"* 35–36, 134.

9. Benjamin Harrison to W. R. Vaughan, August 17, 1883, in Vaughan, *Vaughan's "Freedmen's Pension Bill,"* 33–35.

10. Vaughan, *Vaughan's "Freedmen's Pension Bill,"* 109; "Why Not Pension Everybody?," *Atlanta Constitution*, July 30, 1891.

11. Hempstead, *Pictorial History of Arkansas*, 972; S. P. Havis to W. R. Vaughan, July 12, 1890, in Vaughan, *Vaughan's "Freedmen's Pension Bill,"* 44–45; "Pensions for the Slaves," *Daily Picayune*, March 7, 1892; Vaughan, "Open Address to the Congressional Committee," in Vaughan, *Vaughan's "Freedmen's Pension Bill,"* 111–14.

12. "Pensioning the Ex-Slaves," *Chicago Tribune*, August 14, 1891, repr. in Vaughan, *Vaughan's "Freedmen's Pension Bill,"* 163–64. The *Bee* joked that should Vaughan's bill be enacted into law, "all the free-born people will be wishing themselves once enslaved." *Bee*, May 1, 1897.

13. *Inter Ocean*, April 27, 1891, quoted in Vaughan, *Vaughan's "Freedmen's Pension Bill,"* 155–56.

14. Vaughan, *Vaughan's "Freedmen's Pension Bill,"* 134–36, 165–66; Davidson, "Encountering," 17; Araujo, *Reparations*, 97.

15. Postel, *Populist Vision*, 173–203; Ali, *In the Lion's Mouth*, 8–9; Mauldin, *Unredeemed Land*, 158–59.

16. Hahn, *Nation under Our Feet*, 431–40; Hild, *Greenbackers*; Gerteis, *Class and the Color Line*; Gaither, *Blacks and the Populist Movement*; Ali, *In the Lion's Mouth*; Frank, *People, No*; Woodward, *Origins of the New South*, 254–58; Goodwyn, *Democratic Promise*, 154–272; Mc-Math, *American Populism*, 83–179; Kazin, *Populist Persuasion*, 27–48.

17. Nembhard, *Collective Courage*, 1–59; Ali, *In the Lion's Mouth*, xiv, 22–23; Hahn, *Nation under Our Feet*, 364–411; Moore, "Black Militancy in Readjuster Virginia"; Pearson, *Readjuster Movement in Virginia*; Dailey, *Before Jim Crow*.

18. Ali, *In the Lion's Mouth*, 18–26, 48–77; Gaither, *Blacks and the Populist Movement*, 1–30; Litwack, *Trouble in Mind*, 175; Goodwyn, *Democratic Promise*, 122; Hahn, *Roots of Southern Populism*, 285; Holmes, "Demise of the Colored Farmers' Alliance"; Miller, "Black Protest and White Leadership."

19. Ali, *In the Lion's Mouth*, 48–77; Postel, *Populist Vision*, 174–80; Gaither, *Blacks and the Populist Movement*, 31–48; Dann, "Black Populism"; Humphrey, "History," 288–92; George, *Progress and Poverty*.

20. *Congressional Record—House*, 51st Cong., 1st Sess. (1890), pp. 6538–44; Richardson, *Death of Reconstruction*, 208–10; Blum, *Reforging the White Republic*, 201–2; White, *Republic for Which It Stands*, 628–29.

21. Ayers, *Promise of the New South*, 256–74; Gaither, *Blacks and the Populist Movement*, 27–30; Ali, *In the Lion's Mouth*, 71–72; *Atlanta Constitution*, September 10, 1891; *Houston Daily Post*, September 12, 1891; Holmes, "Arkansas Cotton Pickers Strike," 111–12; *American Citizen*, September 11, 1891.

22. Hahn, *Nation under Our Feet*, 424–25; Dann, "Black Populism," 65–66; Ayers, *Promise of the New South*, 257–59; "This State Is Safe," *Atlanta Constitution*, September 9, 1891; "Won't Hurt Georgia," *Atlanta Constitution*, September 8, 1891; "The Cotton Pickers' League," *Atlanta Constitution*, September 8, 1891; "Gathering Cotton," *Mobile Daily Register*, September 12, 1891; "The Cotton Pickers' Strike," *New York Times*, September 9, 1891.

23. Ali, *In the Lion's Mouth*, 72–73; "Race Riot in Arkansas," *Richmond Planet*, October 17, 1891; "Nine Negroes Lynched," *Arkansas Gazette*, October 2, 1891; "Prisoners Lynched," *Mobile Daily Register*, October 3, 1891; "The Arkansas Man Hunt," *Memphis Appeal-Avalanche*, October 3, 1891; "Force Against Force," *Arkansas Gazette*, October 3, 1891; "There Was No Lynching," *Memphis Appeal-Avalanche*, October 5, 1891; Dann, "Black Populism," 65–66; Holmes, "Arkansas Cotton Pickers' Strike," 114–19; Hahn, *Nation under Our Feet*, 424–25.

24. Ali, *In the Lion's Mouth*, 90–92.

25. Ayers, *Promise of the New South*, 274–82; Ali, *In the Lion's Mouth*, 94–112; "The Lesson of the Election," *Georgia Baptist*, repr. in *Progressive Farmer*, October 30, 1894.

26. Woodward, *Origins of the New South*, 321–22; Ali, *In the Lion's Mouth*, 113–67; Kousser, *Shaping of Southern Politics*, 139–81; Gaither, *Blacks and the Populist Movement*, 167; Perman, *Struggle for Mastery*, 9–36, 73–90; Ayers, *Promise of the New South*, 269–74, 283–309; Painter, *Standing at Armageddon*, 216–21.

27. Richardson, *Death of Reconstruction*, 204–45; "The Cotton Pickers' Strike," *New York Times*, September 9, 1891; Tracy, "Menacing Socialism."

28. For important works on Black networks in the nineteenth century, see esp. Hahn, *Nation under Our Feet*; Schermerhorn, *Money over Mastery*; Behrend, *Reconstructing Democracy*; Kaye, *Joining Places*; Penningroth, *Claims of Kinfolk*.

29. Davidson, "Encountering," 18–19; National Ex-Slave Mutual Relief, Bounty, and Pension Association, *Constitution and By-Laws*, in case file 1321, box 13, FOCF.

30. "National Officers Elected," *Nashville American*, September 22, 1897; "A Patent Fraud," *Nashville American*, September 24, 1897; Araujo, *Reparations*, 98; Berry, *My Face*, 46; Hill, "Ex-Slave Pension Movement," 8–9; Fleming, "Ex-Slave Pension Frauds," 5–6; I. H. Dickerson and Callie House, "Onward to Victory!" Advertisement, n.d. [1899], ESPM.

31. L. J. Taylor to Henry Clay Evans, May 30, 1897, ESPM.

32. Wm. C. Baird to G. M. Whiterich, June 8, 1897, case file 1796, box 18, FOCF.

33. Henry Clay Evans to Rev. A. Baccus, November 4, 1897; Henry Clay Evans to Rev. A. Baccus, November 19, 1897; J. L. Davenport, circular, November 20, 1897, all in ESPM.

34. "Negroes Swindled," *Montgomery Advertiser*, September 3, 1899; Betty Patty to [J. L. Davenport], December 2, 1897; Rev. C. P. Jones to [J. L. Davenport], December 9, 1897; Archie Coleman to J. L. Davenport, November 27, 1897; H. W. Mills to J. L. Davenport, November 27, 1897; Alfred Lathan to [J. L. Davenport], December 2, 1897; Emily R. Roundtree to J. L. Davenport, December 3, 1897; Luke Miller to [J. L. Davenport], December 4, 1897; Rev. C. P. Jones to [J. L. Davenport], December 9, 1897; J. A. Davis to Rev. William L. Livingston, December 9, 1897; Rev. Z. P. Smith to J. L. Davenport, December 10, 1897, all in ESPM.

35. Henry Clay Evans to Postmaster of Pacific Missouri, December 4, 1897; Henry Clay Evans to Postmaster of Union City, Tennessee, December 8, 1897; Henry Clay Evans, Circular to Agents of the National Ex-Slave Mutual Relief, Bounty, and Pension Association, December 10, 1897; Henry Clay Evans, Circular, December 10, 1897; Henry Gearing to J. L. Davenport, December 8, 1897, all in ESPM; Petition to Congress blank form, n.d. [1898], case file 1321, box 13, FOCF.

36. Jordan Ellis to [Eugene F. Ware], September n.d., 1902; P. A. Cook to [Eugene F. Ware], February 6, 1903, both in ESPM.

37. Perry Williams to Pension Attorney, February 7, 1898; Allen Hopkins to Henry Clay Evans, September 9, 1899, both in ESPM.

38. S. A. Cuddy to H. Clay Evans, August 1, 1899, in Evans, *ARCP* (1899), 73; S. A. Cuddy to H. Clay Evans, July 23, 1900, in Evans, *ARCP* (1900), 69–70; "A Patent Fraud," *Nashville American*, September 24, 1897.

39. J. J. Porter to Henry Clay Evans, December 18, 1897; R. J. Lowry to Henry Clay Evans, January 11, 1898; Mrs. L. C. Dearmin to [Henry Clay Evans], January 13, 1898; Richard P. Mitchell to [Henry Clay Evans], December 20, 1897; Synthia Shelby to [Henry Clay Evans], December 21, 1897; Buck Bailey to William McKinley, January 11, 1898; H. W. Walker to Henry Clay Evans, February 14, 1898; Rev. E. C. Clark to Henry Clay Evans, March 20, 1898, all in ESPM.

40. Stephen A. Cuddy to Chief of S. E. Division, January 14, 1898, enclosed in Henry Clay Evans to T. R. Hardwick, January 14, 1898; Thomas R. Hardwick to Henry Clay Evans, January 22, 1898, both in ESPM; *Official Register of the United States* (1901), 1015.

41. *Southwestern Christian Advocate,* December 16, 1897; "From Suffolk," *Richmond Planet,* September 24, 1898; "Pension Bill a Fraud," *Afro-American,* April 29, 1899. These editorials coexisted and merged with the broader genre of exposing sensational stories of fraud within the U.S. Pension Bureau. "All Sorts of Crime," *Evening Star,* January 6, 1898.

42. "Negro Pension Scheme Again," *Atlanta Constitution,* January 10, 1898; "Ex-Slaves Want Pensions," *Atlanta Constitution,* February 5, 1898. "Ex-Slaves Are Being Fleeced by Promises of Big Pensions," *Atlanta Constitution,* May 15, 1899; "Negroes Were Badly Fooled," *Atlanta Constitution,* May 18, 1899.

43. I. H. Dickerson, "M'Nairy's Master Stroke For The Ex-Slaves," February 20, 1899, case files, National Ex-Save Mutual Relief, Bounty and Pension Association; I. H. Dickerson and Callie House, "Onward to Victory!" Advertisement, n.d. [1899]; A. L. Steel, Advertisement, n.d. [1899], all in ESPM; Berry, *My Face,* 71; National Ex-Slave Mutual Relief, Bounty, and Pension Association, *Constitution and By-Laws,* in case file 1321, box 13, FOCF; Petition to Congress from the Ex-Slaves of Columbia, Missouri, n.d. [1898], ESPM; Petition to Congress blank form, n.d. [1898], case file 1321, box 13, FOCF.

44. *Home for Aged Negroes.*

45. *Home for Aged Negroes;* Berry, *My Face,* 70–72; Kelly, *Creating a National Home.*

46. Berry, *My Face,* 72–76; I. H. Dickerson, "M'Nairy's Master Stroke for the Ex-Slaves," February 20, 1899, ESPM.

47. Joseph F. Lilis to Henry Clay Evans, August 18, 1899; Rev. W. H. Pender to Henry Clay Evans, September 4, 1899; Rev. T. Parker and Mary Parker to Henry Clay Evans, August 29, 1899, all in ESPM.

48. Henry Clay Evans to J. H. Gallinger, February 4, December 21, 1899, ESPM.

49. W. L. Reid to George A. Dice, May 21, 1899, case file 1796, box 18, FOCF.

50. W. L. Reid to George A. Dice, May 21, 1899, case file 1796, box 18, FOCF; Walter Gorman to Jas. N. Tyner, June 20, 1899, August 16, 30, 1899, all in case file 1321, box 13, FOCF; W. L. Reid to George A. Dice, July 15, 1900, case file 1796, box 18, FOCF.

51. Evans, *ARCP* (1899), 41–42; S. A. Cuddy, "Report of the Law Division," in Evans, *ARCP* (1899), 74–75.

52. Franke, *Repair;* Vaughan, *Vaughan's "Freedmen's Pension Bill,"* 58; Godkin quoted in Stampp and Litwack, *Reconstruction,* 15; White, *Republic for Which It Stands,* 58–60, 192; Stanley, *From Bondage to Contract;* Cohen, *Reconstruction of American Liberalism,* 177–216; Benedict, "Reform Republicans," 75–76; Calhoun, *Conceiving a New Republic.*

53. Sumner, *What Social Classes Owe,* 65–66; Richardson, *Death of Reconstruction,* 183–224; Ring, *Problem South.*

54. N. A. Pless to Commissioner of Pensions, July 14, 1899; Harrison J. Barrett to Henry Clay Evans, August 14, 1899, both in ESPM; W. H. Wills to Harrison J. Barrett, September 15, 1899; Frank M. Taylor to Postmaster General, September 18, 1899, both in case file 1321, box 13, FOCF; Harrison J. Barrett to Henry Clay Evans, September 21, 1899, ESPM; Acting Assistant Attorney General for the Post Office Department to Postmaster of Nashville, September 21, 1899; I. H. Dickerson to A. W. Wills, November 9, 1899, both in case file 1321, box 13, FOCF. The Post Office considered investigating Vaughan's National Ex-Slave Pension Club Association as well but found that the group had apparently already disbanded. Harrison J. Barrett to J. L. Davenport, October 5, 1899, ESPM; Wm. C. Baird to Paul E. Williams, October 20, 1899, case file 1796, box 18, FOCF.

55. I. H. Dickerson to Harrison J. Barrett, September 20, 1899; Callie House to Harrison J. Barrett, September 29, 1899, both in case file 1321, box 13, FOCF.

56. "After the Swindlers," *Atlanta Constitution*, August 12, 1899; "Protecting Ignorant Negroes," *Weekly News and Courier*, September 27, 1899; "Ex-Slave Pension Fraud," *Washington Post*, August 12, 1899; *Army and Navy Journal*, February 3, 1900, p. 522.

57. "Race Gleanings," *Afro-American*, June 3, 1899; "Editorial Comments," *Southwestern Christian Advocate*, September 28, 1899; "Race Items," *People's Recorder*, January 27, 1900; "No Pensions for Ex Slaves," *Colored American*, April 21, 1900.

58. National Ex-Slave Convention, Circular, n.d. [1899]; National Ex-Slave Mutual Relief, Bounty, and Pension Association, *Constitution and By-Laws*, both in case file 1321, box 13, FOCF; I. H. Dickerson and Callie House, "Onward to Victory!" Advertisement, n.d. [1899], ESPM; Callie House to Harrison J. Barrett, November 23, 1899, case file 1321, box 13, FOCF; Berry, *My Face*, 82, 253–54n2; Araujo, *Reparations*, 99–100; Perry, "Prospect of Justice," 68–72.

59. J. E. Purdy to Major A. W. Wills, November 14, 1899; S. A. Jackson, Deposition, November 2, 1899; Acting Assistant Attorney General for the Post Office Department to J. L. Bristow, November 2, 1899; Callie House to Harrison J. Barrett, November 23, 1899, all in case file 1321, box 13, FOCF.

60. N. Smith to Harrison J. Barrett, March 24, 1900; N. Smith to Harrison J. Barrett, March 29, 1900; Callie House to Harrison J. Barrett, April 5, 1900, all in case file 1321, box 13, FOCF; Callie House to Henry Clay Evans, December 13, 1900, ESPM. For other instances of the phrase "bent up with rheumatism," see I. H. Dickerson to Harrison J. Barrett, September 20, 1899; Callie House to Harrison J. Barrett, September 29, 1899; J. B. Mullins to Chas. Emory Smith, March 5, 1901, all in case file 1321, box 13, FOCF.

61. S. 1176, *Congressional Record—Senate*, 56th Cong., 1st Sess. (1899), pp. 180, 183–84; *Pensions for Freedmen*; Callie House to Henry Clay Evans, December 13, 1900, ESPM.

62. A. W. Wills to H. J. Barrett, September 14, 1900; H. Clay Evans to Secretary of the Interior, March 13, 1901; A. W. Wills to Assistant Attorney General for the Post Office Department, August 6, 1901, all in case file 1321, box 13, FOCF; "Convicted," *Nashville Banner*, March 6, 1901; "Dickerson, Head of the Gigantic Ex-Slave Fraud, Is Convicted," *Atlanta Constitution*, March 6, 1901; Berry, *My Face*, 134–35. See also Acting Assistant Attorney General for the Post Office Department to A. W. Wills, September 18, 1900; Harrison J. Barrett to L. F. Livingston, February 26, 1901; Acting Assistant Attorney General for the Post Office Department to A. W. Wills, March 9, 1901; A. W. Wills to G. A. C. Christiancy, April 16, 1901, all in case file 1321, box 13, FOCF; *Nashville American*, April 16, 1901.

63. Orleans County Ex-Slave Mutual Relief, Bounty and Pension Association, Notice, December 9, 1901, case file 1321, box 13, FOCF; "Ex Slaves Pension Fraud," *Colored American*, December 15, 1900; Anna M. Harris to Henry Clay Evans, February 9, 1900, ESPM.

64. J. B. Mullins to President of the United States, March 15, 1901; J. B. Mullins to Chas. Emory Smith, March 5, 1901; Acting Assistant Attorney General for the Post Office Department to J. B. Mullins, March 19, 1901; A. W. Wills to Geo. C. Christiancy, March 30, 1901, all in case file 1321, box 13, FOCF; Berry, *My Face*, 134–35.

65. "National Plea of the Exslave Department National Industrial Association in America," August 13, 1900, case file 1321, box 13, FOCF; "Frauds Are Refused the Mails," *Atlanta Constitution*, October 19, 1901; "Will Oppose Mob Violence," *Washington Post*, February 15,

1902; Davidson, "Encountering," 18–27; J. H. C. Wilson to W. B. Smith, June 4, 1903, case file 1796, box 18, FOCF.

66. Harrison J. Barrett to J. L. Davenport, October 5, 1899, ESPM; Wm. C. Baird to Paul E. Williams, October 20, 1899, case file 1796, box 18, FOCF; Harrison J. Barrett to Henry Clay Evans, February 13, 1900, ESPM; *Colored American*, March 1, 1902; "Vaughn's Justice Party," *Colored American*, April 26, 1902; "Vaughan to Negroes," *Baltimore Sun*, June 10, 1902; Isaiah H. Dickerson, Deposition, May 12, 1902; J. L. Davenport to Thomas Ryan, September 13, 1902, both in ESPM.

67. "New Political Party," *Colored American*, January 17, 1903; "National Industrial Council," *Bee*, January 31, 1903; I. L. Walton, "Pensions and the South," *Colored American*, January 31, 1903; "The Ex-Slave Pension Bill," *Bee*, January 31, 1903; Berry, *My Face*, 149.

68. "Plan to Unite Hangs Fire," *Washington Post*, January 8, 1903; "Hitch among Ex Slaves," *Washington Post*, January 9, 1903; Davidson, "Encountering," 20–21; Berry, *My Face*, 276n14.

69. Davidson, "Encountering," 22–24; "All Praise Hanna," *Bee*, February 14, 1903; "The Ex-Slave Pension Bill," *Bee*, February 7, 1903.

70. "To Pension Ex-Slaves," *Colored American*, February 7, 1903; *Colored American*, February 14, 1903; *Southwest Christian Advocate*, repr. in "Race Gleanings," *Colored American*, February 28, 1903; "The Ex-Slave Pension," *Colored American*, February 28, 1903; Bruce Grit, "In the Public Eye," *Colored American*, March 14, 1903; *Colored American*, March 28, 1903; P. A. Cook to [Eugene F. Ware], February 6, 1903, ESPM.

71. "What Is Hannah [*sic*] Up To?," *Atlanta Constitution*, February 6, 1903; Josiah Ohl, "Senator Hanna Bids Millions for the Support of Negroes," *Atlanta Constitution*, February 5, 1903.

72. "The Slave Pension Bill," *Atlanta Constitution*, February 14, 1903; *Philadelphia Record* quoted in "Hanna's Pension Plan," *Atlanta Constitution*, February 20, 1903; Josiah Ohl, "How D'Armond Ripped Negro Pension," *Atlanta Constitution*, February 14, 1903.

73. "The Slave Pension Bill," *Atlanta Constitution*, February 14, 1903; "Hanna Repudiates Negro," *Washington Post*, August 13, 1903; "Hanna's Name a Bait," *New York Times*, August 13, 1903; Davidson, "Encountering," 24. Interestingly, the number of fraud cases involving impersonation of soldiers seems to have increased in 1903 surrounding the Hanna Bill controversy. See, for instance, Claim of Joseph Scott, no. 1.206.441, CCR, 10:83; Claim of Henry Coleman, no. 1.258.803, CCR, 10:91; Claim of Martin Howard, no. 836.911, CCR, 10:111; Claim of Newton Goodloe, no. 1.034.274, CCR, 10:212.

74. Henry Clay Evans to Eli Torrence, February 7, 1902, ESPM; Berry, *My Face*, 150–51.

75. "What Is Hannah Up To?," *Atlanta Constitution*, February 6, 1903; "Rockefeller, Mark Hanna and Pensions for Negroes," *Atlanta Constitution*, February 11, 1903.

76. "How Negroes Are Duped," *Atlanta Constitution*, September 4, 1901.

77. "Favor Ex-Slave Pensions," *New York Times*, February 8, 1903. As had been the case in the 1870s, the matter of federal pensions to ex-rebels came bound up with the issue of compensating ex-slaveholders. "Consideration for Old Soldiers," 21; "Justice to the South— True History," 323.

78. *Times-Picayune*, December 7, 1896; *Omaha Daily Democrat*, June 20, 1890; Vaughan, *Vaughan's "Freedmen's Pension Bill,"* 56–57; Postel, *Populist Vision*, 193–94; Nugent, *Life Work of Thomas L. Nugent*, 67–68.

79. "Pensioning the Old Slaves," 108–9.

80. Levin, *Searching for Black Confederates*, 6–7, 100–122; "Pensioning the Old Slaves," 108; "Pension Slaves Who Served in the War," 481; Domby, *False Cause*, ch. 4; "Pensions for Faithful Negroes," 284.

81. In all, fourteen Southern states created programs for Confederate veterans and heirs—the eleven states of the Confederacy plus Missouri, Kentucky, and Oklahoma. A few (Alabama in 1867, Georgia in 1870, and North Carolina in 1867) began as programs to support veterans who lost limbs or were blinded and evolved in the 1880s to include indigent Confederate veterans. Many states later extended their programs to include indigent Confederate widows. Marten, *Sing Not War*, 16–17, 203–4; Green, "Protecting Confederate Soldiers and Mothers"; Gorman, "Confederate Pensions"; Morton, "Federal and Confederate Pensions Contrasted."

82. Glasson, *History of Military Pension Legislation*; Glasson, *Federal Military Pensions*; Glasson, "Federal and Confederate Pensions," 280–85; Glasson, "South's Care."

83. United States, *Statutes at Large*, 24:371; "Mexican Pensions: A Measure of Long Delayed Justice," *Atlanta Constitution*, January 18, 1887; Vogel, "Redefining Reconciliation"; "Actual National Obligations," 411–13; Levin, *Searching for Black Confederates*, 57–60; Levine, *Confederate Emancipation*; McCurry, *Confederate Reckoning*, 325–30.

84. Grandin, *End of the Myth*, 137; Blight, *Race and Reunion*, 351–54; Janney, *Remembering the Civil War*, 222–31; Lears, *Rebirth of a Nation*, 207–8; Foster, *Ghosts of the Confederacy*, 145–49; Blair, *Cities of the Dead*, 179–87; Silber, *Romance of Reunion*; McKinley, "Speech before the Legislature," 158–59.

85. "Significant Utterances," *Richmond Planet*, December 24, 1898; "Racial Troubles," *Bee*, December 24, 1898; Alexander, *Army of Lions*. See also "The Blue and the Gray," *Afro-American*, January 7, 1899; "Rebel Pensions," *National Tribune*, February 2, 1899.

86. *Congressional Record—Senate*, 55th Cong., 3d Sess. (1899), pp. 1074–81; Hunt, *Marion Butler and American Populism*, 156–57.

87. "There Are No Rebels Now," *Bee*, February 4, 1899.

88. "Butler's Pension Amendment," *Caucasian*, January 19, 1899; "The Confederate Veterans Break Up Abruptly," *Caucasian*, February 5, 1899; *Congressional Record—Senate*, 55th Cong., 3d Sess. (1899), pp. 1079–80; Vogel, "Redefining Reconciliation," 82–84; J. L. Oxford to Marion Butler, March 13, 1899, repr. in "They Endorse Butler's Amendment," *Caucasian*, March 23, 1899.

89. Broadus, "South and the Pension Bureau," 203–7; Evans, *ARCP* (1899), 67.

90. M. M. Murray, "Pension for Ex-Slaves," *Colored American*, December 28, 1901.

91. "'Rebs' Want Union Pay," *Afro-American*, July 19, 1913; "With the National Lawmakers: Ex-Confederate Pensions," *Afro-American*, March 21, 1903; *Bee*, December 28, 1907; Blight, *Race and Reunion*, 7–15, 383–91; Janney, *Remembering the Civil War*, 266–69.

92. Berry, *My Face*, 171–87; Alfort Tyler to [Commissioner of Pensions], December 3, 1916; Commissioner of Pensions to Alfort Tyler, December 28, 1916; Rolf Harday to [Department of the Interior], January 3, 1917; Commissioner of Pensions to Rolf Harday, January 13, 1917; Tom Edward to Newton D. Baker, January 5, 1917; Sam Sa[w]yer to [Department of the Interior], February 2, 1917; Lawrence Dudley to Commissioner of Pensions, April 24, 1917; Commissioner of Pensions to Lawrence Dudley, April 27, 1917; Sarah Elizabeth Sweeney Buckner to C. C. Tieman, May 3, 1917; Commissioner of Pensions to Sarah Elizabeth Sweeny-Buckner, May 8, 1917, all in ESPM.

93. M. M. Murray, "Pension for Ex-Slaves," *Colored American*, December 28, 1901.

Conclusion

1. "To Abolish Pension Office," *Afro-American*, March 19, 1904; "May Abolish Pension Bureau," *Courier Journal*, March 17, 1904; "To Abolish Pension Office?," *Baltimore Sun*, March 16, 1904; Warner, *ARCP* (1905), 16–17.

2. United States, *Statutes at Large*, 34:879; Warner, *ARCP* (1905), 3–4; Glasson, *Federal Military Pensions*, 246–50; Weber, *Bureau of Pensions*, 17; "Rush for Pensions," *Richmond Planet*, March 16, 1907; *Bee*, February 23, 1907; *Bee*, May 25, 1907; "Pensioners Dying Fast," *Richmond Planet*, February 3, 1906; "Figures on 'Unknown Army,'" *Bee*, April 13, 1907; Warner, *ARCP* (1909), 14.

3. Pearson, *Birth Certificate*; Igo, *Known Citizen*, 55–98; Pearson, "'Age'"; Landrum, "State's Big Family Bible."

4. Vespasian Warner to Solomon Johnson, May 29, 1907; Solomon Johnson, Affidavit, June 3, 1907, both in Emily Johnson file, Co. A, 74th USCT, IA 998.134, IC 1.070.905, WA 956.725, WC 720.642, CWPF.

5. Dr. William Johnson, Affidavit, August 2, 1904; A. C. McClenman et al., Surgeon's Certificate, November 23, 1904; Daniel Drayton, Increase Invalid Pension, January 3, 1905; Daniel Drayton, Increase Invalid Pension, January 22, 1906; A. C. McClenman et al., Surgeon's Certificate, June 10, 1906; Commissioner of Pensions to Daniel Drayton, May 2, 1908; Daniel Drayton, Increase Invalid Pension, April 28, 1908; Daniel Drayton, Affidavit, May 20, 1908, all in Lavina Drayton file, Co. A, 104th, USCT, IA 477.591, IC 968.995, WA 949.378, WC 717.547, CWPF.

6. Johnson, *Soul by Soul*; Robert Roddy, General Affidavit, January 13, 1908, in Virginia Roddy file, Co. I, 63d USCT, IA 970.830, IC 1.065.425, WA 1.146.726, WC 886.293, CWPF.

7. Wright, *Black Boy*, 138–41.

8. The last significant act was that of May 1, 1920, equalizing and increasing various rates of pensions. United States, *Statutes at Large*, 41:585–88. U.S. Treasury Department, *Digest of Appropriations for the Support of the Government of the United States*, 108; Morgan, *ARCP* (1930), 2.

9. Quadagno, *Transformation of Old Age Security*, 48; Orloff, *Politics of Pensions*, 215–39.

10. Brueggemann, "Racial Considerations," 139–40; Sullivan, *Days of Hope*; Sitkoff, *New Deal for Blacks*; Poole, *Segregated Origins of Social Security*, 5; Katznelson, *When Affirmative Action Was White*, 25–52.

11. DeWitt, "Decision to Exclude," 49–53; "Occupations," in *Abstract of the Fifteenth Census of the United States*, Table 12, p. 331.

12. Roosevelt quoted in Quadagno, *Transformation of Old Age Security*, 110–17; Poole, *Segregated Origins of Social Security*, 7–8; Rodems and Shaefer, "Left Out," 386–87; DeWitt, "Decision to Exclude," 56.

13. Poole, *Segregated Origins of Social Security*, 21–25; Piven and Cloward, *Poor People's Movements*, 30–31; Casebeer, "Unemployment Insurance"; Quadagno, "Welfare Capitalism."

14. The Social Security Act also allocated funds for public health work, created a program to aid the blind, and established four other important programs designed to protect poor and disabled children. These included Maternal and Child Welfare, Services for Crippled Children, Child Welfare Services, and Vocational Rehabilitation. Poole, *Segregated Origins of Social Security*, 7–8; DeWitt, "Decision to Exclude," 51–52.

15. Brueggemann, "Racial Considerations," 149; Skocpol, "Limits," 296; Tani, *States of Dependency*, 9. Much of the literature on the "two-track welfare state" explores discriminatory policies and practices based on gender. See Gordon, *Pitied but Not Entitled*; Nelson, "Origins"; Mink, "Lady and the Tramp"; Skocpol, *Protecting Soldiers and Mothers*; Mettler, *Dividing Citizens*; Kessler-Harris, "In the Nation's Image"; Kessler-Harris, *In Pursuit of Equity*; Katz, "American Welfare State."

16. Poole, *Segregated Origins of Social Security*, 25–27; Manning, *Troubled Refuge*; Manning, "Working for Citizenship."

17. For scholars who regard the racism of Southern representatives as the decisive motivation behind the exclusion of agricultural and domestic workers, see Brown, *Race, Money*; Lieberman, "Race, Institutions," 514–15; Williams, *Constraint of Race*; Katznelson, *When Affirmative Action Was White*, 25–52; Quadagno, *Transformation of Old Age Security*; Quadagno, *Color of Welfare*. Mary Poole's important book on the racial dimensions of Social Security argues that the act ultimately discriminated on the basis of race, although that was not the explicit intention of Southern members of Congress. Rather, the act was "made discriminatory through a shifting web of alliances of white policymakers that crossed regions and political parties," orchestrated by the team of liberal white reformers appointed by President Roosevelt. Poole, *Segregated Origins of Social Security*, 5–6, 42.

18. Davies and Derthick, "Race and Social Welfare Policy"; Alston and Ferrie, *Southern Paternalism*, 49–74; Fields, "Ideology and Race," 156–69.

19. Poole, *Segregated Origins of Social Security*, 36–42; Rodems and Shaefer, "Left Out," 387–89.

20. Edwin E. Witte, "Statement of Edwin E. Witte, Executive Director, President's Committee on Economic Security—Continued," in *Economic Security Act*, 198; Henry Morgenthau, "Testimony of Henry Morgenthau before the House Ways and Means Committee," *Economic Security Act*, 897–911; Poole, *Segregated Origins of Social Security*, 42–43; DeWitt, "Decision to Exclude," 57–59; Davies and Derthick, "Race and Social Welfare Policy," 224–26. Rodems and Shaefer find that no compulsory UI system specifically included agricultural workers at its inception, though most were included in later amendments. Such was the case with Great Britain, which left agricultural workers out of its UI program created in 1911 but later included them in 1935. Rodems and Shaefer, "Left Out," 398–400.

21. Perkins, *Roosevelt I Knew*, 297–98; DeWitt, "Decision to Exclude," 58.

22. Poole, *Segregated Origins of Social Security*, 28–60; Zelizer, *On Capitol Hill*, 23; DeWitt, "Decision to Exclude," 56–64; Witte, *Development of the Social Security Act*, 143–45.

23. George E. Haynes, "Statement of George E. Haynes, Executive Secretary Department of Race Relations, Federal Council of Churches," in *Economic Security Act*, 479–91.

24. Charles H. Houston, "Statement of Charles H. Houston, Representing the National Association for the Advancement of Colored People," in *Economic Security Act*, 640–47.

25. Poole, *Segregated Origins of Social Security*, 49–50; Lieberman, *Shifting the Color Line*, 48–56.

26. Poole, *Segregated Origins of Social Security*, 50–53; Tani, *States of Dependency*, 39.

27. Katznelson, *When Affirmative Action Was White*, 30–35; Poole, *Segregated Origins of Social Security*, 17–18; Bedell, "Employment and Income," 598.

28. Jones, *End to the Neglect*, 11–12.

29. Political scientists have begun conceptualizing what they call a "policy feedback theory," whereby policies are seen as having a determinative effect on politics. More universal programs with clear and easily attainable benefits—including Medicare and (present-day) Social Security—are shown to empower citizens who in turn become more active and engaged in the political process. Other policies, stigmatizing and discriminatory by design, work to undermine beneficiaries' sense of worth, rights, and citizenship, and thereby forestalling the potential for mass politics. Campbell, "Policy Makes Mass Politics."

Epilogue

1. Boston Blackwell, Arkansas Narratives, vol. 2, pt. 1, pp. 168–74, *BIS*; Escott, *Slavery Remembered*, 189.

2. Yetman, *Voices from Slavery*, 1–6.

3. Shaw, "Using the WPA Ex-Slave Narratives"; Yetman, "Background"; Botkin, "Slave as His Own Interpreter"; Woodward, "History from Slave Sources"; Escott, "Art and Science"; Johnson, *Soul by Soul*, 226n24; Cantrell, "WPA Sources"; Spindel, "Assessing Memory"; Soapes, "Federal Writers' Project Slave Interviews"; Blassingame, "Using the Testimony of Ex-Slaves."

4. Baptist, *Half Has Never Been Told*, 445–46n4.

5. Silber, *This War Ain't Over*.

6. J. F. Boone, Arkansas Narratives, vol. 2, pt. 1, pp. 210–13; George Greene, Arkansas Narratives, vol. 2, pt. 3, pp. 104–11; Omelia Thomas, Arkansas Narratives, vol. 2, pt. 6, pp. 298–99; Enoch Beel, Arkansas Narratives, vol. 2, pt. 1, pp. 135–36, all in *BIS*. For accounts that express pride and relief in securing a military pension, see Elizabeth Hines, Arkansas Narratives, vol. 2, pt. 3, pp. 273–75; Solomon Lambert, Arkansas Narratives, vol. 2, pt. 4, pp. 229–34; Patsey Moore, Arkansas Narratives, vol. 2, pt. 5, pp. 123–24; James Spikes, Arkansas Narratives, vol. 2, pt. 6, pp. 212–13; J. Roberts, Arkansas Narratives, vol. 2, pt. 6, p. 53; Jennie Washington, Arkansas Narratives, vol. 2, pt. 7, pp. 57–59; "Soldier" Williams, Arkansas Narratives, vol. 2, pt. 7, pp. 191–92; Lucy Withers, Arkansas Narratives, vol. 2, pt. 7, pp. 222–23; Tom Yates, Arkansas Narratives, vol. 2, pt. 7, p. 252; Susan Dale Sanders, Kentucky Narratives, vol. 7, pp. 43–44; Joe Higgerson, Missouri Narratives, vol. 10, pp. 173–78; Hannah Jones, Missouri Narratives, vol. 10, pp. 214–17; Charles H. Anderson, Ohio Narratives, vol. 12, pp. 1–5; Emma Grisham, Tennessee Narratives, vol. 15, pp. 28–30; Henry H. Buttler, Texas Narratives, vol. 16, pt. 1, pp. 179–81, all in *BIS*.

7. Nannie Eaves, Kentucky Narratives, vol. 7, p. 60; Lizzie Barnett, Arkansas Narratives, vol. 2, pt. 1, p. 112–14, both in *BIS*. On the generational divide, see esp. Litwack, *Trouble in Mind*; Mitchell, *Raising Freedom's Child*.

8. Kretz, "People."

9. Sabe Rutledge, South Carolina Narratives, vol. 14, pt. 4, pp. 59–70; Charlie Davis, South Carolina Narratives, pt. 1, pp. 250–53; Emma Jeter, South Carolina Narratives, pt. 3, pp. 33–34; Sena Moore, South Carolina Narratives, pt. 3, pp. 209–12, all in *BIS*; Shaw, "Using the WPA Ex-Slave Narratives," 652–53.

10. Jeff Bailey, Arkansas Narratives, vol. 2, pt. 1, p. 87; Richard Crump, Arkansas Narratives, vol. 2, pt. 2, pp. 62–66; Laura Thornton, Arkansas Narratives, vol. 2, pt. 6, pp. 322–29; Thomas Johns, Texas Narratives, vol. 16, pt. 2, pp. 201–4, all in *BIS*.

Bibliography

Abbreviations

GPO   Government Printing Office
RG   Record Group

Archival Collections

Henry E. Huntington Library, San Marino, Calif.
  James Milo Alexander Papers
National Archives and Records Administration, Washington, D.C.
  RG 15 Records of the Department of Veterans Affairs
  RG 28 Records of the Post Office Department
  RG 46 Records of the United States Senate
  RG 94 Records of the Adjutant General's Office
  RG 105 Records of the Bureau of Refugees, Freedmen, and Abandoned Lands
  RG 217 Records of the U.S. General Accounting Office
  RG 233 Records of the United States House of Representatives
New York Public Library, New York, N.Y.
  U.S. Sanitary Commission Records, Series 1, Medical Committee Archives, 1861–1865
Southern Historical Collection, University of North Carolina, Chapel Hill, N.C.
  Everard Green Baker Papers
  Franklin A. Hudson Diary

Newspapers and Periodicals

Afro-American (Baltimore)
American Citizen (Kansas City, Kan.)
Arkansas Gazette
Army and Navy Journal
The Atchison Daily Globe (Kan.)
The Atlanta Constitution
The Baltimore Sun
Bangor Daily Whig & Courier (Maine)
The Bee (Washington, D.C.)
Brownlow's Knoxville Whig (Knoxville)
Buffalo Courier
The Caucasian (Clinton, N.C.)
The Charleston Daily News
The Charlotte Democrat

Chicago Tribune
Christian Recorder
Clarion-Ledger (Jackson, Miss.)
The Colored American (Washington, D.C.)
Commonwealth (Boston)
The Courier Journal (Louisville)
Daily Arkansas Gazette (Little Rock)
The Daily Cleveland Herald
The Daily Constitution (Atlanta)
The Daily Dispatch (Richmond)
The Daily Inter Ocean (Chicago)
The Daily Mississippian (Jackson)
The Daily News and Herald (Savannah)
The Daily Phoenix (Columbia)

The Daily State Journal (Richmond)
The Democratic Advocate
  (Westminster, Md.)
Edgefield Advertiser (S.C.)
Evening Star (Washington, D.C.)
Fort Smith Weekly New Era (Ark.)
The Gazette (Raleigh)
The Georgia Baptist (Augusta)
The Greensboro Patriot (N.C.)
Harper's Weekly
Herald and Tribune (Jonesborough, Tenn.)
The Hinds County Gazette (Raymond,
  Miss.)
Houston Daily Post
Knoxville Daily Chronicle
Memphis Appeal-Avalanche
Memphis Daily Appeal
Meridian Mercury (Miss.)
Milwaukee Daily Sentinel
Missionary Record (Charleston)
Mobile Daily Register
The Montgomery Advertiser
Morning Republican (Little Rock)
The Nashville American
Nashville Banner
Nashville Union and American
Natchez Democrat
The National Republican (Washington, D.C.)
National Savings Bank
The National Tribune (Washington, D.C.)
The New National Era
The New Orleans Daily Democrat
New Orleans Republican
The New South (Port Royal, S.C.)
New York Daily Herald

New York Herald
New York Times
The News and Observer (Raleigh)
North Alabamian (Tuscumbia)
North American and United States Gazette
  (Philadelphia)
Omaha Daily Democrat
The People's Recorder (Columbia)
Philadelphia Record
The Progressive Farmer (Winston-Salem)
Public Ledger (Memphis)
Richmond Dispatch
Richmond Planet
The Semi-Weekly Clarion (Jackson, Miss.)
Semi-Weekly Louisianian (New Orleans)
Soldier's Friend
South Carolina Leader (Charleston)
The South-Western (Shreveport)
Southwestern Christian Advocate
  (New Orleans)
St. Louis Globe-Democrat
St. Louis Post-Dispatch
The Sun (New York)
The Times-Democrat (New Orleans)
The Times-Picayune (New Orleans)
Union Springs Herald (Ala.)
Vicksburg Daily Times
Vicksburg Herald
Washington Law Reporter
Washington Post
Weekly Georgia Telegraph (Macon)
Weekly Inter Ocean (Chicago)
Weekly Louisianian (New Orleans)
Weekly News and Courier (Charleston)
Wilmington Morning Star (N.C.)

Government Publications

Abstract of the Fifteenth Census of the United States. Washington, D.C.: GPO, 1933.
Ancrum, Sallie, Invalid Pensions. 49th Cong., 1st Sess. (1886), H. Report No. 1792.
Annual Register of the Department of the Interior. Washington, D.C.: GPO, 1881–1898.
Annual Report of the Secretary of War. Washington, D.C.: GPO, 1877.
Annual Report of the Secretary of War. Washington, D.C.: GPO, 1879.
Annual Report of the Secretary of War. Washington, D.C.: GPO, 1880.
Annual Report of the Secretary of War. Washington, D.C.: GPO, 1881.

Annual Report of the Secretary of War. Washington, D.C.: GPO, 1882.

Annual Report of the Secretary of War. Washington, D.C.: GPO, 1883.

Annual Report of the Secretary of War. Washington, D.C.: GPO, 1884.

Annual Report of the Secretary of War. Washington, D.C.: GPO, 1885.

Annual Report of the Secretary of War. Washington, D.C.: GPO, 1886.

Annual Report of the Secretary of War. Washington, D.C.: GPO, 1887.

Annual Report of the Secretary of War. Washington, D.C.: GPO, 1888.

Answer to Resolution on Suspension or Mustering out of Brigadier General George W. Balloch. 42d Cong., 2d Sess. (1872), H. Exec. Doc. No. 38.

Atkinson, H. M. *Annual Report of the Commissioner of Pensions to the Secretary of the Interior for the Fiscal Year Ended June 30, 1875.* Washington, D.C.: GPO, 1875.

Baber, George, ed. *Decisions of the Department of the Interior in Cases Relating to Pension Claims.* Vol. 3. Washington, D.C.: GPO, 1890.

———, ed. *Decisions of the Department of the Interior in Cases Relating to Pension Claims.* Vol. 4. Washington, D.C.: GPO, 1891.

Baker, J. H. *Annual Report of the Commissioner of Pensions to the Secretary of the Interior for the Fiscal Year Ended June 30, 1872.* Washington, D.C.: GPO, 1872.

———. *Annual Report of the Commissioner of Pensions to the Secretary of the Interior for the Fiscal Year Ended June 30, 1873.* Washington, D.C.: GPO, 1873.

———. "Report of the Commissioner of Pensions." In *Report of Secretary of Interior, 1871, and Reports of Subordinate Officers.* 42d Cong., 2d Sess. (1871), H. Exec. Doc. No. 1-5.

Barrett, Joseph H. "Report of the Commissioner of Pensions." In *Message of the President of the United States and Accompanying Documents.* Washington, D.C.: GPO, 1865.

———. "Report of the Commissioner of Pensions." In *Report of Secretary of Interior, 1866, and Reports of Subordinate Officers.* 39th Cong., 2d Sess. (1866), H. Exec. Doc. No. 1.

———. "Report of the Commissioner of Pensions." In *Report of Secretary of Interior, 1872, and Reports of Subordinate Officers.* 40th Cong., 2d Sess. (1867), H. Exec. Doc. No. 1.

Bentley, J. A. *Annual Report of the Commissioner of Pensions to the Secretary of the Interior for the Fiscal Year Ended June 30, 1876.* Washington, D.C.: GPO, 1876.

———. *Annual Report of the Commissioner of Pensions to the Secretary of the Interior for the Fiscal Year Ended June 30, 1877.* Washington, D.C.: GPO, 1877.

———. *Annual Report of the Commissioner of Pensions to the Secretary of the Interior for the Fiscal Year Ended June 30, 1878.* Washington, D.C.: GPO, 1878.

———. *Annual Report of the Commissioner of Pensions to the Secretary of the Interior for the Fiscal Year Ended June 30, 1879.* Washington, D.C.: GPO, 1879.

Bixler, John W., ed. *Decisions of the Department of the Interior in Appealed Pension and Bounty-Land Claims.* Vol. 10. Washington, D.C.: GPO, 1900.

———, ed. *Decisions of the Department of the Interior in Appealed Pension and Bounty-Land Claims.* Vol. 12. Washington, D.C.: GPO, 1902.

———, ed. *Decisions of the Department of the Interior in Appealed Pension and Bounty-Land Claims.* Vol. 13. Washington, D.C.: GPO, 1903.

———, ed. *Decisions of the Department of the Interior in Appealed Pension and Bounty-Land Claims.* Vol. 14. Washington, D.C.: GPO, 1904.

———, ed. *Decisions of the Department of the Interior in Appealed Pension and Bounty-Land Claims.* Vol. 15. Washington, D.C.: GPO, 1905.

Black, John C. *Annual Report of the Commissioner of Pensions to the Secretary of the Interior for the Fiscal Year Ended June 30, 1885.* Washington, D.C.: GPO, 1885.

————. *Annual Report of the Commissioner of Pensions to the Secretary of the Interior for the Fiscal Year Ended June 30, 1886.* Washington, D.C.: GPO, 1886.

————. *Annual Report of the Commissioner of Pensions to the Secretary of the Interior for the Fiscal Year Ended June 30, 1887.* Washington, D.C.: GPO, 1887.

————. *Annual Report of the Commissioner of Pensions to the Secretary of the Interior for the Fiscal Year Ended June 30, 1888.* Washington, D.C.: GPO, 1888.

————. *Annual Report of the Commissioner of Pensions to the Secretary of the Interior for the Fiscal Year Ended June 30, 1889.* Washington, D.C.: GPO, 1889.

Bounty for Slaves Who Enlisted in Army. 42d Cong., 2d sess. (1872), H. Exec. Doc. No. 264.

Bounty to Colored Soldiers. 41st Cong., 2d Sess. (1870), H. Exec. Doc. No. 241.

Browning, O. H. *Report of Secretary of Interior, 1872, and Reports of Subordinate Officers.* 40th Cong., 2d Sess. (1867), H. Exec. Doc. No. 1.

Bureau of the Census, U.S. Department of Commerce, Fifteenth Census of the United States: 1930. Washington, D.C.: GPO, 1933.

————. U.S. Department of Commerce, Sixteenth Census of the United States: 1940. Washington, D.C.: GPO, 1943.

Charges against General O. O. Howard, Administrator of Freedmen's Bureau. 41st Cong., 2d Sess. (1870), H. Report No. 121.

Civil Rights Cases, 109 U.S. 3 (1883).

Condition of Affairs of the Freedmen's Bureau. 42d Cong., 3d Sess. (1872), H. Exec. Doc. No. 109.

Conway, Thomas W. *The Freedmen of Louisiana: Final Report of The Bureau of Free Labor, Department of The Gulf, To Major General E. R. S. Canby.* New Orleans: New Orleans Times Book and Job Office, 1865.

Cox, Christopher C. "Report of the Commissioner of Pensions." In *Report of Secretary of Interior, 1868, and Reports of Subordinate Officers.* 40th Cong., 3d Sess. (1868), H. Exec. Doc. No. 1.

Cox, J. D. *Report of Secretary of Interior, 1869, and Reports of Subordinate Officers.* 41st Cong., 2d Sess. (1869), H. Exec. Doc. No. 1-3.

————. *Report of Secretary of Interior, 1870, and Reports of Subordinate Officers.* 41st Cong., 3d Sess. (1870), H. Exec. Doc. No. 1-4.

Decisions of the Department of the Interior in Cases Relating to Pension Claims. Vol. 1. Washington, D.C.: GPO, 1887.

Dudley, Wm. W. *Annual Report of the Commissioner of Pensions to the Secretary of the Interior for the Fiscal Year Ended June 30, 1881.* Washington, D.C.: GPO, 1881.

————. *Annual Report of the Commissioner of Pensions to the Secretary of the Interior for the Fiscal Year Ended June 30, 1882.* Washington, D.C.: GPO, 1882.

————. *Annual Report of the Commissioner of Pensions to the Secretary of the Interior for the Fiscal Year Ended June 30, 1883.* Washington, D.C.: GPO, 1883.

————. *Annual Report of the Commissioner of Pensions to the Secretary of the Interior for the Fiscal Year Ended June 30, 1884.* Washington, D.C.: GPO, 1884.

Eaton, John. *Extracts from Reports of Superintendents of the Freedmen. Compiled by Rev. Joseph Warren, D.D. Second Series–June 1864.* Vicksburg: Freedmen Press Print, 1864.

———. *Grant, Lincoln, and the Freedmen: Reminiscences of the Civil War, with Special Reference to the Work for the Contrabands and Freedmen of the Mississippi Valley.* New York: Longman, Green, 1907.

———. *Report of the General Superintendent, Freedmen Department of the Tennessee and State of Arkansas for 1864.* Memphis, 1865.

Economic Security Act: Hearings before the Committee on Finance United States Senate Seventy-Fourth Congress First Session on S. 1130. Washington, D.C.: GPO, 1935.

Estimates from Paymaster-General and Adjutant-General for Collection and Payment of Bounty, Prize Money, and Other Claims of Colored Soldiers. 45th Cong., 2d Sess. (1878), S. Exec. Doc. No. 57.

Evans, H. Clay. *Annual Report of the Commissioner of Pensions to the Secretary of the Interior for the Fiscal Year Ended June 30, 1897.* Washington, D.C.: GPO, 1897.

———. *Annual Report of the Commissioner of Pensions to the Secretary of the Interior for the Fiscal Year Ended June 30, 1898.* Washington, D.C.: GPO, 1898.

———. *Annual Report of the Commissioner of Pensions to the Secretary of the Interior for the Fiscal Year Ended June 30, 1899.* Washington, D.C.: GPO, 1899.

———. *Annual Report of the Commissioner of Pensions to the Secretary of the Interior for the Fiscal Year Ended June 30, 1900.* Washington, D.C.: GPO, 1900.

———. *Annual Report of the Commissioner of Pensions to the Secretary of the Interior for the Fiscal Year Ended June 30, 1901.* Washington, D.C.: GPO, 1901.

Freedmen's Bureau. *Officers' Manual: Bureau of Refugees, Freedmen, and Abandoned Lands.* Washington, D.C.: GPO, 1866.

French, E. B. "Report of the Second Auditor." In *Annual Report of the Secretary of the Treasury on the State of Finances for the Year 1878.* Washington, D.C.: GPO, 1878.

[Fry, James B.] *Final Report Made to the Secretary of War, by the Provost Marshal General of the Operations of the Bureau of the Provost Marshal General of the U.S., from the Commencement of the Business of the Bureau, March 17, 1863 to March 17, 1866, the Bureau Terminating by Law August 28, 1866.* Washington, D.C.: GPO, 1866.

General Instructions to Special Examiners of the United States Pension Office. Washington, D.C.: GPO, 1881.

Gill, Charles R. "Report of the Commissioner of Pensions upon House Resolution of 2nd March, 1876, relative to claims for pensions of Colored Applicants residing in Mississippi." In Committee on Invalid Pensions, 44th Cong., 1st Sess. (1876).

Granting Pension to Mary Norman. 49th Cong., 1st Sess. (1886), S. Report No. 871.

Harlan, James. "Report of the Secretary of the Interior." In *Message of the President of the United States and Accompanying Documents.* Washington, D.C.: GPO, 1865.

Home for Aged Negroes from Funds Due Dead Negro Soldiers. 55th Cong., 3d Sess. (1899), H. Report No. 1795.

Howard, O. O. "Report of the Commissioner Bureau Refugees, Freedmen, Etc." In *Report of the Secretary of War.* Washington, D.C.: GPO, 1871.

———. "Report of the Commissioner of Bureau of Refugees, Freedmen, and Abandoned Lands." In *Annual Report of the Secretary of War.* Washington, D.C.: GPO, 1867.

———. "Report of the Commissioner of Bureau of Refugees, Freedmen, and Abandoned Lands." In *Annual Report of the Secretary of War*. Washington, D.C.: GPO, 1869.

———. "Report of the Commissioner of Bureau of Refugees, Freedmen, and Abandoned Lands." In *Annual Report of the Secretary of War*. Washington, D.C.: GPO, 1870.

———. *Statement of Br. Maj. Gen. O.O. Howard before the Committee on Education and Labor: In Defense against the Charges Presented by Hon. Fernando Wood: And Argument of Edgar Ketchum, Esq., Of Counsel for Gen. Howard in Summing Up the Case Upon the Testimony before the Committee*. New York: Bradstreet, 1870.

Inaugural Address of Grover Cleveland, President of the United States, March 4, 1893. Washington, D.C.: GPO, 1893.

Increase of Pension for Harriet Tubman Davis. 55th Cong., 3d Sess. (1899), S. Report No. 1619.

Instructions to Examining Surgeons for Pensions. Washington, D.C.: GPO, 1882.

Instructions to Examining Surgeons for Pensions. Washington, D.C.: GPO, 1884.

Invalid Pensions, Dixon, Nancy. 44th Cong., 2d Sess. (1887), H. Report No. 81.

Invalid Pensions, Douglas, Eliza. 50th Cong., 1st Sess. (1888), H. Report No. 1068.

Irregular Practices of Pension Attorneys. 48th Cong., 1st Sess. (1884), H. Exec. Doc. No. 172.

Laws in Relation to Freedmen. 39th Cong., 2d Sess. (1867), S. Exec. Doc. No. 6.

Lochren, Wm. *Annual Report of the Commissioner of Pensions to the Secretary of the Interior for the Fiscal Year Ended June 30, 1893*. Washington, D.C.: GPO, 1893.

———. *Annual Report of the Commissioner of Pensions to the Secretary of the Interior for the Fiscal Year Ended June 30, 1894*. Washington, D.C.: GPO, 1894.

———. *Annual Report of the Commissioner of Pensions to the Secretary of the Interior for the Fiscal Year Ended June 30, 1895*. Washington, D.C.: GPO, 1895.

Mellen, William P. *Report Relative to Leasing Abandoned Plantations and Affairs of the Freed People in First Special Agency*. Washington, D.C.: McGill & Witherow, 1864.

Message of President on Refugees, Freedmen, and Abandoned Lands. 39th Cong., 1st Sess. (1866), H. Exec. Doc. No. 120.

Message of the President of the United States and Accompanying Documents. Washington, D.C.: GPO, 1865.

Morgan, E. W. *Annual Report of the Bureau of Pensions to the Secretary of the Interior 1930*. Washington, D.C.: GPO, 1930.

Murphy, D. I. *Annual Report of the Commissioner of Pensions to the Secretary of the Interior for the Fiscal Year Ended June 30, 1896*. Washington, D.C.: GPO, 1896.

Norman, Mary, Invalid Pensions, 2 pts. 49th Cong., 1st Sess. (1886), H. Report No. 3203.

Norman, Mary, Invalid Pensions. 49th Cong., 1st Sess. (1886), H. Report No. 1107.

Official Journal of the Proceedings of the Convention: For Framing a Constitution for the State of Louisiana. New Orleans: J. B. Roudanez & Company, printers to the Convention, 1868.

Official Opinions of the Attorneys General of the United States: Advising the President and Heads of Departments, in Relation to Their Official Duties. Washington, D.C.: GPO, 1881.

Official Register of the United States. Washington, D.C.: GPO, 1901.

Payne, Eugene B., ed. *Digest of Decisions of the Department of the Interior in Appealed Pension and Bounty-Land Claims*. Washington, D.C.: GPO, 1905.

Pension to Eliza Douglass. 50th Cong., 1st Sess. (1888), S. Report No. 49.

Pension to Washington Grigsby. 51st Cong., 2d Sess. (1891), S. Report No. 2466.

Pensions for Freedmen. 56th Cong., 1st Sess. (1900), S. Report No. 75.

Pensions for Heirs of Colored Soldiers who Served in War of Rebellion. 47th Cong., 2d Sess. (1883), H. Report No. 1883.

Petition of Colored Citizens of Arkansas, Soldiers in Late War, Praying Repeal of Certain Laws Relating to Manner of Paying Bounties to Colored Soldiers, etc. 44th Cong., 1st Sess. (1876), S. Report No. 224.

President's Veto of Bill to Pension Mary Norman. 49th Cong., 1st Sess. (1886), H. Exec. Doc. No. 325.

Randolph, Thomas P., and Edward P. Hall. *The Pension Attorney's Guide.* Washington, D.C.: GPO, 1892.

Raum, Green B. *Annual Report of the Commissioner of Pensions to the Secretary of the Interior for the Fiscal Year Ended June 30, 1891.* Washington, D.C.: GPO, 1891.

————. *Annual Report of the Commissioner of Pensions to the Secretary of the Interior for the Fiscal Year Ended June 30, 1892.* Washington, D.C.: GPO, 1892.

Report of the Board of Managers of the National Home for Disabled Volunteer Soldiers for the Fiscal Year ended June 30, 1899. Washington, D.C.: GPO, 1900.

Report of Commissioner of Bureau of Refugees, Freedmen, and Abandoned Lands. 39th Cong., 1st Sess. (1865), H. Exec. Doc. No. 11.

Report of Commissioners of Freedmen's Bureau. 39th Cong., 1st Sess. (1866), H. Exec. Doc. No. 70.

Report of the Joint Committee on Reconstruction. 4 parts. Washington, D.C.: GPO, 1866.

Report of Secretary of Interior, 1871, and Reports of Subordinate Officers. 42d Cong., 2d Sess. (1871), H. Exec. Doc. No. 1-5.

Report of the Secretary of War. 39th Cong., 2d Sess. (1866), H. Exec. Doc. No. 1.

Report of the Secretary of War. 40th Cong., 2d Sess. (1867), H. Exec. Doc. No. 1.

Report of the Secretary of War. 40th Cong., 3d Sess. (1868), H. Exec. Doc. No. 1.

Report of the Secretary of War. 41st Cong., 2d Sess. (1869), H. Exec. Doc. No. 1–2.

Report of the Secretary of War. 43d Cong., 1st Sess. (1873), H. Exec. Doc. No. 1-1.

Report of the Secretary of War. 43d Cong., 1st Sess. (1874), H. Exec. Doc. No. 1.

Report of the Secretary of War. 44th Cong., 2d Sess. (1876), H. Exec. Doc. No. 1.

Revised Statutes of the United States, Passed at the First Session of the Forty-Third Congress, 1873–'74. 2d ed. Washington, D.C.: GPO, 1878.

Reynolds, Jno. M., ed. *Digest of Decisions and Opinions Relating to Pensions and Bounty Land.* Washington, D.C.: GPO, 1897.

Secretary of War, Transmitting Certain Developments Connected with Bureau of Refugees, Freedmen and Abandoned Lands. 43d Cong., 1st Sess. (1873), H. Exec. Doc. No. 10-2.

South Carolina State Board of Health. *Annual Report of the State Board of Health of South Carolina for the Fiscal Year Ending October 31, 1882.* Columbia, S.C.: Charles A. Calvo Jr., 1882.

————. *Annual Report of the State Board of Health of South Carolina for the Fiscal Year Ending October 31, 1883.* Columbia, S.C.: Charles A. Calvo Jr., 1883.

————. *Annual Report of the State Board of Health of South Carolina for the Fiscal Year Ending October 31, 1894.* Columbia, S.C.: Charles A. Calvo Jr., 1894.

Tanner, James. *Annual Report of the Commissioner of Pensions to the Secretary of the Interior for the Fiscal Year Ended June 30, 1889.* Washington, D.C.: GPO, 1889.

Testimony Taken or Investigation of Condition of Pension Bureau. 46th Cong., 3d Sess. (1881), H. Report No. 387.

To Distribute Certain Unclaimed Pay and Bounty Moneys Belonging to Colored Soldiers.
46th Cong., 2d Sess. (1880), S. Report No. 359.

To Provide for Payment of Bounties, etc., to Colored Soldiers. 44th Cong., 1st Sess. (1876),
S. Exec. Doc. No. 46.

Townsend, E. D. "Annual Report of the Adjutant General on the Operations of the
Freedmen's Branch." In *Report of the Secretary of War.* 44th Cong., 2d Sess. (1876),
H. Exec. Doc. No. 1.

———. "Report of the Freedmen's Branch of the Adjutant-General's Office." In *Report of
the Secretary of War.* Washington, D.C.: GPO, 1876.

United States. *The Statutes at Large, Treaties, and Proclamations of the United States of
America,* vols. 1–41. Boston: Little, Brown, 1789–1921.

U.S. Congress. *Congressional Globe.* 38th–42d Cong. Washington, D.C.: GPO, 1864–1873.

———. *Congressional Record.* 44th–55th Cong. Washington, D.C.: GPO, 1876–1899.

———. *Journal of the House of Representatives.* 49th Cong., 2d Sess. Washington, D.C.:
GPO, 1887.

———. *Select Committee to Investigate the Causes of the Removal of the Negroes from
the Southern States to the Northern States, Report and Testimony of the Select Committee
of the United States Senate to Investigate the Causes of the Removal of the Negroes from
the Southern States to the Northern States: In Three Parts.* Washington, D.C.: GPO, 1880.

U.S. Treasury Department. *Digest of Appropriations for the Support of the Government of the
United States for the Service of the Fiscal Year Ending June 30, 1931.* Washington, D.C.:
GPO, 1930.

Van Aernam, H. "Report of the Commissioner of Pensions." In *Report of Secretary of Interior,
1870, and Reports of Subordinate Officers.* 41st Cong., 3d Sess. (1870), H. Exec. Doc. No. 1-4.

Veto Message on Bill to Amend Act to Establish Bureau for Relief of Freedmen and Refugees.
39th Cong., 1st Sess. (1866), S. Exec. Doc. No. 25.

Walker, Calvin B. *A Treatise on the Practice of the Pension Bureau, Governing the Adjudication
of Army and Navy Pensions, Being the Unwritten Practice Formulated.* Washington, D.C.:
GPO, 1882.

———, ed. *A Digest of the Laws of the United States Governing the Granting of Army and Navy
Pensions and Bounty-Land Warrants; Decisions of the Secretary of the Interior and Rulings and
Orders of the Commissioner of Pensions Thereunder.* Washington, D.C.: GPO, 1882.

Warner, Vespasian. *Annual Report of the Commissioner of Pensions to the Secretary of the
Interior for the Fiscal Year Ended June 30, 1905.* Washington, D.C.: GPO, 1905.

———. *Annual Report of the Commissioner of Pensions to the Secretary of the Interior for
the Fiscal Year Ended June 30, 1909.* Washington, D.C.: GPO, 1909.

Work of Late Bureau of Refugees, Freedmen, and Abandoned Lands. 44th Cong., 1st Sess.
(1875), H. Exec. Doc. No. 144.

Published Primary Sources

"Actual National Obligations." *Confederate Veteran* 6, no. 9 (September 1898): 411–13.

Alvord, John Watson. *Letters from the South, Relating to the Condition of Freedmen:
Addressed to Major General O. O. Howard, Commissioner Bureau R., F., and A. L.*
Washington, D.C.: Howard University Press, 1870.

Andrews, William L., ed. *Slave Narratives after Slavery*. New York: Oxford University Press, 2011.

Baber, George. "Our Pension System." *North American Review* 150, no. 402 (May 1890): 663–64.

Barrier, J. M. "Tuberculosis among Our Negroes in Louisiana." *New Orleans Medical and Surgical Journal* 55 (October 1902): 226–33.

Baxter, J. H. *Statistics, Medical and Anthropological, of the Provost-Marshal-General's Bureau, Derived from Records of the Examination for Military Service in the Armies of the United States during the Late War of the Rebellion*. 2 vols. Washington, D.C.: GPO, 1875.

Bellows, Henry W. "Report concerning Provision required for the Relief and Support of Disabled Soldiers and Sailors and their Dependents." In *Documents of the U.S. Sanitary Commission*, edited by U.S. Sanitary Commission. vol. 2, doc. 95 (December 15, 1865).

Bergeron, Paul H., ed. *The Papers of Andrew Johnson, Volume 8, May–August 1865*. Knoxville: University of Tennessee Press, 1989.

Berlin, Ira, Thavolia Glymph, Steven F. Miller, Joseph P. Reidy, Leslie S. Rowland, and Julie Saville, eds. *The Wartime Genesis of Free Labor: The Lower South*. Ser. 1, vol. 3 of *Freedom: A Documentary History of Emancipation, 1861–1867*. New York: Cambridge University Press, 1990.

Berlin, Ira, Steven F. Miller, Joseph P. Reidy, and Leslie S. Rowland, eds. *The Wartime Genesis of Free Labor: The Upper South*. Ser. 1, vol. 2, of *Freedom: A Documentary History of Emancipation, 1861–1867*. New York: Cambridge University Press, 1993.

Berlin, Ira, Joseph P. Reidy, and Leslie S. Rowland, eds. *The Black Military Experience*. Ser. 2, vol. 1 of *Freedom: A Documentary History of Emancipation, 1861–1867*. New York: Cambridge University Press, 1982.

Berlin, Ira, and Leslie S. Rowland, eds. *Families and Freedom: A Documentary History of African-American Kinship in the Civil War Era*. New York: New Press, 1997.

Brady, C. M. "The Negro as a Patient." *New Orleans Medical and Surgical Journal* 56 (December 1903): 431–45.

Broadus, Thomas A. "The South and the Pension Bureau." *American Monthly Review of Reviews: An International Magazine* 23 (January–June 1901): 203–7.

Brown, E. M. "Some Observations from the Medical Examiner's End of the Pension Bureau." In *Transactions of the National Association of United States Examining Surgeons*. Vol. 3. Rochester: Burnett Printing Company, 1905.

Brown, John. *Slave Life in Georgia: A Narrative of the Life, Sufferings, and Escape of John Brown, a Fugitive Slave, Now in England*, edited by Louis Alexis Chamerovzow. London: W. M. Watts, 1855.

Bruce, Henry Clay. *The New Man: Twenty-Nine Years a Slave, Twenty-Nine Years a Free Man; Recollections of H. C. Bruce*. York, Penn.: P. Anstadt & Sons, 1895.

The Campaign Text Book. Why the People Want a Change. The Republican Party Reviewed: Its Sins of Commission and Omission. New York: Democratic National Committee, 1876.

Clark, S. N. "Some Weak Places in Our Pension System." *Forum* 26 (1898): 306–20.

Coffin, Charles Carleton. *The Boys of '61: Or, Four Years of Fighting: Personal Observation with the Army and Navy, from the First Battle of Bull Run to the Fall of Richmond*. Rev. ed. Boston: Page Company, 1896.

"Consideration for Old Soldiers." *Confederate Veteran* 1, no. 1 (1893): 21.

Crummell, Alexander. *Africa and America: Addresses and Discourses.* Springfield, Mass.: Willey, 1891.

Curtis, Frank B., and William H. Webster, eds. *A Digest of the Laws of the United States Governing the Granting of Army and Navy Pensions and Bounty-Land Warrants; Decisions of the Secretary of the Interior and Rulings and Orders of the Commissioner of Pensions Thereunder.* Washington, D.C.: GPO, 1885.

Ellis, Thomas. *Leaves from the Diary of an Army Surgeon; or, Incidents of Field, Camp, and Hospital Life.* New York: John Bradburn, 1863.

Fisk, Clinton Bowen. *Plain Counsels for Freedmen: In Sixteen Brief Lectures.* Boston: American Tract Society, 1866.

Forman, Jacob Gilbert. *The Western Sanitary Commission: A Sketch of Its Origin, History, Labors for the Sick and Wounded of the Western Armies, and Aid Given to Freedmen and Union Refugees, with Incidents of Hospital Life.* St. Louis: R. P. Studley, 1864.

Freedman's Savings and Trust Company. *Charter and By-Laws.* New York: Wm. C. Bryant, 1865.

George, Henry. *Progress and Poverty: An Inquiry into the Cause of Industrial Depressions and of Increase of Want with Increase of Wealth: The Remedy.* New York: D. Appleton, 1879.

Gould, Benjamin A. *Investigations of the Military and Anthropological Statistics of American Soldiers.* New York: Hurd & Houghton for the U.S. Sanitary Commission, 1869.

Hahn, Steven, Steven F. Miller, Susan E. O'Donovan, John C. Rodrigue, and Leslie S. Rowland, eds. *Land and Labor, 1865.* Ser. 3, vol. 1 of *Freedom: A Documentary History of Emancipation, 1861–1867.* Chapel Hill: University of North Carolina Press, 2008.

Harriss, Juriah. "What Constitutes Unsoundness in the Negro?" *Savannah Journal of Medicine* 1, no. 3 (September 1858): 145–52; 1, no. 5 (January 1859): 289–95; 2, no. 1 (May 1859): 10–16.

Hayden, René, Anthony E. Kaye, Kate Masur, Steven F. Miller, Susan E. O'Donovan, Leslie S. Rowland, and Stephen A. West, eds. *Land and Labor, 1866–1867.* Ser. 3, vol. 2 of *Freedom: A Documentary History of Emancipation, 1861–1867.* Chapel Hill: University of North Carolina Press, 2013.

Heard, William H. *From Slavery to the Bishopric in the A.M.E. Church: An Autobiography.* Philadelphia: A.M.E. Book Concern, 1924.

Hempstead, Fay. *A Pictorial History of Arkansas, from Earliest Times to the Year 1890.* St. Louis: N. D. Thompson, 1890.

Hepworth, George H. *The Whip, Hoe, and Sword: or, The Gulf Department in '63.* Boston: Walker, Wise, 1864.

Higginson, Thomas Wentworth. *Army Life in a Black Regiment.* Boston: Fields, Osgood, 1870.

Hoffman, Frederick L. *Race Traits and Tendencies of the American Negro.* Publications of the American Economic Association. Vol. 11. New York: Macmillan, 1896.

Hough, Theodore, and William Thompson Sedgwick. *The Human Mechanism: Its Physiology and the Sanitation of Its Surroundings.* Boston: Ginn, 1906.

Howard, Oliver Otis. *Autobiography of Oliver Otis Howard: Major General United States Army.* 2 vols. New York: Baker & Taylor, 1907.

Humphrey, R. M. "History of the Colored Farmers' Alliance and Co-operative Union." In *The Farmers' Alliance History and Agricultural Digest,* edited by Nelson A. Dunning, 288–92. Washington, D.C.: National Farmers' Alliance, 1891.

Hunt, Sandford B. "The Negro as a Soldier." *Anthropological Review* 7, no. 24 (January 1869): 40–54.

———. "The Negro as a Soldier." *Quarterly Journal of Psychological Medicine and Medical Jurisprudence* 1 (October 1867): 161–86.

Jones, Claudia. *An End to the Neglect of the Problems of the Negro Woman!* New York: National Women's Commission CPUSA, 1949.

"Justice to the South—True History." *Confederate Veteran* 1, no. 11 (1893): 323.

McKinley, William. "Speech before the Legislature in Joint Assembly at the State Capitol, Atlanta, Georgia, December 14, 1898." In *Speeches and Addresses of William McKinley: from March 1, 1897, to May 30, 1900*. New York: Doubleday & McClure, 1900.

Miller, J. F. "The Effects of Emancipation upon the Mental and Physical Qualifications of the Negro in the South." *North Carolina Medical Journal* 38 (November 1896): 285–94.

Moore, Frank, ed. *The Rebellion Record: A Diary of American Events, with Documents, Narratives, Illustrative Incidents, Poetry, Etc.* 11 vols. New York: G. Putnam's Sons, 1861–68.

Morton, M. B. "Federal and Confederate Pensions Contrasted." *Forum* 16 (1893): 68–74.

National Ex-Slave Mutual Relief, Bounty, and Pension Association. *Constitution and By-Laws of Governing the National, State, and Local Associations of the National Ex-Slave Mutual Relief, Bounty, and Pension Association*. Nashville, 1900.

Nordhoff, Charles. *The Freedmen of South-Carolina: Some Account of Their Appearance, Character, Condition, and Peculiar Customs*. New York: Charles T. Evans, 1863.

Nugent, Catherine, ed. *Life Work of Thomas L. Nugent*. Stephenville, Tex.: Catherine Nugent, 1896.

"Pension Slaves Who Served in the War." *Confederate Veteran* 21, no. 10 (October 1913): 481.

"Pensioning the Old Slaves." *Confederate Veteran* 11, no. 3 (March 1903): 108–9.

"Pensions for Faithful Negroes." *Confederate Veteran* 29, no. 8 (August 1921): 284.

Perkins, Frances. *The Roosevelt I Knew*. New York: Viking, 1946.

Perkins, Stephen H. *Report on the Pension Systems, and Invalid Hospitals of France, Prussia, Austria, Russia and Italy, with Some Suggestions upon the Best Means of Disposing of Our Disabled Soldiers*. New York: W. C. Bryant, 1863.

Proceedings of the National Conference of Colored Men of the United States, Held in the State Capitol at Nashville Tennessee, May 6, 7, 8 and 9, 1879. Washington, D.C.: R. H. Darby, 1879.

Raff, George W. *The War Claimant's Guide: A Manual of Laws, Regulations, Instructions, Forms and Official Decisions*. Cincinnati: Robert Clarke, 1866.

Rapp, S. A., ed. *A Complete Digest of Laws in Relation to Bounty*. Washington, D.C.: W. H. & O. H. Morrison, 1872.

Redkey, Edwin S., ed. *A Grand Army of Black Men: Letters from African-American Soldiers in the Union Army, 1861–1865*. New York: Cambridge University Press, 1992.

Reelin, Frank A. *Life and Public Services of Martin R. Delany: Sub-Assistant Commissioner, Bureau Relief of Refugees, Freedmen, and of Abandoned Lands, and Late Major 104th U.S. Colored Troops*. Boston: Lee and Shepard, 1883.

Rogers, Seth. "Letters of Dr. Seth Rogers." *Proceedings of the Massachusetts Historical Society* 43, 3rd Series (February 1910): 338–98.

Sears, Richard D., ed. *Camp Nelson, Kentucky: A Civil War History*. Lexington: University Press of Kentucky, 2002.

Sloane, William M. "Pensions and Socialism." *Century* 42, no. 2 (June 1891): 179–88.

Smalley, Eugene V. "United States Pension Office." *The Century Illustrated Monthly Magazine* 28 (1884): 427–34.

Smith, James Lindsay. *Autobiography of James L. Smith, Including, Also, Reminiscences of Slave Life, Recollections of the War, Education of Freedmen, Causes of the Exodus, etc.* Norwich, Conn.: The Bulletin, 1881.

Stillé, Charles J. *History of the United States Sanitary Commission, Being the General Report of Its Work during the War of the Rebellion.* Philadelphia: J. B. Lippincott, 1866.

Sumner, Charles. *A Bridge from Slavery to Freedom. Speech of Hon. Charles Sumner, on the Bill to Establish a Bureau of Freedmen, in the Senate of the United States, June 13th and 15th, 1864.* Washington, D.C.: H. Polkinhorn & Son, 1864.

Sumner, William Graham. *What Social Classes Owe Each Other.* New York: Harper & Brothers, 1883.

Taylor, Susie King. *Reminiscences of My Life with the 33rd United States Colored Troops: Late 1st South Carolina Volunteers.* Boston: The author, 1902.

Tracy, Frank Basil. "Menacing Socialism in the Western States." *Forum* (May 1893): 332–42.

"A Tried Watch-Dog Who Will Be Retained." *Puck* (October 30, 1901).

U.S. Sanitary Commission. *Documents of the U.S. Sanitary Commission,* 2 vols. New York, 1866.

———. *Statement of the Object and Methods of the Sanitary Commission.* New York: Wm. C. Bryant, 1863.

Vaughan, Walter R. *Vaughan's "Freedmen's Pension Bill." Being an Appeal in Behalf of Men Released from Slavery. A Plea for American Freedmen and a Rational Proposition to Grant Pensions to Persons of Color Emancipated from Slavery.* Chicago, 1891.

Veazey, Wheelock G., Joseph H. O'Neil, and B. A. Enloe. "Further Views of Pension List Revision." *North American Review* 156, no. 438 (May 1893): 618–30.

Weaver, Clare P., ed. *Thank God My Regiment an African One: The Civil War Diary of Colonel Nathan W. Daniels.* Baton Rouge: Louisiana State University Press, 2000.

Wilson, R. P. C., S. S. Burdett, and William Conant Church. "How Shall the Pension List Be Revised?" *North American Review* 156, no. 437 (April 1893): 416–31.

Witte, Edwin E. *The Development of the Social Security Act: A Memorandum on the History of the Committee on Economic Security and Drafting and Legislative History of the Social Security Act.* Madison: University of Wisconsin Press, 1962.

Wormeley, Katherine Prescott. *The Sanitary Commission of the United States Army: A Succinct Narrative of its Works and Purpose.* New York: USSC, 1864.

Wright, Richard. *Black Boy: (American Hunger); A Record of Childhood and Youth.* Updated ed. New York: Harper Perennial, 2006.

Yeatman, James E. *A Report on the Condition of the Freedmen of the Mississippi, Presented to the Western Sanitary Commission, December 17, 1863.* St. Louis, Mo.: Western Sanitary Commission, 1864.

———. *Suggestions of a Plan of Organization for Freed Labor: And the Leasing of Plantations along the Mississippi River, under a Bureau or Commission to Be Appointed by the Government.* St. Louis, Mo.: Western Sanitary Commission, 1864.

Yetman, Norman R., ed. *Voices from Slavery: 100 Authentic Slave Narratives.* Mineola, N.Y.: Dover, 2000.

Secondary Sources

Abbott, Martin. "Free Land, Free Labor, and the Freedmen's Bureau." *Agricultural History* 30, no. 4 (October 1956): 150–56.

Abel, John H., Jr., and LaWanda Cox. "Andrew Johnson and His Ghost Writers: An Analysis of the Freedmen's Bureau and Civil Rights Veto Messages." *Mississippi Valley Historical Review* 48, no. 3 (December 1961): 460–79.

Abruzzo, Margaret. *Polemical Pain: Slavery, Cruelty, and the Rise of Humanitarianism.* Baltimore: Johns Hopkins University Press, 2011.

Alexander, Shawn Leigh. *An Army of Lions: The Civil Rights Struggle before the NAACP.* Philadelphia: University of Pennsylvania Press, 2012.

Ali, Omar H. *In the Lion's Mouth: Black Populism in the New South, 1886–1900.* Jackson: University Press of Mississippi, 2010.

Alston, Lee J., and Joseph P. Ferrie. *Southern Paternalism and the American Welfare State: Economics, Politics, and Institutions in the South, 1865–1965.* New York: Cambridge University Press, 1999.

Araujo, Ana Lucia. *Reparations for Slavery and the Slave Trade: A Transnational and Comparative History.* London: Bloomsbury, 2017.

Ash, Stephen V. *Firebrand of Liberty: The Story of Two Black Regiments That Changed the Course of the Civil War.* New York: W. W. Norton, 2008.

———. *When the Yankees Came: Conflict & Chaos in the Occupied South, 1861–1865.* Chapel Hill: University of North Carolina Press, 1995.

Ayers, Edward L. *The Promise of the New South: Life after Reconstruction.* New York: Oxford University Press, 1992.

Bailey, N. Louise, Mary L. Morgan, and Carolyn R. Taylor, eds. *Biographical Directory of the South Carolina Senate, 1776–1985.* 3 vols. Columbia: South Carolina Archives Department, 1986.

Baker, Bruce E., and Brian Kelly, eds. *After Slavery: Race, Labor, and Citizenship in the Reconstruction South.* Gainesville: University Press of Florida, 2014.

Balogh, Brian. *The Associational State: American Governance in the Twentieth Century.* Philadelphia: University of Pennsylvania Press, 2015.

———. *A Government Out of Sight: The Mystery of National Authority in Nineteenth-Century America.* New York: Cambridge University Press, 2009.

Bancroft, Frederic. *Slave Trading in the Old South.* Baltimore: J. H. Furst, 1931.

Baptist, Edward E. *The Half Has Never Been Told: Slavery and the Making of American Capitalism.* New York: Basic Books, 2014.

Baradaran, Mehrsa. *The Color of Money: Black Banks and the Racial Wealth Gap.* Cambridge, Mass.: Harvard University Press, 2017.

Barclay, Jenifer L. *The Mark of Slavery: Disability, Race, and Gender in Antebellum America.* Urbana: University of Illinois Press, 2021.

Bardaglio, Peter. *Reconstructing the Household: Families, Sex, and the Law in the Nineteenth-Century South.* New York: Cambridge University Press, 1998.

Barnes, Kenneth C. *Journey of Hope: The Back-to-Africa Movement in Arkansas in the Late 1800s.* Chapel Hill: University of North Carolina Press, 2004.

Barreyre, Nicolas. "The Politics of Economic Crises: The Panic of 1873, the End of Reconstruction, and the Realignment of American Politics." *Journal of the Gilded Age and Progressive Era* 10, no. 4 (October 2011): 403–23.

Baynton, Douglas C. "Defectives in the Land: Disability and American Immigration Policy, 1882–1924." *Journal of American Ethnic History* 24, no. 3 (Spring 2005): 31–44.

———. *Defectives in the Land: Disability and Immigration in the Age of Eugenics.* Chicago: University of Chicago Press, 2016.

———. "Disability and the Justification of Inequality in American History." In *The New Disability History: American Perspectives,* edited by Paul K. Longmore and Lauri Umansky, 33–57. New York: New York University Press, 2001.

Beatty, Bess. *A Revolution Gone Backward: The Black Response to National Politics, 1876–1896.* New York: Greenwood, 1987.

Bedell, Mary S. "Employment and Income of Negro Workers—1940–52." *Monthly Labor Review* (June 1953): 596–601.

Behrend, Justin. *Reconstructing Democracy: Grassroots Black Politics in the Deep South after the Civil War.* Athens: University of Georgia Press, 2017.

Belz, Herman. "Law, Politics, and Race in the Struggle for Equal Pay during the Civil War." *Civil War History* 22, no. 3 (September 1976): 197–213.

Benedict, Michael Les. "Reform Republicans and the Retreat from Reconstruction." In *The Facts of Reconstruction: Essays in Honor of John Hope Franklin,* edited by Eric Anderson and Alfred A. Moss Jr., 53–78. Baton Rouge: Louisiana State University Press, 1991.

Bensel, Richard Franklin. *The Political Economy of American Industrialization, 1877–1900.* New York: Cambridge University Press, 2000.

———. *Sectionalism and American Political Development, 1880–1980.* Madison: University of Wisconsin Press, 1987.

———. *Yankee Leviathan: The Origins of Central State Authority in America, 1859–1877.* New York: Cambridge University Press, 1990.

Bentley, George R. *A History of the Freedmen's Bureau.* Philadelphia: University of Pennsylvania Press, 1955.

Bercaw, Nancy D. *Gendered Freedoms: Race, Rights, and the Politics of Household in the Delta, 1861–1875.* Gainesville: University Press of Florida, 2003.

Berlin, Ira. *The Making of African America: The Four Great Migrations.* New York: Penguin Books, 2010.

Berlin, Ira, and Philip D. Morgan, eds. *The Slaves' Economy: Independent Production by Slaves in the Americas.* Portland, Oreg.: Frank Cass, 1991.

Berlin, Ira, et al. *Slaves No More: Three Essays on Emancipation and the Civil War.* New York: Cambridge University Press, 1992.

Berry, Mary Frances. *Military Necessity and Civil Rights Policy: Black Citizenship and the Constitution, 1861–1868.* Port Washington, N.Y.: Kennikat, 1977.

———. *My Face Is Black Is True: Callie House and the Struggle for Ex-Slave Reparations.* New York: Vintage, 2006.

———. "Negro Troops in Blue and Gray: The Louisiana Native Guards, 1861–1863." *Louisiana History* 8, no. 2 (Spring 1867): 165–90.

Binning, F. Wayne. "Carpetbaggers' Triumph: The Louisiana State Election of 1868." *Louisiana History* 14, no. 1 (Winter 1973): 21–39.

Biographical Directory of the United States Congress. Washington, D.C.: United States Congress, 1998.

Blackmon, Douglas A. *Slavery by Another Name: The Re-Enslavement of Black Americans from the Civil War to World War II*. New York: Anchor Books, 2008.

Blair, William A. *Cities of the Dead: Contesting the Memory of the Civil War in the South, 1865–1914*. Chapel Hill: University of North Carolina Press, 2004.

———. "The Use of Military Force to Protect the Gains of Reconstruction." *Civil War History* 51, no. 4 (December 2005): 388–402.

———. *With Malice toward Some: Treason and Loyalty in the Civil War Era*. Chapel Hill: University of North Carolina Press, 2014.

Blair, William A., and Karen Fisher Younger, eds. *Lincoln's Proclamation: Emancipation Reconsidered*. Chapel Hill: University of North Carolina Press, 2012.

Blanck, Peter, and Chen Song. "Civil War Pension Attorneys and Disability Politics." *University of Michigan Journal of Law Reform* 35, nos. 1 & 2 (Fall 2001–Winter 2002): 137–217.

Blanck, Peter David, and Michael Millender. "Before Disability Civil Rights: Civil War Pensions and the Politics of Disability in America." *Alabama Law Review* 52, no. 1 (Fall 2000): 1–50.

Blassingame, John W. "Using the Testimony of Ex-Slaves: Approaches and Problems." *Journal of Southern History* 41, no. 4 (1975): 473–92.

Blevins, Cameron. *Paper Trails: The US Post and the Making of the American West*. New York: Oxford University Press, 2021.

Blight, David W. *Beyond the Battlefield: Race, Memory, and the American Civil War*. Amherst: University of Massachusetts Press, 2002.

———. *Frederick Douglass: Prophet of Freedom*. New York: Simon & Schuster, 2018.

———. *Frederick Douglass's Civil War: Keeping Faith in Jubilee*. Baton Rouge: Louisiana State University Press, 1989.

———. *Race and Reunion: The Civil War in American Memory*. Cambridge, Mass.: Harvard University Press, 2001.

Blight, David W., and Jim Downs, eds. *Beyond Freedom: Disrupting the History of Emancipation*. Athens: University of Georgia Press, 2017.

Blum, Edward J. *Reforging the White Republic: Race, Religion, and American Nationalism, 1865–1898*. Baton Rouge: Louisiana State University Press, 2005.

Boster, Dea H. *African American Slavery and Disability: Bodies, Property, and Power in the Antebellum South, 1800–1860*. New York: Routledge, 2013.

Botkin, Benjamin A. "The Slave as His Own Interpreter." *Quarterly Journal of Current Acquisitions* 2 (November 1944): 37–63.

Bremner, Robert H. *The Public Good: Philanthropy and Welfare in the Civil War Era*. New York: Alfred A. Knopf, 1980.

Brimmer, Brandi C. "Black Women's Politics, Narratives of Sexual Immorality, and Pension Bureaucracy in Mary Lee's North Carolina Neighborhood." *Journal of Southern History* 80, no. 4 (November 2014): 827–58.

———. *Claiming Union Widowhood: Race, Respectability, and Poverty in the Post-Emancipation South*. Durham, N.C.: Duke University Press, 2020.

———. "'Her Claim for Pension Is Lawful and Just': Representing Black Union Widows in Late-Nineteenth-Century North Carolina." *Journal of the Civil War Era* 1, no. 2 (June 2011): 207–36.

Brown, Elsa Barkley. "To Catch the Vision of Freedom: Reconstructing Southern Black Women's Political History, 1865–1880." In *African American Women and the Vote, 1837–1965*, edited by Ann D. Gordon et al., 66–99. Amherst: University of Massachusetts Press, 1997.

———. "Negotiating and Transforming the Public Sphere: African American Political Life in the Transition from Slavery to Freedom." *Public Culture* 7, no. 1 (Fall 1994): 107–46.

Brown, Michael K. *Race, Money, and the American Welfare State*. Ithaca, N.Y.: Cornell University Press, 1999.

Brueggemann, John. "Racial Considerations and Social Policy in the 1930s." *Social Science History* 26, no. 1 (Spring 2002): 139–77.

Burnham, John C. *Health Care in America: A History*. Baltimore: Johns Hopkins University Press, 2015.

Burnham, Margaret. "An Impossible Marriage: Slave Law and Family Law." *Law and Inequality* 5 (July 1987): 187–225.

Cahill, Cathleen D. *Federal Fathers and Mothers: A Social History of the United States Indian Service, 1869–1933*. Chapel Hill: University of North Carolina Press, 2011.

Calhoun, Charles W. *Conceiving a New Republic: The Republican Party and the Southern Question, 1869–1900*. Lawrence: University Press of Kansas, 2006.

Campbell, Andrea Louise. "Policy Makes Mass Politics." *Annual Review of Political Science* 15 (2012): 333–51.

Cantrell, Andrea. "WPA Sources for African-American Oral History in Arkansas: Ex-Slave Narratives and Early Settlers' Personal Histories." *Arkansas Historical Quarterly* 63, no. 1 (2004): 44–67.

Carpenter, Daniel P. *The Forging of Bureaucratic Autonomy: Reputations, Networks, and Policy Innovation in Executive Agencies, 1862–1928*. Princeton, N.J.: Princeton University Press, 2001.

Casebeer, Kenneth M. "Unemployment Insurance: American Social Wage Labor Organization and Legal Ideology." *Boston College Law Review* 35, issue 2, no. 2 (March 1994): 259–348.

Cassedy, James H. *American Medicine and Statistical Thinking, 1800–1860*. Cambridge, Mass.: Harvard University Press, 1984.

———. "Numbering the North's Medical Events: Humanitarianism and Science in Civil War Statistics." *Bulletin of the History of Medicine* 66 (1992): 210–33.

Cha-Jua, Sundiata Keita, and Clarence Lang. "The 'Long Movement' as Vampire: Temporal and Spatial Fallacies in Recent Black Freedom Studies." *Journal of African American History* 92, no. 2 (Spring, 2007): 265–88.

Cimbala, Paul A. *Under the Guardianship of the Nation: The Freedmen's Bureau and the Reconstruction of Georgia, 1865–1870*. Athens: University of Georgia Press, 1997.

Cimbala, Paul A., and Randall M. Miller, eds. *Freedmen's Bureau and Reconstruction: Reconsiderations*. New York: Fordham University Press, 1999.

Clampitt, Bradley, ed. *The Civil War and Reconstruction in Indian Territory*. Lincoln: University of Nebraska Press, 2015.

Clark, Elizabeth. "'The Sacred Rights of the Weak': Pain, Sympathy, and the Culture of Individual Rights in Antebellum America." *Journal of American History* 82, no. 2 (September 1995): 463–93.

Clark, Kathleen Ann. *Defining Moments: African American Commemoration and Political Culture in the South, 1863–1913*. Chapel Hill: University of North Carolina Press, 2005.

Clarke, Frances. "'Honorable Scars': Northern Amputees and the Meaning of Civil War Injuries." In *Union Soldiers and the Home Front: Wartime Experiences, Postwar Adjustments*, edited by Paul A. Cimbala and Randall Miller, 361–94. New York: Fordham University Press, 2002.

Clemens, Elisabeth S. "Lineages of the Rube Goldberg State: Building and Blurring Public Programs, 1900–1940." In *Rethinking Political Institutions*, edited by Ian Shapiro, Stephen Skowronek, and David Galvin, 380–443. New York: New York University Press, 2006.

Click, Patricia C. *Time Full of Trial: The Roanoke Island Freedmen's Colony, 1862–1867*. Chapel Hill: University of North Carolina Press, 2001.

Clinton, Catherine. *Harriet Tubman: The Road to Freedom*. New York: Little, Brown, 2004.

Cohen, Nancy. *The Reconstruction of American Liberalism, 1865–1914*. Chapel Hill: University of North Carolina Press, 2002.

Cohen, William. *At Freedom's Edge: Black Mobility and the Southern White Quest for Racial Control, 1861–1915*. Baton Rouge: Louisiana State University Press, 1991.

Colby, Ira C. "The Freedmen's Bureau: From Social Welfare to Segregation." *Phylon* 46, no. 3 (1985): 219–30.

Collins, Kathleen. "The Scourged Back." *History of Photography* 9, no. 1 (October 1985): 43–45.

Costa, Dora L. "The Measure of Man and Older Age Mortality: Evidence from the Gould Sample." *Journal of Economic History* 64, no. 1 (March 2004): 1–23.

Cott, Nancy F. *Public Vows: A History of Marriage and the Nation*. Cambridge, Mass.: Harvard University Press, 2000.

Cox, Caroline. *Boy Soldiers of the American Revolution*. Chapel Hill: University of North Carolina Press, 2016.

Cox, John H., and LaWanda Cox. "General O. O. Howard and the 'Misrepresented Bureau.'" *Journal of Southern History* 19, no. 4 (November 1953): 43–56.

Cox, LaWanda. "The Promise of Land for the Freedmen." *Mississippi Valley Historical Review* 45, no. 3 (December 1958): 413–40.

Dailey, Jane. *Before Jim Crow: The Politics of Race in Postemancipation Virginia*. Chapel Hill: University of North Carolina Press, 2000.

Dann, Martin. "Black Populism: A Study of the Colored Farmers' Alliance through 1891." *Journal of Ethnic Studies* 2 (Fall 1974): 58–71.

Dauber, Michele Landis. *The Sympathetic State: Disaster Relief and the Origins of the American Welfare State*. Chicago: University of Chicago Press, 2013.

Davidson, James M. "Encountering the Ex-Slave Reparations Movement from the Grave: The National Industrial Council and National Liberty Party, 1901–1907." *Journal of African American History* 97, no. 1–2 (Winter–Spring 2012): 13–38.

Davies, Gareth, and Martha Derthick. "Race and Social Welfare Policy: The Social Security Act of 1935." *Political Science Quarterly* 112, no. 2 (1997): 217–35.

Davis, Adrienne D. "The Private Law of Race and Sex: An Antebellum Perspective." *Stanford Law Review* 51, no. 2 (January 1999): 221–88.

Davis, Lennard J. *Enforcing Normalcy: Disability, Deafness, and the Body*. New York: Verso, 1995.

Davis, Ronald L. F. *Good and Faithful Labor: From Slavery to Sharecropping in the Natchez District, 1860–1890*. Westport, Conn.: Greenwood, 1982.

de la Fuente, Alejandro, and Ariela J. Gross. *Becoming Free, Becoming Black: Race, Freedom, and Law in Cuba, Virginia, and Louisiana*. New York: Cambridge University Press, 2020.

Dearing, Mary R. *Veterans in Politics: The Story of the G.A.R.* Baton Rouge: Louisiana State University Press, 1952.

DeWitt, Larry. "The Decision to Exclude Agricultural and Domestic Workers from the Social Security Act of 1935." *Social Security Bulletin* 70, no. 4 (2010): 49–68.

Domby, Adam H. *The False Cause: Fraud, Fabrication, and White Supremacy in Confederate Memory*. Charlottesville: University of Virginia Press, 2020.

Downs, Gregory P. *After Appomattox: Military Occupation and the Ends of War*. Cambridge, Mass.: Harvard University Press, 2015.

———. *Declarations of Dependence: The Long Reconstruction of Popular Politics in the South, 1861–1908*. Chapel Hill: University of North Carolina Press, 2011.

———. "Force, Freedom, and the Making of Emancipation." In *Rethinking American Emancipation: Legacies of Slavery and the Quest for Black Freedom*, edited by William A. Link and James J. Broomall, 42–68. New York: Cambridge University Press, 2016.

Downs, Gregory P., and Kate Masur, eds. *The World the Civil War Made*. Chapel Hill: University of North Carolina Press, 2015.

Downs, Jim. "The Continuation of Slavery: The Experience of Disabled Slaves during Emancipation." *Disability Studies Quarterly* 28, no. 3 (Summer 2008).

———. "Emancipating the Evidence: The Ontology of the Freedmen's Bureau Records." In *Beyond Freedom: Disrupting the History of Emancipation*, edited by David W. Blight and Jim Downs, 160–80. Athens: University of Georgia Press, 2017.

———. *Sick from Freedom: African-American Illness and Suffering during the Civil War and Reconstruction*. New York: Oxford University Press, 2012.

Doyle, Don H. *New Men, New Cities, New South: Atlanta, Nashville, Charleston, Mobile, 1860–1910*. Chapel Hill: University of North Carolina Press, 1990.

Du Bois, W. E. B. *Black Reconstruction in America: 1860–1880*. New York: Touchstone, 1995. First published in 1935 by Harcourt, Brace.

———. "Reconstruction and Its Benefits." *American Historical Review* 15, no. 4 (July 1910): 781–99.

———. *The Souls of Black Folk*. New York: Penguin Books, 1996. First published in 1903 by A. C. McClurg.

Edwards, Justene Hill. *Unfree Markets: The Slaves' Economy and the Rise of Capitalism in South Carolina*. New York: Columbia University Press, 2021.

Edwards, Laura F. *Gendered Strife and Confusion: The Political Culture of Reconstruction*. Urbana: University of Illinois Press, 1997.

———. *A Legal History of the Civil War and Reconstruction: A Nation of Rights*. New York: Cambridge University Press, 2015.

———. "'The Marriage Covenant Is at the Foundation of All Our Rights': The Politics of Slave Marriages in North Carolina after Emancipation." *Law and History Review* 14, no. 1 (Spring 1996): 81–124.

———. *The People and Their Peace: Legal Culture and the Transformation of Inequality in the Post-Revolutionary South*. Chapel Hill: University of North Carolina Press, 2009.

———. "Status without Rights: African Americans and the Tangled History of Law and Governance in the Nineteenth-Century U.S. South." *American Historical Review* 112, no. 2 (April 2007): 365–93.

Egerton, Douglas R. *The Wars of Reconstruction: The Brief, Violent History of America's Most Progressive Era*. London: Bloomsbury, 2014.

Eisenstadt, S. N., and Louis Roniger. "Patron-Client Relations as a Model of Structuring Social Exchange." *Comparative Studies in Society and History* 22, no. 1 (January 1980): 42–77.

Ellis, John H. *Yellow Fever and Public Health in the New South*. Lexington: University Press of Kentucky, 1992.

Emberton, Carole. *Beyond Redemption: Race, Violence, and the American South after the Civil War*. Chicago: University of Chicago Press, 2013.

———. "'Only Murder Makes Men': Reconsidering the Black Military Experience." *Journal of the Civil War Era* 2, no. 3 (September 2012): 369–93.

———. "Unwriting the Freedom Narrative: A Review Essay." *Journal of Southern History* 82, no. 2 (May 2016): 377–94.

Engs, Robert F. *Freedom's First Generation: Black Hampton, Virginia, 1861–1890*. New York: Fordham University Press, 2004.

Escott, Paul D. "The Art and Science of Reading WPA Slave Narratives." In *The Slave's Narrative*, edited by Charles T. Davis and Henry Louis Gates Jr., 40–48. New York: Oxford University Press, 1985.

———. *Slavery Remembered: A Record of Twentieth-Century Slave Narratives*. Chapel Hill: University of North Carolina Press, 1979.

Farland, Maria. "W. E. B. DuBois, Anthropometric Science, and the Limits of Racial Uplift." *American Quarterly* 58, no. 4 (December 2006): 1017–44.

Farmer-Kaiser, Mary. *Freedwomen and the Freedmen's Bureau: Race, Gender, and Public Policy in the Age of Emancipation*. New York: Fordham University Press, 2010.

Farmer-Paellmann, Deadria C. "Excerpt from *Black Exodus*." In *Should America Pay? Slavery and the Raging Debate on Reparations*, edited by Raymond Winbush, 22–31. New York: Amistad, 2003.

Faust, Drew Gilpin. *This Republic of Suffering: Death and the American Civil War*. New York: Vintage, 2008.

Fede, Andrew. "Legitimized Violent Slave Abuse in the American South, 1619–1865: A Case Study of Law and Social Change in Six Southern States." *American Journal of Legal History* 29, no. 2 (April 1985): 93–150.

Fehrenbacher, Don E. *The Slaveholding Republic: An Account of the United States Government's Relations to Slavery*. New York: Oxford University Press, 2001.

Feimster, Crystal N. *Southern Horrors: Women and the Politics of Rape and Lynching*. Cambridge, Mass.: Harvard University Press, 2009.

Fett, Sharla M. *Working Cures: Healing, Health, and Power on Southern Slave Plantations*. Chapel Hill: University of North Carolina Press, 2002.

Field, Kendra T. *Growing Up with the Country: Family, Race, and Nation after the Civil War*. New Haven, CT: Yale University Press, 2018.

Fields, Barbara J. "Ideology and Race in American History." In *Region, Race, and Reconstruction: Essays in Honor of C. Vann Woodward*, edited by J. Morgan Kousser and James M. McPherson, 143–77. New York: Oxford University Press, 1982.

Finkenbine, Roy E. "Belinda's Petition: Reparations for Slavery in Revolutionary Massachusetts." *William and Mary Quarterly* 64, no. 1 (2007): 95–104.

———. "Wendell Phillips and 'The Negro's Claim': A Neglected Reparations Document." *Massachusetts Historical Review* 7 (2005): 105–19.

Finley, Randy. "In War's Wake: Health Care and Arkansas Freedmen, 1863–1868." *Arkansas Historical Quarterly* 51, no. 2 (Summer 1992): 135–63.

Fitzgerald, Michael W. "Emancipation and Military Pacification: The Freedmen's Bureau and Social Control in Alabama." In *The Freedmen's Bureau and Reconstruction: Reconsiderations*, edited by Paul A. Cimbala and Randall M. Miller, 45–66. New York: Fordham University Press, 1999.

———. *The Union League Movement in the Deep South: Politics and Agricultural Change during Reconstruction*. Baton Rouge: Louisiana State University Press, 2000.

Fleming, Walter L. *Ex-Slaves Pension Frauds*. Baton Rouge: Ortlier's Printing House, 1910.

Flynn, Charles L., Jr. *White Land, Black Labor: Caste and Class in Late Nineteenth-Century Georgia*. Baton Rouge: Louisiana State University Press, 1983.

Foner, Eric. *The Fiery Trial: Abraham Lincoln and American Slavery*. New York: W. W. Norton, 2010.

———. *Freedom's Lawmakers: A Directory of Black Officeholders during Reconstruction*. Baton Rouge: Louisiana State University Press, 1993.

———. *Reconstruction: America's Unfinished Revolution, 1863–1877*. Updated ed. New York: HarperPerennial Modern Classics, 2014.

———. *The Second Founding: How the Civil War and Reconstruction Remade the Constitution*. New York: W. W. Norton, 2019.

Foster, Gaines M. *Ghosts of the Confederacy: Defeat, the Lost Cause, and the Emergence of the New South, 1865–1913*. New York: Oxford University Press, 1987.

———. "The Limitations of Federal Health Care for Freedmen, 1862–1868." *Journal of Southern History* 48, no. 3 (August 1982): 349–72.

Foucault, Michel. *Discipline and Punish: The Birth of the Prison*. Translated by Alan Sheridan. 2nd ed. New York: Vintage, 1995.

———. *The History of Sexuality, Vol. 1: An Introduction*. Translated by Robert Hurley. New York: Vintage, 1990.

———. *Security, Territory, Population: Lectures at the Collège de France, 1977–78*. Edited by Michel Senellart et al. New York: Picador, 2007.

Fox, Cybelle. *Three Worlds of Relief: Race, Immigration, and the American Welfare State from the Progressive Era to the New Deal*. Princeton, N.J.: Princeton University Press, 2012.

Fox-Amato, Matthew. *Exposing Slavery: Photography, Human Bondage, and the Birth of Modern Visual Politics in America*. New York: Oxford University Press, 2019.

Frank, Thomas. *The People, No: A Brief History of Anti-Populism*. New York: Metropolitan Books, 2020.

Franke, Katherine M. "Becoming a Citizen: Reconstruction Era Regulation of African American Marriages." *Yale Journal of Law and the Humanities* 11, no. 2 (January 1999): 251–309.

———. *Repair: Redeeming the Promise of Abolition*. Chicago: Haymarket Books, 2019.

Frankel, Noralee. *Freedom's Women: Black Women and Families in Civil War Era Mississippi*. Bloomington: Indiana University Press, 1999.

Frankel, Oz. *States of Inquiry: Social Investigations and Print Culture in Nineteenth-Century Britain and the United States*. Baltimore: Johns Hopkins University Press, 2006.

Fraser, Nancy, and Linda Gordon. "Contract versus Charity: Why Is There No Social Citizenship in the United States?" *Socialist Review* 22, no. 3 (July–September 1992): 45–68.

Frederickson, George M. *The Inner Civil War: Northern Intellectuals and the Crisis of the Union*. New York: Harper & Row, 1965.

Fuke, Richard Paul. "Planters, Apprenticeship, and Forced Labor: The Black Family under Pressure in Post-emancipation Maryland." *Agricultural History* 62, no. 4 (Autumn 1988): 54–74.

Gaither, Gerald H. *Blacks and the Populist Movement: Ballots and Bigotry in the New South*. Rev. ed. Tuscaloosa: University of Alabama Press, 2005.

Gamble, Vanessa Northington. *Making a Place for Ourselves: The Black Hospital Movement, 1920–1945*. New York: Oxford University Press, 1995.

Gannon, Barbara A. *The Won Cause: Black and White Comradeship in the Grand Army of the Republic*. Chapel Hill: University of North Carolina Press, 2011.

Genetin-Pilawa, C. Joseph. *Crooked Paths to Allotment: The Fight over Federal Indian Policy after the Civil War*. Chapel Hill: University of North Carolina Press, 2012.

Gerteis, Joseph. *Class and the Color Line: Interracial Class Coalition in the Knights of Labor and the Populist Movement*. Durham, N.C.: Duke University Press, 2007.

Gerteis, Louis. *From Contraband to Freedman: Federal Policy toward Southern Blacks, 1861–1865*. Westport, Conn.: Greenwood, 1973.

Giddings, Paula J. *Ida: A Sword among Lions: Ida B. Wells and the Campaign against Lynching*. New York: HarperCollins, 2008.

Giesberg, Judith Ann. *Civil War Sisterhood: The U.S. Sanitary Commission and Women's Politics in Transition*. Rev. ed. Boston: Northeastern University Press, 2006.

Gilmore, Glenda Elizabeth. *Defying Dixie: The Radical Roots of Civil Rights, 1919–1950*. New York: W. W. Norton, 2009.

Glasson, William H. "Federal and Confederate Pensions in the South." *South Atlantic Quarterly* 9 (1910): 280–85.

———. *Federal Military Pensions in the United States*. New York: Oxford University Press, 1918.

———. *History of Military Pension Legislation in the United States*. New York: Columbia University Press, 1900.

———. "The South's Care for Her Confederate Veterans." *American Monthly Review of Reviews* 36 (1907): 40–47.

Glatthaar, Joseph T. *Forged in Battle: The Civil War Alliance of Black Soldiers and White Officers*. Baton Rouge: Louisiana State University Press, 1990.

Glymph, Thavolia. *Out of the House of Bondage: The Transformation of the Plantation Household*. New York: Cambridge University Press, 2008.

———. *The Women's Fight: The Civil War's Battles for Home, Freedom, and Nation*. Chapel Hill: University of North Carolina Press, 2020.

Glymph, Thavolia, and John J. Kushma, eds. *Essays on the Postbellum Southern Economy*. College Station: Texas A&M University Press, 1985.

Goldberg, Chad Alan. *Citizens and Paupers: Relief, Rights, and Race from the Freedmen's Bureau to Workfare*. Chicago: University of Chicago Press, 2007.

Goodwyn, Lawrence C. *Democratic Promise: The Populist Moment in America*. New York: Oxford University Press, 1976.

Gordon, Linda. *Pitied but Not Entitled: Single Mothers and the History of Welfare, 1890–1935*. New York: Free Press, 1994.

Gordon, Sarah Barringer. *The Mormon Question: Polygamy and Constitutional Conflict in Nineteenth-Century America*. Chapel Hill: University of North Carolina Press, 2002.

Goring, Darlene C. "The History of Slave Marriage in the United States." *John Marshall Law Review* 39, no. 2 (Winter 2006): 299–347.

Gorman, Kathleen. "Confederate Pensions as Southern Social Welfare." In *Before the New Deal: Social Welfare in the South, 1830–1930*, edited by Elna C. Green, 24–39. Athens: University of Georgia Press, 1999.

Gosse, Van. *The First Reconstruction: Black Politics in America from the Revolution to the Civil War*. Chapel Hill: University of North Carolina Press, 2021.

Graeber, David. *The Utopia of Rules: On Technology, Stupidity, and the Secret Joys of Bureaucracy*. Brooklyn, N.Y.: Melville House, 2015.

Grandin, Greg. *The End of the Myth: From the Frontier to the Border Wall in the Mind of America*. New York: Metropolitan Books, 2020.

Grant, Susan-Mary. "Reconstructing the National Body: Masculinity, Disability, and Race in the American Civil War." *Proceedings of the British Academy* 154 (2008): 273–317.

Green, Elna C. "Protecting Confederate Soldiers and Mothers: Pensions, Gender, and the Welfare State in the U.S. South, a Case Study from Florida." *Journal of Social History* 39, no. 4 (Summer 2006): 1079–104.

Gregory, James N. *The Southern Diaspora: How the Great Migration of Black and White Southerners Transformed America*. Chapel Hill: University of North Carolina Press, 2005.

Grimsley, Mark. *The Hard Hand of War: Union Military Policy toward Southern Civilians, 1861–1865*. New York: Cambridge University Press, 1995.

Gross, Ariela J. *Double Character: Slavery and Mastery in the Antebellum Southern Courtroom*. Athens: University of Georgia Press, 2006.

Grossman, James R. *Land of Hope: Chicago, Black Southerners, and the Great Migration*. Chicago: University of Chicago Press, 1989.

Hahn, Steven. "'Extravagant Expectations' of Freedom: Rumour, Political Struggle, and the Christmas Insurrection Scare of 1865 in the American South." *Past & Present* 157 (November 1997): 122–58.

———. *A Nation under Our Feet: Black Political Struggles in the Rural South from Slavery to the Great Migration*. Cambridge, Mass.: Harvard University Press, 2003.

———. *A Nation without Borders: The United States and Its World in an Age of Civil Wars, 1830–1910*. New York: Penguin Books, 2016.

———. *The Roots of Southern Populism: Yeoman Farmers and the Transformation of the Georgia Upcountry, 1850–1890*. New York: Oxford University Press, 1983.

———. "Slave Emancipation, Indian Peoples, and the Projects of a New American Nation-State." *Journal of the Civil War Era* 3, no. 3 (September 2013): 307–30.

Hall, Jacquelyn Dowd. "The Long Civil Rights Movement and the Political Uses of the Past." *Journal of American History* 91, no. 4 (March 2005): 1233–63.

Haller, John S., Jr. *Outcasts from Evolution: Scientific Attitudes of Racial Inferiority, 1859–1900.* 2nd ed. Carbondale: Southern Illinois University Press, 1996.

———. "The Physician versus the Negro: Medical and Anthropological Concepts of Race in the Late Nineteenth Century." *Bulletin of the History of Medicine* 44, no. 2 (March–April 1970): 154–67.

Handley-Cousins, Sarah. *Bodies in Blue: Disability in the Civil War North.* Athens: University of Georgia Press, 2019.

Harmon, John Henry. *The Negro as a Business Man.* College Park, Md.: McGrath, 1969.

Harris, Abram L. *The Negro as Capitalist.* Philadelphia: American Academy of Political and Social Science, 1936.

Hasegawa, Guy R. *Mending Broken Soldiers: The Union and Confederate Programs to Supply Artificial Limbs.* Carbondale: Southern Illinois University Press, 2012.

Herd, Pamela, and Donald P. Moynihan. *Administrative Burden: Policymaking by Other Means.* New York: Russell Sage Foundation, 2019.

Hermann, Janet Sharp. *The Pursuit of a Dream.* New York: Oxford University Press, 1981.

Hild, Matthew. *Greenbackers, Knights of Labor, and Populists: Farmer-Labor Insurgency in the Late-Nineteenth-Century South.* Athens: University of Georgia Press, 2007.

Hill, Walter B., Jr. "The Ex-Slave Pension Movement: Some Historical and Genealogical Notes." *Negro History Bulletin* 59, no. 4 (October–December 1996): 1–7.

Hine, Darlene Clark. *Black Women in White: Racial Conflict and Cooperation in the Nursing Profession, 1890–1950.* Bloomington: Indiana University Press, 1989.

Hodes, Martha. *White Women, Black Men: Illicit Sex in the Nineteenth-Century South.* New Haven, Conn.: Yale University Press, 1997.

Hollandsworth, James, Jr. *The Louisiana Native Guards: The Black Military Experience during the Civil War.* Baton Rouge: Louisiana State University Press, 1995.

Holmes, William F. "The Arkansas Cotton Pickers Strike of 1891 and the Demise of the Colored Farmers's [sic] Alliance." *The Arkansas Historical Quarterly* 32, no. 2 (Summer 1973): 107–19.

———. "The Demise of the Colored Farmers' Alliance." *Journal of Southern History* 41, no. 2 (May 1975): 187–200.

Holt, Thomas. *Black over White: Negro Political Leadership in South Carolina during Reconstruction.* Urbana: University of Illinois Press, 1979.

Humphreys, Margaret. *Intensely Human: The Health of the Black Soldier in the American Civil War.* Baltimore: Johns Hopkins University Press, 2008.

———. *Malaria: Poverty, Race, and Public Health in the United States.* Baltimore: Johns Hopkins University Press, 2001.

———. *Marrow of Tragedy: The Health Crisis of the Civil War.* Baltimore: Johns Hopkins University Press, 2013.

———. *Yellow Fever and the South.* Baltimore: Johns Hopkins University Press, 1992.

Hunt, James L. *Marion Butler and American Populism.* Chapel Hill: University of North Carolina Press, 2003.

Hunter, Tera W. *Bound in Wedlock: Slave and Free Black Marriage in the Nineteenth Century.* Cambridge, Mass.: Harvard University Press, 2017.

———. *To 'Joy My Freedom: Southern Black Women's Lives and Labors after the Civil War.* Cambridge, Mass.: Harvard University Press, 1997.

Hyman, Harold M. *Era of the Oath: Northern Loyalty Tests during the Civil War and Reconstruction.* New York: Octagon Books, 1978.

Igo, Sarah. *The Known Citizen: A History of Privacy in Modern America.* Cambridge, Mass.: Harvard University Press, 2018.

Janney, Caroline E. *Remembering the Civil War: Reunion and the Limits of Reconciliation.* Chapel Hill: University of North Carolina Press, 2015.

Jaynes, Gerald David. *Branches without Roots: The Genesis of the Black Working Class in the American South, 1862–1882.* New York: Oxford University Press, 1986.

Jensen, Laura. *Patriots, Settlers, and the Origins of American Social Policy.* New York: Cambridge University Press, 2003.

Johnson, Russell L. "'Great Injustice': Social Status and the Distribution of Military Pensions after the Civil War." *Journal of the Gilded Age and Progressive Era* 10, no. 2 (April 2011): 137–60.

Johnson, Walter. *River of Dark Dreams: Slavery and Empire in the Cotton Kingdom.* Cambridge, Mass.: Harvard University Press, 2013.

———. *Soul by Soul: Life inside the Antebellum Slave Market.* Cambridge, Mass.: Harvard University Press, 1999.

Jones, Jacqueline. *Labor of Love, Labor of Sorrow: Black Women, Work, and the Family from Slavery to the Present.* Rev. ed. New York: Basic Books, 2010.

Jones, Martha S. *Birthright Citizens: A History of Race and Rights in Antebellum America.* New York: Cambridge University Press, 2018.

Kachun, Mitch. "Before the Eyes of All Nations: African-American Identity and Historical Memory at the Centennial Exposition of 1876." *Pennsylvania History* 65, no. 3 (Summer 1998): 300–323.

Kaczorowski, Robert J. "To Begin the Nation Anew: Congress, Citizenship, and Civil Rights after the Civil War." *American Historical Review* 92, no. 1 (February 1987): 45–68.

Kantrowitz, Stephen. *More Than Freedom: Fighting for Black Citizenship in a White Republic, 1829–1889.* New York: Penguin Books, 2012.

Katz, Michael B. "The American Welfare State and Social Contract in Hard Times." *Journal of Public History* 22, no. 4 (October 2010): 508–29.

———. *In the Shadow of the Poorhouse: A Social History of Welfare in America.* Rev. ed. New York: Basic Books, 1996.

Katznelson, Ira. *When Affirmative Action Was White: An Untold History of Racial Inequality in Twentieth-Century America.* New York: W. W. Norton, 2005.

Kaye, Anthony E. *Joining Places: Slave Neighborhoods in the Old South.* Chapel Hill: University of North Carolina Press, 2007.

Kazin, Michael. *The Populist Persuasion: An American History.* Rev. ed. Ithaca, N.Y.: Cornell University Press, 1998.

———. *War against War: The American Fight for Peace, 1914–1918.* New York: Simon and Schuster, 2017.

Keith, LeeAnna. *The Colfax Massacre: The Untold Story of Black Power, White Terror, and the Death of Reconstruction.* New York: Oxford University Press, 2008.

Keller, Morton. *Affairs of State: Public Life in Late Nineteenth-Century America.* Cambridge, Mass.: Harvard University Press, 1977.

Kelley, Blair L. M. *Right to Ride: Streetcar Boycotts and African American Citizenship in the Era of* Plessy v. Ferguson. Chapel Hill: University of North Carolina Press, 2010.

Kelley, Robin D. G. *Hammer and Hoe: Alabama Communists during the Great Depression.* 2nd ed. Chapel Hill: University of North Carolina Press, 2015.

Kelly, Brian. "Black Laborers, the Republican Party, and the Crisis of Reconstruction in Lowcountry South Carolina." *International Review of Social History* 51, no. 3 (December 2006): 375–414.

———. "Class, Factionalism, and the Radical Retreat: Black Laborers and the Republican Party in South Carolina, 1865–1900." In *After Slavery: Race, Labor, and Citizenship in the Reconstruction South,* edited by Bruce E. Baker and Brian Kelly, 199–220. Gainesville: University Press of Florida, 2014.

———. "Labor and Place: The Contours of Grassroots Black Mobilization in Reconstruction South Carolina." *Journal of Peasant Studies* 35, no. 4 (October 2008): 653–87.

Kelly, Patrick J. *Creating a National Home: Building the Veterans' Welfare State, 1860–1900.* Cambridge, Mass.: Harvard University Press, 1997.

Kendi, Ibram X. *Stamped from the Beginning: The Definitive History of Racist Ideas in America.* New York: Bold Type Books, 2017.

Kennington, Kelly M. *In the Shadow of Dred Scott: St. Louis Freedom Suits and the Legal Culture of Slavery in Antebellum America.* Athens: University of Georgia Press, 2017.

Kerber, Linda K. "The Stateless as the Citizen's Other: A View from the United States." *The American Historical Review* 112, no. 1 (February 2007): 1–34.

Kessler-Harris, Alice. "In the Nation's Image: The Gendered Limits of Social Citizenship in the Depression Era." *Journal of American History* 86, no. 3 (1999): 1251–79.

———. *In Pursuit of Equity: Women, Men, and the Quest for Economic Citizenship in Twentieth-Century America.* New York: Oxford University Press, 2001.

Kettner, James H. *The Development of American Citizenship, 1608–1870.* Chapel Hill: University of North Carolina Press, 1978.

Klingberg, Frank W. *The Southern Claims Commission.* Berkeley: University of California Press, 1955.

———. "The Southern Claims Commission: A Postwar Agency in Operation." *Mississippi Valley Historical Review* 32, no. 2 (September 1945): 195–214.

Kousser, J. Morgan. "Before *Plessy,* before *Brown*: The Development of the Law of Racial Integration in Louisiana and Kansas." In *Toward a Usable Past: Liberty under State Constitutions,* edited by Paul Finkelman and Stephen E. Gottlieb, 213–70. Athens: University of Georgia Press, 2009.

———. *The Shaping of Southern Politics: Suffrage Restriction and the Establishment of the One-Party South, 1880–1910.* New Haven, Conn.: Yale University Press, 1974.

Krauthamer, Barbara. *Black Slaves, Indian Masters: Slavery, Emancipation, and Citizenship in the Native American South.* Chapel Hill: University of North Carolina Press, 2013.

Kretz, Dale. "Pensions and Protest: Former Slaves and the Reconstructed American State." *Journal of the Civil War Era* 7, no. 3 (September 2017): 425–45.

———. "People, Not 'Voices' or 'Bodies,' Make History." *Jacobin* (June 18, 2021).

———. "The Southern Division: Freedpeople, Pensions, and Federal State Building in the Post-Confederate South." In *Revolutions and Reconstructions: Black Politics in the Long Nineteenth Century*, edited by David Waldstreicher and Van Gosse, 198–215. Philadelphia: University of Pennsylvania Press, 2020.

Krowl, Michelle A. "'Her Just Dues': Civil War Pensions of African American Women in Virginia." In *Negotiating Boundaries of Southern Womanhood: Dealing with the Powers That Be*, edited by Janet L. Coryell, 48–70. Columbia: University of Missouri Press, 2000.

Landrum, Shane. "The State's Big Family Bible: Birth Certificates, Personal Identity, and Citizenship in the United States, 1840–1950." PhD diss., Brandeis University, 2014.

Lang, Andrew F. *In the Wake of War: Military Occupation, Emancipation, and Civil War America*. Baton Rouge: Louisiana State University Press, 2017.

Lanza, Michael F. "'One of the Most Appreciated Labors of the Bureau': The Freedmen's Bureau and the Southern Homestead Act." In *Freedmen's Bureau and Reconstruction: Reconsiderations*, edited by Paul A. Cimbala and Randall M. Miller, 67–92. New York: Fordham University Press, 1999.

Laski, Gregory. *Untimely Democracy: The Politics of Progress after Slavery*. New York: Oxford University Press, 2019.

Lawrance, Benjamin N., and Jacqueline Stevens, eds. *Citizenship in Question: Evidentiary Birthright and Statelessness*. Durham, N.C.: Duke University Press, 2017.

Lears, Jackson. *Rebirth of a Nation: The Making of Modern America, 1877–1920*. New York: HarperCollins, 2009.

Lee, Susanna Michele. *Claiming the Union: Citizenship in the Post–Civil War South*. New York: Cambridge University Press, 2014.

LeFlouria, Talitha L. *Chained in Silence: Black Women and Convict Labor in the New South*. Chapel Hill: University of North Carolina Press, 2016.

Levin, Kevin M. *Searching for Black Confederates: The Civil War's Most Persistent Myth*. Chapel Hill: University of North Carolina Press, 2019.

Levine, Bruce. *Confederate Emancipation: Southern Plans to Free and Arm Slaves during the Civil War*. New York: Oxford University Press, 2006.

Levine, Lawrence. *Black Culture and Black Consciousness: Afro-American Folk Thought from Slavery to Freedom*. 30th anniversary ed. New York: Oxford University Press, 2007.

Levy, Jonathan. *Freaks of Fortune: The Emerging World of Capitalism and Risk in America*. Cambridge, Mass.: Harvard University Press, 2014.

Lichtenstein, Alex. *Twice the Work of Free Labor: The Political Economy of Convict Labor in the New South*. New York: Verso, 1996.

Lieberman, Robert C. "The Freedmen's Bureau and the Politics of Institutional Structure." *Social Science History* 18, no. 3 (Autumn 1994): 405–37.

———. "Race, Institutions, and the Administration of Social Policy." *Social Science History* 19, no. 4 (Winter 1995): 511–42.

———. *Shifting the Color Line: Race and the American Welfare State*. Cambridge, Mass.: Harvard University Press, 1998.

Litwack, Leon F. *Been in the Storm So Long: The Aftermath of Slavery*. New York: Vintage Books, 1979.

———. *Trouble in Mind: Black Southerners in the Age of Jim Crow*. New York: Vintage Books, 1998.

Logan, Rayford W. *The Negro in American Life and Thought: The Nadir, 1877–1901*. New York: Dial, 1954.

Logue, Larry M., and Peter Blanck. "'Benefit of the Doubt': African-American Civil War Veterans and Pensions." *Journal of Interdisciplinary History* 38, no. 3 (Winter 2008): 377–99.

———. *Heavy Laden: Union Veterans, Psychological Illness, and Suicide*. New York: Cambridge University Press, 2018.

———. *Race, Ethnicity, and Disability: Veterans and Benefits in Post–Civil War America*. New York: Cambridge University Press, 2010.

Long, Gretchen. *Doctoring Freedom: The Politics of African American Medical Care in Slavery and Emancipation*. Chapel Hill: University of North Carolina Press, 2014.

Longmore, Paul K., and Lauri Umansky. "Disability History: From the Margins to the Mainstream." In *The New Disability History: American Perspectives*, edited by Paul K. Longmore and Lauri Umansky, 1–32. New York: New York University Press, 2001.

Mandle, Jay R. *The Roots of Black Poverty: The Southern Plantation Economy after the Civil War*. Durham, N.C.: Duke University Press, 1978.

Manning, Chandra. "Emancipation as State Building from the Inside Out." In *Beyond Freedom: Disrupting the History of Emancipation*, edited by David W. Blight and Jim Downs, 60–74. Athens: University of Georgia Press, 2017.

———. *Troubled Refuge: Struggling for Freedom in the Civil War*. New York: Alfred A. Knopf, 2016.

———. "Working for Citizenship in Civil War Contraband Camps." *Journal of the Civil War Era* 4, no. 2 (June 2014): 172–204.

Marten, James. *America's Corporal: James Tanner in War and Peace*. Athens: University of Georgia Press, 2014.

———. *Sing Not War: The Lives of Union and Confederate Veterans in Gilded Age America*. Chapel Hill: University of North Carolina Press, 2011.

———. "Those Who Have Borne the Battle: Civil War Veterans, Pension Advocacy, and Politics." *Marquette Law Review* 93, no. 4 (Summer 2010): 1407–13.

Martinez, Jaime Amanda. *Confederate Slave Impressment in the Upper South*. Chapel Hill: University of North Carolina Press, 2013.

Mashaw, Jerry L. *Creating the Administrative Constitution: The Lost One Hundred Years of American Administrative Law*. New Haven, Conn.: Yale University Press, 2012.

———. "Federal Administration and Administrative Law in the Gilded Age." *Yale Law Journal* 119, no. 7 (May 2010): 1362–472.

Mason, Gilbert R., and James Patterson Smith. *Beaches, Blood, and Ballots: A Black Doctor's Civil Rights Struggle*. Jackson: University Press of Mississippi, 2000.

Masur, Kate. *An Example for All the Land: Emancipation and the Struggle over Equality in Washington, D.C.* Chapel Hill: University of North Carolina Press, 2012.

———. *Until Justice Be Done: America's First Civil Rights Movement, from the Revolution to Reconstruction*. New York: W. W. Norton, 2021.

Mathisen, Erik. *The Loyal Republic: Traitors, Slaves, and the Remaking of Citizenship in Civil War America.* Chapel Hill: University of North Carolina Press, 2018.

Mauldin, Erin Stewart. *Unredeemed Land: An Environmental History of Civil War and Emancipation in the Cotton South.* New York: Oxford University Press, 2018.

McClintock, Megan J. "Civil War Pensions and the Reconstruction of Union Families." *Journal of American History* 83, no. 2 (September 1996): 456–80.

McConnell, Stuart. *Glorious Contentment: The Grand Army of the Republic, 1865–1900.* Chapel Hill: University of North Carolina Press, 1992.

McCurry, Stephanie. *Confederate Reckoning: Power and Politics in the Civil War South.* Cambridge, Mass.: Harvard University Press, 2012.

McFeely, William S. *Frederick Douglass.* New York: W. W. Norton, 1991.

———. *Yankee Stepfather: General O. O. Howard and the Freedmen.* New Haven, Conn.: Yale University Press, 1968.

McGuire, Danielle L. *At the Dark End of the Street: Black Women, Rape, and Resistance—A New History of the Civil Rights Movement from Rosa Parks to the Rise of Black Power.* New York: Vintage, 2011.

McKinley, Charles, and Robert W. Frase. *Launching Social Security: A Capture-and-Record Account 1935–1937.* Madison: University of Wisconsin Press, 1970.

McMath, Robert C., Jr. *American Populism: A Social History 1877–1898.* New York: Hill & Wang, 1993.

McMillen, Neil R. *Dark Journey: Black Mississippians in the Age of Jim Crow.* Urbana: University of Illinois Press, 1990.

McMurry, Donald L. "The Bureau of Pensions during the Administration of President Harrison." *Mississippi Valley Historical Review* 13, no. 3 (December 1926): 343–64.

———. "The Political Significance of the Pension Question, 1885–1897." *Mississippi Valley Historical Review* 9, no. 1 (June 1922): 19–36.

McPherson, James M. "Afterward." In *Freedmen's Bureau and Reconstruction: Reconsiderations,* edited by Paul A. Cimbala and Randall M. Miller, 343–49. New York: Fordham University Press, 1999.

Menand, Louis. *The Metaphysical Club: A Story of Ideas in America.* New York: Farrar, Straus and Giroux, 2002.

Mettler, Suzanne. *Dividing Citizens: Gender and Federalism in New Deal Public Policy.* Ithaca, N.Y.: Cornell University Press, 1998.

Metzger, Gillian E. "Administrative Constitutionalism." *Texas Law Review* 91, no. 7 (June 2013): 1897–935.

———. "Ordinary Administrative Law as Constitutional Common Law." *Columbia Law Review* 110, no. 2 (March 2010): 479–536.

Milewski, Melissa. *Litigating across the Color Line: Civil Cases between Black and White Southerners from the End of Slavery to Civil Rights.* New York: Oxford University Press, 2018.

———. "Taking Former Masters to Court: Civil Cases between Former Masters and Slaves in the US South, 1865–1899." *Slavery & Abolition* 40, no. 2 (June 2019): 240–55.

Miller, Brian Craig. *Empty Sleeves: Amputation in the Civil War South.* Athens: University of Georgia Press, 2015.

Miller, Floyd J. "Black Protest and White Leadership: A Note on the Colored Farmers' Alliance." *Phylon* 33 (Summer 1972): 169–74.

Mink, Gwendolyn. "The Lady and the Tramp: Gender, Race, and the Origins of the American Welfare State." In *Women, the State, and Welfare*, edited by Linda Gordon, 92–121. Madison: University of Wisconsin Press, 1990.

Mitchell, Mary Niall. *Raising Freedom's Child: Black Children and Visions of the Future after Slavery*. New York: New York University Press, 2008.

Mitchell, Michele. *Righteous Propagation: African Americans and the Politics of Racial Destiny after Reconstruction*. Chapel Hill: University of North Carolina Press, 2004.

Moore, James T. "Black Militancy in Readjuster Virginia, 1879–1883." *Journal of Southern History* 41, no. 2 (1975): 167–86.

Morris, Thomas D. *Southern Slavery and the Law, 1619–1860*. Chapel Hill: University of North Carolina Press, 1996.

Munden, Kenneth W., and Henry Putney Beers. *The Union: A Guide to Federal Archives Relating to the Civil War*. Washington, D.C.: National Archives and Records Administration, 1998.

Nackenoff, Carol, and Julie Novkov. "Introduction: Statebuilding in the Progressive Era: A Continuing Dilemma in American Political Development." In *Statebuilding from the Margins: Between Reconstruction and the New Deal*, edited by Carol Nackenoff and Julie Novkov, 1–31. Philadelphia: University of Pennsylvania Press, 2014.

Nelson, Barbara. "The Origins of the Two-Channel Welfare State: Workmen's Compensation and Mothers' Aid." In *Women, the State, and Welfare*, edited by Linda Gordon, 123–51. Madison: University of Wisconsin Press, 1990.

Nembhard, Jessica Gordon. *Collective Courage: A History of African American Cooperative Economic Thought and Practice*. University Park: Pennsylvania State University Press, 2014.

Nieman, Donald G. "Andrew Johnson, the Freedmen's Bureau, and the Problem of Equal Rights, 1865–1866." *Journal of Southern History* 44 (August 1978): 399–420.

———. "The Freedmen's Bureau and the Mississippi Black Code." *Journal of Mississippi History* 40 (1978): 91–118.

———. *To Set the Law in Motion: The Freedmen's Bureau and the Legal Rights of Blacks, 1865–1868*. Millwood, N.Y.: KTO, 1979.

———, ed. *From Slavery to Sharecropping: White Land and Black Labor in the Rural South, 1865–1900*. New York: Garland, 1994.

Novak, William J. "The Legal Transformation of Citizenship in Nineteenth-Century America." In *The Democratic Experiment: New Directions in American Political History*, edited by Meg Jacobs, William J. Novak, and Julian E. Zelizer, 85–119. Princeton, N.J.: Princeton University Press, 2003.

———. "The Myth of the 'Weak' American State." *American Historical Review* 113, no. 3 (June 2008): 752–72.

———. *The People's Welfare: Law and Regulation in Nineteenth-Century America*. Chapel Hill: University of North Carolina Press, 1996.

O'Donovan. Susan Eva. *Becoming Free in the Cotton South*. Cambridge, Mass.: Harvard University Press, 2007.

———. "Mapping Freedom's Terrain: The Political and Productive Landscapes of Wilmington, North Carolina." In *After Slavery: Race, Labor, and Citizenship in the Reconstruction South*, edited by Bruce E. Baker and Brian Kelly, 179–82. Gainesville: University Press of Florida, 2014.

————. "Writing Slavery into Freedom's Story." In *Beyond Freedom: Disrupting the History of Emancipation*, edited by David W. Blight and Jim Downs, 26–38. Athens: University of Georgia Press, 2017.

Oakes, James. *Freedom National: The Destruction of Slavery in the United States, 1861–1865*. New York: W. W. Norton, 2013.

Oliver, John William. *History of the Civil War Military Pensions, 1861–1885*. Bulletin of the University of Wisconsin. No. 844, History Series. Madison: University of Wisconsin Press, 1917.

Orloff, Ann Shola. *The Politics of Pensions: A Comparative Analysis of Britain, Canada, and the United States, 1880–1940*. Madison: University of Wisconsin Press, 1993.

Ortiz, Paul. *Emancipation Betrayed: The Hidden History of Black Organizing and White Violence in Florida from Reconstruction to the Bloody Election of 1920*. Berkeley: University of California Press, 2005.

Oshinsky, David M. *Worse Than Slavery: Parchman Farm and the Ordeal of Jim Crow Justice*. New York: Free Press, 1996.

Osthaus, Carl R. *Freedmen, Philanthropy, and Fraud: A History of the Freedmen's Savings Bank*. Urbana: University of Illinois Press, 1976.

Oubre, Claude F. *Forty Acres and a Mule: The Freedmen's Bureau and Black Land Ownership*. 2nd ed. Baton Rouge: Louisiana State University Press, 2012.

Painter, Nell Irvin. *Exodusters: Black Migration to Kansas after Reconstruction*. New York: Knopf, 1976.

————. *Standing at Armageddon: A Grassroots History of the Progressive Era*. Rev. ed. New York: W. W. Norton, 2008.

Parenti, Christian. *The Soft Cage: Surveillance in America from Slavery to the War on Terror*. New York: Basic Books, 2003.

Parrillo, Nicholas R. *Against the Profit Motive: The Salary Revolution in American Government, 1780–1940*. New Haven, Conn.: Yale University Press, 2013.

————. "Introduction: Jerry L. Mashaw's Creative Tension with the Field of Administrative Law." In *Administrative Law from the Inside Out: Essays on Themes in the Work of Jerry L. Mashaw*, edited by Nicholas R. Parrillo, 1–35. New York: Cambridge University Press, 2018.

Parsons, Elaine Frantz. *Ku-Klux: The Birth of the Klan during Reconstruction*. Chapel Hill: University of North Carolina Press, 2015.

Pearson, Charles Chilton. *The Readjuster Movement in Virginia*. New Haven, Conn.: Yale University Press, 1917.

Pearson, Susan J. "'Age Ought to Be a Fact': The Campaign against Child Labor and the Rise of the Birth Certificate." *Journal of American History* 101, no. 4 (March 2015): 1144–65.

————. *The Birth Certificate: An American History*. Chapel Hill: University of North Carolina Press, 2021.

————. "A New Birth of Regulation: The State of the State after the Civil War." *Journal of the Civil War Era* 5, no. 3 (September 2015): 422–39.

————. *The Rights of the Defenseless: Protecting Animals and Children in Gilded Age America*. Chicago: University of Chicago Press, 2011.

Peirce, Paul Skeels. *The Freedmen's Bureau: A Chapter in the History of Reconstruction*. New York: Haskell House, 1971. First published in 1904 by State University of Iowa.

Penningroth, Dylan C. *The Claims of Kinfolk: African American Property and Community in the Nineteenth-Century South*. Chapel Hill: University of North Carolina Press, 2003.

———. "Slavery, Freedom, and Social Claims to Property among African Americans in Liberty County, Georgia, 1850–1880." *Journal of American History* 84, no. 2 (September 1997): 405–35.

Perman, Michael. *Pursuit of Unity: A Political History of the American South*. Chapel Hill: University of North Carolina Press, 2010.

———. *The Road to Redemption: Southern Politics, 1869–1879*. Chapel Hill: University of North Carolina Press, 1985.

———. *Struggle for Mastery: Disfranchisement in the South, 1888–1908*. Chapel Hill: University of North Carolina Press, 2001.

Perrone, Giuliana. "'Back into the Days of Slavery': Slavery, Citizenship, and the Black Family in the Reconstruction Era Courtroom." *Law and History Review*, 37, no. 1 (February 2019): 125–61.

———. *The Problem of Emancipation in the Age of Slavery: Law and Abolition after the U.S. Civil War* (forthcoming).

———. "What, to the Law, Is the Former Slave?" *Slavery and Abolition* 40, no 2. (June 2019): 256–70.

Perry, Miranda Booker. "The Prospect of Justice: African-American Redress and the Ex-Slave Pension Movement, 1865–1937." PhD diss., Howard University, 2012.

Piven, Frances Fox, and Richard A. Cloward. *Poor People's Movements: Why They Succeed, How They Fail*. New York: Vintage Books, 1979.

Pohl, Lynn Marie. "African American Southerners and White Physicians: Medical Care at the Turn of the Twentieth Century." *Bulletin of the History of Medicine* 86, no. 2 (Summer 2012): 178–205.

Poole, Mary. *The Segregated Origins of Social Security: African Americans and the Welfare State*. Chapel Hill: University of North Carolina Press, 2006.

Postel, Charles. *Equality: An American Dilemma, 1866–1896*. New York: Farrar, Straus and Giroux, 2019.

———. *The Populist Vision*. New York: Oxford University Press, 2007.

Powell, Lawrence N. *New Masters: Northern Planters during the Civil War and Reconstruction*. New Haven, Conn.: Yale University Press, 1980.

Quadagno, Jill. *The Color of Welfare: How Racism Undermined the War on Poverty*. New York: Oxford University Press, 1996.

———. *The Transformation of Old Age Security: Class and Politics in the American Welfare State*. Chicago: University of Chicago Press, 1988.

———. "Welfare Capitalism and the Social Security Act of 1935." *American Sociological Review* 49, no. 5 (October 1984): 632–47.

Quigley, Paul, ed. *The Civil War and the Transformation of American Citizenship*. Baton Rouge: Louisiana State University Press, 2018.

Rabinowitz, Howard N. "From Exclusion to Segregation: Health and Welfare Services for Southern Blacks, 1865–1890." *Social Service Review* 48, no. 3 (September 1974): 327–54.

———. *Race Relations in the Urban South, 1865–1890*. New York: Oxford University Press, 1978.

Ranney, Joseph A. *In the Wake of Slavery: Civil War, Civil Rights, and the Reconstruction of Southern Law.* Westport, Conn.: Praeger, 2006.

Ransom, Roger L. "Reconstructing Reconstruction: Options and Limitations to Federal Policies on Land Distribution in 1866–67." *Civil War History* 51, no. 4 (December 2005): 364–77.

Ransom, Roger L., and Richard Sutch. *One Kind of Freedom: The Economic Consequences of Emancipation.* 2nd ed. New York: Cambridge University Press, 2000.

Reed, Adolph, Jr., and Merlin Chowkwanyun. "Race, Class, Crisis: The Discourse of Racial Disparity and Its Analytical Discontents," *Socialist Register* 48 (2012): 149–75.

Regosin, Elizabeth. *Freedom's Promise: Ex-Slave Families and Citizenship in the Age of Emancipation.* Charlottesville: University Press of Virginia, 2002.

Regosin, Elizabeth A., and Donald R. Shaffer. *Voices of Emancipation: Understanding Slavery, the Civil War, and Reconstruction through the U.S. Pension Bureau Files.* New York: New York University Press, 2008.

Reidy, Joseph P. *From Slavery to Agrarian Capitalism in the Cotton Plantation South: Central Georgia, 1800–1880.* Chapel Hill: University of North Carolina Press, 1992.

———. *Illusions of Emancipation: The Pursuit of Freedom and Equality in the Twilight of Slavery.* Chapel Hill: University of North Carolina Press, 2019.

Resch, John Phillips. *Suffering Soldiers: Revolutionary War Veterans, Moral Sentiment, and Political Culture in the Early Republic.* Amherst: University of Massachusetts Press, 1999.

Richardson, Heather Cox. *The Death of Reconstruction: Race, Labor, and Politics in the Post–Civil War North, 1865–1901.* Cambridge, Mass.: Harvard University Press, 2001.

———. *West from Appomattox: The Reconstruction of America after the Civil War.* New Haven, Conn.: Yale University Press, 2007.

Richardson, Joe M. *Christian Reconstruction: The American Missionary Association and Southern Blacks, 1861–1890.* Tuscaloosa: University of Alabama Press, 1986.

Ring, Natalie J. *The Problem South: Region, Empire, and the New Liberal State, 1880–1930.* Athens: University of Georgia Press, 2012.

Roberts, Alaina E. *I've Been Here All the While: Black Freedom on Native Land.* Philadelphia: University of Pennsylvania Press, 2021.

Rockwell, Stephen J. *Indian Affairs and the Administrative State in the Nineteenth Century.* New York: Cambridge University Press, 2010.

Rodems, Richard, and H. Luke Shaefer, "Left Out: Policy Diffusion and the Exclusion of Black Workers from Unemployment Insurance." *Social Science History* 40, no. 3 (Fall 2016): 385–404.

Roediger, David. *Seizing Freedom: Slave Emancipation and Liberty for All.* New York: Verso, 2014.

Rose, Sarah F. *No Right to Be Idle: The Invention of Disability, 1840s–1930s.* Chapel Hill: University of North Carolina Press, 2017.

Rose, Willie Lee. *Rehearsal for Reconstruction: The Port Royal Experiment.* New York: Oxford University Press, 1964.

Rosen, Hannah. *Terror in the Heart of Freedom: Citizenship, Sexual Violence, and the Meaning of Race in the Postemancipation South.* Chapel Hill: University of North Carolina Press, 2009.

Rosenthal, Caitlyn. *Accounting for Slavery: Mastery and Management*. Cambridge, Mass.: Harvard University Press, 2018.

Russell, Marta, and Ravi Malhotra. "Capitalism and the Disability Rights Movement." In *Capitalism and Disability: Selected Writings by Marta Russell*, edited by Keith Rosenthal, 1–10. Chicago: Haymarket Books, 2019.

Ruswick, Brent. *Almost Worthy: The Poor, Paupers, and the Science of Charity in America, 1877–1917*. Bloomington: Indiana University Press, 2013.

Samito, Christian G. *Becoming American under Fire: Irish Americans, African Americans, and the Politics of Citizenship during the Civil War*. Ithaca, N.Y.: Cornell University Press, 2009.

Sanders, Heywood T. "Paying for the 'Bloody Shirt': The Politics of Civil War Pensions." In *Political Benefits: Empirical Studies of American Public Programs*, edited by Barry S. Rundquist, 137–59. Lexington, Mass.: Lexington Books, 1980.

Savage, Kirk. *Standing Soldiers, Kneeling Slaves: Race, War, and Monument in Nineteenth-Century America*. Princeton, N.J.: Princeton University Press, 1997.

Saville, Julie. *The Work of Reconstruction: From Slave to Wage Laborer in South Carolina, 1860–1870*. New York: Cambridge University Press, 1994.

Savitt, Todd L. "Entering a White Profession: Black Physicians in the New South, 1880–1920." *Bulletin of the History of Medicine* 61, no. 4 (Winter 1987): 507–40.

———. *Medicine and Slavery: The Diseases and Health Care of Blacks in Antebellum Virginia*. New ed. Urbana: University of Illinois Press, 2002.

———. *Race and Medicine in Nineteenth- and Early-Twentieth-Century America*. Kent, Ohio: Kent State University Press, 2007.

Schermerhorn, Calvin J. *Money over Mastery, Family over Freedom: Slavery in the Antebellum Upper South*. Baltimore: Johns Hopkins University Press, 2011.

Schmidt, James D. *Free to Work: Labor Law, Emancipation, and Reconstruction, 1815–1880*. Athens: University of Georgia Press, 1998.

———. "'A Full-Fledged Government of Men': Freedmen's Bureau Labor Policy in South Carolina, 1865–1868." In *The Freedmen's Bureau and Reconstruction: Reconsiderations*, edited by Paul A. Cimbala and Randall M. Miller, 219–60. New York: Fordham University Press, 1999.

Schwalm, Leslie A. "A Body of 'Truly Scientific Work': The U.S. Sanitary Commission and the Elaboration of Race in the Civil War Era." *Journal of the Civil War Era* 8, no. 4 (December 2018): 647–76.

———. *Emancipation's Diaspora: Race and Reconstruction in the Upper Midwest America*. Chapel Hill: University of North Carolina Press, 2009.

———. *A Hard Fight for We: Women's Transition from Slavery to Freedom in South Carolina*. Urbana: University of Illinois Press, 1997.

Schwartzberg, Beverly. "'Lots of Them Did That': Desertion, Bigamy, and Marital Fluidity in Late-Nineteenth-Century America." *Journal of Social History* 37 (Spring 2004): 573–600.

Schweninger, Loren. *Appealing for Liberty: Freedom Suits in the South*. New York: Oxford University Press, 2018.

Scott, James C. *Domination and the Arts of Resistance: Hidden Transcripts*. New Haven, Conn.: Yale University Press, 1990.

———. *Seeing Like a State: How Certain Schemes to Improve the Human Condition Have Failed*. New Haven, Conn.: Yale University Press, 1999.

Scott, Rebecca J. "Exploring the Meaning of Freedom: Postemancipation Societies in Comparative Perspective." In *The Abolition of Slavery and the Aftermath of Emancipation in Brazil*, edited by Rebecca J. Scott, Seymour Drescher, Hebe Maria Mattos de Castro, George Reid Andrews, and Robert M. Levine, 1–22. Durham, N.C.: Duke University Press, 1988.

Sefton, James E. *The United States Army and Reconstruction, 1865–1877*. Baton Rouge: Louisiana State University Press, 1967.

Shaffer, Donald R. *After the Glory: The Struggles of Black Civil War Veterans*. Lawrence: University Press of Kansas, 2004.

———. " 'I Do Not Suppose That Uncle Sam Looks at the Skin': African Americans and the Civil War Pension System." *Civil War History* 46, no. 2 (June 2000): 132–47.

Shaw, Stephanie J. "Using the WPA Ex-Slave Narratives to Study the Impact of the Great Depression." *Journal of Southern History* 69, no. 3 (August 2003): 623–58.

Siddali, Silvana. *From Property to Person: Slavery and the Confiscation Acts, 1861–1862*. Baton Rouge: Louisiana State University Press, 2005.

Silber, Nina. *The Romance of Reunion: Northerners and the South, 1865–1900*. Chapel Hill: University of North Carolina Press, 1993.

———. *This War Ain't Over: Fighting the Civil War in New Deal America*. Chapel Hill: University of North Carolina Press, 2020.

Silkenat, David. *Driven from Home: North Carolina's Civil War Refugee Crisis*. Athens: University of Georgia Press, 2016.

———. " 'A Typical Negro': Gordon, Peter, Vincent Colyer, and the Story behind Slavery's Most Famous Photograph." *American Nineteenth Century History* 15, no. 2 (August 2014): 169–86.

Simpson, Brooks D. "Ulysses S. Grant and the Freedmen's Bureau." In *The Freedmen's Bureau and Reconstruction: Reconsiderations*, edited by Paul A. Cimbala and Randall M. Miller, 1–28. New York: Fordham University Press, 1999.

Sitkoff, Harvard. *A New Deal for Blacks: The Emergence of Civil Rights as a National Issue: The Depression Decade*. Rev. ed. New York: Oxford University Press, 2008.

Skocpol, Theda. "America's First Social Security System: The Expansion of Benefits for Civil War Veterans." *Political Science Quarterly* 108, no. 1 (Spring 1993): 85–116.

———. "The Limits of the New Deal System and the Roots of Contemporary Welfare Dilemmas." In *The Politics of Social Policy in the United States*, edited by Margaret Weir, Ann Shola Orloff, and Theda Skocpol, 293–312. Princeton, N.J.: Princeton University Press, 1988.

———. *Protecting Soldiers and Mothers: The Political Origins of Social Policy in the United States*. Cambridge, Mass.: Harvard University Press, 1992.

Skowronek, Stephen. *Building a New American State: The Expansion of National Administrative Capacities, 1877–1920*. Cambridge, Mass.: Harvard University Press, 1982.

Slap, Andrew. *The Doom of Reconstruction: The Liberal Republicans in the Civil War Era*. New York: Fordham University Press, 2006.

Smith, John David, and J. Vincent Lowery, eds. *The Dunning School: Historians, Race, and the Meaning of Reconstruction*. Lexington: University Press of Kentucky, 2013.

Smith, Susan. *Sick and Tired of Being Sick and Tired: Black Women's Health Activism in America, 1890–1950*. Philadelphia: University of Pennsylvania Press, 1995.

Soapes, Thomas F. "The Federal Writers' Project Slave Interviews: Useful Data or Misleading Source." *Oral History Review* 5 (1977): 33–38.

Sommerville, Diane Miller. *Rape and Race in the Nineteenth-Century South*. Chapel Hill: University of North Carolina Press, 2004.

Spindel, Donna J. "Assessing Memory: Twentieth-Century Slave Narratives Reconsidered." *Journal of Interdisciplinary History* 27, no. 2 (1996): 247–61.

Stampp, Kenneth M., and Leon F. Litwack, eds. *Reconstruction: An Anthology of Revisionist Writings*. Baton Rouge: Louisiana State University Press, 1969.

Stanley, Amy Dru. *From Bondage to Contract: Wage Labor, Marriage, and the Market in the Age of Slave Emancipation*. New York: Cambridge University Press, 1998.

Starr, Paul. *The Social Transformation of American Medicine: The Rise of a Sovereign Profession and the Making of a Vast Industry*. New ed. New York: Basic Books, 2008.

Stevenson, Brenda E. "'Us never had no big funerals or weddin's on de place': Ritualizing Black Marriage in the Wake of Freedom." In *Beyond Freedom: Disrupting the History of Emancipation*, edited by David W. Blight and Jim Downs, 39–59. Athens: University of Georgia Press, 2017.

Stowe, Steven M. *Doctoring the South: Southern Physicians and Everyday Medicine in the Mid-Nineteenth Century*. Chapel Hill: University of North Carolina Press, 2004.

Sullivan, Patricia. *Days of Hope: Race and Democracy in the New Deal Era*. Chapel Hill: University of North Carolina Press, 1996.

———. *To Lift Every Voice: The NAACP and the Making of the Civil Rights Movement*. New York: New Press, 2009.

Summers, Mark Wahlgren. *The Ordeal of the Reunion: A New History of Reconstruction*. Chapel Hill: University of North Carolina Press, 2014.

Tani, Karen M. "Administrative Constitutionalism at the 'Borders of Belonging': Drawing on History to Expand the Archive and Change the Lens." *University of Pennsylvania Law Review* 167, no. 7 (June 2019): 1603–30.

———. *States of Dependency: Welfare, Rights, and American Governance, 1935–1972*. New York: Cambridge University Press, 2016.

Taylor, Amy Murrell. *Embattled Freedom: Journeys through the Civil War's Slave Refugee Camps*. Chapel Hill: University of North Carolina Press, 2018.

Teters, Kristopher A. *Practical Liberators: Union Officers in the Western Theater during the Civil War*. Chapel Hill: University of North Carolina Press, 2018.

Thomson, Rosemary Garland. *Extraordinary Bodies: Figuring Physical Disability in American Culture and Literature*. New York: Columbia University Press, 1996.

Torpey, John. *The Invention of the Passport: Surveillance, Citizenship and the State*. New York: Cambridge University Press, 2000.

Trachtenberg, Alan. *The Incorporation of America: Society and Culture in the Gilded Age*. New York: Hill and Wang, 2007.

Trattner, Walter I. *From Poor Law to Welfare State: A History of Social Welfare in America*. 6th ed. New York: Free Press, 1999.

Trotter, Joe William. *Workers on Arrival: Black Labor in the Making of America*. Berkeley: University of California Press, 2019.

Trudeau, Noah Andre. *Like Men of War: Black Troops in the Civil War, 1862–1865*. Boston: Back Bay Books, 1998.

Twitty, Anne. *Before Dred Scott: Slavery and Legal Culture in the American Confluence, 1787–1857*. New York: Cambridge University Press, 2016.

Vogel, Jeffrey E. "Redefining Reconciliation: Confederate Veterans and the Southern Responses to Federal Civil War Pensions." *Civil War History* 51, no. 1 (March 2005): 67–93.

Vorenberg, Michael. "Abraham Lincoln's 'Fellow Citizens'—Before and After Emancipation." In *Lincoln's Proclamation: Emancipation Reconsidered*, edited by William A. Blair and Karen Fisher Younger, 151–69. Chapel Hill: University of North Carolina Press, 2009.

———. *Final Freedom: The Civil War, the Abolition of Slavery, and the Thirteenth Amendment*. New York: Cambridge University Press, 2004.

Wahl, Jenny Bourne. "Legal Constraints on Slave Masters: The Problem of Social Cost." *The American Journal of Legal History* 41, no. 1 (January 1997): 1–24.

Waldrep, Christopher. *African Americans Confront Lynching: Strategies of Resistance from the Civil War to the Civil Rights Era*. Lantham, Md.: Rowman & Littlefield Publishers, 2008.

Waldstreicher, David, and Van Gosse, eds. *Revolutions and Reconstructions: Black Politics in the Long Nineteenth Century*. Philadelphia: University of Pennsylvania Press, 2020.

Wang, Xi. *The Trial of Democracy: Black Suffrage and Northern Republicans, 1860–1910*. Athens: University of Georgia Press, 2012.

Ward, Thomas J., *Black Physicians in the Jim Crow South*. Fayetteville: University of Arkansas Press, 2003.

Warner, John Harley. *The Therapeutic Perspective: Medical Practice, Knowledge, and Identity in America, 1820–1885*. Princeton, N.J.: Princeton University Press, 1997.

Warner, Margaret H. "Public Health in the Old South." In *Science and Medicine in the Old South*, edited by Ronald L. Numbers and Todd L. Savitt, 226–55. Baton Rouge: Louisiana State University Press, 1989.

Washington, Reginald. "The Freedman's Savings and Trust Company and African American Genealogical Research." *Federal Records and African American History* 29, no. 2 (Summer 1997): 170–81.

Washington, Reginald, et al. "Records of the Field Offices of the Freedmen's Branch, Office of the Adjutant General, 1872–1878." *National Archives Microfilm Publications*. Washington, D.C.: U.S. Congress and National Archives and Records Administration, 2006.

Wayne, Michael. *Reshaping the Plantation South: The Natchez District, 1860–1880*. Baton Rouge: Louisiana State University Press, 1982.

Weber, Gustavus A. *The Bureau of Pensions: Its History, Activities and Organization*. Baltimore: Johns Hopkins University Press, 1923.

Wecter, Dixon. *When Johnny Comes Marching Home*. Cambridge, Mass.: Riverside, 1944.

Weiner, Marli F., and Mazie Hough. *Sex, Sickness, and Slavery: Illness in the Antebellum South*. Urbana: University of Illinois Press, 2012.

Welch, Kimberly M. *Black Litigants in the Antebellum American South*. Chapel Hill: University of North Carolina Press, 2018.

Welke, Barbara Young. *Law and the Borders of Belonging in the Long Nineteenth Century*. New York: Cambridge University Press, 2009.

———. *Recasting American Liberty: Gender, Race, Law, and the Railroad Revolution, 1865–1920*. New York: Cambridge University Press, 2001.

West, Elliott. "Reconstructing Race." *Western Historical Quarterly* 34, no. 1 (Spring 2003): 6–26.

White, Howard Ashley. *The Freedmen's Bureau in Louisiana*. Baton Rouge: Louisiana State University Press, 1970.

White, Richard. *The Republic for Which It Stands: The United States during Reconstruction and the Gilded Age, 1865–1896*. New York: Oxford University Press, 2017.

Whites, LeeAnn, and Alecia P. Long, eds. *Occupied Women: Gender, Military Occupation, and the American Civil War*. Baton Rouge: Louisiana State University Press, 2009.

Williams, Chad L. *Torchbearers of Democracy: African American Soldiers in the World War I Era*. Chapel Hill: University of North Carolina Press, 2010.

Williams, Heather Andrea. *Help Me to Find My People: The African American Search for Family Lost in Slavery*. Chapel Hill: University of North Carolina Press, 2012.

Williams, Kidada E. *They Left Great Marks on Me: African American Testimonies of Racial Violence from Emancipation to World War One*. New York: New York University Press, 2012.

Williams, Linda Faye. *The Constraint of Race: Legacies of White Skin Privilege in America*. University Park: Pennsylvania State University Press, 2003.

Williams, Lou Falkner. *The Great South Carolina Ku Klux Klan Trials, 1871–1872*. Athens: University of Georgia Press, 1996.

Willis, Deborah, and Barbara Krauthamer. *Envisioning Emancipation: Black Americans and the End of Slavery*. Philadelphia: Temple University Press, 2013.

Wilson, Sven E. "Prejudice and Policy: Racial Discrimination in the Union Army Disability Pension System, 1865–1906." *American Journal of Public Health* 100, no. S1 (2010): S56–S65.

Witt, John Fabian. *The Accidental Republic: Crippled Workingmen, Destitute Widows, and the Remaking of American Law*. Cambridge, Mass.: Harvard University Press, 2006.

Wood, Marcus. *Blind Memory: Visual Representations of Slavery in England and America, 1780–1865*. New York: Routledge, 2000.

Woodman, Harold D. *New South, New Law: The Legal Foundations of Labor and Credit Relations in the Postbellum South*. Baton Rouge: Louisiana State University Press, 1995.

Woodruff, Nan Elizabeth. *American Congo: The African American Freedom Struggle in the Delta*. Cambridge, Mass.: Harvard University Press, 2003.

Woodward, C. Vann. "History from Slave Sources: A Review Article." *American Historical Review* 79 (April 1974): 470–81.

———. *Origins of the New South, 1877–1913*. 2nd ed. Baton Rouge: Louisiana State University Press, 1971.

Wright, Gavin. *Old South, New South: Revolutions in the Southern Economy since the Civil War*. New York: Basic Books, 1985.

Yetman, Norman R. "The Background of the Slave Narrative Collection." *American Quarterly* 19, no. 3 (Autumn 1967): 534–53.

Zelizer, Julian E. *On Capitol Hill: The Struggle to Reform Congress and Its Consequences, 1948–2000*. New York: Cambridge University Press, 2004.

Index

Note: Page numbers in italics refer to illustrative matter.

CPSIA information can be obtained
at www.ICGtesting.com
Printed in the USA
LVHW101802080922
727889LV00005B/601